Perspectives from the Past

PRIMARY SOURCES IN WESTERN CIVILIZATIONS

Sixth Edition

VOLUME 1

From the Ancient Near East through
the Age of Absolutism

JAMES M. BROPHY · JOSHUA COLE · JOHN ROBERTSON

THOMAS MAX SAFLEY · CAROL SYMES

W · W · NORTON & COMPANY NEW YORK · LONDON

W. W. Norton & Company has been independent since its founding in 1923, when William Warder Norton and Mary D. Herter Norton first published lectures delivered at the People's Institute, the adult education division of New York City's Cooper Union. The firm soon expanded its program beyond the Institute, publishing books by celebrated academics from America and abroad. By mid-century, the two major pillars of Norton's publishing program—trade books and college texts—were firmly established. In the 1950s, the Norton family transferred control of the company to its employees, and today—with a staff of four hundred and a comparable number of trade, college, and professional titles published each year—W. W. Norton & Company stands as the largest and oldest publishing house owned wholly by its employees.

Printed in the United States of America

Editor: Jon Durbin
Editorial assistant: Travis Carr
Production Manager: Jane Searle
Composition: Westchester Publishing Services
Manufacturing: Maple Press
Book Design: Jack Meserole

Acknowledgments and copyrights continue on page 535, which serves as a continuation of the copyright page.

ISBN 978-0-393-26539-2 (v. 1 : pbk.)—ISBN 978-0-393-26540-8 (v. 2 : pbk.)

W. W. Norton & Company, Inc., 500 Fifth Avenue, New York, N.Y. 10110
www.wwnorton.com

W. W. Norton & Company Ltd., Castle House,
75/76 Wells Street, London W1T 3QT

1 2 3 4 5 6 7 8 9 0

ABOUT THE AUTHORS

JAMES M. BROPHY is the Francis H. Squire Professor of history at the University of Delaware, where he has taught since 1992. He received his B.A. from Vassar College and did his graduate training at Eberhard Karls Universität in Tübingen, Germany, and Indiana University, where he took his Ph.D. in modern European history. He is the author of *Capitalism, Politics, and Railroads in Prussia, 1830–1870* (1998) and *Popular Culture and the Public Sphere in the Rhineland, 1800–1850* (2007). He has also published numerous articles on German and European history, which have appeared in such journals as *Past & Present, Journal of Modern History,* and *Historische Zeitschrift.* He regularly teaches the Western civilization survey as well as courses and seminars on historiography, nationalism, modern European history, print culture, and the Holocaust.

JOSHUA COLE is associate professor of history at the University of Michigan. He received his B.A. from Brown University and his M.A. and Ph.D. from the University of California, Berkeley. The author of *The Power of Large Numbers: Population, Politics, and Gender in Nineteenth-Century France* (2000), he has also published articles on French and German social and cultural history in the modern period. His current research is on the legacy of colonial violence in France, Algeria, and Madagascar, with a focus on the problems created by this history of violence in the postcolonial world. He has enjoyed teaching European history in a global context since 1993.

JOHN ROBERTSON received both his M.A. (1976) and his Ph.D. (1981) in ancient history from the University of Pennsylvania. A specialist in the social and economic history of the ancient Near East, he has published several articles in major scholarly journals and contributed articles to such major reference works as the *Anchor Bible Dictionary, Civilizations of the Ancient Near East,* and the *Blackwell Companion to the Ancient Near East.* His book *Iraq: A History* was published in 2015. He has also participated in archaeological excavations in Syria and Greece as well as the American Southwest. Since 1982, he has been a member of the faculty of the department of history at Central Michigan University, where he has taught the history of Western civilization for both the department of history and the university honors program, as well as more specialized courses in the history of the ancient Near East and the Islamic and modern Middle East.

THOMAS MAX SAFLEY teaches the history of early modern Europe at the University of Pennsylvania. A specialist in economic and social history, he has particular research interests in the history of marriage and the family, of poverty and charity, and of labor and business. In addition to numerous articles and reviews, he is the author of *Let No Man Put Asunder: The Control of Marriage in the German Southwest, 1550–1620* (1984), *Charity and Economy in the Orphanages of Early Modern Augsburg* (199_, *Matheus Miller's Memoir: A Merchant's Life* _ *Seventeenth Century* (2000), and *The Childr*_ *boring Poor: Expectation and Experience among* *e Orphans of Early Modern Augsburg* (2004). He is *editor of The Workplace before the Factory: Arti-* *ns and Proletarians, 1500–1800* (1993) and *Child-* *od and Emotion: Across Cultures, 1450–1800* *013*), and he is editor of *The Reformation of Char-* *: The Secular and the Sacred in Early Modern Poor* *lief* (2003), *A Companion to Multiconfessionalism* *the Early Modern World* (2011), and *The History* *Bankruptcy: Economic, Social and Cultural Impli-* *cations in Early Modern Europe* (2013). At the University of Pennsylvania, he regularly teaches the introductory survey of European history and advanced lecture courses on the early modern period. He also offers a broad array of undergraduate and graduate seminars.

CAROL SYMES is the Lynn M. Martin Professorial Scholar at the University of Illinois, Urbana— Champaign, where she is an associate professor of history with appointments in theatre and medieval studies. Educated at Yale and Oxford, she trained for an acting career at the Bristol Old Vic Theatre School (England) and continued to work professionally in theatre while earning the Ph.D. at Harvard, and for several years thereafter. Her research deals with the relationships among premodern performance practices and written records, asking fundamental questions about the transmission of knowledge and the development of communication media and technologies. Her book, *A Common Stage: Theatre and Public Life in Medieval Arras* (2007), won four national awards in three different disciplines, including the Herbert Baxter Adams Prize of the American Historical Association and the John Nicholas Brown Prize from the Medieval Academy of America. Her current book project is a study of the embodied, performative, and material conditions in which medieval texts were negotiated and created. She is the founding executive editor of *The Medieval Globe*, the first academic journal to practice a globalized methodology of medieval studies.

CONTENTS

Preface for Instructors   xii

Preface for Students   xvi

Where to Begin?   xxi

CHAPTER 1 ∽ EARLY CIVILIZATIONS   1

SCULPTED PILLAR AT GOBEKLI TEPE (C. 10,000 B.C.E.)   5

The Instructions of Shuruppag   6

FROM *The Epic of Gilgamesh*   10

FROM The Code of Hammurabi   18

Letters of Royal Women of the Old Babylonian Period   24

FROM The Instruction of Ptah-Hotep   26

FROM The Book of the Dead   33

CHAPTER 2 ∽ PEOPLES, GODS, AND EMPIRES, 1700–500 B.C.E.   37

Akhenaton's *Hymn to the Aton*   40

Treaty between Ramesses II of Egypt and Hattusilis III of Hatti   43

FROM The Middle Assyrian Laws   47

FROM The Book of I Kings: Solomon's Construction of Yahweh's Temple in Jerusalem   50

THE VICTORY STELE OF MERNEPTAH (c. 1210 B.C.E.)   55

HERODOTUS   FROM *The Histories*: Customs of the Persians   56

FROM The Torah: Laws   58

FROM The Book of Isaiah: Prophecies   64

CHAPTER 3   THE CIVILIZATION OF GREECE, 1000–400 B.C.E.   71

HOMER   FROM *The Odyssey*   72

Spartan Society and Values   76

HIPPOCRATES   FROM "On Airs, Waters, and Places"   82

HERODOTUS   FROM *The Histories*: The Second Persian Invasion of Greece   90

THUCYDIDES   FROM *The Peloponnesian Wars*   96

SOPHOCLES   FROM *Antigone*   103

ARISTOPHANES   FROM *Lysistrata*   112

VASE DEPICTING A SLAVE, PERHAPS IN A SCENE FROM A GREEK PLAY (c. 450 B.C.E.)   120

PLATO   FROM "Apology"   121

CHAPTER 4   THE GREEK WORLD EXPANDS, 400–150 B.C.E.   126

PLATO   FROM *The Republic*   128

ARISTOTLE   FROM *Politics*   135

PLUTARCH   FROM "Life of Alexander"   140

HELLENISTIC ARCHITECTURE IN THE NEAR EAST (c. 175 C.E.)   142

EPICTETUS   FROM *The Manual*: Stoicism   143

The Jewish Encounter with Hellenism: The Maccabees' Rebellion   149

CHAPTER 5 ✺ THE CIVILIZATION OF ANCIENT ROME   157

FROM *The Twelve Tables*   158

PLUTARCH   FROM *Lives*   162

CICERO   FROM *On the Laws*   167

VIRGIL   FROM *The Aeneid*   171

TACITUS   FROM *Germania*   173

A MUMMY FROM THE TIME OF THE ROMAN EMPIRE (100 C.E.)   176

TACITUS   FROM *The Speech of Calgacus*   181

CHAPTER 6 ✺ THE TRANSFORMATION OF ROME   183

The Teaching of Jesus According to the Gospel of Matthew   184

The Martyrdom of Perpetua   189

STILICHO AND HIS FAMILY (395 C.E.)   196

ST. AUGUSTINE   FROM *City of God* and *Confessions*   197

FROM *The Theodosian Code: Christian Revisions of the Roman Legal Tradition*   203

ST. BENEDICT   FROM *The Rule*   209

GREGORY OF TOURS   FROM *History of the Franks*   215

CHAPTER 7 ✺ ROME'S THREE HEIRS, 500–950   220

MOSAICS OF JUSTINIAN AND THEODORA, CHURCH OF SAN VITALE, RAVENNA (C. 500 C.E.)   222

PROCOPIUS   FROM *Secret History*   223

MUHAMMAD   FROM *The Qur'an*   228

MASᶜUDI   FROM *The Meadows of Gold*   235

BEDE   FROM *A History of the English Church and People*   239

FROM *The Anglo-Saxon Translation of The Book of Genesis*   243

EINHARD   FROM *The Life of Charlemagne*   248

CHAPTER 8 THE EXPANSION OF EUROPE, 950–1100 253

Pope Gregory VII — Letter to Bishop Hermann of Metz 254
RUNESTONE AT ASPA, SWEDEN 256
RUNESTONE AT KJULA, SWEDEN 257
Anna Comnena — FROM *The Alexiad* 262
FROM *The Song of Roland* 266
FROM The Anonymous of Mainz: A Hebrew Account of the First Crusade 272
Ali Ibn al-Athir — An Arabic Account of the First Crusade 278
FROM The Autobiography of Avicenna 283

CHAPTER 9 THE CONSOLIDATION OF EUROPE, 1100–1250 287

Heloise — Letter to Abelard 288
Guibert of Nogent — On the Uprising of the Laon Commune and the Murder of Bishop Gaudry 295
Anonymous — "The Wife of Orleans" 300
Hildegard of Bingen — Letter to the Clergy of Mainz 303
ECCLESIA AND *SYNAGOGA* FROM THE CATHEDRAL OF STRASBOURG 307
The Magna Carta: The "Great Charter" of 1215 308
Thomas Aquinas — FROM *Summa Theologica* 316

CHAPTER 10 THE MEDIEVAL WORLD, 1250–1350 323

William of Rubruck — FROM *On the Mongols* 324
Ibn Battuta — FROM *The Travels* 330
Pope Boniface VIII — Papal Bull *Unam Sanctam* 335
Dante Alighieri — FROM *The Divine Comedy* 336
THE TRIUMPH OF DEATH (c. 1340) 341
Giovanni Boccaccio — FROM *The Decameron* 342

CHAPTER 11   REBIRTH AND UNREST, 1350–1453   347

GEOFFREY CHAUCER   FROM *The Canterbury Tales: "The Pardoner's Tale"*   348

CHRISTINE DE PISAN   FROM *The Book of the City of Ladies*   366

FROM *The Trial of Jeanne d'Arc*   370

LEON BATTISTA ALBERTI   FROM *I Libri della Famiglia*   374

JAN HUS   FROM *The Church*   380

BARTOLOMEO DE GIANO   FROM "A Letter on the Cruelty of the Turks"   383

CHAPTER 12   INNOVATION AND EXPLORATION, 1453–1533   390

VASCO DA GAMA   Round Africa to India, 1497–1498 C.E.   392

CHRISTOPHER COLUMBUS   Letter on His First Voyage   396

LEONARDO DA VINCI   FROM *The Notebooks*   400

THE SCHOOL OF ATHENS (1509–1511)   403

BALDESAR CASTIGLIONE   FROM *The Book of the Courtier*   404

PORTRAIT OF POPE LEO X AND TWO CARDINALS (1518)   409

GIOVANNI PICO DELLA MIRANDOLA   FROM "Oration on the Dignity of Man"   410

NICCOLÒ MACHIAVELLI   FROM *The Prince*   412

DESIDERIUS ERASMUS OF ROTTERDAM   FROM *Ten Colloquies*   416

SIR THOMAS MORE   FROM *Utopia*   420

CHAPTER 13   THE AGE OF DISSENT AND DIVISION, 1500–1564   426

MARTIN LUTHER   FROM *The Large Catechism*, 1530   427

SEBASTIAN LOTZER   The Twelve Articles of the Peasants of Swabia   432

THE WITTENBERG ALTARPIECE (1547)   433

John Calvin   FROM Draft of Ecclesiastical Ordinances, September and October 1541   437

John Calvin   FROM Catechism of the Church of Geneva, Being a Form of Instruction for Children in the Doctrine of Christ, 1545   442

Saint Ignatius of Loyola   FROM *The Spiritual Exercises*   444

THE MIRACLE OF ST. IGNATIUS OF LOYOLA (C. 1620)   447

Saint Francis Xavier   FROM "Letter from India"   448

Saint Teresa of Ávila   FROM *The Life of Teresa of Jesus*   452

The Council of Trent   455

CHAPTER 14 ❧ EUROPE IN THE ATLANTIC WORLD, 1550–1660   460

CONQUEST OF MEXICO, FLORENTINE CODEX (C. 1555)   462

Giovanni Michiel   FROM A Venetian Ambassador's Report on the St. Bartholomew's Day Massacre   463

Reginald Scot   FROM *Discoverie of Witchcraft*   465

THE PLUNDERING AND BURNING OF A VILLAGE, A HANGING, AND PEASANTS AVENGE THEMSELVES (1633)   473

FROM The Peace of Westphalia   474

Michel Eyquem de Montaigne   FROM "Of Cannibals"   478

THE "ARMADA PORTRAIT" OF QUEEN ELIZABETH (C. 1588)   483

Hugo Grotius   FROM *On the Law of War and Peace*   484

FROM The Religious Peace of Augsburg   489

CHAPTER 15 ❧ EUROPEAN MONARCHIES AND ABSOLUTISM, 1660–1725   491

Jean Bodin   FROM *On Sovereignty*   493

Thomas Mun   FROM *England's Treasure by Forraign Trade. or The Ballance of our Forraign Trade is The Rule of our Treasure*   499

Thomas Hobbes   FROM *Leviathan*   503

SIAMESE EMBASSY TO LOUIS XIV, IN 1686 (1686)   509

Coffee House Society   510

JOHN LOCKE   FROM *Two Treatises of Government*   512

PALACE AND GARDENS OF VERSAILLES (1668)   514

ADAM SMITH   FROM *The Wealth of Nations*   523

CATHERINE THE GREAT   FROM Proposals for a New Code of Law   531

Credits   535

PREFACE FOR INSTRUCTORS

The authors of this text are very pleased to have the opportunity to design and compile this reader, which is the outgrowth of approximately nine decades of combined experience in teaching the history of Western civilization. In the course of acquiring that experience, we were frustrated by what we perceived as serious shortcomings in most of the available supplementary readers. We noted, for example, a frequent overemphasis on political and intellectual history at the expense of social and economic trends, and on elite culture at the expense of sources relating to the experiences of common people and, especially, of women. There is also a tendency to under represent the experiences and perspectives of European societies east of what is today Germany and a lack of attention to the West's important interactions with non-Western peoples and civilizations. We have also wanted to avoid the common practice of presenting texts so abbreviated or disjointed that students are unable to gain a proper appreciation of their contexts or of the nature of the documents from which they are derived. For ancient and medieval sources, this problem is all too often compounded by the use of translations that are either obsolete or rendered in an antiquated idiom that fails to engage students' interest.

In order to address such concerns, we have worked to produce a text that incorporates the following features:

- Selections consist of complete texts or lengthy excerpts of primary documents, ranging from one to eight pages in length and reproduced in authoritative and accessible translations.

- Since images and artifacts are also meaningful primary sources, most chapters of this edition contain visual features (e.g., photographs, paintings, posters, cartoons, sculptures) intended to help students learn how to analyze and interpret visual sources.

- We strive to achieve an appropriate balance of primary sources from the Western canon—works that are illustrative of the origins and development of Western political institutions, intellectual life, and high culture—as well as those that illustrate aspects of social and economic history and daily life in Western societies.

- Selections reflect the experiences and perspectives of women and the dynamics of gender relations, as well as the experiences of commoners and marginalized peoples.

- Selections focus on western civilizations within a broader, global perspective and include ancient Egyptian and Babylonian literature, the Qur'an, and then works of such figures as Ali ibn al-Athir, Ibn Battuta, Edward Morel, Mohandas Gandhi, Frantz Fanon, and Tadataka Kuribayshi.

- In addition to review questions that assist the students in close reading and analysis of individual texts, we include questions designed to link documents (both within and among chapters) in a coherent, pedagogically useful framework. The documents in this reader can thus be used to explore and discuss overarching issues and thematic trends: What are responsibilities and rights of the individual within a local community or broader society, and how have they changed over time? How have people defined their own communities, and how have they viewed outsiders? Who should have power within society, and why? How have people responded to changes in the material world and the environment?

The pedagogical and critical apparatus provided in this reader has been designed to guide the student to an appreciation of the sources but without imparting too much in the way of historical interpretation. For each chapter we have supplied a brief introduction that provides a historical context for the readings and alerts the student to the thematic threads that link them. Each reading in turn has an introduction that supplies an even more specific context. Finally, each selection is accompanied by several questions intended to stimulate analysis and discussion.

For this edition we have included the following new documents:

- The Instructions of Shuruppag
- Treaty between Ramesses II of Egypt and Hattusilis of Hatti
- from The Middle Assyrian Laws
- Aristophanes, from *Lysistrata*
- The Jewish Encounter with Hellenism: The Maccabees' Rebellion
- Virgil, from The *Aeneid*
- Tacitus, from The Speech of Calgacus

- from The Autobiography of Avicenna
- Guibert of Nogent, On the Uprising of the Laon Commune and the Murder of Bishop Gaudry
- Anonymous, "The Wife of Orleans"
- Bartolomeo de Giano, from "A Letter on the Cruelty of the Turks"
- Vasco da Gama, Round Africa to India, 1497–1498 C.E.
- from The Peace of Westphalia
- Thomas Mun, from *England's Treasure by Forraign Trade. or The Ballance of our Forraign Trade is The Rule of our Treasure*

In addition to these features, this Sixth Edition has also been made more affordable and compact to meet the changing needs of instructors and students. Nearly one hundred instructors participated in our online survey, to identify the most essential and highly teachable primary sources from the previous edition, and to offer suggestions of sources that could be included. We have also brought this Sixth Edition into closer alignment with our best-selling survey texts, *Western Civilizations* Eighteenth Edition and *Western Civilizations* Brief Fourth Edition, by Joshua Cole and Carol Symes.

Coordinating a project as complex as this one requires the skills, support, inspiration, and dedication of many people. We therefore wish to express our admiration and profound gratitude to the editorial and marketing staff of W. W. Norton, especially to Travis Carr and Jane Searle, who did a fantastic job of researching sources and pulling the manuscript together; to Bethany Salminen, for her work in securing permissions; and, most especially, to Jon Durbin, who assembled the team, helped us to define and refine our work, organized the project, offered useful insight and judicious criticism, and kept all of us on task and on time. The credit for this reader is as much theirs as ours.

In addition, we would like to thank the following faculty for their valuable input as we developed the Sixth Edition:

- David Adams, Harding University
- Christine Arnold-Lourie, College of Southern Maryland
- Kenneth Atkinson, University of Northern Iowa
- Michelle Barsom, Bainbridge State College
- Jordan Bauer, University of Alabama at Birmingham
- Philippe Beauchamp, Champlain College
- Hilary Bernstein, University of California
- Kurt M. Boughan, The Citadel
- Richard Byington, University of Central Florida
- Amy Colon, SUNY Sullivan

- Trevor Corless, Heritage College
- Christopher Daly, SUNY Albany
- Babette Faehmel, Schenectady County Community College
- Jessica Hammerman, Central Oregon Community College
- David M. Head, John Tyler Community College
- Anthony Heideman, Front Range Community College
- Padhraig Higgins, Mercer County College
- Andrew Kellett, Hartford Community College
- Jacob Latham, University of Tennessee, Knoxville
- John Livingston, William Paterson University
- Marina Maccari-Clayton, University of Tennessee, Knoxville
- Matthew Mingus, University of New Mexico—Gallup
- Aubrey Neal, St. Paul's College
- Stefan Papaioannou, Framingham State University
- Roberta Pergher, Indiana University
- Janet Polasky, University of New Hampshire
- David Porter, Northern Virginia Community College
- Michael Prahl, University of Northern Iowa
- Paula Rieder, Slippery Rock University
- Martin Saltzman, Long Island University
- Wanda L. Scarbro, Pellissippi State Community College
- Kathleen Sheppard, Missouri University of Science and Technology
- Jace Stuckey, Marymount University
- Larissa Taylor, Colby College
- Elisaveta Todorova, University of Cincinnati
- Steven A. Usitalo, Northern State University
- Joseph Western, St. Louis University
- Rebecca Woodham, Wallace Community College

PREFACE FOR STUDENTS

Good Tips for Learning How to Analyze Primary Sources

The purpose of this collection of illustrations and documents is to provide the student with the raw materials of history, the sources, in the form of the objects and written words that survive from the past. Your textbook relies on such documents, known as primary sources, as well as on the works of many past and present historians who have analyzed and interpreted these sources—the secondary literature. In some cases the historians were themselves sources, eyewitnesses to the events they recorded. Authors of textbooks select which facts and interpretations they think you should know, and so the textbook filters what you think about the human past by limiting the information available to you. Textbooks are useful because they provide a coherent historical narrative for students of history, but it is important to remember that they are only an introduction to the rich complexity of human experience over time.

A collection of historical documents and artifacts provides a vital supplement to the textbook, but it also has problems. First, the sources, mostly not intended for us to read and study, exist for the reasons that prompted some people to create them and others to preserve them. These reasons may include a measure of lies, self-deception, or ignorance about what was really happening and being recorded. So we must ask the following questions about any document or object—a treaty, contract, painting, photograph, poem, newspaper article, or sculpture: Why does it exist? What specific purpose did it serve when it was done? Who is its author? What motives prompted the creator to produce this material in this form?

The second major problem is that we, the editors of this collection, have selected, from millions of possible choices, these particular documents and objects, and not others. Even in this process, because of the limitations of space and our own personal experiences, we present a necessarily partial and highly selective view of Western civilization (also because of space limitations, it has been necessary to delete portions from some of the longer sections).* Our purpose is not to repeat what you can find in the textbook but to give you the opportunity to see and discuss how historians, now including you, make history out of documents and objects, and their understanding of why people behave the way they do.

The illustrations in this collection provide a glimpse at the millions of material objects that survive from the past. These churches, buildings, paintings, mosaics, sculptures, photographs, and other items make up an important set of sources for the historian to consider about the past. It is certainly difficult to appreciate an immense building or a small manuscript painting from a photograph. Nevertheless, the editors of this collection include illustrations in the Sixth Edition to make clear the full range of sources that historians utilize. Also, the illustrations in many cases complement the written documents and in every case provide opportunities for a broader discussion of historical questions and the variety of sources that can help answer them.

Before exploring in more detail what documents are, we should be clear about what history is. Simply put, history is what we can say about the human past, in this case about the vast area of Western civilization from its remote origins to the most recent past. We can say, or write, things about the past because people left us their words, in the form of documents, and we can, like detectives, question these sources and then try to understand what happened. Before the written word, there is no history in the strictest sense; instead there are preliterate societies and the tens of thousands of years for which we know only what the anthropologists and archaeologists can tell us from the physical remains of bodies and objects made by human hands. And yet during this time profoundly important human institutions like language, the family, and religion first appeared. History begins with writing because that is when the documentation starts. These accomplishments of our remote ancestors occurred over tens of thousands of years, broken into ages of stone, copper, and bronze. Objects and images, but no words, reveal advances in weapons, art, farming, and other activities.

Although history cannot exist without written documents, we must remember that this evidence is complex and ambiguous. In the first place, it first appears in ancient languages, and the majority of documents in this book were not originally in English. The act of translating the documents into modern English raises another barrier or filter, and we must use our imaginations to recreate the past worlds in which modern words like *liberty, race,* or *sin* had different meanings. One job of the historian is to understand the language of the

---

* We indicate omissions, no matter how brief, with three spaced asterisks (* * *), running them in when the opening, middle, or closing of a paragraph has been deleted and centering them between lines when a full paragraph is dropped. Why asterisks, when ellipsis dots are the standard? Because authors use ellipsis dots, and we want to distinguish our deletions from theirs.

documents in their widest possible contexts. All the authors intended their documents to communicate something, but as time passes, languages and contexts change, and so it becomes more difficult for us to figure out what a document meant then and may mean now. Language is an imperfect way to communicate, but we must make the best of what we have. If we recollect how difficult it is sometimes to understand the events we see and experience, then we can perhaps understand how careful we must be when we interpret someone else's report about an event in the past, especially when that past is far removed in space and time from our experience.

The documents give us the language, or testimony, of witnesses, observers, or people with some point to make. Some documents claim to reveal religious truths and interpreting these claims requires historians to inquire respectfully and sincerely. Historical evidence, like any other, must be examined for flaws, contradictions, lies, and what it tells us that the writer did not necessarily intend to reveal. Like a patient detective, we must question our witnesses with a full awareness of their limited and often-biased perception, piecing together our knowledge of their history with the aid of multiple testimonies and a broad context. Consider the document, whatever it is, as testimony and a piece of a bigger puzzle, many of the remaining pieces of which are missing or broken. It is useful at the beginning to be clear about the simple issues—What type of document is this evidence? Who wrote it? Where and when was it written? Why does it exist? Try to understand the context of the document by relating it to the wider world—how do words by Plato or about the Nazi Party fit with what you already know about ancient Greece or twentieth-century Germany?

When the document, or witness, has been correctly identified and placed in some context, we may then interrogate it further by asking questions about the words before us. Not all documents suggest the same questions, but there are some general questions that apply to nearly every document. One place to begin is to ask, Who or what is left out? Once you see the main point, it is interesting to ask what the documents tell us about people and subjects often left out of the records—women, children, or religious or ethnic minorities, for example. Or, if the document is about a religious minority, we can ask what it tells us about the majority. Take the document and try to turn it inside out by determining the basic assumptions or biases of its author, and then explore what has been intentionally or unintentionally left out. Look for anomalies—pieces of evidence that appear out of place or simply weird; they are often clues to understanding the distances between us and the sources. Another way to ask a fresh question of an old witness is to look beneath the surface and see what else is there. For example, if the document in question seems mainly to offer evidence on religion, ask what it tells us about the economy or contemporary eating habits or whatever else might occur to you. Documents frequently reveal excellent information on topics far from their ostensible subjects, if we remember to ask.

Every document in this collection is some kind of story, either long or short. The stories are almost all nonfiction, at least in theory, but they all have characters; a plot, or story line; and above all a point to the story, the meaning. We have suggested some possible meanings in the sample questions at the end of each document, but these questions are just there to help your thinking or get a discussion going, about the many possible meanings of the documents. You can ask what the meaning was in the document's own time, as well as what we might now see as a meaning that makes sense to us of some pieces of the past. The point of the story in a document may often concern a central issue in history, the process of change. If history is what we can say about the human past, then the most important words describe how change occurs, for example, rapidly, as in revolutions and wars, or more slowly, as in marriage customs or family life. Every document casts some light on human change, and the meaning of the story often relates to why something changed.

History is often at its dullest when a document simply describes a static situation, for example, a law or farming. However, even a good description reveals choices and emphasis. If you ask, Why this law now? Why farm in this way? How did these activities influence human behavior? you can see that the real subject of nearly all documents is human change, on some level. You will find that people can and will strongly disagree about the meaning of a story: they can and will use the same evidence from a document to draw radically different meanings. This is one of the challenges of history and what makes it fun, for some explanations and meanings make more sense than others in the broader context of what you know about an episode or period of history. Argue about meaning, and you will learn something about not only your own biases and values but also the process of sifting facts for good arguments and answers. These skills have a value well beyond the study of history.

The documents and objects in this collection, even the most general works of philosophy or social analysis, reveal the particular and contingent aspects of history. Even the most abstract of these documents and objects comes from a specific time, place, and person and sheds some light on a unique set of circumstances. When history is like the other social sciences (anthropology, economics, sociology, political science, and others), it tries to deal with typical or average people, societies, or behavior. When history is like the other humanities (literature, philosophy, religion, art, and others), it stresses individual people, their quirks and uniqueness. The documents and objects also illustrate the contingent aspect of history, which unlike the social or natural sciences but like the humanities, appears to lack rules or laws. History depends on what people did, subject to the restrictions of their natures, resources, climate, and other natural factors—people with histories of their own! Rerunning this history is not like a movie, and it would never turn out the same way twice, for it is specific and contingent to the way it turned out this time. The documents and objects do not tell a story of an orderly progression from simple to complex societies or from bad to good ones. Instead, history continues, and people cope, or not, with the issues of religious faith, family life, making a living, and creating artifacts and documents. These documents and objects collectively provide perspectives on how experiments in living succeeded or failed. We invite you to use them to learn more about the people of the past than the textbooks can say and to use your imaginations to get these witnesses to answer your questions about the process and meaning of human change.

WHERE TO BEGIN?

A Primary Source Checklist

This checklist is a series of questions that can be used to analyze most of the documents and objects in this reader.

> ✔ What type of document or object is this evidence?
>
> ✔ Why does the document or object exist? What motives prompted the author to create the material in this form?
>
> ✔ Who created this work?
>
> ✔ Who or what is left out—women, children, minorities, members of the majority?
>
> ✔ In addition to the main subject, what other kinds of information can be obtained?
>
> ✔ How do the subjects of the document or object relate to what we know about broader society?
>
> ✔ What was the meaning of the document or object in its own time? What is its meaning for the audience?
>
> ✔ What does the document or object tell us about change or stability in society?

1 ✦ EARLY CIVILIZATIONS

In the history of humankind's sojourn on this planet, no development has been more momentous, or more fraught with consequence, than the emergence of civilization. Exactly what constitutes "civilization" has been debated by scholars for years. But as evidenced by the appearance of states, cities, complex economies, and writing, among other characteristics, civilizations can be said to have arisen independently in several areas across the globe. By far the earliest of them, however, arose in that region of southwestern Asia and northern Africa that we today call the Middle East.

But during the many preceding millennia of the eras that we now refer to as the Paleolithic (literally, "Old Stone Age") and Neolithic ("New Stone Age"), humankind also attained perhaps equally monumental achievements, without which cities and civilizations could never have developed. Those achievements are too numerous to catalogue here, but among the more significant are certainly the harnessing of fire, the creation of technologies for hunting wild animals and foraging for wild plants, and the domestication of those same wild-food sources in the process that resulted in agriculture and herding. The developments made the Neolithic village life possible. With these very early achievements, there also emerged a belief in powers and forces beyond the realm of the purely "natural," powers that, though unseen, might bring abundance or disaster if not properly recognized and, if necessary, propitiated. Such powers might be inherent in the life force of the animals and plants on which early humans depended; they might also lie in some mysterious, unknowable realm inhabited by the dead, including one's ancestors. Until relatively recently, historians had often relegated these so-called prehistoric achievements and ideas to an era of dim savagery that many believed was better left to the scrutiny of anthropologists and archaeologists. Today, however, more and more scholars are embracing the concept of "deep" or "macro" history, in the belief that even though these earliest human societies and achievements date to a preliterate (i.e., before writing) era, we have been mistaken to deny them a place in the unfolding of human "history." Indeed, by calling them "prehistoric," perhaps we have been segregating our "modern" consciousness in the shallow end of the almost immeasurably deeper pool of what constitutes humankind's shared experience on this planet. We surely can embrace such a longer view of "history" while still recognizing the stupendous and rapid amplification of that human experience by the quantum leap ahead by the peoples of what is now the Middle East.

By about 5000 B.C.E.,[1] in what is now eastern Iraq, a Neolithic people to whom archaeologists refer as the Samarrans began to settle in villages where rainfall alone could not support agriculture. Their pioneering efforts in the technology of canal irrigation paved the way for the emergence of cities and, with them, the civilization of ancient Sumer. The world's first cities arose in the floodplain of Lower Mesopotamia, the land between the Tigris and Euphrates rivers (modern-day southern Iraq), more than five thousand years ago, as large population centers governed by administrators powerful enough to organize and direct the construction of large architectural complexes, quite likely temples. These efforts were fueled by agricultural production on an unprecedented scale, entailing the cultivation of thousands of acres of wheat, barley, and other foodstuffs. The floodplain's wondrous fertility could be unleashed only by the profuse application of irrigation water brought from the Euphrates and (perhaps to a lesser extent) the Tigris. Organizing the digging and maintaining of irrigation canals; the plowing, sowing, and harvesting of the fields; and the maintaining of huge herds of livestock was a truly formidable task.

By about 3200 B.C.E., the huge size and increasingly complex administration of these great estates necessitated the creation of a new technology that itself shaped the future of civilization: writing. Primitive pictographs incised on clay tablets evolved into a system that we today refer to as cuneiform (literally, "wedge-shaped") that spread throughout the ancient Near East, where it remained in use for almost three thousand years. The scribes of ancient Mesopotamia (and Anatolia, Syria, Iran, and even Egypt) bequeathed to us a remarkably durable legacy of tens of thousands of records—mostly clay tablets, but also inscriptions on stone monuments and objects. Most of the tablets are detailed accounts of the administration of temples, palaces, and public institutions, tediously dry in themselves but, when reconstructed into coherent archives, crucial evidence of social and economic organization. The remaining records— among them, royal inscriptions, letters, poems, hymns, prayers, law "codes," contracts, and a variety of literary works—provide, at best, tantalizing samples from what was once a vast corpus. Enough has survived, nonetheless, to enable us to reconstruct a complex sequence of dynasties and political configurations in the history of Mesopotamia and the Near East. But perhaps more appealing to our common humanity, these records allow us at least limited insight into the enduring structures of life and the everyday concerns of people who seem to have felt very strongly that their fortune and existence depended utterly on ensuring the continued good favor of their gods. Those gods might bestow on them

---

[1] B.C.E. means "before the common era."

benevolence and plenty or, just as likely, abandon them to destitution and catastrophe, the latter all too often brought by the rampages of "barbarian" invaders or the no less destructive rampages of the normally life-sustaining rivers.

By 2000 B.C.E., the solid foundations of Mesopotamian civilization had been shaken by some major tremors. Imperial dynasties established by the great conqueror Sargon of Akkad and then by the kings of the Third Dynasty of Ur had flourished then ebbed, although the idealized memory of Sargon's rule would inspire future Mesopotamian kings for the next fifteen hundred years. The next four hundred years ushered in chieftains of recently arrived tribal groups known as Amorites, who established themselves in small kingdoms in the urbanized regions of Sumer and Akkad. In time, one of those minor Amorite kingdoms, Babylon, was to establish itself, and its god Marduk, as supreme. With the ascent of its great king Hammurabi shortly after 1800 B.C.E., Babylon took center stage in Lower Mesopotamia (henceforth Babylonia), not to relinquish its leading role there until the era of Alexander the Great's successors. Babylon's rise was possible, though, only because Hammurabi proved himself a master player in an era when (as thousands of cuneiform tablets from the palace of Mari on the Euphrates testify for us) power politics, trade and diplomacy, and competition for prized resources encompassed an arena extending from Anatolia to the Persian Gulf and from Iran to the Mediterranean as far as Crete. His dynasty's fall, around one hundred fifty years later, would come at the hands of a relatively new player, the Hittite rulers of the Anatolian kingdom of Hatti. The Hittites' rise ushered onto the ancient Near Eastern stage speakers and writers of a language that we can identify as Indo-European and as thereby related to the later languages of western Europe (and India). When the curtain eventually lifted again in Babylonia, another new, nonindigenous ruling group, the Kassites, had taken charge. Yet, like the Amorites before them—and the Akkadian kings before them, the Kassites were captured—or, perhaps, captivated—by the enduring traditions and structures of an already ancient Sumerian civilization.

Civilization arose along the Nile River somewhat later than it had in the Tigris-Euphrates floodplain, but Egyptian civilization soon assumed its own distinct form and identity. According to their later traditions, the Egyptians believed that a king named Menes had been the first to unite the two rival kingdoms of Upper Egypt (the long Nile valley) and Lower Egypt (the Nile delta). From a modern vantage point, we detect scant traces of a ruler named Menes in the earliest Egyptian records, and most scholars are convinced that the unification of Egypt was much more complicated than the pulling together of two kingdoms. Nonetheless, by around 3100 B.C.E., what some have identified as the world's first unified nation-state had been created. For the next three thousand years, the people of Egypt regarded the absolute rule of a semidivine king (who by the mid-second millennium B.C.E. came to be known as pharaoh) as the only desirable state of affairs. On his shoulders fell the responsibility of preserving the stability of the cosmos (what the Egyptians called ma'at), an essential ingredient of which was securing the unity of the "Two Lands" of Upper and Lower Egypt. Only the king's vigorous stewardship might avert chaos and calamity. Over time, there developed around the king's person a royal court and hierarchical administration that was served by a class of professional (and mostly male) bureaucrats ("scribes") highly trained in the hieroglyphic script and its hieratic derivative. Through their efforts, the manpower and resources of the kingdom could be marshaled to ensure the king's success, both in this world and the next. It is from the records they have left us—inscribed and painted on temple and tomb walls, or written on papyrus or even flakes of stone—that we glean our hard-won knowledge of ancient Egyptian history and culture.

Neither the grandeur of Egyptian kingship nor the king's preservation of cosmic harmony would have been possible, of course, without the Nile River. As the Greek "father of history" Herodotus so succinctly put it, Egypt is "the river's gift." Until the completion of the Aswan High Dam in the early 1970s, every year, between July and October, the Nile overflowed its banks, bringing life-sustaining water and rich silt that, together with the generative power of the sun, literally resurrected the black land of the Nile Valley. It may well be that in this annual resurrection of the land was born the Egyptian concept of a resurrection and continued existence after death (though only if proper preparations were made and precautions taken). Often, modern observers tend to focus on the Egyptians' supposed morbid preoccupation with death and the hereafter. In part, that perception stems from the accidents of archaeological preservation. Millennia of floods and silt deposits, combined with continued human occupation of town and village sites, have largely obliterated the towns and villages of the ancient Egyptians. Most of what has been left to us are the remains of temples and tombs, built in the low desert where the Nile's floods did not reach; that the remaining records say so much about kings, gods, and death should hardly surprise us. As some of the documents in this chapter make clear, however, the ancient Egyptians did not while away their lives dreamily pining for death.

By 2000 B.C.E., Egypt, like Mesopotamia, had been rocked by adversity, as the disintegration of the Old Kingdom brought, for the first time, the disruption of the divinely ordained, cosmic stability of ma'at that underpinned Egypt's civilization. The reunification forged by the rulers of Thebes (whose god Amun, like Babylon's Marduk, would soon emerge supreme) with the advent of the Middle Kingdom brought renewed strength and cultural vitality, as well as the assertion of Egyptian interests and power as far away as Nubia to the south, Crete to the north, and Palestine to the east. The Middle Kingdom also saw a reassertion of royal traditions and absolutism, though punctuated by the lingering memory of the chaos that had once plagued Egypt. In time, that threat of chaos would again become real: "vile Asiatic" newcomers recently arrived from Palestine into the Nile Delta would assert political control as the Hyksos dynasties of Lower Egypt. Egypt would once again be divided, but now, for the first time, by the abomination of "barbarian" invasion.

SCULPTED PILLAR AT GOBEKLI TEPE (C. 10,000 B.C.E.)

Excavations at the site of Gobekli Tepe (in what is now southeastern Turkey) since the 1990s have revealed an astounding complex of rings of large pillars surrounding two large T-shaped pillars in their centers. The rings are as much as 65 feet in diameter. The tallest pillars stand 16 feet in height, and weigh as much as 10 tons. As the pillar shown above indicates, some of the pillars bear sculpted images of animals. Some observers have gone so far as to refer to the Gobekli complex as the "world's first temple." Equally astonishing, the complex dates to the tenth millennium B.C.E., and seems to have been built by hunter-gatherers, not settled peoples. What might the sculpted pillars such as this one imply about humans' relations with the animal world? Reverence? Worship? Fear? What might the Gobekli complex suggest concerning social organization during the pre-Neolithic era?

The Instructions of Shuruppag

The Sumerian composition known as the Instructions of Shuruppag (also spelled Shuruppak) dates to at least as early as the late third millennium B.C.E. Although historically Shuruppag was a city of ancient Sumer, in this text Shuruppag is the name of a king who here provides wisdom for his son, Ziusudra. (Notably, Ziusudra appears in another celebrated work of Mesopotamian literature, the poem known as Atrahasis, *in which one of the gods instructs him to build a huge boat in which to ride out the Great Flood that the god Enlil had decided to send to wipe out human-kind. In the selection that follows this one, the name of the survivor of the Flood is Utanapishtim.) The Instructions of Shuruppag is also one of the earliest examples of a genre known as Mirrors for Princes, intended to provide sage advice to future rulers.*

From *The Electronic Text Corpus of Sumerian Literature*, J. A. Black, G. Cunningham, J. Ebeling, E. Flückiger-Hawker, E. Robson, J. Taylor, and G. Zólyomi (http://etcsl.orinst.ox.ac .uk/), Oxford 1998–2006.

1–13. In those days, in those far remote days, in those nights, in those faraway nights, in those years, in those far remote years, at that time the wise one who knew how to speak in elaborate words lived in the Land; Šuruppag, the wise one, who knew how to speak with elaborate words lived in the Land. Šuruppag gave instructions to his son; Šuruppag, the son of Ubara-Tutu, gave instructions to his son Zi-ud-sura: My son, let me give you instructions: you should pay attention! Zi-ud-sura, let me speak a word to you: you should pay attention! Do not neglect my instructions! Do not transgress the words I speak! The instructions of an old man are precious; you should comply with them!

14. You should not buy a donkey which brays; it will split (?) your midriff (?).

15–18. You should not locate a field on a road; [. . .] You should not plough a field at a path; [. . .] You should not make a well in your field: people will cause damage on it for you. You should not place your house next to a public square: there is always a crowd (?) there.

19–20. You should not vouch for someone: that man will have a hold on you; and you yourself, you should not let somebody vouch for you: that man will despise (?) you.

21. You should not make an inspection (?) on a man: the flood (?) will give it back (?) to you.

22–27. You should not loiter about where there is a quarrel; you should not let the quarrel make you a witness. You should not let (?) yourself [. . .] in a quarrel. You should not cause a quarrel; [. . .] the gate of the palace [. . .] Stand aside from a quarrel, [. . .] you should not take (?) another road.

28–31. You should not steal anything; you should not [. . .] yourself. You should not break into a house; you should not wish for the money chest (?). A thief is a lion, but after he has been caught, he will be a slave. My son, you should not commit robbery; you should not cut yourself with an axe.

32–34. You should not make a young man best man. You should not [. . .] yourself. You should not play around with a married young woman: the slander could be serious. My son, you should not sit alone in a chamber with a married woman.

35–38. You should not pick a quarrel; you should not disgrace yourself. You should not [. . .] lies; [. . .] You should not boast; then your words will be trusted. You should not deliberate for too long (?); you cannot bear [...] glances.

39–41. You should not eat stolen food with anyone. You should not sink (?) your hand into blood. After you have apportioned the bones, you will be made to restore the ox, you will be made to restore the sheep.

42–43. You should not speak improperly; later it will lay a trap for you.

44–46. You should not scatter your sheep into unknown pastures. You should not hire someone's ox for an uncertain [...] A safe [...] means a safe journey.

47. You should not travel during the night: it can hide both good and evil.

48. You should not buy an onager: it lasts (?) only until the end of the day.

49. You should not have sex with your slave girl: she will chew you up (?).

50. You should not curse strongly: it rebounds on you.

51–52. You should not draw up water which you cannot reach: it will make you weak. . . .

53. You should not drive away a debtor: he will be hostile towards you.

54–57. You should not establish a home with an arrogant man: he will make your life like that of a slave girl. You will not be able to travel through any human dwelling without being shouted at: "There you go! There you go!"

58–59. You should not undo the [...] of the garden's reed fence; "Restore it! Restore it!" they will say to you.

60. You should not provide a stranger (?) with food; you should not wipe out (?) a quarrel.

61–62. My son, you should not use violence (?); [...] You should not commit rape on someone's daughter; the courtyard will learn of it.

63–64. You should not drive away a powerful man; you should not destroy the outer wall. You should not drive away a young man; you should not make him turn against the city.

65–66. The eyes of the slanderer always move around as shiftily as a spindle. You should never remain in his presence; his intentions (?) should not be allowed to have an effect (?) on you.

67. You should not boast in beer halls like a deceitful man: then your words will be trusted.

68–72. Having reached the field of manhood, you should not jump (?) with your hand. The warrior is unique, he alone is the equal of many; Utu is unique, he alone is the equal of many. With your life you should always be on the side of the warrior; with your life you should always be on the side of Utu.

73–75. Šuruppag gave these instructions to his son. Šuruppag, the son of Ubara-Tutu, gave these instructions to his son Zi-ud-sura.

76–82. A second time, Šuruppag gave instructions to his son. Šuruppag, the son of Ubara-Tutu, gave instructions to his son Zi-ud-sura: My son, let me give you instructions: you should pay attention! Zi-ud-sura, let me speak a word to you: you should pay attention! Do not neglect my instructions! Do not transgress the words I speak! The instructions of an old man are precious; you should comply with them!

83–91. The beer-drinking mouth [...] My little one [...] The beer-drinking mouth [...] Ninkasi [...].

92–93. Your own man will not repay (?) it for you. The reedbeds are [...], they can hide (?) slander.

94–96. The palace is like a mighty river: its middle is goring bulls; what flows in is never enough to fill it, and what flows out can never be stopped.

97–100. When it is about someone else's bread, it is easy to say "I will give it to you," but the time of actual giving can be as far away as the sky. If you go after the man who said "I will give it to you," he will say "I cannot give it to you—the bread has just been finished up."

101–102. Property is something to be expanded (?); but nothing can equal my little ones.

103–105. The artistic mouth recites words; the harsh mouth brings litigation documents; the sweet mouth gathers sweet herbs.

106–108. The garrulous liar fills (?) his bread bag; the haughty one brings an empty bag and can fill his empty mouth only with boasting.

109. Who works with leather will eventually (?) work with his own leather.

110. The strong one can escape (?) from anyone's hand.

111–114. The fool loses something. When sleeping, the fool loses something. "Do not tie me up!" he pleads; "Let me live!" he pleads.

115–117. The imprudent decrees fates; the shameless one piles up (?) things in another's lap: "I am such that I deserve admiration."

118. A weak wife is always seized (?) by fate.

119–123. If you hire a worker, he will share the bread bag with you; he eats with you from the same bag, and finishes up the bag with you. Then he will quit working with you and, saying "I have to live on something," he will serve at the palace.

124–125. You tell your son to come to your home; you tell your daughter to go to her women's quarters.

126. You should not pass judgment when you drink beer.

127. You should not worry unduly about what leaves the house.

128–130. Heaven is far, earth is most precious, but it is with heaven that you multiply your goods, and all foreign lands breathe under it.

131–133. At harvest time, at the most priceless time, collect like a slave girl, eat like a queen; my son, to collect like a slave girl, to eat like a queen, this is how it should be.

134–142. Who insults can hurt only the skin; greedy eyes (?), however, can kill. The liar, shouting, tears up his garments. Insults bring (?) advice to the wicked. To speak arrogantly is like an abscess: a herb that makes the stomach sick. . . .

My words of prayer bring abundance. Prayer is cool water that cools the heart. Only (?) insults and stupid speaking receive the attention of the Land.

143–145. Šuruppag gave these instructions to his son. Šuruppag, the son of Ubara-Tutu, gave these instructions to his son Zi-ud-sura.

146–152. A third time, Šuruppag gave instructions to his son. Šuruppag, the son of Ubara-Tutu, gave instructions to his son Zi-ud-sura: My son, let me give you instructions: you should pay attention! Zi-ud-sura, let me speak a word to you: you should pay attention! Do not neglect my instructions! Do not transgress the words I speak! The instructions

of an old man are precious; you should comply with them!

153. You should not beat a farmer's son: he has constructed (?) your embankments and ditches.

154–164. You should not buy a prostitute: she is a mouth that bites. You should not buy a house-born slave: he is a herb that makes the stomach sick. You should not buy a free man: he will always lean against the wall. You should not buy a palace slave girl: she will always be the bottom of the barrel (?). You should rather bring down a foreign slave from the mountains, or you should bring somebody from a place where he is an alien; my son, then he will pour water for you where the sun rises and he will walk before you. He does not belong to any family, so he does not want to go to his family; he does not belong to any city, so he does not want to go to his city.

165–167. My son, you should not travel alone eastwards. Your acquaintance should not [. . .].

168–169. A name placed on another one [. . .]; you should not pile up a mountain on another one.

170–171. Fate is a wet bank; it can make one slip.

172–174. The elder brother is indeed like a father; the elder sister is indeed like a mother. Listen therefore to your elder brother, and you should be obedient to your elder sister as if she were your mother.

175–176. You should not work using only your eyes; you will not multiply your possessions using only your mouth.

177. The negligent one ruins (?) his family.

178–180. The need for food makes some people ascend the mountains; it also brings traitors and foreigners, since the need for food brings down other people from the mountains.

181–182. A small city provides (?) its king with a calf; a huge city digs (?) a house plot (?).

183–188 [. . .] is well equipped. The poor man inflicts all kinds of illnesses on the rich man. The married man is well equipped; the unmarried makes his bed in a haystack (?). He who wishes to destroy a house will go ahead and destroy the house; he who wishes to raise up will go ahead and raise up.

189–192. By grasping the neck of a huge ox, you can cross the river. By moving along (?) at the side of the mighty men of your city, my son, you will certainly ascend (?).

193–201. When you bring a slave girl from the hills, she brings both good and evil with her. The good is in the hands; the evil is in the heart. The heart does not let go of the good; but the heart cannot let go of the evil either. As if it were a watery place, the heart does not abandon the good. Evil is a storeroom [...].

202–203. A loving heart maintains a family; a hateful heart destroys a family.

204–207. To have authority, to have possessions and to be steadfast are princely divine powers. You should submit to the respected; you should be humble before the powerful. My son, you will then survive (?) against the wicked.

208–212. You should not choose a wife during a festival. Her inside is illusory (?); her outside is illusory (?). The silver on her is borrowed; the lapis lazuli on her is borrowed. The dress on her is borrowed; the linen garment on her is borrowed. With [...] nothing (?) is comparable.

213–214. You should not buy a [...] bull. You should not buy a vicious bull; [...] a hole (?) in the cattle-pen [...].

215. One appoints (?) a reliable woman for a good household.

216–217. You should not buy a donkey at the time of harvest. A donkey which eats [...] will [...] with another donkey.

218–219. A vicious donkey hangs its neck; however, a vicious man, my son, [...]

220. A woman with her own property ruins the house.

221. A drunkard will drown the harvest.

222–234. A female burglar (?) [...] ladder; she flies into the houses like a fly. A she-donkey [...] on the street. A sow suckles its child on the street. A woman who pricked herself begins to cry and holds the spindle which pricked (?) her in her hand. She enters every house; she peers into all streets. [...] she keeps saying "Get out!" She looks around (?) from all parapets. She pants (?) where there is a quarrel.[...]

242–244. Nothing at all is to be valued, but life should be sweet. You should not serve things; things should serve you. My son, [...].

246–247. You should not abuse a ewe; otherwise you will give birth to a daughter. You should not throw a lump of earth into the money chest (?); otherwise you will give birth to a son.

248–249. You should not abduct a wife; you should not make her cry (?). The place where the wife is abducted to [...].

250–251. "Let us run in circles (?), saying: "Oh my foot, oh my neck!" Let us with united forces (?) make the mighty bow!"

252–253. You should not kill a [...], he is a child born by [...] You should not kill [...] like [...]; you should not bind him.

254. The wet-nurses in the women's quarters determine the fate of their lord.

255–260. You should not speak arrogantly to your mother; that causes hatred for you. You should not question the words of your mother and your personal god. The mother, like Utu, gives birth to the man; the father, like a god, makes him bright (?). The father is like a god: his words are reliable. The instructions of the father should be complied with.

261. Without suburbs a city has no centre either.

262–263. My son, a field situated at the bottom of the embankments, be it wet or dry, is nevertheless a source of income.

264. It is inconceivable (?) that something is lost forever. . . .

266–271. To get lost is bad for a dog; but terrible for a man. On the unfamiliar way at the edge of the mountains, the gods of the mountains are man-eaters. They do not build houses there as men do; they do not build cities there as men do. . . .

272–273. For the shepherd, he stopped searching, he stopped bringing back the sheep. For the farmer (?), he stopped ploughing the field. . . .

274–276. This gift of words is something which soothes the mind [...]; when it enters the palace, it soothes the mind [...] The gift of many words [...] stars.

277. These are the instructions given by Šuruppag, the son of Ubara-Tutu.

278–280. Praise be to the lady who completed the great tablets, the maiden Nisaba, that Šuruppag, the son of Ubara-Tutu, gave his instructions!

REVIEW QUESTIONS

1. What does this text suggest about the role and status of women in Sumerian society?
2. What does it suggest about sources of tension and conflict in ancient Mesopotamia?
3. Can you find parallels between ancient Sumerian social values and those we see in societies globally today?

FROM *The Epic of Gilgamesh*

With the exception of the Hebrew Bible, The Epic of Gilgamesh is the most celebrated literary work of the ancient Near East. Although Gilgamesh almost certainly was an actual ruler of the Sumerian city of Uruk in the early third millennium B.C.E., the Akkadian epic that developed around him (elements of which can be found in even earlier Sumerian stories about him) is most prized today not as a historical source for his era but as one of world literature's earliest and most profound statements on the human condition, and especially on the inescapability of human mortality. The epic also contains by far the most detailed account of the Flood that is to be found in Mesopotamian literature. (In fact, the discovery of a cuneiform tablet containing this story, with its obvious parallels to the story of Noah and the Flood in the biblical Book of Genesis, helped to foster continued archaeological expeditions to Iraq in the late nineteenth and early twentieth centuries.)

From *The Epic of Gilgamesh: A New Translation, Analogues, Criticism,* translated by Benjamin R. Foster (New York: Norton, 2001), pp. 77, 81–82, 84–91.

FROM **Tablet IX**

Gilgamesh was weeping bitterly for Enkidu, his friend,
As he roamed the steppe:

Shall I not die too? Am I not like Enkidu?
Oh woe has entered my vitals!
I have grown afraid of death, so I roam the steppe.
Having come this far, I will go on swiftly
Towards Utanapishtim, son of Ubar-Tutu.

[*To reach Utanapishtim, who corresponds to Atrahasis in the first reading in this chapter, Gilgamesh must undertake a dangerous journey that culmi-nates in a voyage by boat across a sea of lethal water. Finally, he reaches the far shore, where an amazed Utanapishtim has watched him coming.*]

*   *   *

FROM **Tablet X**

Utanapishtim said to him, to Gilgamesh:

Why are your cheeks emaciated, your face cast down,
Your heart wretched, your features wasted,
Woe in your vitals,
Your face like a traveler's from afar,
Your features weathered by cold and sun,

Why are you clad in a lion skin, roaming the steppe?

[Gilgamesh tells Utanapishtim his mission, wallowing in the luxury of self-pity on the difficulties of his quest.]

Gilgamesh said to him, to Utanapishtim:

> My cheeks would not be emaciated, nor my face cast down,
> Nor my heart wretched, nor my features wasted,
> Nor would there be woe in my vitals,
> Nor would my face be like a traveler's from afar,
> Nor would my features be weathered by cold and sun,
> Nor would I be clad in a lion skin, roaming the steppe,
> But for my friend, swift wild donkey, mountain onager, panther of the steppe,
> But for Enkidu, my friend, swift wild donkey, mountain onager, panther of the steppe,
> He who stood by me as we ascended the mountain,
> Seized and killed the bull that came down from heaven,
> Felled Humbaba who dwelt in the forest of cedars,
> Killed lions at the mountain passes,
> My friend whom I so loved, who went with me through every hardship,
> Enkidu, whom I so loved, who went with me through every hardship,
> The fate of mankind has overtaken him.
> Six days and seven nights I wept for him,
> I would not give him up for burial,
> Until a worm fell out of his nose.
> I was frightened [. . .]
> I have grown afraid of death, so I roam the steppe,
> My friend's case weighs heavy upon me.
> A distant road I roam over the steppe,
> My friend Enkidu's case weighs heavy upon me!
> A distant path I roam over the steppe,
> How can I be silent? How can I hold my peace?

> My friend whom I loved is turned into clay,
> Enkidu, my friend whom I loved, is turned into clay!
> Shall I too not lie down like him,
> And never get up, forever and ever?

Gilgamesh said to him, to Utanapishtim:

> So it is to go find Utanapishtim, whom they call the "Distant One,"
> I traversed all lands,
> I came over, one after another, wearisome mountains,
> Then I crossed, one after another, all the seas.
> Too little sweet sleep has smoothed my countenance,
> I have worn myself out in sleeplessness,
> My muscles ache for misery,
> What have I gained my trials?
> I had not reached the tavern keeper when my clothes were worn out,
> I killed bear, hyena, lion, panther, leopard, deer, ibex, wild beasts of the steppe,
> I ate their meat, I [. . .] their skins.
> Let them close behind me the doors of woe,
> [Let them seal them] with pitch and tar,
> For my part, I [. . .] no amusement,
> For me, [. . .]

Utanapishtim said to him, to Gilgamesh:

> Why, O Gilgamesh, did you prolong woe,
> You who are [formed] of the flesh of gods and mankind,
> You for whom [the gods] acted like fathers and mothers?

*   *   *

FROM **Tablet XI**

[Gilgamesh, whose search for Utanapishtin has been characterized by increasing violence, now finds to his astonishment that there is no battle to be fought; heroics will bring him no further. Now he needs knowledge. He asks Utanapishtim, the wisest man who ever lived, his great question: how

did he alone escape the universal fate of the human race?]

Gilgamesh said to him, to Utanapishtim the Distant One:

As I look upon you, Utanapishtim,
Your limbs are not different, you are just as I am.
Indeed, you are not different at all, you are just as I am!
Yet your heart is drained of battle spirit,
You lie flat on your back, your arm [idle].
You then, how did you join the ranks of the gods and find eternal life?

[In answer, Utanapishtim relates the story of the flood. According to Tablet I, among Gilgamesh's main achievements was bringing back to the human race this hitherto unknown history. The story as told here is abbreviated. In the fuller account, preserved in a Babylonian narrative poem called "Atrahasis," the gods sent the flood because the human race had multiplied to such an extent that their clamor was unbearable to Enlil, the chief god living on earth. After various attempts to reduce the population of the earth were thwarted by Enki (Ea), the god of wisdom and fresh water, Enlil ordered a deluge to obliterate the entire human race. At this point, Utanapishtim takes up the story. He lived at the long-vanished city of Shuruppak and was a favorite of the god Ea, who warned him of the flood, despite his oath not to reveal it. Ea circumvented this by addressing the wall of a reed enclosure Utanapishtim had built near water, perhaps as a place to receive dreams and commands from his god. Utanapishtim is ordered to build a boat. When his fellow citizens ask him what he is about, he is to reply in ambiguous language, foretelling a "shower of abundance" soon.]

Utanapishtim said to him, to Gilgamesh:

I will reveal to you, O Gilgamesh, a secret matter,
And a mystery of the gods I will tell you.
The city Shuruppak, a city you yourself have knowledge of,

Which once was set on the [bank] of the Euphrates,
That aforesaid city was ancient and gods once were within it.
The great gods resolved to send the deluge,
Their father Anu was sworn,
The counselor the valiant Enlil,
Their throne-bearer Ninurta,
Their canal-officer Ennugi,
Their leader Ea was sworn with them.
He repeated their plans to the reed fence:
"Reed fence, reed fence, wall, wall!
Listen, O reed fence! Pay attention, O wall!
O Man of Shuruppak, son of Ubara-Tutu,
Wreck house, build boat,
Forsake possessions and seek life,
Belongings reject and life save!
Take aboard the boat seed of all living things.
The boat you shall build,
Let her dimensions be measured out:
Let her width and length be equal,
Roof her over like the watery depths."
I understood full well, I said to Ea, my lord:
"Your command, my lord, exactly as you said it,
I shall faithfully execute.
What shall I answer the city, the populace, and the elders?"
Ea made ready to speak,
Saying to me, his servant:
"So, you shall speak to them thus:
'No doubt Enlil dislikes me,
I shall not dwell in your city.
I shall not set my foot on the dry land of Enlil,
I shall descend to the watery depths and dwell with my lord Ea.
Upon you he shall shower down in abundance,
A windfall of birds, a surprise of fishes,
He shall pour upon you a harvest of riches,
In the morning cakes in spates,
In the evening grains in rains.'"

[The entire community helps to build the boat. The hull is constructed before the interior framing, as was customary in the ancient world, with cordage used to sew the planks together and to truss the hull for strength. The boat is an enormous cube.

Utanapishtim, here referred to as "Atrahasis,"
loads on his family, his possessions, and every
type of animal, as well as skilled individuals to
keep alive knowledge of arts and crafts.]

At the first glimmer of dawn,
The land was assembling at the gate of
    Atrahasis:
The carpenter carried his axe,
The reed cutter carried his stone,
The old men brought cordage(?),
The young men ran around [. . .],
The wealthy carried the pitch,
The poor brought what was needed of [. . .].
In five days I had planked her hull:
One full acre was her deck space,
Ten dozen cubits, the height of each of her
    sides,
Ten dozen cubits square, her outer dimensions.
I laid out her structure, I planned her design:
I decked her in six,
I divided her in seven,
Her interior I divided in nine.
I drove the water plugs into her,
I saw to the spars and laid in what was needful.
Thrice thirty-six hundred measures of pitch I
    poured in the oven,
Thrice thirty-six hundred measures of tar
    [I poured out] inside her.
Thrice thirty-six hundred measures basket-
    bearers brought aboard for oil,
Not counting the thirty-six hundred measures
    of oil that the offering consumed,
And the twice thirty-six hundred measures of
    oil that the boatbuilders made off with.
For the [builders] I slaughtered bullocks,
I killed sheep upon sheep every day,
Beer, ale, oil, and wine
[I gave out] to the workers like river water,
They made a feast as on New Year's Day,
[. . .] I dispensed ointment with my own
    hand.
By the setting of Shamash, the ship was
    completed.
[Since boarding was(?)] very difficult,
They brought up gangplanks(?), fore and aft,

They came up her sides(?) two-thirds (of her
    height).
[Whatever I had] I loaded upon her:
What silver I had I loaded upon her,
What gold I had I loaded upon her,
What living creatures I had I loaded upon her,
I sent up on board all my family and kin,
Beasts of the steppe, wild animals of the steppe,
    all types of skilled craftsmen I sent up on
    board.
Shamash set for me the appointed time:
"In the morning, cakes in spates,
In the evening, grains in rains,
Go into your boat and caulk the door!"
That appointed time arrived,
In the morning cakes in spates,
In the evening grains in rains,
I gazed upon the face of the storm,
The weather was dreadful to behold!
I went into the boat and caulked the door.
To the caulker of the boat, to Puzur-Amurri the
    boatman,
I gave over the edifice, with all it contained.

[The flood, accompanied by thunder and a fiery
glow, overwhelms the earth. The gods are terrified
by its violence and what they have done.]

At the first glimmer of dawn,
A black cloud rose above the horizon.
Inside it Adad was thundering,
While the destroying gods Shullat and Hanish
    went in front,
Moving as an advance force over hill and plain.
Errakal tore out the mooring posts (of the
    world),
Ninurta came and made the dikes overflow.
The supreme gods held torches aloft,
Setting the land ablaze with their glow.
Adad's awesome power passed over the
    heavens,
Whatever was light was turned into darkness,
[He flooded] the land, he smashed it like a
    [clay pot]!
For one day the storm wind [blew],
Swiftly it blew, [the flood came forth],
It passed over the people like a battle,

No one could see the one next to him,
The people could not recognize one another in
  the downpour.
The gods became frightened of the deluge,
They shrank back, went up to Anu's highest
  heaven.
The gods cowered like dogs, crouching outside.
Ishtar screamed like a woman in childbirth,
And sweet-voiced Belet-ili wailed aloud:
"Would that day had come to naught,
When I spoke up for evil in the assembly of the
  gods!
How could I have spoken up for evil in the
  assembly of the gods,
And spoken up for battle to destroy my people?
It was I myself who brought my people into the
  world,
Now, like a school of fish, they choke up the
  sea!"
The supreme gods were weeping with her,
The gods sat where they were, weeping,
Their lips were parched, taking on a crust.
Six days and seven nights
The wind continued, the deluge and windstorm
  leveled the land.
When the seventh day arrived,
The windstorm and deluge left off their battle,
Which had struggled, like a woman in labor.
The sea grew calm, the tempest stilled, the
  deluge ceased.

*[As the floodwaters recede, Utanapishtim can see
land at the far horizon. The boat is caught on a
mountain.]*

I looked at the weather, stillness reigned,
And the whole human race had turned into
  clay.
The landscape was flat as a rooftop.
I opened the hatch, sunlight fell upon my face.
Falling to my knees, I sat down weeping,
Tears running down my face.
I looked at the edges of the world, the borders
  of the sea,
At twelve times sixty double leagues the
  periphery emerged.
The boat had come to rest on Mount Nimush,

Mount Nimush held the boat fast, not letting it
  move.
One day, a second day Mount Nimush held the
  boat fast, not letting it move.
A third day, a fourth day Mount Nimush held
  the boat fast, not letting it move.
A fifth day, a sixth day Mount Nimush held the
  boat fast, not letting it move.

*[Utanapishtim sends out three birds to see if land
has emerged near the boat. He then quits the boat
and makes an offering to the gods, who crowd
around it, famished.]*

When the seventh day arrived,
I brought out a dove and set it free.
The dove went off and returned,
No landing place came to its view, so it turned
  back.
I brought out a swallow and set it free,
The swallow went off and returned,
No landing place came to its view, so it turned
  back.
I brought out a raven and set it free,
The raven went off and saw the ebbing of the
  waters.
It ate, preened, left droppings, did not turn
  back.
I released all to the four directions,
I brought out an offering and offered it to the
  four directions.
I set up an incense offering on the summit of
  the mountain,
I arranged seven and seven cult vessels,
I heaped reeds, cedar, and myrtle in their
  bowls.
The gods smelled the savor,
The gods smelled the sweet savor,
The gods crowded round the sacrificer like flies.

*[The mother goddess blames Enlil for the flood,
saying her glittering necklace of fly-shaped beads,
which may stand for the rainbow, will memorialize
the human race drowned in the flood.]*

As soon as Belet-ili arrived,
She held up the great fly-ornaments that Anu
  had made in his ardor:

"O gods, these shall be my lapis necklace, lest
  I forget,
I shall be mindful of these days and not forget,
  not ever!
The gods should come to the incense offering,
But Enlil should not come to the incense
  offering,
For he, irrationally, brought on the flood,
And marked my people for destruction!"
As soon as Enlil arrived,
He saw the boat, Enlil flew into a rage,
He was filled with fury at the gods:
"Who came through alive? No man was to sur-
  vive destruction!"
Ninurta made ready to speak,
Said to the valiant Enlil:
"Who but Ea could contrive such a thing?
For Ea alone knows every artifice."

*[Ea's speech urges future limits. Punish but do not
kill; diminish but do not annihilate. He suggests
that in the future less drastic means than a flood
be used to reduce the human population. He
refers to Utanapishtim as Atrahasis, his name in
the independent Babylonian flood story. Enlil
grants Utanapishtim and his wife eternal life but
removes them far away from the rest of the
human race.]*

Ea made ready to speak,
Said to the valiant Enlil:
"You, O valiant one, are the wisest of the
  gods,
How could you, irrationally, have brought on
  the flood?
Punish the wrongdoer for his wrongdoing,
Punish the transgressor for his transgression,
But be lenient, lest he be cut off,
Bear with him, lest he [. . .].
Instead of your bringing on a flood,
Let the lion rise up to diminish the human race!
Instead of your bringing on a flood,
Let the wolf rise up to diminish the human
  race!
Instead of your bringing on a flood,
Let famine rise up to wreak havoc in the land!
Instead of your bringing on a flood,

Let pestilence rise up to wreak havoc in the
  land!
It was not I who disclosed the secret of the great
  gods,
I made Atrahasis have a dream and so he heard
  the secret of the gods.
Now then, make some plan for him."
Then Enlil came up into the boat,
Leading me by the hand, he brought me up
  too.
He brought my wife up and had her kneel
  beside me.
He touched our brows, stood between us to
  bless us:
"Hitherto Utanapishtim has been a human
  being,
Now Utanapishtim and his wife shall become
  like us gods.
Utanapishtim shall dwell far distant at the
  source of the rivers."
Thus it was that they took me far distant and
  had me dwell at the source of the rivers.
Now then, who will convene the gods for your
  sake,
That you may find the eternal life you seek?
Come, come, try not to sleep for six days and
  seven nights.

*[Utanapishtim has challenged Gilgamesh to go
without sleep for a week; if he fails this test, how
could he expect to live forever? Even as he speaks,
Gilgamesh drifts off to sleep.]*

As he sat there on his haunches,
Sleep was swirling over him like a mist.
Utanapishtim said to her, to his wife:

Behold this fellow who seeks eternal life!
Sleep swirls over him like a mist.

*[Utanapishtim's wife, taking pity on Gilgamesh,
urges her husband to awaken him and let him go
home. Utanapishtim insists on a proof of how
long he slept, lest Gilgamesh claim that he had
only dozed. She is to bake him fresh bread every
day and set it beside him, marking the wall for the
day. The bread spoils progressively as Gilgamesh
sleeps for seven days.]*

His wife said to him, to Utanapishtim the Distant
One:

> Do touch him that the man may wake up,
> That he may return safe on the way whence he
> came,
> That through the gate he came forth he may
> return to his land.

Utanapishtim said to her, to his wife:

> Since the human race is duplicitous, he'll
> endeavor to dupe you.
> Come, come, bake his daily loaves, put them
> one after another by his head,
> Then mark the wall for each day he has slept.

She baked his daily loaves for him, put them one
after another by his head,
Then dated the wall for each day he slept.
The first loaf was dried hard,
The second was leathery, the third soggy,
The crust of the fourth turned white,
The fifth was gray with mold, the sixth was fresh,
The seventh was still on the coals when he
touched him, the man woke up.

*[Gilgamesh wakes at last. Claiming at first that he
has scarcely dozed a moment, he sees the bread and
realizes that he has slept for the entire time he was
supposed to remain awake for the test. He gives up
in despair. What course is left for him? Utanapishtim does not answer directly but orders the boatman to take him home. Further, the boatman
himself is never to return. Thus access to Utanapishtim is denied the human race forever. Gilgamesh
is bathed and given clothing that will stay
magically fresh until his return to Uruk.]*

Gilgamesh said to him, to Utanapishtim the
Distant One:

> Scarcely had sleep stolen over me,
> When straightaway you touched me and
> roused me.

Utanapishtim said to him, to Gilgamesh:

> [Up with you], Gilgamesh, count your daily
> loaves,

[That the days you have slept] may be known to
you.
The first loaf is dried hard,
The second is leathery, the third soggy,
The crust of the fourth has turned white,
The fifth is gray with mold,
The sixth is fresh,
The seventh was still in the coals when I
touched you and you woke up.

Gilgamesh said to him, to Utanapishtim the
Distant One:

> What then should I do, Utanapishtim, whither
> should I go,
> Now that the Bereaver has seized my [flesh]?[1]
> Death lurks in my bedchamber,
> And wherever I turn, there is death!

Utanapishtim said to him, to Ur-Shanabi the
boatman:

> Ur-Shanabi, may the harbor [offer] you no [haven],
> May the crossing point reject you,
> Be banished from the shore you shuttled to.
> The man you brought here,
> His body is matted with filthy hair,
> Hides have marred the beauty of his flesh.
> Take him away, Ur-Shanabi, bring him to the
> washing place.
> Have him wash out his filthy hair with water,
> clean as snow,
> Have him throw away his hides, let the sea
> carry them off,
> Let his body be rinsed clean.
> Let his headband be new,
> Have him put on raiment worthy of him.
> Until he reaches his city,
> Until he completes his journey,
> Let his garments stay spotless, fresh and new.

Ur-Shanabi took him away and brought him to
the washing place.
He washed out his filthy hair with water, clean as
snow,

---

[1] "The Bereaver" is an epithet of death. It could also mean
something like "kidnapper."

He threw away his hides, the sea carried them off,
His body was rinsed clean.
He renewed his headband,
He put on raiment worthy of him.
Until he reached his city,
Until he completed his journey,
His garments would stay spotless, fresh and new.

[Gilgamesh and Ur-Shanabi embark on their journey to Uruk. As they push off from the shore, Utanapishtim's wife intervenes, asking her husband to give the hero something to show for his quest. Gilgamesh brings the boat back to shore and waits expectantly. Utanapishtim tells him of a plant of rejuvenation. Gilgamesh dives for the plant by opening a shaft through the earth's surface to the water below. He ties stones to his feet, a technique used in traditional pearl diving in the Gulf. When he comes up from securing the plant, he is on the opposite side of the ocean, where he started from.]

Gilgamesh and Ur-Shanabi embarked on the boat,
They launched the boat, they embarked upon it.
His wife said to him, to Utanapishtim the Distant
    One:

Gilgamesh has come here, spent with exertion,
What will you give him for his homeward
    journey?

At that he, Gilgamesh, lifted the pole,
Bringing the boat back by the shore.
Utanapishtim said to him, to Gilgamesh:

Gilgamesh, you have come here, spent with
    exertion,
What shall I give you for your homeward
    journey?
I will reveal to you, O Gilgamesh, a secret matter,
And a mystery of the gods I will tell you.
There is a certain plant, its stem is like a
    thornbush,
Its thorns, like the wild rose, will prick [your
    hand].
If you can secure this plant, [. . .]
[. . .]

No sooner had Gilgamesh heard this,
He opened a shaft, [flung away his tools].

He tied heavy stones [to his feet],
They pulled him down into the watery depths
    [. . .].
He took the plant though it pricked [his hand].
He cut the heavy stones [from his feet],
The sea cast him up on his home shore.

[Gilgamesh resolves to take the plant to Uruk to experiment on an old man. While Gilgamesh is bathing on the homeward journey, a snake eats the plant and rejuvenates itself by shedding its skin. Gilgamesh gives up. Immense quantities of water have flooded up through the shaft he dug and covered the place. He has left behind his tools so cannot dig another shaft. He has also lost the boat, so there is no going back.]

Gilgamesh said to him, to Ur-Shanabi the boatman:

Ur-Shanabi, this plant is cure for heartache,
Whereby a man will regain his stamina.
I will take it to ramparted Uruk,
I will have an old man eat some and so test the
    plant.
His name shall be "Old Man Has Become
    Young-Again-Man."
I myself will eat it and so return to my carefree
    youth.

At twenty double leagues they took a bite to eat,
At thirty double leagues they made their camp.

Gilgamesh saw a pond whose water was cool,
He went down into it to bathe in the water.
A snake caught the scent of the plant,
[Stealthily] it came up and carried the plant
    away,
On its way back it shed its skin.

Thereupon Gilgamesh sat down weeping,
His tears flowed down his face,
He said to Ur-Shanabi the boatman:

For whom, Ur-Shanabi, have my hands been
    toiling?
For whom has my heart's blood been poured
    out?
For myself I have obtained no benefit,
I have done a good deed for a reptile!

Now, floodwaters rise against me for twenty
    double leagues,
When I opened the shaft, I flung away the tools.
How shall I find my bearings?
I have come much too far to go back, and I
    abandoned the boat on the shore.

*[Upon completing his journey, Gilgamesh invites
Ur-Shanabi to inspect the walls of Uruk.]*

At twenty double leagues they took a bite to eat,
At thirty double leagues they made their camp.
When they arrived in ramparted Uruk,
Gilgamesh said to him, to Ur-Shanabi the
    boatman:

Go up, Ur-Shanabi, pace out the walls of Uruk.
Study the foundation terrace and examine the
    brickwork.
Is not its masonry of kiln-fired brick?

And did not seven masters lay its foundations?
One square mile of city, one square mile of
    gardens,
One square mile of clay pits, a half square mile of
    Ishtar's dwelling,
Three and a half square miles is the measure of
    Uruk!

*   *   *

REVIEW QUESTIONS

1. What kind of figure is Gilgamesh?
2. What becomes of his quest in this epic, and why?
3. What roles do the gods play in the story?
4. When his quest is completed, what is Gilgamesh's view of his fate?

FROM The Code of Hammurabi

Dating to the reign of Hammurabi of Babylon (the conventional dates for which are 1795–1750 B.C.E.), the laws of Hammurabi are not the earliest Mesopotamian compilation of legal rulings known to us. They are, however, the longest and most diverse collection and undoubtedly constitute the single most informative document yet discovered regarding concepts of justice and social regulation in Mesopotamian society. Hammurabi's laws also provide extremely important evidence about the status and rights of women of various social classes in Babylonian society in the early second millennium B.C.E.

From *Law Collections from Mesopotamia and Asia Minor*, edited by Martha T. Roth, SBL Writings from the Ancient World Series, vol. 6 (Atlanta, Ga.: Scholars Press, 1995), pp. 76–135.

When the august god Anu, king of the Anunnaku deities, and the god Enlil, lord of heaven and earth, who determines the destinies of the land, allotted supreme power over all peoples to the god Marduk, the firstborn son of the god Ea, exalted him among the Igigu deities, named the city of Babylon with its august name and made it supreme within the regions of the world, and established for him within it eternal kingship whose foundations are as fixed as heaven and earth, at that time, the gods Anu and Enlil, for the enhancement of the well-being of the people, named me by my name: Hammurabi, the pious prince, who venerates the gods, to make justice prevail in the land, to abolish the wicked and the evil, to prevent the strong from oppressing the weak, to rise like the sun-god Shamash over all humankind, to illuminate the land.

I am Hammurabi, the shepherd, selected by the god Enlil, he who heaps high abundance and plenty, who perfects every possible thing for the city Nippur, the city known as band-of-heaven-and-earth, the pious provider of the Ekur temple;

the capable king, the restorer of the city Eridu, the purifier of the rites of the Eabzu temple;

the onslaught of the four regions of the world, who magnifies the reputation of the city Babylon, who gladdens the heart of his divine lord Marduk, whose days are devoted to the Esagil temple;

*   *   *

When the god Marduk commanded me to provide just ways for the people of the land in order to attain appropriate behavior, I established truth and justice as the declaration of the land, I enhanced the well-being of the people.

*   *   *

1. If a man accuses another man and charges him with homicide but cannot bring proof against him, his accuser shall be killed.

*   *   *

2. If a man charges another man with practicing witchcraft but cannot bring proof against him, he who is charged with witchcraft shall go to the divine River Ordeal,[1] he shall indeed submit to the divine River Ordeal; if the divine River Ordeal should overwhelm him, his accuser shall take full legal possession of his estate; if the divine River

Ordeal should clear that man and should he survive, he who made the charge of witchcraft against him shall be killed; he who submitted to the divine River Ordeal shall take full legal possession of his accuser's estate.

3. If a man comes forward to give false testimony in a case but cannot bring evidence for his accusation, if that case involves a capital offense, that man shall be killed.

*   *   *

6. If a man steals valuables belonging to the god or to the palace, that man shall be killed, and also he who received the stolen goods from him shall be killed.

7. If a man should purchase silver, gold, a slave, a slave woman, an ox, a sheep, a donkey, or anything else whatsoever, from a son of a man or from a slave of a man without witnesses or a contract—or if he accepts the goods for safekeeping—that man is a thief, he shall be killed.

8. If a man steals an ox, a sheep, a donkey, a pig, or a boat—if it belongs either to the god or to the palace, he shall give thirtyfold; if it belongs to a commoner, he shall replace it tenfold; if the thief does not have anything to give, he shall be killed.

*   *   *

15. If a man should enable a palace slave, a palace slave woman, a commoner's slave, or a commoner's slave woman to leave through the main city-gate, he shall be killed.

16. If a man should harbor a fugitive slave or slave woman of either the palace or of a commoner in his house and not bring him out at the herald's public proclamation, that householder shall be killed.

17. If a man seizes a fugitive slave or slave woman in the open country and leads him back to his owner, the slave owner shall give him 2 shekels of silver.

18. If that slave should refuse to identify his owner, he shall lead him off to the palace, his circumstances shall be investigated, and they shall return him to his owner.

---

[1] The man would take an oath swearing to his innocence before the river god. He then would be required to plunge into the river. If he survived, he was deemed innocent; if he drowned, it was deemed the punishment of the river god, in whose name he had falsely sworn. [Editor]

19. If he should detain that slave in his own house and afterward the slave is discovered in his possession, that man shall be killed.

20. If the slave should escape the custody of the one who seized him, that man shall swear an oath by the god to the owner of the slave, and he shall be released.

21. If a man breaks into a house, they shall kill him and hang him in front of that very breach.

22. If a man commits a robbery and is then seized, that man shall be killed.

*   *   *

53. If a man neglects to reinforce the embankment of the irrigation canal of his field and does not reinforce its embankment, and then a breach opens in its embankment and allows the water to carry away the common irrigated area, the man in whose embankment the breach opened shall replace the grain whose loss he caused.

54. If he cannot replace the grain they shall sell him and his property, and the residents of the common irrigated area whose grain crops the water carried away shall divide (the proceeds).

55. If a man opens his branch of the canal for irrigation and negligently allows the water to carry away his neighbor's field, he shall measure and deliver grain in accordance with his neighbor's yield.

*   *   *

102. If a merchant should give silver to a trading agent for an investment venture, and he incurs a loss on his journeys, he shall return silver to the merchant in the amount of the capital sum.

103. If enemy forces should make him abandon whatever goods he is transporting while on his business trip, the trading agent shall swear an oath by the god and shall be released.

104. If a merchant gives a trading agent grain, wool, oil, or any other commodity for local transactions, the trading agent shall return to the merchant the silver for each transaction; the trading agent shall collect a sealed receipt for each payment in silver that he gives to the merchant.

105. If the trading agent should be negligent and not take a sealed receipt for each payment in silver that he gives to the merchant, any silver that is not documented in a sealed receipt will not be included in the final accounting.

*   *   *

108. If a woman innkeeper should refuse to accept grain for the price of beer but accepts only silver measured by the large weight, thereby reducing the value of beer in relation to the value of grain, they shall charge and convict that woman innkeeper and they shall cast her into the water.

109. If there should be a woman innkeeper in whose house criminals congregate, and she does not seize those criminals and lead them off to the palace authorities, that woman innkeeper shall be killed.

*   *   *

117. If an obligation is outstanding against a man and he sells or gives into debt service his wife, his son, or his daughter, they shall perform service in the house of their buyer or of the one who holds them in debt service for three years; their release shall be secured in the fourth year.

118. If he should give a male or female slave into debt service, the merchant may extend the term beyond the three years, he may sell him; there are no grounds for a claim.

119. If an obligation is outstanding against a man and he therefore sells his slave woman who has borne him children, the owner of the slave woman shall weigh and deliver the silver which the merchant weighed and delivered as the loan and he shall thereby redeem his slave woman.

*   *   *

128. If a man marries a wife but does not draw up a formal contract for her, she is not a wife.

129. If a man's wife should be seized lying with another male, they shall bind them and throw them into the water; if the wife's master allows his wife to live, then the king shall allow his subject (i.e., the other male) to live.

130. If a man pins down another man's virgin wife who is still residing in her father's house, and they seize him lying with her, that man shall be killed; that woman shall be released.

131. If her husband accuses his own wife of adultery, although she has not been seized lying with another male, she shall swear to her innocence by an oath by the god, and return to her house.

132. If a man's wife should have a finger pointed against her in accusation involving another male, although she has not been seized lying with another male, she shall submit to the divine River Ordeal for her husband.

*   *   *

134. If a man should be captured and there are not sufficient provisions in his house, his wife may enter another's house; that woman will not be subject to any penalty.

135. If a man should be captured and there are not sufficient provisions in his house, before his return his wife enters another's house and bears children, and afterwards her husband returns and gets back to his city, that woman shall return to her first husband; the children shall inherit from their father.

136. If a man deserts his city and flees, and after his departure his wife enters another's house—if that man then should return and seize his wife, because he repudiated his city and fled, the wife of the deserter will not return to her husband.

*   *   *

138. If a man intends to divorce his first-ranking wife who did not bear him children, he shall give her silver as much as was her bridewealth and restore to her the dowry that she brought from her father's house, and he shall divorce her.

139. If there is no bridewealth, he shall give her 60 shekels of silver as a divorce settlement.

140. If he is a commoner, he shall give her 20 shekels of silver.

141. If the wife of a man who is residing in the man's house should decide to leave, and she appropriates goods, squanders her household possessions, or disparages her husband, they shall charge

and convict her; and if her husband should declare his intention to divorce her, then he shall divorce her; neither her travel expenses, nor her divorce settlement, nor anything else shall be given to her. If her husband should not declare his intention to divorce her, then her husband may marry another woman and that first woman shall reside in her husband's house as a slave woman.

142. If a woman repudiates her husband, and declares, "You will not have marital relations with me"—her circumstances shall be investigated by the authorities of her city quarter, and if she is circumspect and without fault, but her husband is wayward and disparages her greatly, that woman will not be subject to any penalty; she shall take her dowry and she shall depart for her father's house.

143. If she is not circumspect but is wayward, squanders her household possessions, and disparages her husband, they shall cast that woman into the water.

*   *   *

150. If a man awards to his wife a field, orchard, house, or movable property, and makes out a sealed document for her, after her husband's death her children will not bring a claim against her; the mother shall give her estate to whichever of her children she loves, but she will not give it to an outsider.

151. If a woman who is residing in a man's house should have her husband agree by binding contract that no creditor of her husband shall seize her for his debts—if that man has a debt incurred before marrying that woman, his creditors will not seize his wife; and if that woman has a debt incurred before entering the man's house, her creditors will not seize her husband.

*   *   *

153. If a man's wife has her husband killed on account of (her relationship with) another male, they shall impale that woman.

154. If a man should carnally know his daughter, they shall banish that man from the city.

155. If a man selects a bride for his son and his son carnally knows her, after which he himself then lies with her and they seize him in the act, they shall bind that man and cast him into the water.

156. If a man selects a bride for his son and his son does not yet carnally know her, and he himself then lies with her, he shall weigh and deliver to her 30 shekels of silver; moreover, he shall restore to her whatever she brought from her father's house, and a husband of her choice shall marry her.

157. If a man, after his father's death, should lie with his mother, they shall burn them both.

158. If a man, after his father's death, should be discovered in the lap of the father's principal wife who had borne children, that man shall be disinherited from the paternal estate.

*   *   *

162. If a man marries a wife, she bears him children, and that woman then goes to her fate, her father shall have no claim to her dowry; her dowry belongs only to her children.

163. If a man marries a wife but she does not provide him with children, and that woman goes to her fate—if his father-in-law then returns to him the bridewealth that that man brought to his father-in-law's house, her husband shall have no claim to that woman's dowry; her dowry belongs only to her father's house.

*   *   *

169. If he should be guilty of a grave offense deserving the penalty of disinheritance by his father, they shall pardon him for his first one; if he should commit a grave offense a second time, the father may disinherit his son.

*   *   *

188. If a craftsman takes a young child to rear and then teaches him his craft, he will not be reclaimed.

189. If he should not teach him his craft, that rearling shall return to his father's house.

190. If a man should not reckon the young child whom he took and raised in adoption as equal with his children, that rearling shall return to his father's house.

191. If a man establishes his household by reckoning as equal with any future children the young child whom he took and raised in adoption, but afterwards he has children of his own and then decides to disinherit the rearling, that young child will not depart empty-handed; the father who raised him shall give him a one-third share of his property as his inheritance and he shall depart; he will not give him any property from field, orchard, or house.

*   *   *

195. If a child should strike his father, they shall cut off his hand.

196. If an *awīlu* should blind the eye of another *awīlu*, they shall blind his eye.[2]

197. If he should break the bone of another *awīlu*, they shall break his bone.

198. If he should blind the eye of a commoner or break the bone of a commoner, he shall weigh and deliver 60 shekels of silver.

199. If he should blind the eye of an *awīlu*'s slave or break the bone of an *awīlu*'s slave, he shall weigh and deliver one-half of his value in silver.

200. If an *awīlu* should knock out the tooth of another *awīlu* of his own rank, they shall knock out his tooth.

201. If he should knock out the tooth of a commoner, he shall weigh and deliver 20 shekels of silver.

202. If an *awīlu* should strike the cheek of an *awīlu* who is of status higher than his own, he shall be flogged in the public assembly with 60 stripes of an ox whip.

203. If a member of the *awīlu*-class should strike the cheek of another member of the *awīlu*-class who is his equal, he shall weigh and deliver 60 shekels of silver.

204. If a commoner should strike the cheek of another commoner, he shall weigh and deliver 10 shekels of silver.

---

[2] The most basic meaning of *awīlu* is "man." In this context it seems to represent a free man, probably an owner of private land and with a status higher than that of a "commoner." [Editor]

*   *   *

209. If an *awīlu* strikes a woman of the *awīlu*-class and thereby causes her to miscarry her fetus, he shall weigh and deliver 10 shekels of silver for her fetus.

210. If that woman should die, they shall kill his daughter.

211. If he should cause a woman of the commoner-class to miscarry her fetus by the beating, he shall weigh and deliver 5 shekels of silver.

212. If that woman should die, he shall weigh and deliver 30 shekels of silver.

*   *   *

218. If a physician performs major surgery with a bronze lancet upon an *awīlu* and thus causes the *awīlu*'s death, or opens an *awīlu*'s temple with a bronze lancet and thus blinds the *awīlu*'s eye, they shall cut off his hand.

219. If a physician performs major surgery with a bronze lancet upon a slave of a commoner and thus causes the slave's death, he shall replace the slave with a slave of comparable value.

220. If he opens his (the commoner's slave's) temple with a bronze lancet and thus blinds his eye, he shall weigh and deliver silver equal to half his value.

*   *   *

226. If a barber shaves off the slave-hairlock of a slave not belonging to him without the consent of the slave's owner, they shall cut off that barber's hand.

227. If a man misinforms a barber so that he then shaves off the slave-hairlock of a slave not belonging to him, they shall kill that man and hang him in his own doorway; the barber shall swear, "I did not knowingly shave it off," and he shall be released.

*   *   *

These are the just decisions which Hammurabi, the able king, has established and thereby has directed the land along the course of truth and the correct way of life.

I am Hammurabi, noble king. I have not been careless or negligent toward humankind, granted to my care by the god Enlil, and with whose shepherding the god Marduk charged me. I have sought for them peaceful places, I removed serious difficulties, I spread light over them. With the mighty weapon which the gods Zababa and Ishtar bestowed upon me, with the wisdom which the god Ea allotted to me, with the ability which the god Marduk gave me, I annihilated enemies everywhere, I put an end to wars, I enhanced the well-being of the land, I made the people of all settlements lie in safe pastures, I did not tolerate anyone intimidating them. The great gods having chosen me, I am indeed the shepherd who brings peace, whose scepter is just. My benevolent shade is spread over my city, I held the people of the lands of Sumer and Akkad safely on my lap. They prospered under my protective spirit, I maintained them in peace, with my skillful wisdom I sheltered them.

In order that the mighty not wrong the weak, to provide just ways for the waif and the widow, I have inscribed my precious pronouncements upon my stela and set it up before the statue of me, the king of justice, in the city of Babylon, the city which the gods Anu and Enlil have elevated, within the Esagil, the temple whose foundations are fixed as are heaven and earth, in order to render the judgments of the land, to give the verdicts of the land, and to provide just ways for the wronged.

REVIEW QUESTIONS

1. Of the hundreds of records of litigation that exist from the era of Hammurabi and his successors, not one specifically states that a dispute was resolved in accordance with Hammurabi's laws; some, in fact, record rulings that directly contradict those laws. This has caused some scholars to question why Hammurabi had these laws compiled in the first place. Why do you think Hammurabi had his laws compiled? (Do the prologue and epilogue to the laws provide any clues?)

2. What principles of justice and compensation are evident in these laws, and what kinds of recourse did society have against wrongdoers?
3. What evidence of social classes in Babylonian society do they provide?

4. How did women's rights compare with those of men?
5. What do these laws tell us about Mesopotamian views on sexual activity?
6. What do they tell us about power and authority within Mesopotamian families?

Letters of Royal Women of the Old Babylonian Period

Women's voices are all too infrequently heard in the documents of ancient Mesopotamia. But archeological excavations have recovered major portions of the palace archives (dating to the early second millennium B.C.E.) of the northern Mesopotamian cities of Mari and Karana, including cuneiform tablets containing letters to and from women of the royal houses of both places.

From *Mari and Karana: Two Old Babylonian Cities,* by Stephanie Dalley (Glenview, Ill.: Addison-Wesley Longman, 1984), pp. 104–9.

*   *   *

Speak to Iltani, thus Yasitna-abum your son. May Shamash and Marduk grant that my mother live forever for my sake. My mother called my name, and my heart came alive. Now, do send me a letter saying how you are, and give me new life. Whenever I reread your letter, the duststorms of Adad are forgotten; my heart is replenished with life. The servant boy whom my mother sent to me is far too young. For that servant boy does not keep *me* regularly supplied; it is I who have to keep *him* regularly supplied! Whenever I go on a journey, not even so much as 2 litres of bread for my ration is carried behind me. May my mother send me another servant boy who will be able to carry 10 litres of bread for my ration behind me, and who will be able really to help.

*   *   *

Speak to my lady; thus Belassunu. Ever since the harvest I have written frequently to you, but you have never sent me a reply of any kind. The king had spoken to me saying, "Stay in Zarbat. As soon as I come, Usi-nawir will come with me, and he will let you plead your innocence." Now, why are you silent? He neither lets me plead my innocence nor lets me go. You are near the ruler where you are: write, that they may take me back to the ruler. What have I done wrong? Why have you frowned upon me, and not pleaded my cause? Who will deal with the matter, and who has turned to help me?

*   *   *

Speak to my lord; thus Iltani thy servant. My lord wrote to me about letting go the oxen, sheep and donkeys belonging to Tazabru, saying: "If you do not let them go, I shall cut you into twelve pieces." That is what my lord wrote to me. Why has my lord written my death sentence to me? Only yesterday I spoke to my lord saying it was his own shepherd who had in the past kept his oxen and his sheep; he was pasturing them in Yashibatum. That is what I told my lord. Now, let my lord simply write that they are to take his oxen and sheep away from Yashibatum. If I have taken any of his oxen or sheep, may my lord inflict the punishment on me. Would I, without my lord's permission, would I have laid hands on and taken anything? Why then has my lord written my death sentence?

*   *   *

Speak to Iltani, my sister; thus Lamassani. I am well. The caravan comes regularly. You have never written to me to say how you are. I am still looking for a necklace of lapis lazuli, for which you wrote to me, and I shall send you a serving woman with it, but until now I have not found what you wrote for, and so I have not yet sent a slavegirl. Are you not aware that I am receiving short rations of barley? For in the city of Ashur, barley is expensive and linseed oil is expensive. Your son Sin-rimeni often comes and goes, but you have never mentioned me to him; you have not heaped honour on my head in the household where I am staying. As you must be aware, I am receiving short rations: please provide me with barley and linseed oil.

*   *   *

Speak to Iltani my sister, thus Amat-Shamash your sister. May my divine lord and lady grant that you live forever for my sake. Previously when Aqba-hammu came to Sippar I gave him cause to honour my priessthood, and he honoured me greatly, for he said to me: "When I go back to Karana, write to me and I shall send you a boat full of whatever you need. Offer a prayer for me to your divine lord." Now, I have written, and he has provided me with two servants. But you have not recalled my name; you never even sent me so much as a single jar of perfume; you never said: "Approach and offer a prayer for me to your divine lady." Instead you say: "What do you think I am for?" Apart from you, does a girl who has washed her husband's feet for

one day not send her own sister provisions from then onwards? And the slaves whom my father gave me have grown old. Now, I have sent half a mina of silver to the king. Allow me my claim, and let him send to me slaves that have been captured recently, and who are trustworthy. Now, in recollection of you, I have sent to you five minas of first-rate wool and a basket of "shrimps."

*   *   *

Speak to the lady my mother, thus Erishti-Aya your daughter. May my divine lord and lady grant you long life for my sake. Why didn't you ever wear my dress, but sent it back to me, and made me dishonoured and accursed? I am your daughter, and you are the wife of a king. . . . Your husband and you put me into the cloister; but the soldiers who were taken captive pay me more respect than you! You should pay me respect, and then my divine lord and lady will honour you with the good opinion of the city and its inhabitants. I am sending you a nanny. Do send me something to make me happy, and then I will be happy. Don't neglect me.

*   *   *

Speak to my star, my father and my lord, thus your daughter Kiru. It really was a sign when I spoke to you in the courtyard saying: "You are going away, and so you will not be able to direct the country; the country will become hostile behind you." That is what I said to my father and lord, but he didn't listen to me. . . . Now, if I am truly a woman, may my lord and father pay heed to my words—I am always writing the words of the gods to my father!

*   *   *

About my worries I have written twice to my lord, and my lord has written to me saying: "Go into Ashlakka and don't cry." My lord wrote that to me, and now I have entered Ashlakka and my worries have been fully justified! The wife of Ibal-Addu is queen all right; that woman takes it upon herself to receive personally every delivery for Ashlakka city and its towns. She made me sit in a corner holding my head in my hands like any idiot woman.

Food and drink were regularly put in front of her, while my eyes envied and my mouth watered. She put a strong guard on me, and took no notice at all of appeals in my lord's name. So my fears have been fulfilled here . . . May my lord send someone to fetch me back to my lord, that I may look upon my lord's face.

*   *   *

REVIEW QUESTIONS

1. What kinds of roles and responsibilities did these women have? What needs and concerns do they seem most eager to communicate?
2. What were their relationships with the other members of their families and households?
3. What do these sources reveal about daily life in ancient Mesopotamia?

FROM The Instruction of Ptah-Hotep

In contrast to ancient Mesopotamian laws, no ancient Egyptian law code has survived, although various texts suggest that laws did indeed exist. This document, however, provides an excellent description of proper behavior in personal relations and, implicitly, a sense of Egyptian social values, at least among the elite. Dating perhaps as early as the late Old Kingdom, this text is presented as the instructions of the vizier (the most important royal official under the king himself), Ptah-hotep, to his son.

From *Ancient Egyptian Literature, Vol. I: The Old and Middle Kingdoms,* by Miriam Lichtheim (Berkeley: University of California Press, 1973), pp. 205–9.

Instruction of the Mayor of the city, the Vizier Ptahhotep, under the Majesty of King Isesi, who lives for all eternity. The mayor of the city, the vizier Ptahhotep, said:

O king, my lord!
Age is here, old age arrived,
Feebleness came, weakness grows,
Childlike one sleeps all day.
Eyes are dim, ears deaf,
Strength is waning through weariness,
The mouth, silenced, speaks not,
The heart, void, recalls not the past,
The bones ache throughout.
Good has become evil, all taste is gone,
What age does to people is evil in everything.
The nose, clogged, breathes not,
Painful are standing and sitting.

May this servant be ordered to make a staff of old
   age,
So as to tell him the words of those who heard,
The ways of the ancestors,
Who have listened to the gods.
May such be done for you,
So that strife may be banned from the people,
And the Two Shores may serve you!
Said the majesty of this god:
Instruct him then in the sayings of the past,
May he become a model for the children of the
   great,
May obedience enter him,
And the devotion of him who speaks to him,
No one is born wise.

   Beginning of the formulations of excellent discourse spoken by the Prince, Count, God's Father,

God's beloved, Eldest Son of the King, of his body, Mayor of the city and Vizier, Ptahhotep, in instructing the ignorant in knowledge and in the standard of excellent discourse, as profit for him who will hear, as woe to him who would neglect them. He spoke to his son:

1.   Don't be proud of your knowledge,
     Consult the ignorant and the wise;
     The limits of art are not reached,
     No artist's skills are perfect;
     Good speech is more hidden than
         greenstone,
     Yet may be found among maids at the
         grindstones.

2.   If you meet a disputant in action,
     A powerful man, superior to you,
     Fold your arms, bend your back,
     To flout him will not make him agree with
         you.
     Make little of the evil speech
     By not opposing him while he's in action;
     He will be called an ignoramus,
     Your self-control will match his pile of
         words.

3.   If you meet a disputant in action
     Who is your equal, on your level,
     You will make your worth exceed his by
         silence,
     While he is speaking evilly,
     There will be much talk by the hearers,
     Your name will be good in the mind of the
         magistrates.

4.   If you meet a disputant in action,
     A poor man, not your equal,
     Do not attack him because he is weak,
     Let him alone, he will confute himself.
     Do not answer him to relieve your heart,
     Do not vent yourself against your opponent,
     Wretched is he who injures a poor man,
     One will wish to do what you desire,
     You will beat him through the magistrates'
         reproof.

5.   If you are a man who leads,
     Who controls the affairs of the many,
     Seek out every beneficent deed,
     That your conduct may be blameless.
     Great is justice, lasting in effect,
     Unchallenged since the time of Osiris.
     One punishes the transgressor of laws,
     Though the greedy overlooks this;
     Baseness may seize riches,
     Yet crime never lands its wares;
     In the end it is justice that lasts,
     Man says: "It is my father's ground."

6.   Do not scheme against people,
     God punishes accordingly:
     If a man says: "I shall live by it,"
     He will lack bread for his mouth.
     If a man says: "I shall be rich,"
     He will have to say: "My cleverness has
         snared me."
     If he says: "I will snare for myself,"
     He will be unable to say: "I snared for my
         profit."
     If a man says: "I will rob someone,"
     He will end being given to a stranger.
     People's schemes do not prevail,
     God's command is what prevails;
     Live then in the midst of peace,
     What they give comes by itself.

7.   If you are one among guests
     At the table of one greater than you,
     Take what he gives as it is set before you;
     Look at what is before you,
     Don't shoot many glances at him,
     Molesting him offends the *ka*.[1]
     Don't speak to him until he summons,
     One does not know what may displease;
     Speak when he has addressed you,
     Then your words will please the heart.
     The nobleman, when he is behind food,
     Behaves as his *ka* commands him;
     He will give to him whom he favors,

---

[1] The term *ka* represents a complex concept linked to an individual's life force.

It is the custom when night has come.
It is the *ka* that makes his hands reach out,
The great man gives to the chosen man;
Thus eating is under the counsel of god,
A fool is who complains of it.

8. If you are a man of trust,
Sent by one great man to another,
Adhere to the nature of him who sent you,
Give his message as he said it.
Guard against reviling speech,
Which embroils one great with another;
Keep to the truth, don't exceed it,
But an outburst should not be repeated.
Do not malign anyone,
Great or small, the *ka* abhors it.

9. If you plow and there's growth in the field,
And god lets it prosper in your hand,
Do not boast at your neighbors' side,
One has great respect for the silent man:
Man of character is man of wealth.
If he robs he is like a crocodile in court.
Don't impose on one who is childless,
Neither decry nor boast of it;
There is many a father who has grief,
And a mother of children less content than
  another;
It is the lonely whom god fosters,
While the family man prays for a follower.

10. If you are poor, serve a man of worth,
That all your conduct may be well with the
  god.
Do not recall if he once was poor,
Don't be arrogant toward him
For knowing his former state;
Respect him for what has accrued to him,
For wealth does not come by itself.
It is their law for him whom they love,
His gain, he gathered it himself;
It is the god who makes him worthy
And protects him while he sleeps.

11. Follow your heart as long as you live,
Do no more than is required,

Do not shorten the time of
  "follow-the-heart,"
Trimming its moment offends the *ka*.
Don't waste time on daily cares
Beyond providing for your household;
When wealth has come, follow your heart,
Wealth does no good if one is glum!

12. If you are a man of worth
And produce a son by the grace of god,
If he is straight, takes after you,
Takes good care of your possessions,
Do for him all that is good,
He is your son, your *ka* begot him,
Don't withdraw your heart from him.
But an offspring can make trouble:
If he strays, neglects your counsel,
Disobeys all that is said,
His mouth spouting evil speech,
Punish him for all his talk!
They hate him who crosses you,
His guilt was fated in the womb;
He whom they guide can not go wrong,
Whom they make boatless can not cross.

13. If you are in the antechamber,
Stand and sit as fits your rank,
Which was assigned you the first day.
Do not trespass—you will be turned back,
Keen is the face to him who enters
  announced,
Spacious the seat of him who has been
  called.
The antechamber has a rule,
All behavior is by measure;
It is the god who gives advancement,
He who uses elbows is not helped.

14. If you are among the people,
Gain supporters through being trusted;
The trusted man who does not vent his
  belly's speech,
He will himself become a leader.
A man of means—what is he like?
Your name is good, you are not maligned,
Your body is sleek, your face benign,

One praises you without your knowing.
He whose heart obeys his belly
Puts contempt of himself in place of love,
His heart is bald, his body unanointed;
The great-hearted is god-given,
He who obeys his belly belongs to the enemy.

15.   Report your commission without faltering,
Give your advice in your master's council.
If he is fluent in his speech,
It will not be hard for the envoy to report,
Nor will he be answered, "Who is he to
    know it?"
As to the master, his affairs will fail
If he plans to punish him for it,
He should be silent upon hearing: "I have
    told."

16.   If you are a man who leads,
Whose authority reaches wide,
You should do outstanding things,
Remember the day that comes after.
No strife will occur in the midst of honors,
But where the crocodile enters hatred
    arises.

17.   If you are a man who leads,
Listen calmly to the speech of one who
    pleads;
Don't stop him from purging his body
Of that which he planned to tell.
A man in distress wants to pour out his
    heart
More than that his case be won.
About him who stops a plea
One says: "Why does he reject it?"
Not all one pleads for can be granted,
But a good hearing soothes the heart.

18.   If you want friendship to endure
In the house you enter
As master, brother, or friend,
In whatever place you enter,
Beware of approaching the women!
Unhappy is the place where it is done,
Unwelcome is he who intrudes on them.

A thousand men are turned away from their
    good:
A short moment like a dream,
Then death comes for having known them.
Poor advice is "shoot the opponent,"
When one goes to do it the heart rejects it.
He who fails through lust of them,
No affair of his can prosper.

19.   If you want a perfect conduct,
To be free from every evil,
Guard against the vice of greed:
A grievous sickness without cure,
There is no treatment for it.
It embroils fathers, mothers,
And the brothers of the mother,
It parts wife from husband;
It is a compound of all evils,
A bundle of all hateful things.
That man endures whose rule is rightness,
Who walks a straight line;
He will make a will by it,
The greedy has no tomb.

20.   Do not be greedy in the division,
Do not covet more than your share;
Do not be greedy toward your kin,
The mild has a greater claim than the harsh.
Poor is he who shuns his kin,
He is deprived of interchange.
Even a little of what is craved
Turns a quarreler into an amiable man.

21.   When you prosper and found your house,
And love your wife with ardor,
Fill her belly, clothe her back,
Ointment soothes her body.
Gladden her heart as long as you live,
She is a fertile field for her lord.
Do not contend with her in court,
Keep her from power, restrain her—
Her eye is her storm when she gazes—
Thus will you make her stay in your house.

22.   Sustain your friends with what you have,
You have it by the grace of god;
Of him who fails to sustain his friends

One says, "a selfish *ka*."
One plans the morrow but knows not what
    will be,
The right *ka* is the *ka* by which one is
    sustained.
If praiseworthy deeds are done,
Friends will say, "welcome!"
One does not bring supplies to town,
One brings friends when there is need.

23.   Do not repeat calumny,
    Nor should you listen to it,
    It is the spouting of the hot-bellied.
    Report a thing observed, not heard,
    If it is negligible, don't say anything,
    He who is before you recognizes worth.
    If a seizure is ordered and carried out,
    Hatred will arise against him who seizes;
    Calumny is like a dream against which one
       covers the face.

24.   If you are a man of worth
    Who sits in his master's council,
    Concentrate on excellence,
    Your silence is better than chatter.
    Speak when you know you have a solution,
    It is the skilled who should speak in council;
    Speaking is harder than all other work,
    He who understands it makes it serve.

25.   If you are mighty, gain respect through
      knowledge
    And through gentleness of speech.
    Don't command except as is fitting,
    He who provokes gets into trouble.
    Don't be haughty, lest you be humbled,
    Don't be mute, lest you be chided.
    When you answer one who is fuming,
    Avert your face, control yourself.
    The flame of the hot-heart sweeps across,
    He who steps gently, his path is paved.
    He who frets all day has no happy moment,
    He who's gay all day can't keep house.

26.   Don't oppose a great man's action,
    Don't vex the heart of one who is burdened;

If he gets angry at him who foils him,
The *ka* will part from him who loves him.
Yet he is the provider along with the god,
What he wishes should be done for him.
When he turns his face back to you after
    raging,
There will be peace from his *ka;*
As ill will comes from opposition,
So goodwill increases love.

27.   Teach the great what is useful to him,
    Be his aid before the people;
    If you let his knowledge impress his lord,
    Your sustenance will come from his *ka*.
    As the favorite's belly is filled,
    So your back will be clothed by it,
    And his help will be there to sustain you.
    For your superior whom you love
    And who lives by it,
    He in turn will give you good support.
    Thus will love of you endure
    In the belly of those who love you,
    He is a *ka* who loves to listen.

28.   If you are a magistrate of standing,
    Commissioned to satisfy the many,
    Hew a straight line.
    When you speak don't lean to one side,
    Beware lest one complain:
    "Judges, he distorts the matter!"
    And your deed turns into a judgment of you.

29.   If you are angered by a misdeed,
    Lean toward a man on account of his
      rightness;
    Pass it over, don't recall it,
    Since he was silent to you the first day.

30.   If you are great after having been humble,
    Have gained wealth after having been poor
    In the past, in a town which you know,
    Knowing your former condition,
    Do not put trust in your wealth,
    Which came to you as gift of god;
    So that you will not fall behind one like you,
    To whom the same has happened.

31. Bend your back to your superior,
Your overseer from the palace;
Then your house will endure in its wealth,
Your rewards in their right place.
Wretched is he who opposes a superior,
One lives as long as he is mild,
Baring the arm does not hurt it.
Do not plunder a neighbor's house,
Do not steal the goods of one near you,
Lest he denounce you before you are heard.
A quarreler is a mindless person,
If he is known as an aggressor
The hostile man will have trouble in the
neighborhood.

*   *   *

33. If you probe the character of a friend,
Don't inquire, but approach him,
Deal with him alone,
So as not to suffer from his manner.
Dispute with him after a time,
Test his heart in conversation;
If what he has seen escapes him,
If he does a thing that annoys you,
Be yet friendly with him, don't attack,
Be restrained, don't let fly,
Don't answer with hostility,
Neither part from him nor attack him;
His time does not fail to come,
One does not escape what is fated.

34. Be generous as long as you live,
What leaves the storehouse does not
return;
It is the food to be shared which is coveted,
One whose belly is empty is an accuser;
One deprived becomes an opponent,
Don't have him for a neighbor.
Kindness is a man's memorial
For the years after the function.

35. Know your helpers, then you prosper,
Don't be mean toward your friends,
They are one's watered field,
And greater then one's riches,
For what belongs to one belongs to another.

The character of a son-of-man is profit to
him;
Good nature is a memorial.

36. Punish firmly, chastise soundly,
Then repression of crime becomes an
example;
Punishment except for crime
Turns the complainer into an enemy.

37. If you take to wife a *špnt*[2]
Who is joyful and known by her town,
If she is fickle and likes the moment,
Do not reject her, let her eat,
The joyful brings happiness.

Epilogue

If you listen to my sayings,
All your affairs will go forward;
In their truth resides their value,
Their memory goes on in the speech of men,
Because of the worth of their precepts;
If every word is carried on,
They will not perish in this land.
If advice is given for the good,
The great will speak accordingly;
It is teaching a man to speak to posterity,
He who hears it becomes a master-hearer;
It is good to speak to posterity,
It will listen to it.

If a good example is set by him who leads,
He will be beneficent for ever,
His wisdom being for all time.
The wise feeds his *ba*[3] with what endures,
So that it is happy with him on earth.
The wise is known by his wisdom,
The great by his good actions;
His heart matches his tongue,
His lips are straight when he speaks;

---

[2] No single translation of *špnt* has been agreed upon.
[3] Like *ka*, the term *ba* is a complex concept intimately
related to one's individuality. It is somewhat analogous
to our concept of "soul."

He has eyes that see,
His ears are made to hear what will profit his
    son,
Acting with truth he is free of falsehood.
Useful is hearing to a son who hears;
If hearing enters the hearer,
The hearer becomes a listener,
Hearing well is speaking well.
Useful is hearing to one who hears,
Hearing is better than all else,
It creates good will.
How good for a son to grasp his father's words,
He will reach old age through them.

He who hears is beloved of god,
He whom god hates does not hear.
The heart makes of its owner a hearer or
    non-hearer,
Man's heart is his life-prosperity-health!
The hearer is one who hears what is said,
He who loves to hear is one who does what is
    said.
How good for a son to listen to his father,
How happy is he to whom it is said:
"The son, he pleases as a master of hearing."
The hearer of whom this is said,
He is well-endowed
And honored by his father;
His remembrance is in the mouth of the living,
Those on earth and those who will be.

If a man's son accepts his father's words,
No plan of his will go wrong.
Teach your son to be a hearer,
One who will be valued by the nobles;
One who guides his speech by what he was told,
One regarded as a hearer.
This son excels, his deeds stand out,
While failure follows him who hears not.
The wise wakes early to his lasting gain,
While the fool is hard pressed.

The fool who does not hear,
He can do nothing at all;
He sees knowledge in ignorance,
    Usefulness in harmfulness.

He does all that one detests
And is blamed for it each day;
He lives on that by which one dies,
His food is distortion of speech.
His sort is known to the officials,
Who say: "A living death each day."
One passes over his doings,
Because of his many daily troubles.

A son who hears is a follower of Horus,
It goes well with him when he has heard.
When he is old, has reached veneration,
He will speak likewise to his children,
Renewing the teaching of his father.
Every man teaches as he acts,
He will speak to the children,
So that they will speak to their children:
Set an example, don't give offense,
If justice stands firm your children will live.

                *   *   *

Conceal your heart, control your mouth,
Then you will be known among the officials;
Be quite exact before your lord,
Act so that one will say to him: "He's the son of
    that one."
And those who hear it will say:
"Blessed is he to whom he was born!"
Be deliberate when you speak,
So as to say things that count;
Then the officials who listen will say:
"How good is what comes from his mouth!"
Act so that your lord will say of you:
"How good is he whom his father taught;
When he came forth from his body,
He told him all that was in his mind,
And he does even more than he was told."

Lo, the good son, the gift of god,
Exceeds what is told him by his lord,
He will do right when his heart is straight.
As you succeed me, sound in your body,
The king content with all that was done,
May you obtain many years of life!
Not small is what I did on earth,

I had one hundred and ten years of life
As gift of the king,
Honors exceeding those of the ancestors,
By doing justice for the king,
Until the state of veneration!

*   *   *

1. According to Ptah-hotep, what are the most important virtues in proper human relations?
2. Are those virtues to be applied differently to people of different rank and social class?
3. How much importance is ascribed to the ability to fight physically?

FROM The Book of the Dead

Beginning in the late Old Kingdom, there were inscribed on the walls of the interior chambers of pyramids magical texts that were intended to ensure that the deceased king passed successfully into the next life. In the following centuries, these so-called Pyramid Texts were developed further, and the possibility of proceeding into the next world became less exclusively focused on the king and his immediate family and more inclusive of Egyptians of lesser rank (what some scholars have referred to as the "democratization of death"). From this process emerged the collection of texts that has come to be known (erroneously) as The Book of the Dead. *The following selection has been referred to as the "Protestation of Guiltlessness" or the "Negative Confession." It was to be recited by the deceased as he or she appeared for judgment before the god Osiris and his entourage.*

From *Ancient Near Eastern Texts Relating to the Old Testament*, edited by James B. Pritchard, translated by H. L. Ginsberg (3d ed.; Princeton, N.J.: Princeton University Press, 1969).

*   *   *

What is said on reaching the Broad-Hall of the Two Justices, absolving X [the deceased] of every sin which he has committed, and seeing the faces of the gods:

Hail to thee, O great god, lord of the Two Justices! I have come to thee, my lord, I have been brought that I might see thy beauty. I know thee; I know thy name and the names of the forty-two gods who are with thee in the Broad-Hall of the Two Justices, who live on them who *preserve* evil and who drink their blood on that day of reckoning up character in the presence of Wennofer. Behold, "*Sati-mertifi*, Lord of Justice," is thy name.

I have come to thee; I have brought thee justice; I have expelled deceit for thee.

I have not committed evil against men.
I have not mistreated cattle.
I have not committed sin in the place of truth.
I have not known that which is not.
I have not seen evil. . . .
My name has not reached the Master of the Barque.
I have not blasphemed a god.
I have not *done violence to* a poor man.
I have not done that which the gods abominate.
I have not defamed a slave to his superior.

I have not made anyone sick.

I have not made anyone weep.

I have not killed.

I have given no order to a killer.

I have not caused anyone suffering.

I have not cut down on the food-income in the temples.

I have not damaged the bread of the gods.

I have not taken the loaves of the blessed dead.

I have not had sexual relations with a boy.

I have not defiled myself.

I have neither increased or diminished the grain-measure.

I have not diminished the *aroura*.

I have not falsified a half-*aroura* of land.

I have not added to the weight of the balance.

I have not *weakened* the plummet of the scales.

I have not taken milk from the mouths of children.

I have not driven cattle away from their pasturage.

I have not snared the birds *of* the gods.

I have not caught fish in their marshes.

I have not held up the water in its season.

I have not built a dam against running water.

I have not quenched a fire at its proper time.

I have not neglected the appointed times and their meat-offerings.

I have not driven away the cattle of the god's property.

I have not stopped a god on his procession.

I am pure!—four times. My purity is the purity of that great *benu*-bird which is in Herakleopolis, because I am really that nose of the Lord of Breath, who makes all men to live, on that day of filling out the Eye of Horus in Heliopolis, in the second month of the second season, the last day, in the presence of the lord of this land. I am the one who has seen the filling out of the Eye in Heliopolis. Evil will never happen to me in this land or in this Broad-Hall of the Two Justices, because I know the names of these gods who are in it, the followers of the great god.

O Wide-of-Stride, who comes forth from Heliopolis, I have not committed evil.

O Embracer-of-Fire, who comes forth from Babylon, I have not stolen.

O Nosey, who comes forth from Hermopolis, I have not been covetous.

O Swallower-of-Shadows, who comes forth from the pit, I have not robbed.

O Dangerous-of-Face, who came forth from *Rostau,* I have not killed men.

O *Ruti,* who comes forth from heaven, I have not damaged the grain-measure.

O His-Eyes-are-of-Flint, who comes forth from the shrine, I have not caused *crookedness.*

O Flamer, who comes forth *backward,* I have not stolen the property of a god.

O Breaker-of-Bones, who comes forth from Herakleopolis, I have not told lies.

O *Commander-of-Fire,* who comes forth from Memphis, I have not taken away food.

O Dweller-in-the-Pit, who comes forth from the west, I have not been contentious.

O White-of-Teeth, who comes forth from the Faiyum, I have not trespassed.

O Eater-of-Blood, who comes forth from the execution-block, I have not slain the cattle of the god.

O Eater-of-Entrails, who comes forth from the Thirty, I have not *practised usury.*

O Lord-of-Justice, who comes forth from *Ma'ati,* I have not stolen the *bread-ration.*

O Wanderer, who comes forth from Bubastis, I have not *gossiped.*

O *Aadi,* who comes forth from Heliopolis, my mouth has not gone on unchecked.

O *Djudju*-serpent, who comes forth from Busiris, I have not argued with *some one summoned because of* his property.

O *Wamemti*-serpent, who comes forth from the place of judgment, I have not committed adultery.

O *Maa-Intef,* who comes forth from the Temple of Min, I have not defiled myself.

O Superior-of-the-Nobles, who comes forth from *Imau,* I have not caused terror.

O Wrecker, who comes forth from *the Saite Nome,* I have not trespassed.

O Mischief-Maker, who comes forth from the sanctuary, I have not been overheated.

O Child, who comes forth from the Heliopolitan Nome, I have not been unresponsive to a matter of justice.

O *Ser-kheru,* who comes forth from *Wensi,* I have not been quarrelsome.

O Bastet, who comes forth from the sanctum, I have not winked.

O His-Face-Behind-Him, who comes forth from *Tep-het-djat,* I have not *been perverted;* I have not had sexual relations with a boy.

O Hot-of-Leg, who comes forth from the twilight, I have not swallowed my heart.

O Dark-One, who comes forth from the darkness, I have not been abusive.

O Bringer-of-His-Peace, who comes forth from Sais, I have not been overenergetic.

O Lord-of-Faces, who comes forth from the Heroonpolite Nome, my heart has not been hasty.

O Plan-Maker, who comes forth from *Utenet,* I have not transgressed my color; I have not washed the god.

O Lord-of-Horns, who comes forth from Siut, my voice is not too much about matters.

O *Nefer-tem,* who comes forth from Memphis, I have not committed sins; I have not done evil.

O *Tem-sep,* who comes forth from Busiris, I have not been abusive against a king.

O Acting-with-His-Heart, who comes forth from *Tjebu,* I have not waded in water.

O Flowing-One, who comes forth from Nun, my voice has not been loud.

O Commander-of-the-People, who comes forth from *his shrine,* I have not been abusive against a god.

O *Neheb-nefert,* who comes forth from *the Saite Nome,* I have never made puffings-up.

O *Neheb-kau,* who comes forth from the town, I have not made *discriminations for* myself.

O High-of-Head serpent, who comes forth from the cavern, my portion has not been too large, *not even* in my own property.

O *In-af* serpent, who comes forth from the cemetery, I have not blasphemed against my local god.

WORDS TO BE SPOKEN BY X [the deceased]:

Hail to you, ye gods who are in this Broad-Hall of the Two Justices! I know you; I know your names. I shall not fall for dread of you. Ye have not reported guilt of mine up to this god in whose retinue ye are; no deed of mine has come *from* you. Ye have spoken truth about me in the presence of the All-Lord, because I acted justly in Egypt. I have not been abusive to a god. No deed of mine has come *from* a king who is in his day.

Hail to you who are in the Broad-Hall of the Two Justices, who have no deceit in your bodies, who live on truth and who eat of truth in the presence of Horus, who is in his sun disc. May ye rescue me from Babi, who lives on the entrails *of elders* on that day of the great reckoning. Behold me—I have come to you without sin, without guilt, without evil, without a witness against me, without one against whom I have taken action. I live on truth, and I eat of truth. I have done that which men said and that with which gods are content. I have satisfied a god with that which he desires. I have given bread to the hungry, water to the thirsty, clothing to the naked, and a ferry-boat to him who was marooned. I have provided divine offerings for the gods and mortuary offerings for the dead. So rescue me, you; protect me, you. Ye will not make report against me in the presence of the great god. I am one pure of mouth and pure of hands, one to whom "Welcome, welcome, in peace!" is said by those who see him, because I have heard those great words which the ass discussed with the cat in the house of *the hippopotamus,* when the witness was His-Face-Behind-Him and he gave out a cry. I have seen the splitting of the *ished*-tree in *Rostau.* I am one who has a concern for the gods, who knows the *nature* of their bodies. I have come here to testify to justice and to bring the scales to their proper position in the cemetery.

O thou who art high upon his standard, Lord of the *Atef*-Crown, whose name has been made "Lord of Breath," mayest thou rescue me from thy messengers who give forth uncleanliness and create *destruction,* who have no covering up of their faces, because I have effected justice for the Lord of Justice, being pure—my front is pure, my rear is clean, my middle is in the flowing water of justice; there is no part of me free of justice. . . .

. . . "I will not announce thee," says the doorkeeper of the Broad-Hall of the Two Justices, "unless thou tellest my name." "Understander of Hearts, Searcher of Bodies is thy name." "Then to whom should I announce thee?" "To the god who is in his hour of service." "Thou shouldst tell it to the interpreter of the Two Lands." "Well, who is the interpreter of the Two Lands?" "It is Thoth."

"Come," says Thoth, "why hast thou come?" "I have come here to be announced." "What is thy condition?" "I am pure of sin. I have protected myself from the strife of those who are in their days. I am not among them." "Then to whom shall I announce thee? I shall announce thee to him whose ceiling is of fire, whose walls are living serpents, and whose pavement is water. Who is he?" "He is Osiris." "Then go thou. Behold, thou art announced. Thy bread is the Restored Eye; thy beer is the Restored Eye. Thou hast invocation-offerings upon earth in the Restored Eye." So spoke Osiris to X, the deceased.

Instructions for the Use of the Spell

TO BE DONE IN CONFORMANCE WITH WHAT TAKES PLACE IN THIS BROAD-HALL OF THE TWO JUSTICES. THIS SPELL IS TO BE RECITED WHEN ONE IS CLEAN AND PURE, CLOTHED IN FRESH GARMENTS, SHOD WITH WHITE SANDALS, PAINTED WITH STIBIUM, AND ANOINTED WITH MYRRH, TO WHOM CATTLE, FOWL, INCENSE, BREAD, BEER, AND VEGETABLES HAVE BEEN OFFERED. THEN MAKE THOU THIS TEXT IN WRITING ON A CLEAN PAVEMENT WITH OCHRE SMEARED WITH EARTH UPON WHICH PIGS AND OTHER SMALL CATTLE HAVE NOT TRODDEN. AS FOR HIM ON WHOSE BEHALF THIS BOOK IS MADE, HE SHALL BE PROSPEROUS AND HIS CHILDREN SHALL BE PROSPEROUS, WITHOUT GREED, BECAUSE HE SHALL BE A TRUSTED MAN OF THE KING AND HIS COURTIERS. LOAVES, JARS, BREAD, AND JOINTS OF MEAT SHALL BE GIVEN TO HIM FROM THE ALTAR OF THE GREAT GOD. HE CANNOT BE HELD BACK AT ANY DOOR OF THE WEST, BUT HE SHALL BE USHERED IN WITH the Kings of Upper and Lower Egypt, and he shall be in the retinue of Osiris.

Right and true a million times.

REVIEW QUESTIONS

1. What does this text reveal about the Egyptians' concept of the next life and in particular, about the individual's eligibility for it? Can you detect any parallels in the beliefs of later religious systems?
2. How, ideally, was one to conduct oneself in order to appear blameless before the gods?
3. What does this text have to say about Egyptian social values?

2 ✍ PEOPLES, GODS, AND EMPIRES, 1700–500 B.C.E.

Under the firm hand of the rulers of the Twelfth Dynasty, Egypt had reemerged as a unified, highly centralized monarchy served by an efficient corps of royal bureaucrats. By the seventeenth century B.C.E., however, that stability was shaken as "vile Asiatics" migrated from Palestine into the Nile Delta and asserted their own political authority as the Hyksos dynasties of Lower Egypt. With the onset of its Second Intermediate Period, then, Egypt was once again divided, but for the first time under the abominable yoke of "barbarian" conquerors. Once again, the unity of the "Two Lands" of Upper and Lower Egypt would be restored by the prowess of the rulers of Amun's city of Thebes, who expelled the foreigners, chased them back into Palestine, and subsequently, perhaps as insurance against a repetition of such an abomination, conquered and ruled most of the eastern Mediterranean seaboard from the Sinai to Syria as well as the region of Nubia, ranging into the interior of Africa.

The zenith of Egypt's New Kingdom Empire coincides with the era of the Late Bronze Age, a cosmopolitan age of unprecedented internationalism. As reflected vividly in the diplomatic correspondence found at the short-lived capital at Amarna as well as in the preserved cargo of a shipwreck discovered off the coast of Turkey at Ulu Burun, kings from Babylonia to Cyprus negotiated favors and offered their daughters in marriage. Maritime traders plied the sea routes of the Aegean and the eastern Mediterranean, carrying ingots of bronze, tusks of ivory, disks of blue glass, and pottery containers filled with valuable oils and resins. Envoys and ambassadors trudged well-worn caravan tracks, bearing messages from kings offering alliances to other kings or from local princes supplicating the pharaoh or informing him of depredations by outlaws. At the top of royal wish lists was the gold of Nubia, which the pharaoh had the power to dispense to royal "brothers" in Babylonia, Assyria, Hatti, Mittani, Alashiya (Cyprus), or Ahhiyawa (perhaps Mycenaean Greece). Many pounds of that same gold were expended on the burial of a short-lived pharaoh named Tutankhamun, whose abandoned birth name of Tutankhaten testifies to the genius (or psychosis) of his predecessor, regarded by some experts as the first ruler to espouse monotheism, a religious system based on a single god (in this instance, the sun as personified in its disk, or aten). Later Egyptians would condemn Akhenaten's "revolution" as heresy and attempt to eradicate his memory. Only well after the internationalism of the Late Bronze Age had been disrupted and Egypt itself had become a "broken reed" would the Hebrews (perhaps not totally unrelated to those outlaws mentioned above) develop the concept of monotheism, a concept that eventually was to become one of the most central and enduring structures of civilization throughout the West, and the world.

The period 1200–1100 B.C.E. is a watershed in the history of the ancient Near East. Before 1200, the region enjoyed a vibrant internationalism set against the backdrop of competing great kingdoms, some of them with substantial empires. By 1100, most of those great kingdoms had disappeared—in some instances suddenly, perhaps even catastrophically; among them were the Hittite kingdom of Anatolia, the Kassite kingdom of Babylonia, the kingdom of Alashiya on Cyprus, and Mycenaean Greece. Others were in decline—most notably New Kingdom Egypt, whose empire in Syria and Palestine had waned and whose dynastic unity was dissolving. Scholars today still debate the impact of the invasion of the "Sea Peoples" on these events. In one prominent view, their invasions were the most catastrophic event to befall the ancient Near East prior to the arrival of Alexander's armies. Others see their arrival, though certainly shattering, as but one event in a concatenation of causes, both external and internal, that brought down the great Late Bronze Age kingdoms, ushered in a new configuration of states and peoples, and contributed to the ascendancy of iron over bronze as the preferred metal of technology.

Within the new configuration emerged peoples whose contributions to later Western and world civilizations were both profound and enduring. Among the Sea Peoples, memory of the Philistines has endured the longest, perhaps because the region in which they settled took on their name as Palestine. The Hebrew Bible depicts them as a potent and incorrigible threat to the early Israelites, and the ensuing animosity undoubtedly contributed to the modern (and surely unjustified) connotation of "philistine" as crude and unsophisticated. To their north, the long-established Canaanite craftsmen and traders of Tyre, Sidon, and Beirut whom the Greeks came to identify as Phoenicians established far-flung colonies and commercial routes along which their goods and reputation were carried to the Straits of Gibraltar and beyond. As part of their enterprise, they refined and disseminated a new technology (likely inspired by Egyptian hieroglyphs) that eventually would revolutionize both literacy and society—alphabetic writing. Meanwhile, emerging to the west of the Phoenicians were several tribal kingdoms of the Aramaeans, perhaps the most powerful of which was centered on the ancient city of Damascus. In time, Aramaean peoples spread across the Middle Eastern landscape as far away as Babylonia, bringing with them their language, Aramaic, and an alphabetic writing system that would eventually supplant the ancient cuneiform system. Aramaic became the official language of the

Persian Empire; it was the language spoken by Jesus Christ, and it remained the dominant spoken language throughout the Middle East until supplanted by Arabic in the wake of the Arab/Islamic conquests many centuries later.

The ancient Hebrews, or Israelites, had an impact on the shaping of Western civilization that dwarfs their impact on the history and culture of their own time. They emerged from almost total obscurity late during the second millennium B.C.E., in circumstances about which historians and archaeologists have yet to reach consensus and continually struggle to understand. According to the (hardly objective or verifiable) accounts in the Hebrew Bible, they came to dominate the area of modern Israel/Palestine under two kings, David and Solomon, whose reigns together encompassed less than a century (approximately 1000–920 B.C.E.). The civil war that erupted on Solomon's death left the previously united Hebrew monarchy irreparably divided into its two constituent parts: Israel in the north and Judah in the south.

Within a few centuries, however, both of these kingdoms, and most of the rest of the Middle East as well, were overcome by the reasserted might of Mesopotamian and then Persian Empires. The Assyrians destroyed Israel in 722 B.C.E. and by 650 had conquered virtually all of the Middle East, their kings celebrating their brutal conquests in vivid accounts that can shock even twenty-first-century sensibilities. One of their successors to imperial dominion, the Chaldaean king Nebuchadnezzar of Babylonia, captured Judah's capital, Jerusalem, in 587 and deported much of its population to Babylon— an event that began the Diaspora, the "dispersion" that has so dominated the experience of the Jewish people since that time. With Cyrus and his successors came the greatest of all ancient Near Eastern empires, that of the Achaemenid Persians, who developed a system and mentality of universal dominion that later empires emulated for centuries to come.

It was probably during the Captivity in Babylon that the displaced people of Judah (in Hebrew, yehudim—the word came to be "Jews") undertook in earnest the process of compiling and editing their ancient laws and traditions. The body of writings that was developed over the next several centuries—the Hebrew Bible, known in Christian tradition as the Old Testament—is, along with the New Testament, arguably the most influential corpus of literature in human history. Without a doubt, it is the ancient Near East's most significant contribution to the shaping of Western civilization. Its impact on the formation of later Islamic civilization worldwide, through its contribution to the teachings of the prophet Muhammad as reflected in the Qur'an, is likewise beyond measuring. Furthermore, for the nearly two millennia before the archaeological rediscovery of ancient Mesopotamian civilization in the mid-nineteenth century and the decipherment of the cuneiform and hieroglyphic scripts, the Bible was the chief fount of knowledge of human history from the creation of the world (which some scholars, using Biblical evidence, dated to exactly 4004 B.C.E.) to the rise of the Greeks.

The theory of evolution and the modern discoveries of historians and archaeologists have undermined the historical value of much of the Bible's narrative.

Obviously, then, it is not in the accuracy of their historical accounts that the Hebrews have had their greatest influence on later civilization. Rather, their singular contribution lies in the unique perspective that dominated their sense of their own history: their special relationship with a divine being who chose them as his own people and established with them a covenant that promised them his support and protection. In return, they pledged to accept only him as their exclusive deity and to govern their behavior, both cultic and social, in accordance with a body of explicitly defined regulations handed down by him and him alone. The working out of this covenant in the historical experience of the Hebrew people provided the developmental context for concepts that became central to the tradition of Western civilization: divinely revealed law as the basis of the relationship between God and humankind; and a monotheism founded on humankind's exclusive acceptance of a single, universal Supreme Being and Creator who demands justice and righteousness but is also capable of mercy and compassion. These concepts today remain at the heart of the faiths of the "children of Abraham," the shared monotheistic tradition of Judaism, Christianity, and Islam.

Akhenaton's *Hymn to the Aton*

The nature of the relationship between the king and the gods and the religious focus of the Egyptian royal court took on a significant (though short-lived) new direction during the reign of the New Kingdom pharaoh Amunhotep IV, better known to history by the name he assumed, Akhenaton ("Beloved of the Aton"). Referred to by some today as the heretic pharaoh, Akhenaton tried to redirect worship in the Egyptian royal court to an almost exclusive focus on the Aton, the personification of the sun's power as manifested in the sun disk. Many scholars have seen in this an important precursor of the Hebrews' monotheism centered on their god, Yahweh; some, in fact, have claimed that the Hebrews derived their monotheism from learning of Akhenaton's reform during their captivity in Egypt (as described in the Hebrew Bible's book of Exodus). The following hymn is generally ascribed to Akhenaton himself and shows some interesting parallels to Psalm 104 in the Hebrew Bible.

From *Hymns, Prayers, and Songs: An Anthology of Ancient Egyptian Lyric Poetry*, translated by John L. Foster, SBL Writings from the Ancient World Series, vol. 8 (Atlanta, Ga.: Scholars Press, 1995), pp. 154–58.

In Praise of the living Horakhty who rejoices in the Horizon in his Name of the divine Light which is in the Sundisk, living eternally and forever, the living Aton, Great One who is in the Festival, Lord of all the sundisk circles, Lord of Heaven, Lord of Earth, Living on Maat, Lord of the Two Lands, Nefer-kheper-rê Wa-en-rê, Son of the Sun, Who lives on Maat, Lord of Appearances,

Akhenaton, One Great in his Time; and the Great
Royal Wife, whom he loves, Mistress of the Two
Lands, Nefer-neferu-aten Nefertiti, living, healthy,
flourishing forever and eternity. He says:

i

May you always appear thus gloriously in the
    horizon of the sky,
        O living Aton, origin of life!
Arisen from the eastern horizon,
    you have filled all earth with your splendor;
You are beautiful, great, dazzling, exalted above
    each land,
        yet your rays encompass the lands
            to the limits of all which you have created;
There in the Sun, you reach to their boundaries,
    making them bow to your Son, whom you love;
And though you are far, your rays are over the
    earth,
        and you are in the faces of those who watch
        your journeying.

ii

You go to rest in the western horizon,
    and earth is in a darkness like death,
With the sleepers in bedchambers, heads covered—
    the eye cannot discern its companion;
All their goods might be carried off—
    though they are near—without their knowing.
Every lion comes forth from his doorway,
    insects and snakes bite and sting;
Darkness shrouds, earth is silent—
    he who created them is at rest in his tomb.

iii

Dawn rises shining on the horizon,
    gleams from the sundisk as day.
You scatter the darkness, bestow your sunbeams,
    and the Two Lands offer thanksgiving.
The Sunfolk awaken and stand on their feet,
    for you have raised them up;
Their bodies are bathed, they put on their clothing,
    their arms raised in praise at your appearing.

Throughout the land
    they take up their work.

iv

The herds are at peace in their meadows,
    trees and the vegetation grow green,
Birds fly from their nests,
    their wings spread wide in praise of your
    Person;
All the small beasts leap about on their feet,
    and all who fly up or settle to rest
        live because you have shone upon them.
Ships go downstream or upstream as well,
    each path lies open because of your presence;
The fish in the River dart about in your sight,
    and your beams are deep in the Great Green
    Sea.

v

It is you who create the seed in women,
    shape the fluids into human beings,
Make the son alive in the womb of his mother,
    soothe him, ending his tears,
Nurturer from the womb to those given breath
    to bring into life all that he has created.
He descends from the womb to breathe
    on the day of his birth,
And you open his mouth, determine his nature,
    and minister to his needs.

vi

The fledgling in the egg speaks in the shell,
    so you give him breath within it to succor him;
And you have given to him his allotted time
    so that he might break out from the egg
To come forth peeping at that time
    and move about upon his own two feet
        when he emerges from it.

vii

How various are the things you have created,
    and they are all mysterious to the sight!

O sole God, without another of your kind,
   you created the world according to your
   desire,
     while you were alone,
With mankind and cattle and every sort of small
   beast,
   all those upon land, those who go upon feet,
Those who are on high soaring upon their wings,
   the foreign lands of Khor and Kush,
     and all that belongs to Egypt.

viii

You give each person his place in life,
   and you provide for his needs;
Each one has his sustenance,
   and his lifetime is reckoned for him.
Tongues are separated by words,
   the natures of persons as well;
And their skins are made different
   so you can distinguish the peoples.

ix

You create Hapy, the Nile, in the Underworld
   to bring him, at your desire, to nourish the people,
Just as you create them for yourself,
   Lord of them all, who is weary for them,
O Lord of all earth, who shines for them,
   O Aton of day, awesome in majesty.
All the foreign lands are far away,
   yet you make their lives possible,
For you have placed a Hapy in the sky
   that he might come down upon them—
Making waves upon the mountains like those of
   the Great Green Sea
     to water the fields in their villages.

x

How well ordered it is, your governing,
   O Lord of Eternity, Hapy in heaven!
You belong to the foreign peoples,
   to the small beasts of each land who go upon feet.
And Hapy comes from Below to beloved Egypt as
   well,

while your rays are nursing each meadow.
You shine, and they live,
   they grow strong for you;
You fashion the seasons to make all your
   creation flourish—
   the winter for cooling
     and the heat which ripens;
And you have made the sky far off
   in order to shine down from it,
     to watch over all you have created.

xi

You are one alone,
   shining forth in your visible Form as the living
   Aton,
Glorious, giving light,
   far-off yet approaching nearby.
You create the numberless visible forms from
   yourself—you who are one alone—
Cities, towns, fields, the road, the River;
   and each eye looks to you as its shining
   example:
You are in the sun-disk of day,
   overseer of wherever you go and whatever
   shall be;
For you fashion their sight so that you may be
   complete—as they celebrate with one voice
   your creation.

xii

And you are in my heart;
   there is no other who knows you
Except for your son, Akhenaton,
   Nefer-kheper-rê Wa-en-rê.
Let him be wise with your counsel, your strength,
   that the world may approach your condition
     just as when you created it.
You have risen, and they are alive;
   you go to rest, and they die.
For you are the measure of Time itself,
   one lives by means of you.
Eyes shall be filled with beauty until your
   setting; all labor is set aside when you go to
   rest in the West.

Then rise! Let the creatures of earth thrive for the
 king!
And let me hasten on with every footstep
 as I have since you founded the world.
And raise them up for your son
 who came forth from your very body.
The King of Upper and Lower Egypt, who
lives on Truth, Lord of the Two Lands, Nefer-
Kheper-Rê Wa-en-rê, son of the Sun, who lives
on Truth, Lord of Appearances, Akhenaton, one
exalted in his own lifetime; and the Great Royal

Wife, whom he loves, Nefer-nefcru-aton Nefertiti, who lives and flourishes for eternity and
everlasting.

Review Questions

1. What kinds of powers does this hymn ascribe to
the Aton?
2. What is the king's relationship to his newly elevated god?

Treaty between Ramesses II of Egypt
and Hattusilis III of Hatti

*During the Egyptian New Kingdom era of the Late Bronze Age, Egypt's imperial
aspirations in Syria faced no greater threat than that from the kings of Hatti (more
commonly known as the Hittites), whose center of power was in Anatolia (modern
Turkey). Around 1274 B.C.E., the great pharaoh Ramesses II had fought a great,
though inconclusive, chariot battle against the Hittites at Kadesh in Syria. In the
decades following, however, the emergence of new threats in the region led Ramesses
to conclude a treaty of peace with his Hittite counterpart, Hattusilis III. The following selection is a translation of the Egyptian version; the Hittite version has also been
preserved. Both versions, however, were translations of an original that would have
been composed in Akkadian, the language of Babylonia that was the lingua franca of
Late Bronze Age international relations.*

From *Ancient Near Eastern Texts Relating to the Old Testament*, edited by James B. Pritchard,
translated by John A. Wilson (3d ed.; Princeton, N.J.: Princeton University Press, 1969),
pp. 199–201.

Year 21, 1st month of the second season, day 21,
under the majesty of the King of Upper and Lower
Egypt: User-maat-Re; Son of Re: Ramses Meri-
Amon, given life forever, beloved of Amon-Re;
Har-akhti; Ptah, South-of-His-Wall, Lord of Life of
the Two Lands; Mut, the Lady of Ishru; and Khonsu
Neferhotep; appearing on the Horus-Throne of the
Living, like his father Har-akhti forever and ever.

On this day, while his majesty was in the town
of Per-Ramses Meri-Amon, doing the pleasure of
his father Amon-Re; Har-akhti; Atum, Lord of the

Two Lands, the Heliopolitan; Amon of Ramses
Meri-Amon; Ptah of Ramses Meri-Amon; and
[Seth], the Great of Strength, the Son of Nut, according as they give him an eternity of jubilees and an
infinity of years of peace, while all lands and all foreign countries are prostrate under his soles forever—
there came the Royal Envoy and Deputy . . . Royal
Envoy . . . [User-maat-Re] Setep-en-[Re] . . . [Tar]-
Teshub, and the Messenger of Hatti, . . . -silis, carrying [the *tablet of silver which*] the Great Prince
of Hatti, Hattusilis [caused] to be brought to

Pharaoh—life, prosperity, health!—in order to beg [peace from *the majesty of* User-maat-Re] Setep-en-Re, the Son of Re: Ramses Meri-Amon, [given] life forever and ever, like his father Re every day.

Copy of the tablet of silver which the Great Prince of Hatti, Hattusilis, caused to be brought to Pharaoh—life, prosperity, health!—by the hand of his envoy Tar-Teshub, and his envoy Ra-mose, in order to beg peace from the majesty of [User-maat-Re], Son of Re: Ramses Meri-Amon, the bull of rulers, who has made his frontier where he wished in very land.

Preamble

The regulations which the Great Prince of Hatti, Hattusilis, the powerful, the son of Mursilis, the Great Prince of Hatti, the powerful, the son of the son of Suppi[luliumas, the Great Prince of Hatti, the] powerful, made upon a tablet of silver for User-maat-Re, the great ruler of Egypt, the powerful, the son of Men-maat-Re, the great ruler of Egypt, the powerful, the son of Men-pehti-Re, the great ruler of Egypt, the powerful; the good regulations of peace and of brotherhood, giving peace . . . forever.

Former Relations

Now from the beginning of the limits of eternity, as for the situation of the great ruler of Egypt with the Great Prince of Hatti, the god did not permit hostility to occur between them, through a regulation. But in the time of Muwatallis, the Great Prince of Hatti, my brother, he fought with [Ramses Meri-Amon], the great ruler of Egypt. But hereafter, from this day, behold Hattusilis, the Great Prince of Hatti, [is *under*] a regulation for making permanent the situation which the Re and Seth made for the land of Egypt with the land of Hatti, in order not to permit hostility to occur between them forever.

The Present Treaty

Behold, Hattusilis, the Great Prince of Hatti, has set himself in a regulation with User-maat-Re Setep-en-Re, the great ruler of Egypt, beginning from this day, to cause that good peace and brotherhood occur between us forever, while he is in brotherhood with me and he is at peace with me, and I am in brotherhood with him and I am at peace with him forever.

Now since Muwatallis, the Great Prince of Hatti, my brother, went in pursuit of his fate, and Hattusilis sat as Great Prince of Hatti upon the throne of his father, behold, I have come to be with Ramses Meri-Amon, the great ruler of Egypt, for *we are* [*together in*] *our* peace and our brotherhood. It is better than the peace or the brotherhood which was formerly in the land.

Behold, I, as the Great Prince of Hatti, am with [Ramses Meri-Amon], in good peace and in good brotherhood. The children of the children [of] the Great Prince of Hatti *are* in brotherhood and peace with the children of the children of [Ra]mses Meri-[Amon], the great ruler of Egypt, for they are in our situation of brotherhood and our situation [of peace. *The land of Egypt*], with the land of Hatti, [*shall be*] at peace and in brotherhood like unto us forever. Hostilities shall not occur between them forever.

Mutual Renunciation of Invasion

The Great Prince of Hatti shall not trespass against the land of Egypt forever, to take anything from it. And User-maat-Re Setep-en-Re, the great ruler of Egypt, shall not trespass against the land [of Hatti, to take] from it forever.

Reaffirmation of Former Treaties

As to the traditional regulation which had been here in the time of Suppiluliumas, the Great Prince of Hatti, as well as the traditional regulation which had been in the time of Muwatallis, the Great Prince of Hatti, my father, I seize hold of it. Behold, Ramses Meri-Amon, the great ruler of Egypt, seizes hold of [*the regulation which he makes*] together with us, beginning from this day. We seize hold of it, and we act in this traditional situation.

A Defensive Alliance—for Egypt

If another enemy come against the lands of User-maat-Re, the great ruler of Egypt, and he send to the Great Prince of Hatti, saying: "Come with me as reinforcement against him," the Great Prince of Hatti shall [come to him and] the Great Prince of Hatti shall slay his enemy. However, if it is not the desire of the Great Prince of Hatti to go (himself), he shall send his infantry and his chariotry, and he shall slay his enemy. Or, if Ramses Meri-Amon, [the great ruler of Egypt], is enraged against servants belonging to him, and they commit another offence against him, and he go to slay them, the Great Prince of Hatti shall act with him [to *slay*] everyone [against whom] they shall be enraged.

A Defensive Alliance—for Hatti

But [if] another enemy [come] against the Great Prince [of Hatti, User]-maat-[Re] Setep-en-Re, [the great ruler of Egypt, shall] come to him as reinforcement to slay his enemy. If it is (not) the desire of Ramses Meri-Amon, the great ruler of Egypt, to come, he shall . . . Hatti, [and he shall send his infantry and his] chariotry, besides returning answer to the land of Hatti. Now if the servants of the Great Prince of Hatti trespass against him, and Ramses Meri-Amon. . . .

The Contingency of Death?

. . . the [land] of Hatti and the land [of Egypt] . . . the life. *Should it be that* I shall go [in] pursuit of my fate, *then* Ramses Meri-[Amon], the great ruler of Egypt, living forever, *shall go and come* [*to*] the [land of] Hatti, . . . to cause . . . , to make him lord for them, to make User-maat-Re Setep-en-[Re], the great ruler of Egypt, silent with his mouth forever. Now after he . . . the land of Hatti, and he *returns* . . . the Great Prince of Hatti, as well as the. . . .

Extradition of Refugees to Egypt

[If a great man flee from the land of Egypt and come to] the Great Prince of Hatti, or a town belonging to the lands of Ramses Meri-Amon, the great ruler of Egypt, and they come to the Great Prince of Hatti, the Great Prince of Hatti shall not receive them. The Great Prince of Hatti shall cause them to be brought to User-maat-Re Setep-en-Re, the great ruler of Egypt, their lord, [because] of it. Or if a man or two men—no matter who—flee, and they come to the land of Hatti to be servants of someone else, they shall not be left in the land of Hatti; they shall be brought to Ramses Meri-Amon, the great ruler of Egypt.

Extradition of Refugees to Hatti

Or if a great man flee from the land of Hatti and [come to User]-maat-[Re] Setep-en-Re, the [great] ruler of Egypt, or a town or a district or a . . . belonging to the land of Hatti, and they come to Ramses Meri-Amon, the great ruler of Egypt, (then) User-maat-Re Setep-en-Re, the great ruler of Egypt, shall not receive them. Ramses Meri-Amon, the great ruler of Egypt, shall cause them to be brought to the Prince [*of Hatti*]. They shall not be left. Similarly, if a man or two men—[no] matter who—flee, and they come to the land of Egypt to be servants of other people, User-maat-Re Setep-en-Re, the great ruler of Egypt, shall not leave them. He shall cause them to be brought to the Great Prince of Hatti.

The Divine Witnesses to the Treaty

As for these words of the regulation [*which*] the Great Prince of Hatti [*made*] with Ramses [Meri-Amon], the great ruler [of Egypt], in writing upon this tablet of silver—as for these words, a thousand gods of the male gods and of the female gods of them of the land of Hatti, together with a thousand gods of the male gods and of the female gods of them of the land of Egypt, are with me as witnesses [*hearing*] these words: the Re, the lord of the sky; the Re of the town of Arinna; Seth, the lord of the sky; Seth of Hatti; Seth of the town of Arinna; Seth of the town of Zippalanda; Seth of the town of Pe(tt)iyarik; Seth of the town of Hissas(ha)pa; Seth of the town of Sarissa; Seth of the town of Aleppo; Seth of the town of Lihzina; Seth of the town . . . ; . . . ; Seth of the town of *Sahpin; Antaret* of the land of Hatti; the god of Zithari(as); the god of *Karzis*; the god of Hapantaliyas; the goddess of the town of Karahna; the goddess of . . . ; the Queen of the Sky; the gods, the lords of oaths; this goddess, the Lady of the Ground; the Lady of the Oath, Ishara; the Lady (*of the*) mountains and the rivers of the land of Hatti; the gods of the land of Kizuwadna; Amon; the Re; Seth; the male gods; the female gods; the mountains; and the rivers of the land of Egypt; the sky; the earth; the great sea; the winds; and the clouds.

Curses and Blessings for this Treaty

As for these words which are on this tablet of silver of the land of Hatti and of the land of Egypt—as for him who shall not keep them, a thousand gods of the land of Hatti, together with a thousand gods of the land of Egypt, shall destroy his house, his land, and his servants. But, as for him who shall keep these words which are on this tablet of silver, whether they are Hatti or whether they are Egyptians, and they are not *neglectful of* them, a thousand gods of the land of Hatti, together with a thousand gods of the land of Egypt, shall cause that he be well, shall cause that he live, together with his houses and his (land) and his servants.

Extradition of Egyptians from Hatti

If a man flee from the land of Egypt—or two or three—and they come to the Great Prince of Hatti, the Great Prince of Hatti shall lay hold of them, and he shall cause that they be brought back to User-maat-Re Setep-en-Re, the great ruler of Egypt. But, as for the man who shall be brought to Ramses Meri-Amon, the great ruler of Egypt, do not cause that his crime be raised against him; do not cause that his house or his wives or his children be destroyed; [do not cause that] he be [slain]; do not cause that injury be done to his eyes, to his ears, to his mouth, or to his legs; do not let any [crime be raised] against him.

Extradition of Hittites from Egypt

Similarly, if men flee from the land of Hatti—whether he be one or two or three—and they come to User-maat-Re Setep-en-Re, the great ruler of Egypt, let Ramses Meri-Amon, the [great] ruler [of Egypt], lay hold [of them and cause] that they be brought to the Great Prince of Hatti, and the Great Prince of Hatti shall not raise their crime against them, and they shall not destroy his house or his wives or his children, and they shall not slay him, and they shall not do injury to his ears, to his eyes, to his mouth, or to his legs, and they shall not raise any crime against him.

Description of the Tablet

What is in the middle of the tablet of silver. On its front side: figures consisting of an image of Seth embracing an image of the Great Prince [of Hatti], surrounded by a border with the words: "the seal of Seth, the ruler of the sky; the seal of the regulation which Hattusilis made, the Great Prince of Hatti, the powerful, the son of Mursilis, the Great Prince of Hatti, the powerful." What is within that which surrounds the figures: the seal [of *Seth*. What is on] its other side: figures consisting of a female image of [the] goddess of Hatti embracing a female image of the Princess of Hatti, surrounded by a border with the words: "the seal of the Re of the town of Arinna, the lord of the land; the seal of Putu-hepa, the Princess of the land of Hatti, the daughter of the land of Kizuwadna, the [*priestess*] of [*the town of*] Arinna, the Lady of the Land, the servant of the goddess." What is within the surrounding (frame) of the figures: the seal of the Re of Arinna, the lord of every land.

REVIEW QUESTIONS

1. To what extent are relations between monarchs represented as family ties?
2. Can you find evidence of the extent to which international relations were sanctioned by divine authority?

FROM **The Middle Assyrian Laws**

The middle of the fourteenth century B.C.E. marks the beginning of what scholars identify as the Middle Assyrian period (to distinguish this era from the earlier Old Assyrian period [ca. 1950–1750 B.C.E.] and the later great age of Assyrian empire, the Neo-Assyrian period [ca. 900–609 B.C.E.]). It was during the Middle Assyrian period that the kings of Assyria (in what is now northern Iraq) emerged to become one of the major powers whose rivalry—and diplomacy—characterized the Late Bronze Age of the Middle East. During the late thirteenth century B.C.E., the great Middle Assyrian king Tukulti-Ninurta I even conquered the city of Babylon (an achievement celebrated in a text known as the Tukulti-Ninurta Epic) and posed a major threat to the Hittite kings in central Anatolia. Among our most useful sources for understanding ancient Mesopotamian society during this era is a text known as the Middle Assyrian Laws. As the following excerpt reflects, these laws deal significantly with the status of—and regulations concerning—women and sexual activity. They also provide interesting parallels and contrasts with the laws of Hammurabi of Babylon, which date several centuries earlier.

From *Law Collections from Mesopotamia and Asia Minor*, edited by Martha T. Roth, SBL Writings from the Ancient World Series, vol. 6 (Atlanta, Ga.: Scholars Press, 1995), pp. 76–135.

*   *   *

4. If either a slave or a slave woman should receive something from a man's wife, they shall cut off the slave's or slave woman's nose and ears; they shall restore the stolen goods; the man shall cut off his own wife's ears. But if he releases his wife and does not cut off her ears, they shall not cut off the nose and ears of the slave or slave woman, and they shall not restore the stolen goods.

*   *   *

7. If a woman should lay a hand upon a man and they prove the charges against her, she shall pay 1,800 shekels of lead; they shall strike her 20 blows with rods.

8. If a woman should crush a man's testicle during a quarrel, they shall cut off one of her fingers. And even if the physician should bandage it, but the second testicle then becomes infected along with it and becomes . . . , or she should crush the second testicle during the quarrel—they shall gouge out both her . . .

9. If a man lays a hand upon a woman, attacking her like a rutting bull, and they prove the charges against him and find him guilty, they shall cut off one of his fingers. If he should kiss her, they shall draw his lower lip across the blade of an ax and cut it off.

*   *   *

12. If a wife of a man should walk along the main thoroughfare and should a man seize her and say to her, "I want to have sex with you!"—she shall not consent but she shall protect herself; should he seize her by force and fornicate with her—whether they discover him upon the woman or witnesses later prove the charges against him that he fornicated with the woman—they shall kill the man; there is no punishment for the woman.

13. If the wife of a man should go out of her own house, and go to another man where he resides, and should he fornicate with her knowing that she is the wife of a man, they shall kill the man and the wife.

14. If a man should fornicate with another man's wife either in an inn or in the main thoroughfare,

knowing that she is the wife of a man, they shall treat the fornicator as the man declares he wishes his wife to be treated. If he should fornicate with her without knowing that she is the wife of a man, the fornicator is clear; the man shall prove the charges against his wife and he shall treat her as he wishes.

15. If a man should seize another man upon his wife and they prove the charges against him and find him guilty, they shall kill both of them; there is no liability for him. If he should seize him and bring him either before the king or the judges, and they prove the charges against him and find him guilty—if the woman's husband kills his wife, then he shall also kill the man; if he cuts off his wife's nose, he shall turn the man into a eunuch and they shall lacerate his entire face; but if he wishes to release his wife, he shall release the man.

16. If a man should fornicate with the wife of a man . . . by her invitation, there is no punishment for the man; the husband shall impose whatever punishment he chooses upon his wife. If he should fornicate with her by force and they prove the charges against him and find him guilty, his punishment shall be identical to that of the wife of the man.

*   *   *

23. If a man's wife should take another man's wife into her house and give her to a man for purposes of fornication, and the man knows that she is the wife of a man, they shall treat him as one who has fornicated with the wife of another man; and they treat the female procurer just as the woman's husband treats his fornicating wife. And if the woman's husband intends to do nothing to his fornicating wife, they shall do nothing to the fornicator or to the female procurer; they shall release them. But if the man's wife does not know what was intended, and the woman who takes her into her house brings the man in to her by deceit, and he then fornicates with her—if, as soon as she leaves the house, she should declare that she has been the victim of fornication, they shall release the woman, she is clear; they shall kill the fornicator and the female procurer. But if the woman should not so

declare, the man shall impose whatever punishment on his wife he wishes; they shall kill the fornicator and the female procurer.

24. If a man's wife should withdraw herself from her husband and enter into the house of another Assyrian, either in that city or in any of the nearby towns, to a house which he assigns to her, residing with the mistress of the household staying overnight three or four nights, and the householder is not aware that it is the wife of a man who is residing in his house, and later that woman is seized, the householder whose wife withdrew herself from him shall mutilate his wife and not take her back. As for the man's wife with whom his wife resided, they shall cut off her ears; if he pleases, her husband shall give 12,600 shekels of lead as her value, and, if he pleases, he shall take back his wife. However, if the householder knows that it is a man's wife who is residing in his house with his wife, he shall give "triple." And if he should deny that he knew of her status, he shall declare, "I did not know," they shall undergo the divine River Ordeal. And if the man in whose house the wife of a man resided should refuse to undergo the divine River Ordeal, he shall give "triple"; if it is the man whose wife withdrew herself from him who should refuse to undergo the divine River Ordeal, he in whose house she resided is clear; he shall bear the expenses of the divine River Ordeal. However, if the man whose wife withdrew herself from him does not mutilate his wife, he shall take back his wife; no sanctions are imposed.

*   *   *

37. If a man intends to divorce his wife, if it is his wish, he shall give her something; if that is not his wish, he shall not give her anything, and she shall leave emptyhanded.

*   *   *

40. Wives of a man, or widows, or any Assyrian women who go out into the main thoroughfare shall not have their heads bare. Daughters of a man with either a cloth or garments shall veil their heads. When they go about in the main thoroughfare during the daytime, they shall be veiled. A concubine who goes about in the main thoroughfare with her

mistress is to be veiled. A married *qadiltu*-woman is to be veiled when she goes about in the main thoroughfare, but an unmarried one is to leave her head bare in the main thoroughfare, she shall not be veiled. A prostitute shall not be veiled, her head shall be bare. Whoever sees a veiled prostitute shall seize her, secure witnesses, and bring her to the palace entrance. They shall not take away her jewelry, but he who has seized her takes her clothing; they shall strike her 50 blows with rods; they shall pour hot pitch over her head. And if a man should see a veiled prostitute and release her, and does not bring her to the palace entrance, they shall strike that man 50 blows with rods; the one who informs against him shall take his clothing; they shall pierce his ears, thread them on a cord, tie it at his back; he shall perform the king's service for one full month. Slave women shall not be veiled, and he who should see a veiled slave woman shall seize her and bring her to the palace entrance; they shall cut off her ears; he who seizes her shall take her clothing. If a man should see a veiled slave woman but release her and not seize her, and does not bring her to the palace entrance, and they then prove the charges against him and find him guilty, they shall strike him 50 blows with rods; they shall pierce his ears, thread them on a cord, tie it at his back; the one who informs against him shall take his garments; he shall perform the king's service for one full month.

*   *   *

53. If a woman aborts her fetus by her own action and they then prove the charges against her and find her guilty, they shall impale her, they shall not bury her. If she dies as a result of aborting her fetus, they shall impale her, they shall not bury her. If any persons should hide that woman because she aborted her fetus . . .

*   *   *

55. If a man forcibly seizes and rapes a maiden who is residing in her father's house, who is not betrothed, whose womb is not opened, who is not married, and against whose father's house there is no outstanding claim—whether within the city or in the countryside, or at night whether in the main thoroughfare, or in a granary, or during the city festival—the father of the maiden shall take the wife of the fornicator of the maiden and hand her over to be raped; he shall not return her to her husband, but he shall take (and keep) her; the father shall give his daughter who is the victim of fornication into the protection of the household of her fornicator. If he, the fornicator, has no wife, the fornicator shall give "triple" the silver as the value of the maiden to her father; her fornicator shall marry her; he shall not reject her. If the father does not desire it so, he shall receive "triple" silver for the maiden, and he shall give his daughter in marriage to whomever he chooses.

56. If a maiden should willingly give herself to a man, the man shall so swear; they shall have no claim to his wife; the fornicator shall pay "triple" the silver as the value of the maiden; the father shall treat his daughter in whatever manner he chooses.

*   *   *

59. In addition to the punishments for a man's wife that are written on the tablet, a man may whip his wife, pluck out her hair, mutilate her ears, or strike her, with impunity.

REVIEW QUESTIONS

1. What principles of justice and compensation are evident in these laws, and what kinds of recourse did society have against wrongdoers?
2. How did women's rights compare with those of men?
3. What do these laws tell us about Mesopotamian views about responsibility for sexual activity?
4. What do they tell us about power and authority within Mesopotamian families?
5. Can you detect parallels or differences between provisions in the Middle Assyrian Laws and provisions in the Code of Hammurabi, which you examined in Chapter 1?

FROM The Book of I Kings: Solomon's Construction of Yahweh's Temple in Jerusalem

As recounted in the following selection from the First Book of Kings, 5–8, in the Hebrew Bible, the crowning achievement of the reign of the Israelite king Solomon was the building of the great temple of Yahweh in Jerusalem, perhaps sometime during the later tenth century B.C.E. That temple was part of a larger palace complex, no archaeological evidence of which has yet been recovered. This helps explain why modern historians have been compelled to reassess the biblical accounts of the great power and extent of David's and Solomon's kingdom. Nonetheless, Solomon's First Temple, later destroyed by the Babylonians under Nebuchadnezzar in the sixth century B.C.E. (the Second Temple, rebuilt by Herod the Great in the first century B.C.E., was destroyed by the Romans in the first century C.E.),[1] became the central locus of ritual and worship in early Judaism and is an overriding reason for modern Israel's adamant refusal to share sovereignty over Jerusalem today.

From *Contemporary English Version* by American Bible Society (New York: American Bible Society, 1995).

King Hiram of Tyre had always been friends with Solomon's father David. When Hiram learned that Solomon was king, he sent some of his officials to meet with Solomon. Solomon sent a message back to Hiram: "Remember how my father David wanted to build a temple where the LORD his God could be worshiped? But enemies kept attacking my father's kingdom, and he never had the chance. Now, thanks to the LORD God, there is peace in my kingdom and no trouble or threat of war anywhere. The LORD God promised my father that when his son became king, he would build a temple for worshiping the LORD. So I've decided to do that. I'd like you to have your workers cut down cedar trees in Lebanon for me. I will pay them whatever you say and will even have my workers help them. We both know that your workers are more experienced than anyone else at cutting lumber."

Hiram was so happy when he heard Solomon's request that he said, "I am grateful that the LORD gave David such a wise son to be king of that great nation!" Then he sent back his answer: "I received your message and will give you all the cedar and pine logs you need. My workers will carry them down from Lebanon to the Mediterranean Sea. They will tie the logs together and float them along the coast to wherever you want them. Then they will untie the logs, and your workers can take them from there. To pay for the logs, you can provide the grain I need for my household." Hiram gave Solomon all the cedar and pine logs he needed. In return, Solomon gave Hiram about one hundred twenty-five thousand bushels of wheat and about one thousand one hundred gallons of pure olive oil each year. The LORD kept his promise and made Solomon wise. Hiram and Solomon signed a treaty and never went to war against each other.

---

[1] C.E. means "common era."

Solomon ordered thirty thousand people from all over Israel to cut logs for the temple, and he put Adoniram in charge of these workers. Solomon divided them into three groups of ten thousand. Each group worked one month in Lebanon and had two months off at home. He also had eighty thousand workers to cut stone in the hill country of Israel, seventy thousand workers to carry the stones, and over three thousand assistants to keep track of the work and to supervise the workers. He ordered the workers to cut and shape large blocks of good stone for the foundation of the temple. Solomon's and Hiram's men worked with men from the city of Gebal, and together they got the stones and logs ready for the temple.

Solomon's workers started building the temple during Ziv, the second month of the year. It had been four years since Solomon became king of Israel, and four hundred eighty years since the people of Israel left Egypt. The inside of the LORD's temple was ninety feet long, thirty feet wide, and forty-five feet high. A fifteen-foot porch went all the way across the front of the temple. The windows were narrow on the outside but wide on the inside. Along the sides and back of the temple, there were three levels of storage rooms. The rooms on the bottom level were seven and a half feet wide, the rooms on the middle level were nine feet wide, and those on the top level were ten and a half feet wide. There were ledges on the outside of the temple that supported the beams of the storage rooms, so that nothing was built into the temple walls. Solomon did not want the noise of hammers and axes to be heard at the place where the temple was being built. So he had the workers shape the blocks of stone at the quarry.

The entrance to the bottom storage rooms was on the south side of the building, and stairs to the other rooms were also there. The roof of the temple was made out of beams and cedar boards. The workers finished building the outside of the temple. Storage rooms seven and a half feet high were all around the temple, and they were attached to the temple by cedar beams.

The LORD told Solomon: "If you obey my commands and do what I say, I will keep the promise I made to your father David. I will live among my people Israel in this temple you are building, and I will not desert them."

So Solomon's workers finished building the temple. The floor of the temple was made out of pine, and the walls were lined with cedar from floor to ceiling. The most holy place was in the back of the temple, and it was thirty feet square. Cedar boards standing from floor to ceiling separated it from the rest of the temple. The temple's main room was sixty feet long, and it was in front of the most holy place. The inside walls were lined with cedar to hide the stones, and the cedar was decorated with carvings of gourds and flowers.

The sacred chest was kept in the most holy place. This room was thirty feet long, thirty feet wide, and thirty feet high, and it was lined with pure gold. There were also gold chains across the front of the most holy place. The inside of the temple, as well as the cedar altar in the most holy place, was covered with gold. Solomon had two statues of winged creatures made from olive wood to put in the most holy place. Each creature was fifteen feet tall and fifteen feet across. They had two wings, and the wings were seven and a half feet long. Solomon put them next to each other in the most holy place. Their wings were spread out and reached across the room. The creatures were also covered with gold. The walls of the two rooms were decorated with carvings of palm trees, flowers, and winged creatures. Even the floor was covered with gold. The two doors to the most holy place were made out of olive wood and were decorated with carvings of palm trees, flowers, and winged creatures. The doors and the carvings were covered with gold. The door frame came to a point at the top. The two doors to the main room of the temple were made out of pine, and each one had two sections so they could fold open. The door frame was shaped like a rectangle and was made out of olive wood. The doors were covered with gold and were decorated with carvings of palm trees, flowers, and winged creatures. The inner courtyard of the temple had walls made out of three layers of cut stones with one layer of cedar beams.

Work began on the temple during Ziv, the second month of the year, four years after Solomon became king of Israel. Seven years later the workers finished building it during Bul, the eighth month of the year. It was built exactly as it had been planned. Solomon's palace took thirteen years to build.

Forest Hall was the largest room in the palace. It was one hundred fifty feet long, seventy-five feet wide, and forty-five feet high, and was lined with cedar from Lebanon. It had four rows of cedar pillars, fifteen in a row, and they held up forty-five cedar beams. The ceiling was covered with cedar. Three rows of windows on each side faced each other, and there were three doors on each side near the front of the hall. Pillar Hall was seventy-five feet long and forty-five feet wide. A covered porch supported by pillars went all the way across the front of the hall. Solomon's throne was in Justice Hall, where he judged cases. This hall was completely lined with cedar. The section of the palace where Solomon lived was behind Justice Hall and looked exactly like it. He had a similar place built for his wife, the daughter of the king of Egypt.

From the foundation all the way to the top, these buildings and the courtyard were made out of the best stones carefully cut to size, then smoothed on every side with saws. The foundation stones were huge, good stones—some of them fifteen feet long and others twelve feet long. The cedar beams and other stones that had been cut to size were on top of these foundation stones. The walls around the palace courtyard were made out of three layers of cut stones with one layer of cedar beams, just like the front porch and the inner courtyard of the temple.

Hiram was a skilled bronze worker from the city of Tyre. His father was now dead, but he also had been a bronze worker from Tyre, and his mother was from the tribe of Naphtali. King Solomon asked Hiram to come to Jerusalem and make the bronze furnishings to use for worship in the LORD's temple, and he agreed to do it. Hiram made two bronze columns twenty-seven feet tall and about six feet across. For the top of each column, he also made a bronze cap seven and a half feet high. The caps were decorated with seven rows of designs that looked like chains, with two rows of designs that looked like pomegranates. The caps for the columns of the porch were six feet high and

were shaped like lilies. The chain designs on the caps were right above the rounded tops of the two columns, and there were two hundred pomegranates in rows around each cap. Hiram placed the two columns on each side of the main door of the temple. The column on the south side was called Jachin, and the one on the north was called Boaz. The lily-shaped caps were on top of the columns. This completed the work on the columns.

Hiram also made a large bowl called the Sea. It was seven and a half feet deep, about fifteen feet across, and forty-five feet around. Two rows of bronze gourds were around the outer edge of the bowl, ten gourds to every eighteen inches. The bowl itself sat on top of twelve bronze bulls with three bulls facing outward in each of four directions. The sides of the bowl were four inches thick, and its rim was like a cup that curved outward like flower petals. The bowl held about eleven thousand gallons.

Hiram made ten movable bronze stands, each one four and a half feet high, six feet long, and six feet wide. The sides were made with panels attached to frames decorated with flower designs. The panels themselves were decorated with figures of lions, bulls, and winged creatures. Each stand had four bronze wheels and axles and a round frame twenty-seven inches across, held up by four supports eighteen inches high. A small bowl rested in the frame. The supports were decorated with flower designs, and the frame with carvings.

The side panels of the stands were square, and the wheels and axles were underneath them. The wheels were about twenty-seven inches high and looked like chariot wheels. The axles, rims, spokes, and hubs were made out of bronze. Around the top of each stand was a nine-inch strip, and there were four braces attached to the corners of each stand. The panels and the supports were attached to the stands, and the stands were decorated with flower designs and figures of lions, palm trees, and winged creatures. Hiram made the ten bronze stands from the same mold, so they were exactly the same size and shape. Hiram also made ten small bronze bowls, one for each stand. The bowls were six feet across and could hold about two hundred thirty gallons. He put five stands on the south side of the temple, five stands on the north side, and the large bowl at the southeast corner of the temple. Hiram made pans for hot ashes, and also shovels and sprinkling bowls.

This is a list of the bronze items that Hiram made for the LORD's temple: two columns; two bowl-shaped caps for the tops of the columns; two chain designs on the caps; four hundred pomegranates for the chain designs; ten movable stands; ten small bowls for the stands; a large bowl; twelve bulls that held up the bowl; pans for hot ashes, and also shovels and sprinkling bowls. Hiram made these bronze things for Solomon near the Jordan River between Succoth and Zarethan by pouring melted bronze into clay molds. There were so many bronze things that Solomon never bothered to weigh them, and no one ever knew how much bronze was used.

Solomon gave orders to make the following temple furnishings out of gold: the altar; the table that held the sacred loaves of bread; ten lamp-stands that went in front of the most holy place; flower designs; lamps and tongs; cups, lamp snuff-ers, and small sprinkling bowls; dishes for incense; fire pans; and the hinges for the doors to the most holy place and the main room of the temple. After the LORD's temple was finished, Solomon put into its storage rooms everything that his father David had dedicated to the LORD, including the gold and the silver.

The sacred chest had been kept on Mount Zion, also known as the city of David. But Solomon decided to have the chest moved to the temple while everyone was in Jerusalem, celebrating the Festival of Shelters during Ethanim, the seventh month of the year. Solomon called together the important leaders of Israel. Then the priests and the Levites carried to the temple the sacred chest, the sacred tent, and the objects used for worship. Solomon and a crowd of people walked in front of the chest, and along the way they sacrificed more sheep and cattle than could be counted.

The priests carried the chest into the most holy place and put it under the winged creatures, whose wings covered the chest and the poles used for carrying it. The poles were so long that they could be seen from right outside the most holy place, but not from anywhere else. And they stayed there from then on. The only things kept in the chest were the two flat stones Moses had put there when the LORD made his agreement with the people of Israel at Mount Sinai, after bringing them out of Egypt. Suddenly a cloud filled the temple as the priests were leaving the most holy place. The LORD's glory was in the cloud, and the light from it was so bright that the priests could not stay inside to do their work. Then Solomon prayed:

"Our LORD, you said that you
would live in a dark cloud.
Now I have built a glorious temple
where you can live forever."

Solomon turned toward the people standing there. Then he blessed them and said: "Praise the LORD God of Israel! Long ago he brought his people out of Egypt. He later kept his promise to make my father David the king of Israel. The LORD also said that he had not chosen the city where his temple would be built. So when David wanted to build a temple for the LORD God of Israel, the LORD said, 'It's good that you want to build a temple where I can be worshiped. But you're not the one to do it. Your son will build a temple to honor me.' The LORD has done what he promised. I am the king of Israel like my father, and I've built a temple for the LORD our God. I've also made a place in the temple for the sacred chest. And in that chest are the two flat stones on which is written the solemn agreement the LORD made with our ancestors when he led them out of Egypt."

Solomon stood facing the altar with everyone standing behind him. Then he lifted his arms toward heaven and prayed: "LORD God of Israel, no other god in heaven or on earth is like you! You never forget the agreement you made with your people, and you are loyal to anyone who faithfully obeys your teachings. My father David was your servant, and today you have kept every promise you made to him. LORD God of Israel, you promised my father that someone from his family would always be king of Israel, if they do their best to obey you, just as he did. Please keep this promise you made to your servant David.

"There's not enough room in all of heaven for you, LORD God. How could you possibly live on earth in this temple I have built? But I ask you to answer my prayer. This is the temple where you have chosen to be worshiped. Please watch over it day and night and listen when I turn toward it and pray. I am your servant, and the people of Israel belong to you. So whenever any of us look toward this temple and pray, answer from your home in heaven and forgive our sins.

"Suppose someone accuses a person of a crime, and the accused has to stand in front of the altar in your temple and say, 'I swear I am innocent!' Listen from heaven and decide who is right. Then punish the guilty person and let the innocent one go free.

"Suppose your people Israel sin against you, and then an enemy defeats them. If they come to this temple and beg for forgiveness, listen from your home in heaven. Forgive them and bring them back to the land you gave their ancestors.

"Suppose your people sin against you, and you punish them by holding back the rain. If they turn toward this temple and pray in your name and stop sinning, listen from your home in heaven and forgive them. The people of Israel are your servants, so teach them to live right. And please send rain on the land you promised them forever.

"Sometimes the crops may dry up or rot or be eaten by locusts or grasshoppers, and your people will be starving. Sometimes enemies may surround their towns, or your people will become sick with deadly diseases. Listen when anyone in Israel truly feels sorry and sincerely prays with arms lifted toward your temple. You know what is in everyone's heart. So from your home in heaven answer their prayers, according to the way they live and what is in their hearts. Then your people will worship and obey you for as long as they live in the land you gave their ancestors. Foreigners will hear about you and your mighty power, and some of them will come to live among your people Israel. If any of them pray toward this temple, listen from your home in heaven and answer their prayers. Then everyone on earth will worship you, just like your people Israel, and they will know that I have built this temple to honor you.

"Our LORD, sometimes you will order your people to attack their enemies. Then your people will turn toward this temple I have built for you in your chosen city, and they will pray to you. Answer their prayers from heaven and give them victory.

"Everyone sins. But when your people sin against you, suppose you get angry enough to let their enemies drag them away to foreign countries. Later, they may feel sorry for what they did and ask your forgiveness. Answer them when they pray toward this temple I have built for you in your chosen city, here in this land you gave their ancestors. From your home in heaven, listen to their sincere prayers and do what they ask. Forgive your people no matter how much they have sinned against you. Make the enemies who defeated them be kind to them. Remember, they are the people you chose and rescued from Egypt that was like a blazing fire to them.

"I am your servant, and the people of Israel belong to you. So listen when any of us pray and cry out for your help. When you brought our ancestors out of Egypt, you told your servant Moses to say to them, 'From all people on earth, the LORD God has chosen you to be his very own.'"

When Solomon finished his prayer at the altar, he was kneeling with his arms lifted toward heaven. He stood up, turned toward the people, blessed them, and said loudly: "Praise the LORD! He has kept his promise and given us peace. Every good thing he promised to his servant Moses has happened. The LORD our God was with our ancestors to help them, and I pray that he will be with us and never abandon us. May the LORD help us obey him and follow all the laws and teachings he gave our ancestors. I pray that the LORD our God will remember my prayer day and night. May he help everyone in Israel each day, in whatever way we need it. Then every nation will know that the LORD is the only true God. Obey the LORD our God and follow his commands with all your heart, just as you are doing today."

Solomon and the people dedicated the temple to the LORD by offering twenty-two thousand cattle and one hundred twenty thousand sheep as sacrifices to ask the LORD's blessing. On that day, Solomon dedicated the courtyard in front of the temple and made it acceptable for worship. He offered the sacrifices there because the bronze altar in front of the temple was too small. Solomon and the huge crowd celebrated the Festival of Shelters at the

THE VICTORY STELE OF MERNEPTAH (C. 1210 B.C.E.)

Around 1210 B.C.E., the pharaoh Merneptah, son of Ramesses II, commissioned a stele (a sculpted and inscribed commemorative stone monument) to celebrate his military success in repelling and defeating numerous enemies from Libya and lands to the north who had threatened his realm. But what has drawn the most attention from scholars is Merneptah's claim, inscribed near the bottom of the stela, that "Israel is laid waste; his seed is not." In the view of most scholars, this stele provides the earliest datable evidence of an entity known as "Israel." In the inscription, "Israel" is identified with the hieroglyphic symbol indicating a people rather than an established kingdom or geographic locale. What might this suggest concerning the nature and existence of "Israel" during the Late Bronze Age? Can you link this evidence to any of the accounts from the Hebrew Bible (Old Testament)?

temple for seven days. There were people from as far away as the Egyptian Gorge in the south and Lebo-Hamath in the north. Then on the eighth day, he sent everyone home. They said good-by and left, very happy, because of all the good things the LORD had done for his servant David and his people Israel.

*   *   *

REVIEW QUESTIONS

1. How are the wealth, skills, and products of the cities of Phoenicia represented in this selection?
2. Why did Solomon cause the temple to be built?
3. How is the temple intended to be a link between Yahweh and his people?

HERODOTUS

FROM *The Histories:* Customs of the Persians

The Greek historian Herodotus, who wrote during the fifth century B.C.E., has long been lauded as the father of history (although some would call him the grandfather and accord Thucydides the appellation father*). Although modern historians are quite aware of Herodotus's own prejudices and gullibility, his* Histories *nonetheless remains our most important source for the history of the Persian invasions of Greece in 490 and 480–479 B.C.E. As background for that story, Herodotus also furnished a virtual travelogue of the peoples, places, and customs of the fifth century B.C.E. world. (In fact, his description of Egyptian customs remains an often-cited source on techniques of mummification.) In the following selection, Herodotus reports his knowledge of the customs of the Persians.*

From *Herodotus: The Histories*, edited by Walter Blanco and Jennifer Tolbert Roberts, translated by Walter Blanco (New York: Norton, 1992), pp. 48–50.

*   *   *

These are the customs I know the Persians to observe. They are not allowed to build statues, temples, and altars, and in fact they accuse those who do of silliness, in my opinion because unlike the Greeks, they don't think of the gods as having human form. It is their custom to climb to the mountaintops and sacrifice to Zeus, which is the name they give to the full circle of the sky. They sacrifice to the sun and the moon and the earth, as well as to fire, water, and air. At first, they sacrificed only to these, but they later learned to sacrifice to the Heavenly Aphrodite—they learned this from the Assyrians and the Arabians. The Assyrians call

Aphrodite Mylitta, the Arabians call her Alilat, and the Persians call her Mitra.

This is the way the Persians sacrifice to the above-mentioned gods: they make no altars and light no fires when they are about to sacrifice. They don't pour libations or play the flute or wear garlands or sprinkle barley on their victims. Whenever someone wants to sacrifice to one of the gods, he leads the victim to a ritually pure place and invokes the god while wearing his turban wreathed, preferably, with myrtle. It is not allowed for the sacrificer to pray, in private, for good things for himself. Instead, he prays for the well-being of all the Persians and of the king, for the sacrificer, after all, is included among all the Persians. When he has cut up the sacrificial victim into pieces and then boiled the meat, he spreads out the tenderest grass—preferably clover—and then places all of the meat on top of it. When he has arranged the meat piece by piece, a Magus stands near and chants a hymn on the origin of the gods—anyway, that's the kind of hymn they say it is. It is not their custom to perform a sacrifice without a Magus. The sacrificer waits a little while, then carries away the meat and does whatever he wants with it.

The day of all days they celebrate the most is their own birthday. On that day, the right thing to do is to serve a bigger meal than on any other day. On that day, their rich people serve up oxen, horses, camels, and donkeys that have been roasted whole in ovens, while their poor people serve smaller cattle, like sheep and goats. They eat few main dishes, but lots of appetizers, one after another, and for this reason the Persians say that the Greeks eat a main course and then stop when they are still hungry since after dinner nothing worth mentioning is brought out, though they wouldn't stop eating if it was. They love wine, but they are not allowed to vomit or to urinate in front of someone else. But though they have to be careful about that, they are accustomed to deliberate about their most important affairs when they are drunk, and then, on the next day, when they are sober, the master of the house they have been deliberating in proposes the decision that pleased them most. If they like it even when they are sober, they adopt it, but if not, they let it go. If they ever come to a provisional decision while sober, though, they then get drunk and reconsider it.

This is how you can tell if people who happen to meet each other on the street are social equals: instead of a verbal greeting, they kiss each other on the lips. If one is of slightly lower rank, they kiss each other's cheeks. If one is of a much lower rank, though, he prostrates himself and pays homage to the other. After themselves, Persians have the highest respect for the people who live closest to them, and next highest for those next closest, and so on. In accordance with this principle, they have the least respect for those who live farthest away. They consider themselves to be the best of people by far and others to share worth proportionally, so the people who live the farthest away are the worst. Subject nations ruled each other even under Median rule. That is, the Medes ruled over everything, but especially over those nearest to them, while those, in turn, ruled their neighbors, and so on. The Persians rank nations according to the same principle, by which each nation has a surrogate rule over the next one.

Nevertheless, the Persians are more inclined than other people to adopt foreign customs. For example, they wear Median clothes in the belief that they are more attractive than their own, and they wear Egyptian breastplates into war. They seek out and learn about all kinds of delights, and they even learned from the Greeks to have sex with boys. Each Persian man has many lawfully wedded wives, but many more mistresses.

Second only to being brave in battle, a man is considered manly if he has many sons to show for himself, and every year the king sends gifts to the man who shows off the most sons. They believe that there is strength in numbers. They educate their sons from the age of five to the age of twenty in only three things: horseback riding, archery, and telling the truth. The boy does not come into the presence of his father until he is five years old—until then he lives with the women. This is done so that if he should die while he is growing up he won't cause any grief to his father.

I approve of that custom, and I also approve of the one that forbids even the king to put someone to death on the basis of only one charge, and that forbids any Persian to do any of his house-hold slaves any irreparable harm on the basis of one charge either. If, however, he finds on review that there are more and greater offenses than services, then he may give way to anger.

They say that no one has yet killed his own father or mother. It is inevitable, they say, that any such child who has ever been born will be found on investigation to have been either a changeling or a bastard. They say that it just isn't likely that a true parent will be killed by his own child.

Whatever they are not allowed to do, they are also not allowed to talk about. They consider lying to be the most disgraceful of all things. After that, it is owing money—for many reasons, but mostly, they say, because it is necessary for somebody who owes money to tell lies.

No citizen who is an albino or who has leprosy is allowed into the city or to mingle with other Persians. They say that he has committed some offense against the sun. Foreigners who catch these diseases are driven out of the country by posses. Even white doves are driven out, charged with the same offense.

They don't spit, urinate, or wash their hands in rivers, or allow anyone else to, for they especially revere rivers.

The Persians don't notice it, though we do, but this also happens to be true of them: their names, which refer to their physical characteristics or to their social importance, all end in the same letter, which the Dorians call san and which the Ionians call sigma. If you look into it, you will find that Persian names end in this letter—not some here and some there, but *all* of them.

I am able to say these things with certainty because I know them for a fact. There are things about the dead, though, which are concealed or referred to obliquely—for example that the corpse of a Persian man is not buried until it has been torn at by a bird or a dog. I know for sure, though, that the Magi practice this—because they do it openly—and that the Persians cover a corpse with wax before putting it in the ground. The Magi are very different from other people, including the Egyptian priests. The Egyptian priests refrain from killing any living thing, except what they ritually sacrifice. The Magi, however, will kill everything but dogs and people with their own hands. In fact, they make a point of killing things, and go around killing ants and snakes and anything else that creeps, crawls, and flies. Well, that's how they've been practicing this custom since the beginning, so let it stay that way.

*   *   *

REVIEW QUESTIONS

1. How would you judge Herodotus's general opinion of Persian customs and values? Does he find things to admire about them?
2. Do any of his observations suggest to you that he might have been taken in by someone else's stories?

FROM The Torah: Laws

Modern scholars question the historicity of the Bible's account of the Hebrew Exodus, when thousands supposedly migrated from Egypt under the leadership of a man named Moses. The Egyptian records make no mention of such an event, nor is there any other evidence of it outside the biblical account. The impact of the Exodus story on the self-concept of the early Jewish people as having been chosen by God (who has identified himself by then as Yahweh) and whose fate is bound to their acceptance of him, is, however, immeasurable. As they made their way through the barren wilderness of the Sinai Desert, the Hebrews received from Yahweh a set of laws—the Decalogue, or Ten Commandments. These laws were to govern both their relationship with him and their behavior among themselves. In subsequent books of the Pentateuch (the first five books of the Hebrew Bible, the authorship of which was traditionally ascribed to Moses), these laws were expanded and elaborated on to form the basis of the Torah, the corpus of biblical law. The Torah remains today the very core of Judaism and of Jewish self-identity as a people chosen by God.

From *Contemporary English Version* by American Bible Society (New York: American Bible Society, 1995).

FROM **The Book of Exodus**

Moses led the people out of the camp to meet God, and they stood at the foot of the mountain. Mount Sinai was covered with smoke because the LORD had come down in a flaming fire. Smoke poured out of the mountain just like a furnace, and the whole mountain shook. The trumpet blew louder and louder. Moses spoke, and God answered him with thunder. The LORD came down to the top of Mount Sinai and told Moses to meet him there. Then he said, "Moses, go and warn the people not to cross the boundary that you set at the foot of the mountain. They must not cross it to come and look at me, because if they do, many of them will die. Only the priests may come near me, and they must obey strict rules before I let them. If they don't, they will be punished." Moses replied, "The people cannot come up the mountain. You warned us to stay away because it is holy." Then the LORD told Moses, "Go down and bring Aaron back here with you. But the priests and people must not try to push their way through, or I will rush at them like a flood!" After Moses had gone back down, he told the people what the LORD had said.

God said to the people of Israel:

I am the LORD your God, the one who brought you out of Egypt where you were slaves.

Do not worship any god except me.

Do not make idols that look like anything in the sky or on earth or in the ocean under the earth. Don't bow down and worship idols. I am the LORD your God, and I demand all your love. If you reject me, I will punish your families for three or four generations. But if you love me and obey my laws, I will be kind to your families for thousands of generations.

Do not misuse my name. I am the LORD your God, and I will punish anyone who misuses my name. Remember that the Sabbath Day belongs to me. You have six days when you can do your work, but the seventh day of each week belongs to me, your God. No one is to work on that day—not you, your children, your slaves, your animals, or the foreigners who live in your towns. In six days I made the sky, the earth, the oceans, and everything in them, but on the seventh day I rested. That's why I made the Sabbath a special day that belongs to me.

Respect your father and your mother, and you will live a long time in the land I am giving you.

Do not murder.

Be faithful in marriage.

Do not steal.

Do not tell lies about others.

Do not want anything that belongs to someone else. Don't want anyone's house, wife or husband, slaves, oxen, donkeys or anything else.

*   *   *

The LORD told Moses to say to the people of Israel: "With your own eyes, you saw me speak to you from heaven. So you must never make idols of silver or gold to worship in place of me. Build an altar out of earth, and offer on it your sacrifices of sheep, goats, and cattle. Wherever I choose to be worshiped, I will come down to bless you. If you ever build an altar for me out of stones, do not use any tools to chisel the stones, because that would make the altar unfit. And don't build an altar that requires steps; you might expose yourself when you climb up."

The LORD gave Moses the following laws for his people:

If you buy a Hebrew slave, he must remain your slave for six years. But in the seventh year you must set him free, without cost to him. If he was single at the time you bought him, he alone must be set free. But if he was married at the time, both he and his wife must be given their freedom. If you give him a wife, and they have children, only the man himself must be set free; his wife and children remain the property of his owner.

But suppose the slave loves his wife and children so much that he won't leave without them. Then he must stand beside either the door or the doorpost at the place of worship, while his owner punches a small hole through one of his ears with a sharp metal rod. This makes him a slave for life. A young woman who was sold by her father doesn't gain her freedom in the same way that a man does. If she doesn't please the man who bought her to be his wife, he must let her be bought back. He cannot sell her to foreigners; this would break the contract he made with her. If he selects her as a wife for his son, he must treat her as his own daughter. If the man later marries another woman, he must continue to provide food and clothing for the one he bought and to treat her as a wife. If he fails to do any of these things, she must be given her freedom without cost.

Death is the punishment for murder. But if you did not intend to kill someone, and I, the LORD, let it happen anyway, you may run for safety to a place that I have set aside. If you plan in advance to murder someone, there's no escape, not even by holding on to my altar. You will be dragged off and killed. Death is the punishment for attacking your father or mother.

Death is the punishment for kidnapping. If you sell the person you kidnapped, or if you are caught with that person, the penalty is death.

Death is the punishment for cursing your father or mother.

Suppose two of you are arguing, and you hit the other with either a rock or your fist, without causing a fatal injury. If the victim has to stay in bed, and later has to use a stick when walking outside, you must pay for the loss of time and do what you can to help until the injury is completely healed. That's your only responsibility.

Death is the punishment for beating to death any of your slaves. However, if the slave lives a few days after the beating, you are not to be punished. After all, you have already lost the services of that slave who was your property.

Suppose a pregnant woman suffers a miscarriage as the result of an injury caused by someone who is fighting. If she isn't badly hurt, the one who injured her must pay whatever fine her husband demands and the judges approve. But if she is seriously injured, the payment will be life for life, eye for eye, tooth for tooth, hand for hand, foot for foot, burn for burn, cut for cut, and bruise for bruise. If you hit one of your slaves and cause the loss of an eye, the slave must be set free. The same law applies if you knock out a slave's tooth—the slave goes free.

A bull that kills someone with its horns must be killed and its meat destroyed, but the owner of the bull isn't responsible for the death.

Suppose you own a bull that has been in the habit of attacking people, but you have refused to keep it fenced in. If that bull kills someone, both you and the bull must be put to death by stoning. However, you may save your own life by paying whatever fine is demanded. This same law applies if the bull gores someone's son or daughter. If the bull kills a slave, you must pay the slave owner thirty pieces of silver for the loss of the slave, and the bull must be killed by stoning.

Suppose someone's ox or donkey is killed by falling into an open pit that you dug or left uncovered on your property. You must pay for the dead animal, and it becomes yours.

If your bull kills someone else's, yours must be sold. Then the money from your bull and the meat from the dead bull must be divided equally between you and the other owner.

If you refuse to fence in a bull that is known to attack others, you must pay for any animal it kills, but the dead animal will belong to you.

*   *   *

Suppose you borrow an animal from a neighbor, and it gets injured or dies while the neighbor isn't around. Then you must replace it. But if something happens to the animal while the owner is present, you do not have to replace it. If you had leased the animal, the money you paid the owner will cover any harm done to it.

Suppose a young woman has never been married and isn't engaged. If a man talks her into having sex, he must pay the bride price and marry her. But if her father refuses to let her marry the man, the bride price must still be paid. Death is the punishment for witchcraft.

Death is the punishment for having sex with an animal.

Death is the punishment for offering sacrifices to any god except me.

Do not mistreat or abuse foreigners who live among you. Remember, you were foreigners in Egypt.

Do not mistreat widows or orphans. If you do, they will beg for my help, and I will come to their rescue. In fact, I will get so angry that I will kill your men and make widows of their wives and orphans of their children.

Don't charge interest when you lend money to any of my people who are in need. Before sunset you must return any coat taken as security for a loan, because that is the only cover the poor have when they sleep at night. I am a merciful God, and when they call out to me, I will come to help them.

Don't speak evil of me or of the ruler of your people. Don't fail to give me the offerings of grain and wine that belong to me. Dedicate to me your first-born sons and the first-born of your cattle and sheep. Let the animals stay with their mothers for seven days, then on the eighth day give them to me, your God.

You are my chosen people, so don't eat the meat of any of your livestock that was killed by a wild animal. Instead, feed the meat to dogs.

Don't spread harmful rumors or help a criminal by giving false evidence.

Always tell the truth in court, even if everyone else is dishonest and stands in the way of justice. And don't favor the poor, simply because they are poor. If you find an ox or a donkey that has wandered off, take it back where it belongs, even if the owner is your enemy.

If a donkey is overloaded and falls down, you must do what you can to help, even if it belongs to someone who doesn't like you. Make sure that the poor are given equal justice in court. Don't bring false charges against anyone or sentence an innocent person to death. I won't forgive you if you do.

Don't accept bribes. Judges are blinded and justice is twisted by bribes.

Don't mistreat foreigners. You were foreigners in Egypt, and you know what it is like.

Plant and harvest your crops for six years, but let the land rest during the seventh year. The poor are to eat what they want from your fields, vineyards, and olive trees during that year, and when they have all they want from your fields, leave the rest for wild animals.

Work the first six days of the week, but rest and relax on the seventh day. This law is not only for you, but for your oxen, donkeys, and slaves, as well as for any foreigners among you.

*   *   *

FROM **The Book of Leviticus**

If you curse your father or mother, you will be put to death, and it will be your own fault.

If any of you men have sex with another man's wife, both you and the woman will be put to death.

Having sex with one of your father's wives disgraces him. So both you and the woman will be put to death, just as you deserve. It isn't natural to have sex with your daughter-in-law, and both of you will be put to death, just as you deserve. It's disgusting for men to have sex with one another, and those who do will be put to death, just as they deserve. It isn't natural for a man to marry both a mother and her daughter, and so all three of them will be burned to death. If any of you have sex with an animal, both you and the animal will be put to death, just as you deserve.

If you marry one of your sisters, you will be punished, and the two of you will be disgraced by being openly forced out of the community. If you have sex with a woman during her monthly period, both you and the woman will be cut off from the people of Israel. The sisters of your father and mother are your own relatives, and you will be punished for having sex with any of them. If you have sex with your uncle's wife, neither you nor she will ever have any children. And if you marry your sister-in-law, neither of you will ever have any children. Obey my laws and teachings. Or else the land I am giving you will become sick of you and throw you out. The nations I am chasing out did these disgusting things, and I hated them for it, so don't follow their example. I am the LORD your God, and I have promised you their land that is rich with milk and honey. I have chosen you to be different from other people. That's why you must make a difference between animals and birds that I have said are clean and unclean—this will keep you from becoming disgusting to me. I am the LORD, the holy God. You have been chosen to be my people, and so you must be holy too. If you claim to receive messages from the dead, you will be put to death by stoning, just as you deserve.

*   *   *

Suppose some of your people become so poor that they have to sell themselves and become your slaves. Then you must treat them as servants, rather than as slaves. And in the Year of Celebration they are to be set free, so they and their children may return home to their families and property. I brought them out of Egypt to be my servants, not to be sold as slaves. So obey me, and don't be cruel to the poor.

If you want slaves, buy them from other nations or from the foreigners who live in your own country, and make them your property. You can own them, and even leave them to your children when you die, but do not make slaves of your own people or be cruel to them.

*   *   *

Faithfully obey my laws, and I will send rain to make your crops grow and your trees produce fruit. Your harvest of grain and grapes will be so abundant, that you won't know what to do with it all. You will eat and be satisfied, and you will live in safety. I will bless your country with peace, and you will rest without fear. I will wipe out the dangerous animals and protect you from enemy attacks. You will chase and destroy your enemies, even if there are only five of you and a hundred of them, or only a hundred of you and ten thousand of them. I will treat you with such kindness that your nation will grow strong, and I will also keep my promises to you. Your barns will overflow with grain each year. I will live among you and never again look on you with disgust. I will walk with you—I will be your God, and you will be my people. I am the LORD your God, and I rescued you from Egypt, so that you would never again be slaves. I have set you free; now walk with your heads held high.

If you disobey me and my laws, and if you break our agreement, I will punish you terribly, and you will be ruined. You will be struck with incurable diseases and with fever that leads to blindness and depression. Your enemies will eat the crops you plant, and I will turn from you and let you be destroyed by your attackers. You will even run at the very rumor of attack. Then, if you still refuse to obey me, I will punish you seven times for each of your sins, until your pride is completely crushed. I will hold back the rain, so the sky above you will be like iron, and the ground beneath your feet will be like copper. All of your hard work will be for nothing—and there will be no harvest of grain or fruit.

If you keep rebelling against me, I'll punish you seven times worse, just as your sins deserve! I'll send wild animals to attack you, and they will gobble down your children and livestock. So few of you will be left that your roads will be deserted.

If you remain my enemies after this, I'll remain your enemy and punish you even worse. War will break out because you broke our agreement, and if you escape to your walled cities, I'll punish you with horrible diseases, and you will be captured by your enemies. You will have such a shortage of bread, that ten women will be able to bake their bread in the same oven. Each of you will get only a few crumbs, and you will go hungry.

Then if you don't stop rebelling, I'll really get furious and punish you terribly for your sins! In fact, you will be so desperate for food that you will eat your own children. I'll destroy your shrines and tear down your incense altars, leaving your dead bodies piled on top of your idols. And you will be disgusting to me. I'll wipe out your towns and your places of worship and will no longer be pleased with the smell of your sacrifices. Your land will become so desolate that even your enemies who settle there will be shocked when they see it. After I destroy your towns and ruin your land with war, I'll scatter you among the nations.

While you are prisoners in foreign lands, your own land will enjoy years of rest and refreshment, as it should have done each seventh year when you lived there. In the land of your enemies, you will tremble at the rustle of a leaf, as though it were a sword. And you will become so weak that you will stumble and fall over each other, even when no one is chasing you. Many of you will die in foreign lands, and others of you will waste away in sorrow as the result of your sins and the sins of your ancestors.

Then suppose you realize that I turned against you and brought you to the land of your enemies because both you and your ancestors had stubbornly sinned against me. If you humbly confess what you have done and start living right, I'll keep the promise I made to your ancestors Abraham, Isaac, and Jacob. I will bless your land and let it rest during the time that you are in a foreign country, paying for your rebellion against me and my laws.

No matter what you have done, I am still the LORD your God, and I will never completely reject you or become absolutely disgusted with you there in the land of your enemies. While nations watched, I rescued your ancestors from Egypt so that I would be their God. Yes, I am your LORD, and I will never forget our agreement.

*   *   *

FROM **The Book of Deuteronomy**

Suppose a man starts hating his wife soon after they are married. He might tell ugly lies about her, and say, "I married this woman, but when we slept together, I found out she wasn't a virgin."

If this happens, the bride's father and mother must go to the town gate to show the town leaders the proof that the woman was a virgin. Her father will say, "I let my daughter marry this man, but he started hating her and accusing her of not being a virgin. But he is wrong, because here is proof that she was a virgin!" Then the bride's parents will show them the bed sheet from the woman's wedding night.

The town leaders will beat the man with a whip because he accused his bride of not being a virgin. He will have to pay her father one hundred pieces of silver and will never be allowed to divorce her.

But if the man was right and there is no proof that his bride was a virgin, the men of the town will take the woman to the door of her father's house and stone her to death.

This woman brought evil into your community by sleeping with someone before she got married, and you must get rid of that evil by killing her.

People of Israel, if a man is caught having sex with someone else's wife, you must put them both to death. That way, you will get rid of the evil they have done in Israel.

If a man is caught in town having sex with an engaged woman who isn't screaming for help, they both must be put to death. The man is guilty of having sex with a married woman. And the woman is guilty because she didn't call for help, even though she was inside a town and people were nearby. Take them both to the town gate and stone them to death. You must get rid of the evil they brought into your community. If an engaged woman is raped out in the country, only the man will be put to death. Do not punish the woman at all; she has done nothing wrong, and certainly nothing deserving death. This crime is like murder, because the woman was alone out in the country when the man attacked her. She screamed, but there was no one to help her.

Suppose a woman isn't engaged to be married, and a man talks her into sleeping with him. If they are caught, they will be forced to get married. He must give her father fifty pieces of silver as a bride-price and can never divorce her. A man must not marry a woman who was married to his father. This would be a disgrace to his father.

REVIEW QUESTIONS

1. According to the Torah, what is Yahweh's relationship to his chosen people?
2. How are these chosen people to set themselves apart from other peoples? How are they to relate to them?
3. As reflected in these laws, what are the principal values and modes of acceptable behavior in Hebrew society?
4. What kinds of principles of compensation do these laws reflect, and how do they compare with the principles of compensation reflected in the laws of Hammurabi (see Chapter 1)?
5. What kinds of attitudes toward sexual behavior do these laws reflect? How is that behavior regulated?
6. What status and rights do women possess in the context of these laws?
7. What does Yahweh promise in return for obedience to his laws? For disobedience to them?

FROM The Book of Isaiah: Prophecies

The Book of Isaiah contains the writings of at least two different authors, separated in time by about one hundred fifty years: a prophet named Isaiah, from Jerusalem, whose career spanned the latter half of the eighth century B.C.E., and an unknown prophet, referred to now as the Second Isaiah, whose writings are included here. The Second Isaiah's career was in Babylon and encompassed the later part of the exile there (587–539 B.C.E.) as well as the conquest of Babylon by the Persian King Cyrus the Great. In the Second Isaiah's writings, Yahweh has assumed a role much larger than that of the exclusive God of a chosen people.

From *Contemporary English Version* by American Bible Society (New York: American Bible Society, 1995).

*   *   *

People of Israel,
I have chosen you
as my servant.
I am your Creator.
You were in my care
even before you were born.
Israel, don't be terrified!
You are my chosen servant,
my very favorite. I will bless the thirsty land
by sending streams of water;
I will bless your descendants
by giving them my Spirit.
They will spring up like grass or like willow trees
near flowing streams.
They will worship me
and become my people.
They will write my name
on the back of their hands. I am the LORD
  All-Powerful,
the first and the last,
the one and only God.
Israel, I have rescued you!
I am your King.
Can anyone compare with me?
If so, let them speak up
and tell me now.
Let them say what has happened
since I made my nation

long ago,
and let them tell
what is going to happen. Don't tremble with fear!
Didn't I tell you long ago?
Didn't you hear me?
I alone am God—
no one else is a mighty rock.
Those people who make idols
are nothing themselves,
and the idols they treasure
are just as worthless.
Worshipers of idols are blind,
stupid, and foolish.
Why make an idol or an image
that can't do a thing?
Everyone who makes idols
and all who worship them
are mere humans,
who will end up
sadly disappointed.
Let them face me in court
and be terrified.

*   *   *

People of Israel,
you are my servant,
so remember all of this.
Israel, I created you,
and you are my servant.

I won't forget you. Turn back to me!
I have rescued you
and swept away your sins
as though they were clouds.

Tell the heavens and the earth
to start singing!
Tell the mountains
and every tree in the forest
to join in the song!
The LORD has rescued his people;
now they will worship him.

Israel, I am your LORD.
I am your source of life,
and I have rescued you.
I created everything
from the sky above
to the earth below.
I make liars of false prophets
and fools of fortunetellers.
I take human wisdom
and turn it into nonsense.
I will make the message
of my prophets come true.
They are saying, "Jerusalem
will be filled with people,
and the LORD will rebuild
the towns of Judah."
I am the one who commands
the sea and its streams
to run dry.
I am also the one who says,
"Cyrus will lead my people
and obey my orders.
Jerusalem and the temple
will be rebuilt."

The LORD said to Cyrus, his chosen one:
I have taken hold
of your right hand
to help you capture nations
and remove kings from power.
City gates will open for you;
not one will stay closed.
As I lead you,
I will level mountains and break the iron bars

on bronze gates of cities.
I will give you treasures
hidden in dark
and secret places.
Then you will know that I,
the LORD God of Israel,
have called you by name.
Cyrus, you don't even know me!
But I have called you by name
and highly honored you because of Israel,
my chosen servant.
Only I am the LORD!
There are no other gods.
I have made you strong,
though you don't know me.
Now everyone from east to west
will learn that I am the LORD.
No other gods are real.
I create light and darkness,
happiness and sorrow.
I, the LORD, do all of this.

                    *   *   *

The clay doesn't ask,
"Why did you make me this way?
Where are the handles?"
Children don't have the right
to demand of their parents,
"What have you done
to make us what we are?"
I am the LORD, the Creator,
the holy God of Israel.
Do you dare question me
about my own nation
or about what I have done?
I created the world
and covered it with people;
I stretched out the sky
and filled it with stars.
I have done the right thing
by placing Cyrus in power,
and I will make the roads easy
for him to follow.
I am the LORD All-Powerful!
Cyrus will rebuild my city
and set my people free

without being paid a thing.
I, the LORD, have spoken.

*   *   *

Anyone who makes idols
will be confused
and terribly disgraced.
But Israel, I, the LORD,
will always keep you safe
and free from shame.

The LORD alone is God!
He created the heavens
and made a world
where people can live,
instead of creating
an empty desert.
The LORD alone is God;
there are no others.
The LORD did not speak
in a dark secret place
or command Jacob's descendants
to search for him in vain.
The LORD speaks the truth,
and this is what he says
to every survivor
from every nation:
"Gather around me!
Learn how senseless it is
to worship wooden idols
or pray to helpless gods.
"Why don't you get together
and meet me in court?
Didn't I tell you long ago
what would happen?
I am the only God!
There are no others.
I bring about justice,
and have the power to save.
"I invite the whole world
to turn to me and be saved.
I alone am God!
No others are real.
I have made a solemn promise,
one that won't be broken:
Everyone will bow down

and worship me.
They will admit that I alone
can bring about justice.
Everyone who is angry with me
will be terribly ashamed
and will turn to me.
I, the LORD, will give
victory and great honor
to the people of Israel."

City of Babylon,
You are delicate
and untouched,
but that will change.
Surrender your royal power
and sit in the dirt.
Start grinding grain!
Take off your veil.
Strip off your fancy clothes
and cross over rivers. You will suffer the shame
of going naked,
because I will take revenge,
and no one can escape. I am the LORD
    All-Powerful,
the holy God of Israel.
I am their Savior.
Babylon, be silent!
Sit in the dark.
No longer will nations
accept you as their queen.
I was angry with my people.
So I let you take their land
and bring disgrace on them.
You showed them no mercy,
but were especially cruel
to those who were old.
You thought that you
would be queen forever.
You didn't care what you did;
it never entered your mind
that you might get caught.
You think that you alone
are all-powerful,
that you won't be a widow
or lose your children.
All you care about is pleasure,

but listen to what I say.
Your magic powers and charms
will suddenly fail,
then you will be a widow
and lose your children.
You hid behind evil
like a shield and said,
"No one can see me!"
You were fooled by your wisdom
and your knowledge;
you felt sure that you alone
were in full control.
But without warning,
disaster will strike—
and your magic charms
won't help at all.
Keep using your magic powers
and your charms
as you have always done.
Maybe—just maybe—
you will frighten somebody!
You have worn yourself out,
asking for advice
from those who study the stars
and tell the future
month after month.
Go ask them how to be saved
from what will happen.
People who trust the stars
are as helpless
as straw
in a flaming fire.
No one can even keep warm, sitting by a fire
that feeds only on straw.
These are the fortunetellers
you have done business with
all of your life.
But they don't know
where they are going,
and they can't save you.

People of Israel,
you come from Jacob's family
and the tribe of Judah. You claim to worship me,
the LORD God of Israel,
but you are lying.

You call Jerusalem your home
and say you depend on me,
the LORD All-Powerful,
the God of Israel.
Long ago I announced
what was going to be,
then without warning,
I made it happen.
I knew you were stubborn
and hardheaded.
And I told you these things,
so that when they happened
you would not say,
"The idols we worship did this."
You heard what I said,
and you have seen it happen.
Now admit that it's true!
I will show you secrets
you have never known.

*   *   *

By the power of his Spirit
the LORD God has sent me
with this message:
People of Israel,
I am the holy LORD God,
the one who rescues you.
For your own good,
I teach you,
and I lead you
along the right path.
How I wish that you
had obeyed my commands!
Your success and good fortune
would then have overflowed
like a flooding river.
Your nation would be blessed
with more people
than there are grains of sand
along the seashore.
And I would never have let
your country be destroyed.
Now leave Babylon!
Celebrate as you go.
Be happy and shout
for everyone to hear,

"The LORD has rescued
his servant Israel!
He led us through the desert
and made water flow from a rock
to satisfy our thirst.
But the LORD has promised
that none who are evil
will live in peace."
Everyone, listen,
even you foreign nations
across the sea.
The LORD chose me
and gave me a name
before I was born.
He made my words pierce
like a sharp sword
or a pointed arrow;
he kept me safely hidden
in the palm of his hand.
The LORD said to me,
"Israel, you are my servant;
and because of you
I will be highly honored."
I said to myself,
"I'm completely worn out;
my time has been wasted.
But I did it for the LORD God,
and he will reward me."
Even before I was born,
the LORD God chose me
to serve him and to lead back
the people of Israel.
So the LORD has honored me
and made me strong.
Now the LORD says to me,
"It isn't enough for you
to be merely my servant.
You must do more than lead back
survivors
from the tribes
of Israel.
I have placed you here as a light
for other nations;
you must take my saving power
to everyone on earth."
Israel, I am the holy LORD God,

the one who rescues you.
You are slaves of rulers
and of a nation
who despises you. Now this is what I promise:
Kings and rulers will honor you
by kneeling at your feet.
You can trust me! I am your LORD,
the holy God of Israel,
and you are my chosen ones.

This is what the LORD says:
I will answer your prayers
because I have set a time
when I will help
by coming to save you.
I have chosen you
to take my promise of hope
to other nations. You will rebuild the country
from its ruins,
then people will come
and settle there.
You will set prisoners free
from dark dungeons
to see the light of day.
On their way home,
they will find plenty to eat,
even on barren hills.
They won't go hungry
or get thirsty;
they won't be bothered
by the scorching sun
or hot desert winds.
I will be merciful
while leading them along
to streams of water.
I will level the mountains
and make roads.
Then my people will return
from distant lands
in the north and the west
and from the city of Syene.

Tell the heavens and the earth
to celebrate and sing;
command every mountain
to join in the song.

The LORD's people have suffered,
but he has shown mercy
and given them comfort.
The people of Zion said,
"The LORD has turned away
and forgotten us."
The LORD answered,
"Could a mother forget a child
who nurses at her breast?
Could she fail to love an infant
who came from her own body?
Even if a mother could forget,
I will never forget you.
A picture of your city
is drawn on my hand.
You are always in my thoughts!
Your city will be built faster
than it was destroyed—those who attacked it
will retreat and leave.
Look around! You will see
your people coming home.
As surely as I live,
I, the LORD, promise
that your city with its people
will be as lovely as a bride
wearing her jewelry."

Jerusalem is now in ruins!
Nothing is left of the city.
But it will be rebuilt
and soon overcrowded;
its cruel enemies
will be gone far away.
Jerusalem is a woman
whose children were born
while she was in deep sorrow over the loss of her
    husband.
Now those children
will come and seek room
in the crowded city,
and Jerusalem will ask,
"Am I really their mother?
How could I have given birth
when I was still mourning
in a foreign land?
Who raised these children?

Where have they come from?"
The LORD God says:
"I will soon give a signal
for the nations
to return your sons
and your daughters
to the arms of Jerusalem.
The kings and queens
of those nations
where they were raised
will come and bow down.
They will take care of you
just like a slave
taking care of a child.
Then you will know
that I am the LORD.
You won't be disappointed
if you trust me."

Has anyone believed us
or seen the mighty power
of the LORD in action?
Like a young plant or a root
that sprouts in dry ground,
the servant grew up
obeying the LORD.
He wasn't some handsome king.
Nothing about the way he looked
made him attractive to us.
He was hated and rejected;
his life was filled with sorrow
and terrible suffering.
No one wanted to look at him.
We despised him and said,
"He is a nobody!"
He suffered and endured
great pain for us,
but we thought his suffering
was punishment from God.
He was wounded and crushed
because of our sins;
by taking our punishment,
he made us completely well.
All of us were like sheep
that had wandered off.
We had each gone our own way,

but the LORD gave him
the punishment we deserved.
He was painfully abused,
but he did not complain.
He was silent like a lamb
being led to the butcher,
as quiet as a sheep
having its wool cut off.
He was condemned to death
without a fair trial.
Who could have imagined
what would happen to him?
His life was taken away
because of the sinful things
my people had done. He wasn't dishonest
    or violent,
but he was buried in a tomb
of cruel and rich people. The LORD decided
    his servant
would suffer as a sacrifice
to take away the sin
and guilt of others.
Now the servant will live
to see his own descendants. He did everything
the LORD had planned.

By suffering, the servant
will learn the true meaning
of obeying the LORD.
Although he is innocent,
he will take the punishment
for the sins of others,
so that many of them
will no longer be guilty.
The LORD will reward him
with honor and power
for sacrificing his life.
Others thought he was a sinner,
but he suffered for our sins
and asked God to forgive us.

REVIEW QUESTIONS

1. According to the Second Isaiah, what now is the dominion of the Hebrews' God?
2. What role has Israel now assumed in relation to the other nations of the earth?
3. Does a messiah figure emerge in this document?
4. What is God's judgment of Babylon?

3 ❧ THE CIVILIZATION OF GREECE, 1000–400 B.C.E.

By the time that the uncharacteristically allied city-states of Hellas (Greece) had to face invasion by the massive forces of the Achaemenid Persian emperor Darius in 490 B.C.E., the much more ancient civilizations of Mesopotamia and Egypt (not to mention India and China) had been thriving for thousands of years. By 500 B.C.E., both Babylon and Egypt—in fact, the entire Near East—had fallen under the sway of the Persian Empire, which could boast of one of the more sophisticated imperial systems of antiquity and resources vastly superior to those of the upstarts from the Aegean, located on the empire's far western periphery. The Greeks themselves, from the Persian perspective, undoubtedly seemed to be a disorganized, belligerent, even barbarian people who were no real threat to continued Persian dominion.

Nonetheless, only eleven years after the Persians' first invasion, the Greeks had vanquished and expelled not only the invasion of Darius but also a second, even more massive invasion under the son and successor of Darius, Xerxes. The Greeks' improbable success came to be seen as one of the first events in the process by which the West, over many centuries, defined itself as an entity distinct from and, in its own eyes, generally superior to the East.

Scholars today recognize (as did ancient Greek writers) the tremendous debt the early Greeks owed to the older civilizations of the ancient Near East and Egypt. Indeed, to be aware of that debt, we need look no further than early Greek statuary and temple architecture, with their obviously Egyptian inspiration, or the Greek alphabet, borrowed from the Phoenicians, with whom the Greeks traded. However, within the unique context of early Greek society, political development, and culture, a number of concepts and issues emerged that have remained at the heart of the ongoing development of Western civilization and have had significant impact on the non-Western civilizations that, in the past two centuries, have increasingly been confronted with the ideas and values of the West. What are the appropriate roles and rights of the individual in society? To what does the individual owe primary allegiance, the dictates of conscience or the laws of the state? How should a state be properly organized and governed, and by whom? What ought to be the respective roles of men and women in society? Do divine forces govern natural phenomena and human history? Indeed, do gods or a god even exist? Some have claimed that much of the history of Western culture subsequent to the era of the Greek city-states has centered on the continuing endeavor to answer these and other questions that the Greeks raised.

The Greeks took some giant steps in addressing these questions. In fact, they made perhaps their most significant contributions to that endeavor during the relatively brief "golden age" that accompanied Athens' rise to preeminence among the city-states after the defeat of the Persians. Classical Greek civilization achieved its loftiest heights in Athens during the decades prior to Athens' disastrous defeat by Sparta and its allies at the end of the Peloponnesian War. Less than seventy years later, Athens, Sparta, and the other previously independent city-states were compelled to cede their autonomy to the hegemony of the Macedonian king Philip II, whose son Alexander would inaugurate a new era during which the affairs of those city-states would take a backseat to the Hellenistic kingdoms. Nonetheless, the relatively brief zenith of the classical Greek city-states would, in time, be recognized as vastly out of proportion to their influence on the later course of Western civilization.

HOMER

FROM *The Odyssey*

The actual existence of the poet named Homer, and of the Trojan War about which he wrote, is still debated among scholars. The influence of the epic poems, the Iliad *and the* Odyssey, *that the later Greeks attributed to him is not. For the warrior aristocracy whose interests and tastes these poems reflected and for whom they were recited as entertainment, Homer's tales of the Greeks' siege of Troy and of the exploits of Odysseus and his men on their way home after that siege provided a vivid model of heroic values and behavior in a world where the gods intruded their designs regularly into human affairs. In the following selection from The* Odyssey, *the main hero, Odysseus, on his long and dangerous journey back to Ithaca on the Greek mainland after the Greeks have sacked Troy, has reached the land of Phaeacia. Its king, Alcinous, is determined to act as his worthy host.*

From *The Odyssey of Homer,* translated by Samuel Butler (London: Longmans, Green, & Co., 1900).

Now when the child of morning, rosy-fingered Dawn, appeared, Alcinous and Odysseus both rose, and Alcinous led the way to the Phaeacian place of assembly, which was near the ships. When they got there they sat down side by side on a seat of polished stone, while Athene took the form of one of Alcinous' servants, and went round the town in order to help Odysseus to get home. She went up to the citizens, man by man, and said: "Aldermen and town councilors of the Phaeacians, come to the assembly all of you and listen to the stranger who has just come off a long voyage to the house of King Alcinous. He looks like an immortal god."

With these words she made them all want to come, and they flocked to the assembly till seats and standing room were alike crowded. Everyone was struck with the appearance of Odysseus, for Athene had beautified him about the head and shoulders, making him look taller and stouter than he really was, that he might impress the Phaeacians favorably as being a very remarkable man, and might come off well in the many trials of skill to which they would challenge him. Then, when they were got together, Alcinous spoke:

"Hear me," said he, "aldermen and town councilors of the Phaeacians, that I may speak even as I am minded. This stranger, whoever he may be, has found his way to my house from somewhere or other either east or west. He wants an escort and wishes to have the matter settled. Let us then get one ready for him, as we have done for others before him. Indeed, no one who ever yet came to my house has been able to complain of me for not speeding him on his way soon enough. Let us draw a ship into the sea—one that has never yet made a voyage—and man her with two and fifty of our smartest young sailors. Then when you have made fast your oars each by his own seat, leave the ship and come to my house to prepare a feast. I will supply you with everything. I am giving these instructions to the young men who will form the crew. As regards you aldermen and town councilors, you will join me in entertaining our guest in the cloisters. I can take no excuses, and we will have Demodocus to sing to us; for there is no bard like him, whatever he may choose to sing about."

Alcinous then led the way, and the others followed after, while a servant went to fetch Demodocus. The fifty-two picked oarsmen went to the seashore as they had been told, and when they got there they drew the ship into the water, got her mast and sails inside her, bound the oars to the thole-pins with twisted thongs of leather, all in due course, and spread the white sails aloft. They moored the vessel a little way out from land, and then came on shore and went to the house of King Alcinous. The outhouses, yards, and all the precincts were filled with crowds of men in great multitudes both old and young; and Alcinous killed them a dozen sheep, eight full-grown pigs, and two oxen. These they skinned and dressed so as to provide a magnificent banquet.

A servant presently led in the famous bard Demodocus, whom the muse had dearly loved, but to whom she had given both good and evil, for though she had endowed him with a divine gift of song, she had robbed him of his eyesight. Pontonous set a seat for him among the guests, leaning it up against a bearing-post. He hung the lyre for him on a peg over his head, and showed him where he was to feel for it with his hands. He also set a fair table with a basket of victuals by his side, and a cup of wine from which he might drink whenever he was so disposed.

The company then laid their hands upon the good things that were before them, but as soon as they had had enough to eat and drink, the muse inspired Demodocus to sing the feats of heroes, and more especially a matter that was then in the mouths of all men, to wit, the quarrel between Odysseus and Achilles, and the fierce words that they heaped on one another as they sat together at a banquet. But Agamemnon was glad when he heard his chieftains quarreling with one another, for Apollo had foretold him this at Pytho when he crossed the stone floor to consult the oracle. Here was the beginning of the evil that by the will of Zeus fell both upon Danaans and Trojans.

Thus sang the bard, but Odysseus drew his purple mantle over his head and covered his face, for he was ashamed to let the Phaeacians see that he was weeping. When the bard left off singing, he wiped the tears from his eyes, uncovered his face, and, taking his cup, made a drink offering to the gods; but when the Phaeacians pressed Demodocus to sing further, for they delighted in his lays, then Odysseus again drew his mantle over his head and wept bitterly. No one noticed his distress except Alcinous, who was sitting near him, and heard the heavy sighs that he was heaving. So he at once said, "Aldermen and town councilors of the Phaeacians, we have had enough now, both of the feast and of the minstrelsy that is its due accompaniment. Let us proceed therefore to the athletic sports so that our guest on his return home may be able to tell his friends how much we surpass all other nations as boxers, wrestlers, jumpers, and runners."

With these words he led the way, and the others followed after. A servant hung Demodocus' lyre on its peg for him, led him out of the cloister, and set him on the same way as that along which all the chief men of the Phaeacians were going to see the sports; a crowd of several thousands of people followed them, and there were many excellent competitors for all the prizes. Acroneos, Ocyalus, Elatreus, Nauteus, Prymneus, Anchialus, Eretmeus, Ponteus, Proreus, Thoon, Anabesineus, and Amphialus son of Polyneus son of Tecton. There was also Euryalus son of Naubolus, who was like Ares himself, and was the best looking man among the Phaeacians except Laodamas. Three sons of Alcinous—Laodamas, Halios, and Clytoneus—competed also.

The foot races came first. The course was set out for them from the starting post, and they raised a dust upon the plain as they all flew forward at the same moment. Clytoneus came in first by a long way; he left everyone else behind him by the length of the furrow that a couple of mules can plow in a fallow field. They then turned to the painful art of wrestling, and here Euryalus proved to be the best man. Amphialus excelled all the others in jumping, while at throwing the disc there was no one who could approach Elatreus. Alcinous' son Laodamas was the best boxer, and he it was who presently said, when they had all been diverted with the games, "Let us ask the stranger whether he excels in any of these sports. He seems very powerfully built; his thighs, calves, hands, and neck are of prodigious strength, nor is he at all old, but he has suffered much

lately, and there is nothing like the sea for making havoc with a man, no matter how strong he is."

"You are quite right, Laodamas," replied Euryalus, "go up to your guest and speak to him about it yourself."

When Laodamas heard this he made his way into the middle of the crowd and said to Odysseus, "I hope, sir, that you will enter yourself for some one or other of our competitions if you are skilled in any of them—and you must have gone in for many a one before now. There is nothing that does anyone so much credit all his life long as the showing himself a proper man with his hands and feet. Have a try therefore at something, and banish all sorrow from your mind. Your return home will not be long delayed, for the ship is already drawn into the water, and the crew is found."

Odysseus answered, "Laodamas, why do you taunt me in this way? My mind is set rather on cares than contests; I have been through infinite trouble, and am come among you now as a suppliant, praying your king and people to further me on my return home."

Then Euryalus reviled him outright and said: "I gather, then, that you are unskilled in any of the many sports that men generally delight in. I suppose you are one of those grasping traders that go about in ships as captains or merchants, and who think of nothing but of their outward freights and homeward cargoes. There does not seem to be much of the athlete about you."

"For shame, sir!" answered Odysseus, fiercely. "You are an insolent fellow—so true is it that the gods do not grace all men alike in speech, person, and understanding. One man may be of weak presence, but heaven has adorned him with such a good conversation that he charms everyone who sees him; his honeyed moderation carries his hearers with him so that he is leader in all assemblies of his fellows, and wherever he goes he is looked up to. Another may be as handsome as a god, but his good looks are not crowned with discretion. This is your case. No god could make a finer looking fellow than you are, but you are a fool. Your ill-judged remarks have made me exceedingly angry, and you are quite mistaken, for I excel in a great many athletic exercises.

Indeed, so long as I had youth and strength, I was among the first athletes of the age. Now, however, I am worn out by labor and sorrow, for I have gone through much both on the field of battle and by the waves of the weary sea. Still, in spite of all this I will compete, for your taunts have stung me to the quick."

So he hurried up without even taking his cloak off, and seized a disc, larger, more massive and much heavier than those used by the Phaeacians when disc-throwing among themselves. Then, swinging it back, he threw it from his brawny hand, and it made a humming sound in the air as he did so. The Phaeacians quailed beneath the rushing of its flight as it sped gracefully from his hand, and flew beyond any mark that had been made yet. Athene, in the form of a man, came and marked the place where it had fallen. "A blind man, sir," said she, "could easily tell your mark by groping for it— it is so far ahead of any other. You may make your mind easy about this contest, for no Phaeacian can come near to such a throw as yours."

Odysseus was glad when he found he had a friend among the lookers-on, so he began to speak more pleasantly. "Young men," said he, "come up to that throw if you can, and I will throw another disc as heavy or even heavier. If anyone wants to have a bout with me let him come on, for I am exceedingly angry. I will box, wrestle, or run, I do not care what it is, with any man of you all except Laodamas, but not with him because I am his guest, and one cannot compete with one's own personal friend. At least I do not think it a prudent or a sensible thing for a guest to challenge his host's family at any game, especially when he is in a foreign country. He will cut the ground from under his own feet if he does. But I make no exception as regards anyone else, for I want to have the matter out and know which is the best man.

"I am a good hand at every kind of athletic sport known among mankind. I am an excellent archer. In battle I am always the first to bring a man down with my arrow, no matter how many more are taking aim at him alongside of me. Philoctetes was the only man who could shoot better than I could when we Achaeans were before Troy and in practice. I far excel everyone else in the whole world, of those who still eat bread upon the face of the earth, but I should not like to shoot against the mighty dead, such as Heracles, or Eurytus the Oechalian—men who could shoot against the gods themselves. This in fact was how Eurytus came prematurely by his end, for Apollo was angry with him and killed him because he challenged him as an archer. I can throw a dart farther than anyone else can shoot an arrow. Running is the only point in respect of which I am afraid some of the Phaeacians might beat me, for I have been brought down very low at sea; my provisions ran short, and therefore I am still weak."

They all held their peace except King Alcinous, who began: "Sir, we have had much pleasure in hearing all that you have told us, from which I understand that you are willing to show your prowess, as having been displeased with some insolent remarks that have been made to you by one of our athletes, and which could never have been uttered by anyone who knows how to talk with propriety. I hope you will apprehend my meaning, and will explain to anyone of your chief men who may be dining with yourself and your family when you get home, that we have an hereditary aptitude for accomplishments of all kinds. We are not particularly remarkable for our boxing, nor yet as wrestlers, but we are singularly fleet of foot and are excellent sailors. We are extremely fond of good dinners, music, and dancing; we also like frequent changes of linen, warm baths, and good beds. So now, please, some of you who are the best dancers set about dancing, that our guest on his return home may be able to tell his friends how much we surpass all other nations as sailors, runners, dancers, and minstrels. Demodocus has left his lyre at my house, so run some one or other of you and fetch it for him."

*   *   *

REVIEW QUESTIONS

1. What does this selection reveal about the Greek ideal of masculine behavior?
2. What does it reveal about attitudes concerning hospitality?

Spartan Society and Values

Among all the Greek city-states, Sparta (also referred to by some authors as Lace-daemon) was distinguished by the military ethic that governed virtually every aspect of its society. The life of the Spartan citizen was geared toward maintaining a constant state of military preparedness. For this achievement, no sacrifice was too great, as was heroically demonstrated by the Spartans who defended the pass at Thermopylae against the Persians in 480 B.C.E. The following selections shed light on the values and organization of Spartan society. The first, "The Spartan Creed," is the work of the Spartan poet Tyrtaeus, whose poetry continued to inspire Spartan warriors long after his death. The second selection is a description of Spartan laws and customs by Xenophon, an Athenian follower of the philosopher Socrates. Xenophon is known best for his work the Anabasis, *which describes the retreat, which he led, of a mercenary army stranded in Persian territory circa 400 B.C.E.*

Tyrtaeus: "The Spartan Creed"*

I would not say anything for a man nor take
account of him
for any speed of his feet or wrestling skill he
   might have,
not if he had the size of a Cyclops and strength
   to go with it,
not if he could outrun Bóreas, the North Wind
   of Thrace,
not if he were more handsome and gracefully
   formed than Tithónos,
or had more riches than Midas had, or Kínyras
   too,
not if he were more of a king than Tantalid
   Pelops,
or had the power of speech and persuasion
   Adrastos had,
not if he had all splendors except for a fighting
   spirit.
For no man ever proves himself a good man in war
unless he can endure to face the blood and the
   slaughter,
go close against the enemy and fight with his
   hands.

---

* From *Greek Lyrics*, translated by Richmond Lattimore
  (Chicago: University of Chicago Press, 1960).

Here is courage, mankind's finest possession,
   here is
the noblest prize that a young man can endeavor
   to win,
and it is a good thing his city and all the people
   share with him
when a man plants his feet and stands in the
   foremost spears
relentlessly, all thought of foul flight completely
   forgotten,
and has well trained his heart to be steadfast
   and to endure,
and with words encourages the man who is
   stationed beside him.
Here is a man who proves himself to be valiant
   in war.
With a sudden rush he turns to flight the rugged
   battalions
of the enemy, and sustains the beating waves of
   assault.
And he who so falls among the champions and
   loses his sweet life,
so blessing with honor his city, his father, and
   all his people,
with wounds in his chest, where the spear that
   he was facing has transfixed
that massive guard of his shield, and gone
   through his breastplate as well,

why, such a man is lamented alike by the young
   and the elders,
and all his city goes into mourning and grieves for
   his loss.

His tomb is pointed to with pride, and so are his
   children,
and his children's children, and afterward all the
   race that is his.
His shining glory is never forgotten, his name is
   remembered,
and he becomes an immortal, though he lies
   under the ground,
when one who was a brave man has been killed by
   the furious War God
standing his ground and fighting hard for his
   children and land.
But if he escapes the doom of death, the destroyer
   of bodies,
and wins his battle, and bright renown for the
   work of his spear,
all men give place to him alike, the youth and the
   elders,
and much joy comes his way before he goes down
   to the dead.
Aging, he has reputation among his citizens. No one
tries to interfere with his honors or all he deserves;
all men withdraw before his presence, and yield
   their seats to him,
the youth, and the men his age, and even those
   older than he.
Thus a man should endeavor to reach this high
   place of courage
with all his heart, and, so trying, never be backward in war.

Xenophon: from "The Laws and Customs of the Spartans"*

*   *   *

   But reflecting once how Sparta, one of the least populous of states, had proved the most powerful and celebrated city in Greece, I wondered by what means this result had been produced. When I proceeded, however, to contemplate the institutions of the Spartans, I wondered no longer.

   Lycurgus, who made the laws for them, by obedience to which they have flourished, I not only admire, but consider to have been in the fullest sense a wise man; for he rendered his country preëminent in prosperity, not by imitating other states, but by making ordinances contrary to those of most governments.

   With regard, for example, to the procreation of children, that I may begin from the beginning, other people feed their young women, who are about to produce offspring, and who are of the class regarded as well brought up, on the most moderate quantity of vegetable food possible, and on the least possible quantity of meat, while they either keep them from wine altogether, or allow them to use it only when mixed with water; and as the greater number of the men engaged in trades are sedentary, so the rest of the Greeks think it proper that their young women should sit quiet and spin wool. But how can we expect that women thus treated should produce a vigorous progeny? Lycurgus, on the contrary, thought that female slaves were competent to furnish clothes; and, considering that the production of children was the noblest duty of the free, he enacted, in the first place, that the female should practice bodily exercises no less than the male sex; and he thus appointed for the women contests with one another, just as for the men, expecting that when both parents were rendered strong a stronger offspring would be born from them.

   Observing, too, that the men of other nations, when women were united to husbands, associated with their wives during the early part of their intercourse without restraint, he made enactments quite at variance with this practice; for he ordained that a man should think it shame to be seen going in to his wife, or coming out from her. When married people meet in this way, they must feel stronger desire for the company of one another, and whatever offspring is produced must thus be rendered far more robust than if the parents were satiated with each other's society.

---

* From *Xenophon's Minor Works*, translated by J. S. Watson (Bell: Bohn Classical Library, 1878).

In addition to these regulations, he also took from the men the liberty of marrying when each of them pleased, and appointed that they should contract marriages only when they were in full bodily vigour, deeming this injunction also conducive to the production of an excellent offspring. Seeing also that if old men chanced to have young wives, they watched their wives with the utmost strictness, he made a law quite opposed to this feeling; for he appointed that an old man should introduce to his wife whatever man in the prime of life he admired for his corporeal and mental qualities, in order that she might have children by him. If, again, a man was unwilling to associate with his wife, and yet was desirous of having proper children, he made a provision also with respect to him, that whatever women he saw likely to have offspring, and of good disposition, he might, on obtaining the consent of her husband, have children by her. Many similar permissions he gave; for the women are willing to have two families, and the men to receive brothers to their children, who are equal to them in birth and standing, but have no claim to share in their property.

Let him who wishes, then, consider whether Lycurgus, in thus making enactments different from those of other legislators, in regard to the procreation of children, secured for Sparta a race of men eminent for size and strength.

Having given this account of the procreation of children, I wish also to detail the education of those of both sexes. Of the other Greeks, those who say that they bring up their sons best set slaves over them to take charge of them, as soon as the children can understand what is said to them, and send them, at the same time, to schoolmasters, to learn letters, and music, and the exercises of the palaestra. They also render their children's feet delicate by the use of sandals, and weaken their bodies by changes of clothes; and as to food, they regard their appetite as the measure of what they are to take. But Lycurgus, instead of allowing each citizen to set slaves as guardians over his children, appointed a man to have the care of them all, one of those from whom the chief magistrates are chosen; and he is called the paedonomus. He invested this man

with full authority to assemble the boys, and, if he found that any one was negligent of his duties, to punish him severely. He assigned him also some of the grown-up boys as whip-carriers, that they might inflict whatever chastisement was necessary; so that great dread of disgrace, and great willingness to obey, prevailed among them.

Instead, also, of making their feet soft with sandals, he enacted that they should harden them by going without sandals; thinking that, if they exercised themselves in this state, they would go up steep places with far greater ease, and descend declivities with greater safety; and that they would also leap, and skip, and run faster unshod, if they had their feet inured to doing so, than shod. Instead of being rendered effeminate, too, by a variety of dresses, he made it a practice that they should accustom themselves to one dress throughout the year; thinking that they would thus be better prepared to endure cold and heat.

As to food, he ordained that they should exhort the boys to take only such a quantity as never to be oppressed with overeating, and not to be strangers to living somewhat frugally; supposing that, being thus brought up, they would be the better able, if they should be required, to support toil under a scarcity of supplies, would be the more likely to persevere in exertion, should it be imposed on them, on the same quantity of provisions, and would be less desirous of sauces, more easily satisfied with any kind of food, and pass their lives in greater health. He also considered that the fare which rendered the body slender would be more conducive to increasing its stature than that which expanded it with nutriment. Yet that the boys might not suffer too much from hunger, Lycurgus, though he did not allow them to take what they wanted without trouble, gave them liberty to steal certain things to relieve the cravings of nature; and he made it honourable to steal as many cheeses as possible. That he did not give them leave to form schemes for getting food because he was at a loss what to allot them, I suppose no one is ignorant; as it is evident that he who designs to steal must be wakeful during the night, and use deceit, and lay plots; and, if he would gain anything of consequence, must employ spies. All these things, therefore, it is plain that he taught the children from a desire to render them more dexterous in securing provisions, and better qualified for warfare.

Some one may say, "Why, then, if he thought it honourable to steal, did he inflict a great number of whiplashes on him who was caught in the act?" I answer, that in other things which men teach, they punish him who does not follow his instructions properly; and that the Spartans accordingly punished those who were detected as having attempted to steal in an improper manner. These boys he gave in charge to others to whip them at the altar of Diana Orthia; designing to show by this enactment that it is possible for a person, after enduring pain for a short time, to enjoy pleasure with credit for a long time. It is also shown by this punishment that, where there is need of activity, the inert person benefits himself the least, and occasions himself most trouble.

In order, too, that the boys, in case of the paedonomus being absent, may never be in want of a president, he appointed that whoever of the citizens may happen at any time to be present is to assume the direction of them, and to enjoin whatever he may think advantageous for them, and punish them if they do anything wrong. By doing this, Lycurgus has also succeeded in rendering the boys much more modest; for neither boys nor men respect any one so much as their rulers. And that if, on any occasion, no full-grown man happen to be present, the boys may not even in that case be without a leader, he ordained that the most active of the grown-up youths take the command of each band; so that the boys there are never without a superintendent.

It appears to me that I must say something also of the boys as objects of affection; for this has likewise some reference to education. Among the other Greeks, a man and boy either form a union, as among the Boeotians, and associate together, or, as among the Eleians, the men gain the favour of the youths by means of attentions bestowed upon them; but there are some of the Greeks who prohibit the suitors for the boys' favours from having the least conversation with them. But Lycurgus, acting contrary to all these people also, thought proper, if any man, being himself such as he ought to be, admired the disposition of a youth, and made it his object to render him a faultless friend, and to enjoy his society, to bestow praise upon him, and regarded this as the most excellent kind of education; but if any man showed that his affections were fixed only on the bodily attractions of a youth, Lycurgus, considering this as most unbecoming, appointed that at Lacedaemon suitors for the favours of boys should abstain from intimate connexion with them, not less strictly than parents abstain from such intercourse with their children, or children of the same family from that with one another. That such a state of things is disbelieved by some, I am not surprised; for in most states the laws are not at all adverse to the love of youths; but Lycurgus, for his part, took such precautions with reference to it.

*   *   *

Lycurgus, then, having found the Spartans, like the other Greeks, taking their meals at home, and knowing that most were guilty of excess at them, caused their meals to be taken in public, thinking that his regulations would thus be less likely to be transgressed. He appointed them such a quantity of food, that they should neither be overfed nor feel stinted. Many extraordinary supplies are also furnished from what is caught in hunting, and for these the rich sometimes contribute bread; so that the table is never without provisions, as long as they design the meal to last, and yet is never expensive.

Having put a stop likewise to all unnecessary drinking, which weakens alike the body and the mind, he gave permission that every one should drink when he was thirsty, thinking that the drink would then be most innoxious and most pleasant. When they take their meals together in this manner, how can any one ruin either himself or his family by gluttony or drunkenness? In other states, equals in age generally associate together, and with them modesty has but very little influence; but Lycurgus, at Sparta, mixed citizens of different ages, so that the younger are for the most part instructed by the experience of the older. It is a custom at these public meals, that whatever any one has done to his honour in the community is related; so that insolence, or disorder from intoxication, or any indecency in conduct or language, has there no opportunity of showing itself. The practice of taking meals away from home is also attended with these advantages, that the people are obliged to walk in taking their departure homewards, and to be careful that they may not stagger from the effects of wine, knowing that they will not remain where they dined, and that they must conduct themselves in the night just as in the day; for it is not allowable for any one who is still liable to military duty to walk with a torch.

As Lycurgus observed, too, that those who, after taking food, exercise themselves, become well-complexioned, plump, and robust, while those who are inactive are puffy, unhealthy-looking, and feeble, he did not neglect to give attention to that point; and as he perceived that when any one engages in labour from his own inclination, he proves himself to have his body in efficient condition, he ordered that the oldest in each place of exercise should take care that those belonging to it should never be overcome by taking too much food. With regard to this matter, he appears to me to have been by no means mistaken; for no one would easily find men more healthy, or more able-bodied, than the Spartans; for they exercise themselves alike in their legs, in their hands, and in their shoulders.

*   *   *

From acquiring money by unjust means, he prohibited them by such methods as the following. He instituted, in the first place, such a kind of money, that, even if but ten minae came into a house, it could never escape the notice either of masters or of servants; for it would require much room, and a carriage to convey it. In the next place, gold and silver are searched after, and, if they are discovered anywhere, the possessor of them is punished. How, then, could gain by traffic be an object of pursuit, in a state where the possession of money occasions more pain than the use of it affords pleasure?

That at Sparta the citizens pay the strictest obedience to the magistrates and laws, we all know. I suppose, however, that Lycurgus did not attempt to establish such an excellent order of things, until he had brought the most powerful men in the state to be of the same mind with regard to it. I form my opinion on this consideration, that, in other states, the more influential men are not willing even to appear to fear the magistrates, but think that such fear is unbecoming free men but in Sparta, the most powerful men not only put themselves under the magistrates, but even count it an honour to humble themselves before them, and to obey, when they are called upon, not walking, but running; supposing that if they themselves are the first to pay exact obedience, others will follow their example; and such has been the case. It is probable, also, that the chief men established the offices of the Ephors[1] in conjunction with Lycurgus, as they must have been certain that obedience is of the greatest benefit, alike in a state, and in an army, and in a family; and they doubtless considered that the greater power magistrates have, the greater effect will they produce on the citizens in enforcing obedience. The Ephors, accordingly, have full power to impose a fine on whomsoever they please, and to exact the fine without delay; they have power also to degrade magistrates even while they are in office, and to put them in prison, and to bring them to trial for their life. Being possessed of such authority, they do not, like the magistrates in other states, always permit those who are elected to offices to rule during the whole year as they choose, but, like despots and presidents in gymnastic contests, punish on the instant whomsoever they find acting at all contrary to the laws.

Though there were many other excellent contrivances adopted by Lycurgus, to induce the citizens to obey the laws, the most excellent of all appears to me to be, that he did not deliver his laws to the people until he had gone, in company with the most eminent of his fellow-citizens, to Delphi, and consulted the god whether it would be more beneficial and advantageous for Sparta to obey the

---

[1] The five magistrates elected annually to govern the Spartan state. [Editor]

laws which he had made. As the god replied that it would be more beneficial in every way, he at once delivered them, deciding that it would be not only illegal, but impious, to disobey laws sanctioned by the oracle.

It is deserving of admiration, too, in Lycurgus, that he made it a settled principle in the community, that an honourable death is preferable to a dishonourable life; for whoever pays attention to the subject will find that fewer of those who hold this opinion die than of those who attempt to escape danger by flight. Hence we may say with truth, that safety attends for a much longer period on valour than on cowardice; for valour is not only attended with less anxiety and greater pleasure, but is also more capable of assisting and supporting us. It is evident, too, that good report accompanies valour; for almost everybody is willing to be in alliance with the brave.

How he contrived that such sentiments should be entertained, it is proper not to omit to mention. He evidently, then, intended a happy life for the brave, and a miserable one for the cowardly. In other communities, when a man acts as a coward, he merely brings on himself the name of coward, but the coward goes to the same market, and sits or takes exercise, if he pleases, in the same place with the brave men; at Sparta, however, every one would be ashamed to admit a coward into the same tent with him, or to allow him to be his opponent in a match at wrestling. Frequently, too, a person of such character, when they choose opposite parties to play at ball, is left without any place, and in forming a chorus he is thrust into the least honourable position. On the road he must yield the way to others, and at public meetings he must rise up, even before his juniors. His female relatives he must maintain at home, and they too must pay the penalty of his cowardice, since no man will marry them. He is also not allowed to take a wife, and must at the same time pay the customary fine for being a bachelor. He must not walk about with a cheerful expression, or imitate the manners of persons of blameless character; else he will have to receive whipping from his betters. Since, then, such

disgrace is inflicted on cowards, I do not at all wonder that death is preferred at Sparta to a life so dishonourable and infamous.

Lycurgus seems to me to have provided also, with great judgment, how virtue might be practised even to old age; for by adding to his other enactments the choice of senators at an advanced stage of life, he caused honour and virtue not to be disregarded even in old age.

It is worthy of admiration in him, too, that he attached consideration to the old age of the well-deserving; for by making the old men arbiters in the contest for superiority in mental qualifications, he rendered their old age more honourable than the vigour of those in the meridian of life. This contest is deservedly held in the greatest esteem among the people, for gymnastic contests are attended with honour, but they concern only bodily accomplishments; the contest for distinction in old age involves a decision respecting merits of the mind. In proportion, therefore, as the mind is superior to the body, so much are contests for mental eminence more worthy of regard than those concerning bodily superiority.

Is it not highly worthy of admiration, also, in Lycurgus, that when he saw that those who are dis-inclined to practice virtue are not qualified to increase the power of their country, he obliged all the citizens of Sparta to cultivate every kind of virtue publicly. As private individuals, accordingly, who practise virtue, are superior in it to those who neglect it, so Sparta is naturally superior in virtue to all other states, as it is the only one that engages in a public cultivation of honour and virtue. Is it not also deserving of commendation, that, when other states punish any person that injures another, Lycurgus inflicted no less punishment on any one that openly showed himself unconcerned with becoming as good a man as possible? He thought, as it appears, that by those who make others slaves, or rob them, or steal anything, the individual sufferers only are injured, but that by the unprincipled and cowardly whole communities are betrayed; so that he appears to me to have justly imposed the heaviest penalties on such characters.

He also imposed on his countrymen an obligation, from which there is no exception, of practising every kind of political virtue; for he made the privileges of citizenship equally available to all those who observed what was enjoined by the laws, without taking any account either of weakness of body or scantiness of means; but if any one was too indolent to perform what the laws prescribed, Lycurgus appointed that he should be no longer counted in the number of equally privileged citizens.

That these laws are extremely ancient is certain; for Lycurgus is said to have lived in the time of the Heracleidae; but, ancient as they are, they are still very new to other communities; for, what is the most wonderful of all things, all men extol such institutions, but no state thinks proper to imitate them.

The regulations which I have mentioned are beneficial alike in peace and in war; but if any one wishes to learn what he contrived better than other legislators with reference to military proceedings, he may attend to the following particulars.

In the first place, then, the Ephors proclaim the age limits for the citizen draft to the army; artisans (non-citizens) are also called by the same order to serve supplying the troops. For the Spartans provide themselves in the field with an abundance of all those things which people use in a city; and of whatever instruments an army may require in common, orders are given to bring some on waggons, and others on beasts of burden, as by this arrangement anything left behind is least likely to escape notice.

For engagements in the field he made the following arrangements. He ordered that each soldier should have a purple robe and a brass shield; for he thought that such a dress had least resemblance to that of women, and was excellently adapted for the field of battle, as it is soonest made splendid, and is longest in growing soiled. He permitted also those above the age of puberty to let their hair grow, as he thought that they thus appeared taller, more manly, and more terrifying in the eyes of the enemy. . . .

*   *   *

REVIEW QUESTIONS

1. According to these readings, what was the pre-eminent role of the individual citizen within Spartan society?
2. What was the purpose of education among the Spartans?
3. What was the proper role of women in Spartan society? Why?
4. What values governed Spartan life?

HIPPOCRATES

FROM "On Airs, Waters, and Places"

One of the classical Greek philosopher-scientists whose names have become almost household words today is Hippocrates of Cos, the "father of medicine," in whose name modern physicians are obligated (in the "Hippocratic oath") to apply rational, humane treatment to the care and healing of their patients. Hippocrates himself was born around 460 B.C.E. on the Aegean island of Cos. During his career, he established a school of medical thought that focused on natural medicine, attention to personal hygiene, and simple common sense in emphasizing a rational (rather than magical, superstition-bound) approach to the study and care of the human body. By the second century C.E., Greek and Latin writers ascribed to Hippocrates a substantial body of written works dealing with human physiology; the diagnosis of illness; and the influence of lifestyle, diet, and environment on health. Scholars today continue to debate their authorship, but their contribution to later Western (and Islamic) civilizations is incalculable, not only in the realm of medicine, but also—as the selection below reflects—in shaping later, often destructive assumptions that linked supposedly innate superiorities and inferiorities of other human societies to their environment, climate, and lifestyle. In some instances, the judgments that the "Hippocratic" authors reached parallel more modern notions of ethnocentrism and racism—other elements of later Western thought that, like rationalism and democracy, can be traced to Classical roots.

In the following selection, Hippocrates first defines the criteria for assessing the impact of environment on human health—among them, winds, water quality, terrain, and personal habits and lifestyle of the inhabitants. Then, the author uses these criteria to assess and contrast the qualities of peoples inhabiting different regions of the world known to him.

From The Internet Classics Archive, translated by Francis Adams, http://classics.mit.edu// Hippocrates/airwatpl.html.

Part 1

Whoever wishes to investigate medicine properly, should proceed thus: in the first place to consider the seasons of the year, and what effects each of them produces for they are not at all alike, but differ much from themselves in regard to their changes. Then the winds, the hot and the cold, especially such as are common to all countries, and then such as are peculiar to each locality. We must also consider the qualities of the waters, for as they differ from one another in taste and weight, so also do they differ much in their qualities. In the same manner, when one comes into a city to which he is a stranger, he ought to consider its situation, how it lies as to the winds and the rising of the sun; for its influence is not the same whether it lies to the north or the south, to the rising or to the setting sun. These things one ought to consider most attentively, and concerning the waters which the inhabitants use, whether they be marshy and soft, or hard, and running from elevated and rocky situations, and then if saltish and unfit for cooking; and the ground, whether it be naked and deficient in water, or wooded and well watered, and whether it lies in a hollow, confined situation, or is elevated and cold; and the mode in which the inhabitants live, and what are their pursuits, whether they are fond of drinking and eating to excess, and given to indolence, or are fond of exercise and labor, and not given to excess in eating and drinking.

Part 2

From these things he must proceed to investigate everything else. For if one knows all these things well, or at least the greater part of them, he cannot miss knowing, when he comes into a strange city, either the diseases peculiar to the place, or the particular nature of common diseases, so that he will not be in doubt as to the treatment of the diseases, or commit mistakes, as is likely to be the case provided one had not previously considered these matters. And in particular, as the season and the year advances, he can tell what epidemic diseases will attack the city, either in summer or in winter, and what each individual will be in danger of experiencing from the change of regimen. For knowing the changes of the seasons, the risings and settings of the stars, how each of them takes place, he will be able to know beforehand what sort of a year is going to ensue. Having made these investigations, and knowing beforehand the seasons, such a one must be acquainted with each particular, and must succeed in the preservation of health, and be by no means unsuccessful in the practice of his art. And if it shall be thought that these things belong rather to meteorology, it will be admitted, on second thoughts, that astronomy contributes not a little, but a very great deal, indeed, to medicine. For with the seasons the digestive organs of men undergo a change.

*   *   *

Part 12

I wish to show, respecting Asia and Europe, how, in all respects, they differ from one another, and concerning the figure of the inhabitants, for they are different, and do not at all resemble one another. To treat of all would be a long story, but I will tell you how I think it is with regard to the greatest and most marked differences. I say, then, that Asia differs very much from Europe as to the nature of all things, both with regard to the productions of the earth and the inhabitants, for everything is produced much more beautiful and large in Asia; the country is milder, and the dispositions of the inhabitants also are more gentle and affectionate. The cause of this is the temperature of the seasons, because it lies in the middle of the risings of the sun towards the east, and removed from the cold (and heat), for nothing tends to growth and mildness so much as when the climate has no predominant quality, but a general equality of temperature prevails. It is not everywhere the same with regard to Asia, but such parts of the country as lie intermediate between the heat and the cold, are the best supplied with fruits and trees, and have the most genial climate, and enjoy the purest waters, both celestial and terrestrial. For neither are they much burnt up by the heat, nor dried up by the drought and want of rain, nor do they suffer from the cold; since they are well watered from abundant showers and snow, and the fruits of the season, as might be supposed, grow in abun-

dance, both such as are raised from seed that has been sown, and such plants as the earth produces of its own accord, the fruits of which the inhabitants make use of, training them from their wild state and transplanting them to a suitable soil; the cattle also which are reared there are vigorous, particularly prolific, and bring up young of the fairest description; the inhabitants too, are well fed, most beautiful in shape, of large stature, and differ little from one another either as to figure or size; and the country itself, both as regards its constitution and mildness of the seasons, may be said to bear a close resemblance to the spring. Manly courage, endurance of suffering, laborious enterprise, and high spirit, could not be produced in such a state of things either among the native inhabitants or those of a different country, for there pleasure necessarily reigns. For this reason, also, the forms of wild beasts there are much varied. Thus it is, as I think, with the Egyptians and Libyans.

Part 13

But concerning those on the right hand of the summer risings of the sun as far as the Palus Maeotis (for this is the boundary of Europe and Asia), it is with them as follows: the inhabitants there differ far more from one another than those I have treated of above, owing to the differences of the seasons and the nature of the soil. But with regard to the country itself, matters are the same there as among all other men; for where the seasons undergo the greatest and most rapid changes, there the country is the wildest and most unequal; and you will find the greatest variety of mountains, forests, plains, and meadows; but where the seasons do not change much there the country is the most even; and, if one will consider it, so is it also with regard to the inhabitants; for the nature of some is like to a country covered with trees and well watered; of some, to a thin soil deficient in water; of others, to fenny and marshy places; and of some again, to a plain of bare and parched land. For the seasons which modify their natural frame of body are varied, and the greater the varieties of them the greater also will be the differences of their shapes.

Part 14

I will pass over the smaller differences among the nations, but will now treat of such as are great either from nature, or custom; and, first, concerning the Macrocephali. There is no other race of men which have heads in the least resembling theirs. At first, usage was the principal cause of the length of their head, but now nature cooperates with usage. They think those the most noble who have the longest heads. It is thus with regard to the usage: immediately after the child is born, and while its head is still tender, they fashion it with their hands, and constrain it to assume a lengthened shape by applying bandages and other suitable contrivances whereby the spherical form of the head is destroyed, and it is made to increase in length. Thus, at first, usage operated, so that this constitution was the result of force: but, in the course of time, it was formed naturally; so that usage had nothing to do with it; for the semen comes from all parts of the body, sound from the sound parts, and unhealthy from the unhealthy parts. If, then, children with bald heads are born to parents with bald heads; and children with blue eyes to parents who have blue eyes; and if the children of parents having distorted eyes squint also for the most part; and if the same may be said of other forms of the body, what is to prevent it from happening that a child with a long head should be produced by a parent having a long head? But now these things do not happen as they did formerly, for the custom no longer prevails owing to their intercourse with other men. Thus it appears to me to be with regard to them.

Part 15

As to the inhabitants of Phasis [along the eastern shore at the Black Sea], their country is fenny, warm, humid, and wooded; copious and severe rains occur there at all seasons; and the life of the inhabitants is spent among the fens; for their dwellings are constructed of wood and reeds, and are erected amidst the waters; they seldom practice walking either to the city or the market, but sail about, up and down, in canoes constructed out of single trees, for there are many canals there. They drink the hot and stagnant waters, both when rendered putrid by the sun, and when swollen with rains. The Phasis itself is the most stagnant of all rivers, and runs the smoothest; all the fruits which spring there are unwholesome, feeble and imperfect growth, owing to the redundance of water, and on this account they do not ripen, for much vapor from the waters overspreads the country. For these reasons the Phasians have shapes different from those of all other men; for they are large in stature, and of a very gross habit of body, so that not a joint nor vein is visible; in color they are sallow, as if affected with jaundice. Of all men they have the roughest voices, from their breathing an atmosphere which is not clear, but misty and humid; they are naturally rather languid in supporting bodily fatigue. The seasons undergo but little change either as to heat or cold; their winds for the most part are southerly, with the exception of one peculiar to the country, which sometimes blows strong, is violent and hot, and is called by them the wind cenchron. The north wind scarcely reaches them, and when it does blow it is weak and gentle. Thus it is with regard to the different nature and shape of the inhabitants of Asia and Europe.

Part 16

And with regard to the pusillanimity and cowardice of the inhabitants, the principal reason the Asiatics are more unwarlike and of gentler disposition than the Europeans is, the nature of the seasons, which do not undergo any great changes either to heat or cold, or the like; for there is neither excitement of the understanding nor any strong change of the body whereby the temper might be ruffled and they be roused to inconsiderate emotion and passion, rather than living as they do always in the state. It is changes of all kinds which arouse understanding of mankind, and do not allow them to get into a torpid condition. For these reasons, it appears to me, the Asiatic race is feeble, and further, owing to their laws; for monarchy prevails in the greater part of Asia, and where men are not their own masters nor independent, but are the slaves of others, it is not a matter of consideration with them how they may acquire military discipline, but how they may seem not to be warlike, for the dangers are not equally shared, since they must serve as soldiers, perhaps endure fatigue, and die for their masters, far from their children, their wives, and other friends; and whatever noble and manly actions they may perform lead only to the aggrandizement of their masters, whilst the fruits which they reap are dangers and death; and, in addition to all this, the lands of such persons must be laid waste by the enemy and want of culture. Thus, then, if any one be naturally warlike and courageous, his disposition will be changed by the institutions. As a strong proof of all this, such Greeks or barbarians in Asia as are not under a despotic form of government, but are independent, and enjoy the fruits of their own labors, are of all others the most warlike; for these encounter dangers on their own account, bear the prizes of their own valor, and in like manner endure the punishment of their own cowardice. And you will find the Asiatics differing from one another, for some are better and others more dastardly; of these differences, as I stated before, the changes of the seasons are the cause. Thus it is with Asia.

Part 17

In Europe there is a Scythian race, called Sauromatae, which inhabits the confines of the Palus Maeotis, and is different from all other races. Their women mount on horseback, use the bow, and throw the javelin from their horses, and fight with their enemies as long as they are virgins; and they do not lay aside their virginity until they kill three of their enemies, nor have any connection with men until they perform the sacrifices according to law. Whoever takes to herself a husband, gives up riding on horseback unless the necessity of a general expedition obliges her. They have no right breast; for while still of a tender age their mothers heat strongly a copper instrument constructed for this very purpose, and apply it to the right breast, which is burnt up, and its development being arrested, all the strength and fullness are determined to the right shoulder and arm.

Part 18

As the other Scythians have a peculiarity of shape, and do not resemble any other, the same observation applies to the Egyptians, only that the latter are oppressed by heat and the former by cold. What is called the Scythian desert is a prairie, rich in meadows, high-lying, and well watered; for the rivers which carry off the water from the plains are large. There live those Scythians which are called Nomades, because they have no houses, but live in wagons. The smallest of these wagons have four wheels, but some have six; they are covered in with felt, and they are constructed in the manner of houses, some having but a single apartment, and some three; they are proof against rain, snow, and winds. The wagons are drawn by yokes of oxen, some of two and others of three, and all without horns, for they have no horns, owing to the cold. In these wagons the women live, but the men are carried about on horses, and the sheep, oxen, and horses accompany them; and they remain on any spot as long as there is provender for their cattle, and when that fails they migrate to some other place. They eat boiled meat, and drink the milk of mares, and also eat hippace, which is cheese prepared from the milk of the mare. Such is their mode of life and their customs.

Part 19

In respect of the seasons and figure of body, the Scythian race, like the Egyptian, have a uniformity of resemblance, different from all other nations; they are by no means prolific, and the wild beasts which are indigenous there are small in size and few in number, for the country lies under the Northern Bears, and the Rhiphaean mountains, whence the north wind blows; the sun comes very near to them only when in the summer solstice, and warms them but for a short period, and not strongly; and the winds blowing from the hot regions of the earth do not reach them, or but seldom, and with little force; but the winds from the north always blow, congealed, as they are, by the snow, ice, and much water, for these never leave the mountains, which are thereby rendered uninhabitable. A thick fog covers the plains during the day, and amidst it they live, so that winter may be said to be always present with them; or, if they have summer, it is only for a few days, and the heat is not very strong. Their plains are high-lying and naked, not crowned with mountains, but extending upwards under the Northern Bears. The wild beasts there are not large, but such as can be sheltered underground; for the cold of winter and the barrenness of the country prevent their growth, and because they have no covert nor shelter. The changes of the seasons, too, are not great nor violent, for, in fact, they change gradually; and therefore their figures resemble one another, as they all equally use the same food, and the same clothing summer and winter, respiring a humid and dense atmosphere, and drinking water from snow and ice; neither do they make any laborious exertions, for neither body nor mind is capable of enduring fatigue when the changes of the seasons are not great. For these reasons their shapes are gross and fleshy, with ill-marked joints, of a humid temperament, and deficient in tone: the internal cavities, and especially those of the intestines, are full of humors; for the belly cannot possibly be dry in such a country, with such a constitution and in such a climate; but owing to their fat, and the absence of hairs from their bodies, their shapes resemble one another, the males being all alike, and so also with the women; for the seasons being of a uniform temperature, no corruption or deterioration takes place in the concretion of the semen, unless from some violent cause, or from disease.

Part 20

I will give you a strong proof of the humidity (laxity?) of their constitutions. You will find the greater part of the Scythians, and all the Nomades, with marks of the cautery on their shoulders, arms, wrists, breasts, hip-joints, and loins, and that for no other reason but the humidity and flabbiness of their constitution, for they can neither strain with their bows, nor launch the javelin from their shoulder owing to their humidity and atony: but when they are burnt, much of the humidity in their joints is dried up, and

they become better braced, better fed, and their joints get into a more suitable condition. They are flabby and squat at first, because, as in Egypt, they are not swathed (?); and then they pay no attention to horsemanship, so that they may be adepts at it; and because of their sedentary mode of life; for the males, when they cannot be carried about on horseback, sit the most of their time in the wagon, and rarely practise walking, because of their frequent migrations and shiftings of situation; and as to the women, it is amazing how flabby and sluggish they are. The Scythian race are tawny from the cold, and not from the intense heat of the sun, for the whiteness of the skin is parched by the cold, and becomes tawny.

Part 21

It is impossible that persons of such a constitution could be prolific, for, with the man, the sexual desires are not strong, owing to the laxity of his constitution, the softness and coldness of his belly, from all which causes it is little likely that a man should be given to venery; and besides, from being jaded by exercise on horseback, the men become weak in their desires. On the part of the men these are the causes; but on that of the women, they are embonpoint and humidity; for the womb cannot take in the semen, nor is the menstrual discharge such as it should be, but scanty and at too long intervals; and the mouth of the womb is shut up by fat and does not admit the semen; and, moreover, they themselves are indolent and fat, and their bellies cold and soft. From these causes the Scythian race is not prolific. Their female servants furnish a strong proof of this; for they no sooner have connection with a man than they prove with child, owing to their active course of life and the slenderness of body.

Part 22

And, in addition to these, there are many eunuchs among the Scythians, who perform female work, and speak like women. Such persons are called effeminates. The inhabitants of the country attribute the cause of their impotence to a god, and venerate and worship such persons, every one dreading that the like might befall himself; but to me it appears that such affections are just as much divine as all others are, and that no one disease is either more divine or more human than another, but that all are alike divine, for that each has its own nature, and that no one arises without a natural cause. But I will explain how I think that the affection takes its rise. From continued exercise on horseback they are seized with chronic defluxions in their joints owing to their legs always hanging down below their horses; they afterwards become lame and stiff at the hip-joint, such of them, at least, as are severely attacked with it. They treat themselves in this way: when the disease is commencing, they open the vein behind either ear, and when the blood flows, sleep, from feebleness, seizes them, and afterwards they awaken, some in good health and others not. To me it appears that the semen is altered by this treatment, for there are veins behind the ears which, if cut, induce impotence; now, these veins would appear to me to be cut. Such persons afterwards, when they go in to women and cannot have connection with them, at first do not think much about it, but remain quiet; but when, after making the attempt two, three, or more times, they succeed no better, fancying they have committed some offence against the god whom they blame for the affection, they put on female attire, reproach themselves for effeminacy, play the part of women, and perform the same work as women do. This the rich among the Scythians endure, not the basest, but the most noble and powerful, owing to their riding on horseback; for the poor are less affected, as they do not ride on horses. And yet, if this disease had been more divine than the others, it ought not to have befallen the most noble and the richest of the Scythians alone, but all alike, or rather those who have little, as not being able to pay honors to the gods, if, indeed, they delight in being thus rewarded by men, and grant favors in return; for it is likely that the rich sacrifice more to the gods, and dedicate more votive offerings, inasmuch as they have wealth, and worship the gods; whereas the poor, from want, do less in this way, and, moreover, upbraid the gods for not giving them wealth, so that those who have few possessions were more likely to bear the punishments of these offences than the rich. But, as I formerly said, these affections are divine just as much as others, for each springs from a natural cause, and this disease arises among the Scythians from such a cause as I have stated. But it attacks other men in like manner, for whenever men ride much and very frequently on horseback, then many are affected with rheums in the joints, sciatica, and gout, and they are inept at venery. But these complaints befall the Scythians, and they are the most impotent of men for the aforesaid causes, and because they always wear breeches, and spend the most of their time on horseback, so as not to touch their privy parts with the hands, and from the cold and fatigue they forget the sexual desire, and do not make the attempt until after they have lost their virility. Thus it is with the race of the Scythians.

Part 23

The other races in Europe differ from one another, both as to stature and shape, owing to the changes of the seasons, which are very great and frequent, and because the heat is strong, the winters severe, and there are frequent rains, and again protracted droughts, and winds, from which many and diversified changes are induced. These changes are likely to have an effect upon generation in the coagulation of the semen, as this process cannot be the same in summer as in winter, nor in rainy as in dry weather; wherefore, I think, that the figures of Europeans differ more than those of Asiatics; and they differ very much from one another as to stature in the same city; for vitiations of the semen occur in its coagulation more frequently during frequent changes of the seasons, than where they are alike and equable. And the same may be said of their dispositions, for the wild, and unsociable, and the passionate occur in such a constitution; for frequent excitement of the mind induces wildness, and extinguishes sociableness and mildness of disposition, and therefore I think the inhabitants of Europe more courageous than those of Asia; for a climate which is always the same induces indolence, but a changeable climate, laborious exertions both of body and mind; and from rest and indolence cowardice is engendered, and from laborious exertions and pains, courage.

On this account the inhabitants of Europe are more warlike than the Asiatics, and also owing to their institutions, because they are not governed by kings like the latter, for where men are governed by kings there they must be very cowardly, as I have stated before; for their souls are enslaved, and they will not willingly, or readily undergo dangers in order to promote the power of another; but those that are free undertake dangers on their own account, and not for the sake of others; they court hazard and go out to meet it, for they themselves bear off the rewards of victory, and thus their institutions contribute not a little to their courage.

Such is the general character of Europe and Asia.

Part 24

And there are in Europe other tribes, differing from one another in stature, shape, and courage: the differences are those I formerly mentioned, and will now explain more clearly. Such as inhabit a country which is mountainous, rugged, elevated, and well watered, and where the changes of the seasons are very great, are likely to have great variety of shapes among them, and to be naturally of an enterprising and warlike disposition; and such persons are apt to have no little of the savage and ferocious in their nature; but such as dwell in places which are low-lying, abounding in meadows and ill ventilated, and who have a larger proportion of hot than of cold winds, and who make use of warm waters—these are not likely to be of large stature nor well proportioned, but are of a broad make, fleshy, and have black hair; and they are rather of a dark than of a light complexion, and are less likely to be phlegmatic than bilious; courage and laborious enterprise are not naturally in them, but may be engendered in them by means of their institutions. And if there be rivers in the country which carry off the stagnant and rain water from it, these may be wholesome and clear; but if there be no rivers, but the inhabitants drink the waters of fountains, and such as are stagnant and marshy, they must necessarily have prominent bellies and enlarged spleens. But such as inhabit a high country, and one that is level, windy, and well-watered, will be large of stature, and like to one another; but their minds will be rather unmanly and gentle. Those who live on thin, ill-watered, and bare soils, and not well attempered in the changes of the seasons, in such a country they are likely to be in their persons rather hard and well braced, rather of a blond than a dark complexion, and in disposition and passions haughty and self-willed. For, where the changes of the seasons are most frequent, and where they differ most from one another, there you will find their forms, dispositions, and nature the most varied. These are the strongest of the natural causes of difference, and next the country in which one lives, and the waters; for, in general, you will find the forms and dispositions of mankind to correspond with the nature of the country; for where the land is fertile, soft, and well-watered, and supplied with waters from very elevated situations, so as to be hot in summer and cold in winter, and where the seasons are fine, there the men are fleshy, have ill-formed joints, and are of a humid temperament; they are not disposed to endure labor, and, for the most part, are base in spirit; indolence and sluggishness are visible in them, and to the arts they are dull, and not clever nor acute. When the country is bare, not fenced, and rugged, blasted by the winter and scorched by the sun, there you may see the hardy, slender, with well-shaped joints, well-braced, and shaggy; sharp industry and vigilance accompany such a constitution; in morals and passions they are haughty and opinionative, inclining rather to the fierce than to the mild; and you will find them acute and ingenious as regards the arts, and excelling in military affairs; and likewise all the other productions of the earth corresponding to the earth itself. Thus it is with regard to the most opposite natures and shapes; drawing conclusions from them, you may judge of the rest without any risk of error.

REVIEW QUESTIONS

1. Which human groups does Hippocrates consider to be superior? On what basis?
2. Can you discern any parallels between what Hippocrates writes and more recent concepts of "race" and racial inferiority?

HERODOTUS

FROM *The Histories:*

The Second Persian Invasion of Greece

The Greeks' repelling of the Persian invasions of 490 and 480 to 479 B.C.E. can be regarded as one of the earliest events through which the West began to define itself as distinct from the East. Our knowledge of the invasions is derived almost entirely from the account by Herodotus, who wrote only a few decades after the actual events. His description of the war against the Persians is preceded by long discourses (often of questionable reliability) on the history and customs of other peoples who were involved in the war. The following excerpts, however, focus on the fierce resistance of the Spartans during the second invasion, led by the Persian king Xerxes. In the first selection, Xerxes asks the expatriate Spartan Demaratus how the Greeks can possibly stand up to Persia's might. (This is after Herodotus has given an accounting of the composition of the Persian army. According to his figures, it numbered a fantastic—and impossible—2,641,610 warriors.) The following selection is Herodotus's account of the heroic stand of the Spartans under their king, Leonidas, at the mountain pass at Thermopylae.

From *Herodotus: The Histories*, edited by Walter Blanco and Jennifer Tobert Roberts, translated by Walter Blanco (New York: Norton, 1992), pp. 157–77, 191–97.

*   *   *

After the army had been counted and put in battle order, Xerxes wanted to ride past his troops and review them, which he did. He rode past the forces of each nation in his chariot, asking questions while his scribes wrote down the answers until he had gone from one end of the army to the other and reviewed both infantry and cavalry. After he had done this, the ships were dragged down into the sea and Xerxes transferred from his chariot to a Sidonian ship. He sat under a golden awning and sailed along the prows of the ships, asking questions and having answers written down just as he had done with the army. The captains had taken their ships back about four hundred feet from shore, lined them up with their prows facing land, and dropped anchor after posting the marines at their battle sta-

tions in full gear. Xerxes conducted his naval review while sailing between the ships' prows and the shore.

When he had sailed past his fleet and disembarked from his ship, Xerxes summoned Demaratus, son of Ariston, who was accompanying him on the campaign against Greece. As Demaratus approached, Xerxes called out to him and said, "Demaratus, there's something it would give me great pleasure to ask you about right now. You are a Greek, and as far as I can tell from you and the other Greeks who have had conversations with me, your city is by no means the smallest or the weakest. Tell me this, now, are the Greeks going to take up arms and resist? Because I believe that neither all the Greeks nor all the other people who live to the west put together are going to be able to resist my assault—unless they are united, that is. Still, I want to hear from you what you have to say about it."

When Xerxes had finished, Demaratus answered, "Should I tell you the truth, Your Majesty, or just something pleasing?" And Xerxes commanded him to tell the truth—he wouldn't like him any less than before.

When he heard this, Demaratus said, "Since you demand that I tell the truth by all means, Your Majesty, and not something you will later find to be a lie, why then, poverty is congenital to Greece, but bravery is an import, bought with skill and strict rules, and Greece uses bravery to fend off both poverty and despotism. Now, while I praise all Greeks who live in Dorian lands, I'm not really talking about all of them, but solely about the Lacedaemonians. First: there is no way they will ever accept any terms of slavery you bring to Greece. Second: they will oppose you in battle even if all the other Greeks come around to your way of thinking. Don't bother finding out whether there will be enough of them to do it. If there are a thousand, they will fight you, and they will fight you if there are fewer and fight you if there are more."

After Xerxes heard this, he said through his laughter, "What nonsense you talk, Demaratus! A thousand men fighting with an army like this! But come, now, tell me. You say that you yourself used to be king over these people. How would you like to fight with ten men right now? But really, if your citizens are all such as you describe them, then under your laws it would be fitting for you, as their king, to fight with twice that number. If each of them is worth ten men from my army, then I look for you to be worth twenty. That way you can make good on what you've said. Because if they are all like you and the other Greeks who come to talk to me—like you, that is, in size and shape—and you all brag in this way, then see to it that your boast isn't made in vain. Come now, look at it reasonably. How could a thousand, or ten thousand, or fifty thousand men who are all equally free and not ruled by one man stand up to an army this size? Because if there are five thousand of them we will outnumber them by more than a thousand to one! If, like us, they were ruled by one man, they would either surpass themselves through fear of him or they would, under the lash, go up against forces

that outnumbered them. But if they are left to their own devices, they won't do either. Anyway, I think that even if the numbers were the same, it would be hard for the Greeks to fight with just the Persians. We, too, have this quality you speak of. There isn't much of it—it's rare, but there are some of my Persian bodyguard who want to take on three Greeks at a time. You've never come up against them, and that's why you can talk so much drivel."

Demaratus answered, "I knew from the beginning, Your Majesty, that if I told you the truth, you wouldn't like what I had to say. But since you forced me to tell you the whole truth, I told you what the Spartans are like. You, though, more than anyone, know how much I love them now—they who stripped me of my rank and my privileges, who drove me from the city of my fathers and made me an exile while your father welcomed me and gave me an income and a home. A rational man is much more likely to appreciate goodwill than to reject it. As for me, I don't claim to be able to fight with ten men or with two. I wouldn't even willingly fight with one. But if I had to, or if a great cause spurred me on, then I would gladly fight—especially with one of those men who say they're a match for three Greeks. In the same way, when the Lacedaemonians fight one at a time, they are no worse than any other men, but when they fight together, they are the best in the world. Because though they're free, they aren't totally free. Custom is the despot who stands over them, and they secretly fear it more than your people fear you. They do whatever it commands, and its command is always the same: not to run away from any force, however large, but to stay in formation and either prevail or die. If I seem to be talking drivel to you, then I'll keep quiet from now on. I spoke just now only because you made me, but let it be as you think best, Your Majesty."

Although Demaratus answered him in this way, Xerxes didn't get at all angry. Instead, he turned it into a joke and genially sent Demaratus away.

*   *   *

The Spartans sent Leonidas with an advance guard so that the other allies would go to war after seeing them do so and not use any delay on Sparta's part as an excuse for also collaborating with the Persians. Later, after celebrating the Carneian festival, which prevented them from going to battle immediately, they would station a guard in Sparta and march out on the double in full strength. Their allies had the same idea. The Olympic Games were taking place at the same time as these events, so the allies, too, sent their advance guards, never thinking that the battle of Thermopylae would be decided so quickly.

These, then, were their intentions. Meanwhile, when the Greeks at Thermopylae saw the Persians approaching the pass, they panicked and talked about retreat. In general, the Peloponnesians thought they should return to the Peloponnese and guard the Isthmus, but when the Phocians and Locrians became extremely agitated over this idea, Leonidas voted to stay where they were and to dispatch messengers calling on the allies to come to the rescue since they were too few to hold off the Persian army.

While the Greek commanders were discussing their plans, Xerxes sent out a mounted spy to see how many Greeks there were and what they were doing. He had already heard while still in Thessaly that a small army had gathered at Thermopylae, and that it was led by Lacedaemonians under the command of Leonidas, a descendant of Heracles. The horseman could not observe or even see the whole camp as he rode toward it, because some of the men were posted out of sight inside the wall, which they had rebuilt and were guarding. He did see the men outside the wall, though, and their weapons lying nearby. During that watch, the Spartans happened to be stationed outside. He saw some of the men exercising, others combing their long hair. He was amazed at what he saw. He noted their numbers and, after carefully observing everything he could, trotted back unmolested. Nobody pursued him; nobody paid any attention to him at all. When he returned, he told Xerxes everything he had seen.

Xerxes heard it, but he couldn't understand that what they were doing was getting ready to kill or be killed. They seemed to him to be acting so absurdly that he sent for Demaratus, son of Ariston, who was in the camp. When he arrived, Xerxes asked him about everything in detail; he was eager to find out just what the Lacedaemonians were doing. Demaratus said, "I already told you about these men as we were setting out against Greece. You laughed at me for seeing that things would turn out just as they have. I keep trying to tell you the truth, Your Majesty, but it's a struggle. Listen to me now. Those men came here to fight with us for this pass, and that's what they are getting ready to do. It's their way. They comb their hair whenever they are about to risk their lives. But know this: if you defeat these men and the force that remains in Sparta, there are no other people on earth who will take up arms against you, because you are about to face the noblest king and the bravest men in all of Greece."

What he said seemed to Xerxes to be absolutely incredible, and Xerxes asked him for the second time how so few men could do battle with his army. Demaratus said, "Consider me a liar, Your Majesty, if things don't turn out as I say."

That's what he said, but Xerxes didn't believe him.

He let four days go by, expecting the Greeks to run away at any moment. When they had not only not left on the fifth day but seemed to be staying out of sheer reckless effrontery; Xerxes became furious and sent the Medes and Cissians out to attack them, with orders to bring them back into his presence alive. Waves of Medians rushed the Greeks. Many men fell, and others followed in their wake, but none retreated from the overwhelming disaster. The Medes made it clear to everyone and not least to the king himself that he had many troops but few real men. Nevertheless, the battle lasted all day long.

The Medes finally retreated after being thoroughly manhandled. The Persians were the next to attack—the men Xerxes called his Immortals. They were under the command of Hydarnes, and indeed they thought that they would easily prevail, but it was no different for them when they mixed it up with the Greeks from what it had been for the Medes. It was just the same because they were fighting at very close quarters, using spears shorter than the Greeks', and were unable to take advantage of their numerical superiority. The Lacedaemonians fought a battle to remember! Among these men who knew nothing of warfare, they showed in all sorts of ways that they really knew how to fight—like when they turned their backs and pretended to run away, the barbarians would see them running and would chase after them shouting and making noise, and then the Greeks would wheel around and face the barbarians just as they were about to be overtaken and slaughter countless numbers of them.

A few of the Spartans fell there, too.

The Persians couldn't take the pass after attacking it company by company and in every other way, and they finally retreated.

They say that the king, who was observing these assaults, jumped up from his throne three times in fear for his army. That, then, is how the battle went on that day; and the barbarians fought with no more success the next day, either. They attacked in the belief that the small number of Greeks must have suffered so many casualties that they wouldn't even be able to raise their arms to resist. The Greeks, however, stood in formations of tribes and regiments and took turns in the fighting—all except the Phocians, who had been posted on the mountain to guard the trail. The Persians retreated when they didn't see anything different from what they had found the day before.

Xerxes was at a loss as to how to deal with this situation when a Malian, Ephialtes, son of Eurydemus, came to talk to the king in the hope of receiving a large gift. He told Xerxes about the trail leading through the mountains to Thermopylae and thereby doomed the Greek defenders at the pass. Ephialtes later fled to Thessaly in fear of the Lacedaemonians, but at a meeting at Pylae, the Amphyctionic delegates—the Pylagorae—offered a reward for the fugitive. When he returned to Anticyra some time later, he was killed by Athenades, a man from Trachis. Now, Athenades killed Ephialtes for a different reason (which I will talk about in a later narrative), but the Lacedaemonians honored him for it nonetheless.

*   *   *

Xerxes was delighted with what Ephialtes had offered to do, and soon became positively overjoyed. He immediately dispatched Hydarnes and his Immortals, who left camp at dusk, at around the time the lamps are lit.

Malian locals discovered this trail and then guided the Thessalians over it to attack the Phocians after the Phocians had walled up the pass to hold off an invasion. That's how long the Malians have known about this deadly trail! The trail begins where the Asopus issues through the gorge, and its name is the same as the mountain's—the Anopaea. The Anopaea trail runs along the mountain ridge and leaves off at Alpeni, the first town on the Malian side of Locris, at a place called Black Ass Rock and the Cercopian Butts. This is the narrowest part of the pass.

The Persians crossed the Asopus and made their way over the trail through the night, keeping the Oeta Mountains on the right and the mountains of Trachis on the left. They reached the top of the mountain with the glimmering of dawn. As I have already said, a thousand heavily armed Phocians were stationed there to guard the trail and defend their own homeland. The Phocians had voluntarily given their oath to Leonidas to guard that mountain trail, and we know very well who was guarding the pass below.

The Persians could go up the mountain unnoticed because it was covered with oak trees, so the Phocians only found out that the Persians had already gotten up there when, on that perfectly still day, they heard the loud noise of fallen leaves crackling under the tramp of feet. The Phocians sprang up and were putting on their battle gear as the barbarians came in sight. The Persians were astonished to see men putting on their armor. They had thought they would meet with no opposition, and yet here was an army! Hydarnes dreaded that the Phocians might be Spartans, so he asked Ephialtes where they were from. When he was sure of their nationality, he arrayed his Persians for battle. After being showered with arrows thick and fast, the Phocians thought the attack was aimed at them, and they ran up to the very top of the mountain ready to fight to the death; but they were mistaken, because the Persians under Ephialtes and Hydarnes paid no further attention to them and hurried down the mountain.

Meanwhile, Megistias the seer had examined the sacrificial animals and told the Greeks at Thermopylae that they would die at dawn. Also, deserters had told them during the night that the Persians were circling around behind them. Finally, their lookouts ran down from the mountaintops with the news at the dawn's early light. The Greeks then held a meeting, and their opinions were divided between those who would not leave their positions and those who took the opposite view. The two sides parted company: some retreated and scattered into their respective cities; others prepared to take their stand there with Leonidas.

It is said that Leonidas himself sent the others away, concerned lest they be destroyed—while as for him and the Spartans who were with him, they couldn't rightly abandon the post they had come to guard in the first place. I myself am inclined to the view that when Leonidas saw that his allies were balking, unwilling to stay with him and risk their lives, he must have ordered them to retreat, though he himself couldn't go home honorably. He would stay to leave eternal fame behind him, and see to it that Sparta's prosperity was not snuffed out. You see, the Spartans had consulted the Delphic oracle as soon as the war broke out, and the Pythian priestess had prophesied that either the Lacedaemonian people would be uprooted by the barbarians or their king would die. She uttered the prophecy in the following hexameter verses:

But for you, O dwellers in Sparta's wide land,
Either your glorious city shall be sacked by the
  men of Persia
Or, if not, she will mourn the action of Heracles,
The dead ruler over all the land of Lacedaemon.
The strength of bulls and lions cannot resist the
  foe,
For he has the strength of Zeus. No, he will not
  leave off,
I say, until he tears city or king limb from limb.

Leonidas dismissed the allies with this prophecy in mind, and because he wanted to be the only Spartan to win such fame; they did not go home in disarray over a difference of opinion.

For me, not the least evidence for this view is the well-known fact that Leonidas also tried to dismiss the army seer I mentioned—Megistias the Acarnanian, who they say descended from Melampus, and who foretold the future from his sacrificial animals. But although he had been dismissed to keep him from being killed with everyone else, he didn't leave; instead, he sent home his only son, who had gone to war with him.

The allies who had been dismissed obeyed Leonidas and left. Only the Thespians and the Thebans stayed with the Lacedaemonians. The Thebans remained without wanting to because Leonidas, regarding them as hostages, held them against their will. The Thespians, on the other hand, were very willing to stay. Refusing to abandon Leonidas or desert his men, they stayed behind and died along with them. The Thespian commander was Demophilus, son of Diadromes.

Xerxes poured out drink offerings at sunrise. He waited until about midmorning and then began the attack. This plan had been arranged in advance with Ephialtes, because the descent from the mountain would be much quicker, with much less ground to cover, than the march around and the climb up had been. The barbarians under Xerxes moved forward while the Greeks under Leonidas advanced like men who are going out to their deaths; and this time they went much farther out into the wider part of the pass than they had at first. In the first days of battle, concerned with protecting the defending wall, they would only make forays into the narrowest part and fight there. This time, as the two sides grappled with each other beyond the narrow neck of the pass, very many barbarians fell while their company commanders whipped each and every man, driving them constantly forward. Many of them fell into the sea and drowned; many others trampled each other alive; no one cared about the dying. And because they knew that death was coming from the troops who had circled the mountain, the Greeks fought the barbarians with all the strength they had, fought recklessly out of their minds.

Most of their spears were broken by now, so they slaughtered Persians with their swords. That brave man Leonidas fell in the struggle, and other renowned Spartans along with him. I have learned the names of these noble men, as I have learned the names of all the three hundred Spartans who perished. And, indeed, many brave Persians died there, too, two sons of Darius among them—Abrocomes and Hyperanthes, Darius' children by Phratagune, daughter of Artanes. This Artanes was the brother of King Darius, and the son of Hystaspes, son of Arsames. When he married his daughter to Darius, Artanes gave up his whole estate along with her since she was his only child.

Thus two brothers of Xerxes died in the battle.

There was a tremendous crush of Persians and Lacedaemonians around the body of Leonidas, until by sheer courage the Greeks dragged him away after beating back the enemy four times. The fight continued until Ephialtes arrived. The nature of the battle changed as soon as the Greeks realized that he was there. They fell back to the narrow part of the pass and, after ducking behind the wall, massed together on the hillock behind it and dug in—all except the Thebans. This mound is in the pass where the stone lion now stands in honor of Leonidas. The men defended themselves on this hillock with daggers, if they still had them, or with their hands and teeth, while some of the Persians came at them head-on after pulling down and demolishing the wall and others surrounded them and stood there burying them under arrows, spears, and stones.

They say that Dieneces the Spartan stood out even in this company of Lacedaemonians and Thespians. Just before the battle with the Persians, he heard some Trachinian say that when the barbarians shot their arrows the sky was so full of them that the sun was blotted out—that's how many Persians there were. Dieneces wasn't fazed at all. He pooh-poohed the Persian numbers, and is reported to have said that his Trachinian friend had brought good news, because if the Persians blotted out the sun they could have their battle in the shade rather than in the sunlight. They say Dieneces the Spartan left this and other witticisms to be remembered by. After him, they say, two Lacedaemonian brothers, Alpheus and Maron, sons of Orsiphantus, distinguished themselves. The most outstanding Thespian was named Dithyrambus, son of Harmatides.

The men were buried where they fell, along with those who had died before the departure of the men Leonidas had dismissed. There is an epitaph over the mass grave which says:

IN THIS FOUR THOUSAND
PELOPONNESIANS FOUGHT
FOUR MILLION MEN

That epitaph was for all the men. These words commemorate the Spartans alone:

STRANGER GO TELL THE
LACEDAEMONIANS THAT WE WHO LIE
HERE OBEYED THEIR ORDERS

*   *   *

REVIEW QUESTIONS

1. According to Herodotus, why does Xerxes decide to invade Greece? Do he or his generals fear the Greeks at all?
2. What special attributes of the Greeks make it possible for them to resist and eventually defeat the Persian forces?
3. Do the Persians, and Xerxes specifically, possess any flaws that ensure their eventual defeat?
4. How does Herodotus's account of the Spartans at Thermopylae compare with the readings preceding this one?

THUCYDIDES

FROM *The Peloponnesian Wars*

The costly Peloponnesian War of 431–404 B.C.E. was the culmination of years of growing tension between Sparta and its league of allies, on the one hand, and the Athenian Empire on the other. Our principal source for that war is the history written by the Athenian Thucydides, who tended to be much more rigorous than Herodotus in his assessment and use of historical evidence. In the first selection that follows, Thucydides recreates the speech given by the Athenian leader Pericles to honor those Athenians who fell in battle during the war's first year. It has come to be regarded as one of the classic statements of the values of a democracy. The second selection is Thucydides' account of the negotiations several years later between the envoys of the invading Athenian forces and the local authorities of Melos, an Aegean island that Athens was seeking to add to its empire.

From *The Peloponnesian Wars: A New Translation*, translated by Walter Blanco, edited by Walter Blanco and Jennifer Tolbert Roberts (New York: Norton, 1998), pp. 71–76, 227–231.

Pericles' Funeral Speech

That same winter, the Athenians observed an ancestral custom and arranged for the funeral, at the public expense, of the first men to die in the war. They always did it in the following way. Two days beforehand, they would build a tent and lay out the bones and ashes of the dead, and everyone would make whatever offerings he wished to his kin. On the day of the funeral procession, wagons brought in cypress coffins, one for each tribe, with every man's bones to be in the coffin of his tribe. There was one empty bier spread with a coverlet for the missing, the men who could not be found and carried away. Any man, citizen or stranger, could attend the funeral; women who were related to the dead were also present, mourning the dead right up to the grave. The soldiers were buried in the national cemetery, which is in the most beautiful suburb of the city. Those who die in war are always buried there, except for those who died at Marathon, for the Athenians decided that they had shown surpassing courage and buried them right on the battlefield in Marathon. When the coffins are covered with earth, a man who has been chosen by the city for his outstanding reputation and exceptional wisdom delivers a fitting eulogy over the dead. After this, they all depart. Thus are the dead buried, and the custom was observed throughout the whole war whenever it was necessary to do so. Now Pericles, son of Xanthippus, had been chosen to speak over these very first dead, and at the appropriate time, he stepped forward from the gravesite and up onto a podium built high enough so that the largest number of the audience could hear, and spoke as follows:

Most of those who have spoken in this place have praised the man who added this speech to our funeral customs. It was good, they said, for there to be an oration over the fallen men we honor with these rites. As for me, it would have seemed enough to show our respect for brave men who fell in action *with* action—like the one you see us publicly performing here, now, at this national gravesite—and not to risk letting the reputation for courage of so many depend on whether one man speaks well or poorly. For it is hard to say the right thing when people barely agree as to the truth of it. The sympathetic, knowledgeable listener might, perhaps, think that what is said falls short of what he knows and wants to hear. Those who do not know the facts might, from envy, think some things exaggerated if they sound like more than they themselves can do, for praise of others is bearable only insofar as each man thinks he is capable of doing what he hears praised. They therefore begrudge and disbelieve in men who surpass their own abilities.

Nevertheless, since our forefathers thought fit that this should be so, I must observe our customs and try as best I can to satisfy your wishes and your expectations.

I will begin with our ancestors. It is both fitting and right on such an occasion as this to pay them the due regard of memory, because through their courage, they bequeathed this land they always occupied as a free state from one generation to the next down to the present day. They deserve our praise, but our fathers deserve even more because they, with great effort, added the empire we now possess to their inheritance and left it as a legacy for us, the living. We, who are still more or less in the prime of our lives, have enlarged most of that empire and have made our city self-sufficient both for war and peace. I will not go on at length about the things we did in our wars, through which each gain was made; or how our fathers or we ourselves readily defended ourselves against the attacks of hostile Greeks and barbarians alike. You know all that; let it go. But the way of life that brought us to our present state—the constitution, the customs, through which it has become great—these things I will first set forth before going on to the eulogy of these men, because I think it fitting that they be said on this occasion, and right for all this throng of citizens and noncitizens to give them heed.

We practice a politics that does not emulate the customs of our neighbors. On the contrary, we are the models, not the imitators, of others. Because we are governed for the many and not for the few, we go by the name of a democracy. As far as private interests are concerned, everyone has equal access to the law; but you are distinguished in society and chosen for public service not so much by

lot as because of your individual merit. Furthermore, your poverty will not keep you in obscurity if you can do something worthwhile for the city. We are generous towards one another in our public affairs; and though we keep a watchful eye on each other as we go about our daily business, we don't get angry at our neighbor if he does as he pleases, and we don't give him dirty looks, which are painful though they do not kill. Painless as our private lives may be, we are terrified of breaking the laws. We obey them as they are administered by whoever is in power, especially the laws meant to relieve victims of oppression, whether they have been enacted by statute or whether they are the unwritten laws that carry the undisputed penalty of shame.

In addition, we give our minds many a respite from their toils with games and festivals all year long and with the handsome private furnishings whose daily enjoyment dispels the cares of life. Because of its size, all sorts of merchandise comes pouring into our city from all over the world, and foreign goods are no less ours to enjoy than those that are produced right here.

Our approach to military training differs from that of our Spartan opponents in the following ways. We have an open city and do not, by periodically expelling foreigners, keep them from seeing and learning things lest some enemy benefit from what is open to his view. We trust less to our equipment and our guile than to our personal courage in action. When it comes to education, Spartans no sooner reach boyhood than they painfully train to become men, whereas we, who live a more relaxed life, will nevertheless advance to meet the same dangers as they. The proof is that while the Spartans will not march into our land on their own but only with all their allies, we, by ourselves, attacking on foreign soil, usually gain easy victories over men defending their homes. Because we send our own citizens on numerous expeditions by land while simultaneously conducting naval operations, not a single enemy has ever engaged with our whole combined force. Nevertheless, if they should meet with a contingent of our armed forces and defeat some of them somewhere, they boast that they have repelled us all; but if they lose, it is by all of us that they have been vanquished. And since we prefer to run risks with ease of mind rather than with harmful exercise, and with an ingrained rather than an enforced manliness, we do not worry about hardships to come and go to meet them no less boldly than do those who drill incessantly.

This city of ours is amazing for these reasons, but for others as well.

In the first place, we love nobility without ostentation and we have a virile love of knowledge. Furthermore, wealth is for us something to use, not something to brag about. And as to poverty, there is no shame in admitting to it—the real shame is in not taking action to escape from it. Finally, while there are those who manage both the city and their own private business, there are others who, though wrapped up in their work, nevertheless have a thorough knowledge of public affairs. For we are the only people who regard a man who takes no interest in politics to be leading not a quiet life, but a useless one. We are also the only ones who either make governmental decisions or at least frame the issues correctly, because we do not think that action is hampered by public discourse, but by failure to learn enough in advance, through discourse, about what action we need to take. We are especially daring in our analysis and performance of whatever we undertake, whereas for others, ignorance is confidence and reason a drag on action. The bravest men are rightly regarded as those who have the clearest knowledge of pleasure and pain but who do not shrink from danger because of it.

We are also markedly different from most others when it comes to doing good, because we make friends not by receiving favors, but by doing them. The one who does the favor is the firmer friend because his kindness towards the recipient keeps the debt of gratitude unpaid; but the friendship of the debtor has a duller edge because he knows that he reciprocates friendship not by doing favors, but by owing gratitude. And so we alone will also fearlessly help others, not from a calculation of advantage but from the confidence that comes from our freedom.

To sum up, I tell you that this city, taken all in all, is the school of Greece, and as far as I am concerned, any man among us will exhibit a more fully developed personality than men elsewhere and will be able to take care of himself more gracefully and with the quickest of wit. The very strength our city has acquired through our way of life shows that this is not just a speechifying boast for this occasion, but the truth in action. Alone among today's cities, Athens proves stronger than its reputation, and no attacking enemy need be chagrined that he dies at the hands of an inferior, just as no subject state need censure our unworthiness to rule over it. Our power has not gone unnoticed, as you know only too well, and we have given great proofs to those who are living and yet to come as to why we should be the objects of their admiration. We need no more, not a Homer to sing our praises nor any other poet to please us with verses whose plots and fictions are hobbled by the truth. We have forced the earth and all its seas to make way before our daring, establishing an eternal memory everywhere of the vengeance we have taken and the good that we have done, and it was because they could not bear to think of losing such a city as this that these noble men fought and died, and it is fitting that each and every one of us who remain continue the struggle on her behalf.

This is why I have gone on for so long about our city—to teach the lesson that this struggle means more for us than for those who do not have our advantages, and to establish a foundation in fact for the eulogy I will now deliver. . . . But most of it has already been spoken, for the qualities I have extolled in the city were adorned by the valor of these men and of men like them, and it would be true of very few Greeks that words and deeds are so perfectly balanced as it is for these. For me, the end that came to these men makes plain a man's true worth, whether it came as the first sign or as the final confirmation of that worth. These men had human frailties, but it is only right that we emphasize their courage against the enemy in the defense of their fatherland. Their valor for the common good erased any harm done by their private faults. None of these men put off the day of reckoning because, like a coward, he preferred to enjoy the pleasures of his wealth or because he hoped, being poor, that he might yet escape poverty and become rich. They yearned more to take vengeance on their enemies than they did for these things, whatever the danger, and believing that of all the dangers this was the noblest, they chose to punish their foes and relinquish the world, committing their hopes to an uncertain success and relying on themselves alone to enter the action they saw before them. They chose to save themselves by suffering and struggle but never by surrender, to flee disgrace and to withstand the battle with their bodies, and in that brief crisis of chance, at the height not of fear but of glory, they took their leave of us.

These were men worthy of their city! The rest of us must pray that our resolve against the enemy is safer, but we must be determined to be just as courageous. No one needs to harangue you, who know it so well, about how valor consists in driving off our enemies, but you must remember that the greatest gift to the city is not in public speeches but in daily beholding her power in action, in being like lovers to her. Thus when she is great in her glory, you will take it to heart that men knowingly, daringly, reverently built her power by doing what needed to be done, and that even when they perished in one of her enterprises, they did not think that the city was being deprived of their valor, but that they had freely made the handsomest possible investment in her. They offered up their bodies for the common good and took for themselves that undying praise and that most distinctive tomb—not the one in which they lie, but the one in which their fame remains to be eternally remembered in word and deed on every fitting occasion. The whole world is the tomb of famous men. Not just an inscribed tablet in their homeland commemorates them, but an unwritten memorial that lives on not in a monument, but in the minds even of strangers. You must now imitate these men. Think of happiness as freedom and freedom as courage, and do not worry over the dangers of war. It is not the wretched of the earth, for whom there is no hope of improvement, who have reason to be reckless with their lives, but those for whom a change for the worse is a risk they must run for as long as they live and for whom the contrast would be the greatest if they faltered. To a thoughtful man, the knowledge that he is miserable after having proved himself a coward is more painful than a death he hardly feels in strength and comradeship.

Thus, you parents who are here now, I will not weep for you, only console you. You know that you have lived in troubled times. Lucky men, like these here, who have won the handsomest of deaths—for you, a proud grief—have lived for as long as they have been happy. I know it is hard to persuade you of this when you will often be reminded of your sons by the good fortune of others—good fortune in which you yourselves used to exult. And we feel grief not for the deprivation of the good things we have never known, but for what we had grown used to before it was snatched away.

Those who are still of child-bearing age must endure their sorrow in the hope of other children. For them, personally, a new generation will be a way to forget those who are gone; and it will carry the two benefits for the city of preventing underpopulation and of providing security. Those who do not expose their children to the risk of danger along with everyone else are not able to make decisions about equality and justice. To those of you who are past your prime, think of that larger part of your lives in which you were happy as profit. What follows will be short and eased by the good repute of these men. Only the love of honor never grows old, and it is not making money, as some people say, that pleases us most in our useless old age, but the esteem of others.

As to you, the sons and brothers of these men, I foresee that you will have a formidable task before you, because everyone praises those who have passed away, and it will be hard enough for you to be thought of as having fallen just short of their high valor, much less as having equaled it. You see, envy for the living derives from competition, but those who are no longer with us are honored with an unchallengeable good will.

And since I must also make some mention of womanly virtue to those who will now be widows, I will define it in this brief admonition: your greatest fame consists in being no worse than your natures, and in having the least possible reputation among males for good or ill.

I have spoken, in my turn, and according to our custom, what words I could for this occasion, and those who are interred have here been honored, for now, with our deeds. From this day on, the city will rear their children at public expense until they come of age, thus offering a tangible prize to these men and their survivors for their struggle. After all, the people who institute the greatest rewards for excellence will have the best citizens. And now that each of you has mourned your kin to the full, go on your way.

These funeral rites were celebrated that winter, after which the first year of the war came to an end. . . .

The Melian Dialogue

The following summer, Alcibiades sailed to Argos with twenty ships, seized three hundred Argives still suspected of having Spartan sympathies, and then imprisoned them on nearby islands under Athenian control. The Athenians also sent a fleet against the island of Melos. Thirty of the ships were their own, six were from Chios, and two were from Lesbos. Their own troops numbered twelve hundred hoplites, three hundred archers, and twenty mounted archers. There were also about fifteen hundred hoplites from their allies on the islands. The Melians are colonists from Sparta and would not submit to Athenian control like the other islanders. At first, they were neutral and lived peaceably, but they became openly hostile after Athens once tried to compel their obedience by ravaging their land. The generals Cleomedes, son of Lycomedes, and Tisias, son of Tisimachus, bivouacked on Melian territory with their troops, but before doing any injury to the land, they sent ambassadors to hold talks with the Melians. The Melian leadership, however, did not bring these men before the popular assembly. Instead, they asked them to discuss their mission with the council and the privileged voters. The Athenian ambassadors spoke as follows.

"We know that what you are thinking in bringing us before a few voters, and not before the popular assembly, is that now the people won't be deceived after listening to a single long, seductive, and unrefuted speech from us. Well, those of you who are sitting here can make things even safer for yourselves. When we say something that seems wrong, interrupt immediately, and answer, not in a set speech, but one point at a time.—But say first whether this proposal is to your liking."

The Melian councillors said, "There can be no objection to the reasonableness of quiet, instructive talks among ourselves. But this military force, which is here, now, and not off in the future, looks different from instruction. We see that you have come as judges in a debate, and the likely prize will be war if we win the debate with arguments based on right and refuse to capitulate, or servitude if we concede to you."

ATHENIANS: Excuse us, but if you're having this meeting to make guesses about the future or to do anything but look at your situation and see how to save your city, we'll leave. But if that's the topic, we'll keep talking.

MELIANS: It's natural and understandable that in a situation like this, people would want to express their thoughts at length. But so be it. This meeting is about saving our city, and the format of the discussion will be as you have said.

ATHENIANS: Very well.

We Athenians are not going to use false pretenses and go on at length about how we have a right to rule because we destroyed the Persian empire, or about how we are seeking retribution because you did us wrong. You would not believe us anyway. And please do not suppose that you will persuade *us* when you say that you did not campaign with the Spartans although you were their colonists, or that you never did us wrong. No, each of us must exercise what power he really thinks he can, and we know and you know that in the human realm, justice is enforced only among those who can be equally constrained by it, and that those who have power use it, while the weak make compromises.

MELIANS: Since you have ruled out a discussion of justice and forced us to speak of expediency, it would be inexpedient, at least as we see it, for you to eradicate common decency. There has always been a fair and right way to treat people who are in danger, if only to give them some benefit for making persuasive arguments by holding off from the full exercise of power. This applies to you above all, since you would set an example for others of how to take the greatest vengeance if you fall.

ATHENIANS: We're not worried about the end of our empire, if it ever does end. People who rule over others, like the Spartans, are not so bad to their defeated enemies. Anyway, we're not fighting the Spartans just now. What is really horrendous is when subjects are able to attack and defeat their masters.—But you let us worry about all that. We are here to talk about benefiting our empire and saving your city, and we will tell you how we are going to do that, because we want to take control here without any trouble and we want you to be spared for both our sakes.

MELIANS: And just how would it be as much to our advantage to be enslaved, as for you to rule over us?

ATHENIANS You would benefit by surrendering before you experience the worst of consequences, and we would benefit by not having you dead.

MELIANS: So you would not accept our living in peace, being friends instead of enemies, and allies of neither side?

ATHENIANS: Your hatred doesn't hurt us as much as your friendship. That would show us as weak to our other subjects, whereas your hatred would be a proof of our power.

MELIANS: Would your subjects consider you reasonable if you lumped together colonists who had no connection to you, colonists from Athens, and rebellious colonists who had been subdued?

ATHENIANS: They think there's justice all around. They also think the independent islands are strong, and that we are afraid to attack them. So aside from adding to our empire, your subjugation will also enhance our safety, especially since you are islanders and we are a naval power. Besides, you're weaker than the others—unless, that is, you show that you too can be independent.

MELIANS: Don't you think there's safety in our neutrality? You turned us away from a discussion of justice and persuaded us to attend to what was in your interest. Now it's up to us to tell you about what is to our advantage and to try to persuade you that it is also to yours. How will you avoid making enemies of states that are now neutral, but that look at what you do here and decide that you will go after them one day? How will you achieve anything but to make your present enemies seem more attractive, and to force those who had no intention of opposing you into unwilling hostility?

ATHENIANS: We do not think the threat to us is so much from mainlanders who, in their freedom from fear, will be continually putting off their preparations against us, as from independent islanders, like you, and from those who are already chafing under the restraints of rule. These are the ones who are most likely to commit themselves to ill-considered action and create foreseeable dangers for themselves and for us.

MELIANS: Well then, in the face of this desperate effort you and your slaves are making, you to keep your empire and they to get rid of it, wouldn't we, who are still free, be the lowest of cowards if we didn't try everything before submitting to slavery?

ATHENIANS: No, not if you think about it prudently. This isn't a contest about manly virtue between equals, or about bringing disgrace on yourself. You are deliberating about your very existence, about standing up against a power far greater than yours.

MELIANS: But we know that there are times when the odds in warfare don't depend on the numbers. If we give up, our situation becomes hopeless right away, but if we fight, we can still hope to stand tall.

ATHENIANS: In times of danger, hope is a comfort that can hurt you, but it won't destroy you if you back it up with plenty of other resources. People who gamble everything on it (hope is extravagant by nature, you see) know it for what it really is only after they have lost everything. Then, of course, when you can recognize it and take precautions, it's left you flat. You don't want to experience that. You Melians are weak, and you only have one chance. So don't be like all those people who could have saved themselves by their own efforts, but who abandoned their realistic hopes and turned in their hour of need to invisible powers— to prophecies and oracles and all the other nonsense that conspires with hope to ruin you.

MELIANS: As you well know, we too think it will be hard to fight both your power and the fortunes of war, especially with uneven odds. Still, we believe that our fortune comes from god, and that we will not be defeated because we take our stand as righteous men against men who are in the wrong. And what we lack in power will be made up for by the Spartan League. They will have to help us, if only because of our kinship with them and the disgrace they would feel if they didn't. So it's not totally irrational for us to feel hopeful.

ATHENIANS: Well, when it comes to divine good will, we don't think we'll be left out. We're not claiming anything or doing anything outside man's thinking about the gods or about the way the gods themselves behave. Given what we believe about the gods and know about men, we think that both are always forced by the law of nature to dominate everyone they can. We didn't lay down this law, it was there—and we weren't the first to make use of it. We took it as it was and acted on it, and we will bequeath it as a living thing to future generations, knowing full well that if you or anyone else had the same power as we, you would do the same thing. So we probably don't have to fear any disadvantage when it comes to the gods. And as to this opinion of yours about the Spartans, that you can trust them to help you because of their fear of disgrace—well, our blessings on your innocence, but we don't envy your foolishness. The Spartans do the right thing among themselves, according to their local customs. One could say a great deal about their treatment of others, but to put it briefly, they are more conspicuous than anyone else we know in thinking that pleasure

is good and expediency is just. Their mindset really bears no relation to your irrational belief that there is any safety for you now.

MELIANS: But it's exactly because of this expediency that we trust them. They won't want to betray the Melians, their colonists, and prove themselves helpful to their enemies and unreliable to their well-wishers in Greece.

ATHENIANS: But don't you see that expediency is safe, and that doing the right and honorable thing is dangerous? On the whole, the Spartans are the last people to take big risks.

MELIANS: We think they'll take on dangers for us that they wouldn't for others and regard those dangers as less risky, because we are close to the Peloponnese from an operational point of view. Also, they can trust our loyalty because we are kin and we think alike.

ATHENIANS: Men who ask others to come to fight on their side don't offer security in good will but in real fighting power. The Spartans take this kind of thing more into consideration than others, because they have so little faith in their own resources that they even attack their neighbors with plenty of allies. So it's not likely that they'll try to make their way over to an island when we control the sea.

MELIANS: Then maybe they'll send their allies. The sea of Crete is large, and it is harder for those who control the sea to catch a ship than it is for the ship to get through to safety without being noticed. And if that doesn't work, they might turn against your territory or attack the rest of your allies, the ones Brasidas didn't get to. And then the fight would shift from a place where you have no interest to your own land and that of your allies.

ATHENIANS: It's been tried and might even be tried for you—though surely you are aware that we Athenians have never abandoned a siege out of fear of anyone.

But it occurs to us that after saying you were going to talk about saving yourselves, you haven't in any of this lengthy discussion mentioned anything that most people would rely on for their salvation. Your strongest arguments are in the future and depend on hope. What you've actually got is too meager to give you a chance of surviving the forces lined up against you now. You've shown a very irrational attitude—unless, of course, you intend to reach some more prudent conclusion than this after you send us away and begin your deliberations. For surely you don't mean to commit yourselves to that "honor" which has been so destructive to men in clear and present dangers involving "dishonor." Many men who could still see where it was leading them have been drawn on by the allure of this so-called "honor," this word with its seductive power, and fallen with open eyes into irremediable catastrophe, vanquished in their struggle with a fine word, only to achieve a kind of dishonorable honor because they weren't just unlucky, they were fools. You can avoid this, if you think things over carefully, and decide that there is nothing so disgraceful in being defeated by the greatest city in the world, which invites you to become its ally on fair terms—paying us tribute, to be sure, but keeping your land for yourselves. You have been given the choice between war and security. Don't be stubborn and make the wrong choice. The people who are most likely to succeed stand up to their equals, have the right attitude towards their superiors, and are fair to those beneath them.

We will leave now. Think it over, and always remember that you are making a decision about your country. You only have one, and its existence depends on this one chance to make a decision, right or wrong.

Then the Athenians withdrew from the discussion. The Melians, left to themselves, came to the conclusion that had been implied by their responses in the talks. They answered the Athenians as follows: "Men of Athens, our decision is no different from what it was at first. We will not in this brief moment strip the city we have lived in for seven hundred years of its freedom. We will try to save it, trusting in the divine good fortune that has preserved us so far and in the help we expect from the Spartans and from others. We invite you to be our friends, to let us remain neutral, and to leave our territory after making a treaty agreeable to us both."

That was the Melian response. The talks were already breaking up when the Athenians said, "Well, judging from this decision, you seem to us to be the only men who can make out the future more clearly than what you can see, and who gaze upon the invisible with your mind's eye as if it were an accomplished fact. You have cast yourselves on luck, hope, and the Spartans, and the more you trust in them, the harder will be your fall."

REVIEW QUESTIONS

1. What, in Pericles' estimation, are the benefits of democracy?
2. What are the reasons for Athens' greatness?
3. How do the values of Athenian democracy compare with those of Spartan society?
4. How evident are Athens' democratic values in the Athenians' negotiations with the citizens of Melos?

SOPHOCLES

FROM *Antigone*

One of the foremost features of the culture of classical Athens was its focus on the rights, responsibilities, and potential of the individual and its celebration of human intellect and personality. Nowhere is this more evident than in the surviving works of the greatest of the Athenian tragedians, Aeschylus, Sophocles, and Euripides. Sophocles wrote his play Antigone, *from which the following excerpts are taken, shortly before 441 B.C.E. Like so many of the plays of this era,* Antigone *focuses on the nobility of spirit of the human being when faced with terrible conflict. Indeed, one well-known analysis of its impact characterizes it as the only work of literature that expresses "all the principal constants of conflict in the condition of man . . . : the confrontation of men and women; of age and of youth; of society and of the individual; of the living and the dead; of men and of god(s)."*

From *The Antigone of Sophocles,* translated by George Herbert Palmer (Boston: Houghton Mifflin, 1927).

THE PERSONS

CREON, King of Thebes
EURYDICE, his wife
HAEMON, his son, betrothed to Antigone
ANTIGONE, } his nieces, daughters of Oedipus and
ISMENE, } Jocasta, former King and Queen of
} Thebes
WATCHMAN
MESSENGER
SECOND MESSENGER
BOY AND GUARDS, silent persons
CHORUS OF THEBAN ELDERS

The Scene throughout is at Thebes, in front of the palace. The Play begins at daybreak.

ANTIGONE: Ismene, my own sister, of all the woes begun in Oedipus can you imagine any that Zeus will not complete within our lives? There is no grief or crime, no degradation or dishonor, not to be found among the woes of you and me. And what is this new edict issued lately by our captain, people say, to the whole city? Do you know, and did you hear? Or have you failed to learn how on our friends fall evils from our foes?

ISMENE: To me, Antigone, have come no tidings of our friends, for good or ill, since we two lost two brothers, slain in mutual strife the selfsame day. I know the Argive host retreated this last night, but I know nothing further—whether we gain or lose.

ANTIGONE: I guessed as much, and therefore brought you here alone outside the gate to learn the truth.

ISMENE: What is it, then? You seem to hint at some dark tale.

ANTIGONE: Yes. In his order for the burial of our brothers has not Creon honored the one, outraged the other? To Eteocles, they say, he paid each proper rite and custom and laid him in the ground, to be in honor with the dead below. But as for poor dead Polynices' body, they say he has proclaimed among our people that none shall hide it in a grave and mourn, but let it lie unwept, unburied, welcome provision for the birds who watch for such-like prey. These are, they say, the orders our good Creon has proclaimed for you and me—yes, even for me!—and now comes hither to make plain his will to such as do not know. Nor does he treat the matter lightly. But let one do what he forbids, and death by public stoning shall await him in the city. So it stands now, and you must quickly show if you are rightly born or the base child of noble parents.

ISMENE: But, my poor sister, if it has come to this, what further can I do to help or hinder?

ANTIGONE: Think, will you share my toil and strife?

ISMENE: In what bold deed? What is your plan?

ANTIGONE: To try if you with this hand's help will raise that body.

ISMENE: What! Bury him? In opposition to the State?

ANTIGONE: My brother, though, and yours. If you refuse, I will be found no traitor.

ISMENE: Reckless! When Creon too forbids?

ANTIGONE: 'T is not for him to keep me from my own.

ISMENE: Alas! consider, sister, how our father died, hated and scorned, because of self-exposed offences doing his eyes a violence with his own hand. And then his mother and his wife—ah, double title!—with twisted cord ended her life in shame. A third disaster came. Our pair of brothers in a single day, like wretched suicides, wrought out one common ruin by each other's hand. And now once more, when we are the only ones still left, think what a far worse fate we two shall meet if we, defying law, transgress our rulers' will and power. Nay, rather let us bear in mind that we are women, so not fit to strive with men. Moreover, since we are the subjects of those stronger than ourselves, we must obey these orders and orders harsher still. I, then, beseeching those beneath the earth to grant me pardon, seeing I am compelled, will bow to those in power. To act beyond one's sphere shows little wisdom.

ANTIGONE: I will not urge you. No! Nor if hereafter you desire, shall you with my consent give any aid. Be what you will, and I will bury him. Good it would be to die in doing so. Dearly shall I lie with him, with my dear, after my pious sin. And longer must I satisfy those there below than people here, for there I shall lie ever. But you, if you think well, keep disregarding what the gods regard!

ISMENE: I mean no disregard. But to defy the State—it is not in me.

ANTIGONE: Make that, then, your excuse! I will go raise a grave over my dearest brother.

ISMENE: O my poor sister, how I fear for you!

ANTIGONE: Be not disturbed for me. Let your own course be true.

ISMENE: At least do not reveal what you have done. Keep it a secret. I will hide it too.

ANTIGONE: Ha? Speak it out! Far more my enemy if silent than if telling it to all!

ISMENE: Hot heart and chilling deeds!

ANTIGONE: I know I please those I most ought to please.

ISMENE: If you succeed. But you desire what cannot be.

ANTIGONE: Why, then, when strength shall fail me, I will cease.

ISMENE: Best not pursue at all what cannot be.

ANTIGONE: Speak thus, and I shall hate you. And he who died will hate you,—rightly too. Nay, leave me and my rash design to meet our doom, for I shall meet none equal to not dying nobly.

ISMENE: Go, then, if go you must. And yet of this be sure, that mad as is your going, dearly are you loved by those you love.

*   *   *

[*Enter* CREON.]

CREON: Sirs, our city's welfare, though shaken in a heavy surge, the gods have safely righted. Therefore by mandate I have brought you hither, parted from all the rest, because I know full well how in the time of Laïus you steadily respected the power of the throne. So also in the days when Oedipus upheld the State. And even when he fell, you stood around the children of his house with faithful hearts. Since, then, these two have fallen in one day by double doom, smiting and smitten in their own hand's guilt, I take possession of all power and of the throne through being next of kin to the two dead.

It is impossible fully to learn what a man is in heart and mind and judgment until he proves himself by test of office and of laws. For to my thinking he who ordering a great state catches at plans not through their being best, and then through fear holds his lips locked, appears and ever has appeared most base. Him who regards his friend more than his land I count no man at all. I therefore,—all-seeing Zeus bear witness!—never shall keep silence when I see woe coming on my citizens instead of weal. Nor would I ever make that man my friend who is my country's foe; because I know how it is she who saves us, and when we sail with her secure we find true friends.

Such are the principles by which I make this city prosper. And in accord herewith I now have issued public edict touching the sons of Oedipus: ordering that Eteocles, who fell fighting for this city after winning all distinction with his spear, be laid within a grave and given whatever honors meet the brave dead below. But for his brother Polynices, who coming back from exile tried by fire utterly to destroy his native land and his ancestral gods, tried even to taste the blood of his own kin or force them into bondage—this man we have proclaimed throughout the city none shall honor with a grave and none lament, but that his corpse be left unburied, for the birds and dogs to eat, disgraced for all to see. Such is my will. Never by act of mine shall bad men have more honor than the just. But he who is well minded toward this state alike in life or death by me is honored.

*   *   *

CREON: You there, now turning to the ground your face, do you acknowledge or deny you did this thing?

ANTIGONE: I say I did it. I deny not that I did.

CREON: (*To Watchman.*) Then go your way, clear of a heavy charge. [*Exit.*] (*To Antigone.*) Tell me, not at full length but briefly, did you know my edict against doing this?

ANTIGONE: I did. How could I help it? It was plain.

CREON: Yet you presumed to transgress laws?

ANTIGONE: Yes, for it was not Zeus who gave this edict; nor yet did Justice, dwelling with the gods below, make for men laws like these. I did not think such force was in your edicts that the unwritten and unchanging laws of God you, a mere man, could traverse. These are not matters of to-day or yesterday, but are from everlasting. No man can tell at what time they appeared. In view of them I would not, through fear of human will, meet judgment from the gods. That I shall die, I knew,—how fail to know it?—though you had never made an edict. And if before my time I die, I count it gain. For he who lives like me in many woes, how can he fail to find in death a gain? So then for me to meet this doom is not a grief at all. But when my mother's child had died if I had kept his corpse unburied, then I should have grieved. For this I do not grieve. And if I seem to you to have been working folly, it may be he who charges folly is the fool.

CHORUS: Plain is the headstrong temper of this child of headstrong father. She knows not how to bend in times of ill.

CREON: Yet know that spirits very stiff may soonest fail. The strongest iron, baked in the fire overhard, you may see oftenest snap and break. By a little bit, I find, high-mettled steeds are managed. There is no place for pride in one who is dependent. She first set out in crime when she transgressed the established laws; and after that comes further crime in boasting here, laughing at having done so. I am no longer man, she is the man, if such power rests in her unchallenged. Be she my sister's child, or closer to my blood than all who bow before our household Zeus, she and her kin shall not escape the direst doom.

Yes, for I count her sister an equal plotter of this burial. Summon her hither! Even now I saw her in the house raving and uncontrolled. It often happens that the stealthy heart is caught before the act, when in the dark men fashion crooked deeds. But it is hateful, too, when one found out in wrong will give his guilt fine names.

ANTIGONE: Do you desire more than having caught to kill me?

CREON: No, nothing. Having that, I have the whole.

ANTIGONE: Then why delay? For nothing in your words can give me pleasure—and may they never please! So also you mine naturally displease. Yet how could I have gained glory more glorious than by now laying my own brother in the grave? All here would speak approval, did not terror seal their lips. Rulers, so fortunate in much besides, have this advantage too—that they can do and say whatever they may please.

CREON: Of all the race of Cadmus you alone see it so.

ANTIGONE: These also do, but curb their tongues through fear of you.

CREON: And are you not ashamed to act so unlike them?

ANTIGONE: 'T is no disgrace to honor one's own kin.

CREON: Was not he also of your blood who fell, his rival?

ANTIGONE: Mine, by one mother and one father too.

CREON: Why then pay honors which dishonor him?

ANTIGONE: He who is dead would not describe it so.

CREON: Yes, if you give like honor to his impious foe.

ANTIGONE: It was no slave who died. It was his brother.

CREON: Wasting the land. And he defending it.

ANTIGONE: But these are rites called for by Death itself.

CREON: The good and bad should not be like in lot.

ANTIGONE: Who knows if that is pity below?

CREON: A hated man is not beloved, though dead.

ANTIGONE: I take no part in hate. 'T is mine to love.

CREON: Down to the grave, then, if you needs must love, and love those there! But while I live, no woman masters me.

*   *   *

CHORUS: But here is Haemon, the youngest of your sons. Does he come grieving for the fate of his intended bride Antigone, vexed at his vanished nuptials?

[*Enter* HAEMON.]

*   *   *

CREON: Soon we shall know, better than seers could say. My son, because you heard the immutable decree passed on your promised bride, you are not here incensed against your father? Are we not dear to you, do what we may?

HAEMON: My father, I am yours; and with just judgment you may direct, and I shall follow. No marriage shall be counted greater gain than your wise guidance.

CREON: Yes, so it should be settled in your heart, my son, always to take your stand behind your father's judgment. Therefore men pray to rear obedient children and to have them in their homes, to recompense the foe with ill and honor as their father does the friend. If one begets unprofitable children, what shall we say but that he breeds pains for himself, loud laughter for his foes? Do not, my son, at pleasure's bidding, give up your wits for any woman. But know embraces soon grow cold when she who shares the home is false. What ulcer can be worse than the false friend? Then spurn the girl as if she were your foe, and let her seek a husband in the house of Hades. For having found her only, out of all the State, openly disobedient, recreant to that State I will not be, but I will have her life.

Let her appeal to Zeus, the god of kindred; but if I train my kin to be disorderly, I surely shall all those outside my kin. He who in private matters is a faithful man will prove himself upright in public too. But one who wantonly forces the law, and thinks to dictate to the rulers, wins no praise from me. No, whosoever is established by the State should be obeyed, in matters trivial and just or in their opposites. And the obedient man, I should be confident, would govern well and easily be governed, and posted in the storm of spears would hold his ground, a true and loyal comrade. Than lawlessness there is no greater ill. It ruins states, overturns homes, and joining with the spear-thrust breaks the ranks in rout. But in the steady lines what saves most lives is discipline. Therefore we must defend the public order and not at all subject it to a woman. Better be pushed aside, if need be, by a man than to be known as women's subjects.

CHORUS: Unless through age we are at fault, you seem to say with reason what you say.

HAEMON: Father, the gods plant wisdom in mankind, which is of all possessions highest. In what respects you have not spoken rightly I cannot say, and may I never learn; and still it may be possible for some one else to be right too. I naturally watch in your behalf all that men do or say or find to blame. For your eye terrifies the common man and checks the words you might not wish to hear; but it is mine to hear things uttered in the dark. I know how the whole city mourns this maid, as one who of all women least deservedly for noblest deeds meets basest death. "She who, when her brother had fallen in the fight and lay unburied, did not leave him to be torn by savage dogs and birds, is she not worthy to receive some golden honor?" Such guarded talk runs covertly about.

For me, my father, nothing I possess is dearer than your welfare. For what can bring to children greater glory than a successful father's noble name, or to a father than his son's renown? Do not then carry in your heart one fixed belief that what you say and nothing else is right. For he who thinks that he alone is wise, or that he has a tongue and mind no other has, will when laid open be found empty. However wise a man may be, it is no shame to learn, learn much, and not to be too firm. You see along the streams in winter how many trees bend down and save their branches; while those that stand up stiff go trunk and all to ruin. So he who tightly draws his vessel's sheet and will not slack, upsets the boat and ends his course with benches upside down. Be yielding, then, and admit change. For if from me, though younger, an opinion be allowed, I count it best that man should be by nature wise. But if that cannot be,—and usually the scale does not incline so—then it is well to learn from good advisers.

CHORUS: My lord, you ought, when Haemon speaks aright, to learn of him; and Haemon, you of him. For both have spoken well.

CREON: At our age shall we learn from one so young?

HAEMON: Only the truth. Young though I am, do not regard my years more than the facts.

CREON: The fact, you mean, of being gentle to the unruly.

HAEMON: I would not ask for gentleness to wicked persons.

CREON: But is not she tainted with some such ill?

HAEMON: With one accord the men of Thebes say no.

CREON: And shall the city tell me how to rule?

HAEMON: Surely you see how childish are such words!

CREON: Govern this land for others than myself?

HAEMON: No city is the property of one alone.

CREON: Is not the city reckoned his who rules?

HAEMON: Excellent ruling,—you alone, the land deserted!

CREON: He fights, it seems, the woman's battle.

HAEMON: If you are she. Indeed my care is all for you.

CREON: Perverted boy, pressing a cause against your father!

HAEMON: Because I see you causelessly do wrong.

CREON: Do I do wrong in reverencing my office?

HAEMON: It is not reverence to trample on the rights of gods.

CREON: A hateful heart that bends before a woman!

HAEMON: But never will you find me subservient to the base.

CREON: Why, all your argument is urged for her.

HAEMON: Yes, and for you and me, and for the gods below.

CREON: You shall not marry her this side the grave.

HAEMON: So then she dies; but if she dies, destroys another.

CREON: Will you assail me with your threats, audacious boy?

HAEMON: Is it a threat to combat silly schemes?

CREON: To your sorrow you shall teach, while yourself in need of teaching.

HAEMON: But that you are my father, I had counted you ill-taught.

CREON: Be a plaything for your mistress, but trifle not with me!

HAEMON: Will you then speak, and when you speak not listen?

CREON: And has it come to this? But, by Olympus, you shall not lightly heap reproach on insult. Bring me that piece of malice, straight-way to die before my eyes in presence of her bridegroom!

HAEMON: Not in my presence. Do not think it! She shall not die while I am near. And you youself shall see my face no more. Rave on then here with those who will submit!

[*Exit.*]

* * *

CHORUS: So you will put them both to death?

CREON: Not her who had no finger in the business. You say well.

CHORUS: And by what doom do you intend to slay the other?

CREON: Leading her where the ways are clear of humankind, I will shut her up alive in a stone cell, allowing only so much food for expiation that the whole city may escape the stain. And if she calls upon the Grave,—the only god she honors—she may obtain deliverance from death; or else will learn, though late, that honor done the Grave is labor lost.

[*Exit.*]

*   *   *

ANTIGONE: Men of my land, you see me taking my last walk here, looking my last upon the sunshine—never more. No, Hades, who brings all to bed, leads me alive along the strand of Acheron, missing my part in wedding song. Never did bridal hymn hymn me. But I shall be the bride of Acheron.

CHORUS: And yet you will in glory and with praise pass to the secret places of the dead. Not smitten with slow disease, nor meeting the sword's portion, but self-possessed, alone among mankind you go to the Grave alive.

ANTIGONE: I have heard of the pitiful end of the stranger from Phrygia, the daughter of Tantalus, on Mount Sipylus; o'er whom like clinging ivy a rocky growth would creep, and from her wasting form the showers and snow, 't is said, are never absent, but drop upon her neck down from her weeping brows. Most like to her, God brings me to my rest.

CHORUS: Nay, nay! She was a god and sprung from gods. But we are mortals and of human birth. Yet for a mortal maid to win a godlike lot is high renown, whether one live or die.

ANTIGONE: Ah, I am mocked! Why, by our country's gods, taunt me when not yet gone but here before you? O thou my city, and ye great ones of my city, thou spring of Dircé, and thou grove of charioted Thebes, I call on you to witness how all unwept of friends and by what cruel laws I go to that sepulchral mound for an unheard-of burial. Ah, poor me! Having no home with mankind or with corpses, with living or with dead!

CHORUS: Onward pressing to the utmost verge of daring, on the deep foundation stone of Right you fell, my child,—a grievous fall. A father's penalty you pay.

ANTIGONE: Ah, there you touched my bitterest pang, my father's thrice-told woe, and all the doom of the great line of Labdacus. Alas, the horrors of my mother's bed! And the embraces—his very self begetting—of that father and that hapless mother from whom I here, distracted, once was born! To them I go, accursed, unwedded, now to dwell. Alas for you, my brother, who made an ill-starred marriage and in your death stripped me, alive, of all.

CHORUS: In pious actions there is piety. Yet power, when his whose right it is, may nowise be transgressed. Your self-willed temper slew you.

ANTIGONE: Unwept, unfriended, with no bridal song, poor I am led along the appointed way. Never again that sacred ball of fire may I, alas! behold. Yet for my tearless lot not a friend grieves.

CREON: Do you not know that groans and dirges before death would never cease, were it allowed to voice them? Away with her forthwith! And when, as I commanded, you have shut her in the vaulted tomb, leave her alone in solitude, to die if so she must, or let her live her life prisoned in such a home. Thus we are clear of what befalls the maid. Only from dwelling in the light above shall she be hindered.

ANTIGONE: O grave! O bridal chamber! Hollow home, forever holding me! whither I go to join my own; for far the greater number Persephassa has received among the dead, all gone! Last of them I, and most unhappy far, now go below before I reach the limit of my life; yet going, dearly cherish it among my hopes to have my coming welcome to my father, welcome to you, my mother, welcome too to you, my brother. When you all died, with my own hand I washed you, did you service, and poured libations at your graves. But, Polynices, for ministering to your corpse this is my recompense.

Rightly I honored you, the wise will think. Yet had I children, or were my husband mouldering in death, I might not in defiance of my townsmen have taken up the task. And wherefore so? I might have had another husband, had mine died, a child too by another man when I had lost my own; but mother and father hidden in the grave, there is no brother ever to be born. Yet when upon such grounds I held you first in honor, to Creon's eye I seemed to sin and to be over-bold, my brother dear. And now he leads me forth, a captive, deprived of bridal bed and song,—without experience of marriage or the rearing of a child,—that so poor I, cut off from friends but still alive, enter the caverned chambers of the dead.

What ordinance of heaven have I transgressed? Yet why in misery still look to gods or call on them for aid, when even this name of impious I got by piety! No, if such acts are pleasing to the gods, I may by suffering come to know my sin. But if these others rather sin, may they not suffer greater ill than they now wrongly wreak on me.

CHORUS: Still the same winds' same blasts of passion sway her.

CREON: Therefore her guards shall smart for their delay.

ANTIGONE: Ah me! The signal comes that death is nigh!

CHORUS: I cannot bid you hope it will not follow.

ANTIGONE: O city in the land of Thebes! Home of my fathers! And ye, ancestral gods! Men seize me and I cannot stay. Behold, O lords of Thebes, how I, last remnant of the royal line, now suffer, and from whom—I who revered the right.

[ANTIGONE is led away.]

*   *   *

[Enter a messenger.]

MESSENGER: Ye dwellers at the palace of Cadmus and Amphion, there is no human life, however placed, that I can praise or blame. For fortune raises, fortune overthrows, him who is now in good or evil fortune. No seer can tell the destinies of man. Creon was enviable once, I thought, through having saved this land of Cadmus from its foes. Winning full sovereignty he ruled the land, blest too in noble issue. Now all is gone. For when man parts with happiness, I count him not alive, but a mere breathing corpse. Let him have riches in his house, great riches if you

will, and live in royal state; if happiness be absent, I would not pay a puff of smoke for all the rest, when weighed with joy.

CHORUS: What new disaster to our kings come you to tell?

MESSENGER: Dead! And the living caused the death.

CHORUS: Who is the slayer? Who has fallen? Speak!

MESSENGER: Haemon is gone. With violence his blood is shed.

CHORUS: What? By his father's hand, or by his own?

MESSENGER: His own, incensed against his father for the murder.

*   *   *

CHORUS: But lo! Our lord himself draws near, bringing in his arms clear proof—if we may say so—of wrong not wrought by others but by his erring self.

[Enter CREON, bearing the body of HAEMON.]

*   *   *

CREON: Alas, the sins of a presumptuous soul, stubborn and deadly! Ah, ye who see slayers and slain of kindred blood! Woe for my ill-starred plans! Alas, my boy, so young in life and young in sorrow! Woe! Woe! Thou, dead and gone? And by my folly, not thy own!

CHORUS: Ah me! It seems you see the right too late!

CREON: Unhappy I have learned it now. But then some god possessed me, smote on my head a heavy blow, drove me along a brutish path, and so—alas!—o'erthrew my joy and trampled it. Woe, woe, for the wearisome works of man!

[Enter a second messenger.]

SECOND MESSENGER: My lord, 't is having and still getting. You bear one sorrow in your arms; enter the house, and there you soon should see another.

CREON: What is there yet more sorrowful than this?

SECOND MESSENGER: The queen is dead, true mother of the dead here. Poor lady, she has fallen by wounds dealt even now.

CREON: Alas, alas! Insatiate gulf of death! Why, why thus cause my ruin? And cruel messenger, speeding my pain, what is the tale you tell? Why, one already dead you slay anew! What say you, boy? What tidings do you bring? Ah, must the slaughterous ending of my wife follow the death of him?

[*The Scene opens, and the body of* EURYDICE *is disclosed.*]

CHORUS: Here you may see! It shall be hid no longer.

CREON: Ah me! A fresh, a second grief poor I behold. What more has fate in waiting? Just now I took my child in my arms—alas!—and face to face behold another corse. Woe! Woe! unhappy mother! Woe, my child!

SECOND MESSENGER: Crazed, clinging to the altar, and closing her dark eyes, she first bemoaned the glorious grave of Megareus who died before, then this one's end; and with her last breath called down ill on you, the murderer of your children.

CREON: Alas! Alas! Fear thrills me. Will none strike home with two-edged sword? Poor I am steeped in sore distress.

SECOND MESSENGER: You were accused by her who died of causing both the deaths.

CREON: And by what sort of violence did she depart?

SECOND MESSENGER: Her own hand smote herself below the heart, soon as she learned the lamentable ending of her son.

CREON: Ah me! To no one else can this be shifted from my guilty self. 'T was I indeed that killed thee, wretched I! I say the truth, 't was I. Take me, my servants, take me straightway hence, to be no more than nothing.

CHORUS: Wise wishes these, if any way is wise in evil. Briefest is best, when evil clogs our feet.

CREON: Come, then, appear, fairest of fates that brings my final day! O come, best boon, and let me never see another day!

CHORUS: Time will determine that. The present needs our care. Let them whose right it is direct the rest!

CREON: All I desire is summed up in that prayer.

CHORUS: Pray no more now. From his appointed woe man cannot fly.

CREON: Then take away the useless man who by no will of his killed thee, my child, and thee too lying here. Alas poor me, who know not which to look on, where to turn! All in my hands was at cross purposes, and on my head fell fate I could not guide.

CHORUS: Wisdom is far the greater part of peace. The gods will have their dues. Large language, bringing to the proud large chastisement, at last brings wisdom.

*　　*　　*

REVIEW QUESTIONS

1. What is the dilemma with which Antigone is confronted?
2. Where, in her eyes, must her principal allegiance lie?
3. How does the fact that Antigone is a woman affect her treatment by Creon?
4. How do you think this play would have been received by a Spartan audience?

ARISTOPHANES

FROM *Lysistrata*

With eleven of his total of thirty plays having survived from antiquity, Aristophanes is by far the best known and most celebrated of the comic playwrights of classical Athens. His career spanned the later fifth and early fourth centuries B.C.E., *including the final decades of the calamitous Peloponnesian War that pitted Athens and its allies against a coalition led by Sparta. His plays consistently lampooned leading political leaders and cultural figures of Athens as well as Athenian society in general. This is nowhere more evident than in his play* Lysistrata, *which is named for its chief protagonist, an Athenian woman who concocts and then implements a plan to end the war between Athens and Sparta by having the women of both city-states go on a "sex strike"—denying their husbands any sexual activity until the men sit down and bring an end to the war. As the selection below abundantly illustrates, Aristophanes was a master of ribald, bawdy dialogue full of double entendres. But ultimately he points out the folly and futility of war.*

From *Lysistrata*, by Aristophanes, translated by Jack Lindsay (London: Fanfrolico Press, 1926).

As the play begins, Lysistrata consorts with her friends Calonice and Myrrhine, all of them soon joined by a Spartan woman, Lampito.

———

LYSISTRATA: Good day Calonice.
CALONICE: Good day Lysistrata.
    But what has vexed you so? Tell me, child.
    What are these black looks for? It doesn't suit you
    To knit your eyebrows up glumly like that.
LYSISTRATA: Calonice, it's more than I can bear,
    I am hot all over with blushes for our sex.
    Men say we're slippery rogues—
CALONICE: And aren't they right?
LYSISTRATA: Yet summoned on the most tremendous business
    For deliberation, still they snuggle in bed.
CALONICE: My dear, they'll come. It's hard for women, you know,
    To get away. There's so much to do;
    Husbands to be patted and put in good tempers:
    Servants to be poked out: children washed

    Or soothed with lullays or fed with mouthfuls of pap.
LYSISTRATA: But I tell you, here's a far more weighty object.
CALONICE: What is it all about, dear Lysistrata,
    That you've called the women hither in a troop?
    What kind of an object is it?
LYSISTRATA: A tremendous thing!
CALONICE: And long?
LYSISTRATA: Indeed, it may be very lengthy.
CALONICE: Then why aren't they here?
LYSISTRATA: No man's connected with it;
    If that was the case, they'd soon come fluttering along.
    No, no. It concerns an object I've felt over
    And turned this way and that for sleepless nights.
CALONICE: It must be fine to stand such long attention.
LYSISTRATA: So fine it comes to this—Greece saved by Woman!
CALONICE: By Woman? Wretched thing, I'm sorry for it.

LYSISTRATA: Our country's fate is henceforth in
  our hands:
  To destroy the Peloponnesians root and branch
CALONICE: What could be nobler!
LYSISTRATA: Wipe out the Boeotians—
CALONICE: Not utterly. Have mercy on the eels![1]
LYSISTRATA: But with regard to Athens, note I'm
  careful
  Not to say any of these nasty things;
  Still, thought is free. . . . But if the women join us
  From Peloponnesus and Boeotia, then
  Hand in hand we'll rescue Greece.
CALONICE: How could we do
  Such a big wise deed? We women who dwell
  Quietly adorning ourselves in a back-room
  With gowns of lucid gold and gawdy toilets
  Of stately silk and dainty little slippers . . .
LYSISTRATA: These are the very armaments of the
  rescue.
  These crocus-gowns, this outlay of the best
    myrrh,
  Slippers, cosmetics dusting beauty, and robes
  With rippling creases of light.
CALONICE: Yes, but how?
LYSISTRATA: No man will lift a lance against
  another—
CALONICE: I'll run to have my tunic dyed crocus.
LYSISTRATA: Or take a shield—
CALONICE: I'll get a stately gown.
LYSISTRATA: Or unscabbard a sword—
CALONICE: Let me buy a pair of slippers.
LYSISTRATA: Now, tell me, are the women right to
  lag?
CALONICE: They should have turned birds, they
  should have grown wings and flown.
LYSISTRATA: My friend, you'll see that they are
  true Athenians:
  Always too late. Why, there's not a woman
  From the shoreward demes arrived, not one
    from Salamis.
CALONICE: I know for certain they awoke at dawn,
  And got their husbands up if not their boat sails.
LYSISTRATA: And I'd have staked my life the
  Acharnian dames

Would be here first, yet they haven't come
  either!
CALONICE: Well anyhow there is Theagenes' wife
  We can expect—she consulted Hecate.
  But look, here are some at last, and more
    behind them.
  See . . . where are they from?
CALONICE: From Anagyra they come.
LYSISTRATA: Yes, they generally manage to come
  first.
[Enter MYRRHINE.]
MYRRHINE: Are we late, Lysistrata? . . . What is
  that?
  Nothing to say?
LYSISTRATA: I've not much to say for you,
  Myrrhine, dawdling on so vast an affair.
MYRRHINE: I couldn't find my girdle in the dark.
  But if the affair's so wonderful, tell us, what is
    it?
LYSISTRATA: No, let us stay a little longer till
  The Peloponnesian girls and the girls of Boeotia
  Are here to listen.
MYRRHINE: That's the best advice.
  Ah, there comes Lampito.
[*Enter* LAMPITO.]
LYSISTRATA: Welcome Lampito!
  Dear Spartan girl with a delightful face,
  Washed with the rosy spring, how fresh you
    look
  In the easy stride of your sleek slenderness,
  Why you could strangle a bull!
LAMPITO: I think I could.
  It's frae exercise and kicking high behint.[2]
LYSISTRATA: What lovely breasts to own!
LAMPITO: Oo . . . your fingers
  Assess them, ye tickler, wi' such tender chucks
  I feel as if I were an altar-victim.
LYSISTRATA: Who is this youngster?
LAMPITO: A Boeotian lady.
LYSISTRATA: There never was much undergrowth
  in Boeotia,

---

[1] The Boeotian eels were highly esteemed delicacies in
Athens.

[2] The translator has put the speech of the Spartan characters in Scotch dialect which is related to English as much
as was the Spartan dialect to the speech of Athens. The
Spartans, in their character, anticipated the shrewd,
canny, uncouth Scotch highlander of modern times.

Such a smooth place, and this girl takes after it.

CALONICE: Yes, I never saw a skin so primly kept.

LYSISTRATA: This girl?

LAMPITO: A sonsie open-looking jinker!
    She's a Corinthian.

LYSISTRATA: Yes, isn't she
    Very open, in some ways particularly.

LAMPITO: But who's garred this Council o'
    Women to meet here?

LYSISTRATA: I have.

LAMPITO: Propound then what you want o' us.

MYRRHINE: What is the amazing news you have to
    tell?

LYSISTRATA: I'll tell you, but first answer one
    small question.

MYRRHINE: As you like.

LYSISTRATA: Are you not sad your children's fathers
    Go endlessly off soldiering afar
    In this plodding war? I am willing to wager
    There's not one here whose husband is at home.

CALONICE: Mine's been in Thrace, keeping an eye
    on Eucrates
    For five months past.

MYRRHINE: And mine left me for Pylos
    Seven months ago at least.

LAMPITO: And as for mine
    No sooner has he slipped out frae the line
    He straps his shield and he's snickt off again.

LYSISTRATA: And not the slightest glitter of a lover!
    And since the Milesians betrayed us, I've not
        seen
    The image of a single upright man
    To be a marble consolation to us.
    Now will you help me, if I find a means
    To stamp the war out.

MYRRHINE: By the two Goddesses, Yes!
    I will though I've to pawn this very dress
    And drink the barter-money the same day.

CALONICE: And I too though I'm split up like a
    turbot
    And half is hackt off as the price of peace.

LAMPITO: And I too! Why, to get a peep at the shy
    thing
    I'd clamber up to the tip-top o' Taygetus.

LYSISTRATA: Then I'll expose my mighty mystery.
    O women, if we would compel the men

To bow to Peace, we must refrain—

MYRRHINE: From what? O tell us!

LYSISTRATA: Will you truly do it then?

MYRRHINE: We will, we will, if we must die for it.

LYSISTRATA: We must refrain from every depth of
    love. . . .
    Why do you turn your backs?
    Where are you going?
    Why do you bite your lips and shake your
        heads? Why are your faces blanched?
    Why do you weep? Will you or won't you, or
        what do you mean?

MYRRHINE: No, I won't do it. Let the war proceed.

CALONICE: No, I won't do it. Let the war proceed.

LYSISTRATA: You too, dear turbot, you that said
    just now
    You didn't mind being split right up in the least?

CALONICE: Anything else? O bid me walk in fire
    But do not rob us of that darling joy.
    What else is like it, dearest Lysistrata?

LYSISTRATA: And you?

MYRRHINE: O please give me the fire instead.

LYSISTRATA: Lewd to the least drop in the tiniest
    vein,
    Our sex is fitly food for Tragic Poets,
    Our whole life's but a pile of kisses and babies.
    But, hardy Spartan, if you join with me
    All may be righted yet. O help me, help me.

LAMPITO: It's a sair, sair thing to ask of us, by the
    Twa,
    A lass to sleep her lane and never fill
    Love's lack except wi' makeshifts. . . . But let it be.
    Peace maun be thought of first.

LYSISTRATA: My friend, my friend!
    The only one amid this herd of weaklings.

CALONICE: But if—which heaven forbid—we
    should refrain
    As you would have us, how is Peace induced?

LYSISTRATA: By the two Goddesses, now can't you
    see
    All we have to do is idly sit indoors
    With smooth roses powdered on our cheeks,
    Our bodies burning naked through the folds
    Of shining Amorgos' silk, and meet the men
    With our dear Venus-plats plucked trim and
        neat.

Their stirring love will rise up furiously,
They'll beg our arms to open. That's our time!
We'll disregard their knocking, beat them off—
And they will soon be rabid for a Peace.
I'm sure of it.

LAMPITO: Just as Menelaus, they say,
  Seeing the bosom of his naked Helen
  Flang down the sword.

CALONICE: But we'll be tearful fools
  If our husbands take us at our word and leave
  us.

LYSISTRATA: There's only left then, in Pherecrates'
  phrase,
  "To flay a skinned dog"—flay more our flayed
  desires.

CALONICE: Bah, proverbs will never warm a
  celibate.
  But what avail will your scheme be if the men
  Drag us for all our kicking on to the couch?

LYSISTRATA: Cling to the doorposts.

CALONICE: But if they should force us?

LYSISTRATA: Yield then, but with a sluggish, cold
  indifference.
  There is no joy to them in sullen mating.
  Besides we have other ways to madden them;
  They cannot stand up long, and they've no
  delight
  Unless we fit their aim with merry succour.

CALONICE: Well if you must have it so, we'll all
  agree.

LAMPITO: For us I ha' no doubt. We can persuade
  Our men to strike a fair an' decent Peace,
  But how will ye pitch out the battle-frenzy
  O' the Athenian populace?

LYSISTRATA: I promise you
  We'll wither up that curse.

*   *   *

*Later in the play, starved of their husbands'
affections, some of the women try to mutiny, only to
have Lysistrata challenge and cajole them into keeping their oath and staying with their plan. At that
point enters Cinesias, the husband of Lysistrata's
friend and co-conspirator Myrrhine, along with their
infant son. Cinesias is in an obvious state of sexual
"distress."*

*   *   *

LYSISTRATA: A man, a man! I spy a frenzied man!
  He carries Love upon him like a staff.
  O Lady of Cyprus, and Cythera, and Paphos,
  I beseech you, keep our minds and hands to
    the oath.

WOMAN: Where is he, whoever he is?

LYSISTRATA: By the Temple of Chloe.

WOMAN: Yes, now I see him, but who can he be?

LYSISTRATA: Look at him. Does anyone recognise
  his face?

MYRRHINE: I do. He is my husband, Cinesias.

LYSISTRATA: You know how to work. Play with
  him, lead him on,
  Seduce him to the cozening-point—kiss him,
    kiss him,
  Then slip your mouth aside just as he's sure of
    it,
  Ungirdle every caress his mouth feels at
  Save that the oath upon the bowl has locked.

MYRRHINE: You can rely on me.

LYSISTRATA: I'll stay here to help
  In working up his ardor to its height
  Of vain magnificence. . . . The rest to their
    quarters.

[*Enter Cinesias*]
  Who is this that stands within our lines?

CINESIAS: I.

LYSISTRATA: A man?

CINESIAS: Too much a man!

LYSISTRATA: Then be off at once.

CINESIAS: Who are you that thus eject me?

LYSISTRATA: Guard for the day.

CINESIAS: By all the gods, then call Myrrhine
  hither.

LYSISTRATA: So, call Myrrhine hither! Who are
  you?

CINESIAS: I am her husband Cinesias, son of
  Anthros.

LYSISTRATA: Welcome, dear friend! That glorious
  name of yours
  Is quite familiar in our ranks.
  Your wife Continually has it in her mouth.
  She cannot touch an apple or an egg
  But she must say, "This to Cinesias!"

CINESIAS: O is that true?

LYSISTRATA: By Aphrodite, it is.
>   If the conversation strikes on men, your wife
>   Cuts in with, "All are boobies by Cinesias."

CINESIAS: Then call her here.

LYSISTRATA: And what am I to get?

CINESIAS: This, if you want it. . . . See, what I have
>   here. But not to take away.

LYSISTRATA: Then I'll call her.

CINESIAS: Be quick, be quick. All grace is wiped
>   from life
>   Since she went away. O sad, sad am I
>   When there I enter on that loneliness,
>   And wine is unvintaged of the sun's flavour.
>   And food is tasteless. But I've put on weight.

MYRRHINE (ABOVE): I love him O so much! but he
>   won't have it.
>   Don't call me down to him.

CINESIAS: Sweet little Myrrhine!
>   What do you mean? Come here.

MYRRHINE: O no I won't.
>   Why are you calling me? You don't want me.

CINESIAS: Not want you! with this week-old
>   strength of love.

MYRRHINE: Farewell.

CINESIAS: Don't go, please don't go, Myrrhine.
>   At least you'll hear our child. Call your mother,
>   lad.

CHILD: Mummy . . . mummy . . . mummy!

CINESIAS: There now, don't you feel pity for the
>   child?
>   He's not been fed or washed now for six days.

MYRRHINE: I certainly pity him with so heartless
>   a father.

CINESIAS: Come down, my sweetest, come for the
>   child's sake.

MYRRHINE: A trying life it is to be a mother!
>   I suppose I'd better go. [She comes down.]

CINESIAS: How much younger she looks,
>   How fresher and how prettier! Myrrhine,
>   Lift up your lovely face, your disdainful face;
>   And your ankle . . . let your scorn step out its
>   worst;
>   It only rubs me to more ardor here.

MYRRHINE: (PLAYING WITH THE CHILD): You're as
>   innocent as he's iniquitous.
>   Let me kiss you, honey-petting, mother's darling.

CINESIAS: How wrong to follow other women's
>   counsel
>   And let loose all these throbbing voids in
>   yourself
>   As well as in me. Don't you go throb-throb?

MYRRHINE: Take away your hands.

CINESIAS: Everything in the house
>   Is being ruined.

MYRRHINE: I don't care at all.

CINESIAS: The roosters are picking all your web to
>   rags.
>   Do you mind that?

MYRRHINE: Not I.

CINESIAS: What time we've wasted
>   We might have drenched with Paphian
>   laughter, flung
>   On Aphrodite's Mysteries. O come here.

MYRRHINE: Not till a treaty finishes the war.

CINESIAS: If you must have it, then we'll get it done.

MYRRHINE: Do it and I'll come home. Till then
>   I am bound.

CINESIAS: Well, can't your oath perhaps be got
>   around?

MYRRHINE: No . . . no . . . still I'll not say that I
>   don't love you.

CINESIAS: You love me! Then dear girl, let me also
>   love you.

MYRRHINE: You must be joking. The boy's
>   looking on.

CINESIAS: Here, Manes, take the child home! . . .
>   There, he's gone.
>   There's nothing in the way now. Come to the
>   point.

MYRRHINE: Here in the open! In plain sight?

CINESIAS: In Pan's cave.
>   A splendid place.

MYRRHINE: Where shall I dress my hair again
>   Before returning to the citadel?

CINESIAS: You can easily primp yourself in the
>   Clepsydra.

MYRRHINE: But how can I break my oath?

CINESIAS: Leave that to me,
>   I'll take all risk.

MYRRHINE: Well, I'll make you comfortable.

CINESIAS: Don't worry. I'd as soon lie on the grass.

MYRRHINE: No, by Apollo, in spite of all your faults

I won't have you lying on the nasty earth.
[From here MYRRHINE keeps on going off to
    fetch things.]
CINESIAS: Ah, how she loves me.
MYRRHINE: Rest there on the bench,
    While I arrange my clothes. O what a
        nuisance,
    I must find some cushions first.
CINESIAS: Why some cushions?
    Please don't get them!
MYRRHINE: What? The plain, hard wood?
    Never, by Artemis! That would be too vulgar.
CINESIAS: Open your arms!
MYRRHINE: No. Wait a second.
CINESIAS: O. . . .
    Then hurry back again.
MYRRHINE: Here the cushions are.
    Lie down while I—O dear! But what a shame,
    You need more pillows.
CINESIAS: I don't want them, dear.
MYRRHINE: But I do.
CINESIAS: Thwarted affection mine,
    They treat you just like Heracles at a feast
    With cheats of dainties, O disappointing arms!
MYRRHINE: Raise up your head.
CINESIAS: There, that's everything at last.
MYRRHINE: Yes, all.
CINESIAS: Then run to my arms, you golden girl.
MYRRHINE: I'm loosening my girdle now. But
    you've not forgotten?
    You're not deceiving me about the Treaty?
CINESIAS: No, by my life, I'm not.
MYRRHINE: Why, you've no blanket.
CINESIAS: It's not the silly blanket's warmth but
    yours I want.
MYRRHINE: Never mind. You'll soon have both.
    I'll come straight back.
CINESIAS: The woman will choke me with her
    coverlets.
MYRRHINE: Get up a moment.
CINESIAS: I'm up high enough.
MYRRHINE: Would you like me to perfume you?
CINESIAS: By Apollo, no!
MYRRHINE: By Aphrodite, I'll do it anyway.
CINESIAS: Lord Zeus, may she soon use up all the
    myrrh.

MYRRHINE: Stretch out your hand. Take it and rub
    it in.
CINESIAS: Hmm, it's not as fragrant as might be;
    that is,
    Not before it's smeared. It doesn't smell of
        kisses.
MYRRHINE: How silly I am: I've brought you
    Rhodian scents.
CINESIAS: It's good enough, leave it, love.
MYRRHINE: You must be jesting.
CINESIAS: Plague rack the man who first com-
    pounded scent!
MYRRHINE: Here, take this flask.
CINESIAS: I've a far better one.
    Don't tease me, come here, and get nothing
        more.
MYRRHINE: I'm coming. . . . I'm just drawing off
    my shoes. . . .
    You're sure you will vote for Peace?
CINESIAS: I'll think about it.
[She runs off.]
    I'm dead: the woman's worn me all away.
    She's gone and left me with an anguished pulse.
MEN: Baulked in your amorous delight
    How melancholy is your plight.
    With sympathy your case I view;
    For I am sure it's hard on you.
    What human being could sustain
    This unforeseen domestic strain,
    And not a single trace
    Of willing women in the place!
CINESIAS: O Zeus, what throbbing suffering!
MEN: She did it all, the harlot, she
    With her atrocious harlotry.
WOMEN: Nay, rather call her darling-sweet.
MEN: What, sweet? She's a rude, wicked thing.
CINESIAS: A wicked thing, as I repeat.
    O Zeus, O Zeus,
    Canst Thou not suddenly let loose
    Some twirling hurricane to tear
    Her flapping up along the air
    And drop her, when she's whirled around,
    Here to the ground
    Neatly impaled upon the stake
    That's ready upright for her sake.
[He goes out.]

*   *   *

At this point there arrives a herald from Sparta, soon followed by a delegation of Spartan men who have come to Athens desperate to resolve the situation by making peace. Like Cinesias and the Athenian men, they too are in an obvious state of sexual "distress." Their plight is compounded when Lysistrata returns, accompanied by a young, alluring, naked woman named "Reconciliation."

———

[The SPARTAN AMBASSADORS approach.]
CHORUS: Here come the Spartan envoys with long, worried beards.
    Hail, Spartans how do you fare?
    Did anything new arise?
SPARTANS: No need for a clutter o' words. Do ye see our condition?
CHORUS: The situation swells to greater tension. Something will explode soon.
SPARTANS: It's awfu' truly.
    But come, let us wi' the best speed we may
    Scribble a Peace.
CHORUS: I notice that our men
    Like wrestlers poised for contest, hold their clothes
    Out from their bellies. An athlete's malady!
    Since exercise alone can bring relief.
ATHENIANS: Can anyone tell us where Lysistrata is?
    There is no need to describe our men's condition,
    It shows up plainly enough.
CHORUS: It's the same disease.
    Do you feel a jerking throbbing in the morning?
ATHENIANS: By Zeus, yes! In these straits, I'm racked all through.
    Unless Peace is soon declared, we shall be driven
    In the void of women to try Cleisthenes.
CHORUS: Be wise and cover those things with your tunics.
    Who knows what kind of person may perceive you?
ATHENIANS: By Zeus, you're right.
SPARTANS: By the Twa Goddesses,

Indeed ye are. Let's put our tunics on.
ATHENIANS: Hail O my fellow-sufferers, hail Spartans.
SPARTANS: O hinnie darling, what a waefu' thing! If they had seen us wi' our lunging waddies!
ATHENIANS: Tell us then, Spartans, what has brought you here?
SPARTANS: We come to treat o' Peace.
ATHENIANS: Well spoken there!
    And we the same. Let us callout Lysistrata
    Since she alone can settle the Peace-terms.
SPARTANS: Callout Lysistratus too if ye don't mind.
CHORUS: No indeed. She hears your voices and she comes.
[*Enter* LYSISTRATA.]
    Hail, Wonder of all women! Now you must be in turn
    Hard, shifting, clear, deceitful, noble, crafty, sweet, and stern.
    The foremost men of Hellas, smitten by your fascination,
    Have brought their tangled quarrels here for your sole arbitration.
LYSISTRATA: An easy task if the love's raging home-sickness
    Doesn't start trying out how well each other
    Will serve instead of us. But I'll know at once
    If they do. O where's that girl, Reconciliation?
    Bring first before me the Spartan delegates,
    And see you lift no rude or violent hands—
    None of the churlish ways our husbands used.
    But lead them courteously, as women should.
    And if they grudge fingers, guide them by other methods,
    And introduce them with ready tact. The Athenians
    Draw by whatever offers you a grip.
    Now, Spartans, stay here facing me. Here you, Athenians. Both hearken to my words.
    I am a woman, but I'm not a fool.
    And what of natural intelligence I own
    Has been filled out with the remembered precepts
    My father and the city-elders taught me.
    First I reproach you both sides equally
    That when at Pylae and Olympia,

At Pytho and the many other shrines
That I could name, you sprinkle from one cup
The altars common to all Hellenes, yet
You wrack Hellenic cities, bloody Hellas
With deaths of her own sons, while yonder
    clangs
The gathering menace of barbarians.

ATHENIANS: We cannot hold it in much longer now.

LYSISTRATA: Now unto you, O Spartans, do I speak.
Do you forget how your own countryman,
Pericleidas, once came hither suppliant
Before our altars, pale in his purple robes,
Praying for an army when in Messenia
Danger growled, and the Sea-god made earth
    quaver.
Then with four thousand hoplites Cimon
    marched
And saved all Sparta. Yet base ingrates now,
You are ravaging the soil of your preservers.

ATHENIANS: By Zeus, they do great wrong,
Lysistrata.

SPARTANS: Great wrong, indeed. O! What a
luscious wench!

LYSISTRATA: And now I turn to the Athenians.
Have you forgotten too how once the Spartans
In days when you wore slavish tunics, came
And with their spears broke a Thessalian host
And all the partisans of Hippias?
They alone stood by your shoulder on that day.
They freed you, so that for the slave's short skirt
You should wear the trailing cloak of liberty.

SPARTANS: I've never seen a nobler woman
anywhere.

ATHENIANS: Nor I one with such prettily jointing
hips.

LYSISTRATA: Now, brethren twined with mutual
benefactions,
Can you still war, can you suffer such disgrace?
Why not be friends? What is there to prevent
    you?

SPARTANS: We're agreed, gin that we get this
tempting Mole.

LYSISTRATA: Which one?

SPARTANS: That ane we've wanted to get into,
    O for sae lang. . . . Pylos, of course.

ATHENIANS: By Poseidon,
    Never!

LYSISTRATA: Give it up.

ATHENIANS: Then what will we do?
We need that ticklish place united to us–

LYSISTRATA: Ask for some other lurking-hole in
return.

ATHENIANS: Then, ah, we'll choose this snug thing
here, Echinus,
Shall we call the nestling spot? And this back-
    side haven,
These desirable twin promontories, the
    Maliac,
And then of course these Megarean Legs.

SPARTANS: Not that, O surely not that, never that.

LYSISTRATA: Agree! Now what are two legs more
or less?

ATHENIANS: I want to strip at once and plough
my land.

SPARTANS: And mine I want to fertilize at once.

LYSISTRATA: And so you can, when Peace is once
declared.
If you mean it, get your allies' heads together
And come to some decision.

ATHENIANS: What allies?
There's no distinction in our politics:
We've risen as one man to this conclusion;
Every ally is jumping-mad to drive it home.

SPARTANS: And ours the same, for sure.

REVIEW QUESTIONS

1. What does this excerpt tell you about the expected roles and activities of women in late fourth-century B.C.E. Athens?

2. The dialogue here suggests that women might exercise a degree of sexual power over men. But does it indicate that men and women were truly of equal power and status in Athenian society?

3. Aristophanes' *Lysistrata* is generally regarded as one of the masterpieces of Athenian comedy. Given its overtly bawdy sexual content, how would you classify it in terms of twenty-first-century standards?

VASE DEPICTING A SLAVE, PERHAPS IN A SCENE FROM A GREEK PLAY (C. 450 B.C.E.)

Slaves at Athens included a variety of nationalities and were at the bottom of the socio-economic hierarchy. What does the depiction in this vase painting suggest about attitudes toward slaves? How do the physical features and clothing of this slave differ from what you have observed in other works of classical Greek art?

PLATO

FROM *"Apology"*

Our knowledge of the life, personality, and teachings of the late-fifth-century B.C.E. *Athenian philosopher and social critic Socrates is derived almost entirely from the dialogues composed by his most famous student, Plato. In them, Plato recreates Socrates' method of using questions and answers (what today we still refer to as the "Socratic method") to examine and test commonly held opinions. In the following excerpt from the "Apology" (a word that in ancient Greek referred to a defense of one's actions or beliefs, not an expression of contrition or regret), Socrates, on trial before an Athenian jury for allegedly subverting the youth of Athens by converting them to gods of his own invention, defends his career as a teacher. (His eloquence and intellect, in the end, did not save him from condemnation and subsequent execution in 399* B.C.E.*)*

From *The Last Days of Socrates,* translated by Hugh Tredennick (New York: Penguin, 1969), pp. 48–52, 72–76.

*   *   *

Here perhaps one of you might interrupt me and say "But what is it that you do, Socrates? How is it that you have been misrepresented like this? Surely all this talk and gossip about you would never have arisen if you had confined yourself to ordinary activities, but only if your behaviour was abnormal. Tell us the explanation, if you do not want us to invent it for ourselves." This seems to me to be a reasonable request, and I will try to explain to you what it is that has given me this false notoriety; so please give me your attention. Perhaps some of you will think that I am not being serious; but I assure you that I am going to tell you the whole truth.

I have gained this reputation, gentlemen, from nothing more or less than a kind of wisdom. What kind of wisdom do I mean? Human wisdom, I suppose. It seems that I really am wise in this limited sense. Presumably the geniuses whom I mentioned just now are wise in a wisdom that is more than human; I do not know how else to account for it. I certainly have no knowledge of such wisdom, and anyone who says that I have is a liar and wilful slanderer. Now, gentlemen, please do not interrupt me if I seem to make an extravagant claim; for what I am going to tell you is not my own opinion; I am going to refer you to an unimpeachable authority. I shall call as witness to my wisdom (such as it is) the god at Delphi.

You know Chaerephon, of course. He was a friend of mine from boyhood, and a good democrat who played his part with the rest of you in the recent expulsion and restoration. And you know what he was like; how enthusiastic he was over anything that he had once undertaken. Well, one day he actually went to Delphi and asked this question of the god—as I said before, gentlemen, please do not interrupt—he asked whether there was anyone wiser than myself. The priestess replied that there was no one. As Chaerephon is dead, the evidence for my statement will be supplied by his brother, who is here in court.

Please consider my object in telling you this. I want to explain to you how the attack upon my reputation first started. When I heard about the oracle's answer, I said to myself "What does the god mean? Why does he not use plain language? I am only too conscious that I have no claim to wisdom, great or small; so what can he mean by asserting that I am the wisest man in the world? He cannot be telling a lie; that would not be right for him."

After puzzling about it for some time, I set myself at last with considerable reluctance to check the truth of it in the following way. I went to interview a man with a high reputation for wisdom, because I felt that here if anywhere I should succeed in disproving the oracle and pointing out to my divine authority "You said that I was the wisest of men, but here is a man who is wiser than I am."

Well, I gave a thorough examination to this person—I need not mention his name, but it was one of our politicians that I was studying when I had this experience—and in conversation with him I formed the impression that although in many people's opinion, and especially in his own, he appeared to be wise, in fact he was not. Then when I began to try to show him that he only thought he was wise and was not really so, my efforts were resented both by him and by many of the other people present. However, I reflected as I walked away: "Well, I am certainly wiser than this man. It is only too likely that neither of us has any knowledge to boast of; but he thinks that he knows something which he does not know, whereas I am quite conscious of my ignorance. At any rate it seems that I am wiser than he is to this small extent, that I do not think that I know what I do not know."

After this I went on to interview a man with an even greater reputation for wisdom, and I formed the same impression again; and here too I incurred the resentment of the man himself and a number of others.

From that time on I interviewed one person after another. I realized with distress and alarm that I was making myself unpopular, but I felt compelled to put my religious duty first; since I was trying to find out the meaning of the oracle, I was bound to interview everyone who had a reputation for knowledge. And by Dog, gentlemen! (for I must be frank with you) my honest impression was this: it seemed to me, as I pursued my investigation at the god's command, that the people with the greatest reputations were almost entirely deficient, while others who were supposed to be their inferiors were much better qualified in practical intelligence.

I want you to think of my adventures as a sort of pilgrimage undertaken to establish the truth of the oracle once for all. After I had finished with the politicians I turned to the poets, dramatic, lyric, and all the rest, in the belief that here I should expose myself as a comparative ignoramus. I used to pick up what I thought were some of their most perfect works and question them closely about the meaning of what they had written, in the hope of incidentally enlarging my own knowledge. Well, gentlemen, I hesitate to tell you the truth, but it must be told. It is hardly an exaggeration to say that any of the bystanders could have explained those poems better than their actual authors. So I soon made up my mind about the poets too: I decided that it was not wisdom that enabled them to write their poetry, but a kind of instinct or inspiration, such as you find in seers and prophets who deliver all their sublime messages without knowing in the least what they mean. It seemed clear to me that the poets were in much the same case; and I also observed that the very fact that they were poets made them think that they had a perfect understanding of all other subjects, of which they were totally ignorant. So I left that line of inquiry too with the same sense of advantage that I had felt in the case of the politicians.

Last of all I turned to the skilled craftsmen. I knew quite well that I had practically no technical qualifications myself, and I was sure that I should find them full of impressive knowledge. In this I was not disappointed; they understood things which I did not, and to that extent they were wiser than I was. But, gentlemen, these professional experts seemed to share the same failing which I had noticed in the poets; I mean that on the strength of their technical proficiency they claimed a perfect understanding of every other subject, however important; and I felt that this error more than outweighed their positive wisdom. So I made myself spokesman for the oracle, and asked myself whether I would rather be as I was—neither wise with their wisdom nor stupid with their stupidity—or possess both qualities as they did. I replied through myself to the oracle that it was best for me to be as I was.

The effect of these investigations of mine, gentlemen, has been to arouse against me a great deal of hostility, and hostility of a particularly bitter and persistent kind, which has resulted in various malicious suggestions, including the description of me as a professor of wisdom. This is due to the fact that whenever I succeed in disproving another person's claim to wisdom in a given subject, the bystanders assume that I know everything about that subject myself. But the truth of the matter, gentlemen, is pretty certainly this: that real wisdom is the property of God, and this oracle is his way of telling us that human wisdom has little or no value. It seems to me that he is not referring literally to Socrates, but has merely taken my name as an example, as if he would say to us "The wisest of you men is he who has realized, like Socrates, that in respect of wisdom he is really worthless."

That is why I still go about seeking and searching in obedience to the divine command, if I think that anyone is wise, whether citizen or stranger, and when I think that any person is not wise, I try to help the cause of God by proving that he is not. This occupation has kept me too busy to do much either in politics or in my own affairs; in fact, my service to God has reduced me to extreme poverty.

*　　*　　*

Well, gentlemen, for the sake of a very small gain in time you are going to earn the reputation—and the blame from those who wish to disparage our city—of having put Socrates to death, "that wise man"—because they will say I am wise even if I am not, these people who want to find fault with you. If you had waited just a little while, you would have had your way in the course of nature. You can see that I am well on in life and near to death. I am saying this not to all of you but to those who voted for my execution, and I have something else to say to them as well.

No doubt you think, gentlemen, that I have been condemned for lack of the arguments which I could have used if I had thought it right to leave nothing unsaid or undone to secure my acquittal. But that is very far from the truth. It is not a lack of arguments that has caused my condemnation, but a lack of effrontery and impudence, and the fact that I have refused to address you in the way which would give you most pleasure. You would have liked to hear me weep and wail, doing and saying all sorts of things which I regard as unworthy of myself, but which you are used to hearing from other people. But I did not think then that I ought to stoop to servility because I was in danger, and I do not regret now the way in which I pleaded my case; I would much rather die as the result of this defence than live as the result of the other sort. In a court of law, just as in warfare, neither I nor any other ought to use his wits to escape death by any means. In battle it is often obvious that you could escape being killed by giving up your arms and throwing yourself upon the mercy of your pursuers; and in every kind of danger there are plenty of devices for avoiding death if you are unscrupulous enough to stick at nothing. But I suggest, gentlemen, that the difficulty is not so much to escape death; the real difficulty is to escape from doing wrong, which is far more fleet of foot. In this present instance, I, the slow old man, have been overtaken by the slower of the two, but my accusers, who are clever and quick, have been overtaken by the faster: by iniquity. When I leave this court I shall go away condemned by you to death, but they will go away convicted by Truth herself of depravity and wickedness. And they accept their sentence even as I accept mine. No doubt it was bound to be so, and I think that the result is fair enough.

Having said so much, I feel moved to prophesy to you who have given your vote against me; for I am now at that point where the gift of prophecy comes most readily to men: at the point of death. I tell you, my executioners, that as soon as I am dead, vengeance shall fall upon you with a punishment far more painful than your killing of me. You have brought about my death in the belief that through it you will be delivered from submitting your conduct to criticism; but I say that the result will be just the opposite. You will have more critics, whom up till now I have restrained without your knowing it; and being younger they will be harsher to you and will cause you more annoyance. If you expect to stop denunciation of your wrong way of life by putting people to death, there is something amiss with your reasoning. This way of escape is neither possible nor creditable; the best and easiest way is not to stop the mouths of others, but to make yourselves as good men as you can. This is my last message to you who voted for my condemnation.

As for you who voted for my acquittal, I should very much like to say a few words to reconcile you to the result, while the officials are busy and I am not yet on my way to the place where I must die. I ask you, gentlemen, to spare me these few moments; there is no reason why we should not exchange fancies while the law permits. I look upon you as my friends, and I want you to understand the right way of regarding my present position.

Gentlemen of the jury—for *you* deserve to be so called—I have had a remarkable experience. In the past the prophetic voice to which I have become accustomed has always been my constant companion, opposing me even in quite trivial things if I was going to take the wrong course. Now something has happened to me, as you can see, which might be thought and is commonly considered to be a supreme calamity; yet neither when I left home this morning, nor when I was taking my place here in the court, nor at any point in any part of my speech did the divine sign oppose me. In other discussions it has often checked me in the middle of a sentence; but this time it has never opposed me in any part of this business in anything that I have said or done. What do I suppose to be the explanation? I will tell you. I suspect that this thing that has happened to me is a blessing, and we are quite mistaken in supposing death to be an evil. I have good grounds for thinking this, because my accustomed sign could not have failed to oppose me if what I was doing had not been sure to bring some good result.

We should reflect that there is much reason to hope for a good result on other grounds as well. Death is one of two things. Either it is annihilation, and the dead have no consciousness of anything; or, as we are told, it is really a change: a migration of the soul from this place to another. Now if there is no consciousness but only a dreamless sleep, death must be a marvellous gain. I suppose that if anyone were told to pick out the night on which he slept so soundly as not even to dream, and then to compare it with all the other nights and days of his life, and then were told to say, after due consideration, how many better and happier days and nights than this he had spent in the course of his life—well, I think that the Great King himself, to say nothing of any private person, would find these days and nights easy to count in comparison with the rest. If death is like this, then, I call it gain; because the whole of time, if you look at it in this way, can be regarded as no more than one single night. If on the other hand death is a removal from here to some other place, and if what we are told is true, that all the dead are there, what greater blessing could there be than this, gentlemen? If on arrival in the other world, beyond the reach of our so-called justice, one will find there the true judges who are said to preside in those courts, Minos and Rhadamanthys and Aeacus and Triptolemus and all those other half-divinities who were upright in their earthly life, would that be an unrewarding journey? Put it in this way: how much would one of you give to meet Orpheus and Musaeus, Hesiod and Homer? I am willing to die ten times over if this account is true. It would be a specially interesting experience for me to join them there, to meet Palamedes and Ajax the son of Telamon and any other heroes of the old days who met their death through an unfair trial, and to compare my fortunes with theirs—it would be rather amusing, I think—; and above all I should like to spend my time there, as here, in examining and searching people's minds, to find out who is really wise among them, and who only thinks that he is. What would one not give, gentlemen, to be able to question the leader of that great host against Troy, or Odysseus, or Sisyphus, or the thousands of other men and women whom one could mention, to talk and mix and argue with whom would be unimaginable happiness? At any rate I presume that they do not put one to death there for such conduct; because apart from the other happiness in which their world surpasses ours, they are now immortal for the rest of time, if what we are told is true.

You too, gentlemen of the jury, must look forward to death with confidence, and fix your minds on this one belief, which is certain: that nothing can harm a good man either in life or after death, and his fortunes are not a matter of indifference to the gods. This present experience of mine has not come about mechanically; I am quite clear that the time had come when it was better for me to die and be released from my distractions. That is why my sign never turned me back. For my own part I bear no grudge at all against those who condemned me and accused me, although it was not with this kind intention that they did so, but because they thought that they were hurting me; and that is culpable of them. However, I ask them to grant me one favour.

When my sons grow up, gentlemen, if you think that they are putting money or anything else before goodness, take your revenge by plaguing them as I plagued you; and if they fancy themselves for no reason, you must scold them just as I scolded you, for neglecting the important things and thinking that they are good for something when they are good for nothing. If you do this, I shall have had justice at your hands, both I myself and my children.

Now it is time that we were going, I to die and you to live; but which of us has the happier prospect is unknown to anyone but God.

Review Questions

1. What does Socrates identify as his mission?
2. Why might Socrates' activities have seemed subversive to some of the citizens of Athens?
3. What is his attitude toward his own death, and why?

4 ✣ THE GREEK WORLD EXPANDS, 400–150 B.C.E.

While Aristotle was composing his works Ethics *and* Politics, *his former pupil Alexander, the young king of Macedonia, was in the process of rendering his former tutor's discourse on the proper structure of the polis (the traditional Greek city-state) somewhat obsolete. Between 336 and his death in 322 B.C.E., Alexander achieved success almost beyond imagining: the subjugation of the vast Persian Empire, followed by further conquests that took his armies as far east as India. Yet, almost immediately on Alexander's death, his empire began to fragment, and in less than 300 years the Ptolemid, Seleucid, and Antigonid kingdoms all had succumbed to the ascending empires of the Romans from the west and the Parthians from the east. Political and military dominion, then, proved to be ephemeral. Not so fleeting, however, were the influence of Greek culture and urban institutions on the Near East (and the reciprocal influence of Near Eastern and Egyptian cultures on the Greeks) and the devastating impact of the invaders from the west on the previously established state structures of the areas they conquered.*

Historians, and the times during which they write, create history as much as do the great figures and civilizations about which they write. Nowhere is this more evident than in the history of Western perceptions of both Alexander and the new world order that he is claimed to have inaugurated. Until relatively recently, the West has made itself quite comfortable with an idealized image of Alexander the Great as a heroic figure whose conquests were aimed at harmoniously fusing Greek culture with the cultures of the Persian Empire. Likewise, Hellenistic civilization was regarded as mixed, essentially Greek in its inspiration but enriched by its contact with the older Near Eastern cultures. The rise of this point of view, understandably enough, coincided largely with the European colonial ascendancy over the Near and Far East and Africa that began during the nineteenth century C.E. With the disappearance of that colonialism over the past few decades, however, and as previously subject peoples have raised their own voices, there has come a dramatic reevaluation of Hellenistic civilization. The idealized image of a cultural fusion has been replaced with an image of that civilization as more emphatically Greek and of the Greek ruling class of the Hellenistic kingdoms as a colonial presence that was quite determined to maintain its superiority and preserve a large degree of separation from the indigenous peoples. Meanwhile, the political traditions of the regions over which the Greeks ruled continued largely as they had for centuries.

As the Hellenistic world order of large kingdoms took shape, it is not surprising that the traditional institutions and parochial perspectives of the polis were found wanting. This is nowhere more evident than in the development of religion and philosophy in the Hellenistic era. Much of Greek religion had been bound directly to formal cult and ritual within the polis. As the expansion of Greek colonization into the Near Eastern world began to sever the links to the traditional religion of the polis, another kind of religious experience, the mystery religions, became increasingly popular because of their more universal appeal and their promise of salvation and mystical union with a divine presence. In many ways, the spread of these mystery religions established a milieu that later promoted the spread of Christianity in the eastern Mediterranean.

Much of the philosophical thought of Plato and Aristotle had resonated greatest within the political context of the traditional city-state. Although much of the thought of the great Hellenistic philosophers derived from their classical predecessors, it also liberated itself from the confines of the city-state, developing an increasingly universal appeal. Long after the absorption of the Hellenistic kingdoms into the Roman and Parthian empires, the Hellenistic schools of philosophy, and in particular, the Stoic teachings of a divine, universal natural law and the basic brotherhood of human beings, provided rich intellectual capital for the continued development of the legal, political, and spiritual traditions of the West.

In both the broad sweep of its cultural expansion and the increasingly universal appeal of the philosophical doctrines and systems of religious belief of the time, the new world order of the Hellenistic period can justifiably be regarded as the first truly cosmopolitan age. The widespread Greek cultural legacy endowed to the Near East set the stage for the eventual success, during the subsequent era of the Roman Empire, of what became the most successful of the cosmopolitan religions: Christianity.

PLATO

FROM *The Republic*

After the death of his teacher, Socrates, Plato established the Academy, a school of philosophical instruction in an olive grove on the outskirts of Athens. (The fame of this school is apparent in the modern application of the terms academy *and* academic *to institutions of higher learning.) Among the works that Plato produced there was* The Republic, *commonly regarded as one of the most influential statements of political philosophy ever written. Perhaps the central problem that Plato addresses is how to achieve a just society within the framework of the city-state. The following selection, which includes his famous Allegory of the Cave, offers some of his ideas on how to achieve that end.*

From *The Republic*, by Plato, translated by Richard W. Sterling and William C. Scott (New York: Norton, 1985), pp. 146–151, 209–215.

*   *   *

Book V

*   *   *

Now, then, can you think of any of the human arts in which men do not generally excel women? Let's not make a long story out of it by bringing up weaving and baking cakes and boiling vegetables, matters in which women take pride and would be mortified should a man best them in these skills.

You are surely correct in saying that the one sex excels the other in every respect. But it is also true that individually many women are more skilled than many men, even if your general proposition is true.

Then we must conclude that sex cannot be the criterion in appointments to government positions. No office should be reserved for a man just because he is a man or for a woman just because she is a woman. All the capabilities with which nature endows us are distributed among men and women alike. Hence women will have the rightful opportunity to share in every task, and so will men, even though women are the weaker of the two sexes.

Agreed.

Could we then assign all the tasks to the men and none to the women?

How could we propose such thing as that?

Well, then, we shall want to say instead that one woman has the capacity to be a doctor and another not, that one woman is naturally musical and another is unmusical.

Certainly.

Could we deny that there are some women who are warlike and natural athletes while others love neither war nor gymnastic?

I don't think we can.

Again, are there not women who love wisdom and those who do not? Are not some women high-spirited and some not?

There are all these kinds of women, too.

Hence it must also be true that one woman is fit to be a guardian and another unfit. For these are the same criteria we used when we were selecting men as guardians, are they not?

Yes.

As guardians of the state, then, women and men are naturally the same, except that one is weaker and the other stronger.

Apparently.

It follows that women with the requisite qualities must be chosen to live and guard together with men of like qualities since they have the necessary competence and are naturally kin.

By all means.

And the same natures ought to perform the same functions?

Yes.

So we have closed the circle. We agree that we do nothing against nature by educating the guardians' wives in music and gymnastic.

We are agreed.

Since we have legislated in harmony with nature, we have not proposed anything impractical or unattainable. On the contrary, we may say that if anything contradicts nature, it is the way things are done today.

So it appears.

Now we designed our inquiry to test whether our proposals would turn out to be both possible and desirable?

Yes.

Well, I take it we have just established that they are possible.

Yes.

Then we must see if we can agree that they are also desirable.

Clearly.

In preparing a woman to be a guardian, then, we won't prescribe one kind of education for women guardians and another for the men because their natures are the same.

No. There should be no differentiation.

Let me ask you a question.

About what?

About men. Do you think some are better and some worse, or are all alike?

They are certainly not all alike.

Then which do you think will become the better men in the city we are building: the guardians who are being educated in the manner we have prescribed or the cobblers who received instruction in the cobbler's art?

An absurd question.

I understand your answer. You mean that the guardians are the best of our citizens.

By far.

And will not the women guardians be the best of the women?

Yes.

And can we wish for the state anything better than that it should nurture the best possible men and women?

Nothing.

And the education we have prescribed in music and gymnastic will produce this outcome?

Without fail.

Therefore the institutions we have proposed for the state are not only possible, they are the best possible.

Quite so.

Then wearing virtue as a garment, the guardians' wives must go naked and take part alongside their men in war and the other functions of government, and no other duties will be required of them. Owing to the weakness of their gender, however, they shall perform the less burdensome tasks. When they are at their exercises for the body's benefit, any man who laughs at their nakedness will be "gathering unripe fruit," for he does not know what he ridicules nor where his laughter leads. He is ignorant of the fairest words ever spoken: what is beneficial must be beautiful; only the harmful is ugly.

You are right.

Having successfully reached this point in our legislation for women, we could compare ourselves with a swimmer who has surmounted a wave without being drowned by it. Our argument that men and women guardians should pursue all things in common turns out to be consistent in itself, since we have found our proposals to be both possible and beneficial.

That was no small wave, either.

You won't think it was so big when you see what the next one looks like.

Go ahead, then, and let me see.

Here it is. I think that everything we have said so far leads up to the following law.

What law?

That all the women shall belong to all the men and that none shall cohabit privately; that the children should also be raised in common and no child should know its parent nor the parent its child.

A far greater wave, indeed. Your proposal raises questions about both practicability and utility that will provoke the greatest misgivings.

I shouldn't think anyone would want to debate its utility. The desirability of having wives and children in common, were it possible, ought to be self-evident. But I suppose the main subject of dispute would be whether or not it would be possible to establish such a community.

I expect both aspects of the proposal will produce plenty of debate.

I see that you want to entangle me in both questions at once. I hoped for your consent in the matter of utility, so that I could escape from having to discuss it. Then I would only have to consider the question of feasibility.

Your escape efforts have been detected. You won't be allowed to run away, and you will be obliged to defend your case on both counts.

I will pay your penalty. But first, relent a little. Let me go on holiday, like men with lazy minds are wont to do, so that they may entertain themselves with their own thoughts as they walk alone. These men pursue their desires without pausing to inquire how they might be achieved. All such considerations they dismiss in order to spare themselves the trouble of weighing the possible against the impossible. They assume that what they wish is already at hand, giving their imaginations free rein in concocting the details and relishing in advance what they will do when everything is in place. So do idle minds become more idle still. I now yield to this same weakness. I would like to postpone the feasibility issue for later consideration. With your permission, I shall assume the feasibility of my proposal and proceed to inquire how the rulers will arrange the particulars in practice. At the same time, I shall seek to demonstrate that nothing could be more beneficial to our city and its guardians than a successful implementation of our proposal. Let us consider this first, and then we can address the other issue.

Permission granted. Proceed as you suggest.

I suppose that worthy rulers will be prepared to command and worthy helpers ready to obey. In some of their commands the rulers will obey the laws. In those matters of detail that we have left to their discretion their commands will imitate the spirit of the laws.

Presumably they will.

As their lawgiver, you will have selected these men. You will apply the same criteria to select women whose natures are as similar as possible to those of the men. They will live in common houses and eat at common meals. There will be no private property. They will live together, learn together, and exercise together. The necessities of nature, I presume, would see to it that they will also mate with one another. Or is necessity too strong a word?

Not if you mean the necessities of love. They attract and compel most people with far greater force than all geometric necessities posited by the mathematicians.

You are right, Glaucon. But irregularity in sexual relations or in any other matters has no place in a happy city; the rules will not tolerate it.

They would be right.

Then it is evident that we must make marriage a sacred relationship, so far as may be. And those marriages that attain the highest degree of sanctity will produce the best results.

Agreed.

What will produce the best results? You can help me, Glaucon, for I have seen hunting dogs and a number of pedigreed cocks at your house. Have you noticed something about how they mate and breed?

What?

Well, first of all, even though all of them are thoroughbreds, some prove out better than others?

True.

So are you indiscriminate in how you breed them, or do you breed from the best?

From the best.

And which age do you select for the breeding? The young or the old or, so far as possible, those in their prime?

Those in their prime.

And if you failed to supervise the breeding in this way, you would have to expect that the quality of your stock of birds and hounds would deteriorate?

Certainly.

Would it be the same with horses and other animals?

Without doubt.

Well, then, old friend, if the same holds true for human beings, we can see how urgent is our need for rulers with the highest skills.

It does hold true, but what of it?

I say this because the rulers will have to employ many of the kinds of drugs we spoke of earlier. Remember we said that those who can be healed by submitting their bodies to diet and regimen do not need drugs and can be attended by an ordinary doctor. But we know that where it is necessary to prescribe drugs, a physician with greater imagination and audacity will be indispensable.

True, but what is your point?

I mean that the rulers will probably have to resort to frequent doses of lies and mystifications for the benefit of their subjects. You will recall that we said these kinds of lies could be advantageous if used after the manner of medical remedies.

And we were right.

And the right use of this sort of medicine will very often be imperative in matters of marriage and the begetting of children.

How so?

It follows necessarily from the conclusion we reached a moment ago. The best of the men must mate with the best of the women as often as possible. Inferior should mate with inferior as seldom as possible. In order to safeguard the quality of the stock the children of the best unions must be retained for nurture by the rulers, but the others not. And how all this will be managed must be known to none but the rulers, so that the guardian flock will not be divided by dissension.

*   *   *

Book VII

Here allegory may show us best how education—or the lack of it—affects our nature. Imagine men living in a cave with a long passageway stretching between them and the cave's mouth, where it opens wide to the light. Imagine further that since childhood the cave dwellers have had their legs and necks shackled so as to be confined to the same spot. They are further constrained by blinders that prevent them from turning their heads; they can see only directly in front of them. Next, imagine a light from a fire some distance behind them and burning at a higher elevation. Between the prisoners and the fire is a raised path along whose edge there is a low wall like the partition at the front of a puppet stage. The wall conceals the puppeteers while they manipulate their puppets above it.

So far I can visualize it.

Imagine, further, men behind the wall carrying all sorts of objects along its length and holding them above it. The objects include human and animal images made of stone and wood and all other material. Presumably, those who carry them sometimes speak and are sometimes silent.

You describe a strange prison and strange prisoners.

Like ourselves. Tell me, do you not think those men would see only the shadows cast by the fire on the wall of the cave? Would they have seen anything of themselves or of one another?

How could they if they couldn't move their heads their whole life long?

Could they see the objects held above the wall behind them or only the shadows cast in front?

Only the shadows.

If, then, they could talk with one another, don't you think they would impute reality to the passing shadows?

Necessarily.

Imagine an echo in their prison, bouncing off the wall toward which the prisoners were turned. Should one of those behind the wall speak, would the prisoners not think that the sound came from the shadows in front of them?

No doubt of it.

By every measure, then, reality for the prisoners would be nothing but shadows cast by artifacts.

It could be nothing else.

Imagine now how their liberation from bondage and error would come about if something like the following happened. One prisoner is freed from his shackles. He is suddenly compelled to stand up, turn around, walk, and look toward the light. He suffers pain and distress from the glare of the light. So dazzled is he that he cannot even discern the very objects whose shadows he used to be able to see. Now what do you suppose he would answer if he were told that all he had seen before was illusion but that now he was nearer reality, observing real things and therefore seeing more truly? What if someone pointed to the objects being carried above the wall, questioning him as to what each one is? Would he not be at a loss? Would he not regard those things he saw formerly as more real than the things now being shown him?

He would.

Again, let him be compelled to look directly at the light. Would his eyes not feel pain? Would he not flee, turning back to those things he was able to discern before, convinced that they are in every truth clearer and more exact than anything he has seen since?

He would.

Then let him be dragged away by force up the rough and steep incline of the cave's passageway, held fast until he is hauled out into the light of the sun. Would not such a rough passage be painful? Would he not resent the experience? And when he came out into the sunlight, would he not be dazzled once again and unable to see what he calls realities?

He could not see even one of them, at least not immediately.

Habituation, then, is evidently required in order to see things higher up. In the beginning he would most easily see shadows; next, reflections in the water of men and other objects. Then he would see the objects themselves. From there he would go on to behold the heavens and the heavenly phenomena—more easily the moon and stars by night than the sun by day.

Yes.

Finally, I suppose, he would be able to look on the sun itself, not in reflections in the water or in fleeting images in some alien setting. He would look at the sun as it is, in its own domain, and so be able to see what it is really like.

Yes.

It is at this stage that he would be able to conclude that the sun is the cause of the seasons and of the year's turning, that it governs all the visible world and is in some sense also the cause of all visible things.

This is surely the next step he would take.

Now, supposing he recalled where he came from. Supposing he thought of his fellow prisoners and of what passed for wisdom in the place they were inhabiting. Don't you think he would feel pity for all that and rejoice in his own change of circumstance?

He surely would.

Suppose there had been honors and citations those below bestowed upon one another. Suppose prizes were offered for the one quickest to identify the shadows as they go by and best able to remember the sequence and configurations in which they appear. All these skills, in turn, would enhance the ability to guess what would come next. Do you think he would covet such rewards? More, would he envy and want to emulate those who hold power over the prisoners and are in turn reverenced by them? Or would he not rather hold fast to Homer's words that it is "better to be the poor servant of a poor master," better to endure anything, than to believe those things and live that way?

I think he would prefer anything to such a life.

Consider, further, if he should go back down again into the cave and return to the place he was before, would not his eyes now go dark after so abruptly leaving the sunlight behind?

They would.

Suppose he should then have to compete once more in shadow watching with those who never left the cave. And this before his eyes had become accustomed to the dark and his dimmed vision still required a long period of habituation. Would he not be laughed at? Would it not be said that he had made the journey above only to come back with his eyes ruined and that it is futile even to attempt the ascent? Further, if anyone tried to release the prisoners and lead them up and they could get their hands on him and kill him, would they not kill him?

Of course.

Now, my dear Glaucon, we must apply the allegory as a whole to all that has been said so far. The prisoners' cave is the counterpart of our own visible order, and the light of the fire betokens the power of the sun. If you liken the ascent and exploration of things above to the soul's journey through the intelligible order, you will have understood my thinking, since that is what you wanted to hear. God only knows whether it is true. But, in any case, this is the way things appear to me: in the intelligible world the last thing to be seen—and then only dimly—is the idea of the good. Once seen, however, the conclusion becomes irresistible that it is the cause of all things right and good, that in the visible world it gives birth to light and its sovereign source, that in the intelligible world it is itself sovereign and the author of truth and reason, and that the man who will act wisely in private and public life must have seen it.

I agree, insofar as I can follow your thinking.

Come join me, then, in this further thought. Don't be surprised if those who have attained this high vision are unwilling to be involved in the affairs of men. Their souls will ever feel the pull from above and yearn to sojourn there. Such a preference is likely enough if the assumptions of our allegory continue to be valid.

Yes, it is likely.

By the same token, would you think it strange if someone returning from divine contemplation to the miseries of men should appear ridiculous? What if he were still blinking his eyes and not yet readjusted to the surrounding darkness before being compelled to testify in court about the shadows of justice or about the images casting the shadows? What if he had to enter into debate about the notions of such matters held fast by people who had never seen justice itself?

It would not be strange.

Nonetheless, a man with common sense would know that eyesight can be impaired in two different ways by dint of two different causes, namely, transitions from light into darkness and from darkness into light. Believing that the soul also meets with the same experience, he would not thoughtlessly laugh when he saw a soul perturbed and having difficulty in comprehending something. Instead he would try to ascertain whether the cause of its faded vision was the passage from a brighter life to unaccustomed darkness or from the deeper darkness of ignorance toward the world of light, whose brightness then dazzled the soul's eye. He will count the first happy, and the second he will pity. Should he be minded to laugh, he who comes from below will merit it more than the one who descends from the light above.

A fair statement.

If this is true, it follows that education is not what some professors say it is. They claim they can transplant the power of knowledge into a soul that has none, as if they were engrafting vision into blind eyes.

They do claim that.

But our reasoning goes quite to the contrary. We assert that this power is already in the soul of everyone. The way each of us learns compares with what happens to the eye: it cannot be turned away from darkness to face the light without turning the whole body. So it is with our capacity to know; together with the entire soul one must turn away from the world of transient things toward the world of perpetual being, until finally one learns to endure the sight of its most radiant manifestation. This is what we call goodness, is it not?

Yes.

Then there must be some art that would most easily and effectively turn and convert the soul in the way we have described. It would lay no claim to produce sight in the soul's eye. Instead it would assume that sight is already there but wrongly directed; wrongly the soul is not looking where it should. This condition it would be the purpose of the art to remedy.

Such an art might be possible.

Wisdom, then, seems to be of a different order than those other things that are also called virtues of the soul. They seem more akin to the attributes of the body, for when they are not there at the outset, they can be cultivated by exercise and habit. But the ability to think is more divine. Its power is constant and never lost. It can be useful and benign or malevolent and useless, according to the purposes toward which it is directed. Or have you never observed in men who are called vicious but wise how sharp-sighted the petty soul is and how quickly it can pick out those things toward which it has turned its attention? All this shows that we have to do not with poor eyesight but with a soul under compulsion of evil, so that the keener his vision, the more harm he inflicts.

I have seen these things.

Consider then what would happen if such a soul had been differently trained from childhood or had been liberated early from the love of food and similar pleasures that are attached to us at birth like leaden weights. Supposing, I say, he were freed from all these kinds of things that draw the soul's vision downward. If he were then turned and converted to the contemplation of real things, he would be using the very same faculties of vision and be seeing them just as keenly as he now sees their opposites.

That is likely.

And must we not draw other likely and necessary conclusions from all that has been said so far? On the one hand, men lacking education and experience in truth cannot adequately preside over a city. Without a sense of purpose or duty in life they will also be without a sense of direction to govern their public and private acts. On the other hand, those who prolong their education endlessly are also unfit to rule because they become incapable of action. Instead, they suffer themselves to believe that while still living they have already been transported to the Islands of the Blessed.

So our duty as founders is to compel the best natures to achieve that sovereign knowledge we described awhile ago, to scale the heights in order to reach the vision of the good. But after they have reached the summit and have seen the view, we must not permit what they are now allowed to do.

What is that?

Remain above, refusing to go down again among those prisoners to share their labors and their rewards, whatever their worth may be.

Must we wrong them in this way, making them live a worse life when a better is possible?

My friend, you have forgotten again that the law is concerned not with the happiness of any particular class in the city but with the happiness of the city as a whole. Its method is to create harmony among the citizens by persuasion and compulsion, making them share the benefits that each is able to bestow on the community. The law itself produces such men in the city, not in order to let them do as they please but with the intention of using them to bind the city together.

True, I did forget.

Consider further, Glaucon, that in fact we won't be wronging the philosophers who come among us. When we require them to govern the city and be its guardians, we shall vindicate our actions. For we shall say to them that it is quite understandable that men of their quality do not participate in the public life of other cities. After all, there they develop autonomously without favor from the government. It is only just that self-educated men, owing nothing to others for their enlightenment, are not eager to pay anyone for it. But you have been begotten by us to be like kings and leaders in a hive of bees, governing the city for its good and yours. Your education is better and more complete, and you are better equipped to participate in the two ways of life. So down you must go, each in turn, to where the others live and habituate yourselves to see in the dark. Once you have adjusted, you will see ten thousand times better than those who regularly dwell there. Because you have seen the reality of beauty, justice, and goodness, you will be able to know idols and shadows for what they are. Together and wide awake, you and we will govern our city, far differently from most cities today whose inhabitants are ruled darkly as in a dream by men who will fight with each other over shadows and use faction in order to rule, as if that were some great good. The truth is that the city where those who rule are least eager to do so will be the best governed and the least plagued by dissension. The city with the contrary kind of rulers will be burdened with the contrary characteristics.

I agree.

When we tell them this, will our students dis-obey us? Will they refuse to play their role in the affairs of state even when they know that most of the time they will be able to dwell with one another in a better world?

Certainly not. These are just requirements, and they are just men. Yet they will surely approach holding office as an imposed necessity, quite in the opposite frame of mind from those who now rule our cities.

Indeed, old friend. A well-governed city becomes a possibility only if you can discover a better way of life for your future rulers than hold-ing office. Only in such a state will those who rule be really rich, not in gold but with the wealth that yields happiness: a life of goodness and wis-dom. But such a government is impossible if men behave like beggars, turning to politics because of what is lacking in their private lives and hoping to find their good in the public business. When office and the power of governing are treated like prizes to be won in battle the result must be a civil war that will destroy the city along with the office seekers.

True.

Is there any life other than that of true philoso-phers that looks with scorn on political office?

None, by Zeus.

That is why we require that those in office should not be lovers of power. Otherwise there will be a fight among rival lovers.

Right.

Who else would you compel to guard the city? Who else than those who have the clearest under-standing of the principles of good government and who have won distinction in another kind of life preferable to the life of politics?

No one else.

*   *   *

REVIEW QUESTIONS

1. In Plato's view, to whom ought the governing of the state be entrusted?
2. How were these individuals to be educated for such responsibility?
3. Were women to have any possible role in direct-ing the state?
4. How do Plato's ideas compare with the values underlying the democratic system of Athens?
5. Do you see any influence of the Spartan system in Plato's ideas?
6. Does Plato draw any contrasts between the material and immaterial realms?

ARISTOTLE

FROM *Politics*

After twenty years as a student of Plato at the Academy and a subsequent three-year stint as a tutor for Alexander, the young son of King Philip II of Macedonia, Aristotle established his own school, the Lyceum, at Athens and taught there until almost the end of his life. Much of his work is a continuation of Plato's, although, in contrast to Plato's emphasis on the primacy of a world of universal forms or ideas, Aristotle asserted that those ideal forms could not exist independently of the world of matter, which could be directly experienced and observed by human senses. His two most important surviving works are Ethics *and* Politics. Ethics *is his investigation of human character in order to determine what produces a good character and, there-fore, happiness. Aristotle also believed, however, that the greatest degree of human happiness could be achieved only in the context of a properly ordered and governed city-state, the formation and characteristics of which are the focus of* Politics.

From *The Politics of Aristotle,* edited by H. W. C. Davis, translated by Benjamin Jowett (Oxford: Oxford University Press, 1905), pp. 258–61, 264–68.

*   *   *

He who thus considers things in their first growth and origin, whether a state or anything else, will obtain the clearest view of them. In the first place (1) there must be a union of those who cannot exist without each other; for example, of male and female, that the race may continue; and this is a union which is formed, not of deliberate purpose, but because, in common with other animals and with plants, mankind have a natural desire to leave behind them an image of themselves. And (2) there must be a union of natural ruler and subject, that both may be preserved. For he who can foresee with his mind is by nature intended to be lord and master, and he who can work with his body is a subject, and by nature a slave; hence master and slave have the same interest. . . .

Of household management we have seen that there are three parts—one is the rule of a master over slaves, which has been discussed already, another of a father, and the third of a husband. A husband and father rules over wife and children, both free, but the rule differs, the rule over his children being a royal, over his wife a constitutional rule. For although there may be exceptions to the order of nature, the male is by nature fitter for command than the female, just as the elder and full-grown is superior to the younger and more immature. . . .

Now it is obvious that the same principle applies generally, and therefore almost all things rule and are ruled according to nature. But the kind of rule differs; the freeman rules over the slave after another manner from that in which the male rules over the female, or the man over the child; although the parts of the soul are present in all of them, they are present in different degrees. For the slave has no deliberative faculty at all; the woman has, but it is without authority, and the child has, but it is immature. So it must necessarily be with the moral virtues also; all may be supposed to partake of them, but only in such manner and degree as is required by each for the fulfillment of his duty. . . . The courage of a man is shown in commanding, of a woman in obeying. . . . All classes must be deemed to have their special attributes; as the poet says of women, "Silence is a woman's glory," but this is not equally the glory of man. . . .

*   *   *

Next let us consider what should be our arrangements about property; should the citizens of the perfect state have possessions in common or not? . . .

There is always a difficulty in men living together and having things in common, but especially in their having common property. . . . The present arrangement, if improved as it might be by good customs and laws, would be far better, and would have the advantages of both systems. Property should be in a certain sense common, but, as a general rule, private. For when everyone has his separate interest, men will not complain of one another, and they will make more progress, because everyone will be attending to his own business. Yet among good men, and as regards use, "friends," as the proverb says, "will have all things common." . . . For although every human has his own property, some things he will place at the disposal of his friends, while of others he shares the use of them. . . .

Again, how immeasurably greater is the pleasure, when a man feels a thing to be his own! For love of self is a feeling implanted by nature and not given in vain, although selfishness is rightly condemned. This, however is not mere love of self, but love of self in excess, like the miser's love of money; for all, or almost all, men love money, and other such objects in a measure. Furthermore, there is the greatest pleasure in doing a kindness or service to friends or guests or companions, which can only be done when a man has private property. These advantages are lost by the excessive unification of the state.... No one, when men have all things in common, will any longer set an example of liberality or do any liberal action; for liberality consists in the use a man makes of his own property.

Such legislation may have a specious appearance of benevolence. Men readily listen to it, and are easily induced to believe that in some wonderful manner everybody will become everybody's friend, especially when someone is heard denouncing the evils now existing in states, suits about contracts, convictions for perjury, flatteries of rich men, and the like, which are said to arise out of the possession of private property. These evils, however, are due to a very different cause—the wickedness of human nature. Indeed, we see that there is much more quarreling among those who have all things in common, though there are not many of them when compared with the vast numbers who have private property.

Again, we ought to reckon, not only the evils from which the citizens will be saved, but also the advantages which they will lose. The life which they are to lead appears to be quite impracticable. The error of Socrates must be attributed to the false notion of unity from which he starts. Unity there should be, both of the family and of the state, but in some respects only. For there is a point at which a state may attain such a degree of unity as to be no longer a state, or at which, without actually ceasing to exist, it will become an inferior state, like harmony passing into unison, or rhythm which has been reduced to a single foot. The state, as I was saying, is a plurality, which should be united and made into a community by education.... Let us remember that we should not disregard the experience of ages....

*   *   *

... We have next to consider whether there is only one form of government or many; and if many, what they are, and how many; and what are the differences between them.

A constitution is the arrangement of powers in a state, especially of the supreme power, and the constitution is the government. For example, in democracies the people are supreme, but in oligarchies, the few; therefore, we say that the two constitutions are different; and so in other cases. First let us consider what is the purpose of a state and how many forms of government there are by which human society is regulated. We have already said, earlier in this treatise, when drawing a distinction between household management and the rule of a governor, that man is by nature a political animal. And therefore men, even when they do not require one another's help, desire to live together all the same, and are in fact brought together by their common interests in proportion as they severally attain to any measure of wellbeing. Well-being is certainly the chief end of individuals and of states....

The conclusion is evident: governments which have a regard to the common interest are constituted in accordance with strict principles of justice, and are therefore true forms; but those which regard only the interest of the rulers are all defective and perverted forms. For they are despotic, whereas a state is a community of free men.

Having determined these points, we have next to consider how many forms of constitution there are, and what they are; and in the first place what are the true forms, for when they are determined the perversions of them will at once be apparent. The words constitution and government have the same meaning; and the government, which is the supreme authority in states, is necessarily in the hands either of one, or of a few, or of many. The true forms of government, therefore, are those in which the one, or the few, or the many, govern with a view to the common interest; but governments which rule with a view to the private interest, whether of the one, or of the few, or of the many, are perversions. For citizens, if they are truly citizens, ought all to participate in the advantages of a state. We call that form of government in which one rules, and which regards the common interest, kingship or royalty; that in which more than one, but not many, rule, aristocracy. It is so called, either because the rulers are the best men, or because they have at heart the best interest of the state and of the citizens. But when the citizens at large administer the state for the common interest, the government is called by the generic name—constitutional government. And there is a reason for this use of language. One man or a few may excel in virtue; but of virtue there are many kinds. As the number of rulers increases it becomes more difficult for them to attain perfection in every kind, though they may in military virtue, for this is found in the masses. Hence, in a constitutional government the fighting men have the supreme power, and those who possess arms are citizens.

Of the above-mentioned forms, the perversions are as follows: of royalty, tyranny; of aristocracy, oligarchy; of constitutional government, democracy. For tyranny is a kind of monarchy which has in view the interest of the monarch only; oligarchy has in view the interest of the wealthy; democracy, of the needy; none of them the common good of all.

*   *   *

. . . But a state exists for the sake of a good life, and not for the sake of life only. If life only were the object, slaves and brute animals might form a state, but they cannot, for they have no share in happiness or in a life of free choice. Nor does a state exist merely for the sake of alliance and security from injustice, nor yet for the sake of trade and mutual intercourse; for then the Tyrrhenians and the Carthaginians, and all who have commercial treaties with one another, would be citizens of one state. . . . Those who care for good government take into consideration the larger questions of virtue and vice in states. Whence it may be further inferred that virtue must be the serious care of a state which truly deserves the name. Otherwise the community becomes a mere alliance, which differs only in place from alliances of which the members live apart. And law is only a convention, "a surety to one another of justice," as the sophist Lycophron says, and has no real power to make the citizens good and just. . . .

Clearly then a state is not a mere society, having a common place, established for the prevention of crime and for the sake of trade. These are conditions without which a state cannot exist; but all of them

together do not constitute a state, which is a community of families and aggregations of families in well-being for the sake of a perfect and self-sufficing life. Such a community can only be established among those who live in the same place and intermarry. Hence arise in states family connections, brotherhoods, common sacrifices, amusements which draw men together. They are created by friendship, for friendship is the motive of society. The end is the good life, and these are the means towards it. And the state is the union of families and villages having for an end a perfect and self-sufficing life, by which we mean a happy and honorable life.

Our conclusion, then, is that political society exists for the sake of noble actions, and not of mere companionship. And they who contribute most to such a society have a greater share in it than those who have the same or a greater freedom or nobility of birth but are inferior to them in political virtue; or than those who exceed them in wealth but are surpassed by them in virtue. . . .

We maintain that the true forms of government are three, and that the best must be that which is administered by the best, and in which there is one man, or a whole family, or many persons, excelling in virtue, and both rulers and subjects are fitted, the one to rule, the others to be ruled, in such a manner as to attain the most eligible life. We showed at the commencement of our inquiry that the virtue of the good man is necessarily the same as the virtue of the citizen of the perfect state. Clearly then in the same manner, and by the same means through which a man becomes truly good, he will frame a state which will be truly good whether aristocratical, or under kingly rule, and the same education and the same habits will be found to make a good man a good statesman and king. . . .

*   *   *

We have now to inquire what is the best constitution for most states, and the best life for most men, neither assuming a standard of virtue which is above ordinary persons, nor an education which is exceptionally favored by nature and circumstances, nor yet an ideal state which is an inspiration only, but having regard to the life in which the majority are able to share, and to the form of government which states in general can attain. . . . If it was truly said in the *Ethics* that the happy life is the life according to unimpeded virtue and that virtue is a mean, then the life which is a mean and a mean attainable by everyone must be best. And the same criteria of virtue and vice are characteristic of cities and of constitutions; for the constitution is in pattern the life of the city.

Now in all states there are three elements; one class is very rich, another very poor, and a third in the mean. It is admitted that moderation and the mean are best, and therefore it will clearly be best to possess the gifts of fortune in moderation; for in that condition of life men are most ready to listen to reason. . . . Those who have too much of the goods of fortune, strength, wealth, friends, and the like, are neither willing nor able to submit to authority. The evil begins at home; for when they are boys, by reason of the luxury in which they are brought up, they never learn, even at school, the habit of obedience. On the other hand, the very poor, who are in the opposite extreme, are too degraded. So that the one class cannot obey, and can only rule despotically; the other knows not how to command and must be ruled like slaves. Thus arises a city, not of freemen, but of masters and slaves, the one despising, the other envying. Nothing can be more fatal to friendship and good fellowship in states than this; for good fellowship starts from friendship. When men are at enmity with one another, they would rather not even share the same path.

But a city ought to be composed, as far as possible, of equals and similars; and these are generally the middle classes. Wherefore a city which is composed of middle-class citizens is necessarily best constituted with respect to what we call the natural elements of a state. And this class of citizens is most secure in a state, for they do not, like the poor, covet their neighbors' goods; nor do others covet theirs, as the poor covet the goods of the rich. And as they neither plot against others nor are themselves plotted against, they pass through life safely. . . .

Thus it is manifest that the best political community is formed by citizens of the middle class, and that those states are likely to be well administered in which the middle class is large, and if possible larger than both the other classes, or at any rate than either singly, for the addition of the middle class turns the scale and prevents either of the extremes from being dominant. Great then is the good fortune of a state in which the citizens have a moderate and sufficient property. For where some possess much and the rest nothing, there may arise an extreme democracy, or a pure oligarchy; or a tyranny may grow out of either extreme—out of either the most rampant democracy or out of an oligarchy. But it is not so likely to arise out of a middle and nearly equal condition.

Democracies are safer and more permanent than oligarchies, because they have a middle class which is more numerous and has a greater share in the government. For when there is no middle class and the poor greatly exceed in number, troubles arise and the state soon comes to an end. A proof of the superiority of the middle class is that the best legislators have been of a middle rank; for example, Solon, as his own verses testify, and Lycurgus, for he was not a king. . . .

What then is the best form of government, and what makes it the best is evident. Of other states, since we say there are many kinds of democracy and oligarchy, it is not difficult to see which has the first and which the second or any other place in the order of excellence, now that we have determined which is best. For that which is nearest to the best must of necessity be the better, and that which is furthest from it the worse, if we are judging absolutely and not with reference to given conditions. I say "with reference to given conditions," since a particular government may be preferable for some, but another form may be better for others.

*   *   *

REVIEW QUESTIONS

1. In Aristotle's view, what constitutes a state?
2. What is the purpose of the state?

3. Ought women to have any role in the governing of the state?

4. What is Aristotle's view of democracy?

5. Do you find any of Aristotle's views pertinent to government and society of the late twentieth and early twenty-first centuries C.E.?

PLUTARCH

FROM "Life of Alexander"

The biographies produced by Plutarch are an important (though by no means entirely objective or accurate) source of knowledge of the lives of many great figures of the Greek and Roman past. The following selections reveal something of ancient opinion concerning Alexander's character and intentions. To a great extent, they also communicate a view of him that dominated much thinking until relatively recent times.

*   *   *

*Philonicus the Thessalian brought the horse Bucephalus to Philip, offering to sell him for thirteen talents; but when they went into the field to try him, they found him so very vicious and unmanageable, that he reared up when they endeavored to mount him, and would not so much as endure the voice of any of Philip's attendants. Upon which, as they were leading him away as wholly useless and untractable, Alexander, who stood by, said, "What an excellent horse do they lose, for want of skill and boldness to manage him!" Philip at first took no notice of what he said; but when he heard him repeat the same thing several times, and saw he was very frustrated to see the horse sent away, "Do you criticize," said Philip, "those who are older than yourself, as if you knew more, and were better able to manage him then they?" "I could manage this horse," replied Alexander, "better than others do." "And if you do not," said Philip, "what will you forfeit for your rashness?" "I will pay," answered Alexander, "the whole price of the horse." At this

the whole company fell laughing; and as soon as the wager was settled among them, he immediately ran to the horse, and, taking hold of the bridle, turned him directly towards the sun, having, it seems, observed that he was disturbed at and afraid of the motion of his own shadow; then letting him go forward a little, still keeping the reins in his hand, and stroking him gently when he began to grow eager and fiery, . . . with one nimble leap, Alexander securely mounted him, and when he was seated, by little and little drew in the bridle, and curbed him without either striking or spurring him. Presently, when he found him free from all rebelliousness, and only impatient for the course, he let him go at full speed, inciting him now with a commanding voice, and urging him also with his heel. Philip and his friends looked on at first in silence and anxiety for the result, but when he came back rejoicing and triumphing for what he had performed, they all burst out into acclamations of applause; and his father, shedding tears, it is said, for joy, kissed him as he came down from his horse, and in his transport said, "O my son, carve out a kingdom equal to and worthy of yourself, for Macedonia is too small for you."

---

*From *Readings in Ancient History,* vol. 1, edited by William S. Davis (Boston: Allyn and Bacon, 1912).

*   *   *

*After the company had drunk a good deal somebody began to sing the verses of a man named Pranichus . . . which had been written to humiliate and make fun of some Macedonian commanders who had recently been defeated by the barbarians. The older members of the party took offense at this and showed their resentment of both the poet and the singer, but Alexander and those sitting near him listened with obvious pleasure and told the man to continue. Thereupon Cleitus, who had already drunk too much and was rough and hot-tempered by nature, became angrier than ever and shouted that it was not right for Macedonians to be insulted in the presence of barbarians and enemies, even if they had met with misfortune, for they were better men than those who were laughing at them. Alexander retorted that if Cleitus was trying to disguise cowardice as misfortune, he must be pleading his own case. At this Cleitus sprang to his feet and shouted back, "Yes, it was my cowardice that saved your life, you who call yourself the son of the gods, when you were turning your back to Spithridates' sword. And it is the blood of these Macedonians and their wounds which have made you so great that you disown your father Philip and claim to be the son of Ammon!"

These words made Alexander furious. "You scum," he cried out, "do you think that you can keep on speaking of me like this, and stir up trouble among the Macedonians and not pay for it?" "Oh, but we Macedonians do pay for it," Cleitus retorted. "Just think of the rewards we get for all our efforts. It's the dead ones who are happy, because they never lived to see Macedonians being beaten with Median rods, or begging the Persians for an audience with our own king." Cleitus blurted out all this impulsively, whereupon Alexander's friends jumped up and began to abuse him, while the older men tried to calm down both sides. . . . But Cleitus refused to take back anything and he challenged Alexander to speak out whatever he wished to say in front of the company, or else not invite to his table freeborn men who spoke their minds: it would be better for him to spend his time among barbarians and slaves, who would prostrate themselves before his white tunic and his Persian girdle. At this Alexander could no longer control his rage: he hurled one of the apples that lay on the table at Cleitus, hit him, and then looked around for his dagger. One of his body-guards, Aristophanes, had already moved it out of harm's way, and the others crowded around him and begged him to be quiet. But Alexander leaped to his feet and shouted out in the Macedonian tongue for his bodyguard to turn out, a signal that this was an extreme emergency. . . . As Cleitus still refused to give way, . . . Alexander seized a spear from one of his guards, faced Cleitus as he was drawing aside the curtain of the doorway, and ran him through. With a roar of pain and a groan, Cleitus fell, and immediately the king's anger left him. When he came to himself and saw his friends standing around him speechless, he snatched the weapon out of the dead body and would have plunged it into his own throat if the guards had not forestalled him by seizing his hands and carrying him by force to his chamber.

There he spent the rest of the night and the whole of the following day sobbing in an agony of remorse. At last he lay exhausted by his grief, uttering deep groans but unable to speak a word, until his friends, alarmed at his silence, forced their way into his room. He paid no attention to what any of them said, except that when Aristander the diviner reminded him . . . that these events had long ago been ordained by fate, he seemed to accept this assurance.

REVIEW QUESTIONS

1. How would you characterize Plutarch's view of Alexander?
2. Is it completely unbiased?
3. What kind of leader does Alexander appear to be?
4. Does he have any apparent flaws?
5. What, according to Plutarch, were the motives underlying Alexander's conquests?

---

*From *The Age of Alexander,* translated by Ian Scott-Kilvert (New York: Penguin, 1973), pp. 257–58, 307–9.

HELLENISTIC ARCHITECTURE IN THE NEAR EAST (C. 175 C.E.)

In the wake of Alexander's conquests, Greek culture and tastes were adopted by many of the native elites in the Near East. This "treasury" (perhaps a royal mausoleum in actuality) was carved into the sandstone of the city of Petra, now in modern Jordan. In the third and second centuries B.C.E., Petra was the capital of the Nabataean kings, much of whose wealth and power derived from Petra's importance as a major hub for long-distance caravan trade. How does the style of the architecture compare with that of Greek public buildings? What would have inspired non-Greeks to adopt Greek styles?

EPICTETUS

FROM *The Manual:* Stoicism

The school of philosophy known as Stoicism, founded by Zeno of Citium, undoubt-edly has had a more profound impact on the Western intellectual tradition than any other of the Hellenistic schools. In particular, its emphasis on a universal natural order governed by a divine plan greatly influenced the later development of both Roman imperial law and Christian thought. The literary remains of the early devel-opment of Stoic philosophy are quite fragmentary. Much better preserved is the sys-tematic presentation of Stoic principles in The Manual of Epictetus *(60 C.E.–?), as set down probably by his student Arrian.*

From *The Manual of Epictetus*, translated by P. E. Matheson (Oxford: Clarendon Press, 1916).

1. Of all existing things some are in our power, and others are not in our power. In our power are thought, impulse, will to get and will to avoid, and, in a word, everything which is our own doing. Things not in our power include the body, property, reputation, office, and, in a word, everything which is not our own doing. Things in our power are by nature free, unhindered, untrammelled; things not in our power are weak, servile, subject to hindrance, dependent on others. Remember then that if you imagine that what is naturally slavish is free, and what is naturally another's is your own, you will be hampered, you will mourn, you will be put to confusion, you will blame gods and men; but if you think that only your own belongs to you, and that what is another's is indeed another's, no one will ever put compulsion or hindrance on you, you will blame none, you will accuse none, you will do nothing against your will, no one will harm you, you will have no enemy, for no harm can touch you.

Aiming then at these high matters, you must remember that to attain them requires more than ordinary effort; you will have to give up some things entirely, and put off others for the moment. And if you would have these also—office and wealth—it may be that you will fail to get them, just because your desire is set on the former, and you will cer-tainly fail to attain those things which alone bring freedom and happiness.

Make it your study then to confront every harsh impression with the words, "You are but an impres-sion, and not at all what you seem to be." Then test it by those rules that you possess; and first by this—the chief test of all—"Is it concerned with what is in our power or with what is not in our power?" And if it is concerned with what is not in our power, be ready with the answer that it is nothing to you.

2. Remember that the will to get promises attain-ment of what you will, and the will to avoid prom-ises escape from what you avoid; and he who fails to get what he wills is unfortunate, and he who does not escape what he wills to avoid is miserable. If then you try to avoid only what is unnatural in the region within your control, you will escape from all that you avoid; but if you try to avoid dis-ease or death or poverty you will be miserable.

Therefore let your will to avoid have no concern with what is not in man's power; direct it only to things in man's power that are contrary to nature. But for the moment you must utterly remove the will to get; for if you will to get something not in man's power you are bound to be unfortunate; while none of the things in man's power that you could honourably will to get is yet within your reach.

Impulse to act and not to act, these are your concern; yet exercise them gently and without strain, and provisionally.

3. When anything, from the meanest thing upwards, is attractive or serviceable or an object of affection, remember always to say to yourself, "What is its nature?" If you are fond of a jug, say you are fond of a jug; then you will not be disturbed if it be broken. If you kiss your child or your wife, say to yourself that you are kissing a human being, for then if death strikes it you will not be disturbed.

4. When you are about to take something in hand, remind yourself what manner of thing it is. If you are going to bathe put before your mind what happens in the bath—water pouring over some, others being jostled, some reviling, others stealing; and you will set to work more securely if you say to yourself at once: "I want to bathe, and I want to keep my will in harmony with nature," and so in each thing you do; for in this way, if anything turns up to hinder you in your bathing, you will be ready to say, "I did not want only to bathe, but to keep my will in harmony with nature, and I shall not so keep it, if I lose my temper at what happens."

5. What disturbs men's minds is not events but their judgements on events. For instance, death is nothing dreadful, or else Socrates would have thought it so. No, the only dreadful thing about it is men's judgement that it is dreadful. And so when we are hindered, or disturbed, or distressed, let us never lay the blame on others, but on ourselves, that is, on our own judgements. To accuse others for one's own misfortunes is a sign of want of education; to accuse oneself shows that one's education has begun; to accuse neither oneself nor others shows that one's education is complete.

6. Be not elated at an excellence which is not your own. If the horse in his pride were to say, "I am handsome," we could bear with it. But when you say with pride, "I have a handsome horse," know that the good horse is the ground of your pride. You ask then what you can call your own. The answer is—the way you deal with your impressions. Therefore when you deal with your impressions in accord with nature, then you may be proud indeed, for your pride will be in a good which is your own.

7. When you are on a voyage, and your ship is at anchorage, and you disembark to get fresh water, you may pick up a small shellfish or a truffle by the way, but you must keep your attention fixed on the ship, and keep looking towards it constantly, to see if the Helmsman calls you; and if he does, you have to leave everything, or be bundled on board with your legs tied like a sheep. So it is in life. If you have a dear wife or child given you, they are like the shellfish or the truffle, they are very well in their way. Only, if the Helmsman call, run back to your ship, leave all else, and do not look behind you. And if you are old, never go far from the ship, so that when you are called you may not fail to appear.

8. Ask not that events should happen as you will, but let your will be that events should happen as they do, and you shall have peace.

9. Sickness is a hindrance to the body, but not to the will, unless the will consent. Lameness is a hindrance to the leg, but not to the will. Say this to yourself at each event that happens, for you shall find that though it hinders something else it will not hinder you.

10. When anything happens to you, always remember to turn to yourself and ask what faculty you have to deal with it. If you see a beautiful boy or a beautiful woman, you will find continence the faculty to exercise there; if trouble is laid on you, you will find endurance; if ribaldry, you will find patience. And if you train yourself in this habit your impressions will not carry you away.

11. Never say of anything, "I lost it," but say, "I gave it back." Has your child died? It was given back. Has your wife died? She was given back. Has your estate been taken from you? Was not this also given back? But you say, "He who took it from me is wicked." What does it matter to you through whom the Giver asked it back? As long as He gives it you, take care of it, but not as your own; treat it as passers-by treat an inn.

12. If you wish to make progress, abandon reasonings of this sort: "If I neglect my affairs I shall have nothing to live on;" "If I do not punish my son, he will be wicked." For it is better to die of hunger, so that you be free from pain and free from fear, than to live in plenty and be troubled in mind. It is bet-

ter for your son to be wicked than for you to be miserable. Wherefore begin with little things. Is your drop of oil spilt? Is your sup of wine stolen? Say to yourself, "This is the price paid for freedom from passion, this is the price of a quiet mind." Nothing can be had without a price. When you call your slave-boy, reflect that he may not be able to hear you, and if he hears you, he may not be able to do anything you want. But he is not so well off that it rests with him to give you peace of mind.

*　　*　　*

14. It is silly to want your children and your wife and your friends to live for ever, for that means that you want what is not in your control to be in your control, and what is not your own to be yours. In the same way if you want your servant to make no mistakes, you are a fool, for you want vice not to be vice but something different. But if you want not to be disappointed in your will to get, you can attain to that.

Exercise yourself then in what lies in your power. Each man's master is the man who has authority over what he wishes or does not wish, to secure the one or to take away the other. Let him then who wishes to be free not wish for anything or avoid anything that depends on others; or else he is bound to be a slave.

*　　*　　*

16. When you see a man shedding tears in sorrow for a child abroad or dead, or for loss of property, beware that you are not carried away by the impression that it is outward ills that make him miserable. Keep this thought by you: "What distresses him is not the event, for that does not distress another, but his judgement on the event." Therefore do not hesitate to sympathize with him so far as words go, and if it so chance, even to groan with him; but take heed that you do not also groan in your inner being.

17. Remember that you are an actor in a play, and the Playwright chooses the manner of it: if he wants it short, it is short; if long, it is long. If he wants you to act a poor man you must act the part with all your powers; and so if your part be a cripple or a magistrate or a plain man. For your business is to act the character that is given you and act it well; the choice of the cast is Another's.

18. When a raven croaks with evil omen, let not the impression carry you away, but straightway distinguish in your own mind and say, "These portents mean nothing to me; but only to my bit of a body or my bit of property or name, or my children or my wife. But for me all omens are favourable if I will, for, whatever the issue may be, it is in my power to get benefit therefrom."

19. You can be invincible, if you never enter on a contest where victory is not in your power. Beware then that when you see a man raised to honour or great power or high repute you do not let your impression carry you away. For if the reality of good lies in what is in our power, there is no room for envy or jealousy. And you will not wish to be praetor, or prefect or consul, but to be free; and there is but one way to freedom—to despise what is not in our power.

20. Remember that foul words or blows in themselves are no outrage, but your judgement that they are so. So when any one makes you angry, know that it is your own thought that has angered you. Wherefore make it your first endeavour not to let your impressions carry you away. For if once you gain time and delay, you will find it easier to control yourself.

21. Keep before your eyes from day to day death and exile and all things that seem terrible, but death most of all, and then you will never set your thoughts on what is low and will never desire anything beyond measure.

*　　*　　*

26. It is in our power to discover the will of Nature from those matters on which we have no difference of opinion. For instance, when another man's slave has broken the wine-cup we are very ready to say at once, "Such things must happen." Know then that when your own cup is broken, you ought to behave in the same way as when your neighbour's was broken. Apply the same principle to higher matters. Is another's child or wife dead? Not one of us but would say, "Such is the lot of man;" but when one's own dies, straightway one cries, "Alas! miserable am I."

But we ought to remember what our feelings are when we hear it of another.

27. As a mark is not set up for men to miss it, so there is nothing intrinsically evil in the world.

*   *   *

29. . . . Man, consider first what it is you are undertaking; then look at your own powers and see if you can bear it. Do you want to compete in the pentathlon or in wrestling? Look to your arms, your thighs, see what your loins are like. For different men are born for different tasks. Do you suppose that if you do this you can live as you do now—eat and drink as you do now, indulge desire and discontent just as before? Nay, you must sit up late, work hard, abandon your own people, be looked down on by a mere slave, be ridiculed by those who meet you, get the worst of it in everything—in honour, in office, in justice, in every possible thing. This is what you have to consider: whether you are willing to pay this price for peace of mind, freedom, tranquillity. If not, do not come near; do not be, like the children, first a philosopher, then a tax-collector, then an orator, then one of Caesar's procurators. These callings do not agree. You must be one man, good or bad; you must develop either your Governing Principle, or your outward endowments; you must study either your inner man, or outward things—in a word, you must choose between the position of a philosopher and that of a mere outsider.

*   *   *

31. For piety towards the gods know that the most important thing is this: to have right opinions about them—that they exist, and that they govern the universe well and justly—and to have set yourself to obey them, and to give way to all that happens, following events with a free will, in the belief that they are fulfilled by the highest mind. For thus you will never blame the gods, nor accuse them of neglecting you. But this you cannot achieve, unless you apply your conception of good and evil to those things only which are in our power, and not to those which are out of our power. For if you apply your notion of good or evil to the latter, then, as soon as you fail to

get what you will to get or fail to avoid what you will to avoid, you will be bound to blame and hate those you hold responsible. For every living creature has a natural tendency to avoid and shun what seems harmful and all that causes it, and to pursue and admire what is helpful and all that causes it. It is not possible then for one who thinks he is harmed to take pleasure in what he thinks is the author of the harm, any more than to take pleasure in the harm itself. That is why a father is reviled by his son, when he does not give his son a share of what the son regards as good things; thus Polynices and Eteocles were set at enmity with one another by thinking that a king's throne was a good thing. That is why the farmer, and the sailor, and the merchant, and those who lose wife or children revile the gods. For men's religion is bound up with their interest. Therefore he who makes it his concern rightly to direct his will to get and his will to avoid, is thereby making piety his concern. But it is proper on each occasion to make libation and sacrifice and to offer first-fruits according to the custom of our fathers, with purity and not in slovenly or careless fashion, without meanness and without extravagance.

*   *   *

32. . . . Lay down for yourself from the first a definite stamp and style of conduct, which you will maintain when you are alone and also in the society of men. Be silent for the most part, or, if you speak, say only what is necessary and in a few words. Talk, but rarely, if occasion calls you, but do not talk of ordinary things—of gladiators, or horse-races, or athletes, or of meats or drinks—these are topics that arise everywhere—but above all do not talk about men in blame or compliment or comparison. If you can, turn the conversation of your company by your talk to some fitting subject; but if you should chance to be isolated among strangers, be silent. Do not laugh much, nor at many things, nor without restraint.

Refuse to take oaths, altogether if that be possible, but if not, as far as circumstances allow.

Refuse the entertainments of strangers and the vulgar. But if occasions arise to accept them, then strain every nerve to avoid lapsing into the state of the vulgar. For know that, if your comrade has a stain on him, he that associates with him must needs share the stain, even though he be clean in himself.

For your body take just so much as your bare need requires, such as food, drink, clothing, house, servants, but cut down all that tends to luxury and outward show.

Avoid impurity to the utmost of your power before marriage, and if you indulge your passion, let it be done lawfully. But do not be offensive or censorious to those who indulge it, and do not be always bringing up your own chastity. If some one tells you that so and so speaks ill of you, do not defend yourself against what he says, but answer, "He did not know my other faults, or he would not have mentioned these alone."

It is not necessary for the most part to go to the games; but if you should have occasion to go, show that your first concern is for yourself; that is, wish that only to happen which does happen, and him only to win who does win, for so you will suffer no hindrance. But refrain entirely from applause, or ridicule, or prolonged excitement. And when you go away do not talk much of what happened there, except so far as it tends to your improvement. For to talk about it implies that the spectacle excited your wonder.

Do not go lightly or casually to hear lectures; but if you do go, maintain your gravity and dignity and do not make yourself offensive. When you are going to meet any one, and particularly some man of reputed eminence, set before your mind the thought, "What would Socrates or Zeno have done?" and you will not fail to make proper use of the occasion.

When you go to visit some great man, prepare your mind by thinking that you will not find him in, that you will be shut out, that the doors will be slammed in your face, that he will pay no heed to you. And if in spite of all this you find it fitting for you to go, go and bear what happens and never say to yourself, "It was not worth all this"; for that shows a vulgar mind and one at odds with outward things.

In your conversation avoid frequent and disproportionate mention of your own doings or adventures; for other people do not take the same pleasure in hearing what has happened to you as you take in recounting your adventures.

Avoid raising men's laughter; for it is a habit that easily slips into vulgarity, and it may well suffice to lessen your neighbour's respect.

It is dangerous too to lapse into foul language; when anything of the kind occurs, rebuke the offender, if the occasion allow, and if not, make it plain to him by your silence, or a blush or a frown, that you are angry at his words.

34. When you imagine some pleasure, beware that it does not carry you away, like other imaginations. Wait a while, and give yourself pause. Next remember two things: how long you will enjoy the pleasure, and also how long you will afterwards repent and revile yourself. And set on the other side the joy and self-satisfaction you will feel if you refrain. And if the moment seems come to realize it, take heed that you be not overcome by the winning sweetness and attraction of it; set in the other scale the thought how much better is the consciousness of having vanquished it.

35. When you do a thing because you have determined that it ought to be done, never avoid being seen doing it, even if the opinion of the multitude is going to condemn you. For if your action is wrong, then avoid doing it altogether, but if it is right, why do you fear those who will rebuke you wrongly?

*   *   *

37. If you try to act a part beyond your powers, you not only disgrace yourself in it, but you neglect the part which you could have filled with success.

38. As in walking you take care not to tread on a nail or to twist your foot, so take care that you do not harm your Governing Principle. And if we guard this in everything we do, we shall set to work more securely.

39. Every man's body is a measure for his property, as the foot is the measure for his shoe. If you stick to this limit, you will keep the right measure; if you go beyond it, you are bound to be carried away down a precipice in the end; just as with the shoe, if you once go beyond the foot, your shoe puts on gilding, and soon purple and embroidery. For when once you go beyond the measure there is no limit.

40. Women from fourteen years upwards are called "madam" by men. Wherefore, when they see that the only advantage they have got is to be marriageable, they begin to make themselves smart and to set all their hopes on this. We must take pains then to make them understand that they are really honoured for nothing but a modest and decorous life.

41. It is a sign of a dull mind to dwell upon the cares of the body, to prolong exercise, eating, drinking, and other bodily functions. These things are to be done by the way; all your attention must be given to the mind.

42. When a man speaks evil or does evil to you, remember that he does or says it because he thinks it is fitting for him. It is not possible for him to follow what seems good to you, but only what seems good to him, so that, if his opinion is wrong, he suffers, in that he is the victim of deception. In the same way, if a composite judgement which is true is thought to be false, it is not the judgement that suffers, but the man who is deluded about it. If you act on this principle you will be gentle to him who reviles you, saying to yourself on each occasion, "He thought it right."

*   *   *

44. It is illogical to reason thus, "I am richer than you, therefore I am superior to you," "I am more eloquent than you, therefore I am superior to you." It is more logical to reason, "I am richer than you, therefore my property is superior to yours," "I am more eloquent than you, therefore my speech is superior to yours." You are something more than property or speech.

*   *   *

46. On no occasion call yourself a philosopher, nor talk at large of your principles among the multitude, but act on your principles. For instance, at a banquet do not say how one ought to eat, but eat as you ought. Remember that Socrates had so completely got rid of the thought of display that when men came and wanted an introduction to philosophers he took them to be introduced; so patient of neglect was he. And if a discussion arise among the multitude on some principle, keep silent for the most part; for you are in great danger of blurting out some undigested thought. And when someone says to you, 'You know nothing,' and you do not let it provoke you, then know that you are really on the right road. For sheep do not bring grass to their shepherds and show them how much they have eaten, but they digest their fodder and then produce it in the form of wool and milk. Do the same yourself; instead of displaying your principles to the multitude, show them the results of the principles you have digested.

*   *   *

The signs of one who is making progress are: he blames none, praises none, complains of none, accuses none, never speaks of himself as if he were somebody, or as if he knew anything. And if any one compliments him he laughs in himself at his compliment; and if one blames him, he makes no defence. He goes about like a convalescent, careful not to disturb his constitution on its road to recovery, until it has got firm hold. He has got rid of the will to get, and his will to avoid is directed no longer to what is beyond our power but only to what is in our power and contrary to nature. In all things he exercises his will without strain. If men regard him as foolish or ignorant he pays no heed. In one word, he keeps watch and guard on himself as his own enemy, lying in wait for him.

*   *   *

Review Questions

1. As presented in this work, according to what principles is the practitioner of Stoicism to live his life?
2. Why do things happen as they do, and what should the proper Stoic's attitude be?
3. How do the principles of Stoicism contrast with those of Epicureanism?

The Jewish Encounter with Hellenism: The Maccabees' Rebellion

Alexander's conquest of the Persian Empire entailed not only the building of a vast empire, but—and arguably more significantly—an encounter between the Greek culture of the conquerors and the cultures and religious traditions of the conquered. Nowhere was the impact of this encounter more pronounced than in Palestine, where the long-established Jewish population found itself both enticed and repulsed by Greek culture. However, when the Seleucid emperor Antiochus IV attempted to squelch Jewish belief and traditions, and ransacked the great temple at Jerusalem, some of the Jews of Palestine were aroused to rebellion. The following selection is from the first four chapters of First Book of Maccabees, named for the family (also known as the Hasmoneans) who spearheaded what later Jews (including many modern Israelis) came to revere as a heroic war of resistance and national reassertion. As is indicated at the end of the selection, Jews later annually celebrated the restoration of the Temple (dated to 164 B.C.E.) in the festive season commonly known as Hanukkah.

From 1 Maccabees 1:7–4:59, *Revised Standard Version Bible*, National Council of the Churches of Christ in the USA, 1952.

1 Maccabees

1 Macc. 1

*   *   *

And after Alexander had reigned twelve years, he died.

Then his officers began to rule, each in his own place. They all put on crowns after his death, and so did their sons after them for many years; and they caused many evils on the earth.

From them came forth a sinful root, Antiochus Epiphanes, son of Antiochus the king; he had been a hostage in Rome. He began to reign in the one hundred and thirty-seventh year of the kingdom of the Greeks.

In those days lawless men came forth from Israel, and misled many, saying, "Let us go and make a covenant with the Gentiles round about us, for since we separated from them many evils have come upon us." This proposal pleased them, and some of the people eagerly went to the king. He authorized them to observe the ordinances of the Gentiles. So they built a gymnasium in Jerusalem, according to Gentile custom, and removed the marks of circumcision, and abandoned the holy covenant. They joined with the Gentiles and sold themselves to do evil.

When Antiochus saw that his kingdom was established, he determined to become king of the land of Egypt, that he might reign over both kingdoms. So he invaded Egypt with a strong force, with chariots and elephants and cavalry and with a large fleet.

He engaged Ptolemy king of Egypt in battle, and Ptolemy turned and fled before him, and many were wounded and fell. And they captured the fortified cities in the land of Egypt, and he plundered the land of Egypt.

After subduing Egypt, Antiochus returned in the one hundred and forty-third year. He went up against Israel and came to Jerusalem with a strong force. He arrogantly entered the sanctuary and took the golden altar, the lampstand for the light, and all its utensils. He took also the table for the bread of the Presence, the cups for drink offerings, the bowls, the golden censers, the curtain, the crowns, and the gold decoration on the front of the temple; he stripped it all off. He took the silver and the gold, and the costly vessels; he took also the hidden treasures which he found. Taking them all, he departed to his own land.

He committed deeds of murder, and spoke with great arrogance. Israel mourned deeply in every community, rulers and elders groaned, maidens and young men became faint, the beauty of women faded. Every bridegroom took up the lament; she who sat in the bridal chamber was mourning. Even the land shook for its inhabitants, and all the house of Jacob was clothed with shame.

Two years later the king sent to the cities of Judah a chief collector of tribute, and he came to Jerusalem with a large force. Deceitfully he spoke peaceable words to them, and they believed him; but he suddenly fell upon the city, dealt it a severe blow, and destroyed many people of Israel. He plundered the city, burned it with fire, and tore down its houses and its surrounding walls. And they took captive the women and children, and seized the cattle. Then they fortified the city of David with a great strong wall and strong towers, and it became their citadel. And they stationed there a sinful people, lawless men. These strengthened their position; they stored up arms and food, and collecting the spoils of Jerusalem they stored them there, and became a great snare.

It became an ambush against the sanctuary, an evil adversary of Israel continually. On every side of the sanctuary they shed innocent blood; they even defiled the sanctuary. Because of them the residents of Jerusalem fled; she became a dwelling of strangers; she became strange to her offspring, and her children forsook her. Her sanctuary became desolate as a desert; her feasts were turned into mourning, her sabbaths into a reproach, her honor into contempt. Her dishonor now grew as great as her glory; her exaltation was turned into mourning.

Then the king wrote to his whole kingdom that all should be one people, and that each should give up his customs. All the Gentiles accepted the command of the king. Many even from Israel gladly adopted his religion; they sacrificed to idols and profaned the sabbath. And the king sent letters by messengers to Jerusalem and the cities of Judah; he directed them to follow customs strange to the land, to forbid burnt offerings and sacrifices and drink offerings in the sanctuary, to profane sabbaths and feasts, to defile the sanctuary and the priests, to build altars and sacred precincts and shrines for idols, to sacrifice swine and unclean animals, and to leave their sons uncircumcised. They were to make themselves abominable by everything unclean and profane, so that they should forget the law and change all the ordinances. "And whoever does not obey the command of the king shall die."

In such words he wrote to his whole kingdom. And he appointed inspectors over all the people and commanded the cities of Judah to offer sacrifice, city by city. Many of the people, everyone who forsook the law, joined them, and they did evil in the land; they drove Israel into hiding in every place of refuge they had.

Now on the fifteenth day of Chislev, in the one hundred and forty-fifth year, they erected a desolating sacrilege upon the altar of burnt offering. They also built altars in the surrounding cities of Judah, and burned incense at the doors of the houses and in the streets. The books of the law which they found they tore to pieces and burned with fire. Where the book of the covenant was found in the possession of any one, or if any one adhered to the law, the decree of the king condemned him to death. They kept using violence against Israel, against those found month after month in the cities. And on the twenty-fifth day of the month they offered sacrifice on the altar which was upon the altar of burnt offering. According to the decree, they put to death the women who had their children circumcised, and their families and those who circumcised them; and they hung the infants from their mothers' necks.

But many in Israel stood firm and were resolved in their hearts not to eat unclean food. They chose to die rather than to be defiled by food or to profane the holy covenant; and they did die. And very great wrath came upon Israel.

1 Macc. 2

In those days Mattathias the son of John, son of Simeon, a priest of the sons of Joarib, moved from Jerusalem and settled in Modein. He had five sons, John surnamed Gaddi, Simon called Thassi, Judas called Maccabeus, Eleazar called Avaran, and Jonathan called Apphus. He saw the blasphemies being committed in Judah and Jerusalem, and said, "Alas! Why was I born to see this, the ruin of my people, the ruin of the holy city, and to dwell there when it was given over to the enemy, the sanctuary given over to aliens? Her temple has become like a man without honor; her glorious vessels have been carried into captivity. Her babes have been killed in her streets, her youths by the sword of the foe. What nation has not inherited her palaces and has not seized her spoils? All her adornment has been taken away; no longer free, she has become a slave. And behold, our holy place, our beauty, and our glory have been laid waste; the Gentiles have profaned it. Why should we live any longer?" And Mattathias and his sons rent their clothes, put on sackcloth, and mourned greatly.

Then the king's officers who were enforcing the apostasy came to the city of Modein to make them offer sacrifice. Many from Israel came to them; and Mattathias and his sons were assembled. Then the king's officers spoke to Mattathias as follows: "You are a leader, honored and great in this city, and supported by sons and brothers. Now be the first to come and do what the king commands, as all the Gentiles and the men of Judah and those that are left in Jerusalem have done. Then you and your sons will be numbered among the friends of the king, and you and your sons will be honored with silver and gold and many gifts."

But Mattathias answered and said in a loud voice: "Even if all the nations that live under the rule of the king obey him, and have chosen to do his commandments, departing each one from the religion of his fathers, yet I and my sons and my brothers will live by the covenant of our fathers. Far be it from us to desert the law and the ordinances. We will not obey the king's words by turning aside from our religion to the right hand or to the left."

When he had finished speaking these words, a Jew came forward in the sight of all to offer sacrifice upon the altar in Modein, according to the king's command. When Mattathias saw it, he burned with zeal and his heart was stirred. He gave vent to righteous anger; he ran and killed him upon the altar. At the same time he killed the king's officer who was forcing them to sacrifice, and he tore down the altar. Thus he burned with zeal for the law, as Phinehas did against Zimri the son of Salu.

Then Mattathias cried out in the city with a loud voice, saying: "Let every one who is zealous for the law and supports the covenant come out with me!" And he and his sons fled to the hills and left all that they had in the city.

Then many who were seeking righteousness and justice went down to the wilderness to dwell there, they, their sons, their wives, and their cattle, because evils pressed heavily upon them. And it was reported to the king's officers, and to the troops in Jerusalem the city of David, that men who had rejected the king's command had gone down to the hiding places in the wilderness. Many pursued them, and overtook them; they encamped opposite them and prepared for battle against them on the sabbath day. And they said to them, "Enough of this! Come out and do what the king commands, and you will live." But they said, "We will not come out, nor will we do what the king commands and so profane the sabbath day." Then the enemy hastened to attack them. But they did not answer them or hurl a stone at them or block up their hiding places, for they said, "Let us all die in our innocence; heaven and earth testify for us that you are killing us unjustly." So they attacked them on the sabbath, and they died, with their wives and children and cattle, to the number of a thousand persons.

When Mattathias and his friends learned of it, they mourned for them deeply. And each said to his neighbor: "If we all do as our brethren have done and refuse to fight with the Gentiles for our lives and for our ordinances, they will quickly destroy us from the earth." So they made this decision that day: "Let us fight against every man who comes to attack us on the sabbath day; let us not all die as our brethren died in their hiding places."

Then there united with them a company of Hasideans, mighty warriors of Israel, every one who offered himself willingly for the law. And all who became fugitives to escape their troubles joined them and reinforced them. They organized an army, and struck down sinners in their anger and lawless men in their wrath; the survivors fled to the Gentiles for safety. And Mattathias and his friends went about and tore down the altars; they forcibly circumcised all the uncircumcised boys that they found within the borders of Israel. They hunted down the arrogant men, and the work prospered in their hands. They rescued the law out of the hands of the Gentiles and kings, and they never let the sinner gain the upper hand.

Now the days drew near for Mattathias to die, and he said to his sons: "Arrogance and reproach have now become strong; it is a time of ruin and furious anger. Now, my children, show zeal for the law, and give your lives for the covenant of our fathers.

"Remember the deeds of the fathers, which they did in their generations; and receive great honor and an everlasting name. Was not Abraham found faithful when tested, and it was reckoned to him as righteousness? Joseph in the time of his distress kept the commandment, and became lord of Egypt. Phinehas our father, because he was deeply zealous, received the covenant of everlasting priesthood. Joshua, because he fulfilled the command, became a judge in Israel. Caleb, because he testified in the assembly, received an inheritance in the land. David, because he was merciful, inherited the throne of the kingdom for ever. Elijah because of great zeal for the law was taken up into heaven. Hannaniah, Azariah, and Mishael believed and were saved from the flame. Daniel because of his innocence was delivered from the mouth of the lions.

"And so observe, from generation to generation, that none who put their trust in him will lack strength. Do not fear the words of a sinner, for his splendor will turn into dung and worms. Today he will be exalted, but tomorrow he will not be found, because he has returned to the dust, and his plans will perish. My children, be courageous and grow strong in the law, for by it you will gain honor.

"Now behold, I know that Simeon your brother is wise in counsel; always listen to him; he shall be your father. Judas Maccabeus has been a mighty warrior from his youth; he shall command the army for you and fight the battle against the peoples. You shall rally about you all who observe the law, and avenge the wrong done to your people. Pay back the Gentiles in full, and heed what the law commands."

Then he blessed them, and was gathered to his fathers. He died in the one hundred and forty-sixth year and was buried in the tomb of his fathers at Modein. And all Israel mourned for him with great lamentation.

1 Macc. 3

Then Judas his son, who was called Maccabeus, took command in his place. All his brothers and all who had joined his father helped him; they gladly fought for Israel.

He extended the glory of his people. Like a giant he put on his breastplate; he girded on his armor of war and waged battles, protecting the host by his sword. He was like a lion in his deeds, like a lion's cub roaring for prey. He searched out and pursued the lawless; he burned those who troubled his people. Lawless men shrank back for fear of him; all the evildoers were confounded; and deliverance prospered by his hand. He embittered many kings, but he made Jacob glad by his deeds, and his memory is blessed for ever. He went through the cities of Judah; he destroyed the ungodly out of the land; thus he turned away wrath from Israel. He was renowned to the ends of the earth; he gathered in those who were perishing.

But Apollonius gathered together Gentiles and a large force from Samaria to fight against Israel. When Judas learned of it, he went out to meet him, and he defeated and killed him. Many were wounded and fell, and the rest fled. Then they seized their spoils; and Judas took the sword of Apollonius, and used it in battle the rest of his life.

Now when Seron, the commander of the Syrian army, heard that Judas had gathered a large company, including a body of faithful men who stayed with him and went out to battle, he said, "I will make a name for myself and win honor in the kingdom. I will make war on Judas and his companions, who scorn the king's command." And again a strong army of ungodly men went up with him to help him, to take vengeance on the sons of Israel.

When he approached the ascent of Beth-horon, Judas went out to meet him with a small company. But when they saw the army coming to meet them, they said to Judas, "How can we, few as we are, fight against so great and strong a multitude? And we are faint, for we have eaten nothing today." Judas replied, "It is easy for many to be hemmed in by few, for in the sight of Heaven there is no difference between saving by many or by few. It is not on the size of the army that victory in battle depends, but strength comes from Heaven. They come against us in great pride and lawlessness to destroy us and our wives and our children, and to despoil us; but we fight for our lives and our laws. He himself will crush them before us; as for you, do not be afraid of them."

When he finished speaking, he rushed suddenly against Seron and his army, and they were crushed before him. They pursued them down the descent of Beth-horon to the plain; eight hundred of them fell, and the rest fled into the land of the Philistines. Then Judas and his brothers began to be feared, and terror fell upon the Gentiles round about them. His fame reached the king, and the Gentiles talked of the battles of Judas.

When king Antiochus heard these reports, he was greatly angered; and he sent and gathered all the forces of his kingdom, a very strong army. And he opened his coffers and gave a year's pay to his forces, and ordered them to be ready for any need. Then he saw that the money in the treasury was exhausted, and that the revenues from the country were small because of the dissension and disaster which he had caused in the land by abolishing the laws that had existed from the earliest days. He feared that he might not have such funds as he had before for his expenses and for the gifts which he used to give more lavishly than preceding kings. He was greatly perplexed in mind, and determined to go to Persia and collect the revenues from those regions and raise a large fund.

He left Lysias, a distinguished man of royal lineage, in charge of the king's affairs from the river Euphrates to the borders of Egypt. Lysias was also to take care of Antiochus his son until he returned. And he turned over to Lysias half of his troops and the elephants, and gave him orders about all that he wanted done. As for the residents of Judea and Jerusalem, Lysias was to send a force against them to wipe out and destroy the strength of Israel and the remnant of Jerusalem; he was to banish the memory of them from the place, settle aliens in all their territory, and distribute their land. Then the king took the remaining half of his troops and departed from Antioch his capital in the one hundred and forty-seventh year. He crossed the Euphrates river and went through the upper provinces.

Lysias chose Ptolemy the son of Dorymenes, and Nicanor and Gorgias, mighty men among the friends of the king, and sent with them forty thousand infantry and seven thousand cavalry to go into the land of Judah and destroy it, as the king had commanded. so they departed with their entire force, and when they arrived they encamped near Emmaus in the plain. When the traders of the region heard what was said to them, they took silver and gold in immense amounts, and fetters, and went to the camp to get the sons of Israel for slaves. And forces from Syria and the land of the Philistines joined with them.

Now Judas and his brothers saw that misfortunes had increased and that the forces were encamped in their territory. They also learned what the king had commanded to do to the people to cause their final destruction. But they said to one another, "Let us repair the destruction of our people, and fight for our people and the sanctuary." And the congregation assembled to be ready for battle, and to pray and ask for mercy and compassion.

Jerusalem was uninhabited like a wilderness; not one of her children went in or out. The sanctuary was trampled down, and the sons of aliens held the citadel; it was a lodging place for the Gentiles. Joy was taken from Jacob; the flute and the harp ceased to play.

So they assembled and went to Mizpah, opposite Jerusalem, because Israel formerly had a place of prayer in Mizpah. They fasted that day, put on sackcloth and sprinkled ashes on their heads, and rent their clothes. And they opened the book of the law to inquire into those matters about which the Gentiles were consulting the images of their idols. They also brought the garments of the priesthood and the first fruits and the tithes, and they stirred up the Nazirites who had completed their days; and they cried aloud to Heaven, saying, "What shall we do with these? Where shall we take them? Thy sanctuary is trampled down and profaned, and thy priests mourn in humiliation. And behold, the Gentiles are assembled against us to destroy us; thou knowest what they plot against us. How will we be able to withstand them, if thou dost not help us?"

Then they sounded the trumpets and gave a loud shout. After this Judas appointed leaders of the people, in charge of thousands and hundreds and fifties and tens. And he said to those who were building houses, or were betrothed, or were planting vineyards, or were fainthearted, that each should return to his home, according to the law. Then the army marched out and encamped to the south of Emmaus. And Judas said, "Gird yourselves and be valiant. Be ready early in the morning to fight with these Gentiles who have assembled against us to destroy us and our sanctuary. It is better for us to die in battle than to see the misfortunes of our nation and of the sanctuary. But as his will in heaven may be, so he will do."

1 Macc. 4

Now Gorgias took five thousand infantry and a thousand picked cavalry, and this division moved out by night to fall upon the camp of the Jews and attack them suddenly. Men from the citadel were his guides. But Judas heard of it, and he and his mighty men moved out to attack the king's force in Emmaus while the division was still absent from the camp. When Gorgias entered the camp of Judas by night, he found no one there, so he looked for them in the hills, because he said, "These men are fleeing from us."

At daybreak Judas appeared in the plain with three thousand men, but they did not have armor and swords such as they desired. And they saw the camp of the Gentiles, strong and fortified, with cavalry round about it; and these men were trained in war. But Judas said to the men who were with him, "Do not fear their numbers or be afraid when they charge. Remember how our fathers were saved at the Red Sea, when Pharaoh with his forces pursued them. And now let us cry to Heaven, to see whether he will favor us and remember his covenant with our fathers and crush this army before us today. Then all the Gentiles will know that there is one who redeems and saves Israel."

When the foreigners looked up and saw them coming against them, they went forth from their camp to battle. Then the men with Judas blew their trumpets and engaged in battle. The Gentiles were crushed and fled into the plain, and all those in the rear fell by the sword. They pursued them to Gazara, and to the plains of Idumea, and to Azotus and Jamnia; and three thousand of them fell. Then Judas and his force turned back from pursuing them, and he said to the people, "Do not be greedy for plunder, for there is a battle before us; Gorgias and his force are near us in the hills. But stand now against our enemies and fight them, and afterward seize the plunder boldly."

Just as Judas was finishing this speech, a detachment appeared, coming out of the hills. They saw that their army had been put to flight, and that the Jews were burning the camp, for the smoke that was seen showed what had happened. When they perceived this they were greatly frightened, and when they also saw the army of Judas drawn up in the plain for battle, they all fled into the land of the Philistines. Then Judas returned to plunder the camp, and they seized much gold and silver, and cloth dyed blue and sea purple, and great riches. On their return they sang hymns and praises to Heaven, for he is good, for his mercy endures for ever. Thus Israel had a great deliverance that day.

Those of the foreigners who escaped went and reported to Lysias all that had happened. When he heard it, he was perplexed and discouraged, for things had not happened to Israel as he had intended, nor had they turned out as the king had commanded him. But the next year he mustered sixty thousand picked infantrymen and five thousand cavalry to subdue them. They came into Idumea and encamped at Beth-zur, and Judas met them with ten thousand men.

When he saw that the army was strong, he prayed, saying, "Blessed art thou, O Savior of Israel, who didst crush the attack of the mighty warrior by the hand of thy servant David, and didst give the camp of the Philistines into the hands of Jonathan, the son of Saul, and of the man who carried his armor. So do thou hem in this army by the hand of thy people Israel, and let them be ashamed of their troops and their cavalry. Fill them with cowardice; melt the boldness of their strength; let them tremble in their destruction. Strike them down with the sword of those who love thee, and let all who know thy name praise thee with hymns."

Then both sides attacked, and there fell of the army of Lysias five thousand men; they fell in action. And when Lysias saw the rout of his troops and observed the boldness which inspired those of Judas, and how ready they were either to live or to die nobly, he departed to Antioch and enlisted mercenaries, to invade Judea again with an even larger army.

Then said Judas and his brothers, "Behold, our enemies are crushed; let us go up to cleanse the sanctuary and dedicate it." So all the army assembled and they went up to Mount Zion. And they saw the sanctuary desolate, the altar profaned, and the gates burned. In the courts they saw bushes sprung up as in a thicket, or as on one of the mountains. They saw also the chambers of the priests in ruins. Then they rent their clothes, and mourned with great lamentation, and sprinkled themselves with ashes. They fell face down on the ground, and sounded the signal on the trumpets, and cried out to Heaven.

Then Judas detailed men to fight against those in the citadel until he had cleansed the sanctuary. He chose blameless priests devoted to the law, and they cleansed the sanctuary and removed the defiled stones to an unclean place. They deliberated what to do about the altar of burnt offering, which had been profaned. And they thought it best to tear it down, lest it bring reproach upon them, for the Gentiles had defiled it. So they tore down the altar, and stored the stones in a convenient place on the temple hill until there should come a prophet to tell what to do with them. Then they took unhewn stones, as the law directs, and built a new altar like the former one. They also rebuilt the sanctuary and the interior of the temple, and consecrated the courts. They made new holy vessels, and brought the lampstand, the altar of incense, and the table into the temple. Then they burned incense on the altar and lighted the lamps on the lampstand, and these gave light in the temple. They placed the bread on the table and hung up the curtains. Thus they finished all the work they had undertaken.

Early in the morning on the twenty-fifth day of the ninth month, which is the month of Chislev, in the one hundred and forty-eighth year, they rose and offered sacrifice, as the law directs, on the new altar of burnt offering which they had built. At the very season and on the very day that the Gentiles had profaned it, it was dedicated with songs and harps and lutes and cymbals. All the people fell on their faces and worshiped and blessed Heaven, who had prospered them. So they celebrated the dedication of the altar for eight days, and offered burnt offerings with gladness; they offered a sacrifice of deliverance and praise. They decorated the front of the temple with golden crowns and small shields;

they restored the gates and the chambers for the priests, and furnished them with doors. There was very great gladness among the people, and the reproach of the Gentiles was removed. Then Judas and his brothers and all the assembly of Israel determined that every year at that season the days of dedication of the altar should be observed with gladness and joy for eight days, beginning with the twenty-fifth day of the month of Chislev.

REVIEW QUESTIONS

1. How, and why, did Antiochus IV's actions provoke the Jews of Palestine?
2. What evidence do you see of some Jews' assimilation or accommodation with Greek political hegemony and cultural inroads?
3. How strong is the biblical account's view of the alien nature of Greek culture?

5 ✑ THE CIVILIZATION OF ANCIENT ROME

During the same period that the Greeks and Persians were doing battle at Marathon and Thermopylae and Alexander was launching his invasion of the Near East, a new power that in time would supersede them both had begun gradually to emerge in the west. The rise of Rome is one of the most compelling stories of Western civilization: an insignificant settlement, confronted by dangerous enemies and often wracked by internal turmoil, succeeds not only in surviving but also in becoming first the master of Italy, then of the Mediterranean. In only a few centuries, Rome fashioned an empire that extended from Spain to Mesopotamia.

During the march to empire, of course, the Romans sustained casualties. Among them were their early system of government, a republic, and a society that was regulated by a strict code of law and by a tradition that emphasized respect for paternal authority and duty to family, state, and gods. In time, however, the republican system that had brought Rome to greatness was ripped apart by the demands of overseas dominion, to be replaced by rival, power-hungry generals and, eventually, by an emperor whose status eventually went from that of princeps *("first citizen") to* dominus et deus *("lord and god"). As Roman government inexorably changed, so Roman society and values were transformed by the massive infusion of luxury brought by imperial possessions and the influence of Greek culture and philosophical ideas on venerable Roman traditions and behavior. Indeed, of the many parallels that have been drawn between the rise of Rome and the rise of the United States to global domination two millennia later, none has been more jarring, and perhaps more potentially instructive, than the perception of decline brought by the transformation of traditional values in the wake of involvement with the outside world. In both Rome and the United States, we can discern changes brought by the influence of foreign cultures and ideas as their respective dominions expanded; in both cases, the challenge of such changes brought a response, in the form of attempts to reassert the primacy of traditional values and attitudes. This process is nowhere more evident in the Roman world than in the introduction and rapid spread of Christianity and the official Roman response to it. For both Roman and U.S. societies, the balance sheet of benefits and liabilities will surely be discussed for years to come.*

Whatever the conclusions historians and others may reach in such matters, it remains indisputable that the Pax Romana ("Roman peace") over which the Roman emperors presided gave Western civilization the longest period of continuous peace and stability that it had ever seen or has seen since. In the names of our months and the nine planets of our solar system, in the names of some of our important governmental institutions (senate, consulate, diocese), in the architectural style and grandeur of some of our most important public buildings, we find constant reminders that, even with its slavery, gladiatorial games, and vomitoria, the age of imperial Rome remains the great golden age of Western civilization.

FROM The Twelve Tables

Issued by a commission of Roman magistrates in 449 B.C.E., this codification of early Roman law was originally inscribed on twelve bronze plaques that were set up in the Forum in Rome. Our single most important source on the society and economy of early Rome, the Twelve Tables reflect, in relatively unvarnished fashion, the values that dominated life during the early years of the Roman Republic. (To borrow a modern expression, there was not much "kidding around.")

From *Roman Civilization: Selected Readings*, vol. 2, edited by Naphtali Lewis and Meyer Reinhold (New York: Columbia University Press, 1953), pp. 54–67.

Table I
Preliminaries to and Rules for a Trial

If plaintiff summons defendant to court, he shall go. If he does not go, plaintiff shall call witness thereto. Then only shall he take defendant by force.

If defendant shirks or takes to his heels, plaintiff shall lay hands on him.

If disease or age is an impediment, he [who summons defendant to court] shall grant him a team; he shall not spread with cushions the covered carriage if he does not so desire.

For a landowner, a landowner shall be surety; but for a proletarian person, let any one who is willing be his protector. . . .

When parties make a settlement of the case, the judge shall announce it. If they do not reach a settlement, they shall state the outline of their case in the meeting place or Forum before noon.

They shall plead it out together in person. After noon, the judge shall adjudge the case to the party present. If both be present, sunset shall be the time limit [of proceedings].

Table II
Further Enactments on Trials

Action under solemn deposit: 500 *as* pieces is the sum when the object of dispute under solemn deposit is valued at 1,000 in bronze or more, fifty pieces when less. Where the controversy concerns the liberty of a human being, fifty pieces shall be the solemn deposit under which the dispute should be undertaken.

If any of these be impediment for judge, referee, or party, on that account the day of trial shall be broken off.

Whoever is in need of evidence, he shall go on every third day to call out loudly before witness' doorway.

Table III
Execution; Law of Debt

When a debt has been acknowledged, or judgment about the matter has been pronounced in court, thirty days must be the legitimate time of grace. After that, the debtor may be arrested by laying on of hands. Bring him into court. If he does not satisfy the judgment, or no one in court offers himself as surety in his behalf, the creditor may take the defaulter with him. He may bind him either in stocks or in fetters; he may bind him with a weight no more than fifteen pounds, or with less if he shall so desire. The debtor, if he wishes, may live on his own. If he does not live on his own, the person who shall hold him in bonds shall give him one pound of grits for each day. He may give more if he so desires.

Unless they make a settlement, debtors shall be held in bonds for sixty days. During that time they shall be brought before the praetor's court in the meeting place on three successive market days, and the amount for which they are judged liable shall be announced; on the third market day they shall suffer capital punishment or be delivered up for sale abroad, across the Tiber.

On the third market day creditors shall cut pieces. Should they have cut more or less than their due, it shall be with impunity.

Against a stranger, title of ownership shall hold good forever.

Table IV
Patria Potestas: Rights of Head of Family

Quickly kill . . . a dreadfully deformed child.

If a father thrice surrender a son for sale, the son shall be free from the father.

A child born ten months after the father's death will not be admitted into a legal inheritance.

Table V
Guardianship; Succession

Females shall remain in guardianship even when they have attained their majority . . . except Vestal Virgins.

Conveyable possessions of a woman under guardianship of agnates[1] cannot be rightfully acquired by *usucapio*,[2] save such possessions as have been delivered up by her with a guardian's sanction.

According as a person shall will regarding his [household], chattels, or guardianship of his estate, this shall be binding.

If a person dies intestate, and has no self-successor, the nearest agnate kinsman shall have possession of deceased's household.

If there is no agnate kinsman, deceased's clansmen shall have possession of his household.

To persons for whom a guardian has not been appointed by will, to them agnates are guardians.

If a man is raving mad, rightful authority over his person and chattels shall belong to his agnates or to his clansmen.

A spendthrift is forbidden to exercise administration over his own goods. . . . A person who, being insane or a spendthrift, is prohibited from administering his own goods shall be under trusteeship of agnates.

---

[1] Male relatives on the father's side. [Editor]
[2] Length of possession. [Editor]

The inheritance of a Roman citizen-freedman shall be made over to his patron if the freedman has died intestate and without self-successor.

Items which are in the category of debts are not included in the division when they have with automatic right been divided into portions of an inheritance.

Debt bequeathed by inheritance is divided proportionally amongst each heir with automatic liability when the details have been investigated.

Table VI
Acquisition and Possession

When a party shall make bond or conveyance, the terms of the verbal declaration are to be held binding. . . .

A person who has been ordained a free man [in a will, on condition] that he bestow a sum of 10,000 pieces on the heir, though he has been sold by the heir, shall win his freedom by giving the money to the purchaser.

It is sufficient to make good such faults as have been named by word of mouth, and that for any flaws which the vendor had expressly denied, he shall undergo penalty of double damage. . . .

Any woman who does not wish to be subjected in this manner to the hand of her husband should be absent three nights in succession every year. . . .

A person shall not dislodge from a framework a [stolen] beam which has been fixed in buildings or a vineyard. . . . Action [is granted] for double damages against a person found guilty of fixing such [stolen] beam.

Table VII
Rights Concerning Land

Ownership within a five-foot strip [between two pieces of land] shall not be acquired by long usage.

The width of a road [extends] to eight feet where it runs straight ahead, sixteen round a bend. . . .

Persons shall mend roadways. If they do not keep them laid with stone, a person may drive his beasts where he wishes.

If rainwater does damage . . . this must be restrained according to an arbitrator's order.

If a water course directed through a public place shall do damage to a private person, he shall have right of suit to the effect that damage shall be repaired for the owner.

Branches of a tree may be lopped off all round to a height of more than 15 feet. . . . Should a tree on a neighbor's farm be bent crooked by a wind and lean over your farm, action may be taken for removal of that tree.

It is permitted to gather up fruit falling down on another man's farm.

Table VIII
Torts or Delicts

If any person has sung or composed against another person a song such as was causing slander or insult to another, he shall be clubbed to death.

If a person has maimed another's limb, let there be retaliation in kind unless he makes agreement for settlement with him.

If he has broken or bruised a freeman's bone with his hand or a club, he shall undergo penalty of 300 *as* pieces; if a slave's, 150.

If he has done simple harm [to another], penalties shall be 25 *as* pieces.

If a four-footed animal shall be said to have caused loss, legal action . . . shall be either the surrender of the thing which damaged, or else the offer of assessment for the damage.

For pasturing on, or cutting secretly by night, another's crops acquired by tillage, there shall be capital punishment in the case of an adult malefactor . . . he shall be hanged and put to death as a sacrifice to Ceres. In the case of a person under the age of puberty, at the discretion of the praetor either he shall be scourged or settlement shall be made for the harm done by paying double damages.

Any person who destroys by burning any building or heap of corn [grain] deposited alongside a house shall be bound, scourged, and put to death by burning at the stake, provided that he has committed the said misdeed with malice aforethought;

but if he shall have committed it by accident, that is, by negligence, it is ordained that he repair the damage, or, if he be too poor to be competent for such punishment, he shall receive a lighter chastisement.

Any person who has cut down another person's trees with harmful intent shall pay 25 *as* pieces for every tree.

If theft has been done by night, if the owner kill the thief, the thief shall be held lawfully killed.

It is forbidden that a thief be killed by day . . . unless he defend himself with a weapon; even though he has come with a weapon, unless he use his weapon and fight back, you shall not kill him. And even if he resists, first call out.

In the case of all other thieves caught in the act, if they are freemen, they should be flogged and adjudged to the person against whom the theft has been committed, provided that the malefactors have committed it by day and have not defended themselves with a weapon; slaves caught in the act of theft should be flogged and thrown from the Rock; boys under the age of puberty should, at the praetor's discretion, be flogged, and the damage done by them should be repaired.

If a person pleads on a case in theft in which the thief has not been caught in the act, the thief must compound for the loss by paying double damages. . . .

No person shall practice usury at a rate more than one twelfth . . . A usurer is condemned for quadruple amount. . . .

If a patron shall have defrauded his client, he must be solemnly forfeited.

Whosoever shall have allowed himself to be called as witness or shall have been scales-balancer, if he does not as witness pronounce his testimony, he must be deemed dishonored and incapable of acting as witness.

Penalty . . . for false witness . . . a person who has been found guilty of giving false witness shall be hurled down from the Tarpeian Rock. . . .

No person shall hold meetings by night in the city.

Members [of associations] . . . are granted . . . the right to pass any binding rule they like for

themselves provided that they cause no violation of public law.

Table IX
Public Law

*   *   *

The penalty shall be capital punishment for a judge or arbiter legally appointed who has been found guilty of receiving a bribe for giving a decision.

He who shall have roused up a public enemy, or handed over a citizen to a public enemy, must suffer capital punishment.

Putting to death . . . of any man who has not been convicted, whosoever he might be, is forbidden.

Table X
Sacred Law

A dead man shall not be buried or burned within the city.

One must not do more than this [at funerals]; one must not smooth the pyre with an axe. . . .

Women must not tear cheeks or hold chorus of "Alas!" on account of funeral.

When a man is dead one must not gather his bones in order to make a second funeral. An exception [in the case of] death in war or in a foreign land. . . .

Anointing by slaves is abolished, and every kind of drinking bout.

Let there be no costly sprinkling . . . no long garlands . . . no incense boxes. . . .

When a man wins a crown himself or through a chattel or by dint of valor, the crown bestowed on him . . . [may be laid in the grave] with impunity [on the man who won it] or on his father.

To make more than one funeral for one man and to make and spread more than one bier for him . . . this should not occur . . . and a person must not add gold. . . .

But him whose teeth shall have been fastened together with gold, if a person shall bury or burn him along with that gold, it shall be with impunity.

No new pyre or personal burning-mound must be erected nearer than sixty feet to another person's buildings without consent of the owner.

*　　*　　*

Table XI
Supplementary Laws

Intermarriage shall not take place between plebeians and patricians.

*　　*　　*

REVIEW QUESTIONS

1. What can you deduce from this selection about early Roman justice?
2. What are the roles and the rights of the family in early Roman law?
3. How important was corporal punishment in Roman law?

PLUTARCH

FROM *Lives*

By the early second century B.C.E., *Rome's conquests outside Italy, along with its increased exposure to Greek culture, began to have a significant impact on Rome's traditional values. In particular, leaders began to emerge whose individualistic behavior challenged ancient traditions that subjugated the interests of the individual to those of family and state. Plutarch's biography of Cato the Elder (234–149* B.C.E.*), however, presents the life of a Roman leader steeped in traditional values and opposed to the inroads that Greek culture was making into Roman society.*

From *Lives*, by Plutarch, translated by Bernadotte Perrin, vol. 2 (Cambridge, Mass.: Harvard University Press, 1914).

*　　*　　*

FROM **Marcus Cato the Elder**

The family of Marcus Cato, it is said, was of Tusculan origin, though he lived, previous to his career as soldier and statesman, on an inherited estate in the country of the Sabines. His ancestors commonly passed for men of no note whatever, but Cato himself extols his father, Marcus, as a brave man and good soldier. He also says that his grandfather, Cato, often won prizes for soldierly valour, and received from the state treasury, because of his bravery, the price of five horses which had been killed under him in battle. The Romans used to call men who had no family distinction, but were coming into public notice through their own achievements, "new men," and such they called Cato. But he himself used to say that as far as office and distinction went, he was indeed new, but having regard to ancestral deeds of valour, he was oldest of the old. His third name was not Cato at first, but Priscus. Afterwards he got the surname of Cato for his great abilities. The Romans call a man who is wise and prudent, *catus*.

*　　*　　*

His physical body—since he laboured from the very first with his own hands, held to a temperate way of life, and performed military duties—was very serviceable, vigorous, and healthy. His eloquence—a second body, as it were, and an instrument with which to perform not only necessary, but also high and noble services—he developed and perfected in the villages and towns about Rome. There he served as advocate for all who needed him, and got the reputation of being, first a zealous pleader, and then a capable orator. Thenceforth the weight and dignity of his character revealed themselves more and more to those who had dealings with him; they saw that he was bound to be a man of great affairs, and have a leading place in the state. For he not only gave his services in legal contests without fee of any sort, but did not appear to cherish even the reputation won in such contests. For he was more desirous of high reputation in battles and campaigns against the enemy, and while he was yet a mere youth had his breast covered with honourable wounds. He says himself that he made his first campaign when he was seventeen years old, at the time when Hannibal was consuming Italy with the flames of his successes.

In battle, he showed himself effective in hand combat, sure and steadfast of foot, and with a fierce expression. With threatening speech and harsh cries he would advance upon the foe, for he rightly thought, and tried to show others, that often-times such action terrifies the enemy more than does the sword. On the march, he carried his own armour on foot, while a single servant followed in charge of his camp provisions. With this man, it is said, he was never angry, and never scolded him when he served up a meal; he actually assisted in most of such preparations, provided he was free from his military duties. Water was what he drank on his campaigns, except that once in a while, in a raging thirst, he would call for vinegar, or, when his strength was failing, would add a little wine.

Near his fields was the cottage which had once belonged to Manius Curius, a hero of three triumphs. To this he would often go, and the sight of the small farm and the simple dwelling led him to think of their former owner, who, though he had

become the greatest of the Romans, had subdued the most warlike nations, and driven Pyrrhus out of Italy. Nevertheless, he tilled this little patch of ground with his own hands and occupied this cottage, after three triumphs. Here it was that the ambassadors of the Samnites once found him seated at his hearth cooking turnips, and offered him much gold; but he dismissed them, saying that a man whom such a meal satisfied had no need of gold, and for his part he thought that a more honourable thing than the possession of gold was the conquest of its possessors. Cato would go away with his mind full of these things, and on viewing again his own house and lands and servants and way of life, would increase the labours of his hands and reduce his extravagances.

*   *   *

The influence which Cato's oratory won for him increased, and men called him a Roman Demosthenes; but his manner of life was even more talked about and carried abroad. For his oratorical ability set before young men not only a goal which many already were striving eagerly to attain, but a man who worked with his own hands, as his fathers did, and was contented with a cold breakfast, a frugal dinner, simple clothing, and a humble dwelling—one who thought more of rejecting the extras of life than of possessing them. The Roman commonwealth had now grown too large to keep its earlier integrity. The conquest of many kingdoms and peoples had brought a large mixture of customs, and the adoption of ways of life of every sort. It was natural, therefore, that men should admire Cato, when they saw that, whereas other men were broken down by labors and weakened by pleasures, he was victor over both. And this too, not only while he was still young and ambitious, but even in his old age, after consulship and triumph. Then, like some victorious athlete, he persisted in the regimen of his training, and kept his mind unaltered to the last.

He tells us that he never wore expensive clothing; that he drank the same wine as his slaves; that as for fish and meats, he would buy enough for his dinner from the public stalls—and even this for

Rome's sake, that he might strengthen his body for military service. He once inherited an embroidered Babylonian robe, but sold it at once; not a single one of his farm-houses had plastered walls; he never paid much for a slave, since he did not want them to be delicately beautiful, but sturdy workers, such as grooms and herdsmen. And these he thought it his duty to sell when they got old, instead of feeding them when they were useless; and that in general, he thought nothing cheap that one could do without. He said also that he bought lands where crops were raised and cattle herded, not those where lawns were sprinkled and paths swept for pleasure.

These things were thought by some to be the result of the man's stinginess; but others excused them in the belief that he lived in this way only to correct and moderate the extravagance of others. However, for my part, I regard his treatment of his slaves like beasts of burden, using them to the utmost, and then, when they were old, driving them off and selling them, as the mark of a very mean nature, which recognizes no tie between man and man but that of profit.... A kindly man will take good care even of his horses when they are worn out with age, and of his dogs, too, not only in their puppyhood, but when their old age needs nursing....

We should not treat living creatures like shoes or pots and pans, casting them aside when they are bruised and worn out with service; but, if for no other reason, than for the sake of practice in kindness to our fellow men, we should accustom ourselves to mildness and gentleness in our dealings with other creatures. I certainly would not sell even an ox that had worked for me, just because he was old, much less an elderly man, removing him from his habitual place and customary life, as it were from his native land, for a paltry price, useless as he is to those who sell him and as he will be to those who buy him. But Cato, boasting of such things, says that he left in Spain even the horse which had carried him through his military campaign, that he might not tax the city with the cost of its transportation home. Whether these things should be set down to greatness of spirit or littleness of mind, is an open question.

But in other matters, his self-restraint was beyond measure admirable. For instance, when he was in command of an army, he took for himself and his staff not more than three bushels of wheat a month, and for his beasts of burden, less than a bushel and a half of barley a day. He received Sardinia to govern as his province; and whereas his predecessors used to charge the public treasury for their tents, couches, and clothing, ... his simple economy stood out in an incredible contrast. He made no demands whatever upon the public treasury, and made his circuit of the cities on foot, followed by a single public officer, who carried his robe and cup for libations to the gods. And yet, though in such matters he showed himself mild and lenient to those under his authority, in other ways he displayed a dignity and severity proper to the administration of justice. He carried out the edicts of the government in a direct and masterful way so that the Roman power never inspired its subjects with greater fear or affection.

*   *   *

He dealt with the Athenians through an interpreter. He could have spoken to them directly, but he always clung to his native ways, and mocked at those who were lost in admiration of anything that was Greek.

*   *   *

Ten years after his consulship, Cato was a candidate for the censorship. This office towered, as it were, above every other civic honour, and was, in a way, the high point of a political career. The variety of its powers was great, including that of examining into the lives and manners of the citizens. Its creators thought that no one should be left to his own ways and desires, without inspection and review, either in his marrying, having children, ordering his daily life, or in the entertainment of his friends. Thinking that these things revealed a man's real character more than did his public and political career, they set men in office to watch, warn, and chastise, that no one should turn to vices and give up his native and customary way of life. They chose to this office one of the so-called patricians, and one of the plebeians. These officers were called censors, and they had authority to degrade a knight, or to expel a senator who led a wild and disorderly life. They also revised the assessments of property, and arranged the citizens in lists [for military service] according to their social and political classes. There were other great powers also connected with the office.

Therefore, when Cato became a candidate, nearly all the best known and most influential men of the senatorial party united to oppose him. The men of noble parentage among them were moved by jealousy, thinking that nobility of birth would be trampled if men of lowly origin forced their way up to the summits of honour and power; while those who were conscious of base practices and of a departure from ancestral customs, feared the severity of the man, which was sure to be harsh and unyielding in the exercise of power. Therefore, after due consultation and preparation, they put up in opposition to Cato seven candidates for the office, who sought the favour of the people with promises of mild conduct in office, supposing that they wanted to be ruled with a lax and indulgent hand. Cato, on the contrary, showed no inclination to be agreeable whatever, but plainly threatened wrong-doers in his speeches, and loudly cried that the city had need of a great purification. He urged the people, if they were wise, not to choose the most agreeable physician, but the one who was most in earnest. He himself, he said, was such a physician, and so was Valerius Flaccus, of the patricians. With him as colleague, and him alone, he thought he could cut the excessive luxury and effeminacy of the time. As for the rest of the candidates, he saw that they were all trying to force their way into the office in order to administer it badly, since they feared those who would administer it well. And so truly great were the Roman voters, and so worthy of great leaders, that they did not fear Cato's rigour and haughty independence, but rejected those candidates who, it was believed, would do everything to please them, and elected Flaccus to the office along with Cato.

* * *

As censor, Cato paid not the slightest heed to his accusers, but grew still more strict. He cut off the pipes by which people conveyed part of the public water supply into their private houses and gardens; he upset and demolished all buildings that encroached on public land; he reduced the cost of public works to the lowest, and forced the rent of public lands to the highest possible figure. All these things brought much hatred upon him.

* * *

Still, it appears that the people approved of his censorship to an amazing extent. At any rate, after erecting a statue to his honour in the temple of Health, they commemorated in the inscription upon it, not the military commands nor the triumph of Cato, but, as the inscription may be translated, the fact "that when the Roman state was tottering to its fall, he was made censor, and by helpful guidance, wise restraints, and sound teachings, restored it again." . . .

* * *

He was also a good father, a considerate husband, and a household manager of no little talent; nor did he give only a fitful attention to this, as a matter of little or no importance. Therefore, I think I ought to give suitable instances of his conduct in these relations. He married a wife who was of higher birth than she was rich, thinking that, although the rich and the high-born may be alike given to pride, still, women of high birth have such a horror of what is disgraceful that they are more obedient to their husbands in all that is honourable. He used to say that the man who struck his wife or child, laid violent hands on the holiest of holy things. Also that he thought it more praiseworthy to be a good husband than a great senator, and there was nothing more to admire in Socrates of old than that he was always kind and gentle with his shrewish wife and stupid sons. After the birth of his own son, no business could be so urgent, unless it had a public character, as to prevent him from being present when his wife bathed and wrapped the babe. For the mother nursed it herself, and often gave her breast also to the infants of her slaves, that so they might come to cherish a broth-erly affection for her son. As soon as the boy showed signs of understanding, his father took him under his own charge and taught him to read, although he had an accomplished slave, Chilo by name, who was a school-teacher, and taught many boys. Still, Cato thought it not right, as he tells us himself, that his son should be scolded by a slave, or have his ears tweaked when he was slow to learn, still less that he should be indebted to his slave for such a priceless thing as education. He was therefore himself not only the boy's reading-teacher, but his tutor in law, and his athletic trainer, and he taught his son not merely to hurl the javelin and fight in armour and ride the horse, but also to box, to endure heat and cold, and to swim strongly through the eddies and billows of the Tiber. His "History of Rome," as he tells us himself, he wrote out with his own hand and in large characters, that his son might have in his own home an aid to acquaintance with his country's ancient traditions. He declares that his son's presence put him on guard against making indecencies of speech as if in the presence of the Vestal Virgins, and that he never bathed with him. This, indeed, would seem to have been a general taboo with the Romans, for even fathers-in-law avoided bathing with their sons-in-law, because they were ashamed to uncover their nakedness. Afterwards, however, when they had learned from the Greeks their freedom in going naked before men, they in their turn infected the Greeks with the practice of doing so even before women.

*   *   *

He owned many slaves, and usually bought those prisoners of war who were young and still capable of being reared and trained. Not one of his slaves ever entered another man's house unless sent there by Cato or his wife, and when any of them was asked what Cato was doing, he always answered that he did not know. A slave of his was expected either to be busy about the house, or to be asleep, and he preferred the sleepy ones. He thought these gentler than the wakeful ones, and that those who had enjoyed the gift of sleep were better for any kind of service than those who lacked it. In the

belief that his slaves were led into most mischief by their sexual passions, he required that the males should have sex with the female slaves of the house at a fixed price, but should never approach any other woman.

At the outset, when Cato was still poor and in military service, he found no fault at all with what was served up to him, declaring that it was shameful for a man to quarrel with a servant over food and drink. But afterwards, when his circumstances were improved and he used to entertain his friends and colleagues at table, no sooner was the dinner over than he would flog those slaves who had been unsat-isfactory in preparing or serving it. He was always arranging that his slaves should have feuds and disagreements among themselves; harmony among them made him suspicious and fearful of them. He had those who were suspected of some capital offence brought to trial before all their fellow ser-vants, and, if convicted, put to death.

*   *   *

He used to lend money also to those of his slaves who wished it, and they would buy boys with it, and after training and teaching them for a year, at Cato's expense, would sell them again. Many of these boys Cato would retain for himself, counting to the credit of the slave the highest price bid for his boy by outsiders. He tried to persuade his son also to such investments, by saying that it was not the part of a man, but of a widow woman, to lessen his property. But surely Cato was going too far when he said that a man should be admired and glorified like a god if the final inventory of his property showed that he had added to it more than he had inherited.

When he was now well on in years, there came as delegates from Athens to Rome, Carneades the Academic, and Diogenes the Stoic philosopher, to beg the reversal of a certain decision against the Athenian people, which imposed upon them a heavy fine. Upon the arrival of these philosophers, the most studious of the city's youth hastened to wait upon them, and became their devoted and admiring listeners. The charm of Carneades espe-cially, which had boundless power, and a fame not inferior to its power, won large and sympathetic audiences, and filled the city, like a rushing mighty wind, with the noise of his praises. Report spread far and wide that a Greek of amazing talent, who disarmed all opposition by the magic of his eloquence, had infused a tremendous passion into the youth of the city—in consequence of which they gave up their other pleasures and pursuits and were "possessed" about philosophy. The other Romans were pleased at this, and glad to see their young men lay hold of Greek culture and associate with such admirable men. But Cato, at the very outset, when this zeal for discussion came into the city, was distressed—fearing that the young men, by giving this direction to their ambition, should come to love a reputation based on mere words more than one achieved by military deeds. And when the fame of the visiting philosophers rose yet higher in the city, and their first speeches before the Senate were interpreted, at his own instance and request, by so conspicuous a man as Gaius Acilius, Cato determined, on some excuse or other, to rid the city of them all. So he rose in the Senate and condemned the city officials for keeping for so long a time a delegation composed of men who could easily secure anything they wished, so persuasive were they. "We ought," he said, "to make up our minds one way or another, and vote on what the delegation proposes, in order that these men may return to their schools and lecture to the sons of Greece, while the youth of Rome give ear to their laws and officials, as before."

This he did, not, as some think, out of personal hostility to Carneades, but because he was wholly opposed to philosophy, and made mock of all Greek culture and training, out of patriotic Roman zeal. He says, for instance, that Socrates was a mighty talker, who attempted, as best he could, to be his country's tyrant, by abolishing its customs, and by enticing his fellow citizens into opinions contrary to the laws. . . . And seeking to prejudice his son against Greek culture, he declared, in the tone of a prophet or a seer, that Rome would lose her empire when she had become infected with Greek literature. But time has certainly shown the emptiness of this pessimistic declaration, for while the city was at the height of its empire, she made every form of Greek learning and culture her own.

*　　*　　*

Review Questions

1. What were the virtues that Cato prized most highly?
2. What were his reasons for opposing the spread of Greek culture?
3. How did he treat his slaves?
4. What were his attitudes toward women?

Cicero

FROM *On the Laws*

Whereas Cato the Elder epitomizes the traditionalists' resistance to the advances of Greek culture in the late Roman Republic, Cicero (106–43 B.C.E.) is that era's leading representative of Greek ideals. A foremost legal expert and compelling orator, he was a major political figure during the era of the rise of Julius Caesar. He was eventually executed after Caesar's assassination for advocating the restoration of the power of the Roman Senate. His most significant influence on the later Western intellectual tradition, however, lies in his prolific production as a writer. It was largely through his works that Greco-Roman thought was transmitted to later eras. The following selection is from Cicero's On the Laws, *in which, through the mechanism of dialogue that was used so well by earlier Greek philosophers, he propounds his concept of the ideal state.*

From *De Legibus* (*On the Laws*), by Cicero, translated by Clinton W. Keyes (Cambridge, Mass.: Harvard University Press, 1928), pp. 311–91.

*　　*　　*

ATTICUS: Yet if you ask what I expect of you, I consider it a logical thing that, since you have already written a treatise on the constitution of the ideal State, you should also write one on its laws. For I note that this was done by your beloved Plato, whom you admire, revere above all others, and love above all others.

MARCUS: Is it your wish, then, that, as he discussed the institutions of States and the ideal laws, . . . sometimes walking about, sometimes resting— you recall his description—we, in like manner, strolling or taking our ease among these stately poplars on the green and shady river bank, shall discuss the same subjects along somewhat broader lines than the practice of the courts calls for? . . .

MARCUS: And you are wise, for you must understand that in no other kind of discussion can one bring out so clearly what Nature's gifts to man are, what a wealth of most excellent possessions the human mind enjoys, what the purpose is, to strive after and accomplish which we have been born and placed in this world, what it is that unites men, and what natural fellowship there is among them. For it is only after all these things have been made clear that the origin of Law and Justice can be discovered.

ATTICUS: Then you do not think that the science of law is to be derived from the praetor's edict, as the majority do now, or from the Twelve Tables, as people used to think, but from the deepest mysteries of philosophy?

MARCUS: Quite right; for in our present conversation, Pomponius, we are not trying to learn how to protect ourselves legally, or how to answer clients' questions. Such problems may be impor-

tant, and in fact they are; for in former times many eminent men made a specialty of their solution, and at present one person performs this duty with the greatest authority and skill. But in our present investigation we intend to cover the whole range of universal Justice and Law in such a way that our own civil law, as it is called, will be confined to a small and narrow corner. For we must explain the nature of Justice, and this must be sought for in the nature of man; we must also consider the laws by which States ought to be governed; then we must deal with the enactments and decrees of nations which are already formulated and put in writing; and among these the civil law, as it is called, of the Roman people will not fail to find a place. . . .

MARCUS: . . . now let us investigate the origins of Justice.

Well then, the most learned men have determined to begin with Law, and it would seem that they are right, if, according to their definition, Law is the highest reason, implanted in Nature, which commands what ought to be done and forbids the opposite. This reason, when firmly fixed and fully developed in the human mind, is Law. And so they believe that Law is intelligence, whose natural function it is to command right conduct and forbid wrongdoing. . . . Now if this is correct, as I think it to be in general, then the origin of Justice is to be found in Law, for Law is a natural force; it is the mind and reason of the intelligent man, the standard by which Justice and Injustice are measured. But since our whole discussion has to do with the reasoning of the populace, it will sometimes be necessary to speak in the popular manner, and give the name of law to that which in written form decrees whatever it wishes, either by command or prohibition. For such is the crowd's definition of law. But in determining what Justice is, let us begin with that supreme Law which had its origin ages before any written law existed or any State had been established. . . .

*   *   *

MARCUS: I will not make the argument long. Your admission leads us to this: that animal which we call man, endowed with foresight and quick intelligence, complex, keen, possessing memory, full of reason and prudence, has been given a certain distinguished status by the supreme God who created him; for he is the only one among so many different kinds and varieties of living beings who has a share in reason and thought, while all the rest are deprived of it. But what is more divine, I will not say in man only, but in all heaven and earth, than reason? And reason, when it is full grown and perfected, is rightly called wisdom. Therefore, since there is nothing better than reason, and since it exists both in man and God, the first common possession of man and God is reason. But those who have reason in common must also have right reason in common. And since right reason is Law, we must believe that men have Law also in common with the gods. Further, those who share Law must also share Justice; and those who share these are to be regarded as members of the same commonwealth. If indeed they obey the same authorities and powers, this is true in a far greater degree; but as a matter of fact they do obey this celestial system, the divine mind, and the God of transcendent power. Hence we must now conceive of this whole universe as one commonwealth of which both gods and men are members.

*   *   *

MARCUS: The points which are now being briefly touched upon are certainly important; but out of all the material of the philosophers' discussions, surely there comes nothing more valuable than the full realization that we are born for Justice, and that right is based, not upon men's opinions, but upon Nature. This fact will immediately be plain if you once get a clear conception of man's fellowship and union with his fellow-men. For no single thing is so like another, so exactly its counterpart, as all of us are to one another. Nay, if bad habits and false beliefs did not twist the weaker minds and turn them in whatever direction they are inclined, no one would be so like his own self as all men would be like all others. And so, however we may define man, a single definition will apply to all. This is a sufficient proof that there is no difference in kind between man and man; for if there were, one definition could not be applicable to all men; and indeed reason, which alone raises us above the level of the beasts and enables us to draw inferences, to prove and disprove, to discuss and solve problems, and to come to conclusions, is certainly common to us all, and, though varying in what it learns, at least in the capacity to learn it is invariable. For the same things are invariably perceived by the senses, and those things which stimulate the senses, stimulate them in the same way in all men; and those rudimentary beginnings of intelligence to which I have referred, which are imprinted on our minds, are imprinted on all minds alike; and speech, the mind's interpreter, though differing in the choice of words, agrees in the sentiments expressed. In fact, there is no human being of any race who, if he finds a guide, cannot attain to virtue.

*   *   *

MARCUS: The next point, then, is that we are so constituted by Nature as to share the sense of Justice with one another and to pass it on to all men. And in this whole discussion I want it understood that what I shall call Nature is that which is implanted in us by Nature; that, however, the corruption caused by bad habits is so great that the sparks of fire, so to speak, which Nature has kindled in us are extinguished by this corruption, and the vices which are their opposites spring up and are established. But if the judgments of men were in agreement with Nature, so that . . . they considered "nothing alien to them which concerns mankind," then Justice would be equally observed by all. For those creatures who have received the gift of reason from Nature have also received right reason, and therefore they have also received the gift of Law, which is right reason applied to command and prohibition. And if they have received Law, they have received Justice also. Now all men have received reason; therefore all men have received Justice. . . .

Now all this is really a preface to what remains to be said in our discussion, and its purpose is to make it more easily understood that Justice is inherent in Nature. After I have said a few words more on this topic, I shall go on to the civil law, the subject which gives rise to all this discourse. . . .

But you see the direction this conversation is to take; our whole discourse is intended to promote the firm foundation of States, the strengthening of cities, and the curing of the ills of peoples. For that reason I want to be especially careful not to lay down first principles that have not been wisely considered and thoroughly investigated. Of course I cannot expect that they will be universally accepted, for that is impossible; but I do look for the approval of all who believe that everything which is right and honourable is to be desired for its own sake, and that nothing whatever is to be accounted a good unless it is praiseworthy in itself, or at least that nothing should be considered a great good unless it can rightly be praised for its own sake.

*   *   *

MARCUS: Once more, then, before we come to the individual laws, let us look at the character and nature of Law, for fear that, though it must be the standard to which we refer everything, we may now and then be led astray by an incorrect use of terms, and forget the rational principles on which our laws must be based.

QUINTUS: Quite so, that is the correct method of exposition.

MARCUS: Well, then, I find that it has been the opinion of the wisest men that Law is not a product of human thought, nor is it any enactment of peoples, but something eternal which rules the whole universe by its wisdom in command and prohibition. Thus they have been accustomed to say that Law is the primal and ultimate mind of God, whose reason directs all things either by compulsion or restraint. Wherefore that Law which the gods have given to the human race has been justly praised; for it is the reason and mind of a wise lawgiver applied to command and prohibition.

*   *   *

MARCUS: So in the very beginning we must persuade our citizens that the gods are the lords and rulers of all things, and that what is done, is done by their will and authority; that they are likewise great benefactors of man, observing the character of every individual, what he does, of what wrong he is guilty, and with what intentions and with what piety he fulfils his religious duties; and that they take note of the pious and the impious. For surely minds which are imbued with such ideas will not fail to form true and useful opinions. Indeed, what is more true than that no one ought to be so foolishly proud as to think that, though reason and intellect exist in himself, they do not exist in the heavens and the universe, or that those things which can hardly be understood by the highest reasoning powers of the human intellect are guided by no reason at all? In truth, the man that is not driven to gratitude by the orderly courses of the stars, the regular alternation of day and night, the gentle progress of the seasons, and the produce of the earth brought forth for our sustenance—how can such an one be accounted a man at all? And since all things that possess reason stand above those things which are without reason, and since it would be sacrilege to say that anything stands above universal Nature, we must admit that reason is inherent in Nature. Who will deny that such beliefs are useful when he remembers how often oaths are used to confirm agreements, how important to our well-being is the sanctity of treaties, how many persons are deterred from crime by the fear of divine punishment, and how sacred an association of citizens becomes when the immortal gods are made members of it, either as judges or as witnesses?

REVIEW QUESTIONS

1. According to Cicero, what is the source of all law?
2. What is the relationship of civil law to law as Cicero defines it?
3. Do you find in this selection any evidence of a Stoic concept of universal human brotherhood and equality?

VIRGIL

FROM The *Aeneid*

The poet Virgil wrote his great Latin epic, the Aeneid, *in the heady years following the victory of Octavian at Actium in 30 b.c.e. and his ascension as the first Roman emperor, Augustus Caesar. It recounts the adventures of Aeneas, a Trojan hero of the Trojan War who, after Troy's capture, makes his way (via Carthage and other locales) to Italy and becomes the progenitor of the eventual Roman supremacy that the* Aeneid *so vividly and lyrically celebrates. Virgil thus links Rome's greatness to the heroic era of the Trojan War. He also provides a truncated and hardly impartial account of Rome's history from Aeneas's time to Virgil's own day.*

The selection below (from Book 6) is excerpted from a long discourse by Aeneas's dead father, Anchises, during Aeneas's visit to the Underworld, where he is conducted into Anchises' presence. Anchises has brought Aeneas to a spot from which he can point out to his son the spirits of the men whose deeds brought Rome to its pinnacle of greatness.

From *Virgil's Aeneid*, Harvard Classics, Vol. 13, translated by John Dryden (New York: P. F. Collier & Son, 1909), pp. 236–240.

*   *   *

Thus having said, the father spirit leads
The priestess and his son thro' swarms of shades,
And takes a rising ground, from thence to see
The long procession of his progeny.
"Survey," pursued the sire, "this airy throng,
As, offer'd to thy view, they pass along.
These are th' Italian names, which fate will join
With ours, and graff upon the Trojan line.

Observe the youth who first appears in sight,
And holds the nearest station to the light,
Already seems to snuff the vital air,
And leans just forward, on a shining spear:
Silvius is he, thy last-begotten race,
But first in order sent, to fill thy place;
An Alban name, but mix'd with Dardan blood,
Born in the covert of a shady wood:
Him fair Lavinia, thy surviving wife,

Shall breed in groves, to lead a solitary life.
In Alba he shall fix his royal seat,
And, born a king, a race of kings beget.
Then Procas, honor of the Trojan name,
Capys, and Numitor, of endless fame.
A second Silvius after these appears;
Silvius Æneas, for thy name he bears;
For arms and justice equally renown'd,
Who, late restor'd, in Alba shall be crown'd.
How great they look! how vig'rously they wield
Their weighty lances, and sustain the shield!
But they, who crown'd with oaken wreaths appear,
Shall Gabian walls and strong Fidena rear;
Nomentura, Bola, with Pometia, found;
And raise Collatian tow'rs on rocky ground.
All these shall then be towns of mighty fame,
Tho' now they lie obscure, and lands without a
    name.
See Romulus the great, born to restore
The crown that once his injur'd grandsire wore.
This prince a priestess of your blood shall bear,
And like his sire in arms he shall appear.
Two rising crests his royal head adorn;
Born from a god, himself to godhead born:
His sire already signs him for the skies,
And marks the seat amidst the deities.
Auspicious chief! thy race, in times to come,
Shall spread the conquests of imperial Rome—
Rome, whose ascending tow'rs shall heav'n invade,
Involving earth and ocean in her shade;
High as the Mother of the Gods in place,
And proud, like her, of an immortal race.
Then, when in pomp she makes the Phrygian
    round,
With golden turrets on her temples crown'd;
A hundred gods her sweeping train supply;
Her offspring all, and all command the sky.
    "Now fix your sight, and stand intent, to see
Your Roman race, and Julian progeny.
The mighty Cæsar waits his vital hour,
Impatient for the world, and grasps his promis'd
    pow'r.
But next behold the youth of form divine,
Cæsar himself, exalted in his line;
Augustus, promis'd oft, and long foretold,
Sent to the realm that Saturn rul'd of old;

Born to restore a better age of gold.
Afric and India shall his pow'r obey;
He shall extend his propagated sway
Beyond the solar year, without the starry way,
Where Atlas turns the rolling heav'ns around,
And his broad shoulders with their lights are
    crown'd
At his foreseen approach, already quake
The Caspian kingdoms and Mæotian lake:
Their seers behold the tempest from afar,
And threat'ning oracles denounce the war.
Nile hears him knocking at his sev'nfold gates,
And seeks his hidden spring, and fears his
    nephew's fates.
Nor Hercules more lands or labors knew,
Not tho' the brazen-footed hind he slew,
Freed Erymanthus from the foaming boar,
And dipp'd his arrows in Lernæan gore;
Nor Bacchus, turning from his Indian war,
By tigers drawn triumphant in his car,
From Nisus' top descending on the plains,
With curling vines around his purple reins.
And doubt we yet thro' dangers to pursue
The paths of honor, and a crown in view?
But what's the man, who from afar appears?
His head with olive crown'd, his hand a censer
    bears,
His hoary beard and holy vestments bring
His lost idea back: I know the Roman king.
He shall to peaceful Rome new laws ordain,
Call'd from his mean abode a scepter to sustain.
Him Tullus next in dignity succeeds,
An active prince, and prone to martial deeds.
He shall his troops for fighting fields prepare,
Disus'd to toils, and triumphs of the war.
By dint of sword his crown he shall increase,
And scour his armor from the rust of peace.
Whom Ancus follows, with a fawning air,
But vain within, and proudly popular.
Next view the Tarquin kings, th' avenging sword
Of Brutus, justly drawn, and Rome restor'd.
He first renews the rods and ax severe,
And gives the consuls royal robes to wear.
His sons, who seek the tyrant to sustain,
And long for arbitrary lords again,
With ignominy scourg'd, in open sight,

He dooms to death deserv'd, asserting public right.
Unhappy man, to break the pious laws
Of nature, pleading in his children's cause!
Howe'er the doubtful fact is understood,
'Tis love of honor, and his country's good:
The consul, not the father, sheds the blood.
Behold Torquatus the same track pursue;
And, next, the two devoted Decii view:
The Drusian line, Camillus loaded home
With standards well redeem'd, and foreign foes
    o'ercome.
The pair you see in equal armor shine,
Now, friends below, in close embraces join;
But, when they leave the shady realms of night,
And, cloth'd in bodies, breathe your upper light,
With mortal hate each other shall pursue:
What wars, what wounds, what slaughter shall
    ensue!
From Alpine heights the father first descends;
His daughter's husband in the plain attends:
His daughter's husband arms his eastern friends.
Embrace again, my sons, be foes no more;
Nor stain your country with her children's gore!
And thou, the first, lay down thy lawless claim,
Thou, of my blood, who bear'st the Julian name!
Another comes, who shall in triumph ride,
And to the Capitol his chariot guide,
From conquer'd Corinth, rich with Grecian spoils.
And yet another, fam'd for warlike toils,
On Argos shall impose the Roman laws,
And on the Greeks revenge the Trojan cause;
Shall drag in chains their Achillean race;
Shall vindicate his ancestors' disgrace,

And Pallas, for her violated place
Great Cato there, for gravity renown'd,
And conqu'ring Cossus goes with laurels crown'd.
Who can omit the Gracchi? who declare
The Scipios' worth, those thunderbolts of war,
The double bane of Carthage?   Who can see
Without esteem for virtuous poverty,
Severe Fabricius, or can cease t' admire
The plowman consul in his coarse attire?
Tir'd as I am, my praise the Fabii claim;
And thou, great hero, greatest of thy name,
Ordain'd in war to save the sinking state,
And, by delays, to put a stop to fate!
Let others better mold the running mass
Of metals, and inform the breathing brass,
And soften into flesh a marble face;
Plead better at the bar; describe the skies,
And when the stars descend, and when they rise.
But, Rome, 't is thine alone, with awful sway,
To rule mankind, and make the world obey,
Disposing peace and war by thy own majestic
    way;
To tame the proud, the fetter'd slave to free:
These are imperial arts, and worthy thee."

REVIEW QUESTIONS

1. Does Virgil question at all the right of Rome to conquer and rule an empire?
2. How might you contrast Virgil's views on Rome's greatness with the views evidenced in the works of Tacitus decades later?

TACITUS

FROM *Germania*

As the Romans' empire expanded, they came into contact with various peoples. None of them was to have a more significant or enduring influence on the shaping of Western civilization than the Germans, whose chieftains eventually would supplant

Roman authority in western Europe. That at least some Romans had an inkling of the Germans' later importance is evident in the Germania *of the Roman historian Tacitus, who wrote this work at the end of the first century* C.E.

From *The Agricola and Germany of Tacitus*, translated by A. J. Church and W. J. Brodribb (Basingstoke, Eng.: Macmillan, 1877).

*   *   *

For my own part, I agree with those who think that the tribes of Germany are free from all taint of intermarriages with foreign nations, and that they appear as a distinct, unmixed race, like none but themselves. Hence, too, the same physical peculiarities throughout so vast a population. All have fierce blue eyes, red hair, huge frames, fit only for a sudden exertion. They are less able to bear laborious work. Heat and thirst they cannot in the least endure; to cold and hunger their climate and their soil inure them.

Their country, though somewhat various in appearance, yet generally either bristles with forests or reeks with swamps; it is more rainy on the side of Gaul, bleaker on that of Noricum and Pannonia. It is productive of grain, but unfavourable to fruit-bearing trees; it is rich in flocks and herds, but these are for the most part undersized, and even the cattle have not their usual beauty or noble head. It is number that is chiefly valued; they are in fact the most highly prized, indeed the only riches of the people. Silver and gold the gods have refused to them, whether in kindness or in anger I cannot say. I would not, however, affirm that no vein of German soil produces gold or silver, for who has ever made a search? They care but little to possess or use them. You may see among them vessels of silver, which have been presented to their envoys and chieftains, held as cheap as those of clay. The border population, however, value gold and silver for their commercial utility, and are familiar with, and show preference for, some of our coins. The tribes of the interior use the simpler and more ancient practice of the barter of commodities. They like the old and well-known money, coins milled, or showing a two-horse chariot. They likewise prefer silver to gold, not from any special liking, but because a large number of silver pieces is more convenient for use among dealers in cheap and common articles.

Even iron is not plentiful with them, as we infer from the character of their weapons. But few use swords or long lances. They carry a spear with a narrow and short head, but so sharp and easy to wield that the same weapon serves, according to circumstances, for close or distant conflict. As for the horse-soldier, he is satisfied with a shield and spear; the foot-soldiers also scatter showers of missiles, each man having several and hurling them to an immense distance, and being naked or lightly clad with a little cloak. There is no display about their equipment: their shields alone are marked with very choice colours. A few only have corslets, and just one or two here and there a metal or leathern helmet. Their horses are remarkable neither for beauty nor for fleetness. Nor are they taught various evolutions after our fashion, but are driven straight forward, or so as to make one wheel to the right in such a compact body that none is left behind another. On the whole, one would say that their chief strength is in their infantry, which fights along with the cavalry; admirably adapted to the action of the latter is the swiftness of certain foot-soldiers, who are picked from the entire youth of their country, and stationed in front of the line. Their number is fixed,—a hundred from each canton; and from this they take their name among their countrymen, so that what was originally a mere number has now become a title of distinction. Their line of battle is drawn up in a wedge-like formation. To give ground, provided you return to the attack, is considered prudence rather than cowardice. The bodies of their slain they carry off even in indecisive engagements. To abandon your shield is the basest of crimes; nor may a man thus disgraced be present at the sacred rites, or enter their council; many, indeed, after escaping from battle, have ended their infamy with the halter.

They choose their kings by birth, their generals for merit. These kings have not unlimited or arbitrary power, and the generals do more by example than by authority. If they are energetic, if they are conspicuous, if they fight in the front, they lead because they are admired. But to reprimand, to imprison, even to flog, is permitted to the priests alone, and that not as a punishment, or at the general's bidding, but, as it were, by the mandate of the god whom they believe to inspire the warrior. They also carry with them into battle certain figures and images taken from their sacred groves. And what most stimulates their courage is, that their squadrons or battalions, instead of being formed by chance or by a fortuitous gathering, are composed of families and clans. Close by them, too, are those dearest to them, so that they hear the shrieks of women, the cries of infants. *They* are to every man the most sacred witnesses of his bravery—*they* are his most generous applauders. The soldier brings his wounds to mother and wife, who shrink not from counting or even demanding them and who administer both food and encouragement to the combatants.

Tradition says that armies already wavering and giving way have been rallied by women who, with earnest entreaties and bosoms laid bare, have vividly represented the horrors of captivity, which the Germans fear with such extreme dread on behalf of their women, that the strongest tie by which a state can be bound is the being required to give, among the number of hostages, maidens of noble birth. They even believe that the sex has a certain sanctity and prescience, and they do not despise their counsels, or make light of their answers. In Vespasian's days we saw Veleda, long regarded by many as a divinity. In former times, too, they venerated Aurinia, and many other women, but not with servile flatteries, or with sham deification.

*   *   *

Augury and divination by lot no people practise more diligently. The use of the lots is simple. A little bough is lopped off a fruit-bearing tree, and cut into small pieces; these are distinguished by certain marks, and thrown carelessly and at random over a white garment. In public questions the priest of the particular state, in private the father of the family, invokes the gods, and, with his eyes towards heaven, takes up each piece three times, and finds in them a meaning according to the mark previously impressed on them. If they prove unfavourable, there is no further consultation that day about the matter; if they sanction it, the confirmation of augury is still required. For they are also familiar with the practice of consulting the notes and the flight of birds. It is peculiar to this people to seek omens from horses. Kept at the public expense, in these same woods and groves, are white horses, pure from the taint of earthly labour; these are yoked to a sacred car, and accompanied by the priest and the king, or chief of the tribe, who note their neighings and snortings. No species of augury is more trusted, not only by the people and by the nobility, but also by the priests, who regard themselves as the ministers of the gods, and the horses as acquainted with their will. They have also another method of observing auspices, by which they seek to learn the result of an important war. Having taken, by whatever means, a prisoner from the tribe with whom they are at war, they pit him against a picked man of their own tribe, each combatant using the weapons of their country. The victory of the one or the other is accepted as an indication of the issue.

About minor matters the chiefs deliberate, about the more important the whole tribe. Yet even when the final decision rests with the people, the affair is always thoroughly discussed by the chiefs. They assemble, except in the case of a sudden emergency, on certain fixed days, either at new or at full moon; for this they consider the most auspicious season for the transaction of business. Instead of reckoning by days as we do, they reckon by nights, and in this manner fix both their ordinary and their legal appointments. Night they regard as bringing on day. Their freedom has this disadvantage, that they do not meet simultaneously or as they are bidden, but two or three days are wasted in the delays of assembling. When the multitude think proper,

A MUMMY FROM THE TIME OF THE ROMAN EMPIRE (100 C.E.)

This painted and gilded case contains the mummy of a man with the very un-Egyptian name Artemidorus, who died evidently in his early twenties, shortly after 100 C.E. To what extent are classical and Egyptian artistic elements and symbolism mixed in the decoration of this case? Do you see evidence for the survival of ancient Egyptian religious beliefs and traditions under Roman rule? What is your assessment of the skill of the artist who painted Artemidorus's portrait?

they sit down armed. Silence is proclaimed by the priests, who have on these occasions the right of keeping order. Then the king or the chief, according to age, birth, distinction in war, or eloquence, is heard, more because he has influence to persuade than because he has power to command. If his sentiments displease them, they reject them with murmurs; if they are satisfied, they brandish their spears. The most complimentary form of assent is to express approbation with their weapons.

In their councils an accusation may be preferred or a capital crime prosecuted. Penalties are distinguished according to the offence. Traitors and deserters are hanged on trees; the coward, the unwarlike, the man stained with abominable vices, is plunged into the mire of the morass, with a hurdle put over him. This distinction in punishment means that crime, they think, ought, in being punished, to be exposed, while infamy ought to be buried out of sight. Lighter offences, too, have penalties proportioned to them; he who is convicted, is fined in a certain number of horses or of cattle. Half of the fine is paid to the king or to the state, half to the person whose wrongs are avenged and to his relatives. In these same councils they also elect the chief magistrates, who administer law in the cantons and the towns. Each of these has a hundred associates chosen from the people, who support him with their advice and influence.

They transact no public or private business without being armed. It is not, however, usual for anyone to wear arms till the state has recognised his power to use them. Then in the presence of the council one of the chiefs, or the young man's father, or some kinsman, equips him with a shield and a spear. These arms are what the "toga" is with us, the first honour with which youth is invested. Up to this time he is regarded as a member of a household, afterwards as a member of the commonwealth. Very noble birth or great services rendered by the father secure for lads the rank of a chief; such lads attach themselves to men of mature strength and of long approved valour. It is no shame to be seen among a chief's followers. Even in his escort there are gradations of rank, dependent on the choice of the man to whom they are attached. These follow-ers vie keenly with each other as to who shall rank first with his chief, the chiefs as to who shall have the most numerous and the bravest followers. It is an honour as well as a source of strength to be thus always surrounded by a large body of picked youths; it is an ornament in peace and a defence in war. And not only in his own tribe but also in the neighbouring states it is the renown and glory of a chief to be distinguished for the number and valour of his followers, for such a man is courted by embassies, is honoured with presents, and the very prestige of his name often settles a war.

When they go into battle, it is a disgrace for the chief to be surpassed in valour, a disgrace for his followers not to equal the valour of the chief. And it is an infamy and a reproach for life to have survived the chief, and returned from the field. To defend, to protect him, to ascribe one's own brave deeds to his renown, is the height of loyalty. The chief fights for victory; his vassals fight for their chief. If their native state sinks into the sloth of prolonged peace and repose, many of its noble youths voluntarily seek those tribes which are waging some war, both because inaction is odious to their race, and because they win renown more readily in the midst of peril, and cannot maintain a numerous following except by violence and war. Indeed, men look to the liberality of their chief for their war-horse and their blood-stained and victorious lance. Feasts and entertainments, which, though inelegant, are plentifully furnished, are their only pay. The means of this bounty come from war and rapine. Nor are they as easily persuaded to plough the earth and to wait for the year's produce as to challenge an enemy and earn the honour of wounds. Nay, they actually think it tame and stupid to acquire by the sweat of toil what they might win by their blood.

Whenever they are not fighting, they pass much of their time in the chase, and still more in idleness, giving themselves up to sleep and to feasting, the bravest and the most warlike doing nothing, and surrendering the management of the household, of the home, and of the land, to the women, the old men, and all the weakest members of the family. They themselves lie buried in sloth, a strange combination in their nature that the same men should be so fond of idleness, so averse to peace. It is the custom of the states to bestow by voluntary and individual contribution on the chiefs a present of cattle or of grain, which, while accepted as a compliment, supplies their wants. They are particularly delighted by gifts from neighbouring tribes, which are sent not only by individuals but also by the state, such as choice steeds, heavy armour, trappings, and neckchains. We have now taught them to accept money also.

It is well known that the nations of Germany have no cities, and that they do not even tolerate closely contiguous dwellings. They live scattered and apart, just as a spring, a meadow, or a wood has attracted them. Their villages they do not arrange in our fashion, with the buildings connected and joined together, but every person surrounds his dwelling with an open space, either as a precaution against the disasters of fire, or because they do not know how to build. No use is made by them of stone or tile; they employ timber for all purposes, rude masses without ornament or attractiveness. Some parts of their buildings they stain more carefully with a clay so clear and bright that it resembles painting, or a coloured design. They are wont also to dig out subterranean caves, and pile on them great heaps of dung, as a shelter from winter and as a receptacle for the year's produce, for by such places they mitigate the rigour of the cold. And should an enemy approach, he lays waste the open country, while what is hidden and buried is either not known to exist, or else escapes him from the very fact that it has to be searched for.

They all wrap themselves in a cloak which is fastened with a clasp, or, if this is not forthcoming, with a thorn, leaving the rest of their persons bare. They pass whole days on the hearth by the fire. The wealthiest are distinguished by a dress which is not flowing, like that of the Sarmatae and Parthi, but is tight, and exhibits each limb. They also wear the skins of wild beasts; the tribes on the Rhine and Danube in a careless fashion, those of the interior with more elegance, as not obtaining other clothing by commerce. These select certain animals, the hides of which they strip off and vary them with the spotted skins of beasts, the produce of the outer ocean, and of seas unknown to us. The women have the same dress as the men, except that they generally wrap themselves in linen garments, which they embroider with purple, and do not lengthen out the upper part of their clothing into sleeves. The upper and lower arm is thus bare, and the nearest part of the bosom is also exposed.

Their marriage code, however, is strict, and indeed no part of their manners is more praiseworthy. Almost alone among barbarians they are content with one wife, except a very few among them, and then not from sensuality, but because their noble birth procures for them many offers of alliance. The wife does not bring a dower to the husband, but the husband to the wife. The parents and relatives are present, and pass judgment on the marriage-gifts, gifts not meant to suit a woman's taste, nor such as a bride would deck herself with, but oxen, a caparisoned steed, a shield, a lance, and a sword. With these presents the wife is espoused, and she herself in her turn brings her husband a gift of arms. This they count their strongest bond of union, these their sacred mysteries, these their gods of marriage. Lest the woman should think herself to stand apart from aspirations after noble deeds and from the perils of war, she is reminded by the ceremony which inaugurates marriage that she is her husband's partner in toil and danger, destined to suffer and to dare with him alike both in peace and in war. The yoked oxen, the harnessed steed, the gift of arms, proclaim this fact. She must live and die with the feeling that she is receiving what she must hand down to her children neither tarnished nor depreciated, what future daughters-in-law may receive, and may be so passed on to her grandchildren.

Thus with their virtue protected they live uncorrupted by the allurements of public shows or the stimulant of feastings. Clandestine correspondence is equally unknown to men and women. Very rare for so numerous a population is adultery, the punishment for which is prompt, and in the husband's power. Having cut off the hair of the adulteress and stripped her naked, he expels her from the house in the presence of her kinsfolk, and then flogs her through the whole village. The loss of chastity meets with no indulgence; neither beauty, youth, nor wealth will procure the culprit a husband. No one in Germany laughs at vice, nor do they call it the fashion to corrupt and to be corrupted. Still better is the condition of those states in which only maidens are given in marriage, and where the hopes and expectations of a bride are then finally terminated. They receive one husband, as having one body and one life, that they may have no thoughts beyond, no further-reaching desires, that they may love not so much the husband as the married state. To limit the number of their children or to destroy any of their subsequent offspring is accounted infamous, and good habits are here more effectual than good laws elsewhere.

In every household the children, naked and filthy, grow up with those stout frames and limbs which we so much admire. Every mother suckles her own offspring, and never entrusts it to servants and nurses. The master is not distinguished from the slave by being brought up with greater delicacy. Both live amid the same flocks and lie on the same ground till the freeborn are distinguished by age and recognised by merit. The young men marry late, and their vigour is thus unimpaired. Nor are the maidens hurried into marriage; the same age and a similar stature is required; well-matched and vigorous they wed, and the offspring reproduce the strength of the parents. Sisters' sons are held in as much esteem by their uncles as by their fathers; indeed, some regard the relation as even more sacred and binding, and prefer it in receiving hostages, thinking thus to secure a stronger hold on the affections and a wider bond for the family. But every man's own children are his heirs and successors, and there are no wills. Should there be no issue, the next in succession to the property are his brothers and his uncles on either side. The more relatives he has, the more numerous his connections, the more honoured is his old age; nor are there any advantages in childlessness.

It is a duty among them to adopt the feuds as well as the friendships of a father or a kinsman. These feuds are not implacable; even homicide is expiated by the payment of a certain number of cattle and of sheep, and the satisfaction is accepted by the entire family, greatly to the advantage of the state, since feuds are dangerous in proportion to a people's freedom.

No nation indulges more profusely in entertainments and hospitality. To exclude any human being from their roof is thought impious; every German, according to his means, receives his guest with a well-furnished table. When his supplies are exhausted, he who was but now the host becomes the guide and companion to further hospitality, and without invitation they go to the next house. It matters not; they are entertained with like cordiality. No one distinguishes between an acquaintance and a stranger, as regards the rights of hospitality. It is usual to give the departing guest whatever he may ask for, and a present in return is asked with as little hesitation. They are greatly charmed with gifts, but they expect no return for what they give, nor feel any obligation for what they receive.

On waking from sleep, which they generally prolong to a late hour of the day, they take a bath, oftenest of warm water, which suits a country where winter is the longest of the seasons. After their bath they take their meal, each having a separate seat and table of his own. Then they go armed to business, or no less often to their festal meetings. To pass an entire day and night in drinking disgraces no one. Their quarrels, as might be expected with intoxicated people, are seldom fought out with mere abuse, but commonly with wounds and bloodshed. Yet it is at their feasts that they generally consult on the reconciliation of enemies, on the forming of matrimonial alliances, on the choice of chiefs, finally even on peace and war, for they think that at no time is the mind more open to simplicity of purpose or more warmed to noble aspirations. A race without either natural or acquired cunning, they disclose their hidden thoughts in the freedom of the festivity. Thus the sentiments of all having been discovered and laid bare, the discussion is renewed on the following day, and from each occasion its own peculiar advantage is derived. They deliberate when they have no power to dissemble; they resolve when error is impossible.

A liquor for drinking is made out of barley or other grain, and fermented into a certain resemblance to wine. The dwellers on the river-bank also buy wine. Their food is of a simple kind, consisting of wild-fruit, fresh game, and curdled milk. They satisfy their hunger without elaborate preparation and without delicacies. In quenching their thirst they are not equally moderate. If you indulge their love of drinking by supplying them with as much as they desire, they will be overcome by their own vices as easily as by the arms of an enemy.

One and the same kind of spectacle is always exhibited at every gathering. Naked youths who practise the sport bound in the dance amid swords and lances that threaten their lives. Experience gives them skill, and skill again gives grace; profit or pay are out of the question; however reckless their pastime, its reward is the pleasure of the spectators. Strangely enough they make games of hazard a serious occupation even when sober, and so venturesome are they about gaining or losing, that, when every other resource has failed, on the last and final throw they stake the freedom of their own persons. The loser goes into voluntary slavery; though the younger and stronger, he suffers himself to be bound and sold. Such is their stubborn persistency in a bad practice; they themselves call it honour. Slaves of this kind the owners part with in the way of commerce, and also to relieve themselves from the scandal of such a victory.

The other slaves are not employed after our manner with distinct domestic duties assigned to them, but each one has the management of a house and home of his own. The master requires from the slave a certain quantity of grain, of cattle, and of clothing, as he would from a tenant, and this is the limit of subjection. All other household functions are discharged by the wife and children. To strike a slave or to punish him with bonds or with hard labour is a rare occurrence. They often kill them, not in enforcing strict discipline, but on the impulse of passion, as they would an enemy, only it is done with impunity. The freedmen do not rank much above slaves, and are seldom of any weight in the family, never in the state, with the exception of those tribes which are ruled by kings. There indeed they rise above the freeborn and the noble; elsewhere the inferiority of the freedman marks the freedom of the state.

Of lending money on interest and increasing it by compound interest they know nothing—a more effectual safeguard than if it were prohibited.

Land proportioned to the number of inhabitants is occupied by the whole community in turn, and afterwards divided among them according to rank. A wide expanse of plains makes the partition easy. They till fresh fields every year, and they have still more land than enough; with the richness and extent of their soil, they do not laboriously exert themselves in planting orchards, inclosing meadows, and watering gardens. Corn is the only produce required from the earth; hence even the year itself is not divided by them into as many seasons as with us. Winter, spring, and summer have both a meaning and a name; the name and blessings of autumn are alike unknown.

In their funerals there is no pomp; they simply observe the custom of burning the bodies of illustrious men with certain kinds of wood. They do not heap garments or spices on the funeral pile. The weapons of the dead man and in some cases his horse are consigned to the fire. A turf mound forms the tomb. Monuments with their lofty elaborate splendour they reject as oppressive to the dead. Tears and lamentations they soon dismiss; grief and sorrow but slowly. It is thought becoming for women to bewail, for men to remember, the dead.

Such on the whole is the account which I have received of the origin and manners of the entire German people.

*   *   *

REVIEW QUESTIONS

1. As described by Tacitus, what were some of the principal values that governed German society?
2. How did those values compare with values of imperial Roman society as evidenced in some of the preceding readings?
3. Can you discern parallels or contrasts between Tacitus's views on Germans and the earlier views (see Chapter 3) of Hippocrates on the people of Europe?

TACITUS

FROM **The Speech of Calgacus**

*The following selection is from another work by Tacitus—in fact, his first historical work, written around the year 98 c.e.—*The Life and Character of Julius Agricola. *The work as a whole records and celebrates the life of Tacitus's father-in-law, a notable general in the Roman army. It also provides a brief account of the geography of ancient Britain and, as in* Germania, *evidences Tacitus's admiration of its native tribal inhabitants, in this instance, the Britons. Presented below is Tacitus's account of a speech by a Briton chieftain named Calgacus, who exhorts his countrymen to resist the impending Roman invasion that Agricola helped lead.*

From *The Agricola and Germany of Tacitus*, translated by A. J. Church and W. J. Brodribb (London: Macmillan, 1877).

*   *   *

Early in the summer Agricola sustained a domestic affliction in the loss of a son born a year before, a calamity which he endured, neither with the ostentatious fortitude displayed by many brave men, nor, on the other hand, with the tears and grief of a woman. In his sorrow he found one source of relief in war. Having sent on a fleet, which by its ravages at various points might cause a vague and wide-spread alarm, he advanced with a lightly equipped force, including in its ranks some Britons of remarkable bravery, whose fidelity had been tried through years of peace, as far as the Grampian mountains, which the enemy had already occupied. For the Britons, indeed, in no way cowed by the result of the late engagement, had made up their minds to be either avenged or enslaved, and convinced at length that a common danger must be averted by union, had, by embassies and treaties, summoned forth the whole strength of all their states. More than 30,000 armed men were now to be seen, and still there were pressing in all the youth of the country, with all whose old age was yet hale and vigorous, men renowned in war and bearing each decorations of his own. Meanwhile, among the many leaders, one superior to the rest in valour and in birth, Galgacus by name, is said to

have thus harangued the multitude gathered around him and clamouring for battle:—

"Whenever I consider the origin of this war and the necessities of our position, I have a sure confidence that this day, and this union of yours, will be the beginning of freedom to the whole of Britain. To all of us slavery is a thing unknown; there are no lands beyond us, and even the sea is not safe, menaced as we are by a Roman fleet. And thus in war and battle, in which the brave find glory, even the coward will find safety. Former contests, in which, with varying fortune, the Romans were resisted, still left in us a last hope of succour, inasmuch as being the most renowned nation of Britain, dwelling in the very heart of the country, and out of sight of the shores of the conquered, we could keep even our eyes unpolluted by the contagion of slavery. To us who dwell on the uttermost confines of the earth, and of freedom, this remote sanctuary of Britain's glory has up to this time been a defence. Now, however, the furthest limits of Britain are thrown open, and the unknown always passes for something peculiarly grand. But there are no tribes beyond us, nothing indeed but waves and rocks, and the yet more terrible Roman, from whose oppression escape is vainly sought by obedience and submission. Robbers of the world, having by their universal plunder exhausted the land, they rifle the deep. If the enemy be rich, they are rapacious; if he be poor, they lust for dominion; neither the east nor the west has been able to satisfy them. Alone among men they covet with equal eagerness poverty and riches. To robbery, slaughter, plunder, they give the lying name of empire, and where they make a solitude they call it peace.

"Nature has willed that every man's children and kindred should be his dearest objects. Yet these are torn from us by conscriptions to be slaves elsewhere. Our wives and our sisters, even though they may escape violation from the enemy, are dishonoured under the names of friendship and hospitality. Our goods and fortunes they collect for their tribute, our harvests for their granaries. Our very hands and bodies, under the lash and in the midst of insult, are worn down by the toil of clearing forests and morasses. Creatures born to slavery are sold once for all, and are, moreover, fed by their masters; but Britain is daily purchasing, is daily feeding, her own enslaved people. And as in a household the last comer among the slaves is always the butt of his companions, so we in a world long used to slavery, as the newest and the most contemptible, are marked out for destruction. We have neither fruitful plains, nor mines, nor harbours, for the working of which we may be spared. Valour, too, and high spirit in subjects, are offensive to rulers; besides, remoteness and seclusion, while they give safety, provoke suspicion. Since then you cannot hope for quarter, take courage, I beseech you, whether it be safety or renown that you hold most precious. Under a woman's leadership the Brigantes were able to burn a colony, to storm a camp, and had not success issued in supineness, might have thrown off the yoke. Let us, then, a fresh and unconquered people, never likely to abuse our freedom, show forthwith at the very first onset what heroes Caledonia has in reserve.

"Do you suppose that the Romans will be as brave in war as they are licentious in peace? To our strifes and discords they owe their fame, and they turn the errors of an enemy to the renown of their own army, an army, which, composed as it is of every variety of nations, is held together by success

and will be broken up by disaster. These Gauls and Germans, and, I blush to say, these numerous Britons, who, though they lend their lives to support a stranger's rule, have been its enemies longer than its subjects, you cannot imagine to be bound by fidelity and affection. Fear and terror there certainly are, feeble bonds of attachment; remove them, and those who have ceased to fear will begin to hate. All the incentives to victory are on our side. The Romans have no wives to kindle their courage; no parents to taunt them with flight; many have either no country or one far away. Few in number, dismayed by their ignorance, looking around upon a sky, a sea, and forests which are all unfamiliar to them; hemmed in, as it were, and enmeshed, the Gods have delivered them into our hands. Be not frightened by idle display, by the glitter of gold and of silver, which can neither protect nor wound. In the very ranks of the enemy we shall find our own forces. Britons will acknowledge their own cause; Gauls will remember past freedom; the other Germans will abandon them, as but lately did the Usipii. Behind them there is nothing to dread. The forts are ungarrisoned; the colonies in the hands of aged men; what with disloyal subjects and oppressive rulers, the towns are ill-affected and rife with discord. On the one side you have a general and an army; on the other, tribute, the mines, and all the other penalties of an enslaved people. Whether you endure these for ever, or instantly avenge them, this field is to decide. Think, therefore, as you advance to battle, at once of your ancestors and of your posterity."

They received his speech with enthusiasm, and as is usual among barbarians, with songs, shouts and discordant cries.

Review Questions

1. In Tacitus's telling, what are the native Britons' incentives to resist the Roman onslaught?
2. Based on this reading and the preceding selection from Tacitus's *Germania*, how might Tacitus's view of the Roman empire be contrasted with Virgil's in the *Aeneid*?

6 ⚬ THE TRANSFORMATION OF ROME

By 300 C.E., the emperor Diocletian and his colleagues had reorganized the Roman Empire, which now appeared to be more prosperous and stable than it had been for decades. Paganism, a convenient but misleading name for the broad spectrum of ancient beliefs and religions, remained dominant; indeed, Diocletian soon began a vigorous persecution of the Christian sect. But this world was on the verge of a profound change. Starting with the conversion of the emperor Constantine in 312 C.E., Christianity gradually triumphed, becoming the official religion of Rome. Missionary work among the barbarian tribes succeeded in bringing new peoples such as the Franks into the Christian fold. The barbarian kingdoms and the Christian Church, through its bishops and monasteries, transformed the legacies of the ancient world and created the new society of early medieval Europe.

In the centuries before Christianity emerged from persecution, the new faith found adherents because of its promise of salvation, the supportive and caring nature of early Christian communities, and the witness of generations of martyrs. In addition to the texts collected into the New Testament and approved by Church leaders, many other documents reveal both the spirit of the early martyrs and the effects of martyrdom on the people who witnessed it. The account of Perpetua's imprisonment and death in 205 C.E. is a powerful example.

After Christianity became the empire's official religion, Augustine of Hippo (in North Africa) was perhaps the most significant voice of this late Roman world. His many books continued to influence theologians in the medieval and early modern periods and down to our own day. Augustine tried to account for the sack of Rome in 410 C.E. in terms that strengthened Christian beliefs and denied pagans the chance to blame the new religion for the empire's defeats. Augustine, laying the foundations for doctrines on original sin and predestination of the saved and damned, also took on one of the empire's most important social and economic institutions, slavery, and fitted it into Christian belief. Augustine also wrote a spiritual autobiography, the Confessions, *that was a model of self-reflection for many centuries.*

As emperor and high priest of the Roman state cult, Constantine and his successors retained the same legal rights over Christianity that earlier rulers had exercised over pagan cults. This is reflected in the Roman legal system, which was based on imperial decrees and legal commentaries. The fifth-century C.E. *Theodosian Code and the great compilations made under Emperor Justinian in the next century thus show the Christian Roman emperors trying to incorporate the newly official religion into a legal system originally attuned to more ancient values.*

One of Christianity's distinctive institutions, originating in Egypt, was the monastery, and the Rule *of Saint Benedict (d. 547) demonstrates how a community dedicated to poverty, chastity, and obedience organized a common life for people wanting to escape the secular world and its temptations. Not everyone was called to be a nun or a monk, but this style of life defined perfection for Christians after the opportunities for martyrdom waned. The late empire's internal decay encouraged people to abandon the world, but it also attracted its most serious external threat. Tribes such as the Vandals and Visigoths, seeking protection on the frontiers from less Romanized peoples like the Huns, may have weakened an empire they probably wanted to preserve, even as they sought to assimilate and emulate Roman values. The baptism of the Frankish king Clovis was specifically modeled on the story of Constantine's conversion.*

The Teaching of Jesus According to the Gospel of Matthew

Among the eastern religions that gained popularity in the Roman Empire was Judaism, especially that version of it espoused by the followers of an itinerant Jewish preacher named Yeshua (in Latin, Jesus), whose career in Judaea ended with his death by crucifixion sometime around 30 C.E. *The chief records of his life and teachings are contained in the gospels ("good news"), a number of which were composed in the decades after his death. Only four—those of Mark, Matthew, Luke, and John— were later accepted as authoritative. All were originally written in Greek. Jesus himself would have spoken Aramaic and Hebrew.*

From *Contemporary English Version*, by American Bible Society (New York: American Bible Society, 1995).

*   *   *

Years later, John the Baptist started preaching in the desert of Judea. He said, "Turn back to God! The kingdom of heaven will soon be here." John was the one the prophet Isaiah was talking about, when he said,

"In the desert someone
is shouting,
'Get the road ready
for the Lord!
Make a straight path
for him.'"

John wore clothes made of camel's hair. He had a leather strap around his waist and ate grasshoppers and wild honey.

From Jerusalem and all Judea and from the Jordan River Valley crowds of people went to John. They told how sorry they were for their sins, and he baptized them in the river.

Many Pharisees and Sadducees also came to be baptized. But John said to them:

"You bunch of snakes! Who warned you to run from the coming judgment? Do something to show that you have really given up your sins. And don't start telling yourselves that you belong to Abraham's family. I tell you that God can turn these stones into children for Abraham. An ax is ready to cut the trees down at their roots. Any tree that doesn't produce good fruit will be chopped down and thrown into a fire.

"I baptize you with water so that you will give up your sins. But someone more powerful is going to come, and I am not good enough even to carry his sandals. He will baptize you with the Holy Spirit and with fire. His threshing fork is in his hand, and he is ready to separate the wheat from the husks. He will store the wheat in a barn and burn the husks in a fire that never goes out."

Jesus left Galilee and went to the Jordan River to be baptized by John. But John kept objecting and said, "I ought to be baptized by you. Why have you come to me?"

Jesus answered, "For now this is how it should be, because we must do all that God wants us to do." Then John agreed.

So Jesus was baptized. And as soon as he came out of the water, the sky opened, and he saw the Spirit of God coming down on him like a dove. Then a voice from heaven said, "This is my own dear Son, and I am pleased with him."

When Jesus saw the crowds, he went up on the side of a mountain and sat down. Jesus' disciples gathered around him, and he taught them:

"God blesses those people
who depend only on him.
They belong to the kingdom
of heaven! God blesses those people
who grieve.
They will find comfort!
God blesses those people
who are humble.
The earth will belong
to them!
God blesses those people
who want to obey him more than to eat or drink.
They will be given
what they want!
God blesses those people
who are merciful.
They will be treated
with mercy!
God blesses those people
whose hearts are pure.
They will see him!
God blesses those people
who make peace.
They will be called
his children!
God blesses those people
who are treated badly
for doing right.
They belong to the kingdom
of heaven.

"God will bless you when people insult you, mistreat you, and tell all kinds of evil lies about you because of me. Be happy and excited! You will have a great reward in heaven. People did these same things to the prophets who lived long ago.

"You are like salt for everyone on earth. But if salt no longer tastes like salt, how can it make food salty? All it is good for is to be thrown out and walked on.

"You are like light for the whole world. A city built on top of a hill cannot be hidden, and no one would light a lamp and put it under a clay pot. A lamp is placed on a lampstand, where it can give light to everyone in the house. Make your light shine, so that others will see the good that you do and will praise your Father in heaven.

"Don't suppose that I came to do away with the Law and the Prophets. I did not come to do away with them, but to give them their full meaning. Heaven and earth may disappear. But I promise you that not even a period or comma will ever disappear from the Law. Everything written in it must happen. If you reject even the least important command in the Law and teach others to do the same, you will be the least important person in the kingdom of heaven. But if you obey and teach others its commands, you will have an important place in the kingdom. You must obey God's commands better than the Pharisees and the teachers of the Law obey them. If you don't, I promise you that you will never get into the kingdom of heaven.

"You know that our ancestors were told, 'Do not murder' and 'A murderer must be brought to trial.' But I promise you that if you are angry with someone, you will have to stand trial. If you call someone a fool, you will be taken to court. And if you say that someone is worthless, you will be in danger of the fires of hell. So if you are about to place your gift on the altar and remember that someone is angry with you, leave your gift there in front of the altar. Make peace with that person, then come back and offer your gift to God.

"Before you are dragged into court, make friends with the person who has accused you of doing wrong. If you don't, you will be handed over to the judge and then to the officer who will put you in jail. I promise you that you will not get out until you have paid the last cent you owe.

"You know the commandment which says, 'Be faithful in marriage.' But I tell you that if you look at another woman and want her, you are already unfaithful in your thoughts. If your right eye causes you to sin, poke it out and throw it away. It is better to lose one part of your body, than for your whole body to end up in hell. If your right hand causes you to sin, chop it off and throw it away! It is better to lose one part of your body, than for your whole body to be thrown into hell.

"You have been taught that a man who divorces his wife must write out divorce papers for her. But I tell you not to divorce your wife unless she has committed some terrible sexual sin. If you divorce her, you will cause her to be unfaithful, just as any man who marries her is guilty of taking another man's wife.

"You know that our ancestors were told, 'Don't use the Lord's name to make a promise unless you are going to keep it.' But I tell you not to swear by anything when you make a promise! Heaven is God's throne, so don't swear by heaven. The earth is God's footstool, so don't swear by the earth. Jerusalem is the city of the great king, so don't swear by it. Don't swear by your own head. You cannot make one hair white or black. When you make a promise, say only 'Yes' or 'No.' Anything else comes from the devil.

"You know that you have been taught, 'An eye for an eye and a tooth for a tooth.' But I tell you not to try to get even with a person who has done something to you. When someone slaps your right cheek, turn and let that person slap your other cheek. If someone sues you for your shirt, give up your coat as well. If a soldier forces you to carry his pack one mile, carry it two miles. When people ask you for something, give it to them. When they want to borrow money, lend it to them.

"You have heard people say, 'Love your neighbors and hate your enemies.' But I tell you to love your enemies and pray for anyone who mistreats you. Then you will be acting like your Father in heaven. He makes the sun rise on both good and bad people. And he sends rain for the ones who do right and for the ones who do wrong. If you love only those people who love you, will God reward you for that? Even tax collectors love their friends. If you greet only your friends, what's so great about that? Don't even unbelievers do that? But you must always act like your Father in heaven."

*   *   *

"When you pray, don't be like those show-offs who love to stand up and pray in the meeting places and on the street corners. They do this just to look good. I can assure you that they already have their reward.

"When you pray, go into a room alone and close the door. Pray to your Father in private. He knows what is done in private, and he will reward you.

"When you pray, don't talk on and on as people do who don't know God. They think God likes to hear long prayers. Don't be like them. Your Father knows what you need before you ask.

"You should pray like this:

Our Father in heaven,
help us to honor
your name.
Come and set up
your kingdom,
so that everyone on earth
will obey you,
as you are obeyed
in heaven.
Give us our food for today. Forgive us for doing
    wrong,
as we forgive others.
Keep us from being tempted
and protect us from evil.

"If you forgive others for the wrongs they do to you, your Father in heaven will forgive you. But if you don't forgive others, your Father will not forgive your sins.

"When you go without eating, don't try to look gloomy as those show-offs do when they go without eating. I can assure you that they already have their reward. Instead, comb your hair and wash your face. Then others won't know that you are going without eating. But your Father sees what is done in private, and he will reward you.

"Don't store up treasures on earth! Moths and rust can destroy them, and thieves can break in and steal them. Instead, store up your treasures in heaven, where moths and rust cannot destroy them, and thieves cannot break in and steal them. Your heart will always be where your treasure is.

"Your eyes are like a window for your body. When they are good, you have all the light you need. But when your eyes are bad, everything is dark. If the light inside you is dark, you surely are in the dark.

"You cannot be the slave of two masters! You will like one more than the other or be more loyal to one than the other. You cannot serve both God and money.

"I tell you not to worry about your life. Don't worry about having something to eat, drink, or wear. Isn't life more than food or clothing? Look at the birds in the sky! They don't plant or harvest. They don't even store grain in barns. Yet your Father in heaven takes care of them. Aren't you worth more than birds?

"Can worry make you live longer? Why worry about clothes? Look how the wild flowers grow. They don't work hard to make their clothes. But I tell you that Solomon with all his wealth wasn't as well clothed as one of them. God gives such beauty to everything that grows in the fields, even though it is here today and thrown into a fire tomorrow. He will surely do even more for you! Why do you have such little faith? Don't worry and ask yourselves, 'Will we have anything to eat? Will we have anything to drink? Will we have any clothes to wear?' Only people who don't know God are always worrying about such things. Your Father in heaven knows that you need all of these. But more than anything else, put God's work first and do what he wants. Then the other things will be yours as well.

"Don't worry about tomorrow. It will take care of itself. You have enough to worry about today.

"Don't condemn others, and God won't condemn you. God will be as hard on you as you are on others! He will treat you exactly as you treat them.

"You can see the speck in your friend's eye, but you don't notice the log in your own eye. How can you say, 'My friend, let me take the speck out of your eye,' when you don't see the log in your own eye? You're nothing but show-offs! First, take the log out of your own eye. Then you can see how to take the speck out of your friend's eye.

"Don't give to dogs what belongs to God. They will only turn and attack you. Don't throw pearls down in front of pigs. They will trample all over them.

"Ask, and you will receive. Search, and you will find. Knock, and the door will be opened for you. Everyone who asks will receive. Everyone who searches will find. And the door will be opened for everyone who knocks. Would any of you give your hungry child a stone, if the child asked for some bread? Would you give your child a snake if the child asked for a fish? As bad as you are, you still know how to give good gifts to your children. But your heavenly Father is even more ready to give good things to people who ask.

"Treat others as you want them to treat you. This is what the Law and the Prophets are all about.

"Go in through the narrow gate. The gate to destruction is wide, and the road that leads there is easy to follow. A lot of people go through that gate. But the gate to life is very narrow. The road that leads there is so hard to follow that only a few people find it.

"Watch out for false prophets! They dress up like sheep, but inside they are wolves who have come to attack you. You can tell what they are by what they do. No one picks grapes or figs from thornbushes. A good tree produces good fruit, and a bad tree produces bad fruit. A good tree cannot produce bad fruit, and a bad tree cannot produce good fruit. Every tree that produces bad fruit will be chopped down and burned. You can tell who the false prophets are by their deeds.

"Not everyone who calls me their Lord will get into the kingdom of heaven. Only the ones who obey my Father in heaven will get in. On the day of judgment many will call me their Lord. They will say, 'We preached in your name, and in your name we forced out demons and worked many miracles.' But I will tell them, 'I will have nothing to do with you! Get out of my sight, you evil people!'

"Anyone who hears and obeys these teachings of mine is like a wise person who built a house on solid rock. Rain poured down, rivers flooded, and winds beat against that house. But it did not fall, because it was built on solid rock.

"Anyone who hears my teachings and doesn't obey them is like a foolish person who built a house on sand. The rain poured down, the rivers flooded, and the winds blew and beat against that house. Finally, it fell with a crash."

When Jesus finished speaking, the crowds were surprised at his teaching. He taught them like someone with authority, and not like their teachers of the Law of Moses.

*   *   *

REVIEW QUESTIONS

1. What were the chief features of Jesus's teaching, according to these excerpts?
2. How do these teachings challenge the norms of the society in which Jesus lived? How does he represent himself as breaking with tradition?
3. Jesus speaks often of the "kingdom of heaven." What does he seem to mean by this? How might this "kingdom" stand in contrast to the kingdoms and empires that dominated the world in Jesus's own time? How might his teachings have been perceived by those in power?

The Martyrdom of Perpetua

In 203 C.E., a number of Christians were arrested, tried, and convicted by the Roman governor of Carthage (in North Africa). Among them was a young, well-born woman named Vivia (or Vibia) Perpetua, who was accompanied by her slave, Felicitas. Perpetua was nursing a young child at the time, and Felicitas was in the late stages of pregnancy. The following text features a first-hand account of these events in Perpetua's own words, the oldest surviving autobiographical writing associated with a Christian woman. The text has come down to us in both Latin and Greek editions.

From *A Lost Tradition: Women Writers of the Early Church*, by Patricia Wilson-Kastner, G. Ronald Kastner, Ann Millin, Rosemary Rader, and Jeremiah Reedy (Lanham, Md.: United Press of America, 1981), pp. 19–32.

1. If instances of ancient faith which both testified to the grace of God and edified persons were written expressly for God's honor and humans' encouragement, why shouldn't recent events be similarly recorded for those same purposes? For these events will likewise become part of the past and vital to posterity, in spite of the fact that contemporary esteem for antiquity tends to minimize their value. And those who maintain that there is a single manifestation of the one Holy Spirit throughout the ages ought to consider that since a fullness of grace has been decreed for the last days of the world these recent events should be considered of greater value because of their proximity to those days. For "In the last days," says the Lord, "I shall diffuse my spirit over all humanity and their sons and daughters shall prophesy; the young shall see visions, and the old shall dream dreams."[1]

Just as we valued those prophecies so we acknowledge and reverence the new visions which were promised. And we consider the other powers of the Holy Spirit to be instruments of the Church to which that same Spirit was sent to administer all gifts to all people, just as the Lord allotted. For this reason we deem it necessary to disseminate the written accounts for the glory of God, lest anyone with a weak or despairing faith might think that supernatural grace prevailed solely among the ancients who were honored either by their experience of martyrdom or visions. For God always fulfills what he promises, either as proof to nonbelievers or as an added grace to believers.

And so, brothers and dear ones, we share with you those things which we have heard and touched with our hands,[2] so that those of you who were eyewitnesses of these deeds may be reminded of the glory of the Lord, and those of you now learning of it through this narration may associate yourselves with the holy martyrs and, through them, with the Lord Jesus Christ to whom there is glory and honor forever.[3] Amen.

2. Arrested were some young catechumens; Revocatus and Felicitas (both servants), Saturninus, Secundulus, and Vibia Perpetua, a young married woman about twenty years old, of good family and upbringing.[4] She had a father, mother, two brothers (one was a catechumen like herself), and an infant son at the breast. The following account of her martyrdom is her own, a record in her own words of her perceptions of the event.

3. While I was still with the police authorities (she said) my father out of love for me tried to

---

[1] Acts 2:17–18. Cf. Joel 2:28.

[2] I John 1:3. Cf. 1 Cor. 7:17; Rom. 12:3.

[3] I John 1:3.

[4] A catechumen was one receiving instruction in the basic beliefs and teachings of the Christian faith prior to baptism.

dissuade me from my resolution. "Father," I said, "do you see here, for example, this vase, or pitcher, or whatever it is?" "I see it," he said. "Can it be named anything else than what it really is?", I asked, and he said, "No." "So I also cannot be called anything else than what I am, a Christian." Enraged by my words my father came at me as though to tear out my eyes. He only annoyed me, but he left, overpowered by his diabolical arguments.

For a few days my father stayed away. I thanked the Lord and felt relieved because of my father's absence. At this time we were baptized and the Spirit instructed me not to request anything from the baptismal waters except endurance of physical suffering.[5]

A few days later we were imprisoned. I was terrified because never before had I experienced such darkness. What a terrible day! Because of crowded conditions and rough treatment by the soldiers the heat was unbearable. My condition was aggravated by my anxiety for my baby. Then Tertius and Pomponius, those kind deacons who were taking care of our needs, paid for us to be moved for a few hours to a better part of the prison where we might refresh ourselves. Leaving the dungeon we all went about our own business. I nursed my child, who was already weak from hunger. In my anxiety for the infant I spoke to my mother about him, tried to console my brother, and asked that they care for my son.[6] I suffered intensely because I sensed their agony on my account. These were the trials I had to endure for many days. Then I was granted the privilege of having my son remain with me in prison. Being relieved of my anxiety and concern for the infant, I immediately regained my strength. Suddenly the prison became my palace, and I loved being there rather than any other place.

4. Then my brother said to me, "Dear sister, you already have such a great reputation that you could ask for a vision indicating whether you will be condemned or freed." Since I knew that I could speak with the Lord, whose great favors I had already experienced, I confidently promised to do so. I said I would tell my brother about it the next day. Then I made my request and this is what I saw.

There was a bronze ladder of extraordinary height reaching up to heaven, but it was so narrow that only one person could ascend at a time.[7] Every conceivable kind of iron weapon was attached to the sides of the ladder: swords, lances, hooks, and daggers. If anyone climbed up carelessly or without looking upwards, he/she would be mangled as the flesh adhered to the weapons. Crouching directly beneath the ladder was a monstrous dragon who threatened those climbing up and tried to frighten them from ascent.

Saturus went up first. Because of his concern for us he had given himself up voluntarily after we had been arrested. He had been our source of strength but was not with us at the time of the arrest).[8] When he reached the top of the ladder he turned to me and said, "Perpetua, I'm waiting for you, but be careful not to be bitten by the dragon." I told him that in the name of Jesus Christ the dragon could not harm me. At this the dragon slowly lowered its head as though afraid of me. Using its head as the first step, I began my ascent.

At the summit I saw an immense garden, in the center of which sat a tall, grey-haired man dressed like a shepherd, milking sheep. Standing around him were several thousand white-robed people. As he raised his head he noticed me and said, "Welcome, my child." Then he beckoned me to approach and gave me a small morsel of the cheese he was making. I accepted it with cupped hands and ate it. When all those surrounding us said "Amen," I awoke, still tasting the sweet cheese. I immediately told my brother about the vision, and we both realized that we were to experience the sufferings of martyrdom. From then on we gave up having any hope in this world.

5. A few days later there was a rumor that our case was to be heard. My father, completely exhausted

---

[5] Apparently, after baptism, the newly baptized could pray for a special grace or gift. Cf. Tertullian, *De Bapt.* 20.

[6] From the rest of the account, it appears that Perpetua's mother was bringing the child to and from prison.

[7] Cf. Jacob's ladder in Gen. 28:12.

[8] Since Saturus is not listed as a catechumen he was probably the instructor of the others prior to their arrest.

from his anxiety, came from the city to see me, with the intention of weakening my faith. "Daughter", he said, "have pity on my grey head. Have pity on your father if I have the honor to be called father by you, if with these hands I have brought you to the prime of your life, and if I have always favored you above your brothers, do not abandon me to the reproach of men. Consider your brothers; consider your mother and your aunt; consider your son who cannot live without you. Give up your stubbornness before you destroy all of us. None of us will be able to speak freely if anything happens to you."

These were the things my father said out of love, kissing my hands and throwing himself at my feet. With tears he called me not daughter, but woman. I was very upset because of my father's condition. He was the only member of my family who would find no reason for joy in my suffering. I tried to comfort him saying, "Whatever God wants at this tribunal will happen, for remember that our power comes not from ourselves but from God." But utterly dejected, my father left me.

6. One day as we were eating we were suddenly rushed off for a hearing. We arrived at the forum and the news spread quickly throughout the area near the forum, and a huge crowd gathered. We went up to the prisoners' platform. All the others confessed when they were questioned. When my turn came my father appeared with my son. Dragging me from the step, he begged: "Have pity on your son!"

Hilarion, the governor, who assumed power after the death of the proconsul Minucius Timinianus,[9] said, "Have pity on your father's grey head; have pity on your infant son; offer sacrifice for the emperors' welfare." But I answered, "I will not." Hilarion asked, "Are you a Christian?" And I answered, "I am a Christian." And when my father persisted in his attempts to dissuade me, Hilarion ordered him thrown out, and he was beaten with a rod. My father's injury hurt me as much as if I myself had been beaten, and I grieved

because of his pathetic old age. Then the sentence was passed; all of us were condemned to the beasts. We were overjoyed as we went back to the prison cell. Since I was still nursing my child who was ordinarily in the cell with me, I quickly sent the deacon Pomponius to my father's house to ask for the baby, but my father refused to give him up. Then God saw to it that my child no longer needed my nursing, nor were my breasts inflamed. After that I was no longer tortured by anxiety about my child or by pain in my breasts.

7. A few days later while all of us were praying, in the middle of a prayer I suddenly called out the name "Dinocrates." I was astonished since I hadn't thought about him till then. When I recalled what had happened to him I was very disturbed and decided right then that I had not only the right, but the obligation, to pray for him. So I began to pray repeatedly and to make moaning sounds to the Lord in his behalf. During that same night I had this vision: I saw Dinocrates walking away from one of many very dark places. He seemed very hot and thirsty, his face grimy and colorless. The wound on his face was just as it had been when he died. This Dinocrates was my blood-brother who at the age of seven died very tragically from a cancerous disease which so disfigured his face that his death was repulsive to everyone. It was for him that I now prayed. But neither of us could reach the other because of the great distance between. In the place where Dinocrates stood was a pool filled with water, and the rim of the pool was so high that it extended far above the boy's height. Dinocrates stood on his toes as if to drink the water but in spite of the fact that the pool was full, he could not drink because the rim was so high![10]

I realized that my brother was in trouble, but I was confident that I could help him with his problem. I prayed for him every day until we were transferred to the arena prison where we were to fight

---

[9] There is no real information about Minucius Timinianus, but Hilarion is mentioned as an African proconsul by Tertullian, *Ad Scapulam* 3.1. Hilarion was evidently temporarily serving as governor until a new one would be appointed.

[10] The reason Dinocrates was unable to drink the water may have been due to his dying before being baptized. However, Augustine (*De Anima* 1.12) maintained that the boy had committed sins after baptism and had not been cleansed of those sins prior to death.

wild animals on the birthday of Geta Caesar.![11] And I prayed day and night for him, moaning and weeping so that my petition would be granted.

8. On the day that we were kept in chains, I had the following vision: I saw the same place as before, but Dinocrates was clean, well-dressed, looking refreshed. In place of the wound there was a scar, and the fountain which I had seen previously now had its rim lowered to the boy's waist. On the rim, over which water was flowing constantly, there was a golden bowl filled with water. Dinocrates walked up to it and began to drink; the bowl never emptied. And when he was no longer thirsty, he gladly went to play as children do. Then I awoke, knowing that he had been relieved of his suffering.

9. A few days passed. Pudens, the official in charge of the prison (the official who had gradually come to admire us for our persistence), admitted many prisoners to our cell so that we might mutually encourage each other. As the day of the games drew near, my father, overwhelmed with grief, came again to see me. He began to pluck out his beard and throw it on the ground. Falling on his face before me, he cursed his old age, repeating such things as would move all creation. And I grieved because of his old age.

10. The day before the battle in the arena, in a vision I saw Pomponius the deacon coming to the prison door and knocking very loudly. I went to open the gate for him. He was dressed in a loosely fitting white robe, wearing richly decorated sandals. He said to me, "Perpetua, come. We're waiting for you!" He took my hand and we began to walk over extremely rocky and winding paths. When we finally arrived short of breath, at the arena, he led me to the center saying, "Don't be frightened! I'll be here to help you." He left me and I stared out over a huge crowd which watched me with apprehension. Because I knew that I had to fight with the beasts, I wondered why they hadn't yet been turned loose in the arena. Coming towards me was some type of Egyptian, horrible to look at, accompanied by fight-

ers who were to help defeat me. Some handsome young men came forward to help and encourage me. I was stripped of my clothing, and suddenly I was a man. My assistants began to rub me with oil as was the custom before a contest, while the Egyptian was on the opposite side rolling in the sand. Then a certain man appeared, so tall that he towered above the amphitheatre. He wore a loose purple robe with two parallel stripes across the chest; his sandals were richly decorated with gold and silver. He carried a rod like that of an athletic trainer, and a green branch on which were golden apples. He motioned for silence and said, "If this Egyptian wins, he will kill her with the sword; but if she wins, she will receive this branch." Then he withdrew.

We both stepped forward and began to fight with our fists. My opponent kept trying to grab my feet but I repeatedly kicked his face with my heels. I felt myself being lifted up into the air and began to strike at him as one who was no longer earthbound. But when I saw that we were wasting time, I put my two hands together, linked my fingers, and put his head between them. As he fell on his face I stepped on his head. Then the people began to shout and my assistants started singing victory songs. I walked up to the trainer and accepted the branch.[12] He kissed me and said, "Peace be with you, my daughter." And I triumphantly headed towards the Sanavivarian Gate.[13] Then I woke up realizing that I would be contending not with wild animals but with the devil himself. I knew, however, that I would win. I have recorded the events which occurred up to the day before the final contest. Let anyone who wishes to record the events of the contest itself, do so.

11. The saintly Saturus also related a vision which he had and it is recorded here in his own hand. Our suffering had ended (he said), and we were being carried towards the east by four angels

---

[11] This incidental reference to the celebration of games on Geta's birthday helps establish the date of the martydrom somewhere between 200 [and] 205.

[12] The branch was the reward presented to the victor in any kind of official combat or contest.

[13] The Porta Sanavivaria (Gate of Life) was the gate by which the victors would exit. Those who were defeated were carried out through the Porta Libitinensis, which derived its name from the goddess presiding over funeral rites.

whose hands never touched us. And we floated upward, not in a supine position, but as though we were climbing a gentle slope. As we left the earth's atmosphere we saw a brilliant light, and I said to Perpetua who was at my side, "This is what the Lord promised us. We have received his promise."

And while we were being carried along by those four angels we saw a large open space like a splendid garden landscaped with rose trees and every variety of flower. The trees were as tall as cypresses whose leaves rustled gently and incessantly. And there in that garden-sanctuary were four other angels, more dazzling than the rest. And when they saw us they showed us honor, saying to the other angels in admiration, "Here they are! They have arrived."

And those four angels who were carrying us began trembling in awe and set us down. And we walked through a violet-strewn field where we met Jocundus, Saturninus, and Artaxius who were burned alive in that same persecution, and Quintus, also a martyr, who had died in prison. We were asking them where they had been, when the other angels said to us, "First, come this way. Go in and greet the Lord."

12. We went up to a place where the walls seemed constructed of light. At the entrance of the place stood four angels who put white robes on those who entered. We went in and heard a unified voice chanting endlessly, "Holy, holy, holy." We saw a white haired man sitting there who, in spite of his snowy white hair, had the features of a young man. His feet were not visible. On his right and left were four elderly gentlemen and behind them stood many more. As we entered we stood in amazement before the throne. Four angels supported us as we went up to kiss the aged man, and he gently stroked our faces with his hands. The other elderly men said to us, "Stand up." We rose and gave the kiss of peace. Then they told us to enjoy ourselves. I said to Perpetua, "You have your wish." She answered, "I thank God, for although I was happy on earth, I am much happier here right now."

13. Then we went out, and before the gates we saw Optatus the bishop on the right and Aspasius the priest and teacher on the left, both looking sad as they stood there separated from each other. They knelt before us saying, "Make peace between us, for you've gone away and left us this way." But we said to them "Aren't you our spiritual father, and our teacher? Why are you kneeling before us?" We were deeply touched and we embraced them. And Perpetua began to speak to them in Greek and we invited them into the garden beneath a rose tree. While we were talking with them, the angels said to them, "Let them refresh themselves, and if you have any dissensions among you, forgive one another." This disturbed both of them and the angels said to Optatus, "Correct your people who flock to you as though returning from the games, fighting about the different teams." It seemed to us that they wanted to close the gates, and there we began to recognize many of our friends, among whom were martyrs. We were all sustained by an indescribable fragrance which completely satisfied us. Then in my joy, I awoke.

14. The remarkable visions narrated above were those of the blessed martyrs Saturus and Perpetua, just as they put them in writing. As for Secundulus, while he was still in prison God gave him the grace of an earlier exit from this world, so that he could escape combat with the wild beasts. But his body, though not his soul, certainly felt the sword.

15. As for Felicitas, she too was touched by God's grace in the following manner. She was pregnant when arrested, and was now in her eighth month. As the day of the contest approached she became very distressed that her martyrdom might be delayed, since the law forbade the execution of a pregnant woman. Then she would later have to shed her holy and innocent blood among common criminals. Her friends in martyrdom were equally sad at the thought of abandoning such a good friend to travel alone on the same road to hope.

And so, two days before the contest, united in grief they prayed to the Lord. Immediately after the prayers her labor pains began. Because of the additional pain natural for an eighth-month delivery, she suffered greatly during the birth, and one of the prison guards taunted her; "If you're complaining now, what will you do when you'll be thrown to the wild beasts? You didn't think of them when you refused to sacrifice." She answered, "Now it is I who suffer, but then another shall be in me to bear the pain for me, since I am now suffering for him." And she gave birth to a girl whom one of her sisters reared as her own daughter.

16. Since the Holy Spirit has permitted, and by permitting has willed, that the events of the contest be recorded, we have no choice but to carry out the injunction (rather, the sacred trust) of Perpetua, in spite of the fact that it will be an inferior addition to the magnificent events already described. We are adding an instance of Perpetua's perseverance and lively spirit. At one time the prisoners were being treated with unusual severity by the commanding officer because certain deceitful men had intimated to him that the prisoners might escape by some magic spells. Perpetua openly challenged him; "Why don't you at least allow us to freshen up, the most noble of the condemned, since we belong to Caesar and are about to fight on his birthday? Or isn't it to your credit that we should appear in good condition on that day?" The officer grimaced and blushed, then ordered that they be treated more humanely and that her brothers and others be allowed to visit and dine with them. By this time the prison warden was himself a believer.

17. On the day before the public games, as they were eating the last meal commonly called the free meal, they tried as much as possible to make it instead an *agape*.[14] In the same spirit they were exhorting the people, warning them to remember the judgment of God, asking them to be witnesses to the prisoners' joy in suffering, and ridiculing the curiosity of the crowd. Saturus told them, "Won't tomorrow's view be enough for you? Why are you so eager to see something you hate? Friends today, enemies tomorrow! Take a good look so you'll recognize us on that day." Then they all left the prison amazed, and many of them began to believe.

18. The day of their victory dawned, and with joyful countenances they marched from the prison

to the arena as though on their way to heaven. If there was any trembling it was from joy, not fear. Perpetua followed with quick step as a true spouse of Christ, the darling of God, her brightly flashing eyes quelling the gaze of the crowd. Felicitas too, joyful because she had safely survived childbirth and was now able to participate in the contest with the wild animals, passed from one shedding of blood to another: from midwife to gladiator, about to be purified after child-birth by a second baptism. As they were led through the gate they were ordered to put on different clothes; the men, those priests of Saturn, the women, those of the priestesses of Ceres. But that noble woman stubbornly resisted even to the end. She said, "We've come this far voluntarily in order to protect our rights, and we've pledged our lives not to recapitulate [sic] on any such matter as this. We made this agreement with you." Injustice bowed to justice and the guard conceded that they could enter the arena in their ordinary dress. Perpetua was singing victory psalms as if already crushing the head of the Egyptian. Revocatus, Saturninus and Saturus were warning the spectators, and as they came within sight of Hilarion they informed him by nods and gestures: "You condemn us; God condemns you." This so infuriated the crowds that they demanded the scourging of these men in front of the line of gladiators. But the ones so punished rejoiced in that they had obtained yet another share in the Lord's suffering.

19. Whoever said, "Ask and you shall receive," granted to these petitioners the particular death that each one chose. For whenever the martyrs were discussing among themselves their choice of death, Saturus used to say that he wished to be thrown in with all the animals so that he might wear a more glorious crown. Accordingly, at the outset of the show he was matched against a leopard but then called back; then he was mauled by a bear on the exhibition platform. Now Saturus detested nothing as much as a bear and he had already decided to die by one bite from the leopard. Consequently, when he was tied to a wild boar the professional gladiator who had tied the two together was pierced instead and died shortly after the games ended, while Satu-

---

[14] The *agape* or "love feast" was the common meal shared by the early Christian communities. It was the visible expression of the love Christians felt for each other as co-sharers of the love of Christ.

rus was merely dragged about. And when he was tied up on the bridge in front of the bear, the bear refused to come out of his den; and so a second time Saturus was called back unharmed.

20. For the young women the devil had readied a mad cow, an animal not usually used at these games, but selected so that the women's sex would be matched with that of the animal. After being stripped and enmeshed in nets, the women were led into the arena. How horrified the people were as they saw that one was a young girl and the other, her breasts dripping with milk, had just recently given birth to a child. Consequently both were recalled and dressed in loosely fitting gowns.

Perpetua was tossed first and fell on her back. She sat up, and being more concerned with her sense of modesty than with her pain, covered her thighs with her gown which had been torn down one side. Then finding her hair-clip which had fallen out, she pinned back her loose hair thinking it not proper for a martyr to suffer with dishevelled hair; it might seem that she was mourning in her hour of triumph. Then she stood up. Noticing that Felicitas was badly bruised, she went to her, reached out her hands and helped her to her feet. As they stood there the cruelty of the crowds seemed to be appeased and they were sent to the Sanavivarian Gate. There Perpetua was taken care of by a certain catechumen, Rusticus, who stayed near her. She seemed to be waking from a deep sleep (so completely had she been entranced and imbued with the Spirit). She began to look around her and to everyone's astonishment asked, "When are we going to be led out to that cow, or whatever it is." She would not believe that it had already happened until she saw the various markings of the tossing on her body and clothing. Then calling for her brother she said to him and to the catechumen, "Remain strong in your faith and love one another. Do not let our excruciating sufferings become a stumbling block for you."

21. Meanwhile, at another gate Saturus was similarly encouraging the soldier, Pudens. "Up to the present," he said, "I've not been harmed by any of the animals, just as I've foretold and predicted. So that you will now believe completely, watch as I go back to die from a single leopard bite." And so at the end of that contest, Saturus was bitten once by the leopard that had been set loose, and bled so profusely from that one wound that as he was coming back the crowd shouted in witness to his second baptism: "Salvation by being cleansed; Salvation by being cleansed;"[15] And that man was truly saved who was cleansed in this way.

Then Saturus said to Pudens the soldier, "Goodbye, and remember my faith. Let these happenings be a source of strength for you, rather than a cause for anxiety." Then asking Pudens for a ring from his finger, he dipped it into the wound and returned it to Pudens as a legacy, a pledge and remembrance of his death. And as he collapsed he was thrown with the rest to that place reserved for the usual throat-slitting. And when the crowd demanded that the prisoners be brought out into the open so that they might feast their eyes on death by the sword, they voluntarily arose and moved where the crowd wanted them. Before doing so they kissed each other so that their martyrdom would be completely perfected by the rite of the kiss of peace.

The others, without making any movement or sound, were killed by the sword. Saturus in particular, since he had been the first to climb the ladder and was to be Perpetua's encouragement, was the first to die. But Perpetua, in order to feel some of the pain, groaning as she was struck between the ribs, took the gladiator's trembling hand [and] guided it to her throat. Perhaps it was that so great a woman, feared as she was by the unclean spirit, could not have been slain had she not herself willed it.

O brave and fortunate martyrs, truly called and chosen to give honor to our Lord Jesus Christ! And anyone who is elaborating upon, or who reverences or worships that honor, should read these more recent examples, along with the ancient, as sources of encouragement for the Christian community. In this way, there will be new examples of courage witnessing to the fact that even in our day the same Holy Spirit is still efficaciously present, along with

---

[15] One of the customary greetings of good omen before and after the public baths was "Salvum lotum," here used ironically by the crowd in the amphitheater.

STILICHO AND HIS FAMILY (395 C.E.)

The two panels of this ivory diptych (DIP-tick) date to around the year 395 C.E. and they would originally have been joined by hinges, making a portable object that could open and close—or be displayed on a flat surface. On the right is the Roman general Stilicho (c. 359–408), dressed as a conventional Roman soldier; on the left are his wife, Serena (holding a flower), and his young son, Eucherius (holding a book). Stilicho was the son of a Vandal chieftain and an unknown (Roman) woman. Serena came from an aristocratic Roman family and was the adopted niece of the emperor Theodosius I (r. 379–95). At the time of their marriage, Stilicho was the effective ruler of the Western Roman Empire. What do these images reveal about Roman identity and values during a time of intense political and cultural change? What do they suggest about the status and chosen identity of Stilicho himself? How might this object have been used?

the all powerful God the Father and Jesus Christ our Lord, to whom there will always be glory and endless power. Amen.

*   *   *

REVIEW QUESTIONS

1. First-hand accounts of this kind are rare, and it is especially unusual to have a text that preserves the words of a young woman from one of Rome's provinces. How might this document have survived and circulated? What clues to its preservation and audience are given in the text?

2. Perpetua's father is an important figure in this account. What do his interactions with his daughter and with Roman authorities tell us about traditional Roman values, and about the ways that Christianity opposed these values?

3. What can we learn by analyzing Perpetua's visions? In particular, what do you make of the fact that she "became a man" when she was stripped and entered the arena? More generally, what do Perpetua's words and actions reveal about gender roles in Roman provincial society?

ST. AUGUSTINE

FROM *City of God* AND *Confessions*

Augustine (354–430 C.E.) is considered the greatest "father" and theologian of the early Church, second only to Paul of Tarsus in his influence. The son of a pagan father and a Christian mother, he was born in North Africa and educated at Carthage, but his ambitions took him to Italy as a young man. While working as a teacher in Milan, he came under the influence of the city's charismatic bishop, Ambrose, another important Church Father. In 386, after years of deliberation and doubt, he converted to Christianity and was soon appointed bishop of Hippo Regius in his native North Africa. His best-known works are his autobiographical Confessions *and* City of God, *a monumental defense of Christianity published in response to the sack of Rome by the Visigoths in 410 C.E. The following excerpts from the latter book come from the introduction, where Augustine lays out his thesis and begins his analysis of the nature of freedom, sin, and slavery. The short excerpt from the* Confessions *describes a youthful crime that appears to have haunted Augustine throughout his life.*

FROM *City of God,* Book I*

Here, my dear Marcellinus, is the fulfilment of my promise, a book in which I have taken upon myself the task of defending the glorious City of God against those who prefer their own gods to the

---

*From *City of God,* by St. Augustine, translated by Henry Bettenson (New York: Penguin, 1972), pp. 5–9, 874–76.

Founder of that City. I treat of it both as it exists in this world of time, a stranger among the ungodly, living by faith, and as it stands in the security of its everlasting seat. This security it now awaits in steadfast patience, until 'justice returns to judgement'; but it is to attain it hereafter in virtue of its ascendancy over its enemies, when the final victory is won and peace established. The task is long and arduous; but God is our helper.

I know how great is the effort needed to convince the proud of the power and excellence of humility, an excellence which makes it soar above all the summits of this world, which sway in their temporal instability, overtopping them all with an eminence not arrogated by human pride, but granted by divine grace. For the King and Founder of this City which is our subject has revealed in the Scripture of his people this statement of the divine Law, 'God resists the proud, but he gives grace to the humble.' This is God's prerogative; but man's arrogant spirit in its swelling pride has claimed it as its own, and delights to hear this verse quoted in its own praise: 'To spare the conquered, and beat down the proud.'[1]

Therefore I cannot refrain from speaking about the city of this world,[2] a city which aims at dominion, which holds nations in enslavement, but is itself dominated by that very lust of domination. I must consider this city as far as the scheme of this work demands and as occasion serves.

1. THE ENEMIES OF CHRISTIANITY WERE SPARED BY THE BARBARIANS AT THE SACK OF ROME, OUT OF RESPECT FOR CHRIST.

From this world's city there arise enemies against whom the City of God has to be defended, though many of these correct their godless errors and become useful citizens of that City. But many are inflamed with hate against it and feel no gratitude for the benefits offered by its Redeemer. The benefits are unmistakable; those enemies would not today be able to utter a word against the City if, when fleeing from the sword of their enemy, they had not found, in the City's holy places, the safety on which they now congratulate themselves. The barbarians spared them for Christ's sake; and now these Romans assail Christ's name. The sacred places of the martyrs and the basilicas of the apostles bear witness to this, for in the sack of Rome they afforded shelter to fugitives, both Christian and pagan. The bloodthirsty enemy raged thus far, but here the frenzy of butchery was checked; to these refuges the merciful among the enemy conveyed those whom they had spared outside, to save them from encountering foes who had no such pity. Even men who elsewhere raged with all the savagery an enemy can show, arrived at places where practices generally allowed by laws of war were forbidden and their monstrous passion for violence was brought to a sudden halt; their lust for taking captives was subdued.

In this way many escaped who now complain of this Christian era, and hold Christ responsible for the disasters which their city endured. But they do not make Christ responsible for the benefits they received out of respect for Christ, to which they owed their lives. They attribute their deliverance to their own destiny; whereas if they had any right judgement they ought rather to attribute the harsh cruelty they suffered at the hands of their enemies to the providence of God. For God's providence constantly uses war to correct and chasten the corrupt morals of mankind, as it also uses such afflictions to train men in a righteous and laudable way of life, removing to a better state those whose life is approved, or else keeping them in this world for further service.

Moreover, they should give credit to this Christian era for the fact that these savage barbarians showed mercy beyond the custom of war—whether they so acted in general in honour of the name of Christ, or in places specially dedicated to Christ's name, buildings of such size and capacity as to give mercy a wider range. For this clemency our detractors ought rather to give thanks to God; they should have recourse to his name in all sincerity, so as to escape the penalty of everlasting fire, seeing that so many of them assumed his name dishonestly, to escape the penalty of immediate destruction. Among those whom you see insulting Christ's servants with such wanton insolence there are very many who came unscathed through that terrible time of massacre only by passing themselves off as Christ's servants. And now with ungrateful pride and impious madness they oppose his name in the perversity of their hearts, so that they may incur the punishment of eternal darkness; but then they took refuge in that name, though with deceitful lips, so

---

[1] Virgil, *Æneid* VI: 853.
[2] I.e., Rome.

that they might continue to enjoy this transitory light.

2. THAT VICTORS SHOULD SPARE THE VANQUISHED OUT OF RESPECT FOR THEIR GODS IS SOMETHING UNEXAMPLED IN HISTORY.

We have the records of many wars, both before the foundation of Rome and after its rise to power. Let our enemies read their history, and then produce instances of the capture of any city by foreign enemies when those enemies spared any whom they found taking refuge in the temples of their gods. Let them quote any barbarian general who gave instructions, at the storming of a town, that no one should be treated with violence who was discovered in this temple or that. Aeneas saw Priam at the altar,

> polluting with his blood
> The fire which he had consecrated.

And Diomedes and Ulysses

> Slew all the warders of the citadel
> And snatched with bloody hands the sacred
>   image;
> Nor shrank to touch the chaplets virginal
> Of the dread goddess.

And there is no truth in the statement that comes after,

> The Grecian hopes then failed, and ebbed away.[3]

For what in fact followed was the Greek victory, the destruction of Troy by fire and sword, the slaughter of Priam at the altar.

And it was not because Troy lost Minerva that Troy perished. What loss did Minerva herself first incur, that led to her own disappearance? Was it, perhaps, the loss of her guards? There can be no doubt that their death made her removal possible—the image did not preserve the men; the men were preserving the image. Why then did they worship her, to secure her protection for their country and its citizens? She could not guard her own keepers.

3. THE FOLLY OF THE ROMANS IN CONFIDING THEIR SAFETY TO THE HOUSEHOLD GODS WHO HAD FAILED TO PROTECT TROY.

There you see the sorts of gods to whom the Romans gladly entrusted the preservation of their city. Pitiable folly! Yet the Romans are enraged by such criticisms from us, while they are not incensed at the authors of such quotations; in fact they pay money to become acquainted with their works, and they consider that those who merely instruct them in these works merit an official salary and an honoured position in the community. Virgil certainly is held to be a great poet; in fact he is regarded as the best and the most renowned of all poets, and for that reason he is read by children at an early age—they take great draughts of his poetry into their unformed minds, so that they may not easily forget him, for, as Horace[4] remarks,

> New vessels will for long retain the taste
> Of what is first poured into them.

Now in Virgil, Juno is introduced as hostile to the Trojans, and when she urges Aeolus, king of the winds, against them, she says,

> A race I hate sails the Etruscan sea
> Bringing to Italy Troy's vanquished gods,
> And Troy itself.

Ought the Romans, as prudent men, to have entrusted the defence of Rome to gods unable to defend themselves? Juno no doubt spoke like a woman in anger, heedless of what she was saying. But consider what is said by Aeneas himself, who is so often called "the pious."

> Panthus, the priest of Phoebus and the citadel,
> Snatching his conquered gods and his young
>   grandson
> Rushes in frenzy to the door.

---

[3] These are quotations from the *Æneid* of Virgil (70–19 B.C.E.), Augustine's favorite poet.

[4] Quintus Horatius Flaccus (65–8 B.C.E.).

He does not shrink from calling the gods "conquered," and he speaks of them as being entrusted to him, rather than the other way round, when he is told, "To thee, Troy now entrusts her native gods."

If Virgil speaks of such gods as "vanquished," and tells how, after their overthrow, they only succeeded in escaping because they were committed to the care of a man, what folly it is to see any wisdom in committing Rome to such guardians, and in supposing that it could not be sacked while it retained possession of them. To worship "vanquished" gods as protectors and defenders is to rely not on divinities but on defaulters. It is not sensible to assume that Rome would have escaped this disaster had these gods not first perished; the sensible belief is that those gods would have perished long before, had not Rome made every effort to preserve them. Anyone who gives his mind to it can see that it is utter folly to count on invincibility by virtue of the possession of defenders who have been conquered and to attribute destruction to the loss of such guardian deities as these. In fact, the only possible cause of destruction was the choice of such perishable defenders. When the poets wrote and sang of "vanquished gods," it was not because it suited their whim to lie—they were men of sense, and truth compelled them to admit the facts.

But I must deal with this subject in fuller detail in a more convenient place. For the present I will return to the ingratitude of those who blasphemously blame Christ for the disasters which their moral perversity deservedly brought upon them, and I will deal with the subject as briefly as I can. They were spared for Christ's sake, pagans though they were; yet they scorn to acknowledge this. With the madness of sacrilegious perversity they use their tongues against the name of Christ; yet with those same tongues they dishonestly claimed that name in order to save their lives, or else, in places sacred to him, they held their tongues through fear. They were kept safe and protected there where his name stood between them and the enemy's violence. And so they issue from that shelter to assail him with curses of hate.

*   *   *

15. MAN'S NATURAL FREEDOM; AND THE SLAVERY CAUSED BY SIN.

This relationship is prescribed by the order of nature, and it is in this situation that God created man. For he says, "Let him have lordship over the fish of the sea, the birds of the sky . . . and all the reptiles that crawl on the earth."[5] He did not wish the rational being, made in his own image, to have dominion over any but irrational creatures, not man over man, but man over the beasts. Hence the first just men were set up as shepherds of flocks, rather than as kings of men, so that in this way also God might convey the message of what was required by the order of nature, and what was demanded by the deserts of sinners—for it is understood, of course, that the condition of slavery is justly imposed on the sinner. That is why we do not hear of a slave anywhere in the Scriptures until Noah, the just man, punished his son's sin with this word; and so that son deserved this name because of his misdeed, not because of his nature. The origin of the Latin word for slave, *servus*, is believed to be derived from the fact that those who by the laws of war could rightly be put to death by the conquerors, became *servi*, slaves, when they were preserved, receiving this name from their preservation. But even this enslavement could not have happened, if it were not for the deserts of sin. For even when a just war is fought it is in defence of his sin that the other side is contending; and victory, even when the victory falls to the wicked, is a humiliation visited on the conquered by divine judgement, either to correct or to punish their sins. We have a witness to this in Daniel, a man of God, who in captivity confesses to God his own sins and the sins of his people, and in devout grief testifies that they are the cause of that captivity. The first cause of slavery, then, is sin, whereby man was subjected to man in the condition of bondage; and this can only happen by the judgement of God, with whom there is no injustice, and who knows how to allot different punishments according to the deserts of the offenders.

Now, as our Lord above says, "Everyone who commits sin is sin's slave,"[6] and that is why, though

---

[5] Genesis 1:26.
[6] John 8:54.

many devout men are slaves to unrighteous masters, yet the masters they serve are not themselves free men; 'for when a man is conquered by another he is also bound as a slave to his conqueror.' And obviously it is a happier lot to be slave to a human being than to a lust; and, in fact, the most pitiless domination that devastates the hearts of men, is that exercised by this very lust for domination, to mention no others. However, in that order of peace in which men are subordinate to other men, humility is as salutary for the servants as pride is harmful to the masters. And yet by nature, in the condition in which God created man, no man is the slave either of man or of sin. But it remains true that slavery as a punishment is also ordained by that law which enjoins the preservation of the order of nature, and forbids its disturbance; in fact, if nothing had been done to contravene that law, there would have been nothing to require the discipline of slavery as a punishment. That explains also the Apostle's admonition to slaves, that they should be subject to their masters, and serve them loyally and willingly.[7] What he means is that if they cannot be set free by their masters, they themselves may thus make their slavery, in a sense, free, by serving not with the slyness of fear, but with the fidelity of affection, until all injustice disappears and all human lordship and power is annihilated, and God is all in all.

16. EQUITY IN THE RELATION OF MASTER AND SLAVE.

This being so, even though our righteous fathers had slaves, they so managed the peace of their households as to make a distinction between the situation of children and the condition of slaves in respect of the temporal goods of this life; and yet in the matter of the worship of God—in whom we must place our hope of everlasting goods—they were concerned, with equal affection, for all the members of their household. This is what the order of nature prescribes, so that this is the source of the name *paterfamilias,* a name that has become so generally used that even those who exercise unjust rule rejoice to be called by this title. On the other

hand, those who are genuine "fathers of their household" are concerned for the welfare of all in their households in respect of the worship and service of God, as if they were all their children, longing and praying that they may come to the heavenly home, where it will not be a necessary duty to give orders to men, because it will no longer be a necessary duty to be concerned for the welfare of those who are already in the felicity of that immortal state. But until that home is reached, the fathers have an obligation to exercise the authority of masters greater than the duty of slaves to put up with their condition as servants.

However, if anyone in the household is, through his disobedience, an enemy to the domestic peace, he is reproved by a word, or by a blow, or any other kind of punishment that is just and legitimate, to the extent allowed by human society; but this is for the benefit of the offender, intended to readjust him to the domestic peace from which he had broken away. For just as it is not an act of kindness to help a man, when the effect of the help is to make him lose a greater good, so it is not a blameless act to spare a man, when by so doing you let him fall into a greater sin. Hence the duty of anyone who would be blameless includes not only doing no harm to anyone but also restraining a man from sin or punishing his sin, so that either the man who is chastised may be corrected by his experience, or others may be deterred by his example. Now a man's house ought to be the beginning, or rather a small component part of the city, and every beginning is directed to some end of its own kind, and every component part contributes to the completeness of the whole of which it forms a part. The implication is quite apparent, that domestic peace contributes to the peace of the city—that is, the ordered harmony of those who live together in a house in the matter of giving and obeying orders, contributes to the ordered harmony concerning authority and obedience obtaining among the citizens. Consequently it is fitting that the father of a household should take his rules from the law of the city, and govern his household in such a way that it fits in with the peace of the city.

---

[7] Ephesians 6:5.

FROM *Confessions**

4

It is certain, O Lord, that theft is punished by your law, the law that is written in men's hearts and cannot be erased however sinful they are. For no thief can bear that another thief should steal from him, even if he is rich and the other is driven to it by want. Yet I was willing to steal, and steal I did, although I was not compelled by any lack, unless it were the lack of a sense of justice or a distaste for what was right and a greedy love of doing wrong. For of what I stole I already had plenty, and much better at that, and I had no wish to enjoy the things I coveted by stealing, but only to enjoy the theft itself and the sin. There was a pear-tree near our vineyard, loaded with fruit that was attractive neither to look at nor to taste. Late one night a band of ruffians, myself included, went off to shake down the fruit and carry it away, for we had continued our games out of doors until well after dark, as was our pernicious habit. We took away an enormous quantity of pears, not to eat them ourselves, but simply to throw them to the pigs. Perhaps we ate some of them, but our real pleasure consisted in doing something that was forbidden.

Look into my heart, O God, the same heart on which you took pity when it was in the depths of the abyss. Let my heart now tell you what prompted me to do wrong for no purpose, and why it was only my own love of mischief that made me do it. The evil in me was foul, but I loved it. I loved my own perdition and my own faults, not the things for which I committed wrong, but the wrong itself. My soul was vicious and broke away from your safe keeping to seek its own destruction looking for no profit in disgrace but only for disgrace itself.

5

The eye is attracted by beautiful objects, by gold and silver and all such things. There is great pleasure, too, in feeling something agreeable to the touch,

and material things have various qualities to please each of the other senses. Again, it is gratifying to be held in esteem by other men and to have the power of giving them orders and gaining the mastery over them. This is also the reason why revenge is sweet. But our ambition to obtain all these things must not lead us astray from you, O Lord, nor must we depart from what your law allows. The life we live on earth has its own attractions as well, because it has a certain beauty of its own in harmony with all the rest of this world's beauty. Friendship among men, too, is a delightful bond, uniting many souls in one. All these things and their like can be occasions of sin because, good though they are, they are of the lowest order of good, and if we are too much tempted by them we abandon those higher and better things, your truth, your law, and you yourself, O Lord our God. For these earthly things, too, can give joy, though not such joy as my God, who made them all, can give, because *honest men will rejoice in the Lord; upright hearts will not boast in vain.*

When there is an inquiry to discover why a crime has been committed, normally no one is satisfied until it has been shown that the motive might have been either the desire of gaining, or the fear of losing, one of those good things which I said were of the lowest order. For such things are attractive and have beauty, although they are paltry trifles in comparison with the worth of God's blessed treasures. A man commits murder and we ask the reason. He did it because he wanted his victim's wife or estates for himself, or so that he might live on the proceeds of robbery, or because he was afraid that the other might defraud him of something, or because he had been wronged and was burning for revenge. Surely no one would believe that he would commit murder for no reason but the sheer delight of killing? Sallust tells us that Catiline was a man of insane ferocity, "who chose to be cruel and vicious without apparent reason"; but we are also told that his purpose was "not to allow his men to lose heart or waste their skill through lack of practice." If we ask the reason for this, it is obvious that he meant that once he had made himself master of the government by means of this continual violence, he would obtain honour, power, and wealth and would no longer go in fear of the law

* From *Confessions*, by St. Augustine, translated by R. S. Pine-Coffin (New York: Penguin, 1961), pp. 47–49.

because of his crimes or have to face difficulties through lack of funds. So even Catiline did not love crime for crime's sake. He loved something quite different, for the sake of which he committed his crimes.

6

If the crime of theft which I committed that night as a boy of sixteen were a living thing, I could speak to it and ask what it was that, to my shame, I loved in it. I had no beauty because it was a robbery. It is true that the pears which we stole had beauty, because they were created by you, the good God, who are the most beautiful of all beings and the Creator of all things, the supreme Good and my own true Good. But it was not the pears that my unhappy soul desired. I had plenty of my own, better than those, and I only picked them so that I might steal. For no sooner had I picked

them than I threw them away, and tasted nothing in them but my own sin, which I relished and enjoyed. If any part of one of those pears passed my lips, it was the sin that gave it flavour.

*   *   *

REVIEW QUESTIONS

1. How does Augustine interpret the meaning of the sack of Rome? How does he use classical authors to defend his position?
2. How does he justify slavery?
3. What light does he shed on the daily life of Roman slaves?
4. What troubled Augustine about the memory of stealing the pears?

FROM The Theodosian Code: Christian Revisions of the Roman Legal Tradition

This compilation of Roman law was made in Constantinople during the reign of Emperor Theodosius II (r. 408–50), in an attempt to codify and arrange the many disparate senatorial statutes and imperial decisions that made up the Roman legal system. Theodosius also wanted to ensure that these legal traditions were updated to account for the powerful roles played by Christian bishops in Roman governance. The resulting laws also reflect the ways in which the adoption of Christianity had resulted in the creation of new types of criminal law and the enacting of legislation designed to silence or punish "heretics."

From *The Theodosian Code and Novels and the Sirmondian Constitutions*, translated by Clyde Pharr (Princeton, N.J.: Princeton University Press, 1980), pp. 440–51.

Book 16

TITLE 1
THE CATHOLIC FAITH

1. Emperors Valentinian and Valens, Augustuses, to Symmachus, Prefect of the City

If any judge or apparitor [sponsor] should appoint men of the Christian religion as custodians of temples, he shall know that neither his life nor his fortunes will be spared.

Given on the fifteenth day before the kalends of December at Milan in the year of the consulship of Valentinian and Valens Augustuses.—November 17, 365; 364.

2. Emperors Gratian, Valentinian, and Theodosius, Augustuses: An Edict to the People of the City of Constantinople

It is Our will that all the peoples who are ruled by the administration of Our Clemency shall practice that religion which the divine Peter the

Apostle transmitted to the Romans, as the religion which he introduced makes clear even unto this day. It is evident that this is the religion that is followed by the Pontiff Damascus and by Peter, Bishop of Alexandria, a man of apostolic sanctity; that is, according to the apostolic discipline and the evangelic doctrine, we shall believe in the single Deity of the Father, the Son, and the Holy Spirit, under the concept of equal majesty and of the Holy Trinity.

We command that those persons who follow this rule shall embrace the name of Catholic Christians. The rest, however, whom We adjudge demented and insane, shall sustain the infamy of heretical dogmas, their meeting places shall not receive the name of churches, and they shall be smitten first by divine vengeance and secondly by the retribution of Our own initiative, which We shall assume in accordance with the divine judgment.

Given on the third day before the kalends of March at Thessalonica in the year of the fifth consulship of Gratian Augustus and the first consulship of Theodosius Augustus.—February 28, 380.

3. The same Augustuses to Auxonius, Proconsul of Asia

We command that all churches shall immediately be surrendered to those bishops who confess that the Father, the Son, and the Holy Spirit are of one majesty and virtue, of the same glory, and of one splendor; to those bishops who produce no dissonance by unholy distinction, but who affirm the concept of the Trinity by the assertion of three Persons and the unity of the Divinity; to those bishops who appear to have been associated in the communion of Nectarius, Bishop of the Church of Constantinople, and of Timotheus, Bishop of the City of Alexandria in Egypt; to those bishops also who, in the regions of the Orient, appear to be communicants with Pelagius, Bishop of Laodicea, and with Diodorus, Bishop of Tarsus; also, in the Proconsular Province of Asia and in the Diocese of Asia, with Amphilochius, Bishop of Iconium, and with Optimus, Bishop of Antioch; in the Diocese of Pontus, with Helladius, Bishop of Caesarea, and with Otreius of Melitene, and with Gregorius,

Bishop of Nyssa; with Terennius, Bishop of Scythia, and with Marmarius, Bishop of Martianopolis. Those bishops who are of the communion and fellowship of such acceptable priests must be permitted to obtain the Catholic churches. All, however, who dissent from the communion of the faith of those who have been expressly mentioned in this special enumeration shall be expelled from their churches as manifest heretics and hereafter shall be altogether denied the right and power to obtain churches, in order that the priesthood of the true Nicene faith may remain pure, and after the clear regulations of Our law, there shall be no opportunity for malicious subtlety.

Given on the third day before the kalends of August at Heraclea in the year of the consulship of Eucherius and Syagrius.—July 30, 381.

4. Emperors Valentinian, Theodosius, and Arcadius, Augustuses, to Eusignius, Praetorian Prefect

We bestow the right of assembly upon those persons who believe according to the doctrines which in the times of Constantius of sainted memory were decreed as those that would endure forever, when the priests had been called together from all the Roman world and the faith was set forth at the Council of Ariminum by these very persons who are now known to dissent, a faith which was also confirmed by the Council of Constantinople. The right of voluntary assembly shall also be open to those persons for whom We have so ordered. If those persons who suppose that the right of assembly has been granted to them alone should attempt to provoke any agitation against the regulation of Our Tranquillity, they shall know that, as authors of sedition and as disturbers of the peace of the Church, they shall also pay the penalty of high treason with their life and blood. Punishment shall no less await those persons who may attempt to supplicate Us surreptitiously and secretly, contrary to this Our regulation.

Given on the tenth day before the kalends of February at Milan in the year of the consulship of Emperor Designate Honorius and of Evodius.— January 23, 386.

TITLE 2
BISHOPS, CHURCHES, AND CLERICS

1. Emperor Constantine Augustus

We have learned that clerics of the Catholic Church are being so harassed by a faction of heretics that they are being burdened by nominations and by service as tax receivers, as public custom demands, contrary to the privileges granted them. It is Our pleasure, therefore, that if Your Gravity should find any person thus harassed, another person shall be chosen as a substitute for him and that henceforward men of the aforesaid religion shall be protected from such outrages.

Given on the day before the kalends of November in the year of the third consulship of Constantine Augustus and of Licinius Caesar.—October 31, 313(?).

2. The same Augustus to Octavianus, Governor of Lucania [Basilicata] and of Bruttium [Calabra]

Those persons who devote the services of religion to divine worship, that is, those who are called clerics, shall be exempt from all compulsory public services whatever, lest, through the sacrilegious malice of certain persons, they should be called away from divine services.

Given on the twelfth day before the kalends of November in the year of the fifth consulship of Constantine Augustus and the consulship of Licinius Caesar.—October 21, 319; 313.

INTERPRETATION: This law by special ordinance directs that no person whatsoever by sacrilegious ordinance shall presume to make tax collectors or tax gatherers of clerics. The law commands that such clerics shall be free from every compulsory public service, that is, from every duty and servitude, and shall zealously serve the Church.

3. The same Augustus to Bassus, Praetorian Prefect

A constitution was issued which directs that thenceforth no decurion [government official] or descendant of a decurion or even any person provided with adequate resources and suitable to undertake compulsory public services shall take refuge in the name and the service of the clergy, but that in the place of deceased clerics thereafter only those persons shall be chosen as substitutes who have slender fortunes and who are not held bound to such compulsory municipal services. But We have learned that those persons also are being disturbed who became associated with the clergy before the promulgation of the aforesaid law. We command, therefore, that the latter shall be freed from all annoyance, and that the former, who in evasion of public duties have taken refuge in the number of the clergy after the issuance of the law, shall be completely separated from that body, shall be restored to their orders and to the municipal councils, and shall perform their municipal duties.

Posted on the fifteenth day before the kalends of August in the year of the sixth consulship of Constantine Augustus and the consulship of Constantius Caesar.—July 18, 320; 329.

4. The same Augustus to the People

Every person shall have the liberty to leave at his death any property that he wishes to the most holy and venerable council of the Catholic Church. Wills shall not become void. There is nothing which is more due to men than that the expression of their last will, after which they can no longer will anything, shall be free and the power of choice, which does not return again, shall be unhampered.

Posted on the fifth day before the nones of July at Rome in the year of the second consulship of Crispus and Constantine Caesars.—July 3, 321.

5. The same Augustus to Helpidius

Whereas We have learned that certain ecclesiastics and others devoting their services to the Catholic sect have been compelled by men of different religions to the performance of lustral [purifying] sacrifices, We decree by this sanction that, if any person should suppose that those who devote their services to the most sacred law may be forced to the ritual of an alien superstition, he shall be beaten publicly with clubs, provided that his legal status so permits. If, however, the consideration of his honorable rank protects him from such an outrage, he shall sustain the penalty of a very heavy fine, which shall be vindicated to the municipalities.

Given on the eighth day before the kalends of June at Sirmium in the year of the consulship of Severus and Rufinus.—May (December) 25, 323.

6. The same Augustus to Ablavius, Praetorian Prefect

Exemption from compulsory public services shall not be granted by popular consent, nor shall it be granted indiscriminately to all who petition under the pretext of being clerics, nor shall great numbers be added to the clergy rashly and beyond measure, but rather, when a cleric dies, another shall be selected to replace the deceased, one who has no kinship with a decurion family and who has not the wealth of resources whereby he may very easily support the compulsory public services. Thus, if there should be a dispute about the name of any person between a municipality and the clergy, if equity claims him for public service and if he is adjudged suitable for membership in the municipal council through either lineage or wealth, he shall be removed from the clergy and shall be delivered to the municipality. For the wealthy must assume secular obligations, and the poor must be supported by the wealth of the churches.

Posted on the kalends of June in the year of the seventh consulship of Constantine Augustus and the consulship of Constantius Caesar.—June 1, 326; 329.

7. The same Augustus to Valentinus, Governor of Numidia

Lectors [liturgical readers] of the divine scriptures, subdeacons, and the other clerics who through the injustice of heretics have been summoned to the municipal councils shall be absolved, and in the future, according to the practice of the Orient,[1] they shall by no means be summoned to the municipal councils, but they shall possess fullest exemption.

Given on the nones of February at Sofia (Serdica) in the year of the consulship of Gallicanus and Symmachus.—February 5, 330.

---

[1] Rome's eastern provinces.

8. Emperor Constantius Augustus to the Clergy, Greetings

According to the sanction which you are said to have obtained previously, no person shall obligate you and your slaves to new tax payments, but you shall enjoy exemption. Furthermore, you shall not be required to receive quartered persons, and if any of you, for the sake of a livelihood, should wish to conduct a business, they shall possess tax exemption.

Given on the sixth day before the kalends of September in the year of the consulship of Placidus and Romulus.—August 27, 343.

9. The same Augustus to Severianus, Proconsul of Achaea [western Greece]

All clerics must be exempt from compulsory services as decurions and from every annoyance of municipal duties. Their sons, moreover, must continue in the Church, if they are not held obligated to the municipal councils.

Given on the third day before the ides of April in the year of the consulship of Limenius and Catullinus.—April 11, 349.

10. Emperors Constantius and Constans Augustuses to all the Bishops throughout the various provinces.

In order that organizations in the service of the churches may be filled with a great multitude of people, tax exemption shall be granted to clerics and their acolytes, and they shall be protected from the exaction of compulsory public services of a menial nature. They shall by no means be subject to the tax payments of tradesmen, since it is manifest that the profits which they collect from stalls and workshops will benefit the poor. We decree also that their men who engage in trade shall be exempt from all tax payments. Likewise, the exaction of services for the maintenance of the supplementary postwagons shall cease. This indulgence We grant to their wives, children, and servants, to males and females equally, for We command that they also shall continue exempt from tax assessments.

Given on the seventh day before the kalends of June at Constantinople in the year of the sixth consulship of Constantius and the consulship of Constans.—May 26, 353; 320; 346.

11. The same Augustuses to Longinianus, Prefect of Egypt

We formerly sanctioned that bishops and clerics of the Catholic faith who possess nothing at all and are useless with respect to patrimony shall not be summoned to compulsory public services as decurions. But We learn that they are being disturbed in their life of perfection, to no public advantage. Therefore, We direct that their sons also who are not financially responsible and who are found to be below the legal age shall sustain no molestation.

Given on the fourth day before the kalends of March in the year of the seventh consulship of Constantius Augustus and the consulship of Constans Augustus.—February 26, 354; 342.

12. The same Augustuses to their dear friend Severus, Greetings

By a law of Our Clemency We prohibit bishops to be accused in the courts, lest there should be an unrestrained opportunity for fanatical spirits to accuse them, while the accusers assume that they will obtain impunity by the kindness of the bishops. Therefore, if any person should lodge any complaint, such complaint must unquestionably be examined before other bishops, in order that an opportune and suitable hearing may be arranged for the investigation of all concerned.

Given as a letter on the ninth day before the kalends of October.—September 23. Received on the nones of October in the year of the consulship of Arbitio and Lollianus.—October 7, 355.

INTERPRETATION: It is specifically prohibited that any person should dare to accuse a bishop before secular judges, but he shall not delay to submit to the hearing of bishops whatever he supposes may be due him according to the nature of the case, so that the assertions which he makes against the bishop may be decided in a court of other bishops.

13. The same Augustus and Julian Caesar to Leontius

We command that the privileges granted to the Church of the City of Rome and to its clerics shall be firmly guarded.

Given on the fourth day before the ides of November at Milan in the year of the ninth consulship of Constantius Augustus and the second consulship of Julian Caesar.—November 10, 357; 356.

14. The same Augustus and Julian Caesar to Bishop Felix

Clerics shall be protected from every injustice of an undue suit and from every wrong of an unjust exaction, and they shall not be summoned to compulsory public services of a menial nature. Moreover, when tradesmen are summoned to some legally prescribed tax payment, all clerics shall cease to be affected by such a disturbance; for if they have accumulated anything by thrift, foresight, or trading, but still in accordance with honesty, this must be administered for the use of the poor and needy, and whatever they have been able to acquire and collect from their workshops and stalls they shall regard as having been collected for the profit of religion.

(1) Moreover, with respect to their men who are employed in trade, the statutes of the sainted Emperor, that is, of Our father,[2] provided with manifold regulations that the aforesaid clerics should abound in numerous privileges. (2) Therefore, with respect to the aforesaid clerics, the requirement of extraordinary services and all molestation shall cease. (3) Moreover, they and their resources and substance shall not be summoned to furnish supplementary postwagons.

(4) All clerics shall be assisted by the prerogative of this nature, namely, that wives of clerics and also their children and attendants, males and females equally, and their children, shall continue to be exempt forever from tax payments and free from such compulsory public services.

Given on the eighth day before the ides of December at Milan—December 6. Read into the

---

[2] I.e., Constantine.

records on the fifth day before the kalends of January in the year of the ninth consulship of Constantius Augustus and the second consulship of Julian Caesar.—December 28, 357; 356. Or: Read in court proceedings, acta, 2, 8, 1, n. 4.

*   *   *

29. Emperors Arcadius and Honorius, Augustuses, to Hierius, Vicar of Africa

We direct that whatever statutes were enacted by Our fathers at different times with respect to the sacrosanct churches shall remain inviolate and unimpaired. None of their privileges, therefore, shall be altered, and protection shall be granted to all those persons who serve the churches, for We desire that reverence shall be increased in Our time rather than that any of the privileges which were formerly granted should be altered.

Given on the tenth day before the kalends of April at Milan in the year of the consulship of Olybrius and Probinus.—March 23, 395.

30. The same Augustuses to Theodorus, Praetorian Prefect

We decree nothing new by the present sanction; rather, We confirm those privileges that appear to have been granted formerly. We prohibit, therefore, under threat of punishment, that privileges which were formerly obtained through reverence for religion shall be curtailed, so that those who serve the Church may also enjoy fully those special benefits which the Church enjoys.

Given on the day before the kalends of February at Milan in the year of the consulship of Caesarius and Atticus.—January 31, 397.

31. The same Augustuses to Theodorus, Praetorian Prefect

If any person should break forth into such sacrilege that he should invade Catholic churches and should inflict any outrage on the priests and ministers, or on the worship itself and on the place of worship, whatever occurs shall be brought to the notice of the authorities by letters of the municipal senates, magistrates, and curators, and by official reports of the apparitors who are called rural police, so that the names of those who could be recognized may be revealed. Moreover, if the offense is said to have been perpetrated by a multitude, some, if not all, can nevertheless be recognized, and by their confession the names of their accomplices may be disclosed. Thus the governor of the province shall know that the outrage to the priests and ministers of the Catholic Church, to the divine worship, and to the place of worship itself must be punished with a capital sentence against the aforesaid convicted or confessed criminals. The governor shall not wait until the bishop shall demand the avenging of his own injury, since the bishop's sanctity leaves nothing to him except the glory of forgiving. It shall be not only permissible but even laudable for all persons to prosecute as a public crime the atrocious outrages committed against priests and ministers and to exact punishment from such criminals. But if it should be impossible to bring to court a violent multitude by the operation of civil apparitors and by the help of the municipal senates and landholders, in case the multitude protects itself by arms or by the difficulty of the places, the African judges shall prefix the contents of this law to letters which they shall send to the Respectable Count of Africa, and they shall demand the aid of the armed apparitors, in order that the perpetrators of such crimes may not escape.

Given on the seventh day before the kalends of May at Milan in the year of the fourth consulship of Honorius Augustus and the consulship of Eutychianus.—April 25, 398; January 15, 409.

32. The same Augustuses to Caesarius, Praetorian Prefect

If perchance the bishops should suppose that they are in need of clerics, they will more properly ordain them from the number of monks. They shall not incur disfavor by holding those persons who are bound by public and private accounts but shall have those already approved.

Given on the seventh day before the kalends of August in the year of the fourth consulship of Honorius Augustus and the consulship of Eutychianus.—July 26, 398(?).

TITLE 3
MONKS

1. Emperors Valentinian, Theodosius, and Arcadius Augustuses to Tatianus, Praetorian Prefect

If any persons should be found in the profession of monks, they shall be ordered to seek out and to inhabit desert places and desolate solitudes.

Given on the fourth day before the nones of September at Verona in the year of the fourth consulship of Valentinian Augustus and the consulship of Neoterius.—September 2, 390.

2. The same Augustuses to Tatianus, Praetorian Prefect

We direct that the monks to whom the municipalities had been forbidden, since they are strengthened by judicial injustices, shall be restored to their original status, and the aforesaid law shall be repealed. Thus indeed, We revoke such a decree of Our Clemency, and We grant them free ingress into the towns.

Given on the fifteenth day before the kalends of May at Constantinople in the year of the second consulship of Arcadius Augustus and the consulship of Rufinus.—April 17, 392.

* * *

REVIEW QUESTIONS

1. Judging from these laws, what can you conclude about the relationship between the Roman government and the Christian religion after the conversion of Constantine?

2. What groups and individuals emerge as having special legal privileges within the Christian Roman Empire? Which groups and individuals have their rights curtailed?

3. Although the Code was compiled in the Greek-speaking Eastern Roman Empire, it was written in the traditional Latin language of Roman law and bureaucracy. How would you summarize the main assumptions and precepts of Roman legal thought, based on these excerpts from the Code? How do these compare with the older principles of Roman law summarized in the Twelve Tables (p. 158)?

SAINT BENEDICT

FROM *The Rule*

Benedict of Nursia (c. 480–547 C.E.) was a well-born Roman and the founder of an important monastery at Monte Cassino, in south-central Italy. Dissatisfied with other varieties of monasticism, which he critiques in the following excerpt, he drew on Egyptian and Syriac models to formulate a new and very practical set of rules that would structure the daily life, work, and prayer of all the monks within the walls of his monastery, which he conceived as a self-sustaining community that could protect itself from the violence and temptations of the outside world. This Rule continues to form the basis of religious life in Benedictine monasteries around the globe.

From *The Rule of Saint Benedict*, translated by Abbot Gasquet (London: Chatto & Windus, 1909).

Chapter I
Of the Several Kinds of Monks and Their Lives

It is recognized that there are four kinds of monks. The first are the Cenobites: that is, those who live in a monastery under a Rule or an abbot. The second kind is that of Anchorites, or Hermits, who not in the first fervour of conversion, but after long trial in the monastery, and already taught by the example of many others, have learnt to fight against the devil, are well prepared to go forth from the ranks of the brotherhood to the single combat of the desert. They can now, by God's help, safely fight against the vices of their flesh and against evil thoughts singly, with their own hand and arm and without the encouragement of a companion.

The third and worst kind of monks is that of the Sarabites, who have not been tried under any Rule nor schooled by an experienced master, as gold is proved in the furnace, but soft as is lead and still in their works cleaving to the world, are known to lie to God by their tonsure. These in twos or threes, or more frequently singly, are shut up, without a shepherd; not in our Lord's fold, but in their own. The pleasure of carrying out their particular desires is their law, and whatever they dream of or choose this they call holy; but what they like not, that they account unlawful.

The fourth class of monks is called Gyrovagi (or Wanderers). These move about all their lives through various countries, staying as guests for three or four days at different monasteries. They are always on the move and never settle down, and are slaves to their own wills and to the enticements of gluttony. In every way they are worse than the Sarabites, and of their wretched way of life it is better to be silent than to speak.

Leaving these therefore aside, let us by God's help set down a Rule for Cenobites, who are the best kind of monks.

Chapter II
What the Abbot Should Be

An abbot to be fit to rule a monastery should ever remember what he is called, and in his acts illus-trate his high calling. For in a monastery he is considered to take the place of Christ, since he is called by His name as the apostle saith, *Ye have received the spirit of the adoption of sons, whereby we cry, Abba, Father.*[1] Therefore the abbot should neither teach, ordain, nor require anything against the command of our Lord (God forbid!), but in the minds of his disciples let his orders and teaching be mingled with the leaven of divine justice.

The abbot should ever be mindful that at the dread judgment of God there will be inquiry both as to his teaching and as to the obedience of his disciples. Let the abbot know that any lack of goodness, which the master of the family shall find in his flock, will be accounted the shepherd's fault. On the other hand, he shall be acquitted in so far as he shall have shown all the watchfulness of a shepherd over a restless and disobedient flock: and if as their pastor he shall have employed every care to cure their corrupt manners, he shall be declared guiltless in the Lord's judgment, and he may say with the prophet, *I have not hidden Thy justice in my heart; I have told Thy truth and Thy salvation;*[2] *but they contemned and despised me.*[3] And then in the end shall death be inflicted as a meet punishment upon the sheep which have not responded to his care. . . .

Let him make no distinction of persons in the monastery. Let not one be loved more than another, save such as be found to excel in obedience or good works. Let not the free-born be put before the serf-born in religion, unless there be other reasonable cause for it. If upon due consideration the abbot shall see such cause he may place him where he pleases; otherwise let all keep their own places, because *whether bond or free we are all one in Christ,*[4] and bear an equal burden of service under one Lord: *for with God there is no accepting of persons.*[5] For one thing only are we preferred by Him, if we are found better than others in good works and more humble. Let the abbot therefore have

---

[1] Romans 8:15.
[2] Psalms 39:11.
[3] Isaiah 1:2.
[4] 1 Corinthians 9:27.
[5] Ephesians 6:9.

equal love for all, and let all, according to their deserts, be under the same discipline.

The abbot in his teaching should always observe that apostolic rule which saith, *Reprove, entreat, rebuke.*[6] That is to say, as occasions require he ought to mingle encouragement with reproofs. Let him manifest the sternness of a master and the loving affection of a father. He must reprove the undisciplined and restless severely, but he should exhort such as are obedient, quiet and patient, for their better profit. We charge him, however, to reprove and punish the stubborn and negligent. Let him not shut his eyes to the sins of offenders; but, directly they begin to show themselves and to grow, he must use every means to root them up utterly, remembering the fate of Heli, the priest of Silo. To the more virtuous and apprehensive, indeed, he may for the first or second time use words of warning; but in dealing with the stubborn, the hard-hearted, the proud and the disobedient, even at the very beginning of their sin, let him chastise them with stripes and with bodily punishment, knowing that it is written, *The fool is not corrected with words.*[7] And again, *Strike thy son with a rod and thou shalt deliver his soul from death.*[8]

The abbot ought ever to bear in mind what he is and what he is called; he ought to know that to whom more is entrusted, from him more is exacted. Let him recognize how difficult and how hard a task he has undertaken, to rule souls and to make himself a servant to the humours of many. . . .

Chapter III
On Taking Counsel of the Brethren

Whenever any weighty matters have to be transacted in the monastery let the abbot call together all the community and himself propose the matter for discussion. After hearing the advice of the brethren let him consider it in his own mind, and then do what he shall judge most expedient. We ordain that all must be called to council, because

the Lord often reveals to a younger member what is best. And let the brethren give their advice with all humble subjection, and presume not stiffly to defend their own opinion. Let them rather leave the matter to the abbot's discretion, so that all submit to what he shall deem best. As it becometh disciples to obey their master, so doth it behove the master to dispose of all things with forethought and justice.

In all things, therefore, every one shall follow the Rule as their master, and let no one rashly depart from it. In the monastery no one is to be led by the desires of his own heart, neither shall any one within or without the monastery presume to argue wantonly with his abbot. If he presume to do so let him be subjected to punishment according to the Rule.

The abbot, however, must himself do all things in the fear of God and according to the Rule, knowing that he shall undoubtedly have to give an account of his whole government to God, the most just Judge.

If anything of less moment has to be done in the monastery let the abbot take advice of the seniors only, as it is written, *Do all things with counsel, and thou shalt not afterwards repent of it.*[9] . . .

Chapter V
On Obedience

The first degree of humility is prompt obedience. This is required of all who, whether by reason of the holy servitude to which they are pledged, or through fear of hell, or to attain to the glory of eternal life, hold nothing more dear than Christ. Such disciples delay not in doing what is ordered by their superior, just as if the command had come from God. Of such our Lord says, *At the hearing of the ear he hath obeyed me.*[10] And to the teachers He likewise says, *He that heareth you, heareth me.*[11]

For this reason such disciples, surrendering forthwith all they possess, and giving up their own

[6] 2 Timothy 4:2.
[7] Proverbs 23:13.
[8] Proverbs 23:14.

[9] Ecclesiasticus 32:24.
[10] Psalms 17:45.
[11] Luke 10:16.

will, leave unfinished what they were working at, and with the ready foot of obedience in their acts follow the word of command. Thus, as it were, at the same moment comes the order of the master and the finished work of the disciple: with the speed of the fear of God both go jointly forward and are quickly effected by such as ardently desire to walk in the way of eternal life. These take the narrow way, of which the Lord saith, *Narrow is the way which leads to life.*[12] That is, they live not as they themselves will, neither do they obey their own desires and pleasures; but following the command and direction of another and abiding in their monasteries, their desire is to be ruled by an abbot. Without doubt such as these carry out that saying of our Lord, *I came not to do my own will, but the will of Him Who sent me.*[13]

This kind of obedience will be both acceptable to God and pleasing to men, when what is ordered is not done out of fear, or slowly and coldly, grudgingly, or with reluctant protest. Obedience shown to superiors is indeed given to God, Who Himself hath said, *He that heareth you, heareth Me.*[14] What is commanded should be done by those under obedience, with a good will, since *God loveth a cheerful giver.*[15] If the disciple obey unwillingly and murmur in word as well as in heart, it will not be accepted by God, Who considereth the heart of a murmurer, even if he do what was ordered. For a work done in this spirit shall have no reward; rather shall the doer incur the penalty appointed for murmurers if he amend not and make not satisfaction.

Chapter VI
On Silence

Let us do as the prophet says, *I have said, I will keep my ways, that I offend not with my tongue. I have been watchful over my mouth: I held my peace and humbled myself and was silent from speaking even*

good things.[16] Here the prophet shows that, for the sake of silence, we are at times to abstain even from good talk. If this be so, how much more needful is it that we refrain from evil words, on account of the penalty of the sin! Because of the importance of silence, therefore, let leave to speak be seldom given, even to perfect disciples, although their talk be of good and holy matters and tending to edification, since it is written, *In much speaking, thou shalt not escape sin.*[17] The master, indeed, should speak and teach: the disciple should hold his peace and listen.

Whatever, therefore, has to be asked of the prior, let it be done with all humility and with reverent submission. But as to coarse, idle words, or such as move to laughter, we utterly condemn and ban them in all places. We do not allow any disciple to give mouth to them. . . .

Chapter XIX
Of the Manner of Singing the Office

We believe that the Divine Presence is everywhere, and that the eyes of the Lord behold both the good and the bad in all places. Especially do we believe without any doubt that this is so when we assist at the Divine Office. Let us therefore always be mindful of what the prophet says, *Serve ye the Lord in fear;*[18] and again, *Sing ye His praises with understanding;*[19] and, *In the sight of angels I will sing praise to Thee.*[20] Wherefore let us consider how it behoveth us to be in the sight of God and the angels, and so let us take our part in the psalmody that mind and voice accord together.

Chapter XX
On Reverence at Prayer

If, when we wish to obtain some favour from those who have the power to help us, we dare not ask

---

[12] Matthew 7:14.
[13] John 5:30.
[14] Luke 10:16.
[15] 2 Corinthians 9:7.

[16] Psalms 38:2, 3.
[17] Proverbs 18:21.
[18] Psalms 2:11.
[19] Psalms 46:8.
[20] Psalms 137:1.

except with humility and reverence, how much more reason is there that we should present our petitions to the Lord God of the universe in all lowliness of heart and purity of devotion. We may know for certain that we shall be heard, not because we use many words, but on account of the purity of our hearts and our tears of sorrow. Our prayer, therefore, should be short and pure, unless by some inspiration of divine grace it be prolonged. All prayer made by the community in common, however, should be short; and when the prior (that is, the superior) has given the sign, let all rise together. . . .

Chapter XXII
How the Monks Are to Sleep

All shall sleep in separate beds and each shall receive, according to the appointment of his abbot, bedclothes, fitted to the condition of his life. If it be possible let them all sleep in a common dormitory, but if their great number will not allow this they may sleep in tens or twenties, with seniors to have charge of them. Let a candle be constantly burning in the room until morning, and let the monks sleep clothed and girt with girdles or cords; but they are not to have knives by their sides in their beds, lest perchance they be injured whilst sleeping. In this way the monks shall always be ready to rise quickly when the signal is given and hasten each one to come before his brother to the Divine Office, and yet with all gravity and modesty.

The younger brethren are not to have their beds next to each other, but amongst those of the elders. When they rise for the Divine Office let them gently encourage one another, because of the excuses made by those that are drowsy. . . .

Chapter XXXII
Concerning the Iron Tools or Other Goods of the Monastery

Let the abbot appoint brethren, of whose life and moral conduct he is sure, to keep the iron tools, the clothes, or other property of the monastery. To these he shall allot the various things to be kept and collected, as he shall deem expedient. The abbot shall hold a list of these things that, as the brethren succeed each other in their appointed work, he may know what he gives and what he receives back. If any one shall treat the property of the monastery in a slovenly or careless way let him be corrected; if he does not amend let him be subjected to regular discipline.

Chapter XXXIII
Ought Monks to Have Anything of Their Own?

Above all others, let this vice be extirpated in the monastery. No one, without leave of the abbot, shall presume to give, or receive, or keep as his own, anything whatever: neither book, nor tablets, nor pen: nothing at all. For monks are men who can claim no dominion even over their own bodies or wills. All that is necessary, however, they may hope from the Father of the monastery; but they shall keep nothing which the abbot has not given or allowed. All things are to be common to all, as it is written, *Neither did any one say or think that aught was his own.*[21] Hence if any one shall be found given to this most wicked vice let him be admonished once or twice, and if he do not amend let him be subjected to correction. . . .

Chapter XLVIII
Of Daily Manual Labour

Idleness is an enemy of the soul. Because this is so the brethren ought to be occupied at specified times in manual labour, and at other fixed hours in holy reading. We therefore think that both these may be arranged for as follows: from Easter to the first of October, on coming out from Prime, let the brethren labour till about the fourth hour.[22] From the

---

[21] Acts 4:32.
[22] In summer, about 9:00 A.M.

fourth till close upon the sixth hour[23] let them employ themselves in reading. On rising from table after the sixth hour let them rest on their beds in strict silence; but if any one shall wish to read, let him do so in such a way as not to disturb any one else.

Let None be said somewhat before the time, about the middle of the eighth hour,[24] and after this all shall work at what they have to do till evening. If, however, the nature of the place or poverty require them to labour at gathering in the harvest, let them not grieve at that, for then are they truly monks when they live by the labour of their hands, as our Fathers and the Apostles did. Let everything, however, be done with moderation for the sake of the faint-hearted.

From the first of October till the beginning of Lent let the brethren be occupied in reading till the end of the second hour.[25] At that time Tierce shall be said, after which they shall labour at the work enjoined them till None.[26] At the first signal for the Hour of None all shall cease to work, so as to be ready when the second signal is given. After their meal they shall be employed in reading or on the psalms.

On the days of Lent, from the morning till the end of the third[27] hour, the brethren are to have time for reading, after which let them work at what is set them to do till the close of the tenth hour.[28] During these Lenten days let each one have some book from the library which he shall read through carefully. These books are to be given out at the beginning of Lent.

It is of much import that one or two seniors be appointed to go about the monastery at such times as the brethren are free to read, in order to see that no one is slothful, given to idleness or foolish talking instead of reading, and so not only makes no profit himself but also distracts others. If any such be found (which God forbid) let him be corrected once or twice, and if he amend not let him be subjected to regular discipline of such a character that the rest may take warning. Moreover one brother shall not associate with another at unsuitable hours.

On Sunday also, all, save those who are assigned to various offices, shall have time for reading. If, however, any one be so negligent and slothful as to be unwilling or unable to read or meditate, he must have some work given him, so as not to be idle. For weak brethren, or those of delicate constitutions, some work or craft shall be found to keep them from idleness, and yet not such as to crush them by the heavy labour or to drive them away. The weakness of such brethren must be taken into consideration by the abbot....

---

[23] About noon.
[24] About 3:20 P.M.
[25] In winter, about 9 A.M.
[26] About 1:20 P.M.
[27] About 10:00 A.M.
[28] About 2:40 P.M.

REVIEW QUESTIONS

1. How does Benedict justify the need for a new rule to organize religious life? What is wrong with the other varieties of monasticism that he identifies?

2. Although many portions of *The Rule* regulate worship in the monastery, Benedict pays close attention to practical matters: governance, decision making, eating, sleeping, work, relationships. Why would he consider these things so fundamental to monastic spirituality? What do we learn about daily life at Monte Cassino?

3. What can you infer from this source about the world outside the monastery? How might the events of Benedict's lifetime have shaped his *Rule*?

GREGORY OF TOURS

FROM *History of the Franks*

Gregory, bishop of Tours (538–594 c.e.), was descended from a long line of provincial nobles and bishops in Gaul. His History of the Franks *relates how the Franks and other tribes conquered and settled a key area of the Roman Empire, as seen through the eyes of a Gallo-Roman aristocrat. These selections discuss how and why the Frankish chieftain Clovis converted to Roman Christianity in 496 c.e., and his role in solidifying a new dynasty. Barbarian tribes had not yet produced historians or documents, so we must depend on the views of relative outsiders such as Gregory for details on their earliest history.*

From *History of the Franks by Gregory of Tours*, edited by Ernest Brehaut (New York: Columbia University Press, 1944), pp. 36–45.

*   *   *

After these events Childeric died [c. 482 c.e.] and Clovis his son reigned in his stead. In the fifth year of his reign Siagrius, king of the Romans, son of Egidius, had his seat in the city of Soissons which Egidius, who has been mentioned before, once held. And Clovis came against him with Ragnachar, his kinsman, because he used to possess the kingdom, and demanded that they make ready a battle-field. And Siagrius did not delay nor was he afraid to resist. And so they fought against each other and Siagrius, seeing his army crushed, turned his back and fled swiftly to king Alaric at Toulouse. And Clovis sent to Alaric to send him back, otherwise he was to know that Clovis would make war on him for his refusal. And Alaric was afraid that he would incur the anger of the Franks on account of Siagrius, seeing it is the fashion of the Goths to be terrified, and he surrendered him in chains to Clovis' envoys. And Clovis took him and gave orders to put him under guard, and when he had got his kingdom he directed that he be executed secretly.

At that time many churches were despoiled by Clovis' army, since he was as yet involved in hea-then error. Now the army had taken from a certain church a vase of wonderful size and beauty, along with the remainder of the utensils for the service of the church. And the bishop of the church sent messengers to the king asking that the vase at least be returned, if he could not get back any more of the sacred dishes. On hearing this the king said to the messenger: "Follow us as far as Soissons, because all that has been taken is to be divided there and when the lot assigns me that dish I will do what the father asks."

Then when he came to Soissons and all the booty was set in their midst, the king said: "I ask of you, brave warriors, not to refuse to grant me in addition to my share, yonder dish," that is, he was speaking of the vase just mentioned. In answer to the speech of the king those of more sense replied: "Glorious king, all that we see is yours, and we ourselves are subject to your rule. Now do what seems well-pleasing to you; for no one is able to resist your power." When they said this a foolish, envious and excitable fellow lifted his battle-ax and struck the vase, and cried in a loud voice: "You shall get nothing here except what the lot fairly bestows on you." At this all were stupefied, but the king endured the insult with the gentleness of patience, and taking the vase he handed it over to the messenger of the church, nursing the wound deep in his heart.

And at the end of the year he ordered the whole army to come with their equipment of armor, to show the brightness of their arms on the field of March. And when he was reviewing them all carefully, he came to the man who struck the vase, and said to him: "No one has brought armor so carelessly kept as you; for neither your spear nor sword nor ax is in serviceable condition." And seizing his ax he cast it to the earth, and when the other had bent over somewhat to pick it up, the king raised his hands and drove his own ax into the man's head. "This," said he, "is what you did at Soissons to the vase."

Upon the death of this man, he ordered the rest to depart, raising great dread of himself by this action. He made many wars and gained many victories. In the tenth year of his reign he made war on the Thuringi and brought them under his dominion.

Now the king of the Burgundians was Gundevech, of the family of king Athanaric the persecutor, whom we have mentioned before. He had four sons; Gundobad, Godegisel, Chilperic and Godomar. Gundobad killed his brother Chilperic with the sword, and sank his wife in water with a stone tied to her neck. His two daughters he condemned to exile; the older of these, who became a nun, was called Chrona, and the younger Clotilda. And as Clovis often sent embassies to Burgundy, the maiden Clotilda was found by his envoys. And when they saw that she was of good bearing and wise, and learned that she was of the family of the king, they reported this to King Clovis, and he sent an embassy to Gundobad without delay asking her in marriage. And Gundobad was afraid to refuse, and surrendered her to the men, and they took the girl and brought her swiftly to the king. The king was very glad when he saw her, and married her, having already by a concubine a son named Theodoric.

He had a first-born son by queen Clotilda, and as his wife wished to consecrate him in baptism, she tried unceasingly to persuade her husband, saying: "The gods you worship are nothing, and they will be unable to help themselves or any one else. For they are graven out of stone or wood or some metal. And the names you have given them are names of men and not of gods, as Saturn, who is declared to have fled in fear of being banished from his kingdom by his son; as Jove himself, the foul perpetrator of all shameful crimes, committing incest with men, mocking at his kinswomen, not able to refrain from intercourse with his own sister as she herself says: *Jovisque et soror et conjunx.*[1] What could Mars or Mercury do? They are endowed rather with the magic arts than with the power of the divine name. But he ought rather to be worshipped who created by his word heaven and earth, the sea and all that in them is out of a state of nothingness, who made the sun shine, and adorned the heavens with stars, who filled the waters with creeping things, the earth with living things and the air with creatures that fly, at whose nod the earth is decked with growing crops, the trees with fruit, the vines with grapes, by whose hand mankind was created, by whose generosity all that creation serves and helps man whom he created as his own."

But though the queen said this the spirit of the king was by no means moved to belief, and he said: "It was at the command of our gods that all things were created and came forth, and it is plain that your God has no power and, what is more, he is proven not to belong to the family of the gods." Meantime the faithful queen made her son ready for baptism; she gave command to adorn the church with hangings and curtains, in order that he who could not be moved by persuasion might be urged to belief by this mystery. The boy, whom they named Ingomer, died after being baptized, still wearing the white garments in which he became regenerate.

At this the king was violently angry, and reproached the queen harshly, saying: "If the boy had been dedicated in the name of my gods he would certainly have lived; but as it is, since he was baptized in the name of your God, he could not live

---

[1] "And of Jove both sister and wife." Virgil, *Æneid* I: 46–47.

at all." To this the queen said: "I give thanks to the omnipotent God, creator of all, who has judged me not wholly unworthy, that he should deign to take to his kingdom one born from my womb. My soul is not stricken with grief for his sake, because I know that, summoned from this world as he was in his baptismal garments, he will be fed by the vision of God."

After this she bore another son, whom she named Chlodomer at baptism; and when he fell sick, the king said: "It is impossible that anything else should happen to him than happened to his brother, namely, that being baptized in the name of your Christ, he should die at once." But through the prayers of his mother, and the Lord's command, he became well.

The queen did not cease to urge him to recognize the true God and cease worshiping idols. But he could not be influenced in any way to this belief, until at last a war arose with the Alamanni, in which he was driven by necessity to confess what before he had of his free will denied. It came about that as the two armies were fighting fiercely, there was much slaughter, and Clovis's army began to be in danger of destruction. He saw it and raised his eyes to heaven, and with remorse in his heart he burst into tears and cried: "Jesus Christ, whom Clotilda asserts to be the son of the living God, who art said to give aid to those in distress, and to bestow victory on those who hope in thee, I beseech the glory of thy aid, with the vow that if thou wilt grant me victory over these enemies, and I shall know that power which she says that people dedicated in thy name have had from thee, I will believe in thee and be baptized in thy name. For I have invoked my own gods, but, as I find, they have withdrawn from aiding me; and therefore I believe that they possess no power, since they do not help those who obey them. I now call upon thee, I desire to believe thee, only let me be rescued from my adversaries." And when he said this, the Alamanni turned their backs, and began to disperse in flight. And when they saw that their king was killed, they submitted to the dominion of Clovis, saying: "Let not the people perish further, we pray; we are yours now." And he stopped the

fighting, and after encouraging his men, retired in peace and told the queen how he had had merit to win the victory by calling on the name of Christ. This happened in the fifteenth year of his reign.

Then the queen asked saint Remi, bishop of Rheims, to summon Clovis secretly, urging him to introduce the king to the word of salvation. And the bishop sent for him secretly and began to urge him to believe in the true God, maker of heaven and earth, and to cease worshiping idols, which could help neither themselves nor any one else. But the king said: "I gladly hear you, most holy father; but there remains one thing: the people who follow me cannot endure to abandon their gods; but I shall go and speak to them according to your words." He met with his followers, but before he could speak the power of God anticipated him, and all the people cried out together: "O pious king, we reject our mortal gods, and we are ready to follow the immortal God whom Remi preaches." This was reported to the bishop, who was greatly rejoiced, and bade them get ready the baptismal font.

The squares were shaded with tapestried canopies, the churches adorned with white curtains, the baptistery set in order, the aroma of incense spread, candles of fragrant odor burned brightly, and the whole shrine of the baptistery was filled with a divine fragrance: and the Lord gave such grace to those who stood by that they thought they were placed amid the odors of paradise. And the king was the first to ask to be baptized by the bishop. Another Constantine advanced to the baptismal font, to terminate the disease of ancient leprosy and wash away with fresh water the foul spots that had long been borne. And when he entered to be baptized, the saint of God began with ready speech: "Gently bend your neck, Sigamber; worship what you burned; burn what you worshipped."

The holy bishop Remi was a man of excellent wisdom and especially trained in rhetorical studies, and of such surpassing holiness that he equalled the miracles of Silvester. For there is extant a book of his life which tells that he raised a dead man. And so the king confessed all-powerful God in the Trinity, and was baptized in the name of the Father, Son and holy Spirit, and was anointed with the holy ointment with the sign of the cross of Christ. And of his army more than 3000 were baptized. His sister also, Albofled, was baptized, who not long after passed to the Lord. And when the king was in mourning for her, the holy Remi sent a letter of consolation which began in this way: "The reason of your mourning pains me, and pains me greatly, that Albofled your sister, of good memory, has passed away. But I can give you this comfort, that her departure from the world was such that she ought to be envied rather than mourned." Another sister also was converted, Lanthechild by name, who had fallen into the heresy of the Arians, and she confessed that the Son and the holy Spirit were equal to the Father, and was anointed.

At that time the brothers Gundobad and Godegisel were kings of the country about the Rhone and the Saône together with the province of Marseilles. And they, as well as their people, belonged to the Arian sect.[2] And since they were fighting with each other, Godegisel, hearing of the victories of King Clovis, sent an embassy to him secretly, saying: "If you will give me aid in attacking my brother, so that I may be able to kill him in battle or drive him from the country, I will pay you every year whatever tribute you yourself wish to impose." Clovis accepted this offer gladly, and promised aid whenever need should ask. And at a time agreed upon he marched his army against Gundobad. On hearing of this, Gundobad, who did not know of his brother's treachery, sent to him, saying: "Come to my assistance, since the Franks are in motion against us and are coming to our country to take it. Therefore let us be united against a nation hostile to us, lest because of division we suffer in turn what other peoples have suffered." And the other said: "I will come with my army, and will give you aid."

And these three, namely, Clovis against Gundobad and Godegisel, were marching their armies to the same point, and they came with all their warlike equipment to the stronghold named Dijon. And they fought on the river Ouche, and Godegisel joined Clovis, and both armies crushed the people of Gundobad. And he perceived the treachery of his brother, whom he had not suspected, and turned his back and began to flee, hastening along the banks of the Rhone, and he came to the city of Avignon. And Godegisel having won the victory, promised to Clovis a part of his kingdom, and departed quietly and entered Vienne in triumph, as if he now held the whole kingdom.

King Clovis increased his army further, and set off after Gundobad to drag him from his city and slay him. He heard it, and was terrified, and feared that sudden death would come to him. However he had with him Aridius, a man famed for energy and wisdom, and he sent for him and said: "Difficulties wall me in on every side, and I do not know what to do, because these barbarians have come upon us to slay us and destroy the whole country." To this Aridius answered: "You must soften the fierceness of this man in order not to perish. Now if it is pleasing in your eyes, I will pretend to flee from you and to pass over to his side, and when I come to him, I shall prevent his harming either you or this country. Only be willing to do what he demands of you by my advice, until the Lord in his goodness deigns to make your cause successful." And Gundobad said: "I will do whatever you direct."

When he said this, Aridius bade him good-by and departed, and going to King Clovis he said: "Behold I am your humble servant, most pious king, I come to your protection, leaving the wretched Gundobad. And if your goodness condescends to receive me, both you and your children shall have in me a true and faithful servant." Clovis received him very readily, and kept him by him, for he was entertaining in story-telling, ready in counsel, just in judgment, and faithful in what was put in his charge. Then when Clovis with all his army sat around the walls of the city, Aridius said: "O King, if the glory of your loftiness should kindly consent to hear the few words of my lowliness, though you do not need counsel, yet I would utter them with entire faithfulness, and they will be

---

[2] Followers of the bishop Arius (c. 250–336 C.E.) who taught that Jesus was not equal to God the Father in divinity. His teachings were deemed heretical at the First Council of Nicea in 325.

advantageous to you and to the cities through which you purpose to go. Why," said he, "do you keep your army here, when your enemy sits in a very strong place? If you ravage the fields, lay waste the meadows, cut down the vineyards, lay low the olive-yards, and destroy all the produce of the country, you do not, however, succeed in doing him any harm. Send an embassy rather and impose tribute to be paid you every year, so that the country may be safe and you may rule forever over a tributary. And if he refuses, then do whatever pleases you." The king took this advice, and commanded his army to return home. Then he sent an embassy to Gundobad, and ordered him to pay him every year a tribute. And he paid it at once and promised that he would pay it for the future.

Later he regained his power, and now contemptuously refused to pay the promised tribute to King Clovis, and set his army in motion against his brother Godegisel, and shut him up in the city of Vienne and besieged him. And when food began to be lacking for the common people, Godegisel was afraid that the famine would extend to himself, and gave orders that the common people be expelled from the city.

When this was done, there was driven out, among the rest, the artisan who had charge of the aqueduct. And he was indignant that he had been cast out from the city with the rest, and went to Gundobad in a rage to inform him how to burst into the city and take vengeance on his brother. Under his guidance an army was led through the aqueduct, and many with iron crowbars went in front, for there was a vent in the aqueduct closed with a great stone, and when this had been pushed away with crowbars, by direction of the artisan, they entered the city, and surprised from the rear the defenders who were shooting arrows from the wall.

The trumpet was sounded in the midst of the city, and the besiegers seized the gates, and opened them and entered at the same time, and when the people between these two battle lines were being slain by each army, Godegisel sought refuge in the church of the heretics, and was slain there along with the Arian bishop. Finally the Franks who were with Godegisel gathered in a tower. But Gundobad ordered that no harm should be done to a single one of them, but seized them and sent them in exile to king Alaric at Toulouse, and he slew the Burgundian senators who had conspired with Godegisel. He restored to his own dominion all the region which is now called Burgundy. He established milder laws for the Burgundians lest they should oppress the Romans.

*   *   *

REVIEW QUESTIONS

1. According to Gregory, what qualities does a barbarian chieftain need to display in order to succeed? What does this excerpt reveal about the nature of kingship among the Franks?

2. Why does Clovis agree to accept Christianity? What is the role of his wife, Clotilda? What can we infer about the status of women in Frankish society, based on this passage?

3. What is the significance—for Clovis, for his people, and for Gregory—of his conversion? Does it seem to change his nature as a man and a king?

4. What vestiges of the Roman Empire remain in the world of Clovis and his people? What does this source reveal about change and continuity in the former provinces of Rome?

7 ∾ ROME'S THREE HEIRS, 500–950

Roman control over most of the western Mediterranean weakened in the fifth century, and soon Rome itself became the capital of an Ostrogothic kingdom in Italy. A world formerly centered on the "Middle Sea" began to take a different shape. In the eastern Mediterranean, the Roman Empire endured. This state, smaller after the rise of Islam and the loss of North Africa, Egypt, Syria, and Palestine, is now known as the Byzantine Empire. Ancient culture continued to evolve here in the setting of Eastern Orthodox Christianity and a nearly incessant struggle for survival against Slavic, Muslim, and eventually western Christian neighbors.

The Arabian Peninsula, largely neglected by the neighboring Roman and Persian Empires, unified in the seventh century under the influence of Muhammad of Mecca. The new religion of Islam, partially drawing on and extending Jewish and Christian traditions but containing a specific revelation and message for the Arabian peoples, unified Arabia with a mission. Armies spread the new faith as they quickly extended Muslim conquests across Africa to the west and crossed to the Iberian Peninsula. The religion also spread through Mesopotamia, Persia, and northern India to the east. The collected revelations of Muhammad, in the form of the Qur'an, brought a knowledge of the religion as well as the Arabic language to all the new peoples converted into the world of Islam. Islamic scholars and schools preserved much of ancient Greek, Syrian, and Persian culture and soon contributed new insights in the sciences and history. Much of the West's knowledge of ancient Greek thought came through translations of Arabic sources.

In northwestern Europe, the barbarian kingdoms were gradually being converted to Christianity and were becoming the center of a third culture, shaped by the combined influences of Roman civilization and Germanic heritage. European monasteries preserved and copied classical Latin and early Christian texts that became the core of early medieval culture. The religious frontiers between the

Eastern Orthodox, Roman Catholic, and Muslim worlds reflected deep cultural divisions, but all three cultures also preserved parts of the classical legacy which they jointly inherited.

For a time, in the sixth century, the emperor Justinian seemed poised to restore imperial authority in large parts of the West, but his failures and the rise of Islam resulted in a more compact Byzantine state. For nearly a thousand years, Byzantine culture produced distinctive artistic works and writers. In the West there was no Roman emperor until the coronation of Charlemagne in 800. The resurgent Frankish state in the West extended the frontiers of Christendom into the pagan Germanic and Slavic lands to the east. Government depended on the personalities of individual rulers, and in Charlemagne the Franks benefited from the rule of a king who was also interested in sponsoring the revival of learning and the arts. Anglo-Saxon England, remaining outside the Carolingian Empire, also contributed monks and missionaries, as well as a distinctive literature, to this early medieval culture. In the Muslim world, the caliphate of Baghdad presided over a golden age of Arabic culture under Harun al Rashid (786–809). This ruler established contacts with the Christian West and sent Charlemagne an elephant (an animal not seen in Europe since the Romans and a marvel of the age) and a clock, which did not last as long as the elephant.

By about the mid-tenth century, three centers of power had replaced the Roman Empire of late antiquity. Islamic rulers held sway over the southern and eastern shores of the Mediterranean, and in the East a Greek state calling itself a Roman Empire still endured. In the West a distinctly Latin Christendom emerged from the end of Rome and the subsequent barbarian kingdoms, but this civilization was insecure and beset by powerful enemies on all sides.

MOSAICS OF JUSTINIAN AND THEODORA, CHURCH OF SAN VITALE, RAVENNA (C. 500 C.E.)

Justinian (top) holds a communion dish, Theodora (bottom) a chalice. The emperor commissioned these mosaics for an important church in Ravenna, the capital of Byzantine Italy. What does this mosaic suggest about the position of the imperial family in the Church? What does it suggest about the relationships among different powerful groups: the imperial family, the aristocracy, the army, and the clergy?

PROCOPIUS

FROM *Secret History*

Procopius (c. 500–565), bishop of Caesaria, was a scholar active in the service of Justinian (r. 527–65) and the emperor's exact contemporary. He became an official court historian and biographer, and most of his surviving writings present a flattering picture of Justinian's reign and accomplishments. But in the text known as the Secret History—*in the original Greek, the "unpublished writings"—Procopius tells a very different story. The following excerpts explain his rationale for producing (and hiding) this work and present alternative portraits of the "real" Justinian and his wife, the empress Theodora.*

From *Procopius: Secret History*, translated by Richard Atwater (Ann Arbor: University of Michigan Press, 1963), pp. 35–36, 39–49.

*   *   *

In what I have written on the Roman wars up to the present point, the story was arranged in chronological order and as completely as the times then permitted. What I shall write now follows a different plan, supplementing the previous formal chronicle with a disclosure of what really happened throughout the Roman Empire. You see, it was not possible, during the life of certain persons, to write the truth of what they did, as a historian should. If I had, their hordes of spies would have found out about it, and they would have put me to a most horrible death. I could not even trust my nearest relatives. That is why I was compelled to hide the real explanation of many matters glossed over in my previous books.

These secrets it is now my duty to tell and reveal the remaining hidden matters and motives. Yet when I approach this different task, I find it hard indeed to have to stammer and retract what I have written before about the lives of Justinian and Theodora. Worse yet, it occurs to me that what I am now about to tell will seem neither probable nor plausible to future generations, especially as time flows on and my story becomes ancient history. I fear they may think me a writer of fiction, and even put me among the poets.

However, I have this much to cheer me, that my account will not be unendorsed by other testimony: so I shall not shrink from the duty of completing this work.

*   *   *

VII. Outrages of the Blues

The people had since long previous time been divided, as I have explained elsewhere, into two factions, the Blues and the Greens. Justinian, by joining the former party, which had already shown favor to him, was able to bring everything into confusion and turmoil, and by its power to sink the Roman state to its knees before him. Not all the Blues were willing to follow his leadership, but there were plenty who were eager for civil war. Yet even these, as the trouble spread, seemed the most prudent of men, for their crimes were less awful than was in their power to commit. Nor did the Green partisans remain quiet, but showed their resentment as violently as they could, though one by one they were continually punished; which, indeed, urged them each time to further recklessness. For men who are wronged are likely to become desperate.

Then it was that Justinian, fanning the flame and openly inciting the Blues to fight, made the whole Roman Empire shake on its foundation, as if an earthquake or a cataclysm had stricken it, or every city within its confines had been taken by the foe. Everything everywhere was uprooted: nothing was left undisturbed by him. Law and order, throughout the State, overwhelmed by distraction, were turned upside down.

First the rebels revolutionized the style of wearing their hair. For they had it cut differently from the rest of the Romans: not molesting the mustache or beard, which they allowed to keep on growing as long as it would, as the Persians do, but clipping the hair short on the front of the head down to the temples, and letting it hang down in great length and disorder in the back, as the Massageti do. This weird combination they called the Hun haircut.

Next they decided to wear the purple stripe on their togas, and swaggered about in a dress indicating a rank above their station: for it was only by ill-gotten money they were able to buy this finery. And the sleeves of their tunics were cut tight about the wrists, while from there to the shoulders they were of an ineffable fullness; thus, whenever they moved their hands, as when applauding at the theater or encouraging a driver in the hippodrome, these immense sleeves fluttered conspicuously, displaying to the simple public what beautiful and well-developed physiques were these that required such large garments to cover them. They did not consider that by the exaggeration of this dress the meagerness of their stunted bodies appeared all the more noticeable. Their cloaks, trousers, and boots were also different: and these too were called the Hun style, which they imitated.

Almost all of them carried steel openly from the first, while by day they concealed their two-edged daggers along the thigh under their cloaks. Collecting in gangs as soon as dusk fell, they robbed their betters in the open Forum and in the narrow alleys, snatching from passersby their mantles, belts, gold brooches, and whatever they had in their hands. Some they killed after robbing them, so they could not inform anyone of the assault. . . .

Yet all of this disturbed people less than Justinian's offenses against the State. For those who suffer the most grievously from evildoers are relieved of the greater part of their anguish by the expectation they will sometime be avenged by law and authority. Men who are confident of the future can bear more easily and less painfully their present troubles; but when they are outraged even by the government what befalls them is naturally all the more grievous, and by the failing of all hope of redress they are turned to utter despair. And Justinian's crime was that he was not only unwilling to protect the injured, but saw no reason why he should not be the open head of the guilty faction; he gave great sums of money to these young men, and surrounded himself with them: and some he even went so far as to appoint to high office and other posts of honor.

VIII. Character and Appearance of Justinian

Now this went on not only in Constantinople, but in every city: for like any other disease, the evil, starting there, spread throughout the entire Roman Empire. But the Emperor was undisturbed by the trouble, even when it went on continually under his own eyes at the hippodrome. For he was very complacent and resembled most the silly ass, which follows, only shaking its ears, when one drags it by the bridle. As such Justinian acted, and threw everything into confusion.

As soon as he took over the rule from his uncle, his first measure was to spend the public money without restraint, now that he had control of it. He gave much of it to the Huns who, from time to time, entered the state; and in consequence the Roman provinces were subject to constant incursions, for these barbarians, having once tasted Roman wealth, never forgot the road that led to it. And he threw much money into the sea in the form of moles, as if to master the eternal roaring of the breakers. For he jealously hurled stone breakwaters far out from the mainland against the onset of the sea, as if by the power of wealth he could outmatch the might of ocean.

He gathered to himself the private estates of Roman citizens from all over the Empire: some by accusing their possessors of crimes of which they were innocent, others by juggling their owners' words into the semblance of a gift to him of their property. And many, caught in the act of murder and other crimes, turned their possessions over to him and thus escaped the penalty for their sins.

Others, fraudulently disputing title to lands happening to adjoin their own, when they saw they had no chance of getting the best of the argument, with the law against them, gave him their equity in the claim so as to be released from court. Thus, by a gesture that cost him nothing, they gained his favor and were able illegally to get the better of their opponents.

I think this is as good a time as any to describe the personal appearance of the man. Now in physique he was neither tall nor short, but of average height; not thin, but moderately plump; his face was round, and not bad looking, for he had good color, even when he fasted for two days. To make a long description short, he much resembled Domitian, Vespasian's son. He was the one whom the Romans so hated that even tearing him into pieces did not satisfy their wrath against him, but a decree was passed by the Senate that the name of this Emperor should never be written, and that no statue of him should be preserved. And so this name was erased in all the inscriptions at Rome and wherever else it had been written, except only where it occurs in the list of emperors; and nowhere may be seen any statue of him in all the Roman Empire, save one in brass, which was made for the following reason.

Domitian's wife was of free birth and otherwise noble; and neither had she herself ever done wrong to anybody, nor had she assented in her husband's acts. Wherefore she was dearly loved; and the Senate sent for her, when Domitian died, and commanded her to ask whatever boon she wished. But she asked only this: to set up in his memory one brass image, wherever she might desire. To this the Senate agreed. Now the lady, wishing to leave a memorial to future time of the savagery of those who had butchered her husband, conceived this plan: collecting the pieces of Domitian's body, she joined them accurately together and sewed the body up again into its original semblance. Taking this to the statue makers, she ordered them to produce the miserable form in brass. So the artisans forthwith made the image, and the wife took it, and set it up in the street which leads to the Capitol, on the right hand side as one goes there from the Forum: a monument to Domitian and a revelation of the manner of his death until this day.

Justinian's entire person, his manner of expression and all of his features might be clearly pointed out in this statue.

Now such was Justinian in appearance; but his character was something I could not fully describe. For he was at once villainous and amenable; as people say colloquially, a moron. He was never truthful with anyone, but always guileful in what he said and did, yet easily hoodwinked by any who wanted to deceive him. His nature was an unnatural mixture of folly and wickedness. What in olden times a peripatetic philosopher said was also true of him, that opposite qualities combine in a man as in the mixing of colors. I will try to portray him, however, insofar as I can fathom his complexity.

This Emperor, then, was deceitful, devious, false, hypocritical, two-faced, cruel, skilled in dissembling his thought, never moved to tears by either joy or pain, though he could summon them artfully at will when the occasion demanded, a liar always, not only offhand, but in writing, and when he swore sacred oaths to his subjects in their very hearing. Then he would immediately break his agreements and pledges, like the vilest of slaves, whom indeed only the fear of torture drives to confess their perjury. A faithless friend, he was a treacherous enemy, insane for murder and plunder, quarrelsome and revolutionary, easily led to anything evil, but never willing to listen to good counsel, quick to plan mischief and carry it out, but finding even the hearing of anything good distasteful to his ears.

How could anyone put Justinian's ways into words? These and many even worse vices were disclosed in him as in no other mortal: nature seemed to have taken the wickedness of all other men combined and planted it in this man's soul. And besides this, he was too prone to listen to accusations; and too quick to punish. For he decided such cases without full examination, naming the punishment when he had heard only the accuser's side of the matter. Without hesitation he wrote decrees for the plundering of countries, sacking of cities, and slavery of whole nations, for no cause whatever. So that if one wished to take all the calamities which had befallen the Romans before this time and weigh them against his crimes, I think it would be found that more men had been murdered by this single man than in all previous history.

He had no scruples about appropriating other people's property, and did not even think any excuse necessary, legal or illegal, for confiscating what did not belong to him. And when it was his, he was more than ready to squander it in insane display, or give it as an unnecessary bribe to the barbarians. In short, he neither held on to any money himself nor let anyone else keep any: as if his reason were not avarice, but jealousy of those who had riches. Driving all wealth from the country of the Romans in this manner, he became the cause of universal poverty.

Now this was the character of Justinian, so far as I can portray it.

IX. How Theodora Most Depraved of All Courtesans, Won His Love

He took a wife: and in what manner she was born and bred, and, wedded to this man, tore up the Roman Empire by the very roots, I shall now relate. Acacius was the keeper of wild beasts used in the amphitheater in Constantinople; he belonged to the Green faction and was nicknamed the Bearkeeper. This man, during the rule of Anastasius, fell sick and died, leaving three daughters named Comito, Theodora and Anastasia: of whom the eldest was not yet seven years old. His widow took a second husband, who with her undertook to keep up Acacius's family and profession. But Asterius, the dancing master of the Greens, on being bribed by another, removed this office from them and assigned it to the man who gave him the money. For the dancing masters had the power of distributing such positions as they wished.

When this woman saw the populace assembled in the amphitheater, she placed laurel wreaths on her daughters' heads and in their hands, and sent them out to sit on the ground in the attitude of suppliants. The Greens eyed this mute appeal with indifference; but the Blues were moved to bestow on the children an equal office, since their own animal-keeper had just died.

When these children reached the age of girlhood, their mother put them on the local stage, for they were fair to look upon; she sent them forth, however, not all at the same time, but as each one seemed to her to have reached a suitable age. Comito, indeed, had already become one of the leading hetaerae of the day.

Theodora, the second sister, dressed in a little tunic with sleeves, like a slave girl, waited on Comito and used to follow her about carrying on her shoulders the bench on which her favored sister was wont to sit at public gatherings. Now Theodora was still too young to know the normal relation of man with maid, but consented to the unnatural violence of villainous slaves who, following their masters to the theater, employed their leisure in this infamous manner. And for some time in a brothel she suffered such misuse.

But as soon as she arrived at the age of youth, and was now ready for the world, her mother put her on the stage. Forthwith, she became a courtesan, and such as the ancient Greeks used to call a common one, at that: for she was not a flute or harp player, nor was she even trained to dance, but only gave her youth to anyone she met, in utter abandonment. Her general favors included, of course, the actors in the theater; and in their productions she took part in the low comedy scenes. For she was very funny and a good mimic, and immediately became popular in this art. There was no shame in the girl, and no one ever saw her dismayed: no role was too scandalous for her to accept without a blush.

She was the kind of comedienne who delights the audience by letting herself be cuffed and slapped on the cheeks, and makes them guffaw by raising her skirts to reveal to the spectators those feminine secrets here and there which custom veils from the eyes of the opposite sex. With pretended laziness she mocked her lovers, and coquettishly adopting ever new ways of embracing, was able to keep in a constant turmoil the hearts of the sophisticated. And she did not wait to be asked by anyone she met, but on the contrary, with inviting jests and a comic flaunting of her skirts herself tempted all men who passed by, especially those who were adolescent.

On the field of pleasure she was never defeated. Often she would go picnicking with ten young men or more, in the flower of their strength and virility, and dallied with them all, the whole night through. When they wearied of the sport, she would approach their servants, perhaps thirty in number, and fight a duel with each of these, and even thus found no allayment of her craving. Once, visiting the house of an illustrious gentleman, they say she mounted the projecting corner of her dining couch, pulled up the front of her dress, without a blush, and thus carelessly showed her wantonness. And though she flung wide three gates to the ambassadors of Cupid, she lamented that nature had not similarly unlocked the straits of her bosom, that she might there have contrived a further welcome to his emissaries.

Frequently, she conceived, but as she employed every artifice immediately, a miscarriage was straightway effected. Often, even in the theater, in the sight of all the people, she removed her costume and stood nude in their midst, except for a girdle about the groin: not that she was abashed at revealing that, too, to the audience, but because there was a law against appearing altogether naked on the stage, without at least this much of a fig-leaf. Covered thus with a ribbon, she would sink down to the stage floor and recline on her back. Slaves to whom the duty was entrusted would then scatter grains of barley from above into the calyx of this passion flower, whence geese, trained for the purpose, would next pick the grains one by one with their bills and eat. When she rose, it was not with a blush, but she seemed rather to glory in the performance. For she was not only impudent herself, but endeavored to make everybody else as audacious. Often when she was alone with other actors, she would undress in their midst and arch her back provocatively, advertising like a peacock both to those who had experience of her and to those who had not yet had that privilege her trained suppleness.

So perverse was her wantonness that she should have hid not only the customary part of her person, as other women do, but her face as well. Thus those who were intimate with her were straightway recognized from that very fact to be perverts, and any more respectable man who chanced upon her in the Forum avoided her and withdrew in haste, lest the hem of his mantle, touching such a creature, might be thought to share in her pollution. For to those who saw her, especially at dawn, she was a bird of ill omen. And toward her fellow-actresses she was as savage as a scorpion: for she was very malicious.

Later, she followed Hecebolus, a Tyrian who had been made governor of Pentapolis, serving him in the basest of ways; but finally she quarreled with him and was sent summarily away. Consequently, she found herself destitute of the means of life, which she proceeded to earn by prostitution, as she had done before this adventure. She came thus to Alexandria, and then traversing all the East, worked her way to Constantinople; in every city plying a trade (which it is safer, I fancy, in the sight of God not to name too clearly) as if the Devil were determined there be no land on earth that should not know the sins of Theodora.

Thus was this woman born and bred, and her name was a byword beyond that of other common wenches on the tongues of all men.

But when she came back to Constantinople, Justinian fell violently in love with her. At first he kept her only as a mistress, though he raised her to patrician rank. Through him Theodora was able immediately to acquire an unholy power and exceedingly great riches. For she seemed to him the sweetest thing in the world, and like all lovers, he desired to please his charmer with every possible favor and requite her with all his wealth. The extravagance added fuel to the flames of passion. With her now to help spend his money he plundered the people more than ever, not only in the capital, but throughout the Roman Empire. As both of them had for a long time been of the Blue party, they gave this faction almost complete control of the affairs of state.

REVIEW QUESTIONS

1. What reasons does Procopius give for distinguishing between official and secret history? Are these distinctions valid?
2. How might you account for Procopius's extremely negative view of Empress Theodora?
3. After reading these excerpts, do you think that Procopius is a reliable source of information? Why or why not? Even if this is not an accurate portrayal of Justinian and Theodora, what does it reveal about Procopius himself and the world in which he lived?

MUHAMMAD

FROM The Qur'an

The prophet Muhammad (c. 570–632) brought the message of Islam first to the Arab peoples of his home city, Mecca. Muslims, those who submit to the will of the one God (Allah), follow the Qur'an as revealed to Muhammad, which was written down during the Prophet's life. Following are two surahs (chapters) from the Qur'an, an excerpt from number 2, The Cow, and number 47, Muhammad; they are typical of the style and content of the Qur'an.

From *Al-Qur'ān: A Contemporary Translation,* by Ahmed Ali (Princeton, N.J.: Princeton University Press, 2001), pp. 31–39.

2. The Cow

In the name of Allah, most benevolent, ever-merciful.

168. O MEN, eat only the things of the earth
that are lawful and good.
Do not walk in the footsteps of Satan,
your acknowledged enemy.
169. He will ask you to indulge in evil, indecency,
and to speak lies of God you cannot even conceive.
170. When it is said to them:
"Follow what God has revealed,"
they reply: "No, we shall follow only what
our fathers had practiced,"—
even though their fathers had no wisdom
    or guidance!
171. The semblance of the infidels
is that of a man
who shouts to one that cannot hear
more than a call and a cry.
They are deaf, dumb and blind,
and they fail to understand.
172. O believers, eat what is good of the food
We have given you, and be grateful to God,
if indeed you are obedient to Him.
173. Forbidden to you are carrion and blood,

and the flesh of the swine,
and that which has been
consecrated (or killed)
in the name of any other than God.
If one is obliged by necessity
to eat it without intending to transgress,
or reverting to it, he is not guilty of sin;
for God is forgiving and kind.
174. Those who conceal any part of the Scriptures
that God has revealed, and thus make
a little profit thereby,
take nothing but fire as food;
and God will not turn to them on the Day
    of Resurrection,
nor nourish them for growth;
and their doom will be painful.
175. They are those who bartered away
good guidance for error, and pardon for
    punishment:
How great is their striving for the Fire!
176. That is because God has revealed
the Book containing the truth;
but those who are at variance about it
have gone astray in their contrariness.

177. Piety does not lie in turning your face
to East or West:
Piety lies in believing in God,
the Last Day and the angels,
the Scriptures and the prophets,
and disbursing your wealth out of love for God
among your kin and the orphans,
the wayfarers and mendicants,
freeing the slaves, observing your devotional
    obligations,
and in paying the *zakat*[1] and fulfilling a pledge
    you have given,
and being patient in hardship, adversity,
and times of peril.
These are the men who affirm the truth,
and they are those who follow the straight path.
178. O believers, ordained for you is retribution

for the murdered,
(whether) a free man (is guilty)
of (the murder of) a free man, or a slave of a slave,
or a woman of a woman.
But he who is pardoned some of it by his brother
should be dealt with equity,
and recompense (for blood) paid with a grace.
This is a concession from your Lord and a kindness.
He who transgresses in spite of it
shall suffer painful punishment.
179. In retribution there is life (and preservation).
O men of sense, you may haply take heed for
    yourselves.
180. It is ordained that when any one of you
nears death, and he owns goods and chattels,
he should bequeath them equitably
to his parents and next of kin.
This is binding on those who are upright and fear
    God.
181. And any one who changes the will, having
    heard it,
shall be guilty and accountable;
for God hears all and knows every thing.
182. He who suspects wrong or partiality
on the part of the testator
and brings about a settlement,
does not incur any guilt,
for God is verily forgiving and merciful.

183. O believers, fasting is enjoined on you
as it was on those before you,
so that you might become righteous.
184. Fast a (fixed) number of days,
but if someone is ill or is travelling
(he should complete) the number of days (he had
    missed);
and those who find it hard to fast
should expiate by feeding a poor person.
For the good they do with a little hardship is
    better for men.
And if you fast it is good for you,
if you knew.
185. Ramadan is the month in which the Qur'an
    was revealed
as guidance to man and clear proof of the guidance,
and criterion (of falsehood and truth).

---

[1] The practice of giving a portion of one's wealth to the
    poor—one of the Five Pillars of Islam. This does not
    refer to the punishment of blood money.

So when you see the new moon you should fast
   the whole month;
but a person who is ill or travelling
(and fails to do so) should fast on other days,
as God wishes ease and not hardship for you,
so that you complete the (fixed) number (of fasts),
and give glory to God
for the guidance, and be grateful.
186. When My devotees enquire of you about Me,
I am near, and answer the call
of every supplicant when he calls.
It behoves them to hearken to Me
and believe in Me
that they may follow the right path.
187. You are allowed to sleep with your wives
on the nights of the fast:
They are your dress as you are theirs.
God is aware you were cheating yourselves,
so He turned to you and pardoned you.
So now you may have intercourse with them,
and seek what God has ordained for you.
Eat and drink until the white thread
of dawn appears clear from the dark line,
then fast until the night falls;
and abstain from your wives (when you have decided)
to stay in the mosques for assiduous devotion.
These are the bounds fixed by God,
so keep well within them.
So does God make His signs clear to men
that they may take heed for themselves.
188. And do not consume each other's wealth in
   vain,
nor offer it to men in authority with intent
of usurping unlawfully and knowingly
a part of the wealth of others.

189. They ask you of the new moons.
Say: "These are periods set for men (to reckon)
   time,
and for pilgrimage."
Piety does not lie in entering the house through
   the back door,[2]

for the pious man is he who follows the straight path.
Enter the house through the main gate,[3]
and obey God. You may haply find success.
190. Fight those in the way of God who fight you,
but do not be aggressive:
God does not like aggressors.
191. And fight those (who fight you) wheresoever
   you find them,
and expel them from the place
they had turned you out from.
Oppression is worse than killing.
Do not fight them by the Holy Mosque
unless they fight you there.
If they do, then slay them:
Such is the requital for unbelievers.
192. But if they desist, God is forgiving and kind.
193. Fight them till sedition comes to end,
and the law of God (prevails).
If they desist, then cease to be hostile,
except against those who oppress.
194. (Fighting during) the holy month
(if the sanctity) of the holy month (is violated)
is (just) retribution.
So if you are oppressed,
oppress those who oppress you to the same
   degree,
and fear God, and know that God
is with those who are pious
and follow the right path.
195. Spend in the way of God,
and do not seek destruction at your own hands.
So do good;
for God loves those who do good.
196. Perform the pilgrimage and holy visit
   (ᶜUmra, to Mecca)
in the service of God.
But if you are prevented, send an offering
which you can afford as sacrifice,
and do not shave your heads until
the offering has reached the place of sacrifice.
But if you are sick or have ailment of the scalp
(preventing the shaving of hair),

---

[2] It means the same thing as is meant by the English
expression "through the back door," i.e., clandestinely.
Here it has more than one implication, as the verse deals

with the new moon and reckoning "periods," e.g., the
period of fasting, a woman's monthly courses, etc.
[3] That is, seek attainment through the right way.

then offer expiation by fasting
or else giving alms or a sacrificial offering.
When you have security, then those of you who
   wish
to perform the holy visit along with the
   pilgrimage,
should make a sacrifice according to their
   means.
But he who has nothing,
should fast for three days during the pilgrimage
and seven on return, completing ten.
This applies to him whose family does not live
near the Holy Mosque.
Have fear of God, and remember that God
is severe in punishment.

197. Known are the months of pilgrimage.
If one resolves to perform the pilgrimage in these
   months,
let him not indulge in concupiscence, sin or
   quarrel.
And the good you do shall be known to God.
Provide for the journey,
and the best of provisions is piety.
O men of understanding, obey Me.
198. It is no sin to seek the favours of your Lord
   (by trading).
When you start from 'Arafat in a concourse,
remember God at the monument that is sacred
(al-Mashʿar al-haram),
and remember Him as He has shown you the way,
for in the olden days you were a people astray.
199. Then move with the crowd impetuously,
and pray God to forgive you your sins.
God is surely forgiving and kind.
200. When you have finished the rites and
   ceremonies,
remember God as you do your fathers,
in fact with a greater devotion.
There are some who say:
"Give us, O Lord, in the world";
but they will forego their share in the life
   to come.
201. But some there are who pray:
"Give us of good in the world, O Lord,
and give us of good in the life to come,

and suffer us not to suffer the torment of Hell."
202. They are those who will surely have their share
of whatsoever they have earned;
for God is swift at the reckoning.
203. Remember God during the stated days;
but if a person comes away after two days,
it will not be a sin; and if one tarries,
he will not transgress, if he keep away from evil.
Follow the law of God, and remember
that you will have to gather before Him in the end.
204. There is a man who talks well
of the world to your pleasing,
and makes God witness to what is in his heart,
yet he is the most contentious;
205. For when his back is turned
he goes about spreading disorder in the land,
destroying fields and flocks;
but God does not love disorder.
206. Whenever he is told: "Obey God,"
his arrogance leads him to more sin;
and sufficient for him shall be Hell:
How evil a place of wide expanse!
207. And there is a man who is willing to sell
even his soul to win the favour of God;
and God is compassionate to His creatures.
208. O believers, come to full submission to God.
Do not follow in the footsteps of Satan
your acknowledged foe.
209. If you falter even after Our signs
have reached you, then do not forget
that God is all-powerful and all-wise.
210. Are they waiting for God to appear
in the balconies of clouds
with a host of angels,
and the matter to be settled?
But all things rest
with God in the end.

211. Ask the children of Israel
how many a clear sign We had given them.
But if one changes the favour of God
after having received it, then remember,
God is severe in revenge.
212. Enamoured are the unbelievers
of the life of this world,
and scoff at the faithful.

But those who keep from evil and follow the
    straight path
will have a higher place than they
on the Day of Reckoning;
for God gives in measure without number
whomsoever He will.
213. Men belonged to a single community,
and God sent them messengers
to give them happy tidings and warnings,
and sent the Book with them containing the truth
to judge between them in matters of dispute;
but only those who received it differed
after receiving clear proofs,
on account of waywardness
(and jealousies) among them.
Then God by His dispensation showed those who
    believed
the way to the truth about which they were
    differing;
for God shows whom He please
the path that is straight.
214. Do you think you will find your way to Paradise
even though you have not known
what the others before you have gone through?
They had suffered affliction and loss,
and were shaken and tossed about
so that even the Apostle
had to cry out with his followers:
"When will the help of God arrive?"
Remember, the help of God is ever at hand.
215. They ask you of what they should give in charity.
Tell them: "What you can spare of your wealth
as should benefit the parents, the relatives,
the orphans, the needy, the wayfarers,
for God is not unaware of the good deeds that
    you do."
216. Enjoined on you is fighting,
and this you abhor.
You may dislike a thing
yet it may be good for you;
or a thing may haply please you
but may be bad for you.
Only God has knowledge, and you do not know.

217. They ask you of war in the holy month.
Tell them: "To fight in that month is a great sin.

But a greater sin in the eyes of God
is to hinder people from the way of God,
and not to believe in Him,
and to bar access to the Holy Mosque
and turn people out of its precincts;
and oppression is worse than killing.
They will always seek war against you
till they turn you away from your faith, if
    they can.
But those of you who turn back on their faith
and die disbelieving
will have wasted their deeds
in this world and the next.
They are inmates of Hell,
and shall there abide for ever.
218. Surely those who believe,
and those who leave their homes
and fight in the way of God,
may hope for His benevolence,
for God is forgiving and kind.
219. They ask you of (intoxicants,) wine and
    gambling.
Tell them: "There is great enervation though profit
    in them[4]
for men; but their enervation is greater than
    benefit.
And they ask you what they should give.
Tell them: "The utmost you can spare."
So does God reveal His signs: You may haply
    reflect
220. On this world and the next.
And they ask you about the orphans.
Tell them: "Improving their lot is much better;
    and if
you take interest in their affairs, they are your
    brethren;
and God is aware who are corrupt and who are
    honest;
and if He had pleased
He could surely have imposed on you hardship,
for God is all-powerful and all-wise.
221. Do not marry idolatrous women

---

[4] The basic meaning of *ithm* is drunkenness or enervation (*Taj* and Ibn Faris) of which the wine of Paradise is
free.

unless they join the faith.
A maid servant who is a believer
is better than an idolatress
even though you may like her.
And do not marry your daughters to idolaters
until they accept the faith.
A servant who is a believer is better than an
    idolater
even though you may like him.
They invite you to Hell, but God
calls you to Paradise and pardon by His grace.
And He makes His signs manifest that men
may haply take heed.

*   *   *

47. Muhammad

In the name of Allah, most benevolent, ever-merciful.

1. THOSE WHO DISBELIEVE
and obstruct (others) from the way of God
will have wasted their deeds.
2. But those who believe and do the right,
and believe what has been revealed to
    Muhammad,
which is the truth from their Lord,
will have their faults condoned by Him
and their state improved.
3. That is because those who refuse to believe
only follow what is false; but those who believe
follow the truth from their Lord.
That is how God gives men precepts of wisdom.
4. So, when you clash with the unbelievers,
smite their necks until you overpower them,
then hold them in bondage.
Then either free them graciously
or after taking a ransom,
until war shall have come to end.
If God had pleased
He could have punished them (Himself),
but He wills to test some of you through some
    others.
He will not allow the deeds
of those who are killed in the cause of God
to go waste.

5. He will show them the way,
and better their state,
6. And will admit them into gardens
with which he has acquainted them.
7. O you who believe, if you help (in the cause of)
    God
He will surely come to your aid,
and firmly plant your feet.
8. As for the unbelievers, they will suffer
    misfortunes,
and their deeds will be rendered ineffective.
9. That is so as they were averse
to what has been revealed by God,
and their actions will be nullified.
10. Have they not journeyed in the land
and seen the fate of those before them?
Destroyed they were utterly by God;
and a similar (fate) awaits the unbelievers.
11. This is so for God is the friend of those who
    believe
while the unbelievers have no friend.

12. Verily God will admit those who believe and
    do the right
into gardens with streams of water running by.
But the unbelievers revel and carouse
and subsist like beasts, and Hell will be their
    residence.
13. How many were the habitations,
mightier than your city which has turned you out,
which We destroyed;
and they did not have a helper.
14. Can one who stands on a clear proof from his
    Lord,
be like one enamoured of his evil deeds
and follows his inane desires?
15. The semblance of Paradise promised the pious
    and devout
(is that of a garden) with streams of water that will
    not go rank,
and rivers of milk whose taste will not undergo a
    change,
and rivers of wine delectable to drinkers,
and streams of purified honey,
and fruits of every kind in them, and forgiveness
    of their Lord.

Are these like those who will live for ever in the
    Fire
and be given boiling water to drink
which will cut their intestines to shreds?
16. There are some who listen to you; but as soon
    as they go
from you they say to those who were given
    knowledge:
"What is this he is saying now?"
They are those whose hearts
have been sealed by God, and they follow their
    own lusts.
17. But those who are rightly guided will be given
greater guidance by Him, and they will have their
    intrinsic piety.
18. Do they wait for any thing but the Hour
    (of change),
that it may come upon them suddenly?
Its signs have already appeared.
How then will they be warned when it has come
    upon them?
19. Know then, therefore, there is no god but He,
and ask forgiveness for your sins
and those of believing men and women.
God knows your wanderings
and your destination.

20. Those who believe say: "How is it no *Surah*[5]
    was revealed?"
But when a categorical Surah is revealed
that mentions war, you should see those
who are sceptical
staring at you like a man in the swoon of death.
Alas the woe for them!
21. Obedience and modest speech (would have
    been more becoming).
And when the matter has been determined
it is best for them to be true to God.
22. Is it possible that if placed in authority
you will create disorder in the land
and sever your bonds of relationship?
23. They are those who were condemned by God,

whose ears were blocked by Him and their eyes
    blinded.
24. Do they not ponder
on what the Qur'an says?
Or have their hearts been sealed with locks?
25. Those who turn their backs
after the way of guidance has been opened to
    them,
have been surely tempted by Satan
and beguiled by illusory hopes.
26. This was so because they said to those
who disdain what God has revealed:
"We shall obey you in some things."
But God knows their secret intentions well.
27. How will it be when the angels draw out their
    souls
striking their faces and their backs?
28. Because they followed what displeases God,
and they were averse to pleasing Him.
So We nullified their deeds.

29. Do they whose minds are filled with doubt,
    think
that God will not expose their malice?
30. Had We pleased We could have shown them
    to you
that you could know them by their marks,
and recognise them from the way
they twist their words.
Yet God knows all your deeds.
31. We shall try you in order to know
who are the fighters among you,
and who are men of fortitude,
and verify your histories.
32. Surely those who do not believe, and obstruct
    others
from the path of God, and oppose the Prophet
after the way of guidance has been opened
    to them,
will not hurt God in the least,
and He will nullify all that they have done.
33. O you who believe, obey God and the Prophet,
and do not waste your deeds.
34. Those who do not believe and obstruct others
from the way of God, and die disbelieving,

---

[5] A word meaning both "revelation" and a chapter (*surah*)
of the Qur'an.

will not be pardoned by God.

35. So do not become weak-kneed and sue for peace,
for you will have the upper hand
as God is with you and will not overlook your
   deeds.

36. Verily the life of this world
is no more than a sport and frivolity.
If you believe and fear God,
He will give you your reward,
and will not ask for your possessions.

37. If He asks for all you possess and insist upon it,
you will become niggardly,
and it will bring out your malevolence.

38. Beware! You are called to spend in the way of
   God,
yet some among you close their fists.
But he who is niggardly is so for his own self:
God is above need, and it is you who are needy.
If you turn away then God

will bring other people in your place
who, moreover, will not be like you.

*   *   *

REVIEW QUESTIONS

1. What aspects of Muslim belief are revealed in these surahs? What are the obligations of those who submit to Islam? What are their rewards?

2. How do Muhammad's teachings compare with those of Jesus (see pp. 184–188). What do their similarities and differences reveal about the relationships among Judaism, Christianity, and Islam?

3. What do these suras suggest about the historical conditions in which Muhammad and his followers lived?

MAS^CUDI

FROM *The Meadows of Gold*

The Muslim polymath Abu al-Hasan Ali ibn al-Husayn ibn Ali al-Mas^cudi (c. 896–956) was born in Baghdad and traveled widely throughout the Middle East and Asia. Over the course of his extraordinary life, he authored more than thirty books on such varied subjects as philosophy, political science, medicine, astronomy, and law. Only two have survived, and the work originally entitled Meadows of Gold and Mines of Gems *is one of these. Written in classical Arabic, it traces the history of the world from the creation of Adam and Eve to Mas^cudi's own day. The only portion currently translated into English deals with the Abbasid caliphate. The excerpts below focus on the reign of Harun al-Rashid (r. 786–809), a contemporary of Charlemagne, who also figured prominently in the compilation of stories known as* The 1001 Nights.

From *The Meadows of Gold: The Abbasids*, translated and edited by Paul Lunde and Caroline Stone (New York: Kegan Paul International, 1989), pp. 62–67, 71.

Harun al-Rashid and the Death of Hadi

Hadi[1] wished to strip his brother of the title of heir apparent, in order to give it to his own son, Ja'far. He had imprisoned Yahya ibn Khalid, the Barmakid, and wanted to kill him; but Yahya, who was responsible for Harun al-Rashid's interests, said to him one day:

'O Commander of the Faithful, if that thing which I ask heaven to spare us and keep far from us, by granting your majesty long life, should come to pass, do you think, I repeat, do you think that the people would recognize the authority of your son Ja'far, who has not yet reached the age of reason, to lead the prayers, the pilgrimage and the holy wars?'

'No, I don't think so,' he replied.

'Are you not afraid,' continued Yahya, 'that they will raise one of the leading men of your family to the throne, and that the power will pass from your issue to others? You yourself will have stirred up your subjects to break their oath and hold their faith cheap. If, on the other hand, you were to respect the oath of allegiance made to your brother, and if you were to have your son accepted as his heir, it would be the strongest possible position. Then, when Ja'far comes of age, you can ask your brother to yield the supreme power to him.'

'By God,' replied the Caliph, 'you are suggesting a plan that had never occurred to me.'

But later, he determined at all costs to force Harun to give up his rights, with or without his consent, and he severely restrained his movements. Yahya advised his master Harun to ask permission to go out hunting and urged him to spend as much time as possible doing so, since the horoscope cast at the moment of Hadi's birth predicted that his time would be short.

Harun asked and obtained leave to go. He followed the banks of the Euphrates into the region of Hit and Anbar, and then struck inland in the direction of Samawa. Hadi wrote to recall him

---

[1] Abu Abdullah Musa ibn Mahdi al-Hadi, who ruled as caliph from 785–786.

and, when Harun delayed even more, cursed him roundly. It even occurred to Hadi to go in the direction of al-Haditha, but he fell ill there and turned back. His illness took so serious a turn that no one dared go into him, except the youngest eunuchs. He signed to them to bring him his mother Khaizuran and, when she was at his bedside, he said:

'I am going to die tonight, and my brother Harun will immediately succeed me, for you know the sentence pronounced against me by fate at the very moment of my birth at Rayy. I have had to refuse you what you asked and have had to impose my orders upon you, in accordance with the dictates of policy, but to do so always went against the affection which religion demands of a son. Far, however, from having been an ungrateful child, I have never ceased to protect you, nor to be dutiful and loyal.'

Then he took his mother's hand in farewell, laid it on his heart and breathed his last. Hadi, like his brother Harun, was born at Rayy. His death, the accession of Harun al-Rashid and the birth of Ma'mun, all took place on the same night.

The Dream of Mahdi

It is said that one day one of the great men of the dynasty, who was guilty of many crimes, was brought before Hadi. The Caliph reminded him of them, one after another.

'O Commander of the Faithful,' the man replied, 'to make excuses for the things which you accuse me of having done, would mean contradicting you; to accept your charges would be an admission of my guilt. I prefer to say, with the poet:

If what you hope for from punishment is
   satisfaction,
Why deprive yourself of the satisfaction of
   forgiveness?'

Hadi set him free and gave him a present.

A number of chroniclers, learned in the history of this dynasty, relate that Hadi said to his brother Harun al-Rashid:

'It seems to me that you are ceaselessly talking to yourself about the fulfilment of the dream and that you hope for that which is still far from you—but first "you must pluck the thorns from the tragacanth".'[2]

'O Commander of the Faithful,' replied Harun, 'those you have raised shall be laid low and those you have humbled shall be exalted, and the unjust man shall feel his shame. If power comes into my hands, I shall heal him whom you have broken and I shall give to him whom you have refused. Your children shall be set above my children and your sons shall marry my daughters, and thus will I pay my debt to the Imam Mahdi.'

These words melted Hadi's anger and his face shone with joy. He said:

'Harun, that is just what I would have expected of you. Come here.'

Harun rose, kissed his brother's hand and was going back to his place when Hadi said to him:

'No, by the most illustrious shaikh and glorious king, you shall sit nowhere but by me, in the place of honour.' Then he said:

'O treasurer, bring a million dinars to my brother immediately and as soon as the taxes are collected, you are to give him half.'

When Harun wished to withdraw, they led his mount right up to the edge of the carpet.

Amr al-Rumi said:

'I asked Harun al-Rashid about the dream, and he quoted Mahdi's own words:

"I dreamed that I gave a branch of a tree to Hadi and another to Harun. Hadi's branch bore only a few leaves towards the top, while that of Harun, on the other hand, was covered with foliage along all its length."'

Mahdi related his dream to the physician Ibn Ishaq al-Saimari, who interpreted it, saying:

'They will both reign, but the reign of Hadi will be short, while that of Harun will endure longer than that of any other Caliph. His days will be the best of days and his age the best of ages.'

Amr al-Rumi adds that when Harun al-Rashid came to the throne, he married his daughter Hamduna to Ja'far, and his other daughter, Fatima, to Ismail—both sons of Hadi—and that he kept all the promises which he had made to his predecessor.

The Sword Samsama

Abd Allah ibn al-Dahhak relates the following tradition, according to al-Haitham ibn Adi:

'Mahdi had given his son Hadi a famous sword named Samsama, which had belonged to Amr ibn Ma'dikarib. One day, after he had become Caliph, Hadi had this sword brought in and a great basket filled with dinars. Then he ordered his chamberlain:

"Let the poets enter!"

When they had come in, he asked them to choose the sword as subject for their verse. Ibn Yamin of Basra spoke first, and said:

> Hadi, the trustworthy, alone among men
> Possesses the Samsama of Amr al-Zubaidi;
> We have heard that the sword of Amr
> Was the best blade ever closed in a sheath.
> The lightning flash lit it with fire
> And death tempered it with poison, sudden and
>   terrible.
> When you unsheath it, it shines like the sun
> So that a man can scarcely look upon it.
> The temper of its steel flashes on the blade
> Like the ripples of clear water.
> At the moment of striking, what does it matter
> Whether it cuts with the left edge or the right?

"Take the sword and the basket of dinars," said the Caliph. "I give you them both."

Ibn Yamin distributed the contents of the basket to the other poets, saying:

"You came here with me and it is because of me that you have not been rewarded; this sword will take the place of any other fee."

Hadi sent to him later and bought the sword back from him for 50,000 dinars.

The story of this reign, so interesting in spite of its being cut short, is told at length in the *Historical Annals* and the *Intermediate History*.

All help comes from God!

---

[2] A natural gum derived from legumes. The Greek words *tarjos* and *akantha* mean "goat thorn"; thus, to remove the "thorn" from this compound would be impossible.

The Accession of Harun al-Rashid

Allegiance was sworn to Harun, son of Mahdi, at Baghdad, the City of Peace, on a Friday, on the morning after the night that Hadi died. It was the twelfth day before the end of Rabi' 170 AH/786 AD. Harun died in a village called Sanabadh near Tus on a Saturday, the 4th of Jumada II, 193 AH/809 AD. His reign had lasted twenty-three years and six months, or, according to another tradition, twenty-three years, two months and eighteen days. He was twenty-one years and two months old when he became caliph. He died at the age of forty-four years and four months.

As soon as the caliphate came to Harun al-Rashid, he summoned Yahya ibn Khalid, the Barmakid, and said to him:

'My dear little father, it was you who placed me on this throne, it was by your aid and the blessing of heaven—yes, by your happy influence and wise advice! And now I invest you with absolute power.'

And he gave him his seal. This occasion is commemorated in the following lines by Ibrahim al-Mawsili:

Did you not see how the sun was pale and wan
But when Harun took power it blazed with
    light?
This was because of the good fortune of
    Harun,
The generous, the faithful agent of God.
He is the sun's elect, Yahya the sun's vizier.

Raita, the daughter of Abu al-Abbas al-Saffah, died a few months after the accession of Harun al-Rashid or, according to another version, at the end of the reign of Hadi. The mother of both that caliph and Rashid, Khaizuran, died in 173 AH/789 AD and Rashid walked on foot at the head of the funeral procession. The revenues of this princess amounted to 160 million dirhams.

The Last Pilgrimage of Harun al-Rashid

In the year 188 AH/804 AD, Harun al-Rashid went on his last pilgrimage to Mecca. They say that Abu Bakr ibn Ayyash, one of the most highly learned men of the age, said, as Harun al-Rashid was going through Kufa on his return from this pilgrimage:

'Harun al-Rashid will never travel this road again, nor will it be taken by any of the Abbasid Caliphs who come after him.'

'Does this prophecy come from your knowledge of the invisible world?' he was asked.

'Yes,' replied Abu Bakr.

'Is it a revelation from Heaven?'

'Yes.'

'Addressed directly to you?'

'No,' he replied, 'but to Muhammad—may the prayers and peace of God be upon him—and transmitted by him who was murdered in this place.' And with his hand he indicated the place in Kufa where Ali—may God be content with him—was killed.

REVIEW QUESTIONS

1. What are the attributes of a good Caliph? How do Hadi and Harun al-Rashid exemplify these characteristics?

2. What role do dreams and visions play in these historical vignettes? Why might they have been considered important?

3. What do these excerpts tell us about Muslim society under the Abbasid caliphate? What classes of people are represented? What do we learn about them?

BEDE

FROM *A History of the English Church and People*

Bede (d. 735), often known as the Venerable Bede, was an Anglo-Saxon monk from Northumbria (northen England). Known in his own day as "Bede the Computer," he wrote Latin treatises on the accurate calculation of historical time as well as commentaries on the Bible, saints' lives, and histories. His most famous work, excerpted here, tells the story of England's conversion to Christianity and the establishment of what Bede liked to call the "English Church," which he saw as uniting the disparate peoples of Britain, Celtic and Anglo-Saxon, in their allegiance to the Roman pope. The following passages illustrate two of the ways in which English tribal leaders were influenced by Roman missionaries, and eventually persuaded to adopt the Christian religion.

From *Bede: A History of the English Church and People*, translated by Leo Serley-Price and revised by R. E. Latham (New York: Barnes & Noble, 1993), pp. 66–71, 126–29.

The Conversion of Ethelbert, King of Kent

CHAPTER 23: THE HOLY POPE GREGORY SENDS AUGUSTINE AND OTHER MONKS TO PREACH TO THE ENGLISH NATION, AND ENCOURAGES THEM IN A LETTER TO PERSEVERE IN THEIR MISSION [A.D. 596]

In the year of our Lord 582, Maurice, fifty-fourth in succession from Augustus, became Emperor, and ruled for twenty-one years. In the tenth year of his reign, Gregory, an eminent scholar and administrator, was elected Pontiff of the apostolic Roman see, and ruled it for thirteen years, six months, and ten days. In the fourteenth year of this Emperor, and about the one hundred and fiftieth year after the coming of the English to Britain, Gregory was inspired by God to send his servant Augustine with several other God-fearing monks to preach the word of God to the English nation. Having undertaken this task in obedience to the Pope's command and progressed a short distance on their journey, they became afraid, and began to consider returning home. For they were appalled at the idea of going to a barbarous, fierce, and pagan nation, of whose very language they were ignorant. They unanimously agreed that this was the safest course, and sent back Augustine—who was to be consecrated bishop in the event of their being received by the English—so that he might humbly request the holy Gregory to recall them from so dangerous, arduous, and uncertain a journey. In reply, the Pope wrote them a letter of encouragement, urging them to proceed on their mission to preach God's word, and to trust themselves to his aid. This letter ran as follows:

'GREGORY, Servant of the servants of God, to the servants of our Lord. My very dear sons, it is better never to undertake any high enterprise than to abandon it when once begun. So with the help of God you must carry out this holy task which you have begun. Do not be deterred by the troubles of the journey or by what men say. Be constant and zealous in carrying out this enterprise which, under God's guidance, you have undertaken: and be assured that the greater the labour, the greater will be the glory of your eternal reward. When Augustine your leader returns, whom We have appointed your abbot, obey him humbly in all things, remembering that whatever he directs you to do will always be to the good of your souls. May Almighty God protect you with His grace, and grant me to see the result of your labours in our heavenly home. And although my office prevents me from working at your side, yet because I long to do so, I hope to share in your joyful reward. God keep you safe, my dearest sons.

'Dated the twenty-third of July, in the fourteenth year of the reign of the most pious Emperor Maurice Tiberius Augustus, and the thirteenth year after his Consulship: the fourteenth indiction.'

CHAPTER 25: Augustine reaches Britain, and first preaches in the Isle of Thanet before King Ethelbert, who grants permission to preach in Kent [A.D. 597]

Reassured by the encouragement of the blessed father Gregory, Augustine and his fellow-servants of Christ resumed their work in the word of God, and arrived in Britain. At this time the most powerful king there was Ethelbert, who reigned in Kent and whose domains extended northwards to the river Humber, which forms the boundary between the north and south Angles. To the east of Kent lies the large island of Thanet, which by English reckoning is six hundred hides[1] in extent; it is separated from the mainland by a waterway about three furlongs broad called the Wantsum, which joins the sea at either end and is fordable only in two places. It was here that God's servant Augustine landed with companions, who are said to have been forty in number. At the direction of blessed Pope Gregory, they had brought interpreters from among the Franks, and they sent these to Ethelbert, saying that they came from Rome bearing very glad news, which infallibly assured all who would receive it of eternal joy in heaven and an everlasting kingdom with the living and true God. On receiving this

message, the king ordered them to remain in the island where they had landed, and gave directions that they were to be provided with all necessaries until he should decide what action to take. For he had already heard of the Christian religion, having a Christian wife of the Frankish royal house named Bertha, whom he had received from her parents on condition that she should have freedom to hold and practise her faith unhindered with Bishop Liudhard, whom they had sent as her helper in the faith.

After some days, the king came to the island and, sitting down in the open air, summoned Augustine and his companions to an audience. But he took precautions that they should not approach him in a house; for he held an ancient superstition that, if they were practisers of magical arts, they might have opportunity to deceive and master him. But the monks were endowed with power from God, not from the Devil, and approached the king carrying a silver cross as their standard and the likeness of our Lord and Saviour painted on a board. First of all they offered prayer to God, singing a litany for the eternal salvation both of themselves and of those to whom and for whose sake they had come. And when, at the king's command, they had sat down and preached the word of life to the king and his court, the king said: 'Your words and promises are fair indeed; but they are new and uncertain, and I cannot accept them and abandon the age-old beliefs that I have held together with the whole English nation. But since you have travelled far, and I can see that you are sincere in your desire to impart to us what you believe to be true and excellent, we will not harm you. We will receive you hospitably and take care to supply you with all that you need; nor will we forbid you to preach and win any people you can to your religion.' The king then granted them a dwelling in the city of Canterbury, which was the chief city of all his realm, and in accordance with his promise he allowed them provisions and did not withdraw their freedom to preach. Tradition says that as they approached the city, bearing the holy cross and the likeness of our great King and Lord Jesus Christ as was their custom, they sang in unison this litany: 'We pray Thee,

---

[1] *hide*: measurement of land, usually equivalent to about 120 acres.

O Lord, in all Thy mercy, that Thy wrath and anger may be turned away from this city and from Thy holy house, for we are sinners. Alleluia.'

CHAPTER 26: THE LIFE AND DOCTRINE OF THE PRIMITIVE CHURCH ARE FOLLOWED IN KENT: AUGUSTINE ESTABLISHES HIS EPISCOPAL SEE IN THE KING'S CITY

As soon as they had occupied the house given to them they began to emulate the life of the apostles and the primitive Church. They were constantly at prayer; they fasted and kept vigils; they preached the word of life to whomsoever they could. They regarded worldly things as of little importance, and accepted only the necessities of life from those they taught. They practised what they preached, and were willing to endure any hardship, and even to die for the truth which they proclaimed. Before long a number of heathen, admiring the simplicity of their holy lives and the comfort of their heavenly message, believed and were baptized. On the east side of the city stood an old church, built in honour of Saint Martin during the Roman occupation of Britain, where the Christian queen of whom I have spoken went to pray. Here they first assembled to sing the psalms, to pray, to say Mass, to preach, and to baptize, until the king's own conversion to the Faith gave them greater freedom to preach and to build and restore churches everywhere.

At length the king himself, among others, edified by the pure lives of these holy men and their gladdening promises, the truth of which they confirmed by many miracles, believed and was baptized. Thenceforward great numbers gathered each day to hear the word of God, forsaking their heathen rites and entering the unity of Christ's holy Church as believers. While the king was pleased at their faith and conversion, it is said that he would not compel anyone to accept Christianity; for he had learned from his instructors and guides to salvation that the service of Christ must be accepted freely and not under compulsion. Nevertheless, he showed greater favour to believers, because they were fellow-citizens of the kingdom of heaven. And

it was not long before he granted his teachers in his capital of Canterbury a place of residence appropriate to their station, and gave them possessions of various kinds to supply their wants.

The Conversion of Edwin, King of Northumbrians

CHAPTER 13: EDWIN HOLDS A COUNCIL WITH HIS CHIEF MEN ABOUT ACCEPTING THE FAITH OF CHRIST. THE HIGH PRIEST DESTROYS HIS OWN ALTARS [A.D. 627]

When he heard this,[2] the king [Edwin] answered that is was his will as well as his duty to accept the Faith that Paulinus taught, but said that he must still discuss the matter with his principal advisers and friends so that, if they were in agreement with him, they might all be cleansed together in Christ the Fount of Life. Paulinus agreed, and the king kept his promise. He summoned a council of the wise men, and asked each in turn his opinion of this strange doctrine and this new way of worshipping the godhead that was being proclaimed to them.

Coifi, the Chief Priest, replied without hesitation: 'Your Majesty, let us give careful consideration to this new teaching; for I frankly admit that, in my experience, the religion that we have hitherto professed seems valueless and powerless. None of your subjects has been more devoted to the service of our gods than myself; yet there are many to whom you show greater favour, who receive greater honours, and who are more successful in all their undertakings. Now, if the gods had any power, they would surely have favoured myself, who have been more zealous in their service. Therefore, if on examination you perceive that these new teachings are better and more effectual, let us not hesitate to accept them.'

Another of the king's chief men signified his agreement with this prudent argument, and went on to say: 'Your Majesty, when we compare the

---

[2] That is, the assurances of the Roman missionary Paulinus.

present life of man on earth with that time of which we have no knowledge, it seems to me like the swift flight of a single sparrow through the banqueting-hall where you are sitting at dinner on a winter's day with your thanes and counsellors. In the midst there is a comforting fire to warm the hall; outside, the storms of winter rain or snow are raging. This sparrow flies swiftly in through one door of the hall, and out through another. While he is inside, he is safe from the winter storms; but after a few moments of comfort, he vanishes from sight into the wintry world from which he came. Even so, man appears on earth for a little while; but of what went before this life or of what follows, we know nothing. Therefore, if this new teaching has brought any more certain knowledge, it seems only right that we should follow it.' The other elders and counsellors of the king, under God's guidance, gave similar advice.

Coifi then added that he wished to hear Paulinus' teaching about God in greater detail; and when, at the king's bidding, this had been given, he exclaimed: 'I have long realized that there is nothing in our way of worship; for the more diligently I sought after truth in our religion, the less I found. I now publicly confess that this teaching clearly reveals truths that will afford us the blessings of life, salvation, and eternal happiness. Therefore, Your Majesty, I submit that the temples and altars that we have dedicated to no advantage be immediately desecrated and burned.' In short, the king granted blessed Paulinus full permission to preach, renounced idolatry, and professed his acceptance of the Faith of Christ. And when he asked the Chief Priest who should be the first to profane the altars and shrines of the idols, together with the enclosures that surrounded them, Coifi replied: 'I will do this myself; for now that the true God has granted me knowledge, who more suitably than I can set a public example and destroy the idols that I worshipped in ignorance?' So he formally renounced his empty superstitions and asked the king to give him arms and a stallion—for hitherto it had not been lawful for the Chief Priest to carry arms or to ride anything but a mare—and, thus

equipped, he set out to destroy the idols. Girded with a sword and with a spear in his hand, he mounted the king's stallion and rode up to the idols. When the crowd saw him, they thought he had gone mad; but without hesitation, as soon as he reached the temple, he cast into it the spear he carried and thus profaned it. Then, full of joy at his knowledge of the worship of the true God, he told his companions to set fire to the temple and its enclosures and destroy them. The site where these idols once stood is still shown, not far east of York, beyond the river Derwent, and is known today as Goodmanham. Here it was that the Chief Priest, inspired by the true God, desecrated and destroyed the altars that he had himself dedicated.

CHAPTER 14: EDWIN AND HIS PEOPLE ACCEPT THE FAITH, AND ARE BAPTIZED BY PAULINUS [A.D. 627]

So King Edwin, with all the nobility of his kingdom and a large number of humbler folk, accepted the Faith and were washed in the cleansing waters of Baptism in the eleventh year of his reign, which was the year of our Lord 627, and about one hundred and eighty years after the first arrival of the English in Britain. The king's Baptism took place at York on Easter Day, the 12th of April, in the church of Saint Peter the Apostle, which the king had hastily built of timber during the time of his instruction and preparation for Baptism; and in this city he established the see of his teacher and bishop Paulinus. Soon after his Baptism, at Paulinus' suggestion, he gave orders to build on the same site a larger and more noble basilica of stone, which was to enclose the little oratory he had built before. The foundations were laid, and the walls of a square church began to rise around this little oratory; but before they reached their appointed height, the cruel death of the king left the work to be completed by Oswald his successor. Thenceforward for six years, until the close of Edwin's reign, Paulinus preached the word in that province with the king's full consent and approval, and as many as were predestined to eternal life believed and were baptized. . . .

REVIEW QUESTIONS

1. Analyze the two conversion processes that Bede describes. What do they reveal about Anglo-Saxon culture, the role of the king, and the king's relationship with his people?
2. Why, ultimately, did both Ethelbert and Edwin decide to become Christian, according to Bede?

What did they—and their peoples—stand to gain?

3. Compare these conversion experiences with that of Clovis (pp. 215–219). What do the differences and similarities suggest about the cultural ties between the Anglo-Saxons and the Franks?

FROM The Anglo-Saxon Translation of
The Book of Genesis

Following the initial missionary efforts of Latin-speaking emissaries from Rome, the bishops and monastic communities of Anglo-Saxon England became active in developing new ways to spread knowledge of the Christian faith to lay audiences. One powerful mechanism for doing this was to translate portions of the Gospels (the New Testament) or the Hebrew Bible (the Old Testament) into the Anglo-Saxon vernacular. But as this excerpt from an Anglo-Saxon version of Genesis reveals, translation often involves much more than translating words: concepts, customs, social structures, assumptions, and values must also be translated in order to make them comprehensible to a new audience. Comparing the resulting version of the story with that written in the Hebrew Bible reveals a great deal about the Anglo-Saxon worldview and the profound ways in which it differed from that of the ancient Hebrews. As you read, bear in mind that this text was actually written down in verse at about the same time as the epic poem Beowulf.

Genesis 3:1–7 (Revised Standard Version of the Hebrew Bible)*

Now the serpent was more subtle than any other wild creature that the Lord God had made. He said to the woman, "Did God say, 'You shall not eat of any tree of the garden'?" And the woman said to the serpent, "We may eat of the fruit of the trees of the garden; but God said, 'You shall not eat of the fruit

of the tree which is in the midst of the garden, neither shall you touch it, lest you die.'" But the serpent said to the woman, "You will not die. For God knows that when you eat of it your eyes will be opened, and you will be like God, knowing good and evil." So when the woman saw that the tree was good for food, and that it was a delight to the eyes, and that the tree was to be desired to make one wise, she took of its fruit and ate; and she also gave some to her husband, and he ate. Then the eyes of both were opened, and they knew that they were naked; and they sewed fig leaves together and made themselves aprons.

*From *Revised Standard Version Bible*, National Council of the Churches of Christ in the USA, 1952, http://quod.lib.umich.edu/r/rsv/.

The Anglo-Saxon Translation*

442   Then an adversary of God eager in his accoutrements got himself ready: he had an evil sense of purpose. He set on his head a concealing helm and fastened it very tightly and secured it with clasps. He had in him knowledge of plenty of speeches of per-verse words. From there he wound his way upwards and passed through the gates of hell—he had a strong sense of purpose—and hovered aloft, malevolent-minded. He beat down the fire on both sides with his fiend's strength: he meant surreptitiously to seduce, to lead astray and to pervert with wicked deeds the fol-lowers of the Lord, men, so that they would become repugnant to God.

453   He journeyed on then with his fiend's strength until in the kingdom of earth he came upon the perfected Adam, God's wisely created handiwork, and his wife also, a most beautiful woman, so that they could accomplish much good whom mankind's ordaining Lord himself had appointed as his subordinates.

460   And near them stood two trees which were laden with a crop and covered with fruit according as God the Ruler, the high King of heaven, had planted them with his hands in order that thereby the children of men, each person, might choose between good and evil, well-being and woe. Their fruit was not alike. The one was so pleas-ant, beautiful and radiant, graceful and admirable—that was the tree of life. He would be allowed thereafter to live on and to exist in the world in eternity who ate of that fruit, so that age did not harm him after that nor severe sickness, but he would be allowed from then on always to live among pleasures

and to have his existence and the heaven-King's favour here in the world and to have as his pledge assured honours in that high heaven when he should journey there. Then there was the other, entirely black, obscure and dark—that was the tree of death which brought forth much bitterness. Each man soever that tasted of what grew on that tree must needs become aware of the two things, the divergent ways of good and of evil in this world, and thereafter he would have to live by his sweat and in sorrows, forever under punishment. Old age must needs rob him of valorous deeds, of pleasures and of authority, and death be decreed him. For a little while he would enjoy his life and then go to the darkest of realms, into the fire, and would have to minister to fiends there where there will exist for an infinite duration the greatest of all perils for men. That the malignant creature, the devil's secret mes-senger who was contending against God, well knew.

491   He turned himself then into the form of a snake and then wound himself about the tree of death with the cunning of a devil; there he plucked a fruit and went thence back again to where he perceived the heaven-King's handiwork. Then in his first utterance the malignant creature began to question him with lies:

496   'Do you long for anything, Adam, from God above? I have journeyed here from far away on his business; it was not long since that I sat by his very self. He then com-manded me to go on this mission. He com-manded that you should eat of this fruit and he declared that your strength and skill and your mind would grow greater, and your body much more beautiful, your limbs more handsome, and he declared that to you there would prove no want of any wealth in the world. You have now done the will of the heaven-King and your loyal duty to him and

---

*From *Anglo-Saxon Poetry: An Anthology of Old English Poems in Prose Translations with Introduction and Headnotes*, by S. A. J. Bradley (New York: Everyman's Library, 1982), pp. 25–32.

served your Master to his satisfaction and you have made yourself precious to the Lord. I heard him in his splendour praise your deeds and your words and speak about your way of life. Accordingly, you are to carry out what his messengers bring word of here into this country. Broad are the green regions in the world and God, the Ruler of all, sits above in the most exalted realm of the heavens. The Lord of men is unwilling himself to have the hardships of travelling on this mission; rather he sends his subordinate to speak with you. Now he has commanded me to teach you by messages cunning skills. Carry out his bidding confidently. Take this fruit into your hand, bite it and taste it. Within your breast you will become untrammelled and your outward form will become the more beautiful. God the Ruler, your Lord, has sent you this help from the heaven-kingdom.'

522   Adam, the self-determined man, standing there on the earth, spoke out:

523   'When I heard the triumphant Lord, mighty God, speak with stern voice, and when he commanded me to establish myself here and to keep his behests and gave me this wife, this lovely woman, and commanded me take heed that I should not be brought to ruin or utterly betrayed over that tree of death, he declared that he would have to inhabit black hell who of his own volition did anything evil. I do not know whether you come with lies from a hidden motive or whether you are the messenger of the Lord from heaven. You see, I cannot make any sense of your suggestions, of your words and reasons, your mission and declarations. I do know what he, our Saviour, himself enjoined upon me when I saw him last: he commanded me to honour and keep well his word and carry out his precepts. You are not like any of his angels whom I saw before, nor have you shown me any token that my Master has sent to me out of his favour and out of his grace. Therefore I cannot obey

you, and you may go your way. I have a firm trust above in the almighty God who fashioned me here with his arms and with his hands. He is capable of endowing me with every advantage from his high kingdom, even if he did not send his subordinate.'

547   He turned himself, the malevolent creature, to where in earth's domain he saw the woman Eve standing, beautifully formed; and he declared to her that it would prove the greatest harm in the world to all their children thereafter:

551   'I am certain that the Lord God will be incensed against the two of you when I return from this journey along the lengthy road if I personally tell him this message, that you two do not properly act upon whatever message he sends here from the east on this occasion. Now he himself will have to make the journey, according to your answer. His spokesman is not allowed to speak his business, therefore I am certain that in his heart he, the mighty God, is going to be incensed against you. But if you, a compliant woman, will listen to my words then you will be able to think circumspectly about a remedy for it. Consider in your heart that you can fend off punishment from the pair of you, as I shall show you.

564   'Eat of this fruit. Then your eyes will become so clear that you will afterwards be able to see as widely as beyond the whole world and the throne of your Master himself, and henceforth to enjoy his favour. You will be able moreover to manipulate Adam if you command his desire and he trusts in your words. If you tell him truly what an exemplary precept you yourself hold in your bosom, because you have carried out God's bidding and counsel, he will abandon in his heart this distasteful antagonism and his ill response, if we two both talk to him with effect. Coax him carefully so that he carries

out your counsel, lest you should both be forced to prove abhorrent to God your Ruler.

578   'If you achieve that design, most excellent lady, I will conceal from your Master that Adam spoke so much insult and so many contemptible words to me. He accuses me of lies and says that I am a messenger intent upon malicious and hostile things, and not an angel of God. But I know the whole race of angels and the lofty roofs of the heavens so well, so long has been the time I have eagerly served God, my Master, the Lord himself, with loyal resolution. I am not like a devil.'

588   So he led her on with lies and by cunning coaxed on the woman in that mischief until the snake's thinking began to seethe up inside her—the ordaining Lord had defined for her a frailer resolution—so that she began to let her mind go along with those counsels. Therefore she received from the abhorrent foe, against the word of the Lord, the tree of death's injurious fruit. A deed more evil was not defined for men. It is a great wonder that eternal God, the Prince, would ever tolerate it that so many a servant should be led astray by lies as happened because of those counsels.

599   She ate of the fruit then and violated the word and the will of the Ruler of all. Then through the gift of the abhorrent foe who betrayed her with lies and subtly defrauded her, which came to her because of his doings, she was enabled to see far afield so that heaven and earth seemed brighter to her and all this world more beautiful and God's work great and mighty—although she did not view it by means of a human perception, but the destroyer who had lent her the vision assiduously deluded her in her spirit so that she could gaze so widely over the heavenly domain.

609   Then the apostate spoke out of his malevolence; he did not teach her anything at all of profit:

611   'Now you can see for yourself, so I do not need to tell you it, virtuous Eve, that appearances and forms are different since you trusted in my words and carried out my counsels. Now light shines out before you and gracious radiance towards you which I have brought from God, gleaming from out of the heavens. Now you can lay hold on it. Tell Adam what powers of vision you possess through my coming. If even now he carries out my counsels in modest manner, then I shall give him abundance of this light with which, so virtuous, I have adorned you. I shall not reproach him for those blasphemies, even though he is not worthy of being excused for he expressed much that was abhorrent to me.'

623   So must her children live in their turn: when they do something abhorrent they must achieve an amicable settlement, make good the blaspheming of their Master and enjoy his favour from then on.

626   To Adam then she went, the most lovely of women, the most beautiful of wives that might come into the world, because she was the work of the hand of the heaven-King, even though she had then been subtly corrupted and led astray by lies so that they were to prove abhorrent to God through the enemy's scheming and were to lose the esteem and favour of their Master through the devil's devices and to forfeit the kingdom of heaven for many a season. Misery replete will befall the man who does not keep on his guard while he enjoys self-determination.

636   One unblessed apple she carried in her hand, one lay at her heart, the fruit of the tree of death which the Lord of lords had previously forbidden her; and the Prince of glory had uttered this pronouncement, that men, his servants, lay under no necessity of suffering that great death, but he, the holy Lord, granted to each one of his people the kingdom of heaven and copious wealth if

they would let be that one fruit which the abhorrent tree bore on its boughs, filled with bitterness: it was death's tree which the Lord forbade them. Her, then, and the mentality of Eve, the frail mind of woman, he seduced who was hostile to God and in hatred of the heaven-King, so that she believed in his words, carried out his counsels, and accepted in trust that he had brought those precepts from God which he so carefully communicated to her in his words and showed her a sign and gave assurance of his good faith and honest intent. Then she spoke to her master:

655   'Adam, my lord, this fruit is so sweet and delectable in my breast, and this handsome messenger is God's good angel: I see by his apparel that he is the envoy of our Master, the King of heaven. His favour is better for us to win than his enmity. If you spoke anything hurtful to him today he will nevertheless forgive it, if we two are willing to pay him deference. What will it avail you, such detestable quarrelling with your Master's messenger? We need his favour. He can intercede for us with the Ruler of all, the King of heaven. I can see from here where he himself is sitting—it is to the south-east—surrounded with wealth, who shaped the world. I see his angels moving about him on their wings, the hugest of all throngs, of multitudes the most joyous. Who could give me such discernment if God, the Ruler of heaven, had not sent it directly to me? I can hear amply and see so widely into all the world and beyond this spacious creation, I can hear the ethereal merriment in the heavens. My mind has become enlightened within and without since I ate the fruit. I have some of it here in my hands now, virtuous master. I give it to you gladly. I believe that it has come from God, brought by his command—so this messenger has told me with truthful words. It is like nothing else on earth except that, as this envoy says, it has come directly from God.'

684   She talked to him repeatedly and coaxed him the whole day towards the dismal act, that they should violate their Lord's will. The malignant messenger stayed; he foisted desires upon them, enticed them with cunning and audaciously dogged them. The fiend remained very close, who had travelled on the audacious journey along the lengthy road: he meant to make man fall into that great and mortal sin, to misguide people and lead them astray so that they should forgo God's benefaction, the Almighty's gift, possession of the kingdom of heaven. Indeed, the hellish mischief-maker well knew that they must be subject to God's wrath and imprisonment in hell and of necessity undergo that forcible oppression once they had broken God's command, when with lying words he misguided the lovely woman, the most beautiful of wives, into that indiscretion, so that she spoke under his will and became as an instrument to him in misguiding God's handiwork.

704   She talked quite often to Adam, then, this most lovely of women, until the man's mind was changed, so that he put his trust in the promise which the woman expressed to him in her words. Yet she did it out of loyal intent. She did not know that there were to follow so many hurts and terrible torments for humankind because she took to heart what she heard in the counsellings of that abhorrent messenger; but rather she thought that she was gaining the favour of the heavenly King with those words which she presented to the man as a sign, and gave assurance of her good faith until within his breast Adam's determination wavered and his heart began to incline towards her desire. From the woman he accepted hell and departure hence, though it was not so called, but had the name of fruit. Yet it was the sleep of death and the yoke of the devil, hell and death, and the perdition of men, the murder of mankind, that unholy fruit which they took as their food.

REVIEW QUESTIONS

1. Carefully compare this excerpt from the Anglo-Saxon Genesis with the parallel portion of the Hebrew Genesis to which it corresponds. What are the major differences—in length, style, structure, and content?

2. How do these differences constitute historical evidence that can assist in constructing a picture of Anglo-Saxon society in the centuries following the arrival of Roman missionaries?

3. The Anglo-Saxon depiction of Eve, in particular, departs from that of the Hebrew Bible. What does this reveal about the status of women in Anglo-Saxon society?

EINHARD

FROM *The Life of Charlemagne*

The author of this official biography of Charlemagne (r. 768–814) was his close friend and younger contemporary, Einhard (c. 775–840). One of the many able scholars who were attracted to the Carolingian court, Einhard appears to have been an intimate member of Charlemagne's household circle and, after Charlemagne's death, a close associate and supporter of his son, Louis the Pious (r. 814–40). In his efforts to glorify Charlemagne's memory and legacy, he modeled this biography on an earlier life of the first Roman emperor, Augustus Caesar.

From *Two Lives of Charlemagne*, edited by Lewis Thorpe (New York: Penguin, 1969), pp. 73–82.

*   *   *

The Emperor's Private Life

What has gone before is a fair picture of Charlemagne and all that he did to protect and enlarge his kingdom, and indeed to embellish it. I shall now speak of his intellectual qualities, his extraordinary strength of character, whether in prosperity or adversity, and all the other details of his personal and domestic life.

After the death of his father, at the time when he was sharing the kingship with Carloman, Charlemagne bore with such patience this latter's hatred and jealousy that everyone was surprised that he never lost his temper with his brother.

Then, at the bidding of his mother, he married the daughter of Desiderius, the King of the Longobards [Lombards, of northern Italy]. Nobody knows why, but he dismissed this wife after one year. Next he married Hildigard, a woman of most noble family, from the Swabian race. By her he had three sons, Charles, Pepin and Lewis, and the same number of daughters, Rotrude, Bertha and Gisela. He had three more daughters, Theoderada, Hiltrude and Rothaide, two of these by his third wife, Fastrada, who was from the race of Eastern Franks or Germans, and the last by a concubine whose name I cannot remember. Fastrada died and he married Luitgard, from the Alamanni, but she bore him no children. After Luitgard's death, he took four concubines: Madelgard, who bore him a daughter Ruothilde; Gersvinda, of the Saxon race, by whom he had a daughter Adaltrude; Regina, who bore him Drogo and Hugo; and Adallinda, who became the mother of Theodoric.

Charlemagne's own mother, Bertrada, lived with him in high honour to a very great age. He treated her with every respect and never had a cross word with her, except over the divorce of King Desiderius' daughter, whom he had married on her advice. Bertrada died soon after Hildigard, living long enough to see three grandsons and as many granddaughters in her son's house. Charlemagne buried her with great honour in the church of Saint Denis, where his father lay.

He had a single sister, Gisela by name, who from her childhood onwards had been dedicated to the religious life. He treated her with the same respect which he showed his mother. She died a few years before Charlemagne himself, in the nunnery where she had spent her life.

Charlemagne was determined to give his children, his daughters just as much as his sons, a proper training in the liberal arts which had formed the subject of his own studies. As soon as they were old enough he had his sons taught to ride in the Frankish fashion, to use arms and to hunt. He made his daughters learn to spin and weave wool, use the distaff and spindle, and acquire every womanly accomplishment, rather than fritter away their time in sheer idleness.

Of all his children he lost only two sons and one daughter prior to his own death. These were his eldest son Charles, Pepin whom he had made King of Italy, and Rotrude, the eldest of his daughters, who had been engaged to Constantine, the Emperor of the Greeks.[1] Pepin left one son, called Bernard, and five daughters, Adelhaid, Atula, Gundrada, Berthaid and Theoderada. Char-lemagne gave clear proof of the affection which he bore them all, for after the death of Pepin he ordered his grandson Bernard to succeed and he had his granddaughters brought up with his own girls. He bore the death of his two sons and his daughter with less fortitude than one would have expected, considering the

strength of his character; for his emotions as a father, which were very deeply rooted, made him burst into tears.

When the death of Hadrian, the Pope of Rome [r. 772–795] and his close friend, was announced to him, he wept as if he had lost a brother or a dearly loved son. He was firm and steady in his human relationships, developing friendship easily, keeping it up with care and doing everything he possibly could for anyone whom he had admitted to this degree of intimacy.

He paid such attention to the upbringing of his sons and daughters that he never sat down to table without them when he was at home, and never set out on a journey without taking them with him. His sons rode at his side and his daughters followed along behind. Hand-picked guards watched over them as they closed the line of march. These girls were extraordinarily beautiful and greatly loved by their father. It is a remarkable fact that, as a result of this, he kept them with him in his household until the very day of his death, instead of giving them in marriage to his own men or to foreigners, maintaining that he could not live without them. The consequence was that he had a number of unfortunate experiences, he who had been so lucky in all else that he undertook. However, he shut his eyes to all that happened, as if no suspicion of any immoral conduct had ever reached him, or as if the rumour was without foundation.

I did not mention with the others a son called Pepin who was born to Charlemagne by a concubine. He was handsome enough, but a hunchback. At a moment when his father was wintering in Bavaria, soon after the beginning of his campaign against the Huns, this Pepin pretended to be ill and conspired with certain of the Frankish leaders who had won him over to their cause by pretending to offer him the kingship. The plot was discovered and the conspirators were duly punished. Pepin was tonsured and permitted to take up, in the monastery of Prüm, the life of a religious for which he had already expressed a vocation.

Earlier on there had been another dangerous conspiracy against Charlemagne in Germany. All the plotters were exiled, some having their eyes put

---

[1] Constantine II (780–797).

out first, but the others were not maltreated physically. Only three of them were killed. These resisted arrest, drew their swords and started to defend themselves. They slaughtered a few men in the process and had to be destroyed themselves, as there was no other way of dealing with them.

The cruelty of Queen Fastrada is thought to have been the cause of both these conspiracies, since it was under her influence that Charlemagne seemed to have taken actions which were fundamentally opposed to his normal kindliness and good nature. Throughout the remainder of his life he so won the love and favour of all his fellow human beings, both at home and abroad, that no one ever levelled against him the slightest charge of cruelty or injustice.

He loved foreigners and took great pains to make them welcome. So many visited him as a result that they were rightly held to be a burden not only to the palace, but to the entire realm. In his magnanimity he took no notice at all of this criticism, for he considered that his reputation for hospitality and the advantage of the good name which he acquired more than compensated for the great nuisance of their being there.

The Emperor was strong and well built. He was tall in stature, but not excessively so, for his height was just seven times the length of his own feet. The top of his head was round, and his eyes were piercing and unusually large. His nose was slightly longer than normal, he had a fine head of white hair and his expression was gay and good-humoured. As a result, whether he was seated or standing, he always appeared masterful and dignified. His neck was short and rather thick, and his stomach a trifle too heavy, but the proportions of the rest of his body prevented one from noticing these blemishes. His step was firm and he was manly in all his movements. He spoke distinctly, but his voice was thin for a man of his physique. His health was good, except that he suffered from frequent attacks of fever during the last four years of his life, and towards the end he was lame in one foot. Even then he continued to do exactly as he wished, instead of following the advice of his doctors, whom he came positively to dislike after they advised him to stop

eating the roast meat to which he was accustomed and to live on stewed dishes.

He spent much of his time on horseback and out hunting, which came naturally to him, for it would be difficult to find another race on earth who could equal the Franks in this activity. He took delight in steam-baths at the thermal springs, and loved to exercise himself in the water when-ever he could. He was an extremely strong swimmer and in this sport no one could surpass him. It was for this reason that he built his palace at Aachen and remained continuously in residence there during the last years of his life and indeed until the moment of his death. He would invite not only his sons to bathe with him, but his nobles and friends as well, and occasionally even a crowd of his attendants and bodyguards, so that sometimes a hundred men or more would be in the water together.

He wore the national dress of the Franks. Next to his skin he had a linen shirt and linen drawers; and then long hose and a tunic edged with silk. He wore shoes on his feet and bands of cloth wound round his legs. In winter he protected his chest and shoulders with a jerkin made of otter skins or ermine. He wrapped himself in a blue cloak and always had a sword strapped to his side, with a hilt and belt of gold or silver. Sometimes he would use a jewelled sword, but this was only on great feast days or when ambassadors came from foreign peoples. He hated the clothes of other countries, no matter how becoming they might be, and he would never consent to wear them. The only exception to this was one day in Rome when Pope Hadrian entreated him to put on a long tunic and a Greek mantle, and to wear shoes made in the Roman fashion; and then a second time, when Leo, Hadrian's successor, persuaded him to do the same thing. On feast days he walked in procession in a suit of cloth of gold, with jewelled shoes, his cloak fastened with a golden brooch and with a crown of gold and precious stones on his head. On ordinary days his dress differed hardly at all from that of the common people.

He was moderate in his eating and drinking, and especially so in drinking; for he hated to see drunkenness in any man, and even more so in himself and his friends. All the same, he could not go long without food, and he often used to complain that fasting made him feel ill. He rarely gave banquets and these only on high feast days, but then he would invite a great number of guests. His main meal of the day was served in four courses, in addition to the roast meat which his hunters used to bring in on spits and which he enjoyed more than any other food. During his meal he would listen to a public reading or some other entertainment. Stories would be recited for him, or the doings of the ancients told again. He took great pleasure in the books of Saint Augustine and especially in those which are called *The City of God*.

He was so sparing in his use of wine and every other beverage that he rarely drank more than three times in the course of his dinner. In sum-mer, after his midday meal, he would eat some fruit and take another drink; then he would remove his shoes and undress completely, just as he did at night, and rest for two or three hours. During the night he slept so lightly that he would wake four or five times and rise from his bed. When he was dressing and putting on his shoes he would invite his friends to come in. Moreover, if the Count of the Palace told him that there was some dispute which could not be settled without the Emperor's personal decision, he would order the disputants to be brought in there and then, hear the case as if he were sitting in tribunal and pronounce a judgement. If there was any official business to be transacted on that day, or any order to be given to one of his ministers, he would settle it at the same time.

He spoke easily and fluently, and could express with great clarity whatever he had to say. He was not content with his own mother tongue, but took the trouble to learn foreign languages. He learnt Latin so well that he spoke it as fluently as his own tongue; but he understood Greek better than he could speak it. He was eloquent to the point of sometimes seeming almost garrulous.

He paid the greatest attention to the liberal arts; and he had great respect for men who taught them, bestowing high honours upon them. When he was learning the rules of grammar he received tuition from Peter the Deacon of Pisa, who by then was an old man, but for all other subjects he was taught by Alcuin, surnamed Albinus, another Deacon, a man of the Saxon race who came from Britain and was the most learned man anywhere to be found. Under him the Emperor spent much time and effort in studying rhetoric, dialectic and especially astrology. He applied himself to mathematics and traced the course of the stars with great attention and care. He also tried to learn to write. With this object in view he used to keep writing-tablets and note-books under the pillows on his bed, so that he could try his hand at forming letters during his leisure moments; but, although he tried very hard, he had begun too late in life and he made little progress.

Charlemagne practised the Christian religion with great devotion and piety, for he had been brought up in this faith since earliest childhood. This explains why he built a cathedral of such great beauty at Aachen, decorating it with gold and silver, with lamps, and with lattices and doors of solid bronze. He was unable to find marble columns for his construction anywhere else, and so he had them brought from Rome and Ravenna.

As long as his health lasted, he went to church morning and evening with great regularity, and also for early-morning Mass, and the late-night hours. He took the greatest pains to ensure that all church ceremonies were performed with the utmost dignity, and he was always warning the sacristans to see that nothing sordid or dirty was brought into the building or left there. He donated so many sacred vessels made of gold and silver, and so many priestly vestments, that when service time came even those who opened and closed the doors, surely the humblest of all church dignitaries, had no need to perform their duties in their everyday clothes.

He made careful reforms in the way in which the psalms were chanted and the lessons read. He was himself quite an expert at both of these exercises, but he never read the lesson in public and he would sing only with the rest of the congregation and then in a low voice.

He was most active in relieving the poor and in that form of really disinterested charity which the

Greeks call *eleemosyna*. He gave alms not only in his own country and in the kingdom over which he reigned, but also across the sea in Syria, Egypt, Africa, Jerusalem, Alexandria and Carthage. Wherever he heard that Christians were living in want, he took pity on their poverty and sent them money regularly. It was, indeed, precisely for this reason that he sought the friendship of kings beyond the sea, for he hoped that some relief and alleviation might result for the Christians living under their domination.

Charlemagne cared more for the church of the holy Apostle Peter in Rome than for any other sacred and venerable place. He poured into its treasury a vast fortune in gold and silver coinage and in precious stones. He sent so many gifts to the Pope that it was impossible to keep count of them. Throughout the whole period of his reign nothing was ever nearer to his heart than that, by his own efforts and exertion, the city of Rome should regain its former proud position. His ambition was not merely that the church of Saint Peter should remain safe and protected thanks to him, but that by means of his wealth it should be more richly adorned and endowed than any other church. However much he thought of Rome, it still remains true that throughout his whole reign of forty-seven years he went there only four times to fulfil his vows and to offer up his prayers.

These were not the sole reasons for Charlemagne's last visit to Rome. The truth is that the inhabitants of Rome had violently attacked Pope Leo [r. 795–816], putting out his eyes and cutting off his tongue, and had forced him to flee to the King for help. Charlemagne really came to Rome to restore the Church, which was in a very bad state indeed, but in the end he spent the whole winter there. It was on this occasion that he received the title of Emperor and Augustus. At first he was far from wanting this. He made it clear that he would not have entered the cathedral that day at all, although it was the greatest of all the festivals of the Church, if he had known in advance what the Pope was planning to do. Once he had accepted the title, he endured with great patience the jealousy of the so-called Roman Emperors, who were most indignant at what had happened. He overcame their hostility only by the sheer strength of his personality, which was much more powerful than theirs. He was for ever sending messengers to them, and in his dispatches he called them his brothers.

Now that he was Emperor, he discovered that there were many defects in the legal system of his own people, for the Franks have two separate codes of law which differ from each other in many points. He gave much thought to how he could best fill the gaps, reconcile the discrepancies, correct the errors and rewrite the laws which were ill-expressed. None of this was ever finished; he added a few sections, but even these remained incomplete. What he did do was to have collected together and committed to writing the laws of all the nations under his jurisdiction which still remained unrecorded.

At the same time he directed that the age-old narrative poems, barbarous enough, it is true, in which were celebrated the warlike deeds of the kings of ancient times, should be written out and so preserved. He also began a grammar of his native tongue.

*   *   *

REVIEW QUESTIONS

1. According to Einhard, what aspects of Charlemagne's policies and personality made him an effective ruler? Does Einhard seem to be masking any of the emperor's weaknesses? Why?

2. What can we learn from this source about the role and status of women in the Carolingian court?

3. How does this portrait of Charlemagne by an intimate member of his court compare with that of Justinian by Procopius (pp. 223–228)? How would you account for the differences in tone, style, and content?

8 ❧ THE EXPANSION OF EUROPE, 950–1100

The central Middle Ages witnessed tremendous economic growth, which began with agriculture, the basis of the medieval economy. All societies in Europe, North Africa, and western Asia remained overwhelmingly rural and depended on villages of peasants to produce the food and supplies needed to sustain urban life and emerging state bureaucracies. Better technology for vital tools such as plows and harnesses, accurate record keeping, and warming climate all contributed to the improved yields in crops and flocks.

About the year 1000, Christian Europe had only a few small cities, whereas the Muslim world contained many large ones, as did the Byzantine Empire. Most European cities rapidly increased in population in the following centuries, a growth that depended on adequate food supplies, either produced locally or acquired through trade. People living in towns also needed certain rights and liberties to transact business, and urban people wanted secure land ownership; personal liberty, including freedom of travel; and a sound coinage. Merchants did not want to resort to feuds and vendettas to settle their disputes. Kings and lords were prepared to grant some liberties to towns in exchange for money. Urban wealth largely resulted from trade and a modest level of artisan manufactures, especially cloth.

Fending off invaders (like the Vikings) and dispensing justice remained the main tasks of medieval rulers in this era. But secular rulers also had a new rival: the papacy. Beginning in the eleventh century, powerful voices within the Church called for a series of reforms that would not only eradicate perceived abuses of clerical authority but would also strengthen the power of the clergy and aggrandize the role of the Roman pope. Eventually, this reformed Church had the authority to define more closely all Christian liberties and duties, but this was not usually good news for women or for religious or ethnic minorities. Persecution and subjugation were also the result of a new Christian ideology: crusading. In an effort to quell violence within Europe, the papacy took advantage of a call for assistance from the Byzantine emperor Alexius Commenus, urging fractious nobles and landless knights to seek salvation, glory, and treasure overseas. But many crusaders chose to use this mandate closer to home, assaulting and even massacring communities of Jesus. Meanwhile, the rhetoric of crusading entered into popular storytelling traditions and inflamed a parallel discourse of religious warfare within certain Muslim communities.

POPE GREGORY VII

Letter to Bishop Hermann of Metz

Pope Gregory VII (r. 1073–85) wrote this letter to Bishop Hermann of Metz to justify his decision to excommunicate Emperor Henry IV of Germany and to explain his views on the role of the Church in the world. The pope's dispute with Henry IV concerned the emperor's claim to appoint bishops and abbots. The pope considered these appointments to be in the Church's jurisdiction, and other reformers were also troubled by churchmen who became vassals of a secular lord. Homage and fealty for fiefs gave the appearance that secular power was superior to spiritual power. This letter is a concise statement of the reform movement's position.

From *The Correspondence of Pope Gregory VII*, edited by Ephriam Emerton (New York: Columbia University Press, 1969), pp. 166–75.

Gregory to his beloved brother in Christ, Hermann, bishop of Metz, greeting . . .

We know you to be ever ready to bear labor and peril in defense of the truth, and doubt not that this is a gift from God. It is a part of his unspeakable grace and his marvelous mercy that he never permits his chosen ones to wander far or to be completely cast down; but rather, after a time of persecution and wholesome probation, makes them stronger than they were before. On the other hand, just as among cowards one who is worse than the rest is broken down by fear, so among the brave one who acts more bravely than the rest is stirred thereby to new activity. We remind you of this by way of exhortation that you may stand more joyfully in the front ranks of the Christian host, the more confident you are that they are the nearest to God the conqueror.

You ask us to fortify you against the madness of those who babble with accursed tongues about the authority of the Holy Apostolic See not being able to excommunicate King Henry as one who despises the law of Christ, a destroyer of churches and of the empire, a promoter and partner of heresies, nor to release anyone from his oath of fidelity to him; but it has not seemed necessary to reply to this request, seeing that so many and such convincing proofs are to be found in Holy Scripture. Nor do we believe that those who abuse and contradict the truth to their utter damnation do this as much from ignorance as from wretched and desperate folly. And no wonder! It is ever the way of the wicked to protect their own iniquities by calling upon others like themselves; for they think it of no account to incur the penalty of falsehood.

To cite but a few out of the multitude of proofs: Who does not remember the words of our Lord and Savior Jesus Christ: "Thou art Peter and on this rock I will build my Church, and the gates of hell shall not prevail against it. And I will give thee the keys of the kingdom of heaven and whatsoever thou shalt bind on earth shall be bound in heaven and whatsoever thou shalt loose on earth shall be loosed in heaven." Are kings excepted here? Or are they not of the sheep which the Son of God committed to St. Peter? Who, I ask, thinks himself excluded from this universal grant of the power of binding and loosing to St. Peter unless, perchance, that unhappy man who, being unwilling to bear the yoke of the Lord, subjects himself to the burden of the Devil and refuses to be numbered in the flock of Christ? His wretched liberty shall profit him nothing; for if he shakes off from his proud neck the power divinely granted to Peter, so much the heavier shall it be for him in the day of judgment.

This institution of the divine will, this foundation of the rule of the Church, this privilege granted and sealed especially by a heavenly decree to St. Peter, chief of the Apostles, has been accepted and maintained with great reverence by the holy fathers, and they have given to the Holy Roman Church, as well in general councils as in their other acts and writings, the name of "universal mother." They have not only accepted her expositions of doctrine and her instructions in our holy religion, but they have also recognized her judicial decisions. They have agreed as with one spirit and one voice that all major cases, all especially important affairs and the judgments of all churches ought to be referred to her as to their head and mother, that from her there shall be no appeal, that her judgments may not and cannot be reviewed or reversed by anyone.

Thus Pope Gelasius, writing to the emperor Anastasius, gave him these instructions as to the right theory of the principate of the Holy and Apostolic See, based upon divine authority:

Although it is fitting that all the faithful should submit themselves to all priests who perform their sacred functions properly, how much the more should they accept the judgment of that prelate who has been appointed by the supreme divine ruler to be superior to all priests and whom the loyalty of the whole later Church has recognized

as such. Your Wisdom sees plainly that no human capacity whatsoever can equal that of him whom the word of Christ raised above all others and whom the reverend Church has always confessed and still devotedly holds as its Head.

So also Pope Julius, writing to the eastern bishops in regard to the powers of the same Holy and Apostolic See, says:

You ought, my brethren, to have spoken carefully and not ironically of the Holy Roman and Apostolic Church, seeing that our Lord Jesus Christ addressed her respectfully, saying, "Thou art Peter and upon this rock I will build my church, and the gates of hell shall not prevail against it; and I will give thee the keys of the kingdom of heaven." For it has the power, granted by a unique privilege, of opening and shutting the gates of the celestial kingdom to whom it will.

To whom, then, the power of opening and closing Heaven is given, shall he not be able to judge the earth? God forbid! Do you remember what the most blessed Apostle Paul says: "Know ye not that we shall judge angels? How much more things that pertain to this life?"

So Pope Gregory declared that kings who dared to disobey the orders of the Apostolic See should forfeit their office. He wrote to a certain senator and abbot in these words:

If any king, priest, judge or secular person shall disregard this decree of ours and act contrary to it, he shall be deprived of his power and his office and shall learn that he stands condemned at the bar of God for the wrong that he has done. And unless he shall restore what he has wrongfully taken and shall have done fitting penance for his unlawful acts he shall be excluded from the sacred body and blood of our Lord and Savior Jesus Christ and at the last judgment shall receive condign punishment.

Now then, if the blessed Gregory, most gentle of doctors, decreed that kings who should disobey his

RUNESTONE AT ASPA, SWEDEN (SIDE B)

This stone bears inscriptions in two different runic alphabets. Side B (pictured here) records that the stone was erected at the place where an annual assembly (in Norse, the Thing) was traditionally held, and that its sponsor was a woman called þóra (Thora), who was commemorating her husband, Œpir, "who armed his men in the west." It also indicates that their son witnessed the placing of the stone. Side A says simply, "þóra raised this stone in memory of Œpir, her husband."

Stones such as these can be found throughout Scandinavia. They commemorate the extraordinary adventures and travels of Norsemen who went on "viking" (raiding) expeditions as far west as North America and as far to the east as the lands of the Muslim caliphate. Most date from the most intense period of Viking activity, the late ninth to eleventh centuries, and all carry inscriptions in a variety of ancient alphabets whose letters are known as runes. Some of the stones were originally painted in bright colors, and many of the inscriptions are in verse.

RUNESTONE AT KJULA, SWEDEN

The inscription on this stone records that it was raised by Alríkr (Alaric), son of Sigriðr (Sigrid), in memory of his father, a man known as Spjót ("Spear"), famous for attacking and raiding towns in the west—probably England.

Think about the many ways that these runestones function as historical sources. How would you use such information—the practice of erecting these stones, their placement in the landscape, their inscriptions—to reconstruct Norse culture? For example, what do they tell us about the role of women in these societies? What do they indicate about the interactions among far-flung peoples? What do they suggest about the men they commemorate and the families these men left behind?

orders about a hospital for strangers should be not only deposed but excommunicated and condemned in the last judgment, how can anyone blame us for deposing and excommunicating Henry, who not only disregards apostolic judgments, but so far as in him lies tramples upon his mother the Church, basely plunders the whole kingdom and destroys its churches—unless indeed it were one who is a man of his own kind?

As we know also through the teaching of St. Peter in his letter touching the ordination of Clement, where he says: "If any one were friend to those with whom he is not on speaking terms, that man is among those who would like to destroy the Church of God and, while he seems to be with us in the body, he is against us in mind and heart, and he is a far worse enemy than those who are without and are openly hostile. For he, under the forms of friendship, acts as an enemy and scatters and lays waste the Church." Consider then, my best beloved, if he passes so severe a judgment upon him who associates himself with those whom the pope opposes on account of their actions, with what severity he condemns the man himself to whom the pope is thus opposed.

But now, to return to our point: Is not a sovereignty invented by men of this world who were ignorant of God subject to that which the providence of Almighty God established for his own glory and graciously bestowed upon the world? The Son of God we believe to be God and man, sitting at the right hand of the Father as High Priest, head of all priests and ever making intercession for us. He despised the kingdom of this world wherein the sons of this world puff themselves up and offered himself as a sacrifice upon the cross.

Who does not know that kings and princes derive their origin from men ignorant of God who raised themselves above their fellows by pride, plunder, treachery, murder—in short, by every kind of crime—at the instigation of the Devil, the prince of this world, men blind with greed and intolerable in their audacity? If, then, they strive to bend the priests of God to their will, to whom may they more properly be compared than to him who is chief over all the sons of pride? For he, tempting

our High Priest, head of all priests, son of the Most High, offering him all the kingdoms of this world, said: "All these will I give thee if thou wilt fall down and worship me."

Does anyone doubt that the priests of Christ are to be considered as fathers and masters of kings and princes and of all believers? Would it not be regarded as pitiable madness if a son should try to rule his father or a pupil his master and to bind with unjust obligations the one through whom he expects to be bound or loosed, not only on earth but also in heaven? Evidently recognizing this the emperor Constantine the Great, lord over all kings and princes throughout almost the entire earth, as St. Gregory relates in his letter to the emperor Mauritius, at the holy synod of Nicaea took his place below all the bishops and did not venture to pass any judgment upon them but, even addressing them as gods, felt that they ought not to be subject to his judgment but that he ought to be bound by their decisions.

Pope Gelasius, urging upon the emperor Anastasius not to feel himself wronged by the truth that was called to his attention said: "There are two powers, O august Emperor, by which the world is governed, the sacred authority of the priesthood and the power of kings. Of these the priestly is by so much the greater as they will have to answer for kings themselves in the day of divine judgment;" and a little further: "Know that you are subject to their judgment, not that they are to be subjected to your will."

In reliance upon such declarations and such authorities, many prelates have excommunicated kings or emperors. If you ask for illustrations: Pope Innocent excommunicated the emperor Arcadius because he consented to the expulsion of St. John Chrysostom from his office. Another Roman pontiff deposed a king of the Franks, not so much on account of his evil deeds as because he was not equal to so great an office, and set in his place Pippin, father of the emperor Charles the Great, releasing all the Franks from the oath of fealty which they had sworn to him. And this is often done by Holy Church when it absolves fighting men from their oaths to bishops who have been deposed by apostolic authority. So St. Ambrose, a holy man but not bishop of the whole Church, excommunicated the emperor Theodosius the Great for a fault which did not seem to other prelates so very grave and excluded him from the Church. He also shows in his writings that the priestly office is as much superior to royal power as gold is more precious than lead. He says: "The honor and dignity of bishops admit of no comparison. If you liken them to the splendor of kings and the diadem of princes, these are as lead compared to the glitter of gold. You see the necks of kings and princes bowed to the knees of priests, and by the kissing of hands they believe that they share the benefit of their prayers." And again: "Know that we have said all this in order to show that there is nothing in this world more excellent than a priest or more lofty than a bishop."

Your Fraternity should remember also that greater power is granted to an exorcist when he is made a spiritual emperor for the casting out of devils, than can be conferred upon any layman for the purpose of earthly dominion. All kings and princes of this earth who live not piously and in their deeds show not a becoming fear of God are ruled by demons and are sunk in miserable slavery. Such men desire to rule, not guided by the love of God, as priests are, for the glory of God and the profit of human souls, but to display their intolerable pride and to satisfy the lusts of their mind. Of these St. Augustine says in the first book of his Christian doctrine: "He who tries to rule over men—who are by nature equal to him—acts with intolerable pride." Now if exorcists have power over demons, as we have said, how much more over those who are subject to demons and are limbs of demons! And if exorcists are superior to these, how much more are priests superior to them!

Furthermore, every Christian king when he approaches his end asks the aid of a priest as a miserable suppliant that he may escape the prison of hell, may pass from darkness into light and may appear at the judgment seat of God freed from the bonds of sin. But who, layman or priest, in his last moments has ever asked the help of any earthly king for the safety of his soul? And what king or emperor has power through his office to snatch any Christian from the might of the Devil by the sacred rite of baptism, to confirm him among the sons of God and to fortify him by the holy chrism? Or—and this is the greatest thing in the Christian religion—who among them is able by his own word to create the body and blood of the Lord? or to whom among them is given the power to bind and loose in Heaven and upon earth? From this it is apparent how greatly superior in power is the priestly dignity.

Or who of them is able to ordain any clergyman in the Holy Church—much less to depose him for any fault? For bishops, while they may ordain other bishops, may in no wise depose them except by authority of the Apostolic See. How, then, can even the most slightly informed person doubt that priests are higher than kings? But if kings are to be judged by priests for their sins, by whom can they more properly be judged than by the Roman pontiff?

In short, all good Christians, whosoever they may be, are more properly to be called kings than are evil princes; for the former, seeking the glory of God, rule themselves rigorously; but the latter, seeking their own rather than the things that are of God, being enemies to themselves, oppress others tyrannically. The former are the body of the true Christ; the latter, the body of the Devil. The former rule themselves that they may reign forever with the supreme ruler. The power of the latter brings it to pass that they perish in eternal damnation with the prince of darkness who is king over all the sons of pride.

It is no great wonder that evil priests take the part of a king whom they love and fear on account of honors received from him. By ordaining any person whomsoever, they are selling their God at a bargain price. For as the elect are inseparably united to their Head, so the wicked are firmly bound to him who is head of all evil—especially against the good. But against these it is of no use to argue, but rather to pray God with tears and groans that he may deliver them from the snares of Satan, in which they are caught, and after trial may lead them at last into knowledge of the truth.

So much for kings and emperors who, swollen with the pride of this world, rule not for God but for themselves. But since it is our duty to exhort everyone according to his station, it is our care with God's help to furnish emperors, kings and other princes with the weapons of humility that thus they may be strong to keep down the floods and waves of pride. We know that earthly glory and the cares of this world are wont especially to cause rulers to be exalted, to forget humility and, seeking their own glory, strive to excel their fellows. It seems therefore especially useful for emperors and kings, while their hearts are lifted up in the strife for glory, to learn how to humble themselves and to know fear rather than joy. Let them therefore consider carefully how dangerous, even awesome is the office of emperor or king, how very few find salvation therein, and how those who are saved through God's mercy have become far less famous in the Church by divine judgment than many humble persons. From the beginning of the world to the present day we do not find in all authentic records emperors or kings whose lives were as distinguished for virtue and piety as were those of a countless multitude of men who despised the world—although we believe that many of them were saved by the mercy of God. Not to speak of Apostles and Martyrs, who among emperors and kings was famed for his miracles as were St. Martin, St. Antony and St. Benedict? What emperor or king ever raised the dead, cleansed lepers or opened the eyes of the blind? True, Holy Church praises and honors the emperor Constantine, of pious memory, Theodosius and Honorius, Charles and Louis, as lovers of justice, champions of the Christian faith and protectors of churches, but she does not claim that they were illustrious for the splendor of their wonderful works. Or to how many names of kings or emperors has Holy Church ordered churches or altars to be dedicated or masses to be celebrated?

Let kings and princes fear lest the higher they are raised above their fellows in this life, the deeper they may be plunged in everlasting fire. Wherefore it is written: "The mighty shall suffer mighty torments." They shall render unto God an account for all men subject to their rule. But if it is no small labor for the pious individual to guard his own soul, what a task is laid upon princes in the care of so many thousands of souls! And if Holy Church imposes a heavy penalty upon him who takes a single human life, what shall be done to those who send many thousands to death for the glory of this world? These, although they say with their lips, *mea culpa,* for the slaughter of many, yet in their hearts they rejoice at the in-crease of their glory and neither repent of what they have done nor regret that they have sent their brothers into the world below. So that, since they do not repent with all their hearts and will not restore what they have gained by human bloodshed, their penitence before God remains without the fruits of a true repentance.

Wherefore they ought greatly to fear, and they should frequently be reminded that, as we have said, since the beginning of the world and throughout the kingdoms of the earth very few kings of saintly life can be found out of an innumerable multitude, whereas in one single chair of successive bishops—the Roman—from the time of the blessed Apostle Peter nearly a hundred are counted among the holiest of men. How can this be, except because the kings and princes of the earth, seduced by empty glory, prefer their own interests to the things of the Spirit, whereas pious pontiffs, despising vainglory, set the things of God above the things of the flesh. The former readily punish offenses against themselves but are not troubled by offenses against God; the latter quickly forgive those who sin against them but do not easily pardon offenders against God. The former, far too much given to worldly affairs, think little of spiritual things; the latter, dwelling eagerly upon heavenly subjects, despise the things of this world.

All Christians, therefore, who desire to reign with Christ are to be warned not to reign through ambition for wordly power. They are to keep in mind the admonition of that most holy pope Gregory in his book on the pastoral office: "Of all these things what is to be followed, what held fast, except that the man strong in virtue shall come to his office under compulsion? Let him who is without virtue not come to it even though he be urged thereto." If, then, men who fear God come under compulsion with fear and trembling to the Apostolic See where those who are properly ordained become stronger through the merits of the blessed Apostle Peter, with what awe and hesitation should men ascend the throne of a king where even good and humble men like Saul and David become worse! What we have said above is thus stated in the decrees of the blessed pope Symmachus— though we have learned it by experience: "He, that is St. Peter, transmitted to his successors an unfailing endowment of merit together with an inheritance of innocence;" and again: "For who can doubt that he is holy who is raised to the height of such an office, in which if he is lacking in virtue acquired by his own merits, that which is handed down from his predecessor is sufficient. For either he raises men of distinction to bear this burden or he glorifies them after they are raised up."

Wherefore let those whom Holy Church, of its own will and with deliberate judgment, not for fleeting glory but for the welfare of multitudes, has called to royal or imperial rule—let them be obedient and ever mindful of the blessed Gregory's declaration in that same pastoral treatise: "When a man disdains to be the equal of his fellow men, he becomes like an apostate angel. Thus Saul, after his period of humility, swollen with pride, ran into excess of power. He was raised in humility, but rejected in his pride, as God bore witness, saying: 'Though thou wast little in thine own sight, wast thou not made the head of the tribes of Israel?'" and again: "I marvel how, when he was little to himself he was great before God, but when he seemed great to himself he was little before God." Let them watch and remember what God says in the Gospel: "I seek not my own glory," and, "He who would be first among you, let him be the servant of all." Let them ever place the honor of God above their own; let them embrace justice and maintain it by preserving to everyone his right; let them not enter into the counsels of the ungodly, but cling to those of religion with all their hearts.

Let them not seek to make Holy Church their maid-servant or their subject, but recognizing priests, the eyes of God, as their masters and fathers, strive to do them becoming honor.

If we are commanded to honor our fathers and mothers in the flesh, how much more our spiritual parents! If he that curseth his father or his mother shall be put to death, what does he deserve who curses his spiritual father or mother? Let not princes, led astray by carnal affection, set their own sons over that flock for whom Christ shed his blood if a better and more suitable man can be found. By thus loving their own son more than God they bring the greatest evils upon the Church. For it is evident that he who fails to provide to the best of his ability so great and necessary an advantage for our holy mother, the Church, does not love God and his neighbor as befits a Christian man. If this one virtue of charity be wanting, then whatever of good the man may do will lack all saving grace.

But if they do these things in humility, keeping their love for God and their neighbor as they ought, they may count upon the mercy of him who said: "Learn of me, for I am meek and lowly of heart." If they humbly imitate him, they shall pass from their servile and transient reign into the kingdom of eternal liberty.

*   *   *

REVIEW QUESTIONS

1. What does Pope Gregory VII think is the right relationship between the Church and secular authority?
2. How effectively does he use evidence to support his case?
3. How might a supporter of Henry IV answer the pope's arguments?

ANNA COMNENA

FROM *The Alexiad*

Anna Comnena (1083–after 1148), an imperial princess, wrote The Alexiad, *an admiring biography of her father. In this selection, she is describing how Emperor Alexius engaged his mother, Anna Dalassena, in the governance of the Byzantine Empire, with a digression on Anna Dalassena's own qualities. Byzantine royal families allowed women a wide scope for participating in government. Alexius spent much of his reign defending the empire from Turkish advances in Asia Minor, and his request for help from the West was one of the motivations for the First Crusade, the centerpiece of Anna's history.*

From *The Alexiad of Anna Comnena*, edited by E. R. A. Sewter (New York: Penguin, 1969), pp. 116–23.

*   *   *

Gradually and surreptitiously he involved her more and more in state affairs; on occasions he even declared openly that without her brains and good judgement the Empire would not survive. By these means he bound her more closely to himself, but prevented her from attaining her own goal and frustrated it. She had in mind the last stage of life and dreamed of monasteries in which she would drag out her remaining years in the contemplation of wisdom. Such was her intention, the constant aim of her prayers. Despite this longing in her heart, despite the total preoccupation with a higher life, she also loved her son to a quite exceptional degree and wished somehow to bear with him the storms that buffeted the Empire (if I may apply seafaring metaphor to the manifold troubles and tumults to which it was exposed). She desired to guide the ship of state on the best possible course, in fair weather or in tempest (when waves crashed on to it from all sides), especially since the young man had only just taken his seat in the stern and put his hand to the tiller, with no previous experience of storms, winds and waves of such violence. She was constrained, therefore, by a

mother's affection for her son, and governed with him, sometimes even grasping the reins (to change the metaphor) and alone driving the chariot of power—and without accident or error. The truth is that Anna Dalassena was in any case endowed with a fine intellect and possessed besides a really first-class aptitude for governing. On the other hand, she was distracted from it by her love for God. When in the month of August (in the same indiction) Robert's crossing to Epirus compelled Alexius to leave the capital, he brought to light and put into operation his cherished plan: the whole executive power was entrusted to his mother alone and the decision was confirmed publicly in a chrysobull.[1] As it is the historian's duty not merely to summarize the deeds and decrees of good men, but as far as he can to give some details of the former and transmit the latter in full, I myself will set out the terms of this document, omitting only the subtle refinements of the scribe. It ran thus: "When danger is foreseen or some other dreadful occurrence is expected, there is no safeguard stronger than a mother who is understanding and loves her son, for if she gives

---

[1] An imperial decree sealed with gold.

counsel, her advice will be reliable; if she offers prayers, they will confer strength and certain protection. Such at any rate has been the experience of myself, your emperor, in the case of my own revered mother, who has taught and guided and sustained me throughout, from my earliest years. She had a place in aristocratic society, but her first concern was for her son and his faith in her was preserved intact. It was well known that one soul animated us, physically separated though we were, and by the grace of Christ that happy state has persisted to this day. Never were those cold words, 'mine' and 'yours,' uttered between us, and what was even more important, the prayers she poured out during all that time reached the ears of the Lord and have raised me now to the imperial throne. After I took in my hand the imperial sceptre, she found it intolerable that she was not bearing an equal share in my labours, to the interests both of your emperor and of the whole people. But now I am preparing with God's help to do battle with Rome's enemies; with much forethought an army is being recruited and thoroughly equipped; not the least of my cares, however, has been the provision of an efficient organization in financial and civil affairs. Fortunately, an impregnable bulwark for good government has been found—in the appointment of my revered mother, of all women most honoured, as controller of the entire administration. I, your emperor, therefore decree explicitly in this present chrysobull the following: because of her vast experience of secular affairs (despite the very low value she sets upon such matters), whatever she decrees in writing (whether the case be referred to her by the logothete, or by his subordinate officers, or by any other person who prepares memoranda or requests or judgements concerning remissions of public debts) shall have permanent validity as if I myself, your Serene Emperor, had issued them or after dictating them had had them committed to writing. Whatever decisions or orders are made by her, written or unwritten, reasonable or unreasonable, provided that they bear her seal (the Transfiguration and the Assumption), shall be regarded as coming from myself, by the fact that they carry the 'In the

month . . .' of the current logothete.[2] Moreover, with regard to promotions and successions to the tribunals and fiscs, and in the matter of honours, offices and donations of immovable property, my saintly mother shall have full power to take whatever action shall seem good to her. Further, if any persons are promoted to the tribunals or succeed to the fiscs and are honoured with the highest or medium or lowest dignities, they shall thereafter retain these positions on a permanent basis. Again, increases of salary, additional gifts, reductions of tax, economies and diminution of payments shall be settled by her without question. In brief, nothing shall be reckoned invalid which she commands either in writing or by word of mouth, for her words and her decisions shall be reckoned as my own and none of them shall be annulled. In years to come they shall have the force of law permanently. Neither now nor in the future shall my mother be subjected to inquiry or undergo any examination whatsoever at the hands of anybody, whoever he may be. The same provision shall also hold good for her ministers and the chancellor of the time, whether their actions seem to be reasonable or ridiculous. It shall be absolutely impossible in the future to demand account of any action taken by them under the terms of this present chrysobull."

The reader may be surprised by the honour conferred on his mother by the emperor in this matter, since he yielded her precedence in everything, relinquishing the reins of government, as it were, and running alongside as he drove the imperial chariot; only in the title of emperor did he share with her the privileges of his rank. And this despite the fact that he had already passed his boyhood years and was of an age which in the case of men like him is particularly susceptible to the lust for power. Wars against the barbarians, with all their attendant trials and tribulations he was prepared to face himself, but the entire administration of affairs, the choice of civil magistrates, the accounts of the imperial revenues and expenditure he left to his mother. At this point the reader may well censure him for transferring the government

---

[2] Auditor of accounts.

of the Empire to the gynaeconitis,[3] but had he known this woman's spirit, her surpassing virtue, intelligence and energy, his reproaches would soon have turned to admiration. For my grandmother had an exceptional grasp of public affairs, with a genius for organization and government; she was capable, in fact, of managing not only the Roman Empire, but every other empire under the sun as well. She had vast experience and a wide understanding of the motives, ultimate consequences, interrelations good and bad of various courses of action, penetrating quickly to the right solution, adroitly and safely carrying it out. Her intellectual powers, moreover, were paralleled by her command of language. She was indeed a most persuasive orator, without being verbose or long-winded. Nor did the inspiration of the argument readily desert her, for if she began on a felicitous note, she was also most successful in ending her speeches with just the right words. She was already a woman of mature years when she was called upon to exercise imperial authority, at a time of life when one's mental powers are at their best, when one's judgement is fully developed and knowledge of affairs is widest—all qualities that lend force to good administration and government. It is natural that persons of this age should not merely speak with greater wisdom than the young (as the tragic playwright says), but also act in a more expedient way. In the past, when Anna Dalassena was still looked upon as a younger woman, she had impressed everyone as "having an old head on young shoulders"; to the observant her face alone revealed Anna's inherent virtue and gravity. But, as I was saying, once he had seized power my father reserved for himself the struggles and hard labour of war, while she became so to speak an onlooker, but he made her sovereign and like a slave said and did whatever she commanded. He loved her exceedingly and depended on her for advice (such was his affection for her). His right hand he devoted to her service; his ears listened for her bidding. In all things he was entirely subservient, in fact, to her wishes. I can sum up the whole situation thus: he was in theory the emperor,

but she had real power. She was the legislator, the complete organizer and governor, while he confirmed her arrangements, written and unwritten, the former by his signature, the latter by his spoken approval. One might say that he was indeed the instrument of her power—he was not emperor, for all the decisions and ordinances of his mother satisfied him, not merely as an obedient son, but as an attentive listener to her instruction in the art of ruling. He was convinced that she had attained perfection in everything and easily excelled all men of that generation in prudence and understanding of affairs.

Such were the events that marked the beginning of the reign. One could hardly at that stage call Alexius emperor once he had entrusted to her the supreme authority. Another person might yield here to the claims of panegyric and extol the native land of this remarkable woman; he might trace her descent from the Adriani Dalasseni and Charon, while he embarked on the ocean of their achievements. But I am writing history and my fitting task is not to describe her through the family and kinsmen, but by reference to her character, her virtue, and the events which form the proper subject of history. To return once more to my grandmother, I must add this: not only was she a very great credit to her own sex, but to men as well; indeed, she contributed to the glory of the whole human race. The women's quarters in the palace had been the scene of utter depravity ever since the infamous Constantine Monomachos had ascended the throne and right up to the time when my father became emperor had been noted for foolish love intrigues, but Anna effected a reformation; a commendable decorum was restored and the palace now enjoyed a discipline that merited praise. She instituted set times for the singing of sacred hymns, stated hours for breakfast; there was now a special period in which magistrates were chosen. She herself set a firm example to everybody else, with the result that the palace assumed the appearance rather of a monastery under the influence of this really extraordinary woman and her truly saintly character; for in self-control she surpassed the famous women of old, heroines of many a legend, as the

---

[3] I.e., the women's quarters within the palace.

sun outshines all stars. As for her compassion for the poor and her generosity to the needy, no words could do justice to them. Her house was a refuge for penniless relatives, but no less for strangers. Priests and monks she honoured in particular: they shared her meals and no one ever saw her at table without some of them as guests. Her outward serenity, true reflection of character, was respected by angels but terrorized even the demons, and pleasure-loving fools, victims of their own passions, found a single glance from her more than they could bear; yet to the chaste she seemed gentle and gay. She knew exactly how to temper reserve and dignity; her own reserve never gave the impression of harshness or cruelty, nor did her tenderness seem too soft or unrestrained—and this, I fancy, is the true definition of propriety: the due proportion of warm humanity and strict moral principle. She was by nature thoughtful and was always evolving new ideas, not, as some folk whispered, to the detriment of the state; on the contrary, they were wholesome schemes which restored to full vigour the already corrupted empire and revived, as far as one could, the ruined fortunes of the people. In spite of her preoccupation with matters of government, she by no means neglected the duties incumbent on a religious woman, for the greater part of the night was spent by her in the chanting of sacred hymns and she wore herself out with continual prayers and vigils. Nevertheless, at dawn or even at second cockcrow, she was applying herself anew to state business, attending to the choice of magistrates and answering the petitions of suppliants with the help of her secretary Gregory Genesius. Now if some orator had decided to make this the subject of a panegyric, he would no doubt have exalted her and praised her to the skies (as is the way of encomiasts) for her deeds and thoughts and superiority to all others; the famous ones of old, both men and women, who were renowned for their virtue would certainly have been thrown into the shade. But such licence is not for the writer of history. Those who know her virtue, therefore, her dignified character, her never-failing sagacity and the loftiness and sublimity of her spirit, must not blame my history, if I have done less than justice to her great qualities.

*   *   *

Review Questions

1. What does Anna's account reveal about the role of women within the Byzantine court? What does it reveal about the values and culture of the Eastern Roman Empire?
2. How does this picture of women's activities compare with that in Einhard's *Life of Charlemagne* (pp. 248–252)? How does it compare with Procopius's portrait of an earlier Byzantine empress, Theodora (pp. 226–228). How might you explain these differences?
3. What does Anna have to say about the proper way to write history, and about herself as an historian?

FROM *The Song of Roland*

This chanson de geste ("song about great deeds") tells the story of Charlemagne's heroic vassal Roland; his betrayal by his stepfather, Ganelon; and the avenging of his ignominious death at the hands of a Muslim army. Some of the elements that make up this epic may have begun to circulate in Charlemagne's own time, around the year 800, but when the poem was eventually committed to writing, around 1100, it more closely reflected the very recent events of the First Crusade, as well as the culture and values of the warriors from many parts of Europe who spoke the language we call French. (Indeed, the oldest surviving manuscript of the poem was produced in England.) In the following excerpt, news of Roland's death has reached Charlemagne, and now the Frankish and Muslim armies prepare for battle. The Muslim emir (commander) is Baligant.

From *The Song of Roland*, translated by Robert Harrison (New York: Mentor, 1970), pp. 146–56.

226

Dismounting from his horse, the emperor
   [Charlemagne]
has stretched out prone upon the lush green
   grass
and turned his face to meet the rising sun.
With all his heart he prays aloud to God:
3100 "True Father, keep me safe from harm today,
as Thou most certainly protected Jonah
when he was in the body of the whale,
as Thou hath saved the king of Nineveh,
and Daniel from excruciating pain
when he was down within the lions' den,
and all three children in a burning fire!
Allow Thy love to be with me today!
And grant me, in Thy mercy, if it please
   Thee,
the power to avenge my nephew Roland!"
3110 Now having prayed, he rises to his feet
and on his forehead makes the mighty sign.°
The king climbs on his prancing destrier,
his stirrup held by Naimes and Jozeran,

and takes in hand his shield and sharpened
   lance.
His build is rugged, trim, and
   well-proportioned,
his features clean, his bearing confident.
He rides out, seated firmly in the saddle;
from front and rear alike the trumpets sound;
the oliphant booms out above the rest.
3120 The Frenchmen weep with tenderness for
   Roland.

227

With easy grace the emperor rides on,
his flowing beard fanned out upon his
   byrnie.
For love of him, the others do the same:
a hundred thousand Franks are known by
   this.
They pass those hills and soaring rocky
   bluffs,
those sunken glades, those harrowing
   ravines,
then leave behind the passes and the
   wastelands:

3111. *mighty sign:* the sign of the Cross.

they've made their way into the Spanish
    march
and set up camp upon a broad plateau.
3130 The envoys hurry back to Baligant.
A Syrian delivers his report:
"We've had a look at arrogant King Charles.
His men are bold, they have no heart to fail
    him,
so arm yourself—you'll have a battle soon!"
"That's gallantry I hear!" says Baligant.
"To let my pagans know this, sound your
    trumpets."

228

Throughout the host they beat upon the
    drums
and sound those horns and brilliant
    clarions:
the pagans all dismount to arm themselves.
3140 The emir does not intend to lag behind:
he dons a saffron-yellow skirted byrnie
and laces up his jeweled golden casque
and then upon his left side straps his sword.
Through vanity he's given it a name;
because he's heard them speak of Charles's
    sword,
⌊he lets his own be known as "Précieuse."⌋°
This then will be his war cry in the field;
he orders all his knights to sing it out.
He hangs about his neck a great, broad
    shield:
3150 its boss is made of gold with crystal border,
its shoulder strap of roundel-patterned silk.
He grasps his spear, the one he calls Maltet:
its handle was as heavy as a beam,
and its tip alone would overload a mule.
Now Baligant gets on his destrier;
at his stirrup is Marcule of Outremer.
This noble lord° is lengthy in the stride
and narrow-hipped and broad across the
    back;

his chest is deep and beautifully molded,
3160 his shoulders wide, his features very clean,
his look ferocious, and his curly head
as white as flowers in the summertime.
His valor has been proven many times.
God, what a lord, if he were but a
    Christian!
He spurs his horse until the bright blood
    flows
and brings him to a gallop, leaps a ditch
some fifty feet in width, could it be
    measured.
The pagans shout: "This man should hold the
    marches!
No Frenchman who may come to fight with
    him
3170 will fail, to die, whatever he may wish.
King Charles is crazy not to have with-
    drawn." AOI

229

The picture of a baron, the emir
displays a beard as white as any flower;
a man supremely learned in his law,
as well as bold and arrogant in battle.
His son Malprimes is very chivalrous,
robust and tall, the image of his forebears.
He tells his father: "Let us ride, my lord;
if we see Charles at all, I'll be surprised."
3180 Says Baligant: "Oh yes, for he is very brave—
great praise for him is found in many *gestes*—
but since his nephew Roland is no more,
he won't possess the strength to hold us off."
    AOI

230

"Malprimes, fair son," continues Baligant,
"just yesterday brave Roland was brought
    down,
along with valiant, bold Olivier,
the dozen peers, whom Charles once held so
    dear,
and twenty thousand fighting men from
    France.

3146. A line missing from the Oxford ms. and supplied
from V⁴.
3157. *This noble lord*: Baligant.

I wouldn't give a glove for all the rest.
3190 Undoubtedly the emperor's returning:
the Syrian, my messenger, reported
that he has made up ten immense battalions.
The man who sounds the oliphant is brave—
his comrade's clear-voiced trumpet rackets back—
and thus they ride as leaders, up ahead,
in company with fifteen thousand Franks,
the bachelors, whom Charles has called his
    children.
Behind them are at least that many more.
These men will fight with lordly arrogance."
3200 Malprimes says: "I request of you the
stroke."° AOI

231

"Malprimes," says Baligant to him, "my son,
I grant you what you've asked of me just now.
Go out at once and strike against the French.
I'll send along the Persian king Torleu
and Dapamort, another Lycian° king.
If you can blunt that overbearing pride
I'll let you have that section of my country
that lies between Cheirant° and Val
    Marchis."°
The other answers him: "I thank you, sire!"
3210 and stepping forward, he accepts the gift
(a land which once belonged to King Flurit)
at such a time that he will never see it;
nor was he ever seised° of it, nor vested.

232

The emir goes riding through that mighty
    host,
the massive figure of his son behind him.
King Dapamort and King Torleu together
establish quickly thirty battle corps

of chevaliers in numbers past belief;
the smallest one contains some fifty
    thousand.
3220 The first is formed of men from Butentrot,°
the second of big-headed men from
    Misnes—°
along the vertebrae all down their backs
these men have tufted bristles, just like hogs.
    AOI
The third is formed of Nubles and of Blos;
the fourth contains Slavonians and Bruns;°
the fifth is formed of Sorz and of Sorabi;°
the sixth contains Armenians and Moors;
in the seventh are the men from Jericho;
the eighth is formed of blacks; the ninth of
    Gros;
3230 and the tenth is formed of troops from strong
    Balide,
a race of men who never seek the Good. AOI
With all his heart, the emir now swears an
    oath
upon the flesh and wonders of Mohammed:
"Like a madman, Charles of France keeps
    riding on;
unless he turns aside, there'll be a battle,
and he shall have his golden crown no
    more."

233

They make up ten battalions after that.
The first is formed of ugly Canaanites
who made their way cross-country from Val
    Fuit;
3240 the next is formed of Turks; the third of
    Persians;

3200. *the stroke*: the first blow of the battle.
3205. *Lycian*: pertaining to Lycia, a province in south-western Asia Minor.
3208. *Cheirant* is probably Kairouan in Tunisia, a city sacred to the Moslem world. *Val Marchis* may be the city of Marrakech in Morocco.
3213. *seised*: a legal term meaning possessed.

3220. *Butentrot*: a valley in the Taurus Mountains, of southern Asia Minor; its inhabitants at the time of the First Crusade were a tribe of recreant Slavs who had renounced Christianity and had become Moslems.
3221. *Misnes*: the Milceni from Lusatia, a realm lying in the area of eastern Germany and Poland.
3225: *Bruns*: probably the inhabitants of Braunschweig, a province of central Germany.
3226. *Sorabi*: a Slavonic tribe dwelling along the Elbe River in northern Germany.

and the fourth is formed of Petchenegs . . .°
and the fifth is formed of Solteras and Avars°;
and the sixth of Ormaleus and of Eugiez;
and the seventh of the race of Samuel°;
the eighth of men from Bruise°; the ninth,
  Clavers°;
and the tenth of those from Occian Deserta°:
a race that does not serve Almighty God,
you'll never hear of men more infamous;
their skins are every bit as hard as iron,
3250 and thus they have no need for casques or
  hauberks.
In combat they are treacherous and brutal. AOI

234

The emir has drawn up ten battalions more.
The first one is of giants from Malprose;
the next of Huns; the third Hungarians;
and the fourth is formed of men from long
  Baldise;
and the fifth is formed of those from Val
  Peneuse;
and the sixth is formed of . . . Marose°;
and the seventh of the Leus and Astrimoines;
the eighth, Argoilles men; and the ninth,
  Clarbone;
3260 and the tenth is formed of bearded troops
  from Fronde:
a race that has no love for God at all.

The Frankish *geste* counts thirty battle corps,
a mighty force amassed where trumpets
  sound.
The pagans make a brave show as they ride. AOI

235

The emir, a man of vast authority,
commands that they precede him with his
  dragon,
the flags of Termagant and of Mohammed,
and an effigy of villainous Apollo.
Ten Canaanites go riding all around,
3270 in high-pitched voices screaming
  exhortation:
"Whoever wants to have our gods' protection
should pray and offer penitential psalms!"
The pagans let their heads and chins sink
  down
and tilt their shining helmets toward the
  earth.
The French say: "Gluttons, you are soon to
  die!
May utter wrack and ruin be yours today!
Oh Lord of all of us, look after Charles,
and [let us fight]° this battle in his name!" AOI

236

The emir, a man of great sagacity,
3280 now calls upon his son and both the kings:
"My lords and barons, you shall ride ahead
of my battalions; you shall lead them all,
except the finest three. These I'll hold back:
the first, the Turks; the second, Ormaleus;
and the third, the one of giants from
  Malprose.
The men from Occian will stay with me,
so they may go against the French and
  Charles.
If he will fight with me, the emperor
is sure to lose the head from off his torso,
3290 and that's the only 'justice' he shall have."

3241. *Petchenegs:* a barbarian tribe from central Asia that terrorized the civilized world in the eleventh century. The remainder of this line is unknown; the scribe made a blunder and recopied here the end of the preceding line.
3242. *Avars:* a Caucasian tribe that ranged from the Black Sea to the Adriatic and raided northern Italy and southern Germany.
3244. *the race of Samuel:* the Bulgarians who, led by their czar Samuel, invaded the Roman Empire repeatedly in the tenth and eleventh centuries.
3245. *Bruise:* probably the city of Broussa in Asia Minor, a pilgrimage site. *Clavers:* Slavs.
3246. *Occian Deserta:* probably the Theme of Opsicianum, a political and military subdivision of the Byzantine Empire located in northwestern Asia Minor.
3257. Here there is a blank space in the Oxford text, and the other mss. have variant readings.

3278. *let us fight:* a reconstruction of an unintelligible place in the Oxford ms.

237

The hosts are large, the battle corps are
    handsome.
Between them there's no hill nor rise nor
    valley
nor woods nor brake—no place where one
    could hide.
They see each other clearly on the plain.
Says Baligant: "My pagan fighting men,
ride forward, seek them out, and give them
    battle!"
Amborre of Oluferne holds up the ensign.
The pagans bellow out its
    name—"Précieuse!"
"Today will be your downfall," say the
    French,
3300 then loudly they renew the cry "Monjoy!"
The emperor gives word to sound his
    trumpets
and the oliphant, which heartens all the rest.
The pagans say: "This host of Charles looks
    good;
we'll have a brutal, unrelenting fight." AOI

238

The plain is broad, the country flat and open.
Light flashes off those jeweled golden casques
and off those shields and saffron-yellow
    byrnies
and lances with their rolled-up battle flags.
The trumpets sound, their tones are very
    clear;
3310 the oliphant's high note sings out the charge.
The emir just now has called upon his
    brother,
Canabeus, the king of Floredée,
who rules that country clear to Val Sevrée,
and shown him the battalions of King
    Charles:
"Look: there's the pride of celebrated France!
The emperor is riding very fiercely;
he's with those bearded soldiers in the rear.
Across their byrnies they've thrown out their
    beards,

which are as white as snow on top of frost.
3320 These men will fight with lances and with
    swords;
our battle will be vicious and unyielding,
a trial of arms like no one's ever seen."
Then, farther than a peeled switch can be
    thrown,
the emir rides out ahead of his companions
and setting an example tells them this:
"Come, pagans; I'm already on my way!"
He menacingly shook his lance's shaft
and swung its head around to point toward
    Charles. AOI

239

Now Charlemagne, on seeing the emir
3330 and the dragon and the ensign and the flag—
the Arab forces there are so immense,
they've spread out over every bit of land
except for that the emperor is holding—
in ringing tones the king of France calls out:
"French barons, you are splendid fighting
    men;
you've waged so many battles in the field—
you see how vile and base these pagans are,
and all their laws aren't worth a denier.
Their army's huge, my lords, but what's the
    difference?
3340 Whoever will not come with me, get out!"
At this he digs his spurs into his horse
and causes Tencendur to make four leaps.
The Frenchmen say: "This king's a fighting
    man!
Ride on, lord—not a one of us will fail
    you."

240

The day was clear, the sunlight radiant,
the hosts superb, the companies immense;
the lead battalions stand there, face to face.
Count Guinemant, along with Count
    Rabel,
both let their prancing horses' reins fall
    slack

3350 and spur them on. At this, the Frenchmen
    charge
and go to the attack with sharpened spears.
    AOI

241

The count Rabel is a rugged chevalier:
he rakes his horse with spurs of finest gold
and goes to strike Torleu, the Persian king.
No shield nor byrnie can withstand his blow;
he drives his gilded lance into the body
and throws him dead upon a little bush.
The French say: "Help us now, Almighty
    God!
King Charles is in the right—we mustn't fail
    him." AOI

242

3360 And Guinemant accosts a Lycian king.
He shatters his fleuron-emblazoned shield,
and afterward he rips apart his byrnie;
he shoves his pennant deep into the body
and, laugh or cry who will, he drops him
    dead.
And at this stroke, the men from France call
    out:
"Attack them, barons, don't let up at all!
King Charles is in the right against these
    [pagans,]°
and God has left His verdict up to us." AOI

243

Malprimes, who sits upon a pure white horse,
3370 now hurls himself into the crowd of Franks,
repeatedly goes striking mighty blows
and piling corpses one upon the other.
Before the others Baligant calls out:
"My barons, for a long time I have fed° you;
now look: my son goes seeking after Charles,
defying many knights by force of arms—

I'll never ask for any better vassal—
so take your sharpened spears and give him
    help!"
The pagans, moving forward at this word,
3380 strike brutal blows; the carnage is immense.
The fighting is incredible and heavy:
none harsher has occurred before or since.
    AOI

244

The hosts are large, the companies
    aggressive,
and all of the battalions have engaged.
The pagans fight astonishingly well.
God!—so many shafts are snapped in two
and shields destroyed and byrnies stripped of
    mail!
Just look at how the ground about is littered!
Upon the battlefield, the soft green grass
3390 [is all vermillioned by the running blood.]°
The emir encourages his retinue:
"Lay on, my lords, against this Christian
    race!"
The battle is extremely fierce and stubborn;
there's been none harder fought before or
    since.
No truce will be announced until night falls.
    AOI

245

The emir exhorts the members of his race:
"Strike, pagans—that's what you've come
    here for!
I'll make you gifts of pretty, high-born
    women,
and also give you honors, lands, and fiefs."
3400 The pagans say: "For that we'll have to fight."
Attacking with full force, they lose their
    spears;
a hundred thousand swords and more are
    drawn.

3367. *pagans:* this word is supplied from V⁴.
3374. *fed:* of *nurrit,* literally to nourish.

3390. This line, missing from the Oxford ms., is supplied
from V⁴.

Just look at all this grim, relentless slaughter:
whoever stands with them will see a battle.
    AOI

246

The emperor now calls upon his French:
"I hold you dear and trust you, lords and
    barons;
so many battles you have fought for me
and kingdoms overwhelmed and kings
    deposed!
I'm well aware I owe you recompense
3410 in personal assistance, lands, and wealth.
Avenge your sons, your brothers, and your
    heirs
who died at Roncesvals the other evening!
I know you're in the right against the
    pagans."
The Franks reply: "Sire, what you say is true."
Some twenty thousand men who stand
    nearby
swear loyalty to him in unison—
on pain of death or torture they won't fail him.

Not one of them neglects to use his lance;
before long they'll be fighting with their
    swords.
3420 The battle is astonishingly brutal. AOI

REVIEW QUESTIONS

1. Compare and contrast the poem's descriptions of the Christian Franks and the "pagan" Saracens. What do you make of the fact that they are similar in so many respects? Why does the poet admire Baligant in particular (vv. 3156–67)?

2. Scholars are still mystified by the meaning of the letters AOI, which appear after many of the stanzas in the poem's original manuscript, but they almost certainly indicate places where a performer might add a musical interlude or embellishment. What is historically significant about the fact that this poem (or portions of it) functioned as a dramatic entertainment?

3. What can you conclude about the values of this poem's intended audience? How might it have resonated with the first generation of crusaders?

FROM The Anonymous of Mainz: A Hebrew Account of the First Crusade

The summoning of the First Crusade, by Pope Urban II at Clermont in 1095, resulted in widespread enthusiasm in western Europe for an armed expedition to the Muslim east with the aim of recovering Jerusalem. But on the way, some crusaders passing through the Rhineland engaged in massacres of Jewish populations, most notably in the city of Mainz. This Jewish record of the massacre, though anonymous, is close to the original events and bears all the marks of being derived from an eyewitness account of what occurred. The author quotes and paraphrases extensively from Hebrew Scripture, and these passages remain in quotation marks.

From *European Jewry and the First Crusade*, by Robert Chazan (Berkeley: University of California Press, 1987), pp. 225–27, 232–42. Bracketed insertions are Chazan's; insertions in braces are editorial.

Spring, 1096

I shall begin the account of the former persecution. May the Lord protect us and all Israel from persecution.

It came to pass in the year one thousand twenty-eight after the destruction of the Temple that this evil befell Israel. There first arose the princes and nobles and common folk in France, who took counsel and set plans to ascend and "to rise up like eagles" and to do battle and "to clear a way" for journeying to Jerusalem, the Holy City, and for reaching the sepulcher of the Crucified, "a trampled corpse" "who cannot profit and cannot save for he is worthless." They said to one another: "Behold we travel to a distant land to do battle with the kings of that land. 'We take our souls in our hands' in order to kill and to subjugate all those kingdoms that do not believe in the Crucified. How much more so [should we kill and subjugate] the Jews, who killed and crucified him." They taunted us from every direction. They took counsel, ordering that either we turn to their abominable faith or they would destroy us "from infant to suckling." They—both princes and common folk—placed an evil sign upon their garments, a cross, and helmets upon their heads.

When the [Jewish] communities in France heard, they were seized by consternation, fear, and trembling. . . . They wrote letters and sent emissaries to all the [Jewish] communities along the Rhine River, [asking that they] fast and deprive themselves and seek mercy from [God "who] dwells on high," so that he deliver them [the Jews] from their [the crusaders'] hands. When the letters reached the saintly ones who were in that land, they—those men of God, "the pillars of the universe," who were in Mainz—wrote in reply to France. Thus was it written in them [their letters]: "All the [Jewish] communities have decreed a fast. We have done our part. May God save us and save you from 'all distress and hardship.' We are greatly fearful for you. We, however, have less reason to fear [for ourselves], for we have heard not even a rumor [of such developments]." Indeed we did not hear that a decree had been issued and that "a sword was to afflict us mortally."

When the crusaders began to reach this land, they sought funds with which to purchase bread. We gave them, considering ourselves to be fulfilling the verse: "Serve the king of Babylon, and live." All this, however, was of no avail, for our sins brought it about that the burghers in every city to which the crusaders came were hostile to us, for their [the burghers'] hands were also with them [the crusaders] to destroy vine and stock all along the way to Jerusalem.

It came to pass that, when the crusaders came, battalion after battalion, like the army of Sennacherib, some of the princes in the empire said: "Why do we sit thus? Let us also go with them. For every man who sets forth on this journey and undertakes to ascend to the impure sepulcher dedicated to the Crucified will be assured paradise." Then the crusaders along with them [the princes] gathered from all the provinces until they became as numerous "as the sands of the sea," including both princes and common folk. They circulated a report. . . . "Anyone who kills a single Jew will have all his sins absolved." Indeed there was a certain nobleman, Ditmar by name, who announced that he would not depart from this empire until he would kill one Jew—then he would depart. Now when the holy community in Mainz heard this, they decreed a fast. "They cried out mightily to the Lord" and they passed night and day in fasting. Likewise they recited dirges both morning and evening, both small and great. Nonetheless our God "did not turn away from his awesome wrath" against us. For the crusaders with their insignia came, with their standards before our houses. When they saw one of us, they ran after him and pierced him with a spear, to the point that we were afraid even to cross our thresholds.

It came to pass on the eighth of the month of Iyyar {May 3, 1096}, on the Sabbath, the measure of justice began to manifest itself against us. The crusaders and burghers arose first against the saintly ones, the pious of the Almighty in Speyer. They took counsel against them, [planning] to seize them together in the synagogue. But it was revealed to them and they arose [early] on the Sabbath morning and prayed rapidly and left the synagogue.

When they [the crusaders and burghers] saw that their plan for seizing them together was foiled, they rose against them [the Jews] and killed eleven of them. From there the decree began to fulfill that which is said: "Begin at my sanctuary." When Bishop John heard, he came with a large force and helped the [Jewish] community wholeheartedly and brought them indoors and saved them from their [the crusaders' and burghers'] hands. He seized some of the burghers and "cut off their hands." He was a pious one among the nations. Indeed God brought about well-being and salvation through him. R. Moses ben Yekutiel the *parnas*, {a leader}, "stood on the breach" and extended himself on their behalf. Through him all those forcibly converted who remained "here and there" in the empire of Henry returned [to Judaism]. Through the emperor, Bishop John removed the remnant of the community of Speyer to his fortified towns, and the Lord turned to them, for the sake of his great Name. The bishop hid them until the enemies of the Lord passed. They [the Jews] remained there, fasting and weeping and mourning. "They despaired deeply," for every day the crusaders and the gentiles and Emicho—may his bones be ground up—and the common folk gathered against them, to seize them and to destroy them. Through R. Moses the *parnas*, Bishop John saved them, for the Lord inclined his heart to save them without bribery. This was from the Lord, in order to give us there "a remnant and a residue" through him.

*   *   *

It came to pass that, when the saintly ones, the pious of the Almighty, the holy community in Mainz, heard that some of the community of Speyer had been killed and the community of Worms [had been attacked] twice, then their spirit collapsed and "their hearts melted and turned to water." They cried out to the Lord and said: "Ah Lord God of Israel! Are you wiping out the remnant of Israel? Where are all your wondrous deeds about which our ancestors told us, saying: 'Truly the Lord brought you up from Egypt.' But now you have abandoned us, delivering us into the hands of the gentiles for destruction." Then all the leaders of

Israel gathered from the community and came to the archbishop and his ministers and servants and said to them: "What are we to do with regard to the report which we have heard concerning our brethren in Speyer and Worms who have been killed?" They said to them: "Heed our advice and bring all your moneys into our treasury and into the treasury of the archbishop. Then you and your wives and your children and all your retinue bring into the courtyard of the archbishop. Thus will you be able to be saved from the crusaders." They contrived and gave this counsel in order to surrender us and to gather us up and to seize us "like fish enmeshed in a fatal net." In addition, the archbishop gathered his ministers and servants—exalted ministers, nobles and grandees—in order to assist us and to save us from the crusaders. For at the outset it was his desire to save us, but ultimately he failed.

It came to pass on a certain day that a gentile woman came and brought with her a goose that she had raised since it was a gosling. This goose went everywhere that the gentile woman went. She said to all passersby: "Behold this goose understands that I intend to go on the crusade and wishes to go with me." Then the crusaders and burghers gathered against us, saying to us: "Where is your source of trust? How will you be saved? Behold the wonders that the Crucified does for us!" Then all of them came with swords and spears to destroy us. Some of the burghers came and would not allow them [to do so]. At that time they stood . . . and killed along the Rhine River, until they killed one of the crusaders. Then they said: "All these things the Jews have caused." Then they almost gathered [against us]. When the saintly ones saw all these things, their hearts melted. They [the Christians] spoke harshly with them, [threatening] to assault and attack us. When they [the Jews] heard their words, they said—from great to small: "If only we might die by the hand of the Lord, rather than die at the hands of the enemies of the Lord. For he is a merciful God, the only king in his universe."

They left their houses empty and came to the synagogue only on the sabbath, that last sabbath prior to our disaster, when "a few" entered to pray. R. Judah ben R. Isaac entered there to pray on that Sabbath. They wept copiously, to the point of exhaustion, for they saw that this was the decree of the King of kings. There was a venerable scholar, R. Baruch ben R. Isaac, and he said to us: "Know that a decree has truly and surely been enacted against us, and we will not be able to be saved. For tonight we—I and my son-in-law Judah—heard the souls praying here loudly, [with a sound] like weeping. When we heard the sound, we thought that perhaps they [those praying] came from the courtyard of the archbishop and that some of the community had returned to pray in the synagogue at midnight out of pain and anguish. We ran to the door of the synagogue, but it was closed. We heard the sound, but we comprehended nothing. We returned home shaken, for our house was close to the synagogue." When we heard these words, we fell on our faces and said: "'Ah Lord God! Are you wiping out the remnant of Israel?'" They went and recounted these incidents to their brethren in the courtyard of the burgrave and in the courtyard of the archbishop. They likewise wept copiously.

It came to pass on the new moon of Sivan that the wicked Emicho—may his bones be ground up on iron millstones—came with a large army outside the city, with crusaders and common folk. For he also said: "It is my desire to go on the crusade." He was our chief persecutor. He had no mercy on the elderly, on young men and young women, on infants and sucklings, nor on the ill. He made the people of the Lord "like dust to be trampled." "Their young men he put to the sword and their pregnant women he ripped open." They camped outside the city for two days. Then the heads of the [Jewish] community said: "Let us send him money, along with our letters, so that the [Jewish] communities along the way will honor him. Perhaps the Lord will treat us with his great loving-kindness." For previously they had liberally spent their moneys, giving the archbishop and the burgrave and their ministers and their servants and the burghers approximately four hundred marks, so that they might aid them. It availed them nothing. We were unlike Sodom and Gomorrah, for in their case ten [righteous] were sought in order to save them. For us neither twenty nor ten were sought.

*   *   *

It came to pass at midday that the wicked Emicho—may his bones be ground up—he and all his army—came, and the burghers opened up to him the gates. Then the enemies of the Lord said one to another: "Behold the gates have been opened by themselves. All this the Crucified has done for us, so that we might avenge his blood on the Jews." They came with their standards to the archbishop's gate, where the children of the sacred covenant were—an army as numerous "as the sands on the seashore." When the saintly and God-fearing saw the huge multitude, they trusted in and cleaved to their Creator. They donned armor and strapped on weapons—great and small—with R. Kalonymous ben Meshullam at their head.

There was a pious one, one of the great men of the generation, Rabbi Menahem ben Rabbi David the *levi*. He said: "All the congregation, sanctify the revered and awesome Name unreservedly." They all replied: . . . [He said]: "All of you must do as did the sons of our ancestor Jacob when he sought to reveal to them the time of redemption, at which point the Divine Presence left him. [Jacob said]: 'Perhaps I too am sullied as was my grandfather Abraham [from whom proceeded Ishmael] or like my father Isaac [from whom proceeded Esau.'] [His sons said to him: 'Hear O Israel! The Lord is our God; the Lord is one.'] [Do] as did our ancestors when they answered and said, as they received the Torah at this very time on Mount Sinai: 'We shall do and hear.'" They then called out loudly: "Hear O Israel! The Lord is our God, the Lord is one." They all then drew near to the gate to do battle with the crusaders and with the burghers. They did battle one with another around the gate. Our sins brought it about that the enemy overcame them and captured the gate. The men of the archbishop, who had promised to assist, fled immediately, in order to turn them over to the enemy, for they are "splintered reeds." Then the enemy came into the courtyard and found R. Isaac ben R. Moses [and others and struck them] a mortal sword blow. Not so for the fifty-three souls who fled with R. Kalonymous through the chambers of the archbishop, exiting into a long room called . . . and remaining there.

*   *   *

When the children of the sacred covenant saw that the decree had been issued and that the enemy had overcome them, they all cried out—young men and old men, young women and children, menservants and maidservants—and wept for themselves and their lives. They said: "We shall suffer the yoke of awe of the sacred. For the moment the enemy will kill us with the easiest of the four deaths—by the sword. But we shall remain alive; our souls [will repose] in paradise, in the radiance of the great light, forever." They all said acceptingly and willingly: "Ultimately one must not question the ways of the Holy One blessed be he and blessed be his Name, who gave us his Torah and commanded us to put to death and to kill ourselves for the unity of his holy Name. Blessed are we if we do his will and blessed are all those who are killed and slaughtered and who die for the unity of his Name. Not only are they privileged to enter the world to come and sit in the circle of the saintly, 'the pillars of the universe.' What is more, they exchange a world of darkness for a world of light, a world of pain for a world of happiness, a transitory world for a world that is eternal and everlasting."

*   *   *

It came to pass that, when the enemy came to the chambers and broke down the doors and found them convulsing, still writhing in their blood, they took their money and stripped them naked. They struck those remaining and left not "a remnant or a residue." Thus they did in all the chambers where there were children of Israel, [children of] the sacred covenant, with the exception of one chamber which was too strong. The enemy did battle against it till evening. When the saintly ones [in that chamber] saw that the enemy was mightier than they were, the men and the women rose up and slaughtered the children. Subsequently, they slaughtered one another. Some fell on their swords or knives. The saintly women threw rocks through the windows. The enemy in turn struck them with rocks. They [the Jewish women] endured all these rocks, until their flesh and faces became shredded. They cursed and

blasphemed the crusaders in the name of the Crucified, the profane and despised, the son of lust: "Upon whom do you rely? 'Upon a trampled corpse!'" Then the crusaders advanced to break down the door.

There was a notable lady, Rachel the daughter of R. Isaac ben R. Asher. She said to her companions: "I have four children. On them as well have no mercy, lest these uncircumcised come and seize them and they remain in their pseudo-faith. With them as well you must sanctify the holy Name." One of her companions came and took the knife. When she saw the knife, she cried loudly and bitterly. She beat her face, crying and saying: "'Where is your steadfast love, O Lord?'" She took Isaac her small son—indeed he was very lovely—and slaughtered him. She . . . said to her companions: "Wait! Do not slaughter Isaac before Aaron." But the lad Aaron, when he saw that his brother had been slaughtered, cried out: "Mother, Mother, do not slaughter me!" He then went and hid himself under a bureau. She took her two daughters, Bella and Matrona, and sacrificed them to the Lord God of Hosts, who commanded us not to abandon pure awe of him and to remain loyal to him. When the saintly one finished sacrificing her three children before our Creator, she then lifted her voice and called out to her son: "Aaron, Aaron, where are you? I shall not have pity or mercy on you either." She pulled him by the leg from under the bureau, where he had hidden, and sacrificed him before the sublime and exalted God. She then put them under her two sleeves, two on one side and two on the other, near her heart. They convulsed near her, until the crusaders seized the chamber. They found her sitting and mourning them. They said to her: "Show us the money which you have under your sleeves." When they saw the slaughtered children, they smote her and killed her. With regard to them and to her it is said: "Mother and babes were dashed to death together." She died with them, as did the [earlier] saintly one with her seven sons. With regard to her it is said: "The mother of the child is happy." The crusaders killed all those in the chamber and stripped them naked. They were still writhing and convulsing in their blood, as they stripped them. "See, O Lord, and behold, how abject I have become."

Subsequently they threw them from the chambers through the windows naked, heap upon heap and mound upon mound, until they formed a high heap. Many of the children of the sacred covenant, as they were thrown, still had life and would signal with their fingers: "Give us water that we might drink." When the crusaders saw this, they would ask them: "Do you wish to sully yourselves [with the waters of the baptism]?" They would shake their heads and would look at their Father in heaven as a means of saying no and would point with their fingers to the Holy One blessed be he. The crusaders then killed them.

All these things were done by those whom we have designated by name. The rest of the community all the more proclaimed the unity of the sacred Name, and all fell in the hands of the Lord.

Then the crusaders began to exult in the name of the Crucified. They lifted their standards and came to the remnant of the community, to the courtyard of the burgrave. They besieged them as well and did battle against them and seized the entranceway to the courtyard and smote them also.

There was a certain man, named Moses ben Helbo. He called to his sons and said to them: "My sons Simon and Helbo. At this moment hell and paradise are open [before you]. Into which do you wish to enter?" They answered him and said: "Bring us into paradise." They stretched forth their necks. The enemy smote them, the father along with the sons.

There was a Torah scroll there in the chamber. The crusaders came into the chamber, found it, and tore it to shreds. When the saintly and pure daughters of royalty [the Jewish women] saw that the Torah had been torn, they called out loudly to their husbands: "Behold, behold the holy Torah. The enemy is tearing it." Then they all, the men and the women, said together: "Woe for the holy Torah, 'perfect in beauty,' 'the delight of our eyes.'

We used to bow before it in the synagogue; we used to kiss it; we used to honor it. How has it now fallen into the hands of the unclean and uncircumcised." When the men heard the words of the saintly women, "they became exceedingly zealous" for the Lord our God and for the holy and beloved Torah. There was there a young man named R. David ben Rabbi Menahem. He said to them: "My brethren, rend your garments over the honor of the Torah." They rent their garments as our teacher commanded. They then found a crusader in a chamber and they all—both men and women—rose up and stoned him. He fell and died. Now when the burghers and crusaders saw that he had died, they did battle against them. They went up on the roof over the place where the children of the covenant were, broke the roof, shot at them with arrows, and pierced them with spears.

*   *   *

I know not how much is missing here. May God save us from this exile. The end of the former persecutions.

REVIEW QUESTIONS

1. According to this account, what factors and motives led to the slaughter of Jews in certain communities? What can you conclude about the conditions in which Jews lived prior to the First Crusade?

2. The anonymous author of this account quotes extensively from the Hebrew Bible. Why? What rhetorical and historical functions might such scriptural passages serve?

3. What does the story about the goose reveal about the crusaders' mind-set? Does this story seem credible? Why or not? Why did the author include it here?

ALI IBN AL-ATHIR

An Arabic Account of the First Crusade

Ali ibn al-Athir (1160–1233) was a historian who may at one time have been in contact with the great leader Salah ad-Din (Saladin, c. 1138–1193), who successfully marshalled Muslim forces against the Christian crusaders. Ibn al-Athir's major work, The Complete History of the World, *includes a description of the events leading up to the First Crusade and provides another valuable perspective on the causes of the crusading movement and the motivations of the crusaders.*

From *Arab Historians of the Crusades*, Arabic sources translated by Francesco Gabrieli, translated from the Italian by E. J. Costello (Berkeley: University of California Press, 1969), pp. 3–12.

The Franks Seize Antioch

The power of the Franks first became apparent when in the year 478/1085–86 they invaded the territories of Islām and took Toledo and other parts of Andalusia, as was mentioned earlier. Then in 484/1091 they attacked and conquered the island of Sicily[1] and turned their attention to the African coast. Certain of their conquests there were won back again but they had other successes, as you will see.

In 490/1097 the Franks attacked Syria. This is how it all began: Baldwin, their King,[2] a kinsman of Roger the Frank who had conquered Sicily, assembled a great army and sent word to Roger saying: 'I have assembled a great army and now I am on my way to you, to use your bases for my conquest of the African coast. Thus you and I shall become neighbours.'

Roger called together his companions and consulted them about these proposals. 'This will be a fine thing both for them and for us!' they declared, 'for by this means these lands will be converted to the Faith!' At this Roger raised one leg and farted loudly, and swore that it was of more use than their advice.[3] 'Why?' 'Because if this army comes here it will need quantities of provisions and fleets of ships to transport it to Africa, as well as reinforcements from my own troops. Then, if the Franks succeed in conquering this territory they will take it over and will need provisioning from Sicily. This will cost me my annual profit from the harvest. If they fail they will return here and be an embarrassment to me here in my own domain. As well as all this Tamīm[4] will say that I have broken faith with him and violated our treaty, and friendly relations and communications between us will be disrupted. As far as we are concerned, Africa is always there. When we are strong enough we will take it.'

He summoned Baldwin's messenger and said to him: 'If you have decided to make war on the Muslims your best course will be to free Jerusalem from

---

[1] This date clearly refers to the end of the Norman conquest.
[2] This Baldwin (*Bardawil*) is a mythical character, compounded of the various Baldwins of Flanders and Jerusalem; or else the first Baldwin is mistakenly thought to have been already a king in the West.

[3] This passage is characteristic of the contempt with which the Muslims usually spoke of their enemies, as well as giving a fairly accurate picture of Roger's political acumen.
[4] The Zirid amīr of Tunisia Tamīm ibn Mu'ízz.

their rule and thereby win great honour. I am bound by certain promises and treaties of allegiance with the rulers of Africa.' So the Franks made ready and set out to attack Syria.

Another story is that the Fatimids of Egypt were afraid when they saw the Seljuqids extending their empire through Syria as far as Gaza, until they reached the Egyptian border and Atsiz[5] invaded Egypt itself. They therefore sent to invite the Franks to invade Syria and so protect Egypt from the Muslims.[6] But God knows best.

When the Franks decided to attack Syria they marched east to Constantinople, so that they could cross the straits and advance into Muslim territory by the easier, land route. When they reached Constantinople, the Emperor of the East refused them permission to pass through his domains. He said: 'Unless you first promise me Antioch, I shall not allow you to cross into the Muslim empire.' His real intention was to incite them to attack the Muslims, for he was convinced that the Turks, whose invincible control over Asia Minor he had observed, would exterminate every one of them. They accepted his conditions and in 490/1097 they crossed the Bosphorus at Constantinople. Iconium and the rest of the area into which they now advanced belonged to Qilij Arslān ibn Sulaimān ibn Qutlumīsh, who barred their way with his troops. They broke through[7] in rajab 490/July 1097, crossed Cilicia,[8] and finally reached Antioch, which they besieged.

When Yaghi Siyān, the ruler of Antioch, heard of their approach, he was not sure how the Christian people of the city would react, so he made the Muslims go outside the city on their own to dig trenches, and the next day sent the Christians out alone to continue the task. When they were ready to return home at the end of the

day he refused to allow them. 'Antioch is yours,' he said, 'but you will have to leave it to me until I see what happens between us and the Franks.' 'Who will protect our children and our wives?' they said. 'I shall look after them for you.' So they resigned themselves to their fate, and lived in the Frankish camp for nine months, while the city was under siege.

Yaghi Siyān showed unparalleled courage and wisdom, strength and judgment. If all the Franks who died had survived they would have overrun all the lands of Islām. He protected the families of the Christians in Antioch and would not allow a hair of their heads to be touched.

After the siege had been going on for a long time the Franks made a deal with one of the men who were responsible for the towers. He was a cuirass-maker called Ruzbih[9] whom they bribed with a fortune in money and lands. He worked in the tower that stood over the river-bed, where the river flowed out of the city into the valley. The Franks sealed their pact with the cuirass-maker, God damn him! and made their way to the water-gate. They opened it and entered the city. Another gang of them climbed the tower with ropes. At dawn, when more than 500 of them were in the city and the defenders were worn out after the night watch, they sounded their trumpets. Yaghi Siyān woke up and asked what the noise meant. He was told that trumpets had sounded from the citadel and that it must have been taken. In fact the sound came not from the citadel but from the tower. Panic seized Yaghi Siyān and he opened the city gates and fled in terror, with an escort of thirty pages. His army commander arrived, but when he discovered on enquiry that Yaghi Siyān had fled, he made his escape by another gate. This was of great help to the Franks, for if he had stood firm for an hour, they would have been wiped out. They entered the city by the gates and sacked it, slaughtering all the Muslims they found there. This happened in jumada I (491/April/May 1098).[10] As for Yaghi Siyān, when the sun rose he

---

[5] A general of the Seljuqid Sultan Malikshāh, who in 1076 attacked Egypt from Palestine.

[6] Of course the Fatimids were also Muslims, but they were heretics and so opposed to the rest of *sunni* [sic] Islām.

[7] At Dorylaeum.

[8] Literally 'the land of the son of Armenus' as the Arab writers call the Lesser Armenia of the Cilician Roupenians.

[9] *Firūz* is an alternative reading.

[10] June 3 according to European sources.

recovered his self control and realized that his flight had taken him several *farsakh*[11] from the city. He asked his companions where he was, and on hearing that he was four *farsakh* from Antioch he repented of having rushed to safety instead of staying to fight to the death. He began to groan and weep for his desertion of his household and children. Overcome by the violence of his grief he fell fainting from his horse. His companions tried to lift him back into the saddle, but they could not get him to sit up, and so left him for dead while they escaped. He was at his last gasp when an Armenian shepherd came past, killed him, cut off his head and took it to the Franks at Antioch.

The Franks had written to the rulers of Aleppo and Damascus to say that they had no interest in any cities but those that had once belonged to Byzantium. This was a piece of deceit calculated to dissuade these rulers from going to the help of Antioch.

The Muslim Attack on the Franks, and Its Results

When Qawām ad-Daula Kerbuqā[12] heard that the Franks had taken Antioch he mustered his army and advanced into Syria, where he camped at Marj Dabiq. All the Turkish and Arab forces in Syria rallied to him except for the army from Aleppo. Among his supporters were Duqāq ibn Tutūsh,[13] the Ata-beg Tughtikīn, Janāh ad-Daula of Hims, Arslān Tash of Sanjār, Sulaimān ibn Artūq and other less important amīrs. When the Franks heard of this they were alarmed and afraid, for their troops were weak and short of food. The Muslims advanced and came face to face with the Franks in front of Antioch. Kerbuqā, thinking that the present crisis would force the Muslims to remain loyal to him, alienated them by his pride and ill-treatment of them. They plotted in secret anger to betray him and desert him in the heat of battle.

After taking Antioch the Franks camped there for twelve days without food. The wealthy ate their horses and the poor ate carrion and leaves from the trees. Their leaders, faced with this situation, wrote to Kerbuqā to ask for safe-conduct through his territory but he refused, saying 'You will have to fight your way out.' Among the Frankish leaders were Baldwin,[14] Saint-Gilles, Godfrey of Bouillon, the future Count of Edessa, and their leader Bohemond of Antioch. There was also a holy man who had great influence over them, a man of low cunning, who proclaimed that the Messiah had a lance buried in the Qusyān, a great building in Antioch:[15] 'And if you find it you will be victorious and if you fail you will surely die.' Before saying this he had buried a lance in a certain spot and concealed all trace of it. He exhorted them to fast and repent for three days, and on the fourth day he led them all to the spot with their soldiers and workmen, who dug everywhere and found the lance as he had told them.[16] Whereupon he cried 'Rejoice! For victory is secure.' So on the fifth day they left the city in groups of five or six. The Muslims said to Kerbuqā: 'You should go up to the city and kill them one by one as they come out; it is easy to pick them off now that they have split up.' He replied: 'No, wait until they have all come out and then we will kill them.' He would not allow them to attack the enemy and when some Muslims killed a group of Franks, he went himself to forbid such behaviour and prevent its recurrence. When all the Franks had come out and not one was left in Antioch, they began to attack strongly, and the Muslims turned and fled. This was Kerbuqā's fault, first because he had treated the Muslims with such

---

[11] One *farsakh* (parasang) is about four miles.

[12] The Turkish amir of Mosul.

[13] The Seljuqid Lord of Damascus, soon to be succeeded by his general, the Ata-beg Tughtikin, whose name comes next on the list and who was to be one of the most active and tenacious opponents of the Crusades during this first phase of conquest.

[14] Baldwin of Le Bourg, later Baldwin II.

[15] The Church of St. Peter in Antioch, called in Byzantine sources Κασσιανός and in Arabic sources *Qusyān*, from the name of the man whose son was raised from the dead by St. Peter.

[16] The Finding of the Sacred Lance, at the instigation of Peter Bartholomew, seen through rationalistic Muslim eyes.

contempt and scorn, and second because he had prevented their killing the Franks. The Muslims were completely routed without striking a single blow or firing a single arrow. The last to flee were Suqmān ibn Artūq and Janāh ad-Daula, who had been sent to set an ambush. Kerbuqā escaped with them. When the Franks saw this they were afraid that a trap was being set for them, for there had not even been any fighting to flee from, so they dared not follow them. The only Muslims to stand firm were a detachment of warriors from the Holy Land, who fought to acquire merit in God's eyes and to seek martyrdom. The Franks killed them by the thousand and stripped their camp of food and possessions, equipment, horses and arms, with which they re-equipped themselves.

The Franks Take Ma'arrat an-Nu'mān

After dealing this blow to the Muslims the Franks marched on Ma'arrat an-Nu'mān and besieged it. The inhabitants valiantly defended their city. When the Franks realized the fierce determination and devotion of the defenders they built a wooden tower as high as the city wall and fought from the top of it, but failed to do the Muslims any serious harm. One night a few Muslims were seized with panic and in their demoralized state thought that if they barricaded themselves into one of the town's largest buildings they would be in a better position to defend themselves, so they climbed down from the wall and abandoned the position they were defending. Others saw them and followed their example, leaving another stretch of wall undefended, and gradually, as one group followed another, the whole wall was left unprotected and the Franks scaled it with ladders. Their appearance in the city terrified the Muslims, who shut themselves up in their houses. For three days the slaughter never stopped; the Franks killed more than 100,000 men and took innumerable prisoners. After taking the town the Franks spent six weeks shut up there, then sent an expedition to 'Arqa, which they besieged for four months. Although they breached the wall in many places they failed to storm it. Munqidh, the ruler of Shaizar, made a treaty with them about 'Arqa and

they left it to pass on to Hims. Here too the ruler Janāh ad-Daula made a treaty with them, and they advanced to Acre by way of an-Nawaqir. However they did not succeed in taking Acre.

The Franks Conquer Jerusalem

Taj ad-Daula Tutūsh[17] was the Lord of Jerusalem but had given it as a feoff to the amīr Suqmān ibn Artūq the Turcoman. When the Franks defeated the Turks at Antioch the massacre demoralized them, and the Egyptians, who saw that the Turkish armies were being weakened by desertion, besieged Jerusalem under the command of al-Afdal ibn Badr al-Jamali.[18] Inside the city were Artūq's sons, Suqmān and Ilghazi, their cousin Sunij and their nephew Yaquti. The Egyptians brought more than forty siege engines to attack Jerusalem and broke down the walls at several points. The inhabitants put up a defence, and the siege and fighting went on for more than six weeks. In the end the Egyptians forced the city to capitulate, in sha'bān 489/August 1096.[19] Suqmān, Ilghazi and their friends were well treated by al-Afdal, who gave them large gifts of money and let them go free. They made for Damascus and then crossed the Euphrates. Suqmān settled in Edessa and Ilghazi went on into Iraq. The Egyptian governor of Jerusalem was a certain Iftikhār ad-Daula, who was still there at the time of which we are speaking.

After their vain attempt to take Acre by siege, the Franks moved on to Jerusalem and besieged it for more than six weeks. They built two towers, one of which, near Sion, the Muslims burnt down, killing everyone inside it. It had scarcely ceased to burn before a messenger arrived to ask for help and to bring the news that the other side of the city had fallen. In fact Jerusalem was taken from the north on the morning of Friday 22 sha'bān 492/15 July 1099. The population was put to the sword by the

---

[17] A Syrian Seljuqid, Malikshāh's brother.
[18] The Fatimid vizier.
[19] If this date were correct the connection with the fall of Antioch would no longer exist. In fact the date given here is wrong: the Egyptians took Jerusalem in August 1098.

Franks, who pillaged the area for a week. A band of Muslims barricaded themselves into the Oratory of David[20] and fought on for several days. They were granted their lives in return for surrendering. The Franks honoured their word, and the group left by night for Ascalon. In the Masjid al-Aqsa the Franks slaughtered more than 70,000 people, among them a large number of Imams and Muslim scholars, devout and ascetic men who had left their homelands to live lives of pious seclusion in the Holy Place. The Franks stripped the Dome of the Rock[21] of more than forty silver candelabra, each of them weighing 3,600 drams, and a great silver lamp weighing forty-four Syrian pounds, as well as a hundred and fifty smaller silver candelabra and more than twenty gold ones, and a great deal more booty. Refugees from Syria reached Baghdād in ramadan, among them the qadi Abu Saʻd al-Hárawi. They told the Caliph's ministers a story that wrung their hearts and brought tears to their eyes. On Friday they went to the Cathedral Mosque and begged for help, weeping so that their hearers wept with them as they described the sufferings of the Muslims in that Holy City: the men killed, the women and children taken prisoner, the homes pillaged. Because of the terrible hardships they had suffered, they were allowed to break the fast.

*   *   *

It was the discord between the Muslim princes, as we shall describe, that enabled the Franks to overrun the country. Abu l-Muzaffar al-Abiwardi[22] composed several poems on this subject, in one of which he says:

> We have mingled blood with flowing tears, and there is no room left in us for pity(?)
> To shed tears is a man's worst weapon when the swords stir up the embers of war.
> Sons of Islām, behind you are battles in which heads rolled at your feet.
> Dare you slumber in the blessed shade of safety, where life is as soft as an orchard flower?
> How can the eye sleep between the lids at a time of disaster that would waken any sleeper?
> While your Syrian brothers can only sleep on the backs of their chargers, or in vultures' bellies!
> Must the foreigners feed on our ignominy, while you trail behind you the train of a pleasant life, like men whose world is at peace?
> When blood has been spilt, when sweet girls must for shame hide their lovely faces in their hands!
> When the white swords' points are red with blood, and the iron of the brown lances is stained with gore!
> At the sound of sword hammering on lance young children's hair turns white.
> This is war, and the man who shuns the whirlpool to save his life shall grind his teeth in penitence.
> This is war, and the infidel's sword is naked in his hand, ready to be sheathed again in men's necks and skulls.
> This is war, and he who lies in the tomb at Medina seems to raise his voice and cry: 'O sons of Hashim!'[23]
> I see my people slow to raise the lance against the enemy: I see the Faith resting on feeble pillars.

---

[20] The *Mihrāb Dawūd*, called the Tower of David in the European sources, in the citadel at Jerusalem. Not to be confused with a small sanctuary of the same name in the Temple precinct.

[21] The rock from which, the Muslims believe, Muhammad ascended into heaven. Over it was built the so-called 'Mosque of Umar', the chief Islamic monument in Jerusalem. It was from this Mosque that the conquerors took their booty. Nearby, but separate from it, is the 'Farthest Mosque' (al-Masjid al-Aqsa), where according to Ibn al-Athir the armies of the Cross showed even greater barbarity. The two sanctuaries are often confused in both Arabic and European sources.

[22] An Iraqi poet of the eleventh and twelfth centuries.

---

[23] The Prophet, who from the tomb raises his voice to rebuke his descendants (the sons of Hashim), that is, the unworthy Caliphs whose opposition to the Crusades is only half-hearted.

For fear of death the Muslims are evading the fire of battle, refusing to believe that death will surely strike them.'

Must the Arab champions then suffer with resignation, while the gallant Persians shut their eyes to their dishonour?

REVIEW QUESTIONS

1. How does Ibn al-Athir describe the behavior and motivations of Roger and his fellow crusad-ers? How does this depiction compare with that of the Anonymous of Mainz (pp. 272–277)?

2. What does Ibn al-Athir reveal about Muslim leaders' immediate responses to the Crusade? What do we learn about divisions within and among various Islamic peoples?

3. This description was written at least a century after the events it describes, at a time when the many of the crusaders' conquests had been reversed. Why do we need to take that into account as we read and extract information from it?

FROM The Autobiography of Avicenna

Almost everything that we know about the early life of the great Persian poly-math Avicenna (Ibn Sina, c. 980–1037) is derived from notes taken by one of his students and eventually incorporated into a History of Learned Men *by the Egyptian scholar Ibn al-Qifti (c. 1172–1248). In the course of his life, Avicenna would author an enormous body of work, including Arabic commentaries on Greek philosophy and logic (especially the works of Aristotle), medical textbooks, encyclopedias of human psychology and physiology, manuals on chemistry and physics, treatises on Muslim theology, and poetry in his native Persian. His extensive learning was revered by generations of scholars all over the medieval world, and Latin translations of some key works had an enormous influence on Christian intellectuals in the wake of the First Crusade (such as the great scholastic theologian Thomas Aquinas: see Chapter 9). In the following passage, Avicenna describes his upbringing in the great Persian city of Bukhara (now in Uzbekistan). Under the rule of the Samanid dynasty—recent converts to Islam—Bukhara came to rival Baghdad as a capital of learning and culture.*

From *Islam: From the Prophet Muhammad to the Capture of Constantinople*, vol. II, translated by Bernard Lewis (New York: Harper & Row, 1974), pp. 177–181.

My father was from Balkh[1] and moved from there to Bukhārā during the reign of Nūḥ ibn Manṣūr.[2] He was employed as an official and administered a village called Kharmaythān, a dependency of Bukhārā and an administrative center. Nearby was a village called Afshana, where he married my mother, who came from there, and settled down. I was born to her there, as was my brother. Later we all moved to

---

[1] An ancient city in what is now Afghanistan.
[2] A Samanid ruler, reigned 977–997.

Bukhārā, where I was given teachers of Qur'ān and polite letters. By the time I was ten years old, I had mastered the Qur'ān and so much of polite letters as to provoke wonderment.

My father was one of those who had responded to propaganda for the Egyptians.[3] . . . He had accepted their teachings on the soul and the mind, as had my brother. They often discussed it with one another. I listened to them and understood what they said, and they tried to win me over to this doctrine. Sometimes they also used to discuss philosophy, geometry, and Indian arithmetic,[4] and my father decided to send me to a certain grocer who knew Indian arithmetic so that I could learn it from him.

Then Abū 'Abdallāh al-Nātilī, who claimed to be a philosopher, came to Bukhārā. My father lodged him in our house in the hope that I would learn something from him. Before he came, I was studying jurisprudence under Ismā'īl al-Zāhid [the Hermit], and I was one of his best pupils. I became proficient in the different methods of questioning and of objection to the respondent, in accordance with the customary procedures. Then, under the guidance of al-Nātilī, I began to read the *Isagoge*.[5] When he told me the definition of *genus*, that is, that which is said of a number of things which differ in species in answer to the question "What is it?" I began to give greater precision to this definition in a way the like of which he had never heard before. He was full of admiration for me and persuaded my father to let me devote myself entirely to learning. Whatever problem he put to me, I resolved better than he could himself. Thus I learned from him the broad principles of logic, but he knew nothing of the subtleties. Then I began to read

books and study commentaries on my own until I mastered logic. I also read the geometry of Euclid, from the beginning to the fifth or sixth figure under the guidance of al-Nātilī, and was then able to cope with the rest of the book on my own. Then I passed to the Almagest.[6] When I had finished with the preliminaries and came to the geometrical figures, al-Nātilī said to me, "Read it on your own and solve the problems yourself, and then explain to me what you have read so that I may show you what is right and what is wrong." The man was not capable of handling this book himself. I therefore began to explain the book by myself. There were many difficult problems which al-Nātilī had not known until the time when I explained them to him and made him understand them.

Eventually al-Nātilī left me. . . . For my part, I busied myself with the study of the *Fuṣūṣ al-Ḥikam*[7] and other commentaries on physics and metaphysics, and the doors of knowledge opened before me. Then I took up medicine and began to read books written on this subject. Medicine is not one of the difficult sciences, and in a very short time I undoubtedly excelled in it, so that physicians of merit studied under me. I also attended the sick, and the doors of medical treatments based on experience opened before me to an extent that cannot be described. At the same time I carried on debates and controversies in jurisprudence. At this point I was sixteen years old.

Then, for a year and a half, I devoted myself to study. I resumed the study of logic and all parts of philosophy. During this time I never slept a whole night through and did nothing but study all day long. I acquired great knowledge. For every problem which I considered, I established firmly the premises of its syllogisms and arranged them in accordance with this knowledge. Then I considered what might be deduced from these premises, and I observed their conditions until the true solution of the problem was demonstrated. Whenever I was

---

[3] The Fatimid Caliphs in Cairo. In other words, Avicenna's father was sympathetic to some Shia teachings, even though he served a Sunni state.

[4] Arithmetic with the zero and positional notation. The Muslims learned this system in India and introduced it to Europe. Hence, the common but inaccurate term "Arabic numerals."

[5] An introduction to Aristotle's *Categories* by the neoplatonist Greek philosopher Porphyrius.

[6] An astronomical treatise by Ptolemy.

[7] A treatise by the Muslim philosopher al-Fārābī. He died in 950.

puzzled by a problem or was unable to establish the middle term of a syllogism, I would go to the mosque, pray, and beg the Creator of All to reveal to me that which was hidden from me and to make easy for me that which was difficult. Then at night I would return home, put a lamp in front of me, and set to work reading and writing. Whenever sleep overcame me or when I felt myself exhausted, I would drink a modest cup to restore my strength and then go on reading. When I dozed, I would dream of the same problem, so that for many problems the solution appeared to me in my sleep. I went on like this until I was firmly grounded in all sciences and mastered them as far as was humanly possible. What I learned then is what I know now, and I have not added to it to this day. Thus I mastered logic, physics, and mathematics.

Then I returned to the study of the divine science. I read the book called *Metaphysics*,[8] but could not understand it, the aim of its author remaining obscure for me. I read the book forty times, until I knew it by heart, but I still could not understand its meaning or its purpose. I despaired of understanding it on my own and said to myself, "There is no way to understand this book." Then one afternoon I happened to be in the market of the booksellers, and a crier was holding a volume in his hand and shouting the price. He offered it to me, and I rejected it impatiently, believing that there was no profit in this science. He persisted and said, "Buy this book from me, it is cheap. I will sell it to you for three dirhams because its owner needs the money." I bought it and found that it was Abu'l-Naṣr al-Fārābī's book, explaining the meaning of the *Metaphysics*.[9] I returned to my house and made haste to read it. Immediately the purposes of this book became clear to me because I already knew it by heart. I was very happy at this, and the next day I gave much alms to the poor in thanksgiving to Almighty God.

The Sultan of Bukhārā at that time was Nūḥ ibn Manṣūr. He was stricken by an illness which baffled the physicians. My name was well-known among them because of the extent of my studies. They mentioned me to the Sultan and asked him to summon me. I appeared before him and joined them in treating him and distinguished myself in his service.

One day I asked his permission to go into their library, look at their books, and read the medical ones. He gave me permission, and I went into a palace of many rooms, each with trunks full of books, back-to-back. In one room there were books on Arabic and poetry, in another books on jurisprudence, and similarly in each room books on a single subject. I read the catalogue of books of the ancients and asked for those I needed. Among these books I saw some the very names of which many people do not know, books which I had never seen before and never saw again.

I therefore read these books, made use of them, and thus knew the rank of every author in his own subject. When I reached the age of eighteen, I had completed the study of all these sciences. At that point my memory was better, whereas today my learning is riper. Otherwise, my knowledge is the same and nothing has been added.

In my neighborhood there lived a man called Abu'l-Ḥasan al-'Arūḍī who asked me to write him an encyclopedic work on science. I compiled the *Majmū'* for him and named it after him. In it I dealt with all sciences other than mathematics. I was then twenty-one years old. . . .

*   *   *

Then my father died, and my situation was transformed. I had to enter the service of the Sultan, and necessity obliged me to leave Bukhārā and move to Gurganj, where Abu'l-Ḥusayn al-Suhaylī, a lover of these sciences, was the vizier.[10] I was presented to the ruler 'Alī ibn al-Ma'mūn. I was then wearing the costume of a jurist. . . . They assigned me a monthly salary suited to one such as myself. Then necessity obliged me to move to Fasā, thence

---

[8] That is, of Aristotle.

[9] A reference to al-Fārābī's *Kitāb al-Ḥurūf*, a commentary on Aristotle's *Metaphysics*.

[10] A vizier of the Khwārazm-Shah. He died in 1027. Gurganj is now Urgench in Turkmenistan.

to Bāvard, thence to Ṭūs, to Shaqqān, to Samanqān, to Jājarm the frontier of Khurāsān, and thence to Gurgān. My objective was the amir Qābūs,[11] but it happened that at this time Qābūs was captured and imprisoned in a fortress where he died. I therefore went toward Dihistān, where I was taken seriously ill and later returned to Gurgān.[12] . . . I composed an ode on my situation, of which here is a verse:

> When I grew great no city could contain me,
> When my price rose I lacked a buyer.

---

[11] Qābūs ibn Vashmgīr, ruler of Gurgān and Tabaristān died 1012.

[12] Here, Avicenna describes an itinerant lifestyle, moving from place to place in Persia, finally setting near the Caspian Sea in what is now northern Iran.

REVIEW QUESTIONS

1. Identify the many personal, political, and intellectual influences that shaped Avicenna's early education. In what ways does he represent himself as a product of these influences? In what ways does he seem to break with them, and with received traditions?

2. What picture of Avicenna's world emerges from this account? How did contemporary circumstances help to advance his own career?

3. We owe this account to one of Avicenna's students, and then to a work of history published two centuries after his death. Why would future scholars cherish this story of Avicenna's coming-of-age? What lessons might they draw from it?

9 ⟡ THE CONSOLIDATION OF EUROPE, 1100–1250

In the wake of the First Crusade, lucrative trade with the Muslim world required reliable contracts to encourage merchants to invest or risk their lives overseas. These contracts rested on a legal framework partly inherited from the Romans but also borrowed from the Byzantines and Muslims and reinvented in the new trading centers. As certain families amassed fortunes in trade and the rest of the population benefited from a general increase in prosperity, the use of written documents in business and family life became more common throughout urban society. Literacy, once useful mainly to the Church, became a valuable money-making skill and generated jobs for copyists and notaries. An ability to manipulate numbers was also valuable.

As the economic and social vitality of the High Middle Ages strengthened the institutions of Church, monarchy, and city governments, people faced the problem of determining the relationships among these different centers of power. The processes of crusade and colonization expanded the frontiers of Western Christendom and brought Europeans into conflicts with their neighbors. By 1300, the papacy in Rome had become the center of a huge ecclesiastical bureaucracy, and new religious orders such as the Cistercians, Franciscans, and Dominicans and an intricate system of canon law buttressed the Church's authority. The university, perhaps the most distinctive legacy of the Middle Ages, supplied the Church with an educated clergy trained in the new disciplines of theology and canon law.

The movement for reforming the church in the eleventh century had raised the issues of clerical celibacy and the proper relations between the Church and the secular world. A series of powerful popes increased the Church's authority by successfully claiming that the Church should not be subordinate to any earthly power. One of the papacy's tools for uniting Western Christendom behind its teachings was the escalating rhetoric of crusading. Eventually, the Church used the Crusades as a way to fight heretics and even political opponents.

Meanwhile, creative minds were finding new answers to old questions about faith. What was happening at the universities often seemed remote from the daily lives of most people, but Saint Thomas Aquinas applied the recently revived tools of Aristotelian logic to basic concerns, in order to harmonize faith and reason. Many artistic developments accompanied all this religious and intellectual fervor, and the great cathedrals and churches rising across Europe are testimony to that society's prosperity and values. However, the increased control exercised by the Church and secular states led to increased restriction of woman's roles and the silencing of their voices. Still, many strong witnesses to female authority survive, and are represented here by Heloise, abbess of the Paraclete, and the polymath Hildegard of Bingen.

HELOISE

Letter to Abelard

Most of what we know about Heloise (c. 1101?–1164) comes from the letters that she exchanged with her former teacher and husband, Peter Abelard. She was the niece of Fulbert, a priest and canon of Notre Dame cathedral in Paris, and had received an excellent education at the royal abbey of Argenteuil. With the exception of Abelard, she was the most famous scholar of her day, and Fulbert had entrusted her to Abelard for further education when she came to live in Paris. But the pair eventually became lovers and were secretly married when Heloise became pregnant. Fulbert, enraged at this betrayal of his trust, had Abelard castrated. Thereafter, Heloise and Abelard separated.

The following is the first of her letters to survive, and it would have been written sometime after the year 1125, when Heloise had become head of a new community of religious women. Abelard, for his part, had failed to make the transition to monastic life and was still making many enemies.

From *Abelard and Heloise: The Letters and Other Writings*, translated by William Levitan, selected songs and poems translated by Stanley Lombardo and Barbara Thorburn (Indianapolis: Hackett Publishing), pp. 49–62.

First Letter
Heloise to Abelard

To her lord, no, her father
To her husband, no, her brother
From his handmaid, no, his daughter
His wife, no, his sister—

To Abelard from Heloise.

The other day, my most beloved,
one of your men brought me a copy
of the letter you wrote as consolation
for your friend.
From what was written at its head I knew at once

that it was yours, and I began to read it
with a warmth as great as the love
with which I hold its writer in my heart.
I hoped that at least by its words
I could be restored to life,
as if by some image
of the one whose real substance I have lost.
Almost every line, I noticed,
was filled with vinegar and gall,
as it told the sad story
of our entrance into monastic life
and the unending crosses which you,
my only one,
have always had to bear.

The letter well fulfilled the promise you made
your friend at its beginning, that he would think
his own troubles small or nothing next to yours.
You wrote of your persecution
at the hands of your teachers,
the supreme betrayal
of the mutilation of your body,
and the enmity and hateful malice
of Alberic and Lotulf, who were once
your fellow students.
You wrote of what happened, through their
    intrigue,
to the glorious book of your *Theology*
and to you yourself
when you were condemned as if to prison.
You wrote of the plots of your abbot and false
    brothers,
the attacks of those spurious apostles
which the same enemies instigated against you,
and the scandal which arose when you gave
the Paraclete[1] its uncustomary name.
And then, when you came to those unbearable
    assaults
which still are launched against you by that tyrant
and by the worst of all monks you call your sons,
you brought the sad story to an end.

No one, I am sure, could read or hear it without
    tears,
and my own grief became fresh with every detail,
and it grows greater still as the danger to you
even now is increasing.
We are all driven to despair of your life,
and every day our hearts beat in fear
of some final word of your death.
So, by that Christ who keeps you for his own even
    now,
we beg of you,
as we are his handmaids and yours,
write to us,
tell us of those storms
in which you find yourself tossed.
We are all you have left: let us share
your grief or your joy.

A community of grief can bring some comfort
to one in need of it, since many shoulders
lighten any burden or even make it
seem to disappear.
If, on the other hand, this storm abates
even just a little, you must write to us quickly
when your letters will bring us more joy.
But whatever it is you write to us about,
it will be no small relief, for in this way
at least you will show you are thinking of us.
Seneca teaches us by his own example
how much joy there is in letters from absent friends,
as he writes to his friend Lucilius:

"I am grateful that you write to me often,
for you show yourself to me in the one way you
    can.
When I receive a letter from you, we are suddenly
    together.
If images of absent friends bring joy,
if they refresh our memory and soothe the ache
of absence even with their false and empty solace,
how much more joy is there in a letter,
which carries the true signature of an absent
    friend?"[2]

---

[1] The monastery for women founded by Heloise and Abelard. Its name reflects its dedication to the Holy Spirit (in Greek, Paraclete).

[2] *Epistulae ad Lucilium* 40.1.

And I am grateful to God that here at least
is a way you can grant us your presence,
one which no malice will hinder,
no obstacle impede,
and no negligence—I beg of you—delay.

You have written your friend a long letter of
    consolation,
addressing his adversities but recounting
your own.
But as you told of them in such detail,
while your mind was on his consolation,
you have worsened our own desolation;
while you were treating his wounds,
you have inflicted new wounds upon us
and have made our old wounds bleed.
I beg of you,
heal these wounds you have made, who are so
    careful
to tend the wounds made by others.
You have done what you ought
for a friend and comrade
and have paid your debt to friendship and
    comradeship.
But you are bound to us by a greater debt,
for we are not your friends but your most loving
    friends,
not your comrades but your daughters—yes,
it is right to call us that, or even use
a name more sacred and more sweet
if one can be imagined.

We need no arguments or testimony
to prove the obligation you have toward us:
if men will keep their silence, the facts will speak
for themselves.
You alone, after God, are the founder of this place,
you alone the builder of this oratory,
you alone the architect of this congregation.
Nothing you have built
is on the foundation of another:[3]
it is all your creation, everything here.
Before you, this was a wilderness,
an empty range for wild beasts and outlaws;

it knew no human settlement and not a house
    stood.
Among these lairs of beasts, these dens of outlaws,
where the name of God was never pronounced,
you raised a tabernacle of the Lord
and dedicated a temple of the Holy Spirit
for him to call his own.
Nothing you brought to the task
was from the wealth of kings and princes,
though you could have had so much at your
    disposal:
it was all to be yours, whatever was done here,
yours alone.
The clerics and students who came flooding here
to learn from you provided all that was needed;
and suddenly, those who were used to living
on the benefices of the Church,
who had learned how to receive offerings
but not how to make them,
who had opened their hands to take
but not to give,
now became prodigal in their gifts
and even pressed them upon you.

Yes, it is yours,
truly yours, this newly planted garden,
whose living shoots are young, still delicate,
and need watering to thrive.[4]
From the nature of women alone the garden is
    tender
and would not be hardy even if it were not new.
Its cultivation, then, must be more careful,
in the way Saint Paul intended when he wrote:

"I have planted, Apollos has watered,
and God has given the increase."[5]

He had planted the Corinthians in the faith
by the doctrine he had preached, and his student
    Apollos
had watered them with his encouragement,
and the grace of God bestowed on them

---

[3] Cf. Rom. 15:20.

[4] Abelard uses similar terms to speak of the Paraclete in
his Sermon 30, which seeks to raise funds for the new
convent.
[5] 1 Cor. 3:6.

the increase of their virtues.
But you are tending another's vine
in a vineyard you have not planted,
and it has turned to bitterness for you,
all your words wasted and vain.[6]
While you lavish your care on another's vine,
remember what you owe your own.
You try to teach rebels and do not succeed;
you are casting pearls of God's word before
    swine.[7]
While you lavish so much on those who defy you,
consider what you owe those who obey.
While you squander so much on your enemies,
think what you owe your daughters.
But leave aside these others for a moment—
remember what you owe *me*,
and all you owe
this whole community of devoted women
you may repay at once to her who is,
with more devotion, your only one.

The wealth of your learning
knows better than the poverty of my own
how many treatises the Fathers have composed—
long, weighty, careful treatises—to teach,
encourage, and, yes, console women in religious
    orders.
That is why, in the tender early time
of my convent life long ago,
your oblivion came as no small surprise to me
when, unpersuaded by any reverence for God,
or any love for me, or any example
set by these same Fathers,
you did not try to console me as I foundered,
overwhelmed in sorrow day after day—
never once, neither by a word when we were
    together
nor a letter when we were apart—
and yet you would know
that you are bound to me by a greater debt,
obliged to me by the sacrament of marriage,
and beholden to me further by what is plain
to everyone:

that I have always held you in my heart
with a love that has no measure.

You know, my dearest,
all the world knows, how much I have lost in you,
how that supreme, that notorious betrayal
robbed me of my very self
when it robbed me of you,
and how incomparably worse than the loss itself
is the pain from the way it happened.
This greater pain must have a greater solace,
and it can come only from you, not from another.
As you alone are the source of my grief,
you alone can grant the grace of consolation.
You alone have the power to make me sad,
to make me happy or to console me,
and you alone owe me this debt,
now above all,
when I have so completely fulfilled your
    commands
in every particular
that, rather than commit a single offense
against you,
I threw myself away at your command.
And the greater irony is that my love
then turned to such insanity
that the one thing it desired above all else
was the one thing it put irrevocably beyond its reach
in that one instant when, at your command,
I changed my habit along with my heart
to show that my body along with my heart
belonged only to you.

I never wanted anything in you
but you alone,
nothing of what you have
but you yourself,
never a marriage, never a dowry,
never any pleasure, any purpose of my own—
as you well know—
but only yours.[8]

---

[6] Cf. Jer. 2:21.
[7] Cf. Matt. 7:6.

[8] In the margin of his own manuscript copy of the letter, the poet Petrarch wrote at this point, "You are acting throughout with gentleness and perfect sweetness, Heloise."

The name of wife may have the advantages
of sanctity and safety, but to me
the sweeter name will always be *lover*
or, if your dignity can bear it,
concubine or *whore*.
Do you imagine
I debased myself to earn your gratitude
and preserve your glorious distinction in the
    world?
You were not so entirely oblivious
when it suited your own purposes in that letter
to your friend,
and did not think it beneath your dignity
to set out at least some of the arguments
I used when I tried to dissuade you
from this marriage of ours and its disastrous bed.
You kept your silence, though, about most of the
    reasons
why I preferred love over marriage,
freedom over a chain.
So I call my God to witness now:
If great Augustus, ruler of the world,
ever thought to honor me by making me his wife
and granted me dominion over the earth,
it would be dearer to me
and more honorable to be called
not his royal consort but your whore.

No man's real worth is measured by his property
    or power:
fortune belongs to one category of things
and virtue to another.[9]
And no woman should think herself any the less
    for sale
if she prefers a rich man to a poor one

in marriage and wants what she would get
in a husband more than the husband himself.
Reward such greed with cash and not devotion,
for she is after property alone
and is prepared to prostitute herself
to an even richer man given the chance.
This is the argument the philosopher
Aspasia used with Xenophon and his wife
in the dialogue of Aeschines the Socratic.
After she set out her argument
aimed at reconciling the pair,
the philosopher capped her proof with this
    conclusion:
"Therefore, if you two are not convinced
that no worthier man exists and no finer woman
    exists
anywhere on earth, then above all else
you will always be seeking that one thing
you think is best—
to have the best of all possible husbands
or the best of all possible wives."[10]

This notion goes beyond philosophy
and should not be called the pursuit of wisdom
but wisdom itself.
There is a blessed delusion among the married,
a happy fantasy that perfect love
keeps their marital ties intact less through the
    restraint
of their bodies than through the chastity
of their hearts.
But what is a delusion for other women,
for me is the manifest truth.
What other women only think about their
    husbands,
I—and the entire world—not only believe
but *know* to be true about you,
and in this way my love is far from any delusion.

---

[9] This argument will find its way into Abelard's *Ethics* (Luscombe 1971, 48): "If this were true [that merit depends on external circumstances], then great wealth could make someone better or more worthy (that is, if wealth in itself could bring about merit or the increase of merit), and the richer men are, the better they could become because out of their abundance of riches they could add more in deeds to their devotion. But to think that wealth can add to real happiness or the worthiness of the soul, or to think that its lack can detract from the merits of the poor is utterly insane."

[10] Cicero, *De Inventione* 1.31.52. Aspasia was the companion (the "concubine or whore," as it were) of the Athenian leader Pericles, widely respected for her character and intellect. In Cicero, Aspasia's words are reported by Socrates, but Heloise has bypassed the middleman and gone straight to the source, the original philosopher herself.

Has there been a philosopher or even a king
whose renown could equal yours?[11]
Has there been any region of the country,
any city, any town that did not boil
with excitement just to see you?
Has there been a single person
who did not come running
to catch a glimpse as you came into sight,
who did not stretch his neck and strain his eyes
to follow you as you left?
Has there been a woman, married or unmarried,
who did not long for you when you were gone
or lust for you when you were present?
Has there been a great lady or even a queen
who did not envy me the pleasures of my bed?

And two things that belonged to you alone
would win the heart of any woman—
your beautiful voice and your gift for writing songs.
These are not common among philosophers,
    I know,
but for you they were amusements, a diversion
from your philosophical work.
You left countless songs,
both in the classical meter of love
and in the rhythms of love as well,
that kept your name on everyone's lips;
and they were of such surpassing sweetness
that their melodies alone would not allow
even the unlettered to forget you.[12]
For this above all, women sighed with love for you.

And since most of the songs told of your love and
    mine,
in what then seemed an instant my name was sung
in every corner of the country,
and the envy of women was kindled against me.[13]
Has there been a grace of mind or body
that you did not possess when you were young?
And is there now, of all the women then
who envied me,
a single one who does not feel compassion
when my own calamity has cut me
from those joys?
Is there any man or woman, even among
our ancient enemies, who is not softened now
by the pity owed to me?

I am entirely guilty; as you know,
I am entirely innocent.
For blame does not reside in the action itself
but in the disposition of the agent,
and justice does not weigh what is done
but what is in the heart.[14]
And what my heart has always been toward you,
you alone can judge, who have put me to the test.
I submit it all for your examination,
and rest my case on your testimony alone.

Now answer me one question if you can:
why, after our entrance into religious life—
which you alone decided, you alone—

---

[11] Petrarch wrote in the margin of his manuscript copy at this point, "About Peter's fame—if love doesn't make her testimony suspect."

[12] The indications here are that these songs were in Latin. The distinction between "meter" and "rhythm" is between verse forms based on syllable quantity (as in classical Latin) and syllable quality or stress accent (as in the accented verse of much medieval Latin poetry). The "classical meter of love," then, is the elegiac couplet, the standard form of classical Latin love poetry. The "unlettered" are those who did not know Latin but who nonetheless found it easy to memorize Abelard's songs because of the qualities Heloise notes. Outside what may be preserved in *The Letters of Two Lovers* . . . , little of Abelard's elegiac poetry addressed to Heloise survives; . . .

[13] Petrarch commented in the margin at this point, "*Muliebriter*—Just like a woman." Far from descending into vanity, however, Heloise is adapting Abelard's own remarks about the role of fame and envy in his life to help confirm a parallel between their experiences. In the next sections, she proceeds to apply to herself the specific language Abelard used about his castration, the examination of his book at the Council of Soissons, and his isolation at St. Gildas of Rhuys, and refers to her own "*calamitas*—calamity."

[14] What evidently has been an issue of mutual concern between them will become central to the doctrine of Abelard's *Ethics*, that intentions alone, not actions in themselves, are subject to moral judgment; see, e.g., *Ethics* (Luscombe 1971, 52): "Indeed, we call an intention good, that is, right in itself; we do not say of an action, however, that it takes on any good in itself but rather that it proceeds from a good intention."

why I have fallen into such neglect
and oblivion with you that I am neither
restored to life with a word when we are together
nor comforted with a letter when we are apart.
Yes, tell me if you can,
and I will tell you
what I, no, what everyone suspects—
that it was appetite and not affection
that connected you to me, your lust and not your
    love;
and that when what you desired suddenly
    became
impossible,
everything you put on for its sake
also disappeared.
My most beloved,
this is not my inference alone but everyone's,
not private and particular to me
but public and universal.
I wish it were just mine alone,
for then your love could find
someone to defend it, someone I could turn to
to relieve the pain I am suffering now.
I wish there were
some plausible excuse I could invent,
for then I could find, in defending you,
some way of covering my own cheapness.

Remember what I ask, I beg of you—
you will find it is small and easy to do:
so long as I am cheated of your presence,
present me with an image of yourself
at least in words,
of which you have an exceptional supply.
I cannot expect your generosity in substance
if I find you miserly in words.
Up to now
I had thought I deserved so much from you
since everything I have done was for your sake
and even now I continue in your service.
It was not any commitment to the religious life
that forced me to the rigors of the convent
when I was the young woman I once was:
it was your command alone.
If even in this
I deserve nothing from you, then you may judge

how all my work here has been wasted.
I can expect no reward from God since it is clear
I have yet done nothing out of love for him.
I followed *you* as you went striding off
to God and to his monastery—
No,
I did not follow: I went first.
Were you haunted by the image of Lot's wife
turning back[15]
when you delivered me up to these vows and holy
    vestments
even before you delivered yourself to God?
That you doubted me in this one thing, my love,
overwhelmed me with grief and shame.
But, as God knows,
I would have followed you
to Vulcan's flames if you commanded it,
and without a moment's hesitation
I would have gone first.

My heart was never my own but was always
with you,
and now even more, if it is not with you
it is nowhere:
without you it cannot exist at all.[16]
Let it be at peace with you, I beg of you.
And it will be at peace with you if you are kind,
if you return grace for grace,[17] small things for
    large,
words for real substance.
My love, I wish your love
had less confidence in me,
so that it would be more careful and concerned.
But now it seems the more secure of me
I have made you feel, the more negligent
you have become.

Recall what I have done, I beg of you.
Remember what you owe me.
In the days
when we shared the pleasures of the flesh,

---

[15] See Gen. 19:26.
[16] Petrarch's marginal comment is *"Amicissime et eleganter*—Written with elegance and the greatest love."
[17] Cf. John 1:16.

no one was sure if I acted out of love or lust.
Now the end confirms the beginning.
I have denied myself all pleasure to follow your
    will:
I kept nothing for myself but to become yours.
If you now give me less when I deserve
so much more,
if you now give me nothing at all,
think what your injustice will be then.
And it is so small a thing I ask and so easy
for you to do.
So, by that God who claims your dedication,
I beg of you,
grant me your presence in the one way you can—
by writing me some word of comfort,
so that at least in this one way
I may be restored to life,
readier and fit for my own service to God.
In the days
when you sought me out for pleasures long ago,
you showered me with letter after letter,
and with your songs you set your Heloise
on the lips of everyone, and every home
and every street re-echoed
Heloise.

Is it not better now to summon me to God
than it once was to call me to your bed?
Think what you owe me, remember what I ask,
I beg of you,
and I will end my long letter
with these brief words—

Farewell, my only one.

REVIEW QUESTIONS

1. What does this letter reveal about gender roles in twelfth-century Europe? How does Heloise herself understand her own role in society?

2. Heloise was known for her beautiful and ornate Latin prose style, and in this letter she quotes from both classical sources and from the Bible. How does she make use of these two cultural legacies?

3. Many (male) scholars of the nineteenth and twentieth centuries alleged that this letter could not have been written by Heloise, or by any woman with a sincere religious vocation. Why would they make such allegations? Do you think they are plausible?

GUIBERT OF NOGENT

On the Uprising of the Laon Commune and the Murder of Bishop Gaudry

The following comes from an extraordinary medieval source: a series of autobiographical reflections written by Guibert, abbot of the small and impoverished monastery of Nogent in northwestern France. Despite his insignificance, Guibert had a high opinion of himself and took a lively—and opinionated—interest in the events of his own time. But because he witnessed few of these events himself, and because he held strong and often strange views, he is not always a reliable narrator. In this passage, he describes what occurred in 1112 when the inhabitants of the nearby city of Laon attempted to counter the power of their bishop by forming a commune: a type of urban association in which all men pledged to support one another's claims to citizenship and free enterprise. In Guibert's telling, this attempt to promote unity actually exacerbated existing tensions among groups of nobility, artisans, merchants, and recently enfranchised serfs. It also enraged the bishop, Gaudry, who claimed to be the lord of Laon and, as such, opposed any alternative form of government. In addition to being a bishop, Gaudry held high political office in the Anglo-Norman kingdom of Henry I and had also served the English king in battle. He was therefore a powerful man in his own right, but he was an outsider to Laon and the region, which was under the influence of the French king, Louis VI. In other words, there was a perfect storm of competing forces brewing in Laon, and they came to a head when the bishop ordered the murder of a prominent citizen of Laon: one of the catalysts for the formation of a commune to check his power.

From *Monodies and On the Relics of Saints: The Autobiography and a Manifesto of a French Monk from the Time of the Crusades*, by Guibert of Nogent, translated by Joseph McAlhany and Jay Rubenstein (New York: Penguin Books, 2011), pp. 127–135.

*   *   *

In consideration of this, the clergy, including the archdeacons, and the nobles, who were always on the lookout for opportunities to get money out of the people, through their intermediaries gave them the option to obtain permission to form a commune, if they should pay a fitting price. "Commune," however, was a new name, and the worst possible one, for what it was:[1] all those in a servile condition would pay their usual debt of servitude to the lords once a year, and if contrary to the terms of the agreement they were in any way delinquent, they would make regular payments as compensation; payment of all other taxes normally inflicted on serfs of all types would be canceled. The people welcomed this opportunity to pay their own ransom, and handed over enormous piles of money to clog so many greedily gaping maws. Showered with such money, they became more peaceful, and gave their firm oath that they would faithfully keep to their bargain.

After the clergy, nobles, and people pledged their mutual assistance, the bishop returned from England with a large sum of money, and angered at those responsible for this revolution, he kept away from the city for some time. . . .

Though he claimed to have been roused to an unyielding animus against those who had conspired to form the commune together with their supporters, the offer of a large pile of gold and silver suddenly quieted all his histrionics. He swore he would uphold the rights of this commune, in the same way as in the city of Noyon and the town of Saint-Quentin, where there were legitimate charters. The king as well,[2] compelled by gifts from the people, swore to this oath. My God, even after they received so much money from the people, even after they had offered their oaths, who could say how many legal disputes they started in order to subvert what they had sworn to, as they sought to return their serfs, once freed from the yoke of customary demands, back to their original condition? For the bishop and nobles possessed an implacable ill will toward the citizens, and since the bishop did not have the power to revoke French liberties as they do in Normandy or England, forgetting his profession as shepherd to his flock, he wilted in the face of insatiable greed. Anybody among the people brought to trial was treated under the law not as a creature of God, but, if I may call it this, a creature of the court, and he would be drained to the last drop of all that he possessed.

*   *   *

---

[1] "Commune" comes from the verb *conjuratio*, meaning an oath of mutual support.

[2] Louis VI of France.

And thus God, upon seeing the magistrates and their subordinates share equally in this wickedness by their deeds or their consent to them, was no longer able to withhold his judgments, and allowed at last the evil designs they had conceived to reach the point of widespread fury. By God's vengeance, the bishop plunged headlong from haughty pride and crashed with a horrendous fall.

Near the end of Lent during the holy days of the Lord's Passion, he summoned the nobles and some clerics, having decided it was time to quash the commune he had sworn to along with the king, whose oath he had procured with bribes. . . .

For on the day when he ought to have performed the most glorious of all the bishop's duties, the consecration of the oil and the absolution of the people's sins, he was not even spotted entering his church. He was plotting with the king's vassals to have the king break the oath he had sworn and bring the laws of the city back to their former state. But the burghers, fearing their own overthrow, promised the king and his men four hundred pounds, or maybe it was more. The bishop in turn asked the nobles to go with him to speak with the king, and they at the same time promised seven hundred pounds. King Louis, son of Philip, a person of such distinction that the majesty of a king seemed the only thing fitting for him, strong in battle, without patience for lengthy negotiations, intrepid in spirit under adversity—although he was a good man in other respects, in this respect he was not altogether equitable, because, as happened in this case as well as others, he listened too much and gave excessive consideration to base persons corrupted by greed. This brought upon him damaging criticism, and upon many others their ruin.

And thus the king's desires, as I said, tilted toward the larger offer, and when contrary to God he ratified this decision, all their oaths (that is, the bishop's and the nobles') were broken, without any respect for honesty or the sanctity of the holy days. . . .

Once the formal agreements to this commune were broken, such furor, such astonishment seized the hearts of the citizens that all craftsmen abandoned their trades, the cobblers and tanners shut their stalls, innkeepers rented no rooms, tavern owners offered nothing for sale, so that their thieving lords could not expect anything to be left over for them. For the bishop and nobles immediately began to take account of everyone's income, and whatever amount could be determined as each individual's contribution to inaugurate the commune was the amount he was required to pay to disband it.

This was done on the day of *Parasceve*, which means "preparation," and on the holy Sabbath—on the days when we receive the body and blood of the Lord—their thoughts were fixed only on homicide on the one side, and perjury on the other. What more? All the designs of the bishop and the nobles during these days were directed toward grinding down the livelihood of those beneath them. But their inferiors, no longer simply angry, but roused to a rabid ferocity, conspired in the death, or rather murder, of the bishop and his accomplices, giving their own oaths in turn. Forty of them swore together, they say, and their plot could not be kept concealed. For word of it reached master Anselm[3] as evening fell that holy Sabbath. He sent a warning to the bishop, who was heading off to bed, not to attend the morning vigil, knowing that if he went he would be killed. But this extraordinarily stupid monster said, "Hah! Could I be killed at the hands of such people?" Although he spoke of them with disdain, he still did not dare arise for morning prayers and enter the church.

The following day, when he was to follow the clergy in procession, he ordered his servants and some soldiers to keep behind him with swords under their clothes. During the procession some small disturbance sprang up, as tends to happen in a crowd, and one of the burghers, thinking the murder plot they had sworn to had been set in motion, emerged from an archway and shouted twice in a loud voice as some kind of signal, "Commune! Commune!" A false alarm, it ceased immediately, but he still brought suspicion onto the opposing faction. When the service of the mass was

---

[3] A renowned teacher and scholar of Laon.

finished, the bishop called out crowds of peasants from the episcopal estates to man the church towers and ordered them to guard his palace, though it was clear that they, too, were no less bitterly opposed to him, since they knew the piles of money he had promised the king would be drained from their own purses.

*   *   *

On that Wednesday, I made my way to him, since by the conflagration he started he had deprived me of my grain supply as well as some shoulders of pork, which are commonly called *bacons.* I urged him to save the city from this terrible storm, but he replied, "What do you think they can accomplish by their unruly behavior? If John, my Moor,[4] dragged by the nose the most powerful man among them, he wouldn't even dare to whimper." . . .

The next day, Thursday, he was spending the afternoon with archdeacon Gautier discussing how to go about exacting money, when suddenly throughout the city sounds of a disturbance rang out, with people shouting, "Commune!" And through the middle of the church of Notre-Dame, . . . an enormous throng of citizens entered the episcopal palace, carrying swords, two-headed axes, bows and hatchets, clubs and lances. Once they realized this was an attempt at revolution, nobles rallied to the bishop from every direction, whom they had sworn to protect in case of such an attack. During this onrush, the castellan Guimar, an older nobleman, very handsome in appearance and innocent in his behavior, was running through the church, armed only with a shield and spear, and as soon as he entered the bishop's courtyard, a certain Raimbert, even though he was his godfather, struck him in the back of the head with a two-headed axe—he was the first to die. Immediately after, Rainier, . . . whom my sister had recently married, was himself stabbed from behind with a lance as he hurried to enter the episcopal palace. He wanted to go up the steps into the bishop's chapel, but while trying was struck down in front of them,

and soon a fire from the palace burned him completely below the groin.

*   *   *

The insolent mob, clamoring before the walls of the courtyard, then attacked the bishop. The bishop along with some of his defenders threw stones and shot arrows, fighting back as long as they could. He was always at his most energetic under arms, and as before so now, but because he had in vain taken up a sword he shouldn't, he perished by the sword.[5] Unable to withstand the audacious onslaught of the people, he put on the clothing of one of his attendants and fled into the church cellar. He hid himself in a small storeroom and thought he would not be found once he was shut up inside by a loyal follower who had blocked up the opening. Running here and there, they shouted not, "Where's the bishop?", but "Where's the villain?" They seized one of his young attendants, but because of his loyalty they could not force out of him anything they wanted. Dragging in another, when they asked where their quarry was, they received the answer with a perfidious nod. After entering the cellar and tearing it apart, they at last found him in the following way.

Theudegaud was a thoroughly sinister man, a dependent of the church of Saint-Vincent and long a subordinate and provost of Enguerrand of Coucy in charge of the crossing tolls at the bridge called Sort. He would keep an eye out for when there were only a few travelers, and after he robbed them of all they had, to ensure they did not have an opportunity to prosecute him, he threw them out into the river with lead weights attached to them. God only knows how many times he did this, since there is no one to tell the number of his thefts and robberies, but the unconstrainable, if I can call it that, wickedness in his heart showed on his horrid face. He had fallen into disfavor with Enguerrand and committed himself fully to the commune at Laon. Thus, a man who once spared no monk, no cleric, no pilgrim—indeed no man or woman at all—was

---

[4] That is, a slave from Muslim Spain or North Africa.

[5] A reference to a proverb quoted in Matthew 26:52: "For all who take the sword will perish by the sword."

in the end the one who would kill the bishop. As a leader and instigator of this criminal undertaking, he spared no effort in tracking down the bishop, whom he hated more than the others.

After they had searched the various containers one by one for him, Theudegaud stopped in front of the cask where the bishop was hiding. He banged on the lid and twice asked, "Who's in there?" Frozen with fear at his knocking, Gaudry could barely open his mouth to say, "A prisoner." The bishop used to call him Isengrin out of mockery for his wolflike appearance (that is what others call wolves), so this criminal man said to him, "Is Lord Isengrin hidden here?"[6] Reviled as a sinner, but still anointed by the Lord, the bishop was dragged by the hair from among the containers, then beaten repeatedly and brought out into the open on the path to the cloister in front of the chaplain Godfrey's house. Even though he begged them for mercy in the most pathetic manner, and swearing on his oath he tried to plead with them—he would never from that day on be their bishop, would give them boundless wealth, would leave the country—their minds were set against him, and they all fell upon him. One man by the name of Bernard, known as de Bruyères, raised up a two-headed axe and savagely dashed the brains out of his holy yet sinful head.

He was slipping from between the hands of those holding him, but before he dropped to the ground, someone struck him from the side through the middle of the nose just under the eyes, and he fell dead. Then they cut off the legs and added many

other wounds to the man they had already killed. Theudegaud noticed a ring on the late bishop's finger, but was not able to pull it off easily, so he cut off the finger from the corpse with a knife and stole the ring. Stripped bare, the bishop was thrown into a corner in front of his chaplain's house. My God, who could reveal how many mocking insults passers-by hurled at him as he lay there, how many clumps of mud, how many rocks, how much dirt covered his body!

REVIEW QUESTIONS

1. Guibert holds strong and complicated opinions about all of the players in this historical drama. What is his attitude toward the bishop? Toward other members of the clergy? Toward the nobility? Toward the common people? What can you conclude about his own values and beliefs? How might these be coloring this story, and how should they make us question the evidence he provides?

2. Based on this account, what did the formation of an urban commune involve? What appear to be the main political, social, and economic benefits for the people of Laon? How does the commune differ from other, more established, forms of power—and why might it be threatening to those in authority?

3. Why does Guibert tell the story of the bishop's murder in such detail? Do you think that this narrative is reliable? Why or why not? What "moral" or conclusions does Guibert want the reader to draw from this story?

---

[6] A reference to the name given to the wolf character in many folktales.

ANONYMOUS

"The Wife of Orleans"

The growing wealth of medieval towns, and the growing power of merchants and citizens, gave rise to new forms of entertainment that embraced these urban lifestyles and values. One very popular type of story was the fabliau: *a short, comic tale told in rhyming vernacular couplets, often composed and performed by traveling entertainers known as* jongleurs *("jugglers"). These little fables lampoon the pretensions of the clergy and of great lords, poke fun at greedy bankers and artisans, and celebrate the pranks of university students and the wiles of women. They therefore provide a window onto a world where access to education, social mobility, and money were challenging the status quo, disrupting gender roles, and creating novel types of social and economic agency.*

From *Cuckolds, Clerics, and Countrymen: Medieval French Fabliaux*, translated by John DuVal (Fayetteville: University of Arkansas Press, 1982), pp. 80–86.

A courtly romance I will tell
Of a bourgeois' wife who used to dwell
In the ancient town of Orléans.
Her husband was from Amiens,
A rich landowner who had made
Money at usury and trade.
He knew the ruses, tricks, and shifts
For getting gold, and once his fists
Closed on a thing, they held it tight.
    There came to town one summer's night
A company of four young scholars
With bookbags hanging from their collars.
These boys were handsome, smart, and portly.
They were big eaters too, and courtly.
The people of the town all said
They were fine fellows, nicely bred.
The plumpest of the four was granted
To be a little bit romantic,
Not proud, but quiet as a mouse.
He frequented the husband's house.
The lady of the house delighted
In his acquaintance and invited
The boy to come and visit her
So often that the usurer

Determined that by some deception
He'd teach this scholar boy a lesson.
    For a long time he had the care
Of his young niece, who was living there.
He secretly called her aside
And promised her that if she spied
Upon the lady and her guest
He'd pay her with a pretty dress.
Meanwhile the scholar strove and pleaded
For friendship till the wife conceded:
She'd give him what he hungered for.
The niece was listening at the door.
She listened well enough to catch
The plot the wife and scholar hatched.
Back to her uncle the young girl ran
To tell him all about their plan.
The plan was, when the husband's work
Called him away, she'd call the clerk.
He'd come to the orchard gate and knock,
And she'd be waiting to unlock
And let him in when evening fell.
These tidings pleased the merchant well.
He called his wife and told her, "My
Affairs have summoned me and I

Must hurry immediately from here.
Take good care of the house my dear.
I don't know how long I'll be gone.
Be a good wife and carry on."
His wife replied, "I will, my Lord."
The husband gave his drivers word
That they would start the journey right
By leaving now. They'd spend the night
At a small inn three miles from there.
The wife did not suspect the snare.
At once she sent the clerk the news.
Meanwhile the rich man worked his ruse,
For when his drivers were in bed,
Back to the meeting place he sped.
That evening, as he lay in wait,
The lady stole to the orchard gate,
Opened it, and welcomed in
And held the man who should have been
Her lover, for she still believed
In what she hoped. She was deceived.
He who deceived her whispered low.
She hardly heard his quick, "Hello."
"I'm glad you're here," the lady said.
Along the orchard path she led
The way. He turned his face aside.
The lady peered around and spied
Beneath his hat where she detected
Something entirely unsuspected.
She hastily concluded that
Her husband hid beneath the hat
And set her mind to outmaneuver
This man who claimed to be her lover.
(Women have known how to deceive
Men ever since the time of Eve.
Not even Argus could guard women.)[1]
With whispered words she welcomed him in:
"It's good to have you by my side.
Be kind to me. I will provide
Some of my funds for you to pay
Your little debts if you will say
Nothing about this. Come, my love,
I'll hide you safely up above

In a small room I have the key to.
Be patient here and I will meet you
After my people have been fed.
When all of them have gone to bed,
I'll lead you to my bed downstairs.
Then nobody will know you're there."
—"Lady," he said, "that's very good."
Lord, how little he understood
Of what his lady thought about.
(A driver, though he plans his route,
Won't get there if the mule won't move.)
The husband's lot will not improve,
For when the merchant's wife had stuck
Him in the attic, she turned the lock
And ran from the house to the orchard gate.
The clerk was there, though she was late.
She hugged and kissed and let him pet her.
This second comer had it better
Than he who reached the orchard first.
She let the one who had it worse
Stay in the upstairs room and stew
And brought the other safely through
The orchard to the hall which led
To the guest-bedroom door. The spread
Was folded back. They both got in.
She urged her scholar to begin
The game of love. He played so well
He wouldn't have given a hazel shell
For any other game, and neither
Would she, for they played well together.
They had good fun while the time sped.
They cuddled and kissed. At last she said,
"My friend, I have to go. Please stay
A little while. Don't go away.
Now I must go and be the lady
And see that the evening meal is ready.
We'll have our own meal by and by
Later tonight, just you and I."
The scholar nodded in assent.
She left him quietly and went
To the eating hall and did her best
To treat her husband's crowd like guests.
The lady put on quite a spread.
The people guzzled wine and fed
Themselves until they almost burst.
They finished and had not dispersed

---

[1] Argus: the hundred-eyed giant whom Juno, wife of the god Jupiter, set to guard Jupiter's concubine, Io. With the help of the god Mercury, Io escaped.

When the lady asked for them to pay
Attention to what she had to say.
Her lord's two nephews were at the table,
A handyman who kept the stable,
A water boy, a cook, two grooms,
And three young girls who cleaned the rooms,
Not to mention the lady's niece.
"Ladies and gentlemen, God give you peace,"
The lady said, "Listen to me;
Lately you may have chanced to see
Hanging around this house a clerk
Who will not let me do my work.
He's begged for love in prose and rhymes.
I told him no a hundred times
Then learned I'd get no rest unless
My tactics changed, so I said yes.
I'd give him what he was begging for
As soon as my lord was out the door.
My husband's gone. God be his guide.
And now this clerk, this thorn in my side,
Has kept his part of the deal all right.
He thinks he's come to spend the night.
He's in the attic, waiting for me.
To each of you I guarantee
The finest wines in my husband's cellar
If you will fix this saucy fellow.
Arise, my people! Up to the attic!
Give him an answer that's emphatic.
Beat him up and beat him down,
Black and blue from toe to crown.
This is the last time in his life
He'll woo a self-respecting wife."

    As soon as the people there had heard,
Up they jumped with one accord.
One took a log, another a stick,
A third a pestle big and thick.
She gave the key. They rushed the stair.
"Don't let him get away from there!
Grab him before he's out the door."
(Some other teller could tell the score
Of all the blows that fell—I couldn't.)
"By God," they shouted, "Mr. Student,
We'll make you smart!" The elder brother
Wrestled him to the floor. The other
Laid hold of his uncle's overcoat
And yanked it over his face and throat

So that he couldn't utter a sound.
Then they really began to pound.
They were not bashful with the sticks.
He couldn't have gotten better licks
If he had paid ten sous apiece.
Both of the nephews and the niece
Sweated to give him many a blow
First above and then below.
It did no good to weep or shout.
Like a dead dog they dragged him out,
Dumped him on a pile of manure,
And clumped back through the kitchen door,
Then set themselves to drinking dry
The best of the husband's wine supply:
Red wines and white the lady poured.
Every laborer drank like a lord.
The lady took good wine and cakes
And a large candle of fine wax
And linen cloths with lace cutwork
And held good council with her clerk
All night until the night was spent.
True love decreed that when he went
She give him gifts of marks and sous.
She begged for other rendezvous
Whenever he could get there to her.

    At last the man in the manure
Moved his muscles to begin
The three-mile crawl back to the inn.
His drivers, when they saw him bruised
Showed much concern. They weren't amused,
But kindly asked him how he was.
"Bad," he said. "Now no more fuss.
Just take me home." He wasn't kidding.
They saddled up and did his bidding.
But after all, it did him good,
And put him out of his bad mood
To know his wife was free from stain.
He snapped his fingers at his pain.
If he survived the day, his wife
Would have his confidence all his life.

    He got home. When his wife perceived
His bruises, she was deeply grieved.
She poured an herb bath, put him in it
And eased his hurt in half a minute.
She asked him what on earth had happened.
"Lady," he said, "I have been destined

To pass through perilous straits alone
Whereby I've broken every bone."
His nephews told about the work
They had accomplished on the clerk
And how she led them to his lair.
"By gosh, she handled this affair
Discreetly and responsibly!"
Never more would the husband be
Suspicious, critical, or spying!
And never would she fail at lying
With him she loved until the day
He went to his own hometown to stay.

REVIEW QUESTIONS

1. The *fabliau* begins by calling this tale "a courtly romance," referring to contemporary aristo-cratic stories of chivalry and knightly deeds— clearly, *not* what "The Wife of Orleans" is about! Why do you think the anonymous author frames the story in this way? What comment may s/he be making about contemporary soci-ety and its literary conventions?

2. What do we learn about the background of the duped husband? Why does the author want the audience to know these details? How might they influence the audience's response(s) to his humiliation?

3. The portrayal of female characters in tales like this one is highly controversial. Many scholars consider this *fabliau* to be openly misogynist, or at least highly critical of women; others see the triumph of the female protagonist as refreshing, liberating. How do you think that a medieval audience might respond to this controversy? Could you argue that this is a feminist story? Why or why not?

HILDEGARD OF BINGEN

Letter to the Clergy of Mainz

Hildegard of Bingen (1098–1179) was a German abbess whose creative genius extended to preaching, founding convents, and above all writing down her visionary prophesies. She was also a prolific composer of sacred songs and plays. Hildegard's remarkable career as an abbess demonstrates one of the few opportunities women had to be in charge of an institution in the medieval world. In this letter to the male clergy of Mainz, Hildegard is objecting to the interdict her convent is experiencing because of a dispute over a burial.

From *The Letters of Hildegard of Bingen*, edited by Joseph L. Baird (Oxford: Oxford University Press, 1994), pp. 76–79.

By a vision, which was implanted in my soul by God the Great Artisan before I was born, I have been compelled to write these things because of the interdict by which our superiors have bound us, on account of a certain dead man buried at our monastery, a man buried without any objection, with his own priest officiating. Yet only a few days after his burial, these men ordered us to remove him from our cemetery. Seized by no small terror, as a result, I looked as usual to the

True Light, and, with wakeful eyes, I saw in my spirit that if this man were disinterred in accordance with their commands, a terrible and lamentable danger would come upon us like a dark cloud before a threatening thunderstorm.

Therefore, we have not presumed to remove the body of the deceased inasmuch as he had confessed his sins, had received extreme unction and communion, and had been buried without objection. Furthermore, we have not yielded to those who advised or even commanded this course of action. Not, certainly, that we take the counsel of upright men or the orders of our superiors lightly, but we would not have it appear that, out of feminine harshness we did injustice to the sacraments of Christ, with which this man had been fortified while he was still alive. But so that we may not be totally disobedient we have, in accordance with their injunction, ceased from singing the divine praises and from participation in Mass, as had been our regular monthly custom.

As a result, my sisters and I have been greatly distressed and saddened. Weighed down by this burden, therefore, I heard these words in a vision: It is improper for you to obey human words ordering you to abandon the sacraments of the Garment of the Word of God, Who, born virginally of the Virgin Mary, is your salvation. Still, it is incumbent upon you to seek permission to participate in the sacraments from those prelates who laid the obligation of obedience upon you. For ever since Adam was driven from the bright region of paradise into the exile of this world on account of his disobedience, the conception of all people is justly tainted by that first transgression. Therefore, in accordance with God's inscrutable plan, it was necessary for a man free from all pollution to be born in human flesh, through whom all who are predestined to life might be cleansed from corruption and might be sanctified by the communion of his body so that he might remain in them and they in him for their fortification. That person, however, who is disobedient to the commands of God, as Adam was, and is completely forgetful of Him must be completely cut off from participation in the sacrament of His body, just as he himself has turned away from Him

in disobedience. And he must remain so until, purged through penitence, he is permitted by the authorities to receive the communion of the Lord's body again. In contrast, however, a person who is aware that he has incurred such a restriction not as a result of anything that he has done, either consciously or deliberately, may be present at the service of the life-giving sacrament, to be cleansed by the Lamb without sin, Who, in obedience to the Father, allowed Himself to be sacrificed on the altar of the cross that he might restore salvation to all.

In that same vision I also heard that I had erred in not going humbly and devoutly to my superiors for permission to participate in the communion, especially since we were not at fault in receiving that dead man into our cemetery. For, after all, he had been fortified by his own priest with proper Christian procedure, and, without objection from anyone, was buried in our cemetery, with all Bingen joining in the funeral procession. And so God has commanded me to report these things to you, our lords and prelates. Further, I saw in my vision also that by obeying you we have been celebrating the divine office incorrectly, for from the time of your restriction up to the present, we have ceased to sing the divine office, merely reading it instead. And I heard a voice coming from the Living Light concerning the various kinds of praises, about which David speaks in the psalm: "Praise Him with sound of trumpet: praise Him with psaltery and harp," and so forth up to this point: "Let every spirit praise the Lord." These words use outward, visible things to teach us about inward things. Thus the material composition and the quality of these instruments instruct us how we ought to give form to the praise of the Creator and turn all the convictions of our inner being to the same. When we consider these things carefully, we recall that man needed the voice of the living Spirit, but Adam lost this divine voice through disobedience. For while he was still innocent, before his transgression, his voice blended fully with the voices of the angels in their praise of God. Angels are called spirits from that Spirit which is God, and thus they have such voices by virtue of their spiritual nature. But Adam lost that angelic voice which he had in paradise, for he fell asleep to that knowledge which he possessed before his sin, just as a person on waking up only dimly remembers what he had seen in his dreams. And so when he was deceived by the trick of the devil and rejected the will of his Creator, he became wrapped up in the darkness of inward ignorance as the just result of his iniquity.

God, however, restores the souls of the elect to that pristine blessedness by infusing them with the light of truth. And in accordance with His eternal plan, He so devised it that whenever He renews the hearts of many with the pouring out of the prophetic spirit, they might, by means of His interior illumination, regain some of the knowledge which Adam had before he was punished for his sin.

And so the holy prophets, inspired by the Spirit which they had received, were called for this purpose: not only to compose psalms and canticles (by which the hearts of listeners would be inflamed) but also to construct various kinds of musical instruments to enhance these songs of praise with melodic strains. Thereby, both through the form and quality of the instruments, as well as through the meaning of the words which accompany them, those who hear might be taught, as we said above, about inward things, since they have been admonished and aroused by outward things. In such a way, these holy prophets get beyond the music of this exile and recall to mind that divine melody of praise which Adam, in company with the angels, enjoyed in God before his fall.

Men of zeal and wisdom have imitated the holy prophets and have themselves, with human skill, invented several kinds of musical instruments, so that they might be able to sing for the delight of their souls, and they accompanied their singing with instruments played with the flexing of the fingers, recalling, in this way, Adam, who was formed by God's finger, which is the Holy Spirit. For, before he sinned, his voice had the sweetness of all musical harmony. Indeed, if he had remained in his original state, the weakness of mortal man would not have been able to endure the power and the resonance of his voice.

But when the devil, man's great deceiver, learned that man had begun to sing through God's inspiration and, therefore, was being transformed to bring back the sweetness of the songs of heaven, mankind's homeland, he was so terrified at seeing his clever machinations go to ruin that he was greatly tormented. Therefore, he devotes himself continually to thinking up and working out all kinds of wicked contrivances. Thus he never ceases from confounding confession and the sweet beauty of both divine praise and spiritual hymns, eradicating them through wicked suggestions, impure thoughts, or various distractions from the heart of man and even from the mouth of the Church itself, wherever he can, through dissension, scandal, or unjust oppression.

Therefore, you and all prelates must exercise the greatest vigilance to clear the air by full and thorough discussion of the justification for such actions before your verdict closes the mouth of any church singing praises to God or suspends it from handling or receiving the divine sacraments. And you must be especially certain that you are drawn to this action out of zeal for God's justice, rather than out of indignation, unjust emotions, or a desire for revenge, and you must always be on your guard not to be circumvented in your decisions by Satan, who drove man from celestial harmony and the delights of paradise.

Consider, too, that just as the body of Jesus Christ was born of the purity of the Virgin Mary through the operation of the Holy Spirit so, too, the canticle of praise, reflecting celestial harmony, is rooted in the Church through the Holy Spirit. The body is the vestment of the spirit, which has a living voice, and so it is proper for the body, in harmony with the soul, to use its voice to sing praises to God. Whence, in metaphor, the prophetic spirit commands us to praise God with clashing cymbals and cymbals of jubilation, as well as other musical instruments which men of wisdom and zeal have invented, because all arts pertaining to things useful and necessary for mankind have been created by the breath that God sent into man's body. For this reason it is proper that God be praised in all things.

And because sometimes a person sighs and groans at the sound of singing, remembering, as it were, the nature of celestial harmony, the prophet, aware that the soul is symphonic and thoughtfully reflecting on the profound nature of the spirit, urges us in the psalm to confess to the Lord with the harp and to sing a psalm to Him with the ten-stringed psaltery. His meaning is that the harp, which is plucked from below, relates to the discipline of the body; the psaltery, which is plucked from above, pertains to the exertion of the spirit; the ten chords, to the fulfillment of the law.

Therefore, those who, without just cause, impose silence on a church and prohibit the singing of God's praises and those who have on earth unjustly despoiled God of His honor and glory will lose their place among the chorus of angels, unless they have amended their lives through true penitence and humble restitution. Moreover, let those who hold the keys of heaven beware not to open those things which are to be kept closed nor to close those things which are to be kept open, for harsh judgment will fall upon those who rule, unless, as the apostle says, they rule with good judgment.

And I heard a voice saying thus: Who created heaven? God. Who opens heaven to the faithful? God. Who is like Him? No one. And so, O men of faith, let none of you resist Him or oppose Him, lest He fall on you in His might and you have no helper to protect you from His judgment. This time is a womanish time, because the dispensation of God's justice is weak. But the strength of God's justice[1] is exerting itself, a female warrior battling against injustice, so that it might fall defeated.

REVIEW QUESTIONS

1. Why does Hildegard need to defend the importance of music? Why would the bishop of Mainz have curtailed the use of music in religious worship at the convent as part of the interdict?
2. What are the sources of Hildegard's authority, according to her letter? How does she use her authority to challenge the decisions of the bishop and clergy of Mainz?
3. Compare this letter with that of Heloise (pp. 288–295). How does it complicate our understanding of gender roles in the twelfth century?

---

[1] In Latin, *justicia* (justice) is a feminine noun.

ECCLESIA AND SYNAGOGA FROM THE CATHEDRAL OF STRASBOURG

These two magnificent statues were sculpted for the cathedral at Strasbourg around the year 1230. Each is larger than life size (about six and a half feet tall), and they would have flanked the entrance to the south transept. Allegorical representations of the Church and the Synagogue were common during the Middle Ages. They were invariably depicted as women (the Latin nouns ecclesia *and* synagoga *are feminine) adorned with certain attributes and posed in distinctive ways. Both of these female figures are beautiful and youthful, but Ecclesia (left) stands proudly erect, wearing a crown, and carrying a victorious banner in the form of cross; her left hand cradles a Eucharistic chalice. Synagoga, in contrast, stands dejectedly, her head bowed and her eyes blindfolded; she holds a broken spear, and an open scroll dangles from her left hand.*

The sculptures, wall paintings, and stained glass of medieval churches helped to communicate complex concepts and stories. What messages do these statues convey? What importance should we attach to the gender of these statues? What did medieval authorities gain by depicting these allegorical figures as women? How might someone such as Hildegard of Bingen (see pp. 303–306) have responded to these figures?

The Magna Carta:
The "Great Charter" of 1215

Magna Carta, issued in June of 1215, was a response to both long-term trends and recent disasters. The barons of England were, most of them, descendants of Norman warriors who had helped their lord, William the Conqueror, subdue and colonize the Anglo-Saxon kingdom after 1066. For nearly a century and a half thereafter, England's strong position vis-à-vis the French king had allowed these men to control lands on both sides of the English Channel. But when John inherited the English throne in 1199, he was forced to contend with the fact that the power of the new French king, Philip Augustus, was growing. Although he had considerable talents as an administrator, he was no warrior; his chief subjects resented both his inability to hold on to Normandy and his tendency to interfere in their affairs. When many of England's bishops, barons, and other lords subsequently rebelled against him, they forced him to put his seal on this contract, which is a curious mixture of lofty ideals and practical details about how John should govern his realm and not infringe on the liberties of his most powerful subjects.

From *Select Documents of English Constitutional History*, edited by George Burton Adams and H. Morse Stephens (Basingstoke: Macmillan, 1901); translation modified and annotated by Carol Symes, with reference to the Latin original.

John, by the grace of God, king of England, lord of Ireland, duke of Normandy and Aquitaine, count of Anjou, to the archbishops, bishops, abbots, earls,[1] barons, justiciars,[2] foresters, sheriffs, reeves,[3] servants, and all bailiffs and his faithful people, greeting. Know that out of respect for God and for the good of our soul and those of all our predecessors and of our heirs; to the honor of God and the exaltation of Holy Church; and the improvement of our kingdom; by the advice of our venerable fathers Stephen, archbishop of Canterbury, primate of all England and Cardinal of the Holy Roman Church, Henry, archbishop of Dublin, William of London, Peter of Winchester, Joscelyn of Bath and Glastonbury, Hugh of Lincoln, Walter of Worcester, William of Coventry, and Benedict of Rochester, bishops; of Master Pandulf, subdeacon and member of the household of the lord Pope, of Brother Aymeric, master of the Knights of the Temple in England; and of the noblemen William Marshall, earl of Pembroke, William, earl of Salisbury, William, earl Warren, William, earl of Arundel, Alan of Galloway, constable of Scotland, Warren Fitz-Gerald, Peter Fitz-Herbert, Hubert de Burgh, seneschal of Poitou, Hugh de Nevil, Matthew Fitz-Herbert, Thomas Bassett, Alan Bassett, Philip d'Albini, Robert de Ropesle, John Marshall, John Fitz-Hugh, and others of our faithful:[4]

1. We have in the first place granted to God, and by this our present charter confirmed, for us and our

---

[1] An Anglo-Saxon word for a nobleman or great lord—as opposed to *baron*, a Norman French word meaning something similar.

[2] A Latin term for judges and court officials.

[3] An Anglo-Saxon term for an elected official; sheriffs are "shire-reeves," reeves with oversight of a shire (an Anglo-Saxon administrative unit).

[4] It is worth noting that nearly all of the noblemen mentioned by name are of Norman descent.

heirs forever, that the English Church shall be free, and shall hold its rights entire and its liberties uninjured; and we will that it thus be ob-served: which is shown by this, that the freedom of elections, which is considered to be most important and especially necessary to the English Church, we, of our pure and spontaneous will, granted, and by our charter confirmed, before the contest between us and our barons had arisen, and obtained a confirmation of it by the Lord Pope Innocent III; which we will observe and which we will shall be observed in good faith by our heirs forever.

We have granted moreover to all free men of our kingdom, for us and our heirs forever, all the liberties written below, to be had and held by themselves and by their heirs from us and from our heirs.

2. If any of our earls or barons, or others holding from us in chief by military service, shall die, and when he has died his heir shall be of full age and owe relief,[5] he shall have his inheritance by the ancient [law of] relief: that is to say, the heir or heirs of an earl [in exchange] for the whole barony of an earl a hundred pounds; the heir or heirs of a baron [in exchange] for a whole barony a hundred pounds; the heir or heirs of a knight, [in exchange] for a whole knight's fee, a hundred shillings at most; and who owes less let him give less according to the ancient custom of fiefs.

3. If moreover the heir of any one of such shall be underage, and shall be in wardship,[6] when he comes of age he shall have his inheritance without relief and without a fine.

4. The custodian of the land of such a minor heir shall not take from the land of the heir any except reasonable products, reasonable customary payments, and reasonable services, and this without destruction or waste of men or of property; and if we shall have committed the custody of the land of any such a one to the sheriff or to any other who is to be responsible to us for its proceeds, and that man shall have caused destruction or waste during

his custody, we will recover damages from him, and the land shall be committed to two legal and discreet men of that fief, who shall be responsible for its proceeds to us or to him to whom we have assigned them; and if we shall have given or sold to anyone the custody of any such land, and he has caused destruction or waste there, he shall lose that custody, and it shall be handed over to two legal and discreet men of that fief who shall be in like manner responsible to us, as is said above.

5. The custodian, moreover, so long as he shall have the custody of the land, must keep up the houses, parks, warrens, fish ponds, mills, and other things pertaining to the land, from the proceeds of the land itself; and he must return to the heir, when he has come to full age, all his land, furnished with ploughs and implements of husbandry according as the time of wainage[7] requires and as the proceeds of the land are able reasonably to sustain.

6. Heirs shall be married without disparity: that is, before the marriage is contracted it shall be announced to the relatives by blood of the heir himself.

7. A widow, after the death of her husband, shall have her marriage portion and her inheritance immediately and without obstruction, nor shall she give anything [in exchange] for her dowry or for her marriage portion, or [in exchange] for her inheritance, which inheritance her husband and she held on the day of the death of her husband; and she may remain in the house of her husband for forty days after his death, within which time her dowry shall be assigned to her.

8. No widow shall be compelled to marry so long as she prefers to live without a husband, provided she gives security that she will not marry without our consent, if she holds [property] from us, or without the consent of her lord from whom she holds [property], if she holds from another.

9. Neither we nor our bailiffs will seize any land or rent for any debt, so long as the chattels of the debtor are sufficient for the payment of the debt;

---

[5] An inheritance tax.

[6] That is, a ward of the crown and under the personal protection of the king.

[7] An Anglo-Saxon term: "carting," or the means of transporting the fruits of the harvest.

nor shall the pledges of a debtor be distrained[8] so long as the principal debtor himself has enough for the payment of the debt; and if the principal debtor fails in the payment of the debt, not having the wherewithal to pay it, the pledges shall be responsible for the debt; and if they wish, they shall have the lands and the rents of the debtor until they shall have been satisfied for the debt which they have before paid for him, unless the principal debtor shall have shown himself to be quit in that respect towards those pledges.

10. If any one has taken anything from the Jews, by way of a loan, [whether] more or less, and dies before that debt is paid, the debt shall not draw interest so long as the heir is under age, from whomsoever he holds; and if that debt falls into our hands, we will take nothing except the chattel contained in the agreement.

11. And if any one dies leaving a debt owing to the Jews, his wife shall have her dowry, and shall pay nothing of that debt; and if there remain minor children of the dead man, necessaries shall be provided for them corresponding to the holding of the dead man; and from the remainder shall the debt be paid, saving the service [owed] to the [debtor's] lords. In the same way debts are to be treated which are owed to others than the Jews.

12. No scutage[9] or aid[10] shall be imposed in our kingdom except by the common council of our kingdom, except for the ransoming of our body, for making our oldest son a knight, and for once marrying our oldest daughter, and for these purposes it shall be only a reasonable aid; in the same way it shall be done concerning the aids [usually paid by merchants] of the city of London.

13. And the city of London shall have all its ancient liberties and free customs, as well by land as by water. Moreover, we will and grant that all other cities and boroughs and villages and ports shall have all their liberties and free customs.

14. And for holding a common council of the kingdom concerning the assessment of an aid otherwise than in the three cases mentioned above, or concerning the assessment of a scutage, we shall cause to be summoned the archbishops, bishops, abbots, earls, and greater barons by our letters, individually; and besides we shall cause to be summoned generally, by our sheriffs and bailiffs all those who hold from us in chief, for [meeting on] a certain day, that is at the end of forty days at least, and for a certain place; and in all the letters of that summons, we will express the cause of the summons; and when the summons has thus been given, the business shall proceed on the appointed day, on the advice of those who shall be present, even if not all of those who were summoned have come.

15. We will not grant to any one, moreover, that he shall take an aid from his free men, except for ransoming his body, for making his oldest son a knight, and for once marrying his oldest daughter; and for these purposes only a reasonable aid shall be taken.

16. No one shall be compelled to perform any greater service for a knight's fief, or for any other free tenement,[11] than is [usually] owed for it.

17. The common pleas shall not follow our court, but shall be held in some certain place.[12]

18. The recognition of *novel disseisin*, *mort d'ancestor*, and *darrein presentment* shall be held only in their own counties and in this manner:[13] we, or (if we are outside of the kingdom) our principal justiciar, will send two justiciars through each county four times a year, who with four knights of each county, elected by the county, shall hold in the

---

[8] Imprisoned or forced to pay: "pledges" in this context means those who have promised to pay the debt in the event that the debtor himself is unable to do so.

[9] A kind of tax.

[10] A loan to the crown, usually a forced loan.

[11] Holding, usually of land.

[12] That is, the king's court should no longer be itinerant, sitting in judgment whenever the king is traveling around the realm, but should instead be convened in a fixed location at certain times.

[13] These Norman French terms are legal neologisms inserted into the Latin text of the charter. *Novel disseisin* refers to the recovery of recently seized land; *mort d'ancestor* ("death of the ancestor") is an inheritance claim; and *darrein presentment* refers to cases concerning nomination to ecclesiastical office.

county, and on the day and in the place of the county court, the aforesaid assizes[14] of the county.

19. And if the aforesaid assizes cannot be held within the day of the county court, a sufficient number of knights and free-holders shall remain from those who were present at the county court on that day to give the judgments, according as the business is more or less.

20. A free man shall not be fined for a small offence, except in proportion to the measure of the offence; and for a great offence he shall be fined in proportion to the magnitude of the offence, saving his freehold;[15] and a merchant in the same way, saving his merchandise; and the villain[16] shall be fined in the same way, saving his wainage, if he shall be at our mercy; and none of the above fines shall be imposed except by the oaths of honest men of the neighborhood.

21. Earls and barons shall only be fined by their peers, and only in proportion to their offence.

22. A cleric shall be fined, like those before mentioned, only in proportion to his lay holding, and not according to the extent of his ecclesiastical benefice.

23. No vill[17] or man shall be compelled to make bridges over the rivers except those which ought to do it of old and rightfully.

24. No sheriff, constable, coroners, or other bailiffs of ours shall hold pleas of our crown.

25. All counties, hundreds, wapentakes, and trithings[18] shall be [valued] at the ancient rents and without any increase, excepting our demesne[19] manors.

26. If any person holding a lay fief from us shall die, and our sheriff or bailiff shall show our letters-patent[20] of our summons concerning a debt which the deceased owed to us, it shall be lawful for our sheriff or bailiff to attach and levy on the chattels of the deceased found on his lay fief, to the value of that debt, in the view of legal men, so nevertheless that nothing be removed thence until the clear debt to us shall be paid; and the remainder shall be left to the executors for the fulfillment of the will of the deceased; and if nothing is owed to us by him, all the chattels shall go to the deceased, saving to his wife and children their reasonable shares.

27. If any free man dies intestate, his chattels shall be distributed by the hands of his near relatives and friends, under the oversight of the Church, saving to each one the debts which the deceased owed to him.

28. No constable or other bailiff of ours shall take anyone's grain or other chattels, without immediately paying for them in money, unless he is able to obtain a postponement at the goodwill of the seller.

29. No constable shall require any knight to give money in place of his ward[21] of a castle if he is willing to furnish that ward in his own person or through another honest man, if he himself is not able to do it for a reasonable cause; and if we shall lead or send him into the army he shall be free from ward in proportion to the amount of time during which he has been in the army through us.

30. No sheriff or bailiff of ours, or anyone else, shall take horses or wagons from any free man for carrying purposes, except by the permission of that free man.

31. Neither we nor our bailiffs will take the wood of another man for castles, or for anything else which we are doing, except by the permission of him to whom the wood belongs.

32. We will not hold the lands of those convicted of a felony for more than a year and a day, after which the lands shall be returned to the lords of the fiefs.

33. All the fish-weirs on the Thames and the Medway [rivers], and throughout all England, shall be done away with, except those on the coast.

---

[14] A Norman French term meaning "sitting" that is, local hearings on minor civil cases.

[15] In other words, his fine cannot be so great as to result in liquidation of his real property.

[16] From the Latin *villanus*, meaning "villager" or even "farmhand."

[17] Community or village.

[18] These are all Anglo-Saxon terms designating successively smaller divisions of land.

[19] A Norman French term referring to lands—domains—from which the king derives revenue directly.

[20] Literally, "open letters," sealed documents whose contents were plainly visible (not secret).

[21] The responsibility for guarding or keeping watch.

34. The writ which is called *præcipe*[22] shall not be given in the future to any one concerning any tenement by which a free man can lose his court.

35. There shall be one measure of wine throughout our whole kingdom, and one measure of ale, and one measure of grain, that is the London quarter, and one width of dyed cloth and of russets and of halbergets,[23] that is two ells within the selvages; of weights, moreover it shall be as of measures.

36. Nothing shall henceforth be given or taken [in exchange] for a writ of inquisition concerning life or limbs, but it shall be given freely and not denied.

37. If any one holds from us by fee farm or by socage or by burgage,[24] and from another he holds land by military service, we will not have the guardianship of the heir or of his land which is of the fief of another, on account of that fee farm, or socage, or burgage; nor will we have the custody of that fee farm, or socage, or burgage, unless that fee farm itself owes military service. We will not have the guardianship of the heir or of the land of anyone who holds land from another by military ser-vice on account of any petty serjeanty[25] which he holds from us by the service of paying to us knives or arrows, or things of that kind.

38. No bailiff in the future shall put any one to his law on his simple affirmation, without credible witnesses brought for this purpose.[26]

39. No free man shall be taken or imprisoned or dispossessed, or outlawed, or banished, or in any way destroyed, nor will we act against him, nor send [anyone] against him, except by the legal judgment of his peers or by the law of the land.

40. To no one will we sell, to no one will we deny or delay right or justice.

41. All merchants shall be safe and secure in going out from England and coming into England and in remaining and going through England, as well by land as by water, for buying and selling, free from all evil tolls, by the ancient and rightful customs, except in time of war, and if they are of a land at war with us; and if such are found in our land at the beginning of war, they shall be attached[27] without injury to their bodies or goods, until it shall be known from us or from our principal justiciar in what way the merchants of our land are treated who shall be then found in the country which is at war with us; and if ours are safe there, the others shall be safe in our land.

42. It is allowed henceforth to any one to go out from our kingdom, and to return, safely and securely, by land and by water, for the sake of their fidelity to us, except in time of war for some short time, for the common good of the kingdom; excepting persons imprisoned and outlawed according to the law of the realm, and people of a land at war with us, and merchants of whom it shall be done as is before said.

43. If any one holds from any escheat,[28] as from the honor of Wallingford, or Nottingham, or Boulogne, or Lancaster, or from other escheats which are in our hands and are baronies, and he dies, his heir shall not give any other relief, nor do to us any other service than he would do to the baron, if that barony was in the hands of the baron; and we will hold it in the same way as the baron held it.

44. Men who dwell outside the forest shall not henceforth come before our justiciars of the forest, on common summons, unless they are in a plea of, or pledges for, any person or persons who are arrested on account of the forest.

45. We will not make [any men] justiciars, constables, sheriffs or bailiffs unless they be such men as know the law of the realm and are well inclined to observe it.

46. All barons who have founded abbeys for which they have charters from kings of England, or ancient tenure, shall have their custody when they have become vacant, as they ought to have.[29]

---

[22] From the Latin command "seize."

[23] Types of cloth: one dyed a dark reddish brown, the other of uncertain texture and hue.

[24] Anglo-Saxon terms, referring to ancient rights and customs of land holding.

[25] A Norman French term meaning "minor military service."

[26] That is, no one should be questioned in a legal matter unless he has been sworn in before legal witnesses.

[27] Arrested or arraigned.

[28] A situation in which the holder of a fief has died without an heir or has been convicted of a crime.

[29] That is, lords who have been granted a controlling interest in abbeys located in their domains are allowed to collect taxes and tithes when the office of the abbot

47. All forests which have been afforested in our time shall be disafforested immediately; and so it shall be concerning river banks which in our time have been fenced in.[30]

48. All the bad customs concerning forests and warrens and concerning foresters and warreners, sheriffs and their servants, river banks and their guardians shall be inquired into immediately in each county by twelve sworn knights of the same county, who shall be elected by the honest men of the same county, and within forty days after the inquisition has been made, they shall be entirely destroyed by them, never to be restored, provided that we be first informed of it, or our justiciar, if we are not in England.

49. We will give back immediately all hostages and charters which have been delivered to us by Englishmen as security for peace or for faithful service.

50. We will remove absolutely from their bailiwicks the relatives of Gerard de Athyes, so that for the future they shall have no bailiwick in England: Engelard de Cygony, Andrew, Peter and Gyon de Chancelles, Gyon de Cygony, Geoffrey de Martin and his brothers, Philip Mark and his brothers, and Geoffrey his nephew and their whole retinue.

51. And immediately after the reëstablishment of peace we will remove from the kingdom all foreign-born soldiers, cross-bow men, sergeants, and mercenaries who have come with horses and arms for the injury of the realm.

52. If any one shall have been dispossessed or removed by us without legal judgment of his peers, from his lands, castles, franchises, or his right, we will restore them to him immediately; and if contention arises about this, then it shall be done according to the judgment of the twenty-five barons, of whom mention is made below concerning the security of the peace. Concerning all those things, however, from which any one has been removed or of which he has been deprived without

legal judgment of his peers by King Henry [II] our father, or by King Richard our brother, which we have in our hand, or which others hold, and which it is our duty to guarantee, we shall have respite according to the usual dispensation of crusaders: excepting those things about which the suit has been begun or the inquisition made by our writ before our assumption of the cross; when, however, we shall return from our journey, or if by chance we desist from the journey, we will immediately show full justice in regard to them.[31]

53. We shall, moreover, have the same respite, and in the same manner, about showing justice in regard to the forests which are to be disafforested or to remain forests, which Henry our father or Richard our brother made into forests; and concerning the custody of lands which are in the fief of another, custody of which we have until now had on account of a fief which any one has held from us by military service; and concerning the abbeys which have been founded in fiefs of others than ourselves, in which the lord of the fief has asserted for himself a right; and when we return, or if we should desist from our journey, we will immediately show full justice to those complaining in regard to them.

54. No one shall be seized nor imprisoned on the appeal of a woman concerning the death of any one except her husband.

55. All fines which have been imposed unjustly and against the law of the land, and all penalties imposed unjustly and against the law of the land are altogether excused, or will be on the judgment of the twenty-five barons of whom mention is made below in connection with the security of the peace, or on the judgment of the majority of them, along with the aforesaid Stephen, archbishop of Canterbury, if he is able to be present, and others whom

---

is vacant. Such lords often had a strong say in the selection of abbots.

[30] Those areas that have been recently declared to be royal forests, and thus the property of the king, should revert to being common land.

[31] This clause and the next, as well as clause 57 below, have to do with seizure of property or other exactions made by John and his immediate predecessors on the grounds that revenue or goods were needed to finance or equip a crusade. Henry II (r. 1154–89) may have taken an oath to go on crusade in order to do just this (he never went). Richard (r. 1189–99) participated in the Third Crusade (1189–92). John himself never went on crusade or seems to have had any intention of doing so.

he may wish to call for this purpose along with him. And if he should not be able to be present, nevertheless the business shall go on without him, provided that if any one or more of the aforesaid twenty-five barons are in a similar suit they should be removed as far as this particular judgment goes, and others who shall be chosen and put upon oath, by the remainder of the twenty-five, shall be substituted for them for this purpose.

56. If we have dispossessed or removed any Welshmen from their lands, or franchises, or other things, without legal judgment of their peers, in England, or in Wales, they shall be immediately returned to them; and if a dispute shall have arisen over this, then it shall be settled in the borderland by judgment of their peers, concerning holdings of England according to the law of England, concerning holdings of Wales according to the law of Wales, and concerning holdings of the borderland according to the law of the borderland. The Welsh shall do the same to us and ours.

57. Concerning all those things, however, from which any one of the Welsh shall have been removed or dispossessed without legal judgment of his peers, by King Henry our father, or King Richard our brother, which we hold in our hands, or which others hold, and we are bound to guarantee to them, we shall have respite till the usual period of crusaders, those being excepted about which suit was begun or inquisition made by our command before our assumption of the cross. When, however, we shall return, or if by chance we shall desist from our journey, we will show full justice to them immediately, according to the laws of the Welsh and the aforesaid parts.

58. We will give back the son of Llewellyn[32] immediately, and all the hostages from Wales and the charters which had been liberated to us as a security for peace.

59. We will act toward Alexander, king of the Scots,[33] concerning the return of his sisters and his hostages, and concerning his franchises and his right, according to the manner in which we shall act toward our other barons of England, unless it ought to be otherwise by the charters which we hold from William his father, formerly king of the Scots, and this shall be by the judgment of his peers in our court.

60. Moreover, all those customs and franchises mentioned above which we have conceded in our kingdom—and which are to be fulfilled, as far as pertains to us, in respect to our men—all men of our kingdom, as well clergy as laymen, shall observe as far as pertains to them, in respect to their men.

61. Since, moreover, for the sake of God, and for the improvement of our kingdom, and for the better quieting of the hostility sprung up lately between us and our barons, we have made all these concessions; wishing them to enjoy these in a complete and firm stability forever, we make and concede to them the security described below; that is to say, that they shall elect twenty-five barons of the kingdom, whom they will, who ought with all their power to observe, hold, and cause to be observed, the peace and liberties which we have conceded to them, and by this our present charter confirmed to them; in this manner, that if we or our justiciar, or our bailiffs, or any one of our servants shall have done wrong in any way toward any one, or shall have transgressed any of the articles of peace or security; and the wrong shall have been shown to four barons of the aforesaid twenty-five barons, let those four barons come to us or to our justiciar, if we are out of the kingdom, laying before us the transgression, and let them ask that we cause that transgression to be corrected without delay. And if we shall not have corrected the transgression or, if we shall be out of the kingdom, if our justiciar shall not have corrected it within a period of forty days, counting from the time in which it has been shown to us or to our justiciar, if we are out of the kingdom; the

---

32 Llywelyn ab Iorwerth, often known as Llewellyn the Great (c. 1172–1240). He was the ruler of Gwynedd (northern Wales) and the *de facto* leader of the Welsh. He had aligned himself with the Norman barons against John, who was holding his son hostage, and used this position to demand certain concessions. The situation was further complicated by the fact that John's illegitimate daughter, Joan, was married to the Welsh prince.

33 Alexander II (r. 1214–49): he, too, took advantage of the situation.

aforesaid four barons shall refer the matter to the remainder of the twenty-five barons, and let these twenty-five barons with the whole community of the country distress and injure us in every way they can; that is to say by the seizure of our castles, lands, possessions, and in such other ways as they can until it shall have been corrected according to their judgment, saving our person and that of our queen, and those of our children; and when the correction has been made, let them devote themselves to us as they did before. And let whoever in the country wishes take an oath that in all the above-mentioned measures he will obey the orders of the aforesaid twenty-five barons, and that he will injure us as far as he is able with them, and we give permission to swear publicly and freely to each one who wishes to swear, and no one will we ever forbid to swear. All those, moreover, in the country who of themselves and their own will are unwilling to take an oath to the twenty-five barons as to distressing and injuring us along with them, we will compel to take the oath by our mandate, as before said. And if any one of the twenty-five barons shall have died or departed from the land or shall in any other way be prevented from taking the above-mentioned action, let the remainder of the aforesaid twenty-five barons choose another in his place, according to their judgment, who shall take an oath in the same way as the others. In all those things, moreover, which are committed to those five and twenty barons to carry out, if perhaps the twenty-five are present, and some disagreement arises among them about something, or if any of them when they have been summoned are not willing or are not able to be present, let that be considered valid and firm which the greater part of those who are present arrange or command, just as if the whole twenty-five had agreed in this; and let the aforesaid twenty-five swear that they will observe faithfully all the things which are said above, and with all their ability cause them to be observed. And we will obtain nothing from any one, either by ourselves or by another by which any of these concessions and liberties shall be revoked or diminished; and if any such thing shall have been obtained, let it be invalid and void, and we will never use it by ourselves or by another.

62. And all ill-will, grudges, and anger sprung up between us and our men, clergy and laymen, from the time of the dispute, we have fully renounced and pardoned to all. Moreover, all transgressions committed on account of this dispute, from Easter in the sixteenth year of our reign [1215] till the restoration of peace, we have fully remitted to all, clergy and laymen, and as far as pertains to us, fully pardoned. And moreover we have caused to be made for them testimonial letters-patent of lord Stephen, archbishop of Canterbury, lord Henry, archbishop of Dublin, and of the aforesaid bishops and of Master Pandulf, in respect to that security and the concessions named above.

63. Wherefore we will and firmly command that the Church of England shall be free, and that the men in our kingdom shall have and hold all the aforesaid liberties, rights and concessions, well and peacefully, freely and quietly, fully and completely, for themselves and their heirs, from us and our heirs, in all things and places, forever, as before said. It has been sworn, moreover, as well on our part as on the part of the barons, that all these things spoken of above shall be observed in good faith and without any evil intent. Witness the above named and many others. Given by our hand in the meadow which is called Runnymede, between Windsor and Staines, on the fifteenth day of June, in the seventeenth year of our reign.

REVIEW QUESTIONS

1. Study the organization of this charter carefully. What does the order of the various clauses reveal about the issues that were most important to the English barons?
2. How would you summarize the barons' main grievances? What would you identify as the most important concessions being granted by the king?
3. What does a close reading of this document reveal about political, social, economic, and ethnic tensions within John's realm—and beyond its borders? What can you conclude about the legal status of "ordinary" men and women in England?

THOMAS AQUINAS

FROM *Summa Theologica*

Thomas Aquinas (c. 1225–1274) was a Dominican theologian, university professor, and author of the Summa Theologica, *the most influential theological work of the Middle Ages.* Theology *was a new term devised to define the recent academic subject of applying the tools of reason to religious truths. This confidence in human ability to understand a reasonable universe working according to God's logical plans and laws is central to the values of medieval humanism. In these sections of the* Summa Theologica, *Thomas analyzes proofs of God's existence and the meaning of humanity's creation. This translation, faithful to the content of the original, rearranges for a modern audience a very formal style of scholastic argument.*

From *St. Thomas Aquinas: Summa Theologica*, edited by Timothy S. McDermott (Westminster, Md.: Christian Classics, 1989), pp. 12–13, 144–49.

*   *   *

There Is a God. There are Five Ways of Proving There is a God:

The first and most obvious way is based on change. We see things changing. Now anything changing is being changed by something else. (For things changing are on the way to realization, whereas things causing change are already realized: they are realizing something else's potential, and for that they must themselves be real. The actual heat of a fire causes wood, already able to be hot, to become actually hot, and so causes change in the wood. Now the actually hot cannot at the same time be potentially hot, but only potentially cold. So what changes cannot as such be causing the change, but must be being changed by something else.) This something else, if itself changing, is being changed by yet another thing; and this last by another. Now we must stop somewhere, otherwise there will be no first cause of the change, and, as a result, no subsequent causes. (Only when acted upon by a first cause do intermediate causes produce a change; if a hand does not move the stick, the stick will not move anything else.) We arrive then at some first cause of change not itself being changed by anything, and this is what everybody understands by *God*.

The second way is based on the very notion of cause. In the observable world causes derive their causality from other causes; we never observe, nor ever could, something causing itself, for this would mean it preceded itself, and this is not possible. But the deriving of causality must stop somewhere; for in the series of causes an earlier member causes an intermediate and the intermediate a last (whether the intermediate be one or many). Now eliminate a cause and you also eliminate its effects: you cannot have a last cause, nor an intermediate one, unless you have a first. Given no stop in the series of causes, no first cause, there will be no intermediate causes and no last effect; which contradicts observation. So one is forced to suppose some first cause, to which everyone gives the name *God*.

The third way is based on what need not be and on what must be, and runs as follows. Some of the things we come across can be but need not be, for we find them springing up and dying away, thus sometimes in being and sometimes not. Now everything cannot be like this, for a thing that need not be, once was not; and if everything need not be, once upon a time there was nothing. But if that were true there would be nothing even now, because something that does not exist can only be brought into being by something already existing. If nothing was in being nothing could be brought into being, and nothing would be in being now, which contradicts observation. Not everything therefore is the sort of thing that need not be; some things must be, and these may or may not owe this necessity to something else. But just as a series of causes must have a stop, so also a series of things which must be and owe this to other things. One is forced to suppose something which must be, and owes this to nothing outside itself; indeed it itself is the cause that other things must be.

The fourth way is based on the gradation observed in things. Some things are better, truer, more excellent than others. Such comparative terms describe varying degrees of approximation to a superlative; for example, things are hotter and hotter the nearer they approach what is hottest. Something therefore is the truest and best and most excellent of things, and hence the most fully in being; for Aristotle says that the truest things are the things most fully in being. Now *when many things possess some property in common, the one most fully possessing it causes it in the others: fire,* as Aristotle says, *the hottest of all things, causes all other things to be hot.* Something therefore causes in all other things their being, their goodness, and whatever other perfection they have. And this is what we call *God.*

The fifth way is based on the guidedness of nature. Goal-directed behaviour is observed in all bodies obeying natural laws, even when they lack awareness. Their behaviour hardly ever varies and practically always turns out well, showing that they truly tend to goals and do not merely hit them by accident. But nothing lacking awareness can tend to a goal except it be directed by someone with

awareness and understanding; the arrow, for example, requires an archer. Everything in nature, therefore, is directed to its goal by someone with understanding, and this we call *God.*

*   *   *

The Genesis of Man

God formed man from the slime of the earth and breathed into his face the breath of life, and man became a living soul. Only what possesses existence and is subject of its own existence—substance—properly exists; all supervening properties exist not as themselves possessing existence but as forms under which a substance exists. Whiteness's existence is really the existence of something as white. This is true of all non-subsistent forms; so, properly speaking, it is not such forms but the things of which they are forms that come into existence. The soul however is a subsistent form and can properly be said both to exist and to come into existence. But since it does not come from pre-existent matter (only bodies do that) it must come by a new creation. Only God can create. All secondary agents presuppose material provided by a primary agent, which they then transform. Since the human soul does not come into existence by transformation of pre-existent matter, it must be produced by God's immediate creation. The soul however is only part of man, and naturally perfect only when united to its body, so it was fittingly created in its body, not before it. If it was a natural species of thing the soul would be a sort of angel; but by nature it is the form of a body, the formal element in an animal. Forms in matter are caused by forms in matter, when composite material things generate one another. The only immaterial thing that can produce something material without needing previous material is God; he alone can create new matter. So Adam's body was formed by God immediately, there being no preceding human body that could generate a body of like species to itself. Because the senses are mainly concentrated in the face, other animals have faces close to the ground to look for food and provender; but men have raised faces so that their senses, especially the finest and most discriminating sense of sight, may experience sense-objects in every direction of heaven and earth. Man's upright carriage also releases his hands for various useful purposes. And since he does not have to use his mouth for gathering food, it is not oblong and hard as in other animals but adapted for speech, the special work of reason. So man's upright carriage is not like that of the plants, for they have their roots (which are their mouths) in the earth.

It is not good for man to be alone; let us make him a help that is like himself. The help God makes for man is not for any sort of work (for there other men would be more help than a woman) but for producing children. In plants, which have no nobler function in life than propagation, the active and passive abilities to propagate are joined at all times. In the higher animals however there is more to life than that, so the active male and passive female partners mate only at certain times, constituting the sort of unity a plant is always. Aristotle called the female *a male manqué.* The particular nature of the active male seed intends to produce a perfect likeness of itself, and when females are conceived this is due to weak seed, or unsuitable material, or external influences like the dampness of the south wind. But this is because nature as a whole intends women; and in this sense they are not manqué but intended by God, the author of nature as a whole. The type of subordination in which servants are managed in their master's interests came in after sin; but the subordination seen in households or cities, where management is for the benefit of the subordinates themselves, would have obtained even without sin. And such is the natural inequality and subordination of women to men, who are by nature more reasonable and discerning. [Some say God should not have produced Eve to be an occasion of sin for Adam, but] if God removed from the world everything which man has made an excuse for sin, the world would be a poor place. What is a general good must not be sacrificed because of some particular abuse, especially since God is powerful enough to turn any evil to good account. Forming Eve from Adam's rib signified companionship, not

domination (so not from his head) nor yet subjection (so not from his feet); and it also symbolized the establishment of the church by the sacraments of blood and water flowing from the side of Christ sleeping on the cross.

Let us make man after our own image and likeness. An image not only resembles, it expresses: however like each other two eggs may be, one does not express the other and is not its image. But the resemblance man bears God derives from God as from an original, so scripture describes man as made to God's image; where the preposition *to* signifies approach to something at a distance, the original in this case being infinitely distant from the image. An image must also resemble its original in species, or in some attribute like shape peculiar to that species, where likeness in species means likeness down to the last thing differentiating the species. Things in general resemble God in existing, some things also in being alive, and some finally in intellectual discernment: the closest likeness to God in creation. Properly speaking then, only creatures with intellect are made to God's image. And the point at which such creatures most closely resemble God is when they imitate his self-understanding and love. So there are three levels to the imaging of God by man: the very nature of mind gives to all men a natural aptitude for understanding and loving God; grace adds to some men an actual if imperfect understanding and love of God; and the glory of heaven brings this to perfection. The principal constituent of God's image in man, mind, is found in both male and female human beings; which is why Genesis says *To God's image he created him (namely, mankind); male and female he created them.* A secondary image of God as beginning and end of creation is however to be found only in male man, the beginning and end of woman: and this is what made St Paul say that *the man is the image and glory of God, and the woman the glory of man, for Adam was not from Eve but Eve from Adam, and Adam was not for Eve, but Eve for Adam.*

That man is made in the image of God's nature implies that all three persons of God are represented in him. In other creatures, and in other parts of man than his mind, there is not the same image or likeness in species to God, but only the sort of trace that all causes leave even in effects unlike in species. Thus we talk of tracks left by animals as traces, fires leave traces of themselves in ashes, and armies traces in the ravaged countryside. An image of the uncreated Trinity can be found in creatures with reason, who utter a word in their minds, and in whose wills a love issues, so representing God in species. In other creatures there is no such word-source or word or love; but a trace of the fact that source, word and love exist in its maker. For a creature's shaping and conditioning indicate that it *comes from* somewhere; its specific form indicates its maker's *word* as a house's shape indicates its architect's idea; and its functional order indicates its maker's *love* as a house's uses indicate what its architect willed. A first image of the Trinity in our minds is found in our activities of thinking out and formulating an inner word from the information we have, and then bursting out from this in a love. But since such activities exist implicitly in their sources [memory, understanding and will], a secondary image of the Trinity exists in our powers and dispositions to act. The kind of word and love we have in our heart varies according to what it is we are conceiving and loving: stone or horse. So God's image is to be found in the conceiving of a word that expresses what we know of God and a love flowing from that; in other words, in the soul attending directly to God. Though the mind can also attend indirectly to God (as to an object seen in a mirror) when, as Augustine says, it remembers and understands and loves itself, and perceives there a trinity: not God indeed, but an image of God; and then moves through that to God.

God made man right. No one can wilfully turn away from happiness, for man wants happiness by nature. So no one seeing God for what he is can wilfully turn his back on God. Plainly then, since Adam sinned, he had not seen God for what he is. The disembodied state of the soul after death differs from its present embodied state in being unnatural; but Adam's state of innocence and man's state after sin differ as integrated and disintegrated states of a soul which has preserved its natural way of existence unimpaired. In the state of innocence, just as now, man's soul was adapted to controlling and perfecting and giving life to his body, but in so fully integrated a way that his body was completely at the service of his soul without hindrance. And since the way of understanding appropriate to a soul that must control and perfect the body's animal life is by recourse to sense-experience, this was also Adam's way of understanding. The things that were made in the beginning were made not only to be themselves but to start other things existing, and that is why they were produced in a state of perfection. Adam was created mature in body, capable of immediate procreation, and mature in soul, capable of immediate education and instruction of others. So he knew all that men normally have to learn, everything implicit in the first self-evident premises, all natural knowledge: *he gave all animals their names.* And since controlling his own and other people's lives also involved knowing life as destined to a goal beyond nature, Adam needed to know the supernatural things required to direct life in that state of innocence, just as nowadays we need the faith. But Adam did not know other things not naturally knowable but not required for directing life: such as men's thoughts, or the indeterminate future, or details like the number of pebbles in some river.

The integrated state of Adam in which his reason was submissive to God, his lower powers to his reason, and his body to his soul, seems to imply that he possessed God's grace from the start; for this is an integration not written into man's nature, otherwise it would have remained after sin. The primary submissiveness of Adam's reason to God must have been more than natural, and therefore due to a gift of grace; for effects cannot be more potent than their cause. In us feeling is partly but not wholly subject to reason: sometimes our feelings pre-empt and hamper reasoned assessment, whilst at other times they presuppose it. In the state of innocence the lower appetites were completely subject to reason, and all feelings presupposed reasoned assessment. Virtues are what dispose our reason towards God and our lower powers towards the standards set by reason; so the very rightness of man's first state required him to possess all virtue. Some virtues, like charity and justice, contain no implication of imperfection, and others, like faith and hope, imply imperfections which were compatible with Adam's state (not yet seeing God and not in full enjoyment of him); so these existed in Adam without qualification, both the dispositions and the acts that proceed from them. But virtues like repentance and compassion that imply imperfections incompatible with Adam's state could only exist inactively, as dispositions to act when required, in the way Aristotle says shame exists in an earnest man.

Let him rule the fishes of the sea and the birds of the sky and the beasts of the earth. In nature the less perfect serve the more perfect: plants feed on the earth, animals on plants, and men on both plants and animals. Moreover, the instincts of animals to behave in certain particular ways is a sort of sharing in man's universal practical sense which can reason out all behaviour. So the subordination of animals to man is natural. To think wild and aggressive animals were originally peaceable, not only to men but also to other animals, is quite irrational. How could man by sinning change the nature of animals from vegetarian to carnivorous? Hostility between animals is natural, but it no more made them insubordinate to man then than it makes them insubordinate to God and his providence now. Man would have been an instrument of that providence then, just as he is now with domesticated animals, giving his tame hawks hens to eat. Instinctively geese follow a leader and bees obey a queen: all animals share by nature in the practical sense we have by reason. And at that time all animals would have obeyed man of their own accord, as the ones he has domesticated do today. Man was master of other things to the measure that he was master of himself. He shares reason with the angels, sense-powers with other animals, natural vital powers with plants, and the body itself with all non-living things. Reason is master, not subject

(so man never had mastery over angels); feelings of aggression and desire man masters to some extent by reason's command (and so in the state of innocence he could command animals); but his own body and vital forces man masters not by command but by use (and so in the state of innocence he could not command plants and non-living things to change their behaviour, but would have had no trouble using their behaviour for his purposes). Of course, disparities existed in that first state: disparities first of all in sex and age, but also in moral and intellectual proficiency (men being free to work to different extents at doing and willing and knowing things), and again in physical strength (since this is influenced by food and climate and the stars one is born under). But none of this would have implied natural defect or sin. Free men exist for their own ends, as Aristotle says; whereas slaves serve others. Such slavery can't exist without suffering: everyone values his own good, and does not willingly cede it exclusively to another. But men can be subordinate to one another and yet remain free, if the good being served is their own or a common good. Such subordination would have existed in the state of innocence, since man is by nature a social animal, and people living a social life need some single authority to look to their common good. If some men are more knowledgeable and just than others the right thing is to use that to the others' benefit.

Death entered the world through sin. Before sin then, man must have been immortal. Not because he was immaterial like angels, or made of a kind of matter that cannot lose its form like the stars of heaven, nor because of some inherent disposition preserving him from his natural mortality like the glorified in heaven, but because God gave his soul supernatural ability to preserve his body from decay as long as it itself remained submissive to God. In the state of innocence man preserved his body from external injury by his own wits, helped by God's providence which so cared for him that nothing dangerous took him by surprise. As Augustine says *Adam was provided with food against hunger, with drink against thirst, and with the tree of life against the ravages of old age.* But the tree of life couldn't be the sole source of immortality. For one thing the tree of life couldn't give the soul its ability to preserve the body from injury; and for another, the potency of any material thing is finite and the effects of the tree of life would wear off in time, after which man would either move on to a life in the spirit or need another dose.

Increase and multiply and fill the earth. Unless there had been reproduction in the state of innocence to propagate the human race, man would have urgently needed to sin, seeing it would have brought such good. For among corruptible things, in which only the species lasts for ever, nature's main aim is the good of the species and its reproduction. Only among incorruptible substances is nature interested in individuals. So man needed to reproduce for the sake of his perishable body; though as regards his imperishable soul man needed nature (or better the author of nature, who alone creates human souls) to be interested in a multitude of individuals for their own sakes. So in the state of innocence reproduction was needed not for conservation of the species but for multiplication of individuals. In the present state of things, when owners multiply, property must be divided up, since, as Aristotle says, common property breeds discord. But in the state of innocence men's wills would have been well enough disposed for them to use their common property in a manner suited to each without danger of discord; as we indeed often see good men doing nowadays.

Some early theologians seeing intercourse besmirched by lust in our present state, thought reproduction would have happened without intercourse in the state of innocence. But this is unreasonable. It is in man's nature, like that of other animals, both before and after sin, to reproduce by intercourse, and nature has provided him with the organs needed for the purpose. In our present state the natural mating of male and female is somewhat disfigured by unbalanced desire, but this would not have happened in the state of innocence where the lower powers obeyed reason. Because animals lack reason, people sometimes say that men become like animals during intercourse, when reason is unable to balance the pleasure and heat of desire. But in the state of innocence nothing would have escaped reason in that way. Yet the pleasure would not have been any less; in fact it would have been greater given the greater purity of nature and sensitivity of body men then had. Rule by reason requires not that the pleasure should be less, but that the desire for it should be within reasonable bounds. Men who eat moderately can take as much pleasure in their food as gluttons do, but their desire doesn't wallow in the pleasure. In the state of innocence there would have been no great esteem for sexual abstinence, which we esteem nowadays not because it reduces fruitfulness but because it tempers lust.

Things beyond nature only faith can teach, and for faith we need authority. So, without God's authority, we can only assert what is in the nature of things. Now scripture tells us God created man right, so that his limbs, for example, would obey his properly ordered will. But a properly ordered will tends only to the behaviour appropriate to one's age. So newly-born infants would only have had power to move their limbs appropriately to their age, sucking the breast and so on. Weakness of seed or unsuitable material are not the only causes of females being conceived, but also external circumstances such as the direction of the wind or an idea in the mind. And this would have been particularly likely in the state of innocence, when the body was more subordinate to the mind, so that the sex of the child could have been decided by the parent. The integrated state in which man was created was a state of our nature, not deriving from the natural constitution of man, but from a gift of God given to human nature as a whole. We know this because its opposite, inherited sin, attaches to nature as a whole and passes from parent to child. When authority is silent we can only believe what accords with nature. Now men naturally learn by sense-experience, so those born in a state of innocence would also have acquired their knowledge over a period of time by discovery and instruction, though without the difficulties we have. And, as infants, they would no more have had mature use of their reason than they had of their bodily limbs.

People who locate Paradise at the equator do so because they think the evenness of day and night produces a temperate climate there, never too cold and never too hot. Aristotle however expressly says that the region is so hot that it is uninhabitable; and this seems more likely, seeing that even countries where the sun never passes directly overhead have excessively hot climates from mere proximity to the sun. In any case we believe Paradise to be situated in the most temperate locality, whether that be on the equator or elsewhere.

*   *   *

REVIEW QUESTIONS

1. What ideas tie together Thomas's five ways of proving there is a God?
2. How does Thomas see the natural relationship between men and women?
3. For Thomas, what is humanity's proper place in nature? Why?

10   THE MEDIEVAL WORLD, 1250–1350

The century between 1250 and 1350 saw the emergence of a new interconnected medieval world, characterized by unprecedented interactions among the peoples of Europe, Asia, and North Africa. The expansion of the Mongol Empire, which reunified China and then spread westward to the threshold of Europe, created the largest land empire in history, encompassing one fifth of the earth's surface and stretching from the Black Sea to the Pacific Ocean. Although the Mongol conquests were hugely destructive, they fostered networks of cultural and commercial exchange that potentially spanned the globe, enabling the extensive travels of William of Rubruck and Ibn Battuta, as well as those of merchant-adventurers like Marco Polo. Although these networks would prove fragile in the face of a large-scale demographic crisis, the Black Death, Europeans were able to establish direct connections with India, China, and the so-called Spice Islands of the Indonesian archipelago.

Europeans' integration with this widening world not only put them into contact with unfamiliar cultures and commodities, it opened up new ways of looking at the world they already knew. New artistic and intellectual responses are exemplified by the poetry of Dante Alighieri (1265–1321), who strove to make his Italian vernacular an instrument for spiritual expression as well as for political and social critique. At the same time, involvement in this wider world placed new pressures on long-term developments within Europe, notably the growing tensions between secular powers and the authority of the papacy. By the early fourteenth century, the papal court would literally be held hostage by the king of France, who moved the papacy from Rome to Avignon. This had a profound impact on everyone in Europe, and it robbed Italy of its major source of power and patronage. Although it merely repeated an old claim—that kings ruled only by divine approval as recognized by the Church—the fact was that the Church now exercised its authority only by bowing to the superior power of a particular king.

The Black Death, the name given to the deadly pandemic caused by the Yersinia pestis *virus*, was another result of the intense connectivity of this era. In the

1330s, it spread quickly from northwestern China to all corners of the Mongol Empire and then to the Mediterranean, Africa, and Europe. By 1350, it had reached Scandinavia and had caused the deaths of 30 to 50 percent of all peoples living in these regions. Its profound impact was discernible through many eyewitness accounts, including that of the Florentine author Giovanni Boccaccio.

WILLIAM OF RUBRUCK

FROM *On the Mongols*

William of Rubruck, a Franciscan monk from Flanders, was sent to the Mongols by Louis IX of France in 1253. The Mongol Empire, established by Chingis, or Genghis, Khan (1167–1227) and extended by his successors, had sent scouting parties as far west as Poland and Hungary. In the first section of this account, William describes Mongol culture. In the second section, he is at the Mongol capital of Caracorum in Mongolia, seeking another audience with Emperor Mangu (r. 1251–59).

From *The Journey of William of Rubruck to the Eastern Parts of the World, 1253–55: As Narrated by Himself,* translated and edited by William Woodville Rockhill (London: Hakluyt Society, 1900), pp. 56–66, 68–83, 235–239.

Commerce and Conquest

The matrons make for themselves most beautiful (luggage) carts, which I would not know how to describe to you unless by a drawing, and I would depict them all to you if I knew how to paint. A single rich Moal or Tartar has quite c or cc such carts with coffers. Baatu has xxvi wives, each of whom has a large dwelling, exclusive of the other little ones which they set up after the big one, and which are like closets, in which the sewing girls live, and to each of these (large) dwellings are attached quite cc carts. And when they set up their houses, the first wife places her dwelling on the extreme west side, and after her the others according to their rank, so that the last wife will be in the extreme east; and there will be the distance of a stone's throw between the *iurt* of one wife and that of another. The *ordu* of a rich Moal seems like a large town, though there

will be very few men in it. One girl will lead xx or xxx carts, for the country is flat, and they tie the ox or camel carts the one after the other, and a girl will sit on the front one driving the ox, and all the others follow after with the same gait. Should it happen that they come to some bad piece of road, they untie them, and take them across one by one. So they go along slowly, as a sheep or an ox might walk.

When they have fixed their dwelling, the door turned to the south, they set up the couch of the master on the north side. The side for the women is always the east side, that is to say, on the left of the house of the master, he sitting on his couch with his face turned to the south. The side for the men is the west side, that is, on the right. Men coming into the house would never hang up their bows on the side of the women

And over the head of the master is always an image of felt, like a doll or statuette, which they call the brother of the master; another similar one is above the head of the mistress, which they call the brother of the mistress, and they are attached to the wall; and higher up between the two of them is a little lank one (*macilenta*), who is, as it were, the guardian of the whole dwelling. The mistress places in her house on her right side, in a conspicuous place at the foot of her couch, a goat-skin full of wool or other stuff, and beside it a very little statuette looking in the direction of the attendants and women. Beside the entry on the women's side is yet another image, with a cow's tit for the women, who milk the cows; for it is part of the duty of the women to milk the cows. On the other side of the entry, toward the men, is another statue with a mare's tit for the men who milk the mares.

And when they have come together to drink, they first sprinkle with liquor this image which is over the master's head, then the other images in order. Then an attendant goes out of the dwelling with a cup and liquor, and sprinkles three times to the south, each time bending the knee, and that to do reverence to the fire; then to the east, and that to do reverence to the air; then to the west to do reverence to the water; to the north they sprinkle for the dead. When the master takes the cup in hand and is about to drink, he first pours a portion on the ground. If he were to drink seated on a horse, he first before he drinks pours a little on the neck or the mane of the horse. Then when the attendant has sprinkled toward the four quarters of the world he goes back into the house, where two attendants are ready with two cups and platters to carry drink to the master and the wife seated near him upon the couch. And when he hath several wives, she with whom he hath slept that night sits beside him in the day, and it becometh all the others to come to her dwelling that day to drink, and court is held there that day, and the gifts which are brought that day are placed in the treasury of that lady. A bench with a skin of milk, or some other drink, and with cups, stands in the entry.

In winter they make a capital drink of rice, of millet, and of honey; it is clear as wine: and wine is carried to them from remote parts. In summer they care only for *cosmos*. There is always *cosmos* near

the house, before the entry door, and beside it stands a guitar-player with his guitar. Lutes and vielles such as we have I did not see there, but many other instruments which are unknown among us. And when the master begins to drink, then one of the attendants cries with a loud voice, "Ha!" and the guitarist strikes his guitar, and when they have a great feast they all clap their hands, and also dance about to the sound of the guitar, the men before the master, the women before the mistress. And when the master has drunken, then the attendant cries as before, and the guitarist stops. Then they drink all around, and sometimes they do drink right shamefully and gluttonly. And when they want to challenge anyone to drink, they take hold of him by the ears, and pull so as to distend his throat, and they clap and dance before him. Likewise, when they want to make a great feasting and jollity with someone, one takes a full cup, and two others are on his right and left, and thus these three come singing and dancing towards him who is to take the cup, and they sing and dance before him; and when he holds out his hand to take the cup, they quickly draw it back, and then again they come back as before, and so they elude him three or four times by drawing away the cup, till he hath become well excited and is in good appetite, and then they give him the cup, and while he drinks they sing and clap their hands and strike with their feet.

The Food of the Tartars

Of their food and victuals you must know that they eat all their dead animals without distinction, and with such flocks and herds it cannot be but that many animals die. Nevertheless, in summer, so long as lasts their *cosmos*, that is to say mare's milk, they care not for any other food. So then if it happens that an ox or a horse dies, they dry its flesh by cutting it into narrow strips and hanging it in the sun and the wind, where at once and without salt it becomes dry without any evil smell. With the intestines of horses they make sausages better than pork ones, and they eat them fresh. The rest of the flesh they keep for winter. With the hides of oxen they make big jars, which they dry in admirable fashion in the smoke. With the hind part of the hide of horses they make most beautiful shoes. With the flesh of a single sheep they give to eat to L men or C; for they cut it up very fine in a platter with salt and water, for they make no other sauce; and then with the point of a knife or a fork which they make for the purpose, like that which we use to eat coddled pears or apples, they give to each of the bystanders a mouthful or two according to the number of the guests. Prior to this, before the flesh of the sheep is served, the master takes what pleases him; and furthermore if he gives to anyone a special piece, it is the custom that he who receives it shall eat it himself, and he may not give it to another; but if he cannot eat it all he carries it off with him, or gives it to his servant if he be present, who keeps it; otherwise he puts it away in his *captargac*, which is a square bag which they carry to put such things in, in which they store away bones when they have not time to gnaw them well, so that they can gnaw them later and that nothing of the food be lost. ✳ ✳ ✳

The Animals They Eat, Their Clothes, and Their Hunting

The great lords have villages in the south, from which millet and flour are brought to them for the winter. The poor procure (these things) by trading sheep and pelts. The slaves fill their bellies with dirty water, and with this they are content. They catch also rats, of which many kinds abound here. Rats with long tails they eat not, but give them to their birds. They eat mice and all kinds of rats which have short tails. There are also many marmots, which are called *sogur*, and which congregate in one hole in winter, xx or xxx together, and sleep for six months; these they catch in great numbers. There are also conies, with a long tail like a cat's, and on the end of the tail they have black and white hairs. They have also many other kinds of small animals good to eat, which they know very well how to distinguish. I saw no deer there. I saw few hares, many gazelles. Wild asses I saw in great numbers, and these are like mules. I saw also

another kind of animal which is called *arcali*, which has quite the body of a sheep, and horns bent like a ram's, but of such size that I could hardly lift the two horns with one hand, and they make of these horns big cups. They have hawks and peregrine falcons in great numbers, which they all carry on their right hand. And they always put a little thong around the hawk's neck, which hangs down to the middle of its breast, by which, when they cast it at its prey, they pull down with the left hand the head and breast of the hawk, so that it be not struck by the wind and carried upward. So it is that they procure a large part of their food by the chase.

Of their clothing and customs you must know, that from Cataia, and other regions of the east, and also from Persia and other regions of the south, are brought to them silken and golden stuffs and cloth of cotton, which they wear in summer. From Ruscia, Moxel, and from greater Bulgaria and Pascatir, which is greater Hungary, and Kerkis, all of which are countries to the north and full of forests, and which obey them, are brought to them costly furs of many kinds, which I never saw in our parts, and which they wear in winter. And they always make in winter at least two fur gowns, one with the fur against the body, the other with the fur outside exposed to the wind and snow; these latter are usually of the skins of wolves or foxes or papions; and while they sit in the dwelling they have another lighter one. The poor make their outside (gowns) of dog and kid (skins).

When they want to chase wild animals, they gather together in a great multitude and surround the district in which they know the game to be, and gradually they come closer to each other till they have shut up the game in among them as in an enclosure, and then they shoot them with their arrows. They make also breeches with furs. The rich furthermore wad their clothing with silk stuffing, which is extraordinarily soft, light and warm. The poor line their clothes with cotton cloth, or with the fine wool which they are able to pick out of the coarser. With this coarser they make felt to cover their houses and coffers, and also for bedding. With wool and a third of horse hair mixed with it they make their ropes. They also make with felt covers, saddle-cloths and rain cloaks; so they use a great deal of wool. You have seen the costume of the men.

How the Men Shave and the Women Adorn Themselves

The men shave a square on the tops of their heads, and from the front corners (of this square) they continue the shaving to the temples, passing along both sides of the head. They shave also the temples and the back of the neck to the top of the cervical cavity, and the forehead as far as the crown of the head, on which they leave a tuft of hair which falls down to the eyebrows. They leave the hair on the sides of the head, and with it they make tresses which they plait together to the ears.

And the dress of the girls differs not from the costume of the men, except that it is somewhat longer. But on the day following her marriage, (a woman) shaves the front half of her head, and puts on a tunic as wide as a nun's gown, but everyway larger and longer, open before, and tied on the right side. For in this the Tartars differ from the Turks; the Turks tie their gowns on the left, the Tartars always on the right. Furthermore they have a head-dress, which they call *bocca*, made of bark, or such other light material as they can find, and it is big and as much as two hands can span around, and is a cubit and more high, and square like the capital of a column. This *bocca* they cover with costly silk stuff, and it is hollow inside, and on top of the capital, or the square on it, they put a tuft of quills or light canes also a cubit or more in length. And this tuft they ornament at the top with peacock feathers, and round the edge (of the top) with feathers from the mallard's tail, and also with precious stones. The wealthy ladies wear such an ornament on their heads, and fasten it down tightly with an amess, for which there is an opening in the top for that purpose, and inside they stuff their hair, gathering it together on the back of the tops of their heads in a kind of knot, and putting it in the *bocca*, which they afterwards tie down tightly under the chin. So it is that when several ladies are riding together, and one sees them from afar, they look like soldiers, helmets on head and lances erect. For this *bocca* looks like a helmet, and the tuft above it is like a lance. And all the women sit their horses astraddle like men. And they tie their gowns with a piece of blue silk stuff at the waist and they wrap another band at the breasts, and tie a piece of white stuff below the eyes which hangs down to the breast. And the women there are wonderfully fat, and she who has the least nose is held the most beautiful. They disfigure themselves horribly by painting their faces. They never lie down in bed when having their children.

The Duties of the Women and Their Work

It is the duty of the women to drive the carts, get the dwellings on and off them, milk the cows, make butter and *gruit*, and to dress and sew skins, which they do with a thread made of tendons. They divide the tendons into fine shreds, and then twist them into one long thread. They also sew the boots, the socks and the clothing. They never wash clothes, for they say that God would be angered thereat, and that it would thunder if they hung them up to dry. They will even beat those they find washing them. Thunder they fear extraordinarily; and when it thunders they will turn out of their dwellings all strangers, wrap themselves in black felt, and thus hide themselves till it has passed away. Furthermore, they never wash their bowls, but when the meat is cooked they rinse out the dish in which they are about to put it with some of the boiling broth from the kettle, which they pour back into it. They also make the felt and cover the houses.

The men make bows and arrows, manufacture stirrups and bits, make saddles, do the carpentering on (the framework of) their dwellings and the carts; they take care of the horses, milk the mares, churn the *cosmos* or mare's milk, make the skins in which it is put; they also look after the camels and load them. Both sexes look after the sheep and goats, sometimes the men, othertimes the women, milking them.

They dress skins with a thick mixture of sour ewe's milk and salt. When they want to wash their hands or head, they fill their mouths with water, which they let trickle on to their hands, and in this way they also wet their hair and wash their heads.

As to their marriages, you must know that no one among them has a wife unless he buys her; so it sometimes happens that girls are well past marriageable age before they marry, for their parents always keep them until they sell them. They observe the first and second degrees of consanguinity, but no degree of affinity; thus (one person) will have at the same time or successively two sisters. Among them no widow marries, for the following reason: they believe that all who serve them in this life shall serve them in the next, so as regards a widow they believe that she will always return to her first husband after death. Hence this shameful custom prevails among them, that sometimes a son takes to wife all his father's wives, except his own mother; for the *orda* of the father and mother always belongs to the youngest son, so it is he who must provide for all his father's wives who come to him with the paternal household, and if he wishes it he uses them as wives, for he esteems not himself injured if they return to his father after death. When then anyone has made a bargain with another to take his daughter, the father of the girl gives a feast, and the girl flees to her relatives and hides there. Then the father says: "Here, my daughter is yours; take her wheresoever you find her." Then he searches for her with his friends till he finds her, and he must take her by force and carry her off with a semblance of violence to his house.

Of Their Justice and Judgments, Death and Burial

As to their justice you must know that when two men fight together no one dares interfere, even a father dare not aid a son; but he who has the worse of it may appeal to the court of the lord, and if anyone touches him after the appeal, he is put to death. But action must be taken at once without any delay, and the injured one must lead him (who has offended) as a captive. They inflict capital punishment on no one unless he be taken in the act or confesses. When one is accused by a number of persons, they torture him so that he confesses. They punish homicide with capital punishment, and also cohabiting with a woman not one's own. By not one's own, I mean not his wife or bondwoman, for with one's slaves one may do as one pleases. They also punish with death grand larceny, but as for petty thefts, such as that of a sheep, so long as one has not repeatedly been taken in the act, they beat him cruelly, and if they administer an hundred blows they must use an hundred sticks: I speak of the case of those beaten under order of authority. In like manner false envoys, that is to say persons who pass themselves off as ambassadors but who are not, are put to death. Likewise sorcerers, of whom I shall however tell you more, for such they consider to be witches.

When anyone dies, they lament with loud wailing, then they are free, for they pay no taxes for the year. And if anyone is present at the death of an adult, he may not enter the dwelling even of Mangu Chan for the year. If it be a child who dies, he may not enter it for a month. Beside the tomb of the dead they always leave a tent if he be one of the nobles, that is of the family of Chingis, who was their first father and lord. Of him who is dead the burying place is not known. And always around these places where they bury their nobles there is a camp with men watching the tombs. I did not understand that they bury treasure with their dead. The Comans raise a great tumulus over the dead, and set up a statue to him, its face to the east, and holding a cup in its hand at the height of the navel. They make also pyramids to the rich, that is to say, little pointed structures, and in some places I saw great tiled covered towers, and in others stone houses, though there were no stones thereabout. Over a person recently dead I saw hung on long poles the skins of xvi horses, four facing each quarter of the world; and they had placed also *cosmos* for him to drink, and meat for him to eat, and for all that they said of him that he had been baptised. Farther east I saw other tombs in shape like great yards covered with big flat stones, some round, some square, and four high vertical stones at the corners facing the four quarters of the world. When anyone sickens he lies on his couch, and places a sign over his dwelling that there is a sick person therein, and that no one shall enter. So no one visits a sick person, save him who serves him. And when anyone from the great *ordu* is ill, they place guards all round the *ordu*, who permit no one to pass those bounds. For they fear lest an evil spirit or some wind should come with those who enter. They call, however, their priests, who are these same soothsayers.

*   *   *

Friar William's Last Audience with Mangu

On Pentecost day (31st May) Mangu Chan called me before him, and also the Tuin with whom I had discussed; but before I went in, the interpreter, master William's son, said to me that we should have to go back to our country, and that I must not raise any objection, for he understood that it was a settled matter. When I came before the Chan, I had to bend the knees, and so did the Tuin beside me, with his interpreter. Then (the Chan) said to me: "Tell me the truth, whether you said the other day, when I sent my secretaries to you, that I was a Tuin." I replied: "My lord, I did not say that; I will tell you what I said, if it pleases you." Then I repeated to him what I had said, and he replied: "I thought full well that you did not say it, for you should not have said it; but your interpreter translated badly." And he held out toward me the staff on which he leaned, saying: "Fear not." And I, smiling, said in an undertone: "If I had been afraid, I should not have come here." He asked the interpreter what I had said, and he repeated it to him. After that he began confiding to me his creed: "We Moal," he said, "believe that there is only one God, by whom we live and by whom we die, and for whom we have an upright heart." Then I said: "May it be so, for without His grace this cannot be." He asked what I had said; the interpreter told him. Then he added: "But as God gives us the different fingers of the hand, so he gives to men divers ways. God gives you the Scriptures, and you Christians keep them not. You do not find (in them, for example) that one should find fault with another, do you?" "No, my lord," I

said; "but I told you from the first that I did not want to wrangle with anyone." "I do not intend to say it," he said, "for you. Likewise you do not find that a man should depart from justice for money." "No, my lord," I said. "And truly I came not to these parts to obtain money; on the contrary I have refused what has been offered me." And there was a secretary present, who bore witness that I had refused an *iascot* and silken cloths. "I do not say it," he said, "for you. God gave you therefore the Scriptures, and you do not keep them; He gave us diviners, we do what they tell us, and we live in peace."

He drank four times, I believe, before he finished saying all this. And I was listening attentively for him to say something else of his creed, when he began talking of my return journey, saying: "You have stayed here a long while; I wish you to go back. You have said that you would not dare take my ambassadors with you; will you take my words, or my letters?" And from that time I never found the opportunity nor the time when I could show him the Catholic Faith. For no one can speak in his presence but so much as he wishes, unless he be an ambassador; for an ambassador can say whatever he chooses, and they always ask if he wishes to say something more. As for me, it was not allowed me to speak more; I had only to listen to him, and reply to his questions. So I answered him that he should make me understand his words, and have them put down in writing, for I would willingly take them as best I could. Then he asked me if I wanted gold or silver or costly clothing. I said: "We take no such things; but we have no travelling money, and without your assistance we cannot get out of your country." He said: "I will have you given all you require while in my possessions; do you want anything more?" I replied: "That suffices us." Then he asked: "How far do you wish to be taken?" I said: "Our power extends to the country of the king of Hermenia; if we were (escorted) that far, it would suffice me." He answered: "I will have you taken that far; after that look out for yourself." And he added: "There are two eyes in the head; but though they be two, they have but one sight, and when one turns its glance there goes the other. You came from Baatu, and so you must go back by way of him." When he had said this, I asked permission of him to speak. "Speak," he said. Then I said: "My lord, we are not men of war. We wish that those should have dominion over the world who rule it most justly, in accordance with the will of God. Our office is to teach men to live after the will of God. For that we have come here, and willingly would we remain here if it pleased you. Since it pleases you that we go back, that must then be. I will go back, and I will carry your letters as well as I can, as you have ordered. I would ask of your majesty that since I shall carry your letters, I may also come back to you with your consent; principally because you have poor slaves at Bolat, who are of our tongue, and who have no priest to teach them and their sons their religion, and willingly would I remain with them." Then he replied: "If your masters should send you back to me (you will be welcome)." I said: "My lord, I know not the will of my masters; but I have their permission to go wherever I wish, where it is needful to preach the word of God; and it seems to me that it is very needful in these parts; so whether he sends back envoys by us or not, if it pleases you I will come back."

Then he remained silent and sat for a long time as if thinking, and the interpreter told me to speak no more. So I waited anxiously for what he would reply. Finally he said: "You have a long way to go, comfort yourself with food, so that you may reach your country in good health." And he had me given to drink, and then I went out from before him, and after that I went not back again. If I had had the power to work by signs and wonders like Moses, perhaps he would have humbled himself.

*   *   *

REVIEW QUESTIONS

1. What valuable insights does William offer about Mongol culture?
2. According to William, how does the role of women in Mongol society compare with that of European women?
3. What ideas about religion determine the outlooks of Mangu and William?

IBN BATTUTA

FROM *The Travels*

Ibn Battuta (1304–c. 1377), from Tangier in Morocco, was an extraordinary traveler whose journeys took him as far as China and India. He wrote extensive accounts of his travels; here he describes Muslim Cairo at its zenith, before the Black Death.

From *The Travels of Ibn Battuta*, A.D. *1325–1354*, edited by H. A. R. Gibb (London: Hakluyt Society, 1958), pp. 41–53.

*   *   *

Commerce

I arrived at length at the city of Miṣr, mother of cities and seat of Pharaoh the tyrant, mistress of broad provinces and fruitful lands, boundless in multitude of buildings, peerless in beauty and splendour, the meeting-place of comer and goer, the stopping-place of feeble and strong. Therein is what you will of learned and simple, grave and gay, prudent and foolish, base and noble, of high estate and low estate, unknown and famous; she surges as the waves of the sea with her throngs of folk and can scarce contain them for all the capacity of her situation and sustaining power. Her youth is ever new in spite of length of days, and the star of her horoscope does not move from the mansion of fortune; her conquering capital (*al-Qāhira*) has subdued the nations, and her kings have grasped the forelocks of both Arab and non-Arab. She has as her peculiar possession the majestic Nile, which dispenses her district from the need of entreating the distillation [of the rain]; her territory is a month's journey for a hastening traveller, of generous soil, and extending a friendly welcome to strangers.

Ibn Juzayy remarks: Of Cairo the poet says—

No common town is Cairo, by thy life! Nay, she
Is heaven on earth for those with eyes to see;
Her youth those boys and maids with lustrous
    eyes,
Kawthar her Nile, her Rawḍa Paradise.

*   *   *

It is said that in Cairo there are twelve thousand water-carriers who transport water on camels, and thirty thousand hirers of mules and donkeys, and that on its Nile there are thirty-six thousand vessels belonging to the Sultan and his subjects, which sail upstream to Upper Egypt and downstream to Alexandria and Damietta, laden with goods and commodities of all kinds. On the bank of the Nile opposite Cairo is the place known as al-Rawḍa ['the Garden'], which is a pleasure park and promenade, containing many beautiful gardens. The people of Cairo are fond of pleasure and amusement. I once witnessed a fête there which was held for al-Malik al-Nāṣir's recovery from a fracture which he had suffered in his hand. All the merchants decorated their bazaars and had rich stuffs, ornaments, and silken fabrics hung up in their shops for several days.

The Mosque of ʿAmr b. al-ʿĀṣ, and the Colleges, Hospital, and Convents

The Mosque of ʿAmr b. al-ʿĀṣ is a noble mosque, highly venerated and widely celebrated. The Friday service is held in it, and the road runs right through it from east to west. To the west of it is the cell where the Imām Abū ʿAbdallāh al-Shāfiʿī used to teach. As for the madrasas in Cairo, they are too many for anyone to count; and as for the Māristān, which is "between the two castles" near the mausoleum of al-Malik al-Manṣūr Qalāʾūn, no description is adequate to its beauties. It is equipped with innumerable conveniences and medicaments, and its revenue is reported to be a thousand dinars a day. The convents too are numerous. The people there call them *khawāniq*, the singular being *khānqa*, and the amīrs in Cairo vie with one another in building them.

Each convent in Cairo is affected to the use of a separate congregation of poor brethren, most of whom are Persians, men of good education and adepts in the "way" of Sufism. Each has a shaikh and a warden, and the organization of their affairs is admirable. It is one of their customs in the matter of their food that the steward of the house comes in the morning to the faqīrs, each of whom then specifies what food he desires. When they assemble for meals, each person is given his bread and soup in a separate dish, none sharing with another. They eat twice a day. They receive winter clothing and summer clothing and a monthly allowance varying from twenty to thirty dirhams each. Every Thursday night they are given sugar cakes, soap to wash their clothes, the price of admission to the bathhouse, and oil to feed their lamps. These men are celibate; the married men have separate convents. Amongst the stipulations required of them are attendance at the five daily prayers, spending the night in the convent, and assembly in mass in a chapel within the convent. Another of their customs is that each one of them sits upon a prayer-carpet reserved for his exclusive use. When they pray the dawn prayer they recite the chapters of *Victory,* of *the Kingdom,* and of *ʿAmma.* After this copies of the Holy Qurʾān are brought, divided into sections, and each faqīr takes a section. After 'sealing' the Qurʾān and reciting a *dhikr,* the Qurʾān-readers give a recital according to the custom of the Easterners. They hold a similar service following the mid-afternoon prayer.

They have a regular ritual for the admission of newcomers. The applicant comes to the gate of the convent and takes up his stand there, with his waist girt, a prayer mat on his shoulder, the staff in his right hand and the jug in his left. The gate-keeper informs the steward of the con-vent that he is there. The steward then comes out to him and asks him from what country he has come, what convents he has stayed in on his way, and who was his spiritual director (*shaikh*). When he has ascertained the truth of his answers, he admits him into the convent, spreads his prayer-mat for him in a place befitting his station, and shows him the lavatory. The newcomer renews his ablutions and, returning to his mat, ungirds his waist, and prays two prostrations, then he clasps the hand of the shaikh and those of the others present, and takes his seat amongst them. Another custom of theirs is that on Fridays the servant collects all their prayer-mats and takes them to the mosque, where he spreads them in readiness for their coming. The faqīrs come out in a body, accompanied by their shaikh, proceed to the mosque, and pray each on his own mat. When they have finished the prayer they recite the Qur'ān according to their custom, and thereafter return in a body to the convent, accompanied by their shaikh.

The Qarāfa of Cairo and Its Sanctuaries

At [Old] Cairo too is [the cemetery called] al-Qarāfa, a place of vast repute for blessed power, whose special virtue is affirmed in a tradition related by al-Qurṭubī amongst others, for it is a part of the amount al-Muqaṭṭam, of which God has promised that it shall be one of the gardens of Paradise. These people build in the Qarāfa beautiful domed chapels and surround them by walls, so that they look like houses, and they construct chambers in them and hire the services of Qur'ān-readers, who recite night and day in beautiful voices. There are some of them who build a religious house or a madrasa by the side of the mausoleum. They go out every Thursday evening to spend

the night there with their children and womenfolk and make a circuit of the famous sanctuaries. They go out also to spend the night there on the night of mid-Sha'bān, and the market-people take out all kinds of eatables.

Among the celebrated sanctuaries is the imposing holy shrine where rests the head of al-Ḥusain b. 'Alī ＊ ＊ ＊. Beside it is a vast convent, of wonderful workmanship, on the doors of which there are silver rings, and plates also on them of the same metal. This shrine is paid its full meed of respect and veneration.

Amongst the monuments is the tomb of the Lady (*Sayyida*) Nafīsa, daughter of Zaid b. 'Alī b. al-Ḥusain b. 'Alī (upon them be peace). She was a woman answered in prayer and zealous in her devotions. This mausoleum is of elegant construction and resplendent brightness, and beside it is a convent which is visited by a great concourse during the days of the feast dedicated to her. Another is the tomb of the Imām Abū 'Abdallāh Muḥammad b. Idrīs al-Shāfi'ī, close by which is a large convent. The mausoleum enjoys an immense revenue and is surmounted by the famous dome, of admirable workmanship and marvellous construction, an exceedingly fine piece of architecture and exceptionally lofty, the diameter of which exceeds thirty cubits. The Qarāfa of Cairo contains also an incalculable number of graves of men eminent for learning and religion, and in it lie a goodly number of the Companions and of the leading figures of both earlier and later generations (God be pleased with them). ＊ ＊ ＊

＊　　＊　　＊

The Egyptian Nile

The Egyptian Nile surpasses all rivers of the earth in sweetness of taste, breadth of channel and magnitude of utility. Cities and villages succeed one another along its banks without interruption and have no equal in the inhabited world, nor is any river known whose basin is so intensively cultivated as that of the Nile. There is no river on earth but it which is called a sea; God Most High has said

"If thou fearest for him, cast him into the *yamm*," thus calling it *yamm*, which means "sea" (*bahr*). It is related in an unimpeachable Tradition that the Prophet of God (God's blessing and peace upon him) reached on the night of his Ascension the Lote-Tree of the Extremity, and lo, at its base were four streams, two outer streams and two inner streams. He asked Gabriel (peace be upon him) what streams these were, and he replied 'The two inner streams flow through Paradise, and as for the two outer streams they are the Nile and Euphrates'. It is also related in the Traditions of the Prophet that the Nile, Euphrates, Saiḥān and Jaiḥān are, each one, rivers of Paradise. The course of the Nile is from south to north, contrary to all the great rivers. One extraordinary thing about it is that it begins to rise in the extreme hot weather, at the time when rivers generally diminish and dry up, and begins to subside at the time when rivers increase in volume and overflow. The river of Sind [Indus] resembles it in this respect, and will be mentioned later. The first beginning of the Nile flood is in Ḥazīrān, that is June; and when its rise amounts to sixteen cubits, the land-tax due to the Sultan is payable in full. If it rises another cubit, there is plenty in that year, and complete well-being. But if it reaches eighteen cubits it does damage to the cultivated lands and causes an outbreak of plague. If it falls short of sixteen by a cubit, the Sultan's land-tax is diminished, and if it is two cubits short the people make solemn prayers for rain and there is the greatest misery.

The Nile is one of the five great rivers of the world, which are the Nile, Euphrates, Tigris, Saiḥūn [Syr Darya] and Jaiḥūn [Amu Darya]; five other rivers rival these, the river of Sind, which is called Panj Āb [i.e. Five Rivers], the river of Hindustān which is called the Kank [or Gang, i.e. Ganges]—to it the Hindus go on pilgrimage, and when they burn their dead they throw the ashes of them into it, and they say that it comes from Paradise—the river Jūn, also in Hindustān, the river Itil [Volga] in the Qifjaq [Kipchak] steppe, on the shore of which is the city of al-Sarā, and the river Sarū in the land of al-Khiṭā [Cathay], on the banks of which is the city of Khān-Bāliq [Pe-king],

whence it descends to the city of al-Khansā [Hang-chow] and from there to the city of al-Zaitūn [Zay-ton] in the land of China. We shall speak of all these in their proper places, if God will. Some distance below Cairo the Nile divides into three sections, and none of these streams can be crossed except by boat, winter or summer. The inhabitants of every township have canals led off the Nile; when it is in flood it fills these and they inundate the cultivated fields.

The Pyramids and Berbās

These are among the marvels which have been celebrated through the course of ages, and there is much talk and theorizing amongst men about them, their significance and the origin of their construction. They aver that all branches of knowledge which came into existence before the Deluge were derived from Hermes the Ancient, who lived in the remotest part of the Saʿīd [Upper Egypt]; he is also called by the name of Khanūkh [Enoch] that is Idrīs (on him be peace). It is said that he was the first to speculate on the movements of the spheres and the celestial bodies, and the first to construct temples and glorify God in them; and that he warned men of the coming of the Deluge, and fearing for the disappearance of knowledge and destruction of the practical arts built the pyramids and berbas, in which he depicted all the practical arts and their tools, and made diagrams of the sciences, in order that they might remain immortalized. It is said also that the seat of learning and kingship in Egypt was the city of Manūf [Memphis], which is one *barīd* from al-Fusṭāṭ. When Alexandria was built, the people removed to it, and it became the seat of learning and kingship until the coming of Islām, when ʿAmr b. al-ʿĀṣ (God be pleased with him) laid out the city of al-Fusṭāṭ, which remains the capital of Egypt to this day.

The pyramids is an edifice of solid hewn stone, of immense height and circular plan, broad at the base and narrow at the top, like the figure of a cone. They have no doorways and the manner of their erection is unknown. One of the tales related about them is that a certain king of Egypt before the

Flood dreamed a dream which filled him with terror and determined him to build these pyra-mids on the western side of the Nile, as a de-pository for the sciences and for the bodies of the kings. He asked the astrologers whether they would be opened in the future at any spot, and they told him that an opening would be made on the north side, and informed him of the exact spot where the opening would begin, and of the sum of money which would be expended in making the opening. He then ordered to be deposited in that place the sum of money which they had told him would be spent in breaching it. By pressing for-ward its construction, he completed it in sixty years, and wrote this inscrip-tion upon them: "We erected these pyramids in the space of sixty years; let him who will, pull them down in the space of six hundred years; yet to pull down is easier than to build." Now when the Caliph-ate devolved upon the Commander of the Faithful al-Ma'mūn, he proposed to pull them down, and although one of the Egyptian shaikhs advised him not to do so he persisted in his design and ordered that they should be breached from the north side. So they set about lighting fires up against them and then sprinkling them with vinegar and battering them with a mangonel, until the breach which is still to be seen in them was opened up. There they found, facing the hole, a sum of money which the Commander of the Faithful ordered to be weighted. He then calculated what had been spent on making the breach, and finding the two sums equal, was greatly astonished. At the same time they found the breadth of the wall to be twenty cubits.

The Sultan of Egypt

The Sultan of Egypt at the time of my entry was al-Malik al-Nāṣir Abu'l-Fatḥ Muḥammad, son of al-Malik al-Manṣūr Saif al-Dīn Qalā'ūn al-Ṣāliḥī. Qalā'ūn was known as al-Alfī ['the Thousand-man'] because al-Malik al-Ṣāliḥ bought him for a

thousand dinars of gold. He came originally from Qifjaq [Kipchak]. Al-Malik al-Nāṣir (God's mercy upon him) was a man of generous character and great virtues, and sufficient proof of his nobility is furnished by his devotion to the service of the two holy sanctuaries of Mecca and Madīna and the works of beneficence which he does every year to assist the pilgrims, in furnishing camels loaded with provisions and water for those without means and the helpless, and for carrying those who cannot keep up with the caravan or are too weak to walk on foot, both on the Egyptian pilgrim-road and on that from Damascus. He also built a great convent at Siryāquṣ, in the outskirts of Cairo. But the convent built by our lord the Commander of the Faithful and Defender of the Faith, the refuge of the poor and needy, Caliph of God upon earth, whose zeal in the Holy War transcends its obli-gations, Abū 'Inān (God be his strength and aid, and grant him the signal victory, and prosper him), in the out-skirts of his sublime residence, the luminous city (God guard it), has no equal to it in the inhabited world for perfection of architecture, beauty of construction, and plaster carving such as none of the Easterners can accomplish. We shall speak in due course of the schools, hospitals, and convents which he (God be his strength) has founded in his land (God guard it and preserve it by the prolonga-tion of his reign). ✴ ✴ ✴

✴   ✴   ✴

REVIEW QUESTIONS

1. Based on this description, how does old Cairo compare with a contemporary European city?
2. According to Ibn Battuta, what are the most important features of a city?
3. How much does the author seem to know about the pyramids and the Nile?

POPE BONIFACE VIII

Papal Bull *Unam Sanctam*

This official statement of papal policy, known as a "bull" from the lead seal (bulla) that carried the pope's insignia, was issued by Boniface VIII (r. 1294–1303) in 1302. Its short title comes from the opening Latin words, "one holy," which capture Boniface's central argument, made in response to a challenge by the French king Philip IV (r. 1285–1314). Philip disputed the papacy's claim to authority over the churches in his realm, and eventually went so far as to claim that the pope should be subordinate to his own superior, secular power.

From *Corpus Iuris Canonici*, vol. 2, edited by E. Friedberg (Leipzig, 1881).

That there is one holy, Catholic and apostolic church we are bound to believe and to hold, our faith urging us, and this we do firmly believe and simply confess; and that outside this church there is no salvation or remission of sins, as her spouse proclaims in the Canticles, "One is my dove, my perfect one. She is the only one of her mother, the chosen of her that bore her"; which represents one mystical body whose head is Christ, while the head of Christ is God. In this church there is one Lord, one faith, one baptism. At the time of the Flood there was one ark, symbolizing the one church. It was finished in one cubit and had one helmsman and captain, namely Noah, and we read that all things on earth outside of it were destroyed. This church we venerate and this alone, the Lord saying through his prophet, "Deliver, O God, my soul from the sword, my only one from the power of the dog." He prayed for the soul, that is himself, the head, and at the same time for the body, which he called the one church on account of the promised unity of faith, sacraments and charity of the church. This is that seamless garment of the Lord which was not cut but fell by lot. Therefore there is one body and one head of this one and only church, not two heads as though it were a monster, namely Christ and Christ's vicar, Peter and Peter's successor, for the Lord said to this Peter, "Feed my sheep." He said "My sheep" in general, not these or those, whence he is understood to have committed them all to Peter. Hence, if the Greeks or any others say that they were not committed to Peter and his successors, they necessarily admit that they are not of Christ's flock, for the Lord says in John that there is one sheepfold and one shepherd.

We are taught by the words of the Gospel that in this church and in her power there are two swords, a spiritual one and a temporal one. For when the apostles said "Here are two swords," meaning in the church since it was the apostles who spoke, the Lord did not reply that it was too many but enough. Certainly anyone who denies that the temporal sword is in the power of Peter has not paid heed to the words of the Lord when he said, "Put up thy sword into its sheath." Both then are in the power of the church, the material sword and the spiritual. But the one is exercised for the church, the other by the church, the one by the hand of the priest, the other by the hand of kings and soldiers, though at the will and suffrance of the priest. One sword ought to be under the other and the temporal authority subject to the spiritual power. For, while the apostle says, "There is no power but from God and those that are ordained of God," they would not be ordained unless one sword was under the other and, being inferior, was led by the other to the highest things. For, according to the blessed

Dionysius,[1] it is the law of divinity for the lowest to be led to the highest through intermediaries. In the order of the universe all things are not kept in order in the same fashion and immediately but the lowest are ordered by the intermediate and inferiors by superiors. But that the spiritual power excels any earthly one in dignity and nobility we ought the more openly to confess in proportion as spiritual things excel temporal ones. Moreover we clearly perceive this from the giving of tithes, from benediction and sanctification, from the acceptance of this power and from the very government of things. For, the truth bearing witness, the spiritual power has to institute the earthly power and to judge it if it has not been good. So is verified the prophecy of Jeremias concerning the church and the power of the church, "Lo, I have set thee this day over the nations and over kingdoms" etc.

Therefore, if the earthly power errs, it shall be judged by the spiritual power, if a lesser spiritual power errs it shall be judged by its superior, but if the supreme spiritual power errs it can be judged only by God not by man, as the apostle witnesses, "The spiritual man judgeth all things and he himself is judged of no man." Although this authority was given to a man and is exercised by a man it is not human but rather divine, being given to Peter at God's mouth, and confirmed to him and to his successors in him, the rock whom the Lord acknowledged when he said to Peter himself "Whatsoever thou shalt bind" etc. Whoever therefore resists this power so ordained by God resists the ordinance of God unless, like the Manicheans,[2] he imagines that there are two beginnings, which we judge to be false and heretical, as Moses witnesses, for not "in the beginnings" but "in the beginning" God created heaven and earth. Therefore we declare, state, define and pronounce that it is altogether necessary to salvation for every human creature to be subject to the Roman Pontiff.

REVIEW QUESTIONS

1. What does Pope Boniface VIII see as the right relation between the Church and secular power?
2. How do his arguments and evidence differ from those of his predecessor Gregory VII (pp. 254–261)?
3. What, in practice, did the last sentence of this bull mean? What are its implications?

---

[1] According to the Acts of the Apostles (17:34), a certain Athenian citizen called Dionysius the Areopagite was converted by the apostle Paul. Centuries later, a body of mystical writings was attributed to him, and he was also misidentified as St. Denis, the first bishop of Paris (d. c. 251 C.E.).

[2] Followers of the third-century visionary Mani, Manicheans were condemned as heretics by the Church. They espoused a dualistic view of the world, in which the good power of God is opposed by the equally powerful forces of evil.

DANTE ALIGHIERI

FROM *The Divine Comedy*

Dante Alighieri (1265–1321), a Florentine poet and part-time politician who was exiled from his native city for his views on the political role of the papacy, completed his masterpiece, The Divine Comedy, *toward the end of his life. Dante's earlier poetry centered on Beatrice, the great love of his life, and her early death changed the direction of his artistic development. Praised as divine after his death, the* Comedy, *beginning sadly in Hell and ending happily in Heaven, consists of one hundred can-*

tos in a then-new poetic style. This complex poem is a window on the values of its age, because Dante allows himself to comment on many aspects of history as he tours Hell, Purgatory, and Paradise, seeing many famous people of the past and of his own present. Canto V describes the fate of the carnal in Hell, as seen by Dante and his guide and master, the Roman poet Virgil.

From *The Divine Comedy*, by Dante Alighieri, translated by John Ciardi (New York: Norton, 1954), pp. 25–29.

*   *   *

Canto V

CIRCLE TWO
THE CARNAL

The Poets leave Limbo and enter the Second Circle. Here begin the torments of Hell proper, and here, blocking the way, sits Minos, the dread and semi-bestial judge of the damned who assigns to each soul its eternal torment. He orders the Poets back; but Virgil silences him as he earlier silenced Charon, and the Poets move on.

They find themselves on a dark ledge swept by a great whirlwind, which spins within it the souls of the Carnal, those who betrayed reason to their appetites. Their sin was to abandon themselves to the tempest of their passions: so they are swept forever in the tempest of Hell, forever denied the light of reason and of God. Virgil identifies many among them. Semiramis is there, and Dido, Cleopatra, Helen, Achilles, Paris, and Tristan. Dante sees Paolo and Francesca swept together, and in the name of love he calls to them to tell their sad story. They pause from their eternal flight to come to him, and Francesca tells their history while Paolo weeps at her side. Dante is so stricken by compassion at their tragic tale that he swoons once again.

So we went down to the second ledge alone;
a smaller circle[1] of so much greater pain
the voice of the damned rose in a bestial moan.

There Minos[2] sits, grinning, grotesque, and hale.
He examines each lost soul as it arrives
and delivers his verdict with his coiling tail.

That is to say, when the ill-fated soul
appears before him it confesses all,[3]
and that grim sorter of the dark and foul

decides which place in Hell shall be its end,
then wraps his twitching tail about himself
one coil for each degree it must descend.

The soul descends and others take its place:
each crowds in its turn to judgment, each
     confesses,
each hears its doom and falls away through
     space.

"O you who come into this camp of woe,"

---

[1] The pit of Hell tapers like a funnel. The circles of ledges accordingly grow smaller as they descend.

[2] Like all the monsters Dante assigns to the various offices of Hell, Minos is drawn from classical mythology. He was the son of Europa and of Zeus, who descended to her in the form of a bull. Minos became a mythological king of Crete, so famous for his wisdom and justice that after death his soul was made judge of the dead. Virgil presents him fulfilling the same office at Aeneas' descent to the underworld. Dante, however, transforms him into an irate and hideous monster with a tail. The transformation may have been suggested by the form Zeus assumed for the rape of Europa—the monster is certainly bullish enough here—but the obvious purpose of the brutalization is to present a figure symbolic of the guilty conscience of the wretches who come before it to make their confessions. Dante freely reshapes his materials to his own purposes.

[3] Just as the souls appeared eager to cross Acheron, so they are eager to confess even while they dread. Dante is once again making the point that sinners elect their Hell by an act of their own will.

cried Minos when he saw me turn away
without awaiting his judgment, "watch where
   you go

once you have entered here, and to whom you
   turn!
Do not be misled by that wide and easy passage!"
And my Guide to him: "That is not your concern;

it is his fate to enter every door.
This has been willed where what is willed must be,
and is not yours to question. Say no more."

Now the choir of anguish, like a wound,
strikes through the tortured air. Now I have come
to Hell's full lamentation,[4] sound beyond sound.

I came to a place stripped bare of every light
and roaring on the naked dark like seas
wracked by a war of winds. Their hellish flight

of storm and counterstorm through time foregone,
sweeps the souls of the damned before its charge.
Whirling and battering it drives them on,

and when they pass the ruined gap of Hell[5]
through which we had come, their shrieks begin
   anew.
There they blaspheme the power of God eternal.

And this, I learned, was the never ending flight
of those who sinned in the flesh, the carnal and
   lusty
who betrayed reason to their appetite.

As the wings of wintering starlings bear them on
in their great wheeling flights, just so the blast
wherries these evil souls through time foregone.

Here, there, up, down, they whirl and, whirling,
   strain
with never a hope of hope to comfort them,
not of release, but even of less pain.

As cranes go over sounding their harsh cry,
leaving the long streak of their flight in air,
so come these spirits, wailing as they fly.

And watching their shadows lashed by wind,
   I cried:
"Master, what souls are these the very air
lashes with its black whips from side to side?"

"The first of these whose history you would know,"
he answered me, "was Empress of many tongues.[6]
Mad sensuality corrupted her so

that to hide the guilt of her debauchery
she licensed all depravity alike,
and lust and law were one in her decree.

She is Semiramis of whom the tale is told
how she married Ninus and succeeded him
to the throne of that wide land the Sultans hold.

The other is Dido;[7] faithless to the ashes
of Sichaeus, she killed herself for love.

---

[4] It is with the second circle that the real tortures of Hell begin.

[5] At the time of the Harrowing of Hell a great earthquake shook the underworld shattering rocks and cliffs. Ruins resulting from the same shock are noted in Canto XII, 34, and Canto XXI, 112 ff. At the beginning of Canto XXIV, the Poets leave the *bolgia* of the Hypocrites by climbing the ruined slabs of a bridge that was shattered by this earthquake.

   Here begin the punishments for the various sins of incontinence (the sins of the She-Wolf). Those are punished who sinned by excess of sexual passion. Since this is the most natural sin and the sin most nearly associated with love, its punishment is the lightest of all to be found in Hell proper. The Carnal are whirled and buffeted endlessly through the murky air (symbolic of the beclouding of their reason by passion) by a great gale (symbolic of their lust).

[6] Semiramis, a legendary queen of Assyria who assumed full power at the death of her husband, Ninus.

[7] Queen and founder of Carthage. She had vowed to remain faithful to her husband, Sichaeus, but she fell in love with Aeneas. When Aeneas abandoned her she stabbed herself on a funeral pyre she had had prepared. According to Dante's own system of punishments, she should be in the Seventh Circle with the suicides. The only clue Dante gives to the tempering of her punish-

The next whom the eternal tempest lashes
is sense-drugged Cleopatra. See Helen there,
from whom such ill arose. And great Achilles,[8]
who fought at last with love in the house of prayer.

And Paris. And Tristan." As they whirled above
he pointed out more than a thousand shades
of those torn from the mortal life by love.

I stood there while my Teacher one by one
named the great knights and ladies of dim time;
and I was swept by pity and confusion.

At last I spoke: "Poet, I should be glad
to speak a word with those two swept together[9]
so lightly on the wind and still so sad."

And he to me: "Watch them. When next they
    pass,
call to them in the name of love that drives

---

ment is his statement that "she killed herself for love."
Dante always seems readiest to forgive in that name.
[8] Achilles is placed among this company because of his passion for Polyxena, the daughter of Priam. For love of her,
he agreed to desert the Greeks and to join the Trojans, but
when he went to the temple for the wedding (according to
the legend Dante has followed), he was killed by Paris.
[9] Paolo and Francesca (PAH-oe-loe: Frahn-CHAY-ska).
Dante's treatment of these two lovers is certainly the
tenderest and most sympathetic accorded any of the
sinners in Hell, and legends immediately began to
grow about this pair.

The facts are these. In 1275 Giovanni Malatesta
(Djoe-VAH-nee Mahl-ah-TEH-stah) of Rimini, called
Giovanni the Lame, a somewhat deformed but brave
and powerful warrior, made a political marriage with
Francesca, daughter of Guido da Polenta of Ravenna.
Francesca came to Rimini and there an amour grew
between her and Giovanni's younger brother Paolo.
Despite the fact that Paolo had married in 1269 and had
become the father of two daughters by 1275, his affair
with Francesca continued for many years. It was sometime between 1283 and 1286 that Giovanni surprised
them in Francesca's bedroom and killed both of them.

Around these facts the legend has grown that Paolo
was sent by Giovanni as his proxy to the marriage, that
Francesca thought he was her real bridegroom and
accordingly gave him her heart irrevocably at first
sight. The legend obviously increases the pathos, but
nothing in Dante gives it support.

and damns them here. In that name they will
    pause."

Thus, as soon as the wind in its wild course
brought them around, I called: "O wearied souls!
if none forbid it, pause and speak to us."

As mating doves that love calls to their nest
glide through the air with motionless raised
    wings,
borne by the sweet desire that fills each breast—

Just so those spirits turned on the torn sky
from the band where Dido whirls across the air;
such was the power of pity in my cry.

"O living creature, gracious, kind, and good,
going this pilgrimage through the sick night,
visiting us who stained the earth with blood,

were the King of Time our friend, we would pray
    His peace
on you who have pitied us. As long as the wind
will let us pause, ask of us what you please.

The town where I was born lies by the shore
where the Po descends into its ocean rest
with its attendant streams in one long murmur.

Love, which in gentlest hearts will soonest bloom
seized my lover with passion for that sweet body
from which I was torn unshriven to my doom.

Love, which permits no loved one not to love,
took me so strongly with delight in him
that we are one in Hell, as we were above.[10]
Love led us to one death. In the depths of Hell

---

[10] At many points of *The Inferno* Dante makes clear the
principle that the souls of the damned are locked so
blindly into their own guilt that none can feel sympa-
thy for another, or find any pleasure in the presence of
another. The temptation of many readers is to interpret this line romantically: i.e., that the love of Paolo
and Francesca survives Hell itself. The more Dantean
interpretation, however, is that they add to one another's anguish (a) as mutual reminders of their sin, and

Caïna waits for him[11] who took our lives."
This was the piteous tale they stopped to tell.

And when I had heard those world-offended lovers
I bowed my head. At last the Poet spoke:
"What painful thoughts are these your lowered
    brow covers?"

When at length I answered, I began: "Alas!
What sweetest thoughts, what green and young
    desire
led these two lovers to this sorry pass."

Then turning to those spirits once again,
I said: "Francesca, what you suffer here
melts me to tears of pity and of pain.

But tell me: in the time of your sweet sighs
by what appearances found love the way
to lure you to his perilous paradise?"

And she: "The double grief of a lost bliss
is to recall its happy hour in pain.
Your Guide and Teacher knows the truth of this.

But if there is indeed a soul in Hell
to ask of the beginning of our love
out of his pity, I will weep and tell:

On a day for dalliance we read the rhyme
of Lancelot,[12] how love had mastered him.
We were alone with innocence and dim time.[13]

Pause after pause that high old story drew
our eyes together while we blushed and paled;
but it was one soft passage overthrew

our caution and our hearts. For when we read
how her fond smile was kissed by such a lover,
he who is one with me alive and dead

breathed on my lips the tremor of his kiss.
That book, and he who wrote it, was a pander.[14]
That day we read no further." As she said this,

the other spirit, who stood by her, wept
so piteously, I felt my senses reel
and faint away with anguish. I was swept

by such a swoon as death is, and I fell,
as a corpse might fall, to the dead floor of Hell.

*   *   *

REVIEW QUESTIONS

1. How does Dante use this poetic format to critique the culture and values of his own time?
2. Why does the poet describe himself as being so affected by the story of Paolo and Francesca? Why would he describe the reading of literature as a dangerous thing—especially in a work such as this?
3. In most of the other rings of Hell, Dante encounters few women; but in this circle, there are many. What does this suggest about Dante's own attitude toward women, or that of his contemporaries?

(b) as insubstantial shades of the bodies for which they once felt such great passion.

[11] Giovanni Malatesta was still alive at the writing. His fate is already decided, however, and upon his death, his soul will fall to Caïna, the first ring of the last circle, where lie those who performed acts of treachery against their kin.

[12] The story exists in many forms. The details Dante makes use of are from an Old French version.

[13] The original simply reads "We were alone, suspecting nothing." "Dim time" is rhyme-forced, but not wholly outside the legitimate implications of the original, I hope. The old courtly romance may well be thought of as happening in the dim ancient days. The apology, of

course, comes after the fact: one does the possible, then argues for justification, and there probably is none.

[14] *Galeotto,* the Italian word for "pander," is also the Italian rendering of the name of Gallehault, who in the French Romance Dante refers to here, urged Lancelot and Guinevere on to love.

THE TRIUMPH OF DEATH (C. 1340)   FRANCESCO TRAINI (?)

This painting is part of a series of frescos decorating the Camposanto, the famous cemetery of Pisa. The frescos are by local tradition attributed to the Pisan painter Francesco Traini. This fresco was probably painted just before the arrival of the bubonic plague in Pisa in 1348, and it incorporates images of death formed in the years of famine and during the epidemics of the early fourteenth century. What overall impression of death does this fresco convey? In particular, find the image of Death and consider her role in the fresco. One of the many striking parts of this fresco is the detail in which the three living riders confront the three corpses. What can we learn about the mentality of a people who commissioned this fresco to decorate a cemetery?

GIOVANNI BOCCACCIO

FROM *The Decameron*

Giovanni Boccaccio (1313–1374) was a native of the city of Florence and a survivor of the Black Death. Around 1351, in the immediate aftermath of the plague, he put together a compilation of one hundred comic tales told in the Florentine dialect and framed them as the amusements devised by a party of ten young people—seven men and three women—who have escaped from the plague-ridden city for a period of ten days. (Hence the title of the collection, which means "ten days.") The following is an excerpt from the preface to this book, in which Boccaccio describes the effects of the plague on the people of Florence.

From *The Decameron: A New Translation*, selected, translated, and edited by Mark Musa and Peter Bondanella (New York: Norton, 1977), pp. 3–10.

FROM Introduction

Whenever, gracious ladies, I consider how compassionate you are by nature, I realize that in your judgment the present work will seem to have had a serious and painful beginning, for it recalls in its opening the unhappy memory of the deadly plague just passed, dreadful and pitiful to all those who saw or heard about it. But I do not wish this to frighten you away from reading any further, as if you were going to pass all of your time sighing and weeping as you read. This horrible beginning will be like the ascent of a steep and rough mountainside, beyond which there lies a most beautiful and delightful plain, which seems more pleasurable to the climbers in proportion to the difficulty of their climb and their descent. And just as pain is the extreme limit of pleasure, so misery ends by unanticipated happiness. This brief pain (I say brief since it contains few words) will be quickly followed by the sweetness and the delight, which I promised you before, and which, had I not promised, might not be expected from such a beginning. To tell the truth, if I could have conveniently led you by any other way than this, which I know is a bitter one, I would have gladly done so; but since it is otherwise impossible to demonstrate how the stories you are

about to read came to be told, I am almost obliged by necessity to write about it this way.

Let me say, then, that thirteen hundred and forty-eight years had already passed after the fruitful Incarnation of the Son of God when into the distinguished city of Florence, more noble than any other Italian city, there came the deadly pestilence. It started in the East, either because of the influence of heavenly bodies or because of God's just wrath as a punishment to mortals for our wicked deeds, and it killed an infinite number of people. Without pause it spread from one place and it stretched its miserable length over the West. And against this pestilence no human wisdom or foresight was of any avail; quantities of filth were removed from the city by officials charged with this task; the entry of any sick person into the city was prohibited; and many directives were issued concerning the maintenance of good health. Nor were the humble supplications, rendered not once but many times to God by pious people, through public processions or by other means, efficacious; for almost at the beginning of springtime of the year in question the plague began to show its sorrowful effects in an extraordinary manner. It did not act as it had done in the East, where bleeding from the nose was a manifest sign of inevitable death, but it began in both men and women with certain swellings either in the groin or under the armpits, some of which grew to the size of a normal apple and others to the size of an egg (more or less), and the people called them *gavoccioli*. And from the two parts of the body already mentioned, within a brief space of time, the said deadly *gavoccioli* began to spread indiscriminately over every part of the body; and after this, the symptoms of the illness changed to black or livid spots appearing on the arms and thighs, and on every part of the body, some large ones and sometimes many little ones scattered all around. And just as the *gavoccioli* were originally, and still are, a very certain indication of impending death, in like manner these spots came to mean the same thing for whoever had them. Neither a doctor's advice nor the strength of medicine could do anything to cure this illness; on the contrary, either the nature of the illness was such that it afforded no cure, or else the doctors were so ignorant that they did not recognize its cause and, as a result, could not prescribe the proper remedy (in fact, the number of doctors, other than the well-trained, was increased by a large number of men and women who had never had any medical training); at any rate, few of the sick were ever cured, and almost all died after the third day of the appearance of the previously described symptoms (some sooner, others later), and most of them died without fever or any other side effects.

This pestilence was so powerful that it was communicated to the healthy by contact with the sick, the way a fire close to dry or oily things will set them aflame. And the evil of the plague went even further: not only did talking to or being around the sick bring infection and a common death, but also touching the clothes of the sick or anything touched or used by them seemed to communicate this very disease to the person involved. What I am about to say is incredible to hear, and if I and others had not witnessed it with our own eyes, I should not dare believe it (let alone write about it), no matter how trustworthy a person I might have heard it from. Let me say, then, that the power of the plague described here was of such virulence in spreading from one person to another

that not only did it pass from one man to the next, but, what's more, it was often transmitted from the garments of a sick or dead man to animals that not only became contaminated by the disease, but also died within a brief period of time. My own eyes, as I said earlier, witnessed such a thing one day: when the rags of a poor man who died of this disease were thrown into the public street, two pigs came upon them, as they are wont to do, and first with their snouts and then with their teeth they took the rags and shook them around; and within a short time, after a number of convulsions, both pigs fell dead upon the ill-fated rags, as if they had been poisoned. From these and many similar or worse occurrences there came about such fear and such fantastic notions among those who remained alive that almost all of them took a very cruel attitude in the matter; that is, they completely avoided the sick and their possessions; and in so doing, each one believed that he was protecting his good health.

There were some people who thought that living moderately and avoiding all superfluity might help a great deal in resisting this disease, and so, they gathered in small groups and lived entirely apart from everyone else. They shut themselves up in those houses where there were no sick people and where one could live well by eating the most delicate of foods and drinking the finest of wines (doing so always in moderation), allowing no one to speak about or listen to anything said about the sick and the dead outside; these people lived, spending their time with music and other pleasures that they could arrange. Others thought the opposite: they believed that drinking too much, enjoying life, going about singing and celebrating, satisfying in every way the appetites as best one could, laughing, and making light of everything that happened was the best medicine for such a disease; so they practiced to the fullest what they believed by going from one tavern to another all day and night, drinking to excess; and often they would make merry in private homes, doing everything that pleased or amused them the most. This they were able to do easily, for everyone felt he was doomed to die and, as a result, abandoned his property, so that most of the houses had become common property, and any stranger who came upon them used them as if he were their rightful owner. In addition to this bestial behavior, they always managed to avoid the sick as best they could. And in this great affliction and misery of our city the revered authority of the laws, both divine and human, had fallen and almost completely disappeared, for, like other men, the ministers and executors of the laws were either dead or sick or so short of help that it was impossible for them to fulfill their duties; as a result, everybody was free to do as he pleased.

Many others adopted a middle course between the two attitudes just described: neither did they restrict their food or drink so much as the first group nor did they fall into such dissoluteness and drunkenness as the second; rather, they satisfied their appetites to a moderate degree. They did not shut themselves up, but went around carrying in their hands flowers, or sweet-smelling herbs, or various kinds of spices; and often they would put these things to their noses, believing that such smells were a wonderful means of purifying the brain, for all the air seemed infected with the stench of dead bodies, sickness, and medicines.

Others were of a crueler opinion (though it was, perhaps, a safer one): they maintained that there was no better medicine against the plague than to flee from it; and convinced of this reasoning, not caring about anything but themselves, men and women in great numbers abandoned their city, their houses, their farms, their relatives, and their possessions and sought other places, and they went at least as far away as the Florentine countryside—as if the wrath of God could not pursue them with this pestilence wherever they went but would only strike those it found within the walls of the city! Or perhaps they thought that Florence's last hour had come and that no one in the city would remain alive.

And not all those who adopted these diverse opinions died, nor did they all escape with their lives; on the contrary, many of those who thought this way were falling sick everywhere, and since they had given, when they were healthy, the bad example of avoiding the sick, they, in turn, were abandoned and left to languish away without care. The fact was that one citizen avoided another, that

almost no one cared for his neighbor, and that relatives rarely or hardly ever visited each other—they stayed far apart. This disaster had struck such fear into the hearts of men and women that brother abandoned brother, uncle abandoned nephew, sister left brother, and very often wife abandoned husband, and—even worse, almost unbelievable—fathers and mothers neglected to tend and care for their children, as if they were not their own.

Thus, for the countless multitude of men and women who fell sick, there remained no support except the charity of their friends (and these were few) or the avarice of servants, who worked for inflated salaries and indecent periods of time and who, in spite of this, were few and far between; and those few were men or women of little wit (most of them not trained for such service) who did little else but hand different things to the sick when requested to do so or watch over them while they died, and in this service, they very often lost their own lives and their profits. And since the sick were abandoned by their neighbors, their parents, and their friends and there was a scarcity of servants, a practice that was almost unheard of before spread through the city: when a woman fell sick, no matter how attractive or beautiful or noble she might be, she did not mind having a manservant (whoever he might be, no matter how young or old he was), and she had no shame whatsoever in revealing any part of her body to him—the way she would have done to a woman—when the necessity of her sickness required her to do so. This practice was, perhaps, in the days that followed the pestilence, the cause of looser morals in the women who survived the plague. And so, many people died who, by chance, might have survived if they had been attended to. Between the lack of competent attendants, which the sick were unable to obtain, and the violence of the pestilence, there were so many, many people who died in the city both day and night that it was incredible just to hear this described, not to mention seeing it! Therefore, out of sheer necessity, there arose among those who remained alive customs which were contrary to the established practices of the time.

It was the custom, as it is again today, for the women, relatives, and neighbors to gather together in the house of a dead person and there to mourn with the women who had been dearest to him; on the other hand, in front of the deceased's home, his male relatives would gather together with his male neighbors and other citizens, and the clergy also came (many of them, or sometimes just a few) depending upon the social class of the dead man. Then, upon the shoulders of his equals, he was carried to the church chosen by him before death with the funeral pomp of candles and chants. With the fury of the pestilence increasing, this custom, for the most part, died out and other practices took its place. And so, not only did people die without having a number of women around them, but there were many who passed away without even having a single witness present, and very few were granted the piteous laments and bitter tears of their relatives; on the contrary, most relatives were somewhere else, laughing, joking, and amusing themselves; even the women learned this practice too well, having put aside, for the most part, their womanly compassion for their own safety. Very few were the dead whose bodies were accompanied to the church by more than ten or twelve of their neighbors, and these dead bodies were not even carried on the shoulders of honored and reputable citizens but rather by gravediggers from the lower classes that were called *becchini*. Working for pay, they would pick up the bier and hurry it off, not to the church the dead man had chosen before his death but, in most cases, to the church closest by, accompanied by four or six churchmen with just a few candles, and often none at all. With the help of these *becchini*, the churchmen would place the body as fast as they could in whatever unoccupied grave they could find, without going to the trouble of saying long or solemn burial services.

The plight of the lower class and, perhaps, a large part of the middle class, was even more pathetic: most of them stayed in their homes or neighborhoods either because of their poverty or their hopes for remaining safe, and every day they fell sick by the thousands; and not having servants or attendants of any kind, they almost always died. Many ended their lives in the public streets, during the day or at night, while many others who died in their homes were discovered dead by their neighbors only by the smell of their decomposing bodies. The city was full of corpses. The dead were usually given the same treatment by their neighbors, who were moved more by the fear that the decomposing corpses would contaminate them than by any charity they might have felt towards the deceased: either by themselves or with the assistance of porters (when they were available), they would drag the corpse out of the home and place it in front of the doorstep where, usually in the morning, quantities of dead bodies could be seen by any passerby; then, they were laid out on biers, or for lack of biers, on a plank. Nor did a bier carry only one corpse; sometimes it was used for two or three at a time. More than once, a single bier would serve for a wife and husband, two or three brothers, a father or son, or other relatives, all at the same time. And countless times it happened that two priests, each with a cross, would be on their way to bury someone, when porters carrying three or four biers would just follow along behind them; and where these priests thought they had just one dead man to bury, they had, in fact, six or eight and sometimes more. Moreover, the dead were honored with no tears or candles or funeral mourners but worse: things had reached such a point that the people who died were cared for as we care for goats today. Thus, it became quite obvious that what the wise had not been able to endure with patience through the few calamities of everyday life now became a matter of indifference to even the most simple-minded people as a result of this colossal misfortune.

So many corpses would arrive in front of a church every day and at every hour that the amount of holy ground for burials was certainly insufficient for the ancient custom of giving each body its individual place; when all the graves were full, huge trenches were dug in all of the cemeteries of the churches and into them the new arrivals were dumped by the hundreds; and they were packed in there with dirt, one on top of another, like a ship's cargo, until the trench was filled.

But instead of going over every detail of the past miseries which befell our city, let me say that the same unfriendly weather there did not, because of this, spare the surrounding countryside any evil; there, not to speak of the towns which, on a smaller scale, were like the city, in the scattered villages and in the fields the poor, miserable peasants and their families, without any medical assistance or aid of servants, died on the roads and in their fields and in their homes, as many by day as by night, and they died not like men but more like wild animals. Because of this they, like the city dwellers, became careless in their ways and did not look after their possessions or their businesses; furthermore, when they saw that death was upon them, completely neglecting the future fruits of their past labors, their livestock, their property, they did their best to consume what they already had at hand. So, it came about that oxen, donkeys, sheep, pigs, chickens and even dogs, man's most faithful companion, were driven from their homes into the fields, where the wheat was left not only unharvested but also unreaped, and they were allowed to roam where they wished; and many of these animals, almost as if they were rational beings, returned at night to their homes without any guidance from a shepherd, satiated after a good day's meal.

Leaving the countryside and returning to the city, what more can one say, except that so great was the cruelty of Heaven, and, perhaps, also that of man, that from March to July of the same year, between the fury of the pestiferous sickness and the fact that many of the sick were badly treated or abandoned in need because of the fear that the healthy had, more than one hundred thousand human beings are believed to have lost their lives for certain inside the walls of the city of Florence whereas, before the deadly plague, one would not have estimated that there were actually that many people dwelling in that city.

Oh, how many great palaces, beautiful homes, and noble dwellings, once filled with families, gentlemen, and ladies, were now emptied, down to the last servant! How many notable families, vast domains, and famous fortunes remained without legitimate heir! How many valiant men, beautiful women, and charming young men, who might have been pronounced very healthy by Galen, Hippocrates, and Aesculapius (not to mention lesser physicians), dined in the morning with their relatives, companions, and friends and then in the evening took supper with their ancestors in the other world!

Reflecting upon so many miseries makes me very sad; therefore, since I wish to pass over as many as I can, let me say that as our city was in this condition, almost emptied of inhabitants, it happened (as I heard it later from a person worthy of trust) that one Tuesday morning in the venerable church of Santa Maria Novella there was hardly any congregation there to hear the holy services ∗ ∗ ∗

∗   ∗   ∗

REVIEW QUESTIONS

1. According to Boccaccio, how did his neighbors explain and respond to the devastations of the Black Death?
2. What does Boccaccio say about the social effects of the plague? How does he describe its effects on the behavior of women, specifically?
3. Given that this account is the preface to a book of mostly bawdy or comic tales, can we take this testimony at face value? Do you think that Boccaccio is a reliable historical source? Why or why not?

11 ∽ REBIRTH AND UNREST, 1350–1453

The fourteenth and fifteenth centuries proved to be a crucial turning point for Europe, both internally and externally—a true period of "rebirth and unrest." The Black Death pandemic that swept the continent at mid-century resulted in population losses that had not occurred in a millennium. The immediate results for many were lower costs of living and higher wages. More striking than the loss of life, perhaps, altered social structures and relations created new opportunities in the forms of expanded trade and prosperity, and posed new challenges to traditional authority. Revolts erupted across Europe. Established governments and groups faced unprecedented questions about the legitimacy of their rule. The rising challengers, especially in the Low Countries and northern Italy, used their newly acquired wealth and confidence not only to challenge for political power but also to patronize new forms of cultural expression. The fourteenth century experienced a new realism in the arts and a new inspiration to scholarship. The first expressions of classicism, that is, a new appreciation for and attention to the authors of classical antiquity, emerged at this point in time and expanded eventually into the cultural program that became known as humanism.

The slow, painful centralization of large territorial states that becomes visible in the fourteenth century stands in sharp contrast to the decentralization fostered by the newly rich. The conflicts among and against these new states increased the general unrest of the period. That unrest had spiritual elements as well. The rise of new, prosperous, and powerful social groups, bringing with them new ambitions, priorities, and values, led to a fundamental revival in religious piety. Individuals, such as Catherine of Siena, and groups, such as the beguines, offer evidence of a widespread yearning for spiritual meaning and fulfillment. Proto-reformers, such as John Wyclif and Jan Hus, levied criticism on an established Christian Church that they believed had become separated from the true inspiration and imperative of the Gospels.

All of these developments, economic and social, cultural and political, received further impetus from what social scientists would call an exogenous shock. The rise of a new and aggressive power in Central Asia and the Middle East, the empire of the Ottoman Turks, unleashed a flood of refugees who brought the remnants of ancient Greek culture into the West, closed established trade routes to the bazaars of the East, and inspired European states with horror.

By the end of the fourteenth century, forces worked upon Europe that would inspire scholars to speak of an end to the Middle Ages and the beginnings of the modern world. The Renaissance, or "rebirth," grew out of all these developments. It began as an Italian phenomenon, occurring between c. 1350 and 1520, that spread to the rest of Europe over the course of the 1500s and early 1600s, although we focus on the early Renaissance in this chapter. Its principal manifestations were the revival of classicism and naturalism in arts and literature, the rise of the modern dynastic state as the dominant political structure, and an economic crisis fueled by industrial change and economic contraction. The following selections capture something of these major developments that represent both continuity and change.

GEOFFREY CHAUCER

FROM *The Canterbury Tales: "The Pardoner's Tale"*

Geoffrey Chaucer (c. 1340–1400) was an English civil servant and poet who, like Boccaccio, survived the Black Death. He never finished his most famous work, The Canterbury Tales, *framed (like Boccaccio's* Decameron*) as a series of stories, in this case told by a diverse group of pilgrims making their way to the shrine of Saint Thomas Becket at Canterbury. One of these pilgrims is a "pardoner," a contemporary slang term for a priest or cleric who makes his living selling indulgences ("pardons") for sins. Here, the Pardoner introduces himself and his cynical attitude toward the people he dupes, then launches into a story that reveals even more about his character. Although Chaucer's language (known as Middle English) may seem difficult at first, you will find that it is quite easy to understand if you read it aloud.*

From *The Canterbury Tales: Nine Tales and the General Prologue: A Norton Critical Edition,* by Geoffrey Chaucer, edited by V. A. Kolve and Glending Olson, (New York: Norton, 1989), pp. 192–207.

The Prologue

"Lordinges," quod he, "in chirches whan I preche,
I peyne me° to han an hauteyn° speche,   *take pains / elevated*
And ringe it out as round as gooth° a belle,   *sounds*
For I can al by rote° that I telle.   *know all by memory*
My theme° is alwey oon,° and evere was—   *text / always the same*
Radix malorum est Cupiditas.[1]
     First I pronounce° whennes° that I come,   *proclaim / whence, from where*
And thanne my bulles[2] shewe I, alle and somme.°   *one and all*
Oure lige lordes seel[3] on my patente,°   *license*
That shewe I first, my body° to warente,°   *person / authorize*
That no man be so bold, ne preest ne clerk,°   *neither priest nor scholar*
Me to destourbe of Cristes holy werk;
And after that thanne telle I forth my tales.
Bulles of popes and of cardinales,
Of patriarkes,° and bishoppes I shewe,   *heads of churches*
And in Latyn I speke a wordes fewe
To saffron with my predicacioun,[4]
And for to stire° hem to devocioun.   *stir*
Thanne shewe I forth my longe cristal stones,°   *glass cases*
Y-crammed ful of cloutes° and of bones—   *rags*
Reliks been they, as wenen they echoon.[5]
Thanne have I in latoun[6] a sholder-boon
Which that was of an holy Jewes shepe.
'Goode men,' seye I, 'tak of my wordes kepe:°   *heed*
If that this boon be wasshe° in any welle,   *washed, dunked*
If cow, or calf, or sheep, or oxe swelle,°   *swell (up)*
That any worm hath ete, or worm y-stonge,[7]
Tak water of that welle, and wash his tonge,
And it is hool° anon;° and forthermore,   *healed / at once*
Of pokkes° and of scabbe and every sore   *pox*
Shal every sheep be hool,° that of this welle   *healed*
Drinketh a draughte. Tak kepe° eek° what I telle: *heed / also*
If that the good-man that the bestes° oweth°   *animals / owns*
Wol every wike,° er° that the cok him croweth,   *week / before*

---

[1] "Avarice (the love of money) is the root of all evil."
[2] Bulls, writs of indulgence for sin, purchasable in lieu of other forms of penance.
[3] Bishop's seal.
[4] "With which to season my preaching." (Saffron is a yellow spice.)
[5] "They are (saints') relics, or so they all suppose."
[6] Latten, a metal like brass.
[7] "Who has eaten any (poisonous) worm, or whom a snake has stung (bitten)."

Fastinge,° drinken of this welle a draughte— (While) fasting
As thilke° holy Jewe[8] bure eldres taughte— that same
His bestes and his stoor° shal multiplye. stock

 And, sires, also it heleth° jalousye: heals
For though a man be falle in jalous rage,
Let maken with this water his potage,[9]
And nevere shal he more his wyf mistriste,° mistrust
Though he the sooth° of hir defaute° wiste°— truth / erring / should know
Al° had she taken° preestes two or three. Even if / taken (as lovers)

 Heer is a miteyn° eek, that ye may see: mitten
He that his hond wol putte in this miteyn,
He shal have multiplying of his greyn° grain
Whan he hath sowen, be it whete° or otes,° wheat / oats
So that he offre pens, or elles grotes.[10]

 Good men and wommen, o° thing warne° I yow: one / tell
If any wight° be in this chirche now, person
That hath doon sinne horrible, that he
Dar° nat for shame of it y-shriven[11] be, Dare
Or any womman, be she yong or old,
That hath y-maked hir housbonde cokewold,° a cuckold
Swich° folk shul have no power ne no grace Such
To offren° to my reliks in this place. To offer (money)
And whoso findeth him out of swich blame,° not deserving such blame
He wol com up and offre a° Goddes name, make an offering in
And I assoille° him by the auctoritee° (will) absolve / authority
Which that by bulle y-graunted was to me.'

 By this gaude° have I wonne,° yeer° by yeer, trick / earned / year
An hundred mark sith I was pardoner.[12]
I stonde lyk a clerk° in my pulpet, scholar
And whan the lewed° peple is doun y-set, ignorant, unlearned
I preche, so as ye han herd bifore,
And telle an hundred false japes° more. tricks, stories
Thanne peyne I me° to strecche forth the nekke, I take pains
And est and west upon the peple I bekke° nod
As doth a dowve,° sitting on a berne.° dove / in a barn
Myn hondes and my tonge goon so yerne° rapidly
That it is joye to see my bisinesse.
Of avaryce and of swich° cursednesse such

---

[8] Jacob.
[9] "Have his soup made with this water."
[10] "Provided that he offers (to me) pennies or else groats (coins worth fourpence)."
[11] Confessed and absolved.
[12] "A hundred marks (coins worth thirteen shillings fourpence) since I became a pardoner."

Is al my preching, for° to make hem free°   *in order / generous*
To yeven hir pens, and namely unto me.[13]
For myn entente° is nat but for to winne,°   *intention / profit*
And nothing° for correccioun of sinne: *not at all*
I rekke° nevere, whan that they ben beried,° *care / buried*
Though that hir soules goon a-blakeberied![14]
For certes,° many a predicacioun°   *certainly / sermon*
Comth ofte tyme of yvel° entencioun: *evil*
Som for plesaunce° of folk and flaterye,   *the entertainment*
To been avaunced by ypocrisye,[15]
And som for veyne glorie,° and som for hate. *vainglory*
For whan I dar non other weyes debate,[16]
Than wol I stinge him[17] with my tonge smerte° *sharp*
In preching, so that he shal nat asterte°   *leap up (to protest)*
To been° defamed falsly, if that he   *At being*
Hath trespased to° my brethren[18] or to me. *wronged*
For, though I telle noght his propre° name, *own*
Men shal wel knowe that it is the same
By signes and by othere circumstances.
Thus quyte° I folk that doon us displesances;° *requite / offenses*
Thus spitte I out my venim under hewe°   *hue, coloring*
Of holynesse, to semen° holy and trewe.   *seem*
  But shortly° myn entente I wol devyse:° *briefly / describe*
I preche of no thing but for coveityse.°   *out of covetousness*
Therfore my theme is yet, and evere was,
Radix malorum est cupiditas.
Thus can I preche agayn° that same vyce   *against*
Which that I use,° and that is avaryce.   *practice*
But though myself be gilty in that sinne,
Yet can I maken other folk to twinne°   *part*
From avaryce, and sore° to repente.   *ardently*
But that is nat my principal entente:
I preche nothing but for coveityse.
Of this matere° it oughte y-nogh suffyse.   *subject*
  Than telle I hem ensamples many oon° *examples many a one*
Of olde stories longe tyme agoon,°   *past*
For lewed° peple loven tales olde;   *unlearned*
Swich° thinges can they wel reporte° and holde.° *Such / repeat / remember*

---

[13] "In giving their pence, and particularly to me."
[14] Blackberrying, i.e., wandering.
[15] To seek advancement through hypocrisy.
[16] "For when I dare enter into contest (argument) no
 other way."
[17] Some enemy.
[18] Fellow pardoners.

What, trowe ye, the whyles I may preche[19]
And winne° gold and silver for° I teche,   *obtain / because*
That I wol live in povert° wilfully?°   *poverty / willingly*
Nay, nay, I thoghte° it nevere, trewely!   *considered*
For I wol preche and begge in sondry° londes;   *various*
I wol nat do no labour with myn hondes,
Ne make baskettes,[20] and live therby,
By cause I wol nat beggen ydelly.°   *without profit*
I wol non of the Apostles counterfete:°   *imitate*
I wol have money, wolle,° chese, and whete,   *wool*
Al° were it yeven of° the povereste page,°   *Even if / given by / servant*
Or of° the povereste widwe° in a village,   *by / poorest widow*
Al sholde hir children sterve for famyne.[21]
Nay! I wol drinke licour° of the vyne,   *liquor, wine*
And have a joly wenche in every toun.
But herkneth,° lordinges, in conclusioun: *listen*
Youre lyking is that I shall telle a tale.
Now have I dronke a draughte of corny° ale,   *malty*
By God, I hope I shal yow telle a thing
That shal by resoun° been at° youre lyking.   *with reason / to*
For though myself be a ful vicious° man,   *evil, vice-ridden*
A moral tale yet I yow telle can,

Which I am wont to preche for to winne.[22]
Now holde youre pees,° my tale I wol beginne."   *peace*

The Tale

In Flaundres whylom was° a compaignye   *once (there) was*
Of yonge folk, that haunteden folye—
As ryot, hasard, stewes, and tavernes,[23]
Where as° with harpes, lutes, and giternes,°   *There where / guitars*
They daunce and pleyen at dees° bothe day and night,   *dice*
And eten also and drinken over hir might,°   *beyond their capacity*
Thurgh which they doon the devel sacrifyse°   *make sacrifice to the devil*
Withinne that develes temple,[24] in cursed wyse,°   *way*

---

[19] "What? do you believe (that) as long as I can preach."
[20] St. Paul was said to have been a basket maker.
[21] "Even though her children should die of hunger."
[22] "Which I am in the habit of preaching, in order to make some money."
[23] "Of young folk who gave themselves up to folly—(such) as excessive revelry, gambling with dice, (visiting) brothels and taverns."
[24] The tavern.

By superfluitee° abhominable.   *excess*
Hir othes° been so grete and so dampnable,°   *oaths, curses / condemnable*
That it is grisly for to here hem swere.
Our blissed Lordes body they totere°—   *tear apart*
Hem thoughte° Jewes rente° him noght y-nough—   *It seemed to them / tore*
And ech° of hem at otheres sinne lough.°   *each / laughed*
And right anon thanne comen tombesteres°   *female tumblers, dancers*
Fetys and smale, and yonge fruytesteres,²⁵
Singeres with harpes, baudes,° wafereres,°   *bawds / girls selling cakes*
Whiche been the verray° develes officeres   *the very*
To kindle and blowe the fyr of lecherye
That is annexed° unto glotonye: *joined (as a sin)*
The Holy Writ take I to my witnesse
That luxurie° is in wyn and dronkenesse.   *lechery*
    Lo, how that dronken Loth° unkindely°   *Lot / unnaturally*
Lay by his doghtres two, unwitingly;°   *unknowingly*
So dronke he was, he niste° what he wroghte.°   *knew not / did*
    Herodes,° whoso wel the stories soghte,°   *Herod / should seek out*
Whan he of wyn was repleet° at his feste,   *replete, full*
Right at his owene table he yaf° his heste°   *gave / command*
To sleen the Baptist John ful giltelees.°   *guiltless (innocent)*
    Senek° seith a good word doutelees: *Seneca*
He seith, he can no difference finde
Bitwix a man that is out of his minde
And a man which that is dronkelewe,°   *drunken*
But that woodnesse, y-fallen in a shrewe,²⁶
Persevereth lenger° than doth dronkenesse.   *Continues longer*
O glotonye,° ful of cursednesse!   *gluttony*
O cause first° of oure confusioun!°   *first cause / ruin*
O original° of oure dampnacioun,   *origin*
Til Crist had boght us with his blood agayn!

Lo, how dere,° shortly for to sayn,°   *costly / to speak briefly*
Aboght was thilke cursed vileinye;²⁷
Corrupt° was al this world for glotonye!   *Corrupted*
Adam oure fader and his wyf also
Fro Paradys to labour and to wo
Were driven for that vyce, it is no drede.°   *doubt*
For whyl that Adam fasted, as I rede,°   *read*
He was in Paradys; and whan that he
Eet of the fruyt defended° on the tree,   *forbidden*

---

²⁵ "Shapely and slender, and young girls selling fruit."
²⁶ "Except that madness, having afflicted a miserable man."
²⁷ "Bought was that same cursed, evil deed."

Anon° he was outcast to wo and peyne.°   *Immediately / pain*
O glotonye, on thee wel oghte us pleyne!²⁸

   O, wiste a man° how manye maladyes   *(if) a man knew*
Folwen of° excesse and of glotonyes,   *Follow on*
He wolde been the more mesurable°   *measured, temperate*
Of his diete, sitting at his table.
Allas! the shorte throte, the tendre mouth,²⁹
Maketh that,° est and west, and north and south,   *Causes*
In erthe, in eir,° in water, men to swinke°   *air / labor*
To gete a glotoun deyntee° mete and drinke!   *dainty*
Of this matere,° O Paul, wel canstow trete:°   *subject / canst thou treat*
"Mete° unto wombe,° and wombe eek unto mete,   *Meat / belly*
Shal God destroyen bothe," as Paulus seith.³⁰
Allas! a foul thing is it, by my feith,
To seye this word, and fouler is the dede,
Whan man so drinketh of the whyte and rede³¹
That of his throte he maketh his privee,°   *privy (toilet)*
Thurgh thilke° cursed superfluitee.°   *that same / excess*

   The apostel,³² weping, seith ful pitously,
"Ther walken manye of whiche yow told have I"—
I seye it now weping with pitous voys—
"They been enemys of Cristes croys,°   *cross*
Of which the ende is deeth: wombe° is her° god!"   *belly / their*
O wombe! O bely! O stinking cod,³³
Fulfild of donge and of corrupcioun!³⁴
At either ende of thee foul is the soun.°   *sound*
How° greet labour and cost is thee to finde!°   *What / to provide for*
Thise cookes, how they stampe,° and streyne,° and
grinde,   *pound / strain*
And turnen substaunce into accident,³⁵
To fulfille al thy likerous talent!°   *lecherous (here, gluttonous) appetite*
Out of the harde bones knokke they
The mary,° for they caste noght° awey   *marrow / nothing*

---

²⁸ "Oh, gluttony, we certainly ought to complain against
   you."
²⁹ "The brief pleasure of swallowing, the mouth accustomed to delicacies."
³⁰ 1 Corinthians 6:13.
³¹ Wines.
³² St. Paul. See Philippians 3:18–19.
³³ "Bag," i.e., the stomach.
³⁴ "Filled up with dung and with decaying matter."
³⁵ "And turn substance into accident" (a scholastic joke:
   substaunce means "essence, essential qualities"; *acci-*
   dent, "external appearances").

That may go thurgh the golet° softe and swote;°   *gullet / sweet*
Of spicerye° of leef, and bark, and rote°   *spices / root(s)*
Shal been his sauce y-maked by delyt,°   *to give pleasure*
To make him yet a newer° appetyt.   *renewed*
But certes, he that haunteth swich delyces[36]
Is deed, whyl that° he liveth in tho° vyces.   *while / those*
    A lecherous thing is wyn, and dronkenesse
Is ful of stryving° and of wrecchednesse.   *quarreling*
O dronke man, disfigured is thy face,
Sour is thy breeth, foul artow° to embrace,   *art thou*
And thurgh thy dronke nose semeth the soun°   *sound*
As though thou seydest ay° "Sampsoun, Sampsoun";[37]   *ever*
And yet, God wot,° Sampsoun drank nevere no wyn.   *knows*
Thou fallest,[38] as it were a stiked swyn;°   *stuck pig*
Thy tonge is lost, and al thyn honest cure,°   *care for decency*
For dronkenesse is verray sepulture°   *the true tomb*
Of mannes wit° and his discrecioun.°   *understanding / discretion*
In whom that° drinke hath dominacioun,   *In him whom*
He can no conscil° kepe, it is no drede.°   *secrets / doubt*
Now kepe yow fro the whyte and fro the rede—
And namely° fro the whyte wyn of Lepe[39]   *especially*
That is to selle° in Fishstrete° or in Chepe.°   *for sale / Fish Street / Cheapside*
This wyn of Spaigne crepeth subtilly
In othere wynes growinge faste by,[40]
Of° which ther ryseth swich fumositee,°   *From / vapor*
That whan a man hath dronken draughtes three
And weneth° that he be at hoom in Chepe,   *thinks*
He is in Spaigne, right at the toune of Lepe,
Nat at The Rochel,° ne at Burdeux toun;°   *La Rochelle / Bordeaux*
And thanne wol he seye, "Sampsoun, Sampsoun."
    But herkneth,° lordinges, o° word I yow preye,   *listen / one*
That alle the sovereyn actes,° dar I seye,   *supreme deeds*
Of victories in the Olde Testament,
Thurgh verray° God, that is omnipotent,   *true*
Were doon in abstinence and in preyere:
Loketh the Bible, and ther ye may it lere.°   *learn*
    Loke Attila,[41] the grete conquerour,

---

[36] "But truly, he that gives himself up to such pleasures."
[37] A witty kind of onomatopoeia—the snoring sound
     seems to say "Samson," who was betrayed.
[38] Down.
[39] Near Cadiz.
[40] The wines sold as French are often mixed with the
     cheaper wines of Spain.
[41] The Hun.

Deyde° in his sleep, with shame and dishonour,　　　　　*Died*
Bledinge ay° at his nose in dronkenesse:　　　　　　　*continually*
A capitayn shoulde live in sobrenesse.
And over al this, avyseth yow right wel°　　　　　　　*be well advised*
What was comaunded unto Lamuel°—　　　　　　　*Lemuel*
Nat Samuel, but Lamuel, seye I—
Redeth the Bible, and finde it expresly
Of wyn-yeving to hem that han justyse.[42]
Namore of this, for it may wel suffyse.
　　And now that I have spoke of glotonye,
Now wol I yow defenden° hasardrye.°　　　　　　　*forbid / gambling at dice*
Hasard is verray moder° of lesinges,°　　　　　　　*the true mother / lies*
And of deceite and cursed forsweringes,°　　　　　　*perjuries*
Blaspheme of Crist, manslaughtre, and wast° also　　*waste*
Of catel° and of tyme; and forthermo,　　　　　　　*goods*
It is repreve° and contrarie of honour　　　　　　　*a reproach*
For to ben holde a commune hasardour.°　　　　　　*gambler*
And ever the hyer° he is of estaat°　　　　　　　　*higher / in social rank*
The more is he y-holden desolaat:°　　　　　　　　*considered debased*
If that a prince useth° hasardrye,　　　　　　　　*practices*
In alle governaunce and policye
He is, as by commune opinioun,
Y-holde the lasse in reputacioun.
　　Stilbon, that was a wys° embassadour,　　　　　*wise*
Was sent to Corinthe in ful greet honour,
For Lacidomie° to make hire alliaunce.°　　　　　　*Lacedaemon (Sparta) / their alliance*
And whan he cam, him happede par chaunce°　　　*it happened by chance*
That alle the grettest° that were of that lond,　　　*greatest (men)*
Pleyinge atte° hasard he hem fond.　　　　　　　　*at (the)*
For which, as sone as it mighte be,°　　　　　　　*could be*
He stal him° hoom agayn to his contree,　　　　　　*stole away*
And seyde, "Ther wol I nat lese° my name,°　　　　*lose / (good) name*
Ne I wol nat take on me so greet defame,°　　　　　*dishonor*
Yow for to allye° unto none hasardours.°　　　　　　*to ally / gamblers*
Sendeth othere wyse embassadours—
For by my trouthe, me were levere dye°　　　　　　*I would rather die*
Than I yow sholde to hasardours allye.
For ye that been so glorious in honours
Shul nat allyen yow with hasardours
As by my wil, ne as by my tretee."°　　　　　　　　*negotiations*
This wyse philosophre, thus seyde he.
　　Loke eek° that to the king Demetrius　　　　　　*also*

---

[42] Concerning the giving of wine to those responsible for
the law (see Proverbs 31.4–5).

The king of Parthes,° as the book seith us,[43]	*Parthia*
Sente him a paire of dees° of gold in scorn,	*dice*
For he hadde used hasard ther-biforn;	
For which he heeld his glorie or his renoun°	*renown*
At no value or reputacioun.	
Lordes may finden other maner pley	
Honeste° y-nough to dryve the day awey.	*Honorable*
Now wol I speke of othes° false and grete	*oaths, curses*
A word or two, as olde bokes trete.	
Gret swering° is a thing abhominable,	*cursing*
And false swering[44] is yet more reprevable.°	*reproachable*
The heighe° God forbad swering at al—	*high*
Witnesse on Mathew—but in special	
Of swering seith the holy Jeremye,°	*Jeremiah*
"Thou shalt swere sooth° thyn othes° and nat lye,	*truly / oaths*
And swere in dome,° and eek in rightwisnesse;"°	*(good) judgment / righteousness*
But ydel° swering is a cursednesse.°	*vain / wickedness*
Bihold and see, that in the first table°	*tablet (of Moses)*
Of heighe Goddes hestes° honurable,	*commandments*
How that the seconde heste of him is this:	
"Tak nat my name in ydel° or amis."°	*in vain / amiss (wrongly)*
Lo, rather° he forbedeth swich° swering	*earlier (in the list) / such*
Than homicyde or many a cursed thing—	
I seye that, as by ordre,° thus it stondeth—	*in terms of the order*
This knoweth, that his hestes understondeth,[45]	
How that the second heste of God is that.	
And forther over,° I wol thee telle al plat°	*moreover / flatly*
That vengeance shal nat parten° from his hous	*depart*
That° of his othes is to° outrageous.	*Who / too*
"By Goddes precious herte," and "By his nayles,"	
And "By the blode of Crist that is in Hayles,[46]	
Seven is my chaunce,[47] and thyn is cink° and treye;"°	*five / three*
"By Goddes armes, if thou falsly pleye,	
This dagger shal thurghout thyn herte go!"	
This fruyt cometh of the bicched bones two—[48]	
Forswering,° ire,° falsnesse, homicyde.	*Perjury / anger*
Now for the love of Crist that for us dyde,	

---

43 The *Policraticus* of John of Salisbury, which also contains the preceding story.
44 I.e., Of oaths.
45 "[He] knows this, who understands His commandments."
46 An abbey in Gloucestershire supposed to possess (as a high relic) some of Christ's blood.
47 Throw.
48 This fruit, i.e., result, comes from the two cursed dice. (Dice were made of bone; hence "bones" here.)

Lete° youre othes, bothe grete and smale.   *Cease*
But, sires, now wol I telle forth my tale.

   Thise ryotoures° three of which I telle,   *rioters, revelers*
Longe erst er° pryme° rong of any belle,   *before / 9 A.M.*
Were set hem° in a taverne for to drinke;   *Had set themselves down*
And as they sat, they herde a belle clinke
Biforn a cors° was° caried to his grave.   *corpse / (which) was (being)*
That oon of hem gan callen to his knave,
"Go bet," quod he, "and axe redily,[49]
What cors is this that passeth heer forby;°   *by here*
And looke that thou reporte his name wel."[50]

   "Sire," quod this boy, "it nedeth never-a-del.°   *it isn't at all necessary*
It was me told, er° ye cam heer two houres.   *before*
He was, pardee,[51] an old felawe° of youres;   *companion*
And sodeynly he was y-slayn to-night,
For-dronke,° as he sat on his bench upright.   *Dead drunk*
Ther cam a privee° theef men clepeth° Deeth,   *secret / call*
That in this contree° al the peple sleeth,°   *region / kills*
And with his spere he smoot his herte atwo,[52]
And wente his wey withouten wordes mo.°   *more*
He hath a thousand slayn this pestilence.°   *(during) this plague*
And maister, er° ye come in his presence,   *before*
Me thinketh° that it were necessarie   *It seems to me*
For to be war° of swich an adversarie: *aware, careful*
Beth redy for to mete him everemore.°   *always*
Thus taughte me my dame,° I sey namore."   *mother*
"By Seinte Marie," seyde this taverner,°   *tavernkeeper*
"The child seith sooth, for he hath slayn this yeer,
Henne° over a myle, withinne a greet village,   *Hence, from here*
Bothe man and womman, child, and hyne,° and page;°   *laborer / servant*
I trowe° his habitacioun be there.   *believe*
To been avysed° greet wisdom it were,   *forewarned*
Er that° he dide a man a dishonour."   *Before*

   "Ye,° Goddes armes," quod° this ryotour,°   *Aye, yes / said / reveler*
"Is it swich peril with him for to mete?
I shal him seke by wey° and eek° by strete,   *road / also*
I make avow to° Goddes digne° bones!   *avow (it) by / worthy*
Herkneth, felawes, we three been al ones:°   *all of one mind*

---

[49] The one of them proceeded to call to his servant-boy,
"Go quickly," he said, "and ask straightway."
[50] Correctly.
[51] A weak form of the oath "by God," based on the French
par dieu.
[52] "And with his spear he struck his heart in two." (Death
was often shown in the visual arts as a hideous skele-
ton menacing men with a spear or arrow.)

Lat ech° of us holde up his hond til other,°   *each / to the other*
And ech of us bicomen otheres° brother,   *the others'*
And we wol sleen° this false traytour Deeth.   *slay*
He shal be slayn, he that so manye sleeth,
By Goddes dignitee,° er it be night."   *worthiness*
   Togidres° han thise three hir trouthes plight°   *Together / plighted their troth*
To live and dyen ech of hem for other,°   *one another*
As though he were his owene y-boren° brother.   *born*
And up they sterte,° al dronken in this rage,°   *leaped / passion*
And forth they goon towardes that village
Of which the taverner hadde spoke biforn,
And many a grisly ooth thanne han they sworn,
And Cristes blessed body they to-rente°—   *tore apart*
Deeth shal be deed, if that they may him hente.°   *seize*
   Whan they han goon nat fully half a myle,
Right° as they wolde han troden° over a style,°   *Just / stepped / stile*
An old man and a povre° with hem mette.   *poor (one)*
This olde man ful mekely° hem grette,°   *meekly / greeted them*
And seyde thus, "Now, lordes, God yow see!"°   *may God protect you*
   The proudest of thise ryotoures three
Answerde agayn, "What, carl,° with sory grace!°   *Hey, fellow / confound you*
Why artow al forwrapped save thy face?[53]
Why livestow° so longe in so greet age?"   *livest thou*
This olde man gan loke in° his visage,   *scrutinized*
   And seyde thus, "For° I ne can nat finde   *Because*
A man, though that I walked into Inde,°   *India*
Neither in citee nor in no village,
That wolde chaunge his youthe for myn age;
And therfore moot° I han myn age stille,   *must*
As longe time as it is Goddes wille.
Ne Deeth, allas! ne wol nat han my lyf.
Thus walke I, lyk° a restelees caityf,°   *like / captive*
And on the ground, which is my modres° gate,   *mother's*
I knokke with my staf bothe erly and late,
And seye, 'Leve° moder, leet me in!   *Dear*
Lo, how I vanish,° flesh, and blood, and skin!   *waste away*
Allas! whan shul my bones been at reste?
Moder, with yow wolde I chaunge° my cheste°   *exchange / chest (of clothes)*
That in my chambre longe tyme hath be,°   *been*
Ye, for an heyre clout° to wrappe me!'   *haircloth (for burial)*
But yet to me she wol nat do that grace,
For which ful pale and welked° is my face.   *withered*
   But sires, to yow it is no curteisye[54]

---

[53] "Why art thou all wrapped up, except for thy face?"
[54] "But, sirs, it is not courteous of you."

To speken to an old man vileinye,°   *rudeness*
But° he trespasse° in worde or elles° in dede.   *Unless / offend / else*
In Holy Writ ye may yourself wel rede,°   *read*
'Agayns° an old man, hoor° upon his heed,   *Before / hoary, white*
Ye sholde aryse.' Wherfor I yeve yow reed:[55]
Ne dooth unto an old man noon harm now,
Namore than that ye wolde men did to yow
In age, if that ye so longe abyde.°   *remain (alive)*
And God be with yow, wher ye go° or ryde;   *walk*
I moot° go thider as° I have to go."   *must / thither where*
    "Nay, olde cherl, by God, thou shalt nat so,"
Seyde this other hasardour° anon;°   *gambler / at once*
"Thou partest° nat so lightly, by Seint John!   *departest*
Thou spak right now of thilke° traitour Deeth   *that same*
That in this contree alle oure frendes sleeth.
Have heer my trouthe,° as° thou art his espye,°   *pledge / since / spy*
Telle wher he is, or thou shalt it abye,°   *pay for*
By God, and by the holy sacrament!
For soothly thou art oon of his assent°   *in league with him*
To sleen us yonge folk, thou false theef!"
    "Now, sires," quod he, "if that yow be so leef°   *desirous*
To finde Deeth, turne up this croked° wey,   *crooked*
For in that grove I lafte° him, by my fey,°   *left / faith*
Under a tree, and there he wol abyde:°   *stay*
Nat for youre boost he wole him nothing hyde.[56]
See ye that ook?° right ther ye shul him finde.   *oak*
God save yow, that boghte agayn° mankinde,   *redeemed*
    And yow amende!"° Thus seyde this olde man.   *make you better*
And everich° of thise ryotoures° ran,   *each / revelers*
Til he cam to that tree, and ther they founde
Of florins° fyne of golde y-coyned° rounde   *florins, coins / coined*
Wel ny an° eighte busshels, as hem thoughte.°   *nearly / it seemed to them*
No lenger thanne° after Deeth they soughte,   *No longer then*
But ech° of hem so glad was of that sighte—   *each*
For that the florins been so faire and brighte—
That doun they sette hem by this precious hord.
The worste of hem he spake the firste word.
    "Brethren," quod he, "take kepe° what that I seye: *heed*
My wit° is greet, though that I bourde° and pleye.   *understanding / jest*
This tresor° hath Fortune unto us yiven°   *treasure / given*
In mirthe and jolitee° our lyf to liven,   *merriment*

---

[55] "'You should stand up (in respect).' Therefore I give
    you (this) advice."
[56] "He won't conceal himself at all because of your
    boasting."

And lightly as it comth, so wol we spende.
Ey! Goddes precious dignitee!° who wende°   *worthiness / would have supposed*
To-day that we sholde han so fair a grace?°   *favor*
But° mighte this gold be caried fro this place   *If only*
Hoom to myn hous—or elles unto youres—
For wel ye woot° that al this gold is oures—   *know*
Thanne were we in heigh felicitee.°   *supreme happiness*
But trewely, by daye it may nat be:°   *be (done)*
Men wolde seyn that we were theves stronge,°   *flagrant*
And for oure owene tresor doon us honge.°   *have us hanged*
This tresor moste y-caried be by nighte,
As wysly° and as slyly° as it mighte.°   *prudently / craftily / can (be)*
Wherfore I rede° that cut° among us alle   *advise / lots, straws*
Be drawe,° and lat se wher the cut wol falle;   *drawn, pulled*
And he that hath the cut with herte blythe
Shal renne° to the toune, and that ful swythe,°   *run / quickly*
And bringe us breed and wyn ful prively.°   *secretly*
And two of us shul kepen° subtilly°   *guard / carefully*
This tresor wel; and if he wol nat tarie,°   *tarry*
Whan it is night we wol this tresor carie,
By oon assent, where as us thinketh best."[57]
That oon of hem the cut broughte in his fest,°   *fist*
And bad hem drawe, and loke wher it wol falle;
And it fil on the yongeste of hem alle,
And forth toward the toun he wente anon.
And also sone as° that he was agon,   *as soon as*
That oon of hem° spak thus unto that other: *The one of them*
"Thou knowest wel thou art my sworne brother;
Thy profit° wol I telle thee anon.   *Something to thy advantage*
Thou woost° wel that oure felawe is agon,°   *knowest / gone*
And heer is gold, and that° ful greet plentee,   *that (in)*
That shal departed° been among us three.   *divided*
But natheles,° if I can shape° it so   *nonetheless / arrange*
That it departed were among us two,
Hadde I nat doon a freendes torn° to thee?"   *turn*
    That other answerde, "I noot° how that may be: *know not*
He woot how that the gold is with us tweye.
What shal we doon? what shal we to him seye?"
    "Shal it be conseil?"° seyde the firste shrewe;° *a secret / wretch*
"And I shal tellen in a wordes fewe
What we shal doon, and bringe it wel aboute."
"I graunte,"° quod that other, "out of doute,[58]   *grant (it)*
That, by my trouthe, I wol thee nat biwreye."°   *betray*

---

[57] "By common assent, wherever seems to us best."
[58] You can be sure.

"Now," quod the firste, "thou woost° wel   *knowest / two*
we be tweye,°
And two of us shul strenger° be than oon.   *stronger*
Looke whan that he is set,° that right anoon°   *has sat down / right away*
Arys° as though thou woldest with him pleye;   *Arise (get up)*
And I shal ryve° him thurgh the sydes tweye°   *stab / through his two sides*
Whyl that thou strogelest° with him as in game,° *strugglest / as if in play*
And with thy dagger looke° thou do the same;   *take heed*
And thanne shall al this gold departed° be,   *divided*
My dere freend, bitwixen me and thee.
Thanne may we bothe oure lustes° al fulfille,   *desires*
And pleye at dees° right at oure owene wille."   *dice*
And thus acorded° been thise shrewes° tweye   *agreed / cursed fellows*
To sleen the thridde, as ye han herd me seye.

    This yongest, which that wente unto the toun,
Ful ofte in herte he rolleth up and doun[59]
The beautee of thise florins newe and brighte.
"O Lord!" quod he, "if so were that I mighte
Have al this tresor to myself allone,
Ther is no man that liveth under the trone°   *throne*
Of God that sholde live so mery as I!"
And atte laste° the feend,° our enemy,   *at (the) last / devil*
Putte in his thought that he shold poyson beye,° *buy poison*
With which he mighte sleen his felawes tweye°— *two companions*
For-why the feend fond him in swich lyvinge[60]
That he had leve° him to sorwe bringe: *permission (from God)*
For this was outrely° his fulle entente,°   *completely / purpose*
To sleen hem bothe, and nevere to repente.
And forth he gooth—no lenger wolde he tarie—
Into the toun, unto a pothecarie,°   *apothecary, pharmacist*
And preyed° him that he him wolde selle   *asked*
Som poyson, that° he mighte his rattes quelle,° *so that / kill his rats*
And eek° ther was a polcat° in his hawe,°   *also / weasel / yard*
That, as he seyde, his capouns° hadde y-slawe,° *capons / killed*
And fayn° he wolde wreke him,° if he mighte,   *gladly / avenge himself*
On vermin, that destroyed° him by nighte.   *were ruining*

    The pothecarie answerde, "And thou shalt have
A thing that, also° God my soule save,   *so (may)*
In al this world ther nis no° creature,   *is not any*
That ete or dronke hath of this confiture°   *mixture*
Noght but the mountance of a corn of whete,[61]

---

[59] Thinks on.
[60] "Because the fiend [the devil] found him living in such
   a way."
[61] "No more than the quantity of a grain of wheat."

That he ne shal his lyf anon° forlete.°　　　*at once / lose*
Ye,° sterve° he shal, and that in lasse whyle°　　*Yes / die / shorter time*
Than thou wolt goon a paas° nat but° a myle,　　*walk at normal pace / only*
This poyson is so strong and violent."
　　This cursed man hath in his hond y-hent°　　*grasped*
This poyson in a box, and sith° he ran　　　*afterward*
Into the nexte strete unto a man
And borwed [of] him large botels° three,　　*bottles (probably of leather)*
And in the two his poyson poured he—
The thridde he kepte clene for his° drinke—　　*his (own)*
For al the night he shoop him° for to swinke°　　*was preparing himself / work*
In caryinge of the gold out of that place.
And whan this ryotour, with sory grace,[62]
Hadde filled with wyn his grete botels three,
To his felawes agayn repaireth° he.　　　*returns*
　　What nedeth it to sermone° of it more?　　*speak*
For right as they hadde cast° his deeth bifore,　　*planned*
Right so they han him slayn, and that anon.°　　*immediately*
And whan that this was doon, thus spak that oon:
"Now lat us sitte and drinke, and make us merie,
And afterward we wol his body berie."°　　　*bury*
And with that word it happed° him, par cas,°　　*befell / by chance*
To take the botel ther° the poyson was,　　*where*
And drank, and yaf° his felawe drink also,　　*gave*
For which anon they storven° bothe two.　　*died*
　　But certes, I suppose that Avicen
Wroot nevere in no canon, ne in no fen,

Mo wonder signes of empoisoning[63]
Than hadde thise wrecches two, er° hir° ending.　　*before / their*
Thus ended been thise homicydes two,
And eek° the false empoysoner° also.°　　*also / poisoner / as well*
　　O cursed sinne of alle cursednesse!
O traytours° homicyde, O wikkednesse!　　*traitorous*
O glotonye, luxurie,° and hasardrye!　　*lechery*
Thou blasphemour of Crist with vileinye°　　*vile speech*
And othes grete, of usage° and of pryde!　　*out of habit*
Allas! mankinde, how may it bityde°　　　*happen*
That to thy Creatour which that thee wroghte,
And with his precious herte-blood thee boghte,°　　*redeemed*
Thou art so fals and so unkinde,° allas!　　*unnatural*

---

[62] Blessed by evil.
[63] "But truly, I would guess that Avicenna—an Arab physician and author—never described, in any treatise or chapter, more terrible symptoms of poisoning."

Now, goode men, God forgeve° yow youre trespas,   *may God forgive*
And ware yow fro° the sinne of avaryce.   *make you beware of*
Myn holy pardoun may yow alle waryce°—   *cure*
So that ye offre nobles or sterlinges,[64]
Or elles silver broches, spones,° ringes.   *spoons*
Boweth youre heed° under this holy bulle!   *head*
Cometh up, ye wyves, offreth of youre wolle!°   *wool*
Youre names I entre heer in my rolle° anon:°   *roll, list / at once*
Into the blisse of hevene shul ye gon.
I yow assoile,° by myn heigh power—   *absolve*
Yow that wol offre°—as clene and eek as cleer°   *make an offering / pure*
As ye were born.—And, lo, sires, thus I preche.
And Jesu Crist, that is our soules leche,°   *healer, doctor*
So graunte° yow his pardon to receyve,   *May He grant*
For that is best; I wol yow nat deceyve.

    But sires, o° word forgat I in my tale: *a, one*
I have relikes and pardon in my male°   *pouch*
As faire as any man in Engelond,
Whiche were me yeven° by the Popes hond.   *given*
If any of yow wol of devocioun°   *out of devotion*
Offren and han myn absolucioun,
Cometh forth anon, and kneleth heer adoun,
And mekely receyveth my pardoun;
Or elles, taketh pardon as ye wende,°   *travel*
Al newe and fresh, at every myles ende—
So that ye offren alwey newe and newe[65]
Nobles or pens,° which that be gode and trewe.   *pence*
It is an honour to everich° that is heer   *every one*
That ye mowe° have a suffisant° pardoner   *may / capable*
T'assoille° yow, in contree as ye ryde,   *To absolve*

For aventures whiche that may bityde.[66]
Peraventure° ther may falle oon or two   *By chance*
Doun of his hors, and breke his nekke atwo.°   *in two*
Look which a seuretee° is it to you alle   *what a security*
That I am in youre felaweship y-falle,
That may assoille yow, bothe more and lasse,°   *great and small*
Whan that the soule shal fro the body passe.
I rede° that oure Host heer shal biginne,   *advise*
For he is most envoluped° in sinne.   *enveloped, wrapped up*
Com forth, sire Hoste, and offre first anon,°   *first now*

---

[64] "As long as you offer nobles [gold coins] or silver pennies."
[65] "As long as you make offering anew each time (of)."
[66] "In respect to things which may befall."

And thou shalt kisse the reliks everichon,°   *every one*
Ye, for a grote:° unbokel° anon thy purs."   *groat (four pence) / unbuckle*
   "Nay, nay," quod° he, "thanne have I Cristes curs!   *said*
Lat be," quod he, "it shal nat be, so theech!°   *as I hope to prosper*
Thou woldest make me kisse thyn olde breech°   *breeches*
And swere it were a relik of a seint,
Thogh it were with thy fundement° depeint!°   *fundament (rectum) / stained*
But by the croys° which that Seint Eleyne° fond,   *(true) Cross / St. Helena*
I wolde I hadde thy coillons° in myn hond   *testicles*
In stede of relikes or of seintuarie.[67]
Lat cutte hem of! I wol thee helpe hem carie.[68]
Thay shul be shryned° in an hogges tord!"°   *enshrined / turd*
   This Pardoner answerde nat a word;
So wrooth° he was, no word ne wolde he seye.   *wroth, angered*
   "Now," quod our Host, "I wol no lenger pleye
With thee, ne with noon other angry man."
But right anon the worthy Knight bigan,
"Whan that he saugh that al the peple lough,°   *laughed*
"Namore of this, for it is right y-nough!°   *quite enough*
Sire Pardoner, be glad and mery of chere;°   *mood*
And ye, sire Host, that been to me so dere,
I prey yow that ye kisse the Pardoner.
And Pardoner, I prey thee, drawe thee neer,
And, as we diden, lat us laughe and pleye."
Anon° they kiste, and riden forth hir weye.°   *At once / (on) their way*

*   *   *

REVIEW QUESTIONS

1. How do the character of the Pardoner and the tale he tells reflect contemporary trends and problems within the late medieval Church and society? What can you discern about Chaucer's attitude toward the sale of indulgences or false relics?

2. How does the Pardoner's Tale reflect the realities of life in the world after the Black Death?

3. Did you find that the reading of Middle English became easier as you became more accustomed to it? How different is this language from our own? What words and phrases are still in use today? What might that reveal about continuities over time?

---

[67] Holy things.
[68] "Have them cut off! I'll help thee carry them."

CHRISTINE DE PISAN

FROM *The Book of the City of Ladies*

Christine de Pisan (1365–after 1429) was the highly educated daughter of a Venetian physician at the court of Charles VI of France. Widowed at an early age, Christine became a writer to support her family, becoming the first professional woman of let-ters. Her most famous work, The Book of the City of Ladies, *is both a historical trea-tise on women and a defense of them. In this selection, the allegorical figure of Lady Rectitude introduces the subject of virtuous women.*

From *The Book of the City of Ladies*, by Christine de Pizan, translated by Earl Jeffrey Rich-ards (New York: Persea Books, 1982), pp. 206–15.

*   *   *

Rectitude Says That Many Women Are Loved for Their Virtues More Than Other Women for Their Prettiness

"If we assumed that women who wished to be loved tried, for this reason, to be pretty, conceited, cute, and vain, then I can show you that such action will not make wise and worthwhile men love them more quickly or better and that, in fact, honest, virtuous, and simple women will more readily and more deeply be loved by men who love honor than pretty women, even if we suppose that these honest women are less beautiful. One could answer that, since women attract men with vir-tue and integrity and since it is bad that men be attracted, it would be better if women were less good. But of course this argument has no validity at all, for one should not neglect the cultivation and advancement of the good in spite of however much fools abuse it, and everyone must do his duty by acting well regardless of what might happen. I will give you an example to prove that women are loved for their virtue and integrity. First I could tell you about the many women who are saints in Paradise who were desired by men because of their honesty.

"Consider Lucretia, whom I spoke to you about before and who was raped: her great integ-rity was the reason why Tarquin became enam-ored, much more so than because of her beauty. For once, when her husband was dining with this Tarquin (who afterward raped her) and with many other knights, the subject of their conver-sation turned to their wives, and each one claimed that his own was the best. In order to discover the truth and to prove which one of their wives was worthy of the highest praise, they got up and rode home, and those women found occupied in the most honest occupation and activity were to be the most celebrated and honored. Lucretia, of all these wives, turned out to be the most hon-estly occupied, for her husband found her, such a wise and upright woman, clothed in a simple gown, sitting at home among her women ser-vants, working in wool, and discoursing on vari-ous subjects. This same Tarquin, the king's son, arrived there with her husband and saw her out-standing honesty, her smile and fair conduct, and her serene manner. He was so captivated by her that he began to plan the folly which he com-mitted later."

Here She Speaks of Queen Blanche, the Mother of Saint Louis, and of Other Good and Wise Ladies Loved for Their Virtue

"The most noble Queen Blanche, mother of Saint Louis, was similarly loved for great learning, prudence, virtue, and goodness by Thibault, the count of Champagne. Even though she had already passed the flower of her youth, this noble count—hearing the wise and good queen speak to him so judiciously after he had gone to war against Saint Louis, sensibly reproving him, telling him he ought not to have acted this way, considering the good deeds her son had done for him—looked at her intently, amazed by her enormous goodness and virtue, and was so overwhelmed by love that he did not know what to do. He did not dare confess his love for fear of death, for he realized that she was so good that she would never consent to his proposition. From that time onward he suffered much grief because of the mad desire which oppressed him. Nevertheless, he told her then not to fear his continuing to wage war against the king and that he wished to be her subject totally, that she should be certain that everything he possessed, body and soul, was entirely subject to her command. So he loved her all his life, from that hour on, and he never stopped loving her in spite of the slight chance he had of ever winning her love. He made his laments to Love in his poems, where he praised his lady most graciously. These beautiful poems of his were put to music in a charming way. He had them inscribed in his bedroom in Provins and also in Troyes, and they appear there to this day. And so I could tell you about many others."

And I, Christine, replied, "Indeed, my lady, I have seen in my own experience several cases similar to the one you mention, for I know of virtuous and wise women who, from what they have confessed to me in lamenting their distress, have been propositioned more frequently after their peak of beauty and youthfulness than when they were in their greatest flower. Concerning this, they have told me, 'Gods! What can this possibly mean? Do these men see in me some foolish behavior which would give them the slightest glimmer of hope that I would agree to commit such foolishness?' But I realize now, from what you say, that their outstanding goodness caused them to be loved. And this is very much against the opinion of many people who claim that an honest woman who intends to be chaste will never be desired or propositioned unless she herself so wishes."

Christine Speaks, and Rectitude Responds in Her Reply to Those Men Who Claim That Women Are Naturally Greedy

"I do not know what more to tell you, my dear lady, for all my questions are answered. It seems to me that you have disproven the slanders put forth by so many men against women. Likewise, what they so often claim is not true, that greed is, among feminine vices, a very natural thing."

She answered, "My dear friend, let me assure you that greed is no more natural in women than it is in men, and God only knows whether men are less greedy! You can see that the latter is in fact the case because considerably more evil occurs and recurs in the world because of the rapacity of different men than because of the greed of women. But, just as I told you before, the fool sees his neighbor's peccadillo and fails to see his own enormous crime. Since one commonly sees women taking delight in collecting cloth and thread and such trifles which go into a household, women are thought to be greedy. I can, however, assure you that there are many women who, were they to possess anything, would not be greedy or stingy in bestowing honors and giving generously where what they have could be used well, just as one poor person would do for an even poorer person in need. Women are usually kept in such financial straits that they guard the little that they can have, knowing they can recover this only with the greatest pain. So some people consider women greedy because some women have foolish husbands, great wastrels of property and gluttons, and the poor women, who know well that their households need what their husbands spend foolishly and that in the end their poor children will have to pay for it, are unable to refrain from speaking to their husbands and from urging them to spend less. Thus, such behavior is not at all avarice or greed, but is a sign of great prudence. Of course I am referring to those women who act with discretion. One sees so much quarreling in these marriages because the husbands do not like such urging and so blame their wives for something which they should praise them for. It is clear from the alms which these women so freely give that the vice of avarice is not to be found in them. God knows how many prisoners, even in the lands of the Saracens, how many destitute and needy noblemen and others have been and are every day, in this world here below, comforted and helped by women and their property."

And I, Christine, then said, "Indeed, my lady, your remarks remind me that I have seen women show themselves honorable in prudent generosity, and today I am acquainted with women who rejoice when they can say, 'See, the money is put to good use there, and no greedy man can hoard it away in some coffer.' For although Alexander the Great was said to be generous, I can tell you that I never saw any examples of it."

Rectitude then began to laugh and said, "Indeed, my friend, the ladies of Rome were not greedy when their city was gravely afflicted with war, when the public treasury was completely spent on warriors. The Romans had terrible trouble finding money to finance a large army which they had to raise. But the ladies, with their liberality—even the widows—collected all their jewels and property together, sparing nothing, and freely gave them to the princes of Rome. The ladies received great praise for this deed, and afterward their jewels were given back to them, and quite rightly so, for they had saved Rome."

Here She Speaks of the Rich and Generous Lady Named Busa

"In the *Faits des Romains* the generosity of a rich and upright woman named Busa, or Paulina, is

described. She lived in Apuleia during the time when Hannibal was ravaging the Romans with fire and arms, despoiling almost all of Italy of men and goods. Many Romans retreated after the great defeat at the battle of Cannae, where Hannibal won such a noble victory, and they fled the battlefield wounded or injured. But this valiant Lady Busa received as many as she could take in, until she sheltered some ten thousand in her household, for she was extremely wealthy and had them cared for at her expense. All of them, having been helped by her wealth as much as by the aid and comfort she afforded them, were able to return to Rome and put the army back on its feet, for which she was highly praised. So do not doubt, dear friend, that I could tell you more about the endless generosity, bounty, and liberality of women.

"And even without going back to look for historical examples, how many other examples of the generosity of ladies from your own time could be mentioned! Was not the generosity great which was shown by the Dame de la Rivière, named Marguerite, who is still alive and was formerly the wife of Monsieur Burel de la Rivière, first chamberlain of the wise King Charles? On one occasion among others it happened that this lady, as she was always wise, valiant, and well-bred, was attending a very fine celebration which the duke of Anjou, later king of Sicily, was holding in Paris. At this celebration there were a large number of noble ladies and knights and gentlemen in fine array. This lady, who was young and beautiful, realized while she watched the noble knights assembled there, that a most noteworthy knight of great fame among those then living, named Emerion de Poumiers, was missing from the company of knights. She, of course, allowed that this Sir Emerion was too old to remember her, but his goodness and valiance made the lady remember him, and she felt there could be no more beautiful an ornament for such an assembly than so noteworthy and famous a man, even if he were old, so she inquired where the missing knight was. She was told that he was in prison in the Châtelet in Paris because of a debt of five hundred francs that he had incurred during his frequent travels in arms. 'Ah!' said the noble lady, 'what a shame for this kingdom to suffer a single hour of such a man imprisoned for debt!' Whereupon she removed the gold chaplet which she was wearing on her rich and fair head and replaced it with a chaplet of periwinkle on her blond hair. She gave the gold chaplet to a certain messenger and said, 'Go and give this chaplet as a pledge for what he owes, and let him be freed immediately and come here.' This was done and she was highly praised for it."

She Speaks Here of the Princesses and Ladies of France

Then I, Christine, spoke again. "My lady, since you have recalled a lady from my own time and since you have come to the history of the ladies of France and of those ladies still living, let me ask you whether you think it is a good idea to lodge some of them in our City. For why should they be forgotten, and foreign women as well?"

She replied, "I can answer you, Christine, that there are certainly a great many virtuous ladies of France, and I would be more than pleased if they were among our citizens. First of all, the noble queen of France, Isabella of Bavaria, will not be refused, reigning now by the grace of God, and in whom there is not a trace of cruelty, extortion, or any other evil vice, but only great love and good will toward her subjects.

"We can equally praise the fair, young, good, and wise duchess of Berry, wife of Duke John, son of the late King John of France and brother of wise King Charles. In the flower of her youth this noble duchess conducted herself so chastely, so sensibly, and so wisely that all the world praised and reputed her for her excellent virtue.

"What could I say about Valentina Visconti, the duchess of Orléans, wife of Duke Louis, son of Charles, the wise king of France, and daughter of the duke of Milan? What more could be said about such a prudent lady? A lady who is strong and constant in heart, filled with devotion to her lord and good teaching for her children, well-informed in government, just toward all, sensible in her conduct, and virtuous in all things—and all this is well known.

"What more could be said concerning the duchess of Burgundy, wife of Duke John, son of Philip, the son of the late King John of France? Is she not extraordinarily virtuous, loyal to her lord, kind in heart and manners, excellent in her morals and lacking a single vice?

"Is not the countess of Clermont, daughter of the duke of Berry mentioned above from his first marriage, and wife of Count John of Clermont, son of the duke of Bourbon and heir to the duchy, is she not everything which every lofty princess must be, devoted to her love, well-bred in everything, beautiful, wise, and good? In short, her virtues shine forth in her good conduct and honorable bearing.

"And what about that one woman among others whom you love singularly as much for the goodness of her virtues as for the favors she has extended to you and to whom you are much beholden, the noble duchess of Holland and countess of Hainault, daughter of the late Duke Philip of Burgundy mentioned above, and sister of the present duke? This lady should be ranked among the most perfect ladies, loyal hearted, most prudent, wise in government, charitable, supremely devoted to God, and, in short, wholly good.

"Should not the duchess of Bourbon also be recalled among princesses known for their honor and laudability in all things?

"What more shall I tell you? I would need much time to recount all their great virtues.

"The good and beautiful countess of Saint-Pol, noble and upright, daughter of the duke of Bar, second cousin of the king of France, should also be ranked among the good women.

"Similarly the woman whom you love, Anne, daughter of the late count of La Marche and sister of the present duke, married to Ludwig of Bavaria, brother of the queen of France, does not discredit the company of women endowed with grace and praise, for her excellent virtues are well-known to God and the world.

"In spite of the slanderers, there are so many good and beautiful women among the ranks of countesses, baronesses, ladies, maidens, bourgeois women, and all classes that God should be praised who upholds them all. May He correct those women with shortcomings! Do not think otherwise, for I assure you of its truth, even if many jealous and slanderous people say the opposite."

And I, Christine, replied, "My lady, hearing this from you is a supreme joy for me."

She answered, "My dear friend, it seems to me I have now more than adequately executed my office in the City of Ladies. I have built it up with beautiful palaces and many fair inns and mansions. I have populated it for your sake with noble ladies and with such great numbers of women from all classes that it is already completely filled. Now let my sister Justice come to complete the rest, and this should satisfy you."

Christine Addresses Herself to All Princesses and to All Women

"Most excellent, revered, and honored princesses of France and of all lands, and all ladies and maidens, and, indeed, all women who have loved and do love and will love virtue and morality, as well as all who have died or who are now living or who are to come, rejoice and exult in our new City which, thanks to God, is already formed and almost finished and populated. Give thanks to God who has

led me to undertake this great labor and the desirable task of establishing for you honorable lodging within city walls as a perpetual residence for as long as the world endures. I have come this far hoping to reach the conclusion of my work with the aid and comfort of Lady Justice, who, in accordance with her promise, will unfailingly help me until the City is finished and wholly completed. Now, my most honored ladies, pray for me."

*   *   *

REVIEW QUESTIONS

1. Christine was outspokenly critical of the ways that women were represented by the male authors of her own day, notably Boccaccio. How might she have responded to the depictions of women in the *Decameron* or even in Dante's *Divine Comedy* in Chapter 10?
2. How does Christine use history to make her case for women?
3. What does Christine see as the correct way for men and women to relate in society?

FROM *The Trial of Jeanne d'Arc*

Jeanne d'Arc appeared on the scene in 1429 as French fortunes in the Hundred Years' War were at their lowest. Taking command of the Dauphin's army, and then lifting the siege of Orleans, she had him crowned as Charles VII at Rheims and revived the French cause. Captured by the Burgundians and then sold to their English allies, Jeanne was tried as a heretic and eventually burned at the stake in Rouen in May of 1431. Although she was dead before the age of twenty, Jeanne's career is a remarkable episode in the history of France and of late medieval women. The following excerpts from her trial include some of Jeanne's own words and reveal the concerns of the prosecutors.

From *The Trial of Jeanne d'Arc*, edited by W. P. Barrett (London: Routledge and Paul, 1931), pp. 50–51, 68–70, 73–74, 125–26, 318–19.

*   *   *

First Inquiry after the Oath

When she had thus taken the oath the said Jeanne was questioned by us about her name and her surname. To which she replied that in her own country she was called Jeannette, and after she came to France, she was called Jeanne. Of her surname she said she knew nothing. Consequently she was questioned about the district from which she came. She replied she was born in the village of Domrémy, which is one with the village of Greux; and in Greux is the principal church.

Asked about the name of her father and mother, she replied that her father's name was Jacques d'Arc, and her mother's Isabelle.

Asked where she was baptized, she replied it was in the church of Domrémy.

Asked who were her godfathers and godmothers, she said one of her godmothers was named Agnes, another Jeanne, another Sibylle; of her godfathers, one was named Jean Lingué, another Jean Barrey: she had several other godmothers, she had heard her mother say.

Asked what priest had baptized her, she replied that it was master Jean Minet, as far as she knew.

Asked if he was still living, she said she believed he was.

Asked how old she was, she replied she thought nineteen. She said moreover that her mother taught her the Paternoster, Ave Maria, and Credo; and that no one but her mother had taught her her Credo.

*   *   *

Asked whether the voice which spoke to her was that of an angel, or of a saint, male or female, or straight from God, she answered that the voice was the voice of St. Catherine and of St. Margaret. And their heads were crowned in a rich and precious fashion with beautiful crowns. "And to tell this," she said, "I have God's permission. If you doubt it, send to Poitiers where I was examined before."

Asked how she knew they were these two saints, and how she knew one from the other, she answered she knew well who they were, and easily distinguished one from the other.

Asked how she knew one from the other, she answered she knew them by the greeting they gave her. She said further that a good seven years have passed since they undertook to guide her. She said also she knows the saints because they tell her their names.

Asked if the said saints are dressed in the same cloth, she answered: "I will tell you no more now; I have not leave to reveal it. If you do not believe me, send to Poitiers!" She said also that there were some revelations made directly to the king of France, and not to those who question her.

Asked if the saints are the same age, she answered that she had not leave to say.

Asked if the saints spoke at the same time, or one after another, she answered: "I have not leave to tell you; nevertheless I have always had counsel from both."

Asked which one appeared first, she answered: "I did not recognize them immediately; I knew well enough once, but I have forgotten; if I had leave I would gladly tell you. It is written down in the register at Poitiers." She added that she had received comfort from St. Michael.

Asked which of the apparitions came to her first, she answered that St. Michael came first.

Asked whether it was a long time ago that she first heard the voice of St. Michael, she answered: "I do not speak of St. Michael's voice, but of his great comfort."

Asked which was the first voice which came to her when she was about thirteen, she answered that it was St. Michael whom she saw before her eyes; and he was not alone, but accompanied by many angels from heaven. She said also that she came into France only by the instruction of God.

Asked if she saw St. Michael and these angels corporeally and in reality, she answered: "I saw them with my bodily eyes as well as I see you; and when they left me, I wept; and I fain would have had them take me with them too."

Asked in what form St. Michael appeared, she answered: "There is as yet no reply to that, for I have not had leave to answer."

Asked what St. Michael said to her the first time, she answered: "You will get no further reply to-day." She said the voices told her to answer boldly. She said she had indeed once told her king everything that had been revealed to her, since it concerned him. She said, however, that she had not yet leave to reveal what St. Michael said. She added that she wished her examiner had a copy of the book at Poitiers, provided that God desired it.

Asked if the voices told her not to tell her revelations without their permission, she answered: "I will not answer you further about that; and what I have permission to, that I will gladly answer. If the voices forbade me, I did not understand."

Asked what sign she gives that this revelation comes from God, and that it is St. Catherine and St. Margaret who speak to her, she answered: "I have told you often enough that it is St. Catherine and St. Margaret; believe me if you will."

Asked if it is forbidden for her to tell, she answered: "I have not quite understood whether that is permitted or not."

Asked how she can distinguish such points as she will answer, and such as she will not, she answered that on some points she had asked permission, and on some points she had received it. Furthermore she said she would rather be torn asunder by horses than have come to France without God's leave.

Asked if God ordered her to wear a man's dress, she answered that the dress is a small, nay, the least thing. Nor did she put on man's dress by the advice of any man whatsoever; she did not put it on, nor did she do aught, but by the command of God and the angels.

Asked whether it seemed to her that this command to assume male attire was lawful, she answered: "Everything I have done is at God's command; and if He had ordered me to assume a different habit, I should have done it, because it would have been His command."

Asked if she did it at the order of Robert de Baudricourt she said no.

Asked if she thought she had done well to take man's dress, she answered that everything she did at God's command she thought well done, and hoped for good warrant and succour in it.

Asked if, in this particular case, by taking man's dress, she thought she had done well, she answered that she had done nothing in the world but by God's commands.

Asked whether, when she saw the voice coming to her, there was a light, she answered that there was a great deal of light on all sides, as was most fitting. She added to the examiner that not all the light came to him alone!

*   *   *

Asked whether, when she went to Orleans, she had a standard or banner, in French *estandart ou banière,* and what colour it was, she answered she had a banner, with a field sown with lilies; the world was depicted on it, and two angels, one at each side; it was white, of white linen or boucassin, and on it were written, she thought, these names, JHESUS MARIA; and it was fringed with silk.

Asked if these names JHESUS MARIA were written above, or below, or at the side, she answered, at the side, she believed.

Asked which she preferred, her standard or her sword, she answered she much preferred her standard to her sword.

Asked who persuaded her to have this painting on her standard, she answered: "I have told you often enough that I have done nothing but by God's command." She said also that she herself bore the standard, when attacking the enemy, so as not to kill anyone; she never has killed anyone, she said.

Asked what force her king gave her when he set her to work, she answered that he gave her 10 or 12,000 men; and she went first to Orleans, to the fortress of Saint-Loup, and then to the fortress of the Bridge.

Asked to which fortress she ordered her men to retire, she says she does not remember. She added that she was confident of raising the siege of Orleans, for it had been revealed to her, and she had told the king so before going there.

Asked whether, when the assault was to be made, she did not tell her men that she would receive arrows, crossbolts and stones hurled by catapults or cannons, she answered no; there were a hundred wounded, or more. But she had indeed told her men not to fear and they would raise the siege. She said also that at the assault upon the fortress of the Bridge she was wounded in the neck by an arrow or crossbolt; but she received great comfort from St. Margaret, and was better in a fortnight. But she did not on account of that give up her riding or work.

Asked if she knew beforehand that she would be wounded, she answered that she did indeed, and she had told her king so; but that notwithstanding she would not give up her work. And it was revealed to her by the voices of the two saints, namely the blessed Catherine and Margaret. She added that she herself was the first to plant the ladder against the said fortress of the Bridge; and as she was raising the ladder she was wounded in the neck with the crossbolt, as she had said.

*   *   *

Asked on the subject of the woman's dress offered her so that she might hear Mass, she answered that she would not put it on till it should please Our Lord. And if it be that she must be brought to judgment she requests the Lords of the Church to grant her the mercy of a woman's dress and a hood for her head; she would die rather than turn back from what Our Lord commanded her: she firmly believed God would not let her be brought so low, or be presently without His help or miracle.

Asked why, if she wore man's dress at God's bidding, she asked for a woman's robe in the event of her death, she answered: "It is enough for me that it be long."

Asked if her godmother, who saw the fairies, was held to be a wise woman, she answered that she was held and reputed to be an honest woman, and not a witch or sorceress.

Asked whether her saying she would take a woman's dress if they would let her go would please God, she answered that if she were given permission to go in woman's dress she would immediately put on man's dress and do what Our Lord bade her. So she had formerly answered: and nothing would induce her to swear not to take up arms or to wear man's dress, to accomplish our Lord's will.

Asked about the age of the garments worn by St. Catherine and St. Margaret, she answered: "You already have my reply on this matter, and you will get none other from me. I have answered you as best I can."

Asked if she did not believe heretofore that the fairies were evil spirits, she answered she knew nothing of that.

Asked how she knew that St. Catherine and St. Margaret hated the English, she answered: "They love those whom God loves, and hate whom He hates."

Asked if God hated the English, she answered that of God's love or His hatred for the English, or of what He would do to their souls, she knew nothing, but she was certain that, excepting those who died there, they would be driven out of France, and God would send victory to the French and against the English.

Asked if God was for the English when they were prospering in France, she answered that she knew not whether God hated the French, but she believed it was His will to suffer them to be beaten for their sins, if they were in a state of sin.

*   *   *

The Trial for Relapse

On Monday following, the day after Holy Trinity Sunday, we the said judges repaired to Jeanne's prison to observe her state and disposition. * * *

Now because the said Jeanne was wearing a man's dress, a short mantle, a hood, a doublet and other garments used by men (which at our order she had recently put off in favour of woman's dress), we questioned her to find out when and for what reason she had resumed man's dress and rejected woman's clothes. Jeanne said she had but recently resumed man's dress and rejected woman's clothes.

Asked why she had resumed it, and who had compelled her to wear it, she answered that she had taken it of her own will, under no compulsion, as she preferred man's to woman's dress.

She was told that she had promised and sworn not to wear man's dress again, and answered that she never meant to take such an oath.

Asked for what reason she had assumed male costume, she answered that it was more lawful and convenient for her to wear it, since she was among men, than to wear woman's dress. She said she had resumed it because the promises made to her had not been kept, which were to permit her to go to Mass and receive her Saviour, and to take off her chains.

Asked whether she had not abjured and sworn in particular not to resume this male costume, she answered that she would rather die than be in chains, but if she were allowed to go to Mass, if her chains were taken off and she were put in a gracious prison and were given a woman as companion, she would be good and obey the Church.

As we her judges had heard from certain people that she had not yet cut herself off from her illusions and pretended revelations, which she had previously renounced, we asked her whether she had not since Thursday heard the voices of St. Catherine and St. Margaret. She answered yes.

Asked what they told her, she answered that they told her God had sent her word through St. Catherine and St. Margaret of the great pity of this treason by which she consented to abjure and recant in order to save her life; that she had damned herself to save her life. She said that before Thursday they told her what to do and say then, which she did. Further her voices told her, when she was on the scaffold or platform before the people, to answer the preacher boldly. The said Jeanne declared that he was a false preacher, and had accused her of many things she had not done. She said that if she declared God had not sent her she would damn herself, for in truth she was sent from God. She said that her voices had since told her that she had done a great evil in declaring that what she had done was wrong. She said that what she had declared and recanted on Thursday was done only for fear of the fire.

Asked if she believed her voices to be St. Catherine and St. Margaret, she answered yes, and they came from God.

Asked to speak truthfully of the crown which is mentioned above, she replied: "In everything, I told you the truth about it in my trial, as well as I could."

*   *   *

REVIEW QUESTIONS

1. Why do the prosecutors seem preoccupied with the issues of Jeanne's dress and appearance?
2. On what grounds is Jeanne being tried for heresy? What are her crimes, according to the tribunal?
3. In what other ways can legal testimony such as this be used as a historical evidence source? What are the potential pitfalls and limitations of such sources?

LEON BATTISTA ALBERTI

FROM *I Libri della Famiglia*

Leon Battista Alberti (1404–1474) embodied the Renaissance universal man. Born the illegitimate son of a Florentine merchant, he was an athlete, polymath, and artist. He earned a degree in canon law at the University of Bologna in 1428 and migrated to Rome, where he entered papal service. It was there, in 1438, that he began to write On the Family. *Written in the form of a dialogue among the members of the Alberti family, gathered at the deathbed of Leon Battista's father in 1421, it examines the ideal family as a unit for the begetting and rearing of children, for the amassing and maintaining of fortunes, and for the accumulation and exercise of power. It was also a sly exercise in satire, insofar as it indirectly criticizes his brothers and uncles for violating his father's dying wish that Leon Battista be treated as a legitimate member of the family.*

From *I Libri della Famiglia*, translated by Renée Neu Watkins (Columbia: University of South Carolina Press, 1969).

*   *   *

XIII

Lionardo: If I had children, you may be sure I should think about them, but my thoughts would be untroubled. My first consideration would only be to make my children grow up with good character and virtue. Whatever activities suited their taste would suit me. Any activity which is not dishonest is not displeasing to an honorable mind. The activities which lead to honor and praise belong to honorable and wellborn men. Certainly I will admit that every son cannot achieve all that his father might wish. If he does something he is able to do, however, I like that better than to have him strike out in a direction where he cannot follow through. I also think it is more praiseworthy for a man, even if he does not altogether succeed, to do his best in some field rather than sit inactive, inert, and idle. There is an old saying which our ancestors often repeated: "Idleness is the mother of vice." It is an ugly and hateful thing to see a man keep himself forever useless, like that idle fellow who when they asked him why he spent all day as if condemned to sit or lie on public benches, answered "I am waiting to get fat." The man who heard him was disgusted, and asked him rather to try to fatten up a pig, since at least something useful might come of it. Thus quite correctly he showed him what an idle fellow amounts to, which is less than a pig.

I'll go further, Adovardo. However rich and noble a father may be, he should try to have his son learn, besides the noble skills, some occupation which is not degrading. By means of this occupation in case of misfortune he can live honestly by his own labor and the work of his hands. Are the vicissitudes of this world so little or so infrequent that we can ignore the possibility of adverse circumstances? Was not the son of Perseus, king of Macedonia, seen sweating and soiled in a Roman factory, employed in making his living with heavy and painful labor? If the instability of things could thus transport the son of a famous and powerful king to such depths of poverty and need, it is right for us private citizens as well as for men of higher station to provide against every misfortune. If none in our house ever had to devote himself to such laboring occupations, thank fortune for it, and let us make sure that none will have to in the future. A wise and foresightful pilot, to be able to survive in adverse storms, carries more rope, anchors, and sheets than he needs for good weather. So let the father see that his sons enjoy some praiseworthy and useful activity. In this matter let him consider first of all the honesty of the work, and then adapt his course to what he knows his son can actually accomplish, and finally try to choose a field in which, by applying himself, the young man can hope to earn a reputation.

*   *   *

Battista: Whatever you think. The only question we have is what are the things that make a family fortunate. Go on with what you have to say and we shall listen.

*   *   *

Lionardo: In our discussion we may establish four general precepts as sound and firm foundation for all the other points to be developed or added. I shall name them. In the family the number of men must not diminish but augment; possessions must not grow less, but more; all forms of disgrace are to be shunned—a good name and fine reputation is precious and worth pursuing; hatreds, enmities, rancor must be carefully avoided, while good will, numerous acquaintances, and friendships are something to look for, augment, and cultivate.

*   *   *

If a family is not to fall for these reasons into what we have described as the most unfortunate condition of decline, but is to grow, instead, in fame and in the prosperous multitude of its youth, we must persuade our young men to take wives. We must use every argument for this purpose, offer incentive, promise reward, employ all our wit, persistence, and cunning. A most appropriate reason for taking a wife may be found in what we were saying before, about the evil of sensual indulgence, for the condemnation of such things may lead young men to desire honorable satisfactions. As other incentives, we may also speak to them of the delights of this primary and natural companionship of marriage. Children act as pledges and securities of marital love and kindness. At the same time they offer a focus for all a man's hopes and desires. Sad, indeed, is the man who has labored to get wealth and power and lands, and then has no true heir and perpetuator of his memory. No one can be more suited than a man's true and legitimate sons to gain advantages by virtue of his character, position, and authority, and to enjoy the fruits and rewards of his labor. If a man leaves such heirs, furthermore, he need not consider himself wholly dead and gone. His children keep his own position and his true image in the family. Dido, the Phoenician, when Aeneas left her, his mistress, cried out with tears, among her great sorrows no desire above this one: "Ah, had I but a small Aeneas now, to play beside me." As you were first poisoned, wretched and abandoned woman, by that man whose fatal and consuming love you did embrace, so another little Aeneas might by his similar face and gestures have offered you some consolation in your grief and anguish.

*   *   *

When, by the urging and counsel of their elders and of the whole family, young men have arrived at the point of marriage, their mothers and other female relatives and friends, who have known the virgins of the neighborhood from earliest childhood and know the way their upbringing has

formed them, should select all the well-born and well-brought-up girls and present that list to the new groom-to-be. He can then choose the one who suits him best. The elders of the house and all of the family shall reject no daughter-in-law unless she is tainted with the breath of scandal or bad reputation. Aside from that, let the man who will have to satisfy her satisfy himself. He should act as do wise heads of families before they acquire some property—they like to look it over several times before they actually sign a contract. It is good in the case of any purchase and contract to inform oneself fully and to take counsel. One should consult a good number of persons and be very careful in order to avoid belated regrets. The man who has decided to marry must be still more cautious. I recommend that he examine and anticipate in every way, and consider for many days, what sort of person it is he is to live with for all his years as husband and companion. Let him be minded to marry for two purposes: first to perpetuate himself in his children, and second to have a steady and constant companion all his life. A woman is needed, therefore, who is likely to bear children and who is desirable as a perpetual mate.

*   *   *

To sum up this whole subject in a few words, for I want above all to be brief on this point, let a man get himself new kinsmen of better than plebeian blood, of a fortune more than diminutive, of a decent occupation, and of modest and respectable habits. Let them not be too far above himself, lest their greatness overshadow his own honor and position. Too high a family may disturb his own and his family's peace and tranquillity, and also, if one of them falls, you cannot help to support him without collapsing or wearing yourself out as you stagger under a weight too great for your arms and your strength. I also do not want the new relatives to rank too low, for while the first error puts you in a position of servitude, the second causes expense. Let them be equals, then, and, to repeat, modest and respectable people.

*   *   *

We have, as I said, made the house numerous and full of young people. It is essential to give them something to do now, and not let them grow lazy. Idleness is not only useless and generally despised in young men, but a positive burden and danger to the family. I do not need to teach you to shun idleness, when I know you are hard workers and active. I do encourage you to continue as you are doing in every sort of activity and hard discipline that you may attain excellence and deserve fame. Only think this matter over and consider whether any man, even if he is not necessarily ambitious of gaining glory but merely a little shy of falling into disgrace, can ever be, in actuality or even if we merely try to imagine him, a man not heartily opposed to idleness and to mere sitting. Who has ever dreamed he might reach any grace or dignity without hard work in the noblest arts, without assiduous efforts, without plenty of sweat poured out in manly and strenuous exertions? Certainly a man who would wish for the favor of praise and fame must avoid and resist idleness and inertia just as he would do major and hateful enemies. There is nothing that leads more quickly to dishonor and disgrace than idleness. The lap of the idler has always been the nest and lair of vice. Nothing is so harmful and pestilent in public and private life as the lazy and passive citizen. From idleness springs lasciviousness; from lasciviousness comes a contempt for the law; from disobedience to law comes ruin and the destruction of the country itself. To the extent that men tolerate the first resistance of men's will to the customs and ways of the country, their spirits soon turn to arrogance, pride, and the harmful power of avarice and greed. Thieves, murderers, adulterers, and all sorts of criminals and evil men run wild.

*   *   *

To this I might add that man ought to give some reward to God, to satisfy him with good works in return for the wonderful gifts which He gave to the spirit of man exalting and magnifying it beyond that of all other earthly beings. Nature, that is, God, made man a composite of two parts, one celestial and divine, the other most beautiful and noble among mortal things. He provided him with a form and a body suited to every sort of movement, so as to enable him to perceive and to flee from that which threatened to harm and oppose him. He

gave him speech and judgment so that he would be able to seek after and to find what he needed and could use. He gave him movement and sentiment, desire and the power of excitement, so that he might clearly appreciate and pursue useful things and shun those harmful and dangerous to him. He gave him intelligence, teachability, memory and reason, qualities divine in themselves and which enable man to investigate, to distinguish, to know what to avoid and what to desire in order best to preserve himself. To these great gifts, admirable beyond measure, God added still another power of the spirit and mind of man, namely moderation. As a curb on greed and on excessive lusts, he gave him modesty and the desire for honor. Further, God established in the human mind a strong tie to bind together human beings in society, namely justice, equity, liberality, and love. These are the means by which a man can gain the favor and praise of other men, as well as the mercy and grace of the creator. Beyond this, God filled the manly breast with powers that make man able to bear fatigue, adversity, and the hard blows of fortune. He is able to undertake what is difficult, to overcome sorrow, not even to fear death—such are his qualities of strength, of endurance and fortitude, such can be his contempt for transitory things. These are qualities which enable us to honor and serve God as fully as we should, with piety, with moderation, and with every other perfect and honorable deed. Let us agree, then, that man was not born to languish in idleness but to labor and create magnificent and great works, first for the pleasure and glory of God, and second for his own enjoyment of that life of perfect virtue and its fruit, which is happiness.

*   *   *

Let men seek their own happiness first, and they will obtain the happiness of their family also. As I have said, happiness cannot be gained without good works and just and righteous deeds. Works are just and good which not only do no harm to anyone, but which benefit many. Works are righteous if they are without a trace of the dishonorable or any element of dishonesty. The best works are those which benefit many people. Those are most virtuous, perhaps, which cannot be pursued without strength and nobility. We must give ourselves to manly effort, then, and follow the noblest pursuits.

It seems to me, before we dedicate ourselves to any particular activity, it would be wise to think over and examine the question of what is our easiest way to reach or come near to happiness. Not every man easily attains happiness. Nature did not make all men of the same humor, or of the same intelligence or will, or equally endowed with skill and power. Rather nature planned that where I might be weak, you would make good the deficiency, and in some other way you would lack the virtue found in another. Why this? So that I should have need of you, and you of him, he of another, and some other of me. In this way one man's need for another serves as the cause and means to keep us all united in general friendship and alliance. This may, indeed, have been the source and beginning of republics. Laws may have begun thus rather than as I was saying before; fire and water alone may not have been the cause of so great a union among men as society gives them. Society is a union sustained by laws, by reason, and by custom.

Let us not digress. To decide which is the most suitable career for himself, a man must take two things into account: the first is his own intelligence, his mind and his body, everything about himself; and the second, the question requiring close consideration, is that of outside supports, the help and resources which are necessary or useful and to which he must have early access, welcome, and free right of use if he is to enter the field for which he seems more suited than for any other. Take an example: if a man wished to perform great feats of arms while he knew he was himself but a weak fellow, not very robust, incapable of bearing up through dust and storm and sun, this would not be the right profession for him to pursue. If I, being poor, longed to devote my life to letters, though I had not the money to pay the considerable expenses attached to such a career, again this would be a poor choice of career. If you are equipped with numerous relatives, plenty of friends, abundant wealth, and if you possess within yourself intelligence, eloquence, and such tact as to keep you out of any rough or awkward situations,

and you decide to dedicate yourself to civic affairs, you might do extremely well.

*   *   *

We should also consider at this point how much reward and profit, how much honor and fame, you can gain from any work or achievement you undertake to perform. The only condition is that you surpass everyone else in the field. In every craft the most skilled master, as you know, gains most riches and has the best position and the greatest stature among his companions. Think how even in so humble a profession as shoemaking men search out the best among the cobblers. If it is true of the humblest occupations that the most skilled practitioners are ever most in demand and so become most famous, consider whether in the highest professions the opposite suddenly holds true. In fact you will find it still more to the point to be the best in these, or at least one of the best. If you succeed in these fields, you know that you have been given a greater portion of happiness than other men. If you are learned, you realize the misfortune of the ignorant. You know, in addition, that the unhappiest lot falls to those who, being ignorant, desire still to appear learned.

*   *   *

Consider in your own mind what a boon to know more than others and to put the knowledge to good use at the right time and place. If you think it over, I am sure you will realize that in every field a man who would appear to be valuable must be valuable in fact. Now we have stated this much: that youth should not be wasted but should be directed to some honorable kind of work, that a man should do his utmost in that work, and that he should choose the field which will be most helpful to his family and bring him most fame. A career should suit our own nature and the state of our fortunes, and should be pursued in such a way that we may never, by our own fault at least, fall short of the first rank.

Riches, however, are for nearly everyone the primary reason for working at all. They are also most useful in making it possible to persevere in our undertakings until we win approval and attain public favor, position, and fame. This is the time, therefore, to explain how wealth is acquired and how it is kept. It was also one of the four things which we said were necessary to bring about and to preserve contentment in a family. Now, then, let us begin to accumulate wealth. Perhaps the present moment, as the evening grows dark, is just right for this subject, for no occupation seems less attractive to a man of large and liberal spirit than the kind of labor by which wealth is in fact gathered. If you will count over in your imagination the actual careers that bring great profits, you will see that all basically concern themselves with buying and selling or with lending and collecting the returns. Having neither petty nor vulgar minds, I imagine you probably find these activities, which are solely directed to making a profit, somewhat below you. They seem entirely to lack honor and distinction.

*   *   *

Those who thus dismiss all mercenary activities are wrong, I believe. If the pursuit of wealth is not as glorious as are other great pursuits, yet a man is not contemptible if, being unsuited by nature to achieve anything much in other finer fields of work, he devotes himself to this kind of activity. Here, it may be, he knows he is not inadequately equipped to do well. Here everyone admits he is very useful to the republic and still more to his own family. Wealth, if it is used to help the needy, can gain a man esteem and praise. With wealth, if it is used to do great and noble things and to show a fine magnanimity and splendor, fame and dignity can be attained. In emergencies and times of need we see every day how useful is the wealth of private citizens to the country itself. From public funds alone it is not always possible to pay the wages of those whose arms and blood defend the country's liberty and dignity. Nor can republics increase their glory and their might without enormous expenditure.

*   *   *

Why have I gone on at length on these topics? Only to show you that, among occupations, there are quite a few, both honorable and highly esteemed, by means of which wealth in no small measure may be gained. One of these occupations, as you

know, is that of merchant. You can easily call to mind other similar careers which are both honorable and highly profitable. You want to know, then, what they are. Let us run through them. We shall spread out all the occupations before us and choose the best among them, then we shall try to define how they make us wealthy and prosperous. Occupations that do not bring profit and gain will never make you rich. Those that bring frequent and large profits are the ones that make you rich. The only system for becoming rich, by our own industry and by the means that luck, friends, or anyone's favor can give us, is to make profits. And how do men grow poor? Ill fortune certainly plays a part, this I admit, but excluding fortune, let us speak here of industry. If riches come through profits, and these through labor, diligence, and hard work, then poverty, which is the reverse of profit, will follow from the reverse of these virtues, namely from neglect, laziness, and sloth. These are the fault neither of fortune nor of others, but of oneself. One grows poor, also, by spending too much. Prodigality dissipates wealth and throws it away. The opposite of prodigality, the opposite of neglect, are carefulness and conscientiousness, in short, good management. Good management is the means to preserve wealth. Thus we have found out that to become rich one must make profits, keep what one has gained, and exercise rational good management.

*   *   *

REVIEW QUESTIONS

1. What, according to Alberti, is the role and nature of a father?
2. How is a father's authority different from other kinds of authority?
3. What is the role of education in the formation of human nature?
4. How does this view differ from that of other authors?
5. What is Alberti's definition of honor?
6. What is its relationship to the family? Why is it so important to Alberti?
7. How might Alberti define the family?

JAN HUS

FROM *The Church*

Jan Hus (c. 1373–1415) was a Czech preacher and writer active in Prague. Influenced by the writings of the English theologian John Wyclif (c. 1330–1384), he called for radical reforms in the Church. Summoned under safe conduct to the Council of Constance, he was nevertheless accused of heresy, convicted, and burned at the stake. Hus thus became a national martyr in his native Bohemia, which remained for decades in rebellion against the Catholic Church. This chapter from his book The Church *expresses his opinions on the papacy.*

From *The Church by John Hus*, edited by David S. Schaff (New York: Scribner's, 1915).

Chapter XII
Christ the True Roman Pontiff upon Salvation Depends

To the honor of our Lord Jesus Christ, which honor and also Christ the aforesaid doctors nowhere mention in their writing, this conclusion is proved, namely, "to be subject to the Roman pontiff is necessary for salvation for every human being."[1] From this it is clear, that no one can be saved unless he is meritoriously subject to Jesus Christ. But Christ is the Roman pontiff, just as he is the head of the universal church and every particular church. Therefore the conclusion is a true one. The consequence is clear from the major premise. And the minor premise is clear from the things said above and from what is said in I Peter 2:25, "For ye were sometime going astray like sheep but are now returned unto the shepherd and bishop of your souls," and also from Heb. 7:22: "By so much also hath Jesus become the surety of a better covenant and they indeed have been made free, many in number, according to the law because that by death they are hindered from continuing. But this man, because

he continueth forever, hath his priesthood unchangeable, wherefore also he is able to save to the uttermost, drawing near through himself to the Lord and always living to intercede for us. For such a high priest became us holy, guileless, undefiled, separated from sinners and made higher than the heavens, who needeth not daily like those priests, to offer up sacrifices first for his own sins and then for the sins of the people, for this he did once for all when he offered himself."

Truly this is the most holy and chief Roman pontiff, sitting at God's right hand and dwelling with us, for he said: "And lo, I am with you all the days, even unto the consummation of the age," Matt. 28:20. For that person, Christ, is everywhere present, since he is very God whose right it is to be everywhere without limitation. He is the bishop, who baptizes and takes away the sins of the world, John 1:29. He is the one who joins in marriage so that no man may put asunder: "What God hath joined together let not man put asunder," Matt. 19:6. He is the one who makes us priests: "He made us a kingdom and priests," Rev. 1:6. He performs the sacrament of the eucharist, saying: "This is my body," Luke 22:19. This is he who confirms his faithful ones: "I will give you a mouth of wisdom which all your adversaries will not be able to withstand or gainsay," Luke 21:15. He it is who feeds his sheep by his word and example and by the food of

---

[1] From Boniface VIII's bull *Unam sanctam*. The expression in the next sentence, "meritoriously," refers to the mediæval doctrine of merit in proportion to our good works.

his body. All these things, however, he does on his part indefectibly, because he is a holy priest, guileless, undefiled, separated from sinners and made higher than the heavens. He is the bishop holding supreme guardianship over his flock, because he sleeps not nor is he, that watches over Israel, weary. He is the pontiff who in advance makes the way easy for us to the heavenly country. He is the pope—*papa*—because he is the wonderful Prince of Peace, the Father of the future age. For, indeed, such a pontiff became us who, since he was in the form of God, did not think it robbery to be equal with God but emptied himself, taking upon him the form of a servant, because he humbled himself by being made obedient unto death, even the death of the cross. Wherefore God hath highly exalted and given him a name which is above every name, that at the name of Jesus every knee should bow, of things in heaven, of things on the earth, and things in hell [Phil. 2:6 *sqq.*].

To this the conclusion follows, namely: "To be subject to the Roman pontiff is necessary for salvation for every human being." But there is no other such pontiff except the Lord Jesus Christ himself, our pontiff. . . .

Chapter XIII
The Pope Not the Head of the Church but Christ's Vicar

Further, the aforesaid doctors lay down in their writing that "the pope is head of the Roman church and the college of cardinals the body, and that they are very successors and princes of the apostle Peter and the college of Christ's other apostles in ecclesiastical office for the purpose of discerning and defining all catholic and church matters, correcting and purging all errors in respect to them and, in all these matters, to have the care of all the churches and of all the faithful of Christ. For in order to govern the church throughout the whole world it is fitting there should always continue to be such manifest and true successors in the office of Peter, the prince of the apostles, and of the college of the other apostles of Christ. And such successors cannot be found or procured on the earth

other than the pope, the existing head, and the college of cardinals, the existing body, of the aforesaid Roman church." . . .

I assume that the pope stands for that spiritual bishop who, in the highest way and in the most similar way, occupies the place of Christ, just as Peter did after the ascension. But if any person whatsoever is to be called pope—whom the Western church accepts as Roman bishop—appointed to decide as the final court ecclesiastical cases and to teach the faithful whatever he wishes, then there is an abuse of the term, because according to this view, it would be necessary in cases to concede that the most unlettered layman or a female, or a heretic and antichrist, may be pope. This is plain, for Constantine II, an unlettered layman, was suddenly ordained a priest and through ambition made pope and then was deposed and all the things which he ordained were declared invalid, about A.D. 707. And the same is plain from the case of Gregory, who was unlettered and consecrated another in addition to himself. And as the people were displeased with the act, a third pope was superinduced. Then these quarrelling among themselves, the emperor came to Rome and elected another as sole pope. As for a female, it is plain in the case of Agnes, who was called John Anglicus,[2] and of her Castrensis, 5:3, writes: "A certain woman sat in the papal chair two years and five months, following Leo. She is said to have been a girl, called Agnes, of the nation of Mainz, was led about by her paramour in a man's dress in Athens and named John Anglicus. She made such progress in different studies that, coming to Rome, she read the trivium to an audience of great teachers. Finally, elected pope, she was with child by her paramour, and, as she was proceeding from St. Peter's to the Lateran, she had the pains of labor in a narrow street between the Colosseum and St. Clement's and gave birth to a child. Shortly afterward she died there and was buried. For this reason it is said that all the popes avoid this street. Therefore, she is not put down in the catalogue of popes."

As for a heretic occupying the papal chair we have an instance in Liberius, of whom Castrensis

---

[2] The alleged female Pope Agnes (John VIII, about 855), whom Hus refers again and again in his writings.

writes, . . . that at Constantius's command he was exiled for three years because he wished to favor the Arians. At the counsel of the same Constantius, the Roman clergy ordained Felix pope who, during the sessions of a synod condemned and cast out two Arian presbyters, Ursacius and Valens, and when this became known, Liberius was recalled from exile, and being wearied by his long exile and exhilarated by the reoccupation of the papal chair, he yielded to heretical depravity; and when Felix was cast down, Liberius with violence held the church of Peter and Paul and St. Lawrence so that the clergy and priests who favored Felix were murdered in the church, and Felix was martyred, Liberius not preventing.

As for antichrist occupying the papal chair, it is evident that a pope living contrary to Christ, like any other perverted person, is called by common consent antichrist. In accordance with John 2:22, many are become antichrists. And the faithful will not dare to deny persistently that it is possible for the man of sin to sit in the holy place. Of him the Saviour prophesied when he said: "When ye see the abomination of desolation, which is spoken of by Daniel, standing in the holy place." Matt. 24:15. The apostle also says: "Let no man beguile you in any wise, for it will not be except the falling away come first and the man of sin be revealed, the son of perdition; he that opposeth and exalteth himself against all that is called God or is worshipped; so that he sitteth in the temple of God setting himself forth as God," II Thess. 2:3–4. And it is apparent from the *Chronicles* how the papal dignity has sunk. . . .

. . . No pope is the most exalted person of the catholic church but Christ himself; therefore no pope is the head of the catholic church besides Christ. The conclusion is valid reasoning from description to the thing described. Inasmuch as the head of the church is the capital or chief person of the church, yea, inasmuch as the head is a name of dignity and of office—dignity in view of predestination, and office in view of the administration of the whole church—it follows that no one may reasonably assert of himself or of another without revelation that he is the head of a particular holy church, although if he live well he ought to hope that he is a member of the holy catholic church, the

bride of Christ. Therefore, we should not contend in regard to the reality of the incumbency whether any one, whoever he may be, living with us is the head of a particular holy church but, on the ground of his works, we ought assume that, if he is a superior, ruling over a particular holy church, then he is the superior in that particular church, and this ought to be assumed of the Roman pontiff, unless his works gainsay it, for the Saviour said: "Beware of false prophets which come unto you in sheep's clothing but inwardly they are ravening wolves. By their fruits ye shall know them." Matt. 7:15. Also John 10:38: "Believe the works." . . .

In the same way, it is not of necessity to salvation for all Christians, living together, that they should believe expressly that any one is head of any church whatsoever unless his evangelical life and works plainly moved them to believe this. For it would be all too much presumption to affirm that we are heads of any particular church which perhaps might be a part of holy mother church. How, therefore, may any one of us without revelation presume to assert of himself or of another that he is the head, since it is said truly, Ecclesiasticus 9, that "no one knows, so far as predestination goes, whether one is worthy of love or hatred."

Likewise, if we examine in the light of the feeling and influence with which we influence inferiors and, on the other hand, examine by the mirror of Scripture, according to which we should regulate our whole life, then we would choose rather to be called servants and ministers of the church than its heads. For it is certain that if we do not fulfil the office of a head, we are not heads, as Augustine, *de decem chordis* says: that a perverse husband is not the head of his wife, much less is a prelate of the church, who alone from God could have a dignity of this kind, the head of a particular church in case he fall away from Christ.[3]

Therefore, after Augustine has shown that a truly Christian wife ought to mourn over the fornication of her husband, not for carnal reasons, but

---

[3] Not an exact quotation. The inference is drawn by Hus. The Sermon on the Ten Strings, Psalms 144:9, has much to say on the relation of husband and wife on the basis of "Thou shalt not commit adultery."

out of love and for the chastity due to the man Christ—he says consequentially that Christ speaks in the hearts of good women, where the husband does not hear, and he goes on to say: "Mourn over the injuries done by thy husband, but do not imitate them that he may rather imitate you in that which is good. For in that wherein he does wrong, do not regard him as thy head but me, thy Lord." And he proves that this ought to be the case and says: "If he is the head in that wherein he does wrong and the body follow its head, they both go over the precipice. But that the Christian may not follow this bad head, let him keep himself to the head of the church, Christ, to whom he owes his chastity, to whom he yields his honor, no longer a single man but now a man wedded to his mother, the church." Blessed, therefore, be the head of the church, Christ, who cannot be separated from his bride which is his mystical body, as the popes have often been separated from the church by heresy.

But some of the aforesaid doctors say that the pope is the bodily head of the church militant and this head ought always to be here with the church, but in this sense Christ is not the bodily head. Here is meant that the same difficulty remains, namely, that they prove the first part of the statement. For it remains for them to prove that the pope is the head of holy church, a thing they have not proved. And, before that, it remains for them to prove that Christ is not the bodily head of the church militant, inasmuch as Christ is a bodily person, because the man who is the head of the church militant, who is Christ, is present through all time with his church

unto the consummation of the age, in virtue of his divine personality. Similarly, he is present by grace, giving his body to the church to be eaten in a sacramental and spiritual way. Wherefore, is not that bridegroom, who is the head of the church, much more present with us than the pope, who is removed from us two thousand miles and incapable of influencing of himself our feeling or movements? Let it suffice, therefore, to say, that the pope may be the vicar of Christ and may be so to his profit, if he is a faithful minister predestinated unto the glory of the head, Jesus Christ.[4]

* * *

REVIEW QUESTIONS

1. What sources of authority in the Church does Hus accept? Which does he deny?
2. How do Hus's arguments compare with those that Gregory VII and Boniface VIII raised in defense of papal authority (see pp. 254–261 and 335–336)?
3. In what ways was Hus a threat to the organized Church? In what ways was he an asset?

---

[4] The same thought is expressed in Reply to Palecz, *Mon.*, 1:321: "God gave Christ to be the head over the militant church, that he might preside over it most excellently without any hindrance of local distance . . . and pour into it, as the head pours into the body, movement, feeling and a gracious life whether there be no pope or a woman be pope."

BARTOLOMEO DE GIANO

FROM "A Letter on the Cruelty of the Turks"

We know very little of the life of Bartolomeo de Giano, a Franciscan friar of the mid-fifteenth century. What little we do know must be derived from the letter that preserves his name in history. The dates of his birth and death are unknown, though he is generally assumed to have been born at the end of the fourteenth century in or near the town of Giano, in Umbria. At some point in early life, Bartolomeo entered the Order of Friars Minor as a Conventual, because he is listed by Bernardino of L'Aquila among the famous men of his country. In 1402, he seems to have become an Observant Franciscan, following the example of the great preacher, Bernardino of Siena. Bartolomeo seems to have spent the early portion of his career at Foligno, where he became a Master of Theology and is reported to have preached regularly on the necessity of Christian peace and modesty. All of this changed in 1431, when he and five other friars, including Albert of Sarteano, the addressee of his letter, were chosen by Pope Eugenius IV for a mission to Constantinople. There he was to negotiate with the Byzantine Emperor John VIII Paleologus to facilitate the participation of Orthodox Christians in the coming Council of Florence. Due to his erudition and eloquence, it is reported, Bartolomeo convinced both the Byzantine Emperor and the Greek patriarch Joseph II to attend the council. He is reported to have accompanied them to Italy in 1437–1438, then returned to Constantinople to found a Franciscan friary. In 1444, Eugenius named Bartolomeo Vicar to the Minister General of the Eastern province of the Franciscan Order. At this point, the historical record ceases but for a rumor that he spent the final years of his life in the Franciscan convent of S. Francesco del Monte in Perugia to which he is said to have brought books written in Greek and translated into Latin. In 1438, during or shortly after his first mission to Constantinople, he wrote to his companion, Albert of Sarteano, at that time preaching in Venice, to urge the necessity of a crusade to counter the growing threat posed to Christendom by the expansion of the Ottoman Turks.

From "A Letter on the Cruelty of the Turks," by Bartolomeo de Giano, translated by W. L. North, in *Patrologia Graeca*, Vol. 158, edited by J. P. Migne (Paris: J. P. Migne, 1857–66), cols. 1055–68.

To the venerable religious and my outstanding brother, Friar Abbot of Sartiano of the order of the Friars who preaches to the Venetians and is his father in Christ Jesus, who should be greatly beloved.

For a long time now, my venerable father, I have longed to see, to speak, and to embrace your person but this grace has not yet been granted to me. For when I am traveling in the West, you head for the East, and when I seek you in the East, you return to your homeland in the West. But all this, I suppose, has happened through God's plan, since, as I have heard, your preaching—as usual—brought no small benefit this year in Venice. But now I would wish with fervent desire that when, with the Lord's favor, the union of both churches is celebrated, you visit these and farther distant regions with your usual lessons of preaching, knowledge, and life. Indeed, we think that a tremendous harvest of souls can be accomplished by the friars. For although Greece has been lost as has all of Turkey (which is elsewhere called Asia where the seven churches mentioned in the Apocalypse are and where Teucer, the enemy of Christ, reigns), at the present time innumerable Christian peoples still remain beyond the Black Sea, governing themselves under the Greek rite to this very day. First, there is to the East of Trebizond the not insignificant kingdom of the Georgians, i.e., of Georgia, where King Alexander rules today. And who can traverse under the open sky the homeland of the Russians and the Ruthenians to the marshes of Meotis (which is called the Sea of Habbakuk when interpreted)? I leave out Circasia, Vogaria, Mingrillia, Wallachia,

Patras on the sea, though at present these are under the Greek rite. I'll say nothing about the Armenians, whom, I hope, you will soon see coming to Italy along with our father Jacob so as to be led back to the Catholic faith. They are far more eager than other nations for ready conversion and for receiving the truth and most favorably inclined to the Latins. Furthermore, you know from experience that innumerable Christians are scattered in the Caesian mountains and here and there in Persia and Scythia, where the houses of our brethren stand devoid of friars, and that some are still living even among the Tartars. I therefore think that your personality and others like yours would be not without benefit—indeed, they would be most appropriate in those regions—once the sacred union is celebrated, if God should permit it.

Oh, but why do I recall these things when it is far more pleasant to weep than to hope for anything good for the aforementioned peoples? It is far more pleasing to weep, I say, and to shout to the stars, that the ever merciful Most High may look down upon these regions that should be liberated—in the midst of which we almost are—and not instead gaze upon the peoples' sins for so long that the name of Christianity is snuffed out in the North and East. Alas! each day Christians are lost and the Devil's followers grow in number and strength of arms. For in Turkey and in Greece there is scarcely a city, fort, or village in which—and scarcely a day on which—the most holy name of Christ is denied and Muhammad, the son of the devil, exalted. And this happens not only because of fear and threats but also because of delights and honor. And this will perhaps surprise you: this is done by those who concern themselves with wealth, honor, and with the prudence of the world! But passing over past evils in silence—since I believe no tongue capable of recounting them—I shall touch briefly on what I have recently seen with my own eyes so that you may know and lament it with me and so that if you find anyone not utterly devoid of piety, you may compel them to weep as well.

I think you can recall, beloved Father, that when we left Venice, destined for these parts by our Lord Pope, at the same time that you arrived there,

having just returned from Jerusalem, news spread there over the next few days that the Hungarians had burned some Turkish ships and killed many of them. These things, I declare, were all true. But I do not know if you later heard that the Turk himself, enraged by this, came there in person with a great army and carried off, it is said, more than sixty thousand souls from the kingdom of Rascia, Hungary's neighbor. It is uncertain as to whether any of them now remember Christ. Does this surprise you? You should instead wonder and lament much more what has for the last twenty-five or thirty years been reckoned to our own shame and no small damage: that each year the Turk seizes no less than ten to fifteen thousand souls (and I am stating a lower number so that you may believe it)? And if you would believe it, I would say that the Turk has compelled five hundred thousand to deny Christ Jesus with threats and blandishments. Truly I would be not a little surprised if even one Christian is still found in these parts. For the city of Corinth alone gains thousands and thousands of ducats each year as the toll for the captives passing from Gallipoli into Turkey. Oh sins of Christians, where are you heading? Where are you taking yourselves? To what servitude, to what shame do you compel yourselves to be subject?

*   *   *

Three great mountains of heads have been made there from the dead men who refused to give themselves up peacefully. Their bodies, meanwhile, have been rolled up upon the slopes of the mountains—a horrific food for wolves, dogs, and birds. Priests and monks, young and old, were led away in iron fetters tied to the backs of horses, at least as long as they were able to walk. But the rest of the crowd, including women and children, were herded by dogs without any mercy or piety. If one of them slowed down, unable to walk further because of thirst or pain, O Good Jesus! she immediately ended her life there in torment, cut in half. So great was the multitude of the dead, as I learned from the aforementioned brother who told me with his conscience as his witness, that this brother, after deliberating within himself over whether or not to recite the *De profundis* for each of the dead and being unable to do so because of the multitude of the dead, finally said, weeping, the prayer *Inclina*. Nor did this perhaps happen just in one place, as one might think, but over the entire course of the twenty days' journey that the aforementioned captives had made and especially in Adrianople where outside the dwellings so great a quantity of bodies lay consumed, partially rotted, partially devoured by dogs, that it would seem unbelievable to anyone who had not seen it with their own eyes. Meanwhile, some of the dying are cast out in the sight of the Latin merchants, and if any of them did try to bury or remove them from there it was more because of the stench than their piety, and not was even this allowed on any conditions, unless they paid first. Oh!! I shall call these people blessed unless they died in despair! For they were crying out loud with weak wailing as children and infants, youths and virgins, men and women, were captured, driven along, and killed. Thou Who art in Heaven, are You seeing all this? Are You moved even a little by piety? O blessed Virgin, O holy men and women of God, where is our hope, our trust in you? Or perhaps we were deceived, because our faith is empty and false? No! Blessed I would call these people, I say, if they should have patiently endured hunger, thirst, travail, pain, servitude, and death. Yet why should I call them blessed when they constantly deny the faith of Christ, especially youths of both sexes who are turned from the faith and converted to a hostility towards Christians with such great ease that they may almost begin to believe, if it is possible, even the elect are led into error. Oh the depths of God's wisdom and knowledge! How incomprehensible are His judgments and untraceable are His ways! Oh, how many and what great people are in the world, I believe, who seem in both fact and name to be Christians but who, if this coal of persecution should heat them— or rather the mild sweetness of the flesh should entreat them—would deny Christ and say with Peter: *I do not know him.* Oh, would that we not encounter such a testing, such an experience, such a furnace, and if it is going to consume, let it not make its trial in our age, saving God's will! Indeed,

many who believe that they will be immoveable columns and are believed by others to be so, we shall see, or perhaps be seen, to be in a wretched state of ruined wretchedly. I am a liar if I do not know many religious persons of diverse orders who most fervently preach Christ today but tomorrow shall foully renounce Him. This is why I think that no one should trust in themselves but all should be afraid. But let us return to our initial theme.

*   *   *

Often do we say these things, often do we lament them, and on these and similar lamentable deeds we consume no small portion of our time, although we would rather die than see the latest evils that each day consume more and more of our race. But what arouses and confirms even greater sorrow is the fact that we have absolutely no one with whom we can share these things and [thereby] lighten the punishment. For if any Christians either stay in or visit these parts, they burn with so much lust for temporal gain that they either do not give any thought to these things or—horrible to say— they secretly desire them. Behold! They fill their purses from Turkish profits and enrich themselves on the blood of Christians.

*   *   *

For you see, it just was two hundred years or so ago that all of Asia down to Antioch and beyond was inhabited by Christian peoples. Now, little by little this fire has consumed Asia so that now you shall find but few Christians there unless they be Slavs dedicated to the service of the Turks. I exclude Syria, the Holy Land, Armenia, Arabia, and the surrounding countries up to Alexandria which obviously have not been Christian by and large for a long time now. Nor shall I speak of Egypt, Ethiopia, Persia and—greater than all the rest—all of Africa, where you shall find hardly a single Christian except perhaps some merchants. And yet it is asserted that all the aforementioned were Christian countries. But these [Christian nations] have now been laid to rest by the length of time [under Muslim rule].

It was only eighty years ago or so that not a single Turk was found in Greece. They even crossed over carried by the Christians themselves and have filled that entire country. Indeed, unless it is provided with some swift remedy, Greece shall soon become like Arabia or Egypt. I am speaking of a broad and populous country adorned by the most glorious cities which have all been, for the time being at least, reduced to nothingness, so to speak, since they have been emptied of their inhabitants. It is the land where Alexander the Great ruled, and where there are the cities of Athens, Corinth, Sparta, Thessalonika, and Philippi . . . cities that now it is painful to see.

What I have described is nothing in comparison with the following deeds that have or will occur there unless someone pays attention and offers help. Where, I ask you, are the countries now of Dalmatia, Croatia, Bosnia, Rascia, Bulgaria, Albania, and Wallachia—not insignificant kingdoms that were despoiled of their inhabitants in just a few years? I come now to Hungary from which, it is said, three hundred thousand (though I would say more truly six hundred thousand) souls have been carried off in just a few days.

Don't you believe that what I fear could happen, namely that by the just judgment of God this fire shall advance so far that it could occupy the border of [European] Christians? What then are those wretched Christians doing now? What are their princes doing? What about the pastors of the Church? Do they not sleep or do they suffer instead from lethargy so that they simply await Christendom to be consumed bit by bit? They play around—or rather hurt themselves—with lances and dances! And in the meantime, the Turk snuffs out the name of Christ and has already sworn, has already vowed himself to his own God, not to remain at peace under any agreement, unless he hears the praises of Muhammad sung in all of Hungary as soon as possible.

*   *   *

Now, venerable father, wait to hear something else amazing and not a little delightful: it is said that the Turks do not have weapons! And if you consider this to be impossible when they have despoiled so many Christians countries, take a look at the merchants from Italy—Latins, Venetians,

Genoese, and others. Because of their great piety and grace and contrary to what is just and unjust, these merchants bring galleys and ships there loaded not with iron but with steel in such great abundance that I can scarcely believe that steel would be found in any Italian city at such a good price and in such great quantities as it is found in Gallipoli, Pera, and Adrianople! I am a liar if I have not seen it with my own eyes and in the galleys on which it came. But hear how they excuse themselves—they do not sell it to the Turks but only to the Jews and the Greeks. It is they, therefore, who later give the steel to the Turks with their own hands. And this, so that the Turks may make sharper swords to spill the guts of Christians! O how much God's piety endures! How long do you intend to delay your vengeance?! You are perhaps amazed at how troubled are Venice, Genoa, and the other Italian cities? Surely you should wonder more why they are not completely destroyed. Indeed, over the last forty days we have seen mules loaded with steel led from this city to Adrianople where the Turks themselves foully mock the Christians, saying openly: *Look at your blindness, you wretches: you offer us arms so that we may completely destroy you!* What do you think of that, beloved brother!? On this point alone why do you not openly proclaim this disaster to those in the city in which you preach? But I know without a doubt what you are doing. You cry out but are not heard. But the scourge of God is at hand which justly whips sinners. But you want us now to return to the Tartars.

In this very year around the month of August when the Turk was destroying Hungary, many here claimed that a new emperor was elected, though I do not confirm this because I have not seen it. You are more familiar with these matters because, when fighting with the Poles for the kingdom of Hungary, he conquered them and killed innumerable people—I mean Christians. Then, the Tartars, who are the Poles neighbors, perceived that the Christian peoples were involved in wars and invaded Poland. What they did there, I have no words to describe. Ask them yourself, if some people have come from there.

Such are the princes' fortifications! Such are their plans! Such is their warfare against the infidel! Alas, for the wretches who should and can help but do not do so. Nor did they lack advance notice. For I sent brethren [to them] on behalf of the majority and wrote more than thirty letters long before the month of December when that man was preparing an army against them. And these letters I sent to the emperor and the dukes—they had them, they read them but they did not care, as the results themselves show. That trumpet of God, Friar James, was also proclaiming this before the kings and princes and was declaring these injuries to their faces, saying: *Behold, you wretches, foreigners despoil your homeland, dishonor your wives in your presence, and lead your brothers and sons off in chains—and yet you do not care.* But when they heard these words and the like, they laughed and seemed without feeling. And what is more, our lord, the most holy Pope, even sent them eternal gifts, namely the indulgence of their sins, if any would take up arms against the infidel.

When, oh when, therefore, shall these miserable Christians be roused [to action]? When shall that time come? Shall I see it with mine own eyes before I die? This is my hope but it is a very weak one and has truly waned and is now all but despair. Where is the glorious kingdom of the Franks now, which in ancient times drove the Saracens from Hispania? Where is the great power of the English? These two have been consumed [fighting] against one another. Where now is the king of Aragon, terror of the infidel? Where are the other powers and Christian princes? . . .

*   *   *

But, really, the most important reason that moved me to write these things to you is this: so that you, who burn with the piety of Christ and a zeal for souls and who blossom with learning and eloquence, may shape and adorn this letter that I have prepared for you, and compose it with due piety and gravity so that it may be worthy to stand in the sight of kings and princes, if they perchance should hear and at some point be turned to avenge the injury done to Jesus Christ.

But unless you shall decide the opposite, anyone will recognize that a text is all the more likely to lend itself to believability as it has been written not with carefully composed and ornate eloquence but in a simple style. But this matter I leave entirely to your judgment. . . .

*   *   *

It therefore seems abundantly clear—to conclude this summary briefly—that the time is now unmistakably upon us when he shall destroy the Christians or be utterly destroyed by them. I am profoundly afraid of the first of these; may God Himself grant the other instead. Yet we should not give up hope. For a rumor is said to be widespread among the Saracens and Turks that the time of their destruction is at hand, indeed already past, as certain of their prophets say. But because of their alms and piety towards the poor—and this is true—it has been delayed for the moment and shall yet be deferred a little longer.

*   *   *

Why delay any longer? Look, here is what you seek. But why do I waste time and breath on such things? Since no one but God Himself can illuminate their eyes and move their hearts, all human exhortation is rendered void. Yet on this matter, fathers and brothers, when this news comes to your ears, rouse God, I beg you, with your cries, rouse Him with your sighs, disturb the saints, male and female alike, with your prayers, hasten through cities and towns, call the people, gather an assembly and pierce the hearts of small and great alike concerning these events. For thus these people may abstain from sin for a time, persist in diligent prayer, and set their minds to works of piety, so that pious and merciful God, who is now roused to anger because of man's sins, may be calmed by these good works and may look down briefly upon the Christian people, infuse love into their hearts, and give holy union and peace to prelates and princes. For when the Devil, the inventor and kindler of all evils who has hitherto sown so many stumbling blocks in Christ's Church, is dragged off to Tartarus, confounded, then the Church's faithful shall be exultant and the infidel shall blush for shame, be confounded, and give way: the Turks who today deride and mock Christ and the Christians. And if with the Lord's favor, this sacred union is celebrated, cross the sea, my brothers, in safety (I mean those who are suitable and willing) for within your gaze there shall be much land overflowing with eternal fruits. And beloved brother, I invite you all the more confidently as I know the secrets of your heart. Amen.

From Constantinople, 12 December 1438

Yours completely,
Brother Bartholomew de Jano of the order of Friars Minor, although unworthy.

REVIEW QUESTIONS

1. What threat do the Ottoman Turks pose to Christians in the East?
2. Given that many, even most, eastern Christians are Greek and offer no obedience to the Pope in Rome, why is Bartolomeo so concerned about them?
3. What is the importance of Constantinople in Bartolomeo's eyes?
4. What should western Christians do to support their co-religionaries in the East?
5. What makes this "crusade" different from those intended to reclaim the Holy Land for Christianity?

12 ∾ INNOVATION AND EXPLORATION, 1453–1533

This chapter takes up both the Renaissance at its height and the intensification of contact between Europe and the rest of the world. We have already witnessed the impact that closer relations between Europeans and Muslims around the Fall of Constantinople had on launching the early Renaissance. Equally important was the rise of the printing press that would enable the cultural and intellectual transmissions that took place during this period, which included maps, geographies, and histories, to be shared widely around Europe. Ultimately, the transmission and spread of this information spurred explorations along the western coast of Africa, the Atlantic Ocean, and around the globe leading to encounters and exchanges that would forever change Europe and all the regions of the world.

As noted in Chapter 11, scholars have traditionally viewed the Renaissance as a period of great change and have identified the following several characteristics: 1) scholars and artists revived classical antiquity as a subject of study and emulation; 2) the state emerged as a subject that could be studied and used by those seeking power; 3) the notion that the ideal ("universal") man was well rounded in physical and intellectual endeavors; and 4) the notion that achievement mattered more than lineage. Scholars in recent decades, however, argue that while there were indeed some new cultural and intellectual developments during this period, much of the political, cultural, and social changes that took place were part of longer developments that had been underway for centuries. Many of the selections in this chapter take on the characteristics of the Renaissance in a longer context.

Exploration, expansion, and exploitation intensified and increased as a result of these short and long term historic developments, leading to what historians refer to as the "Age of Exploration." One recalls the well-known stories of the attempt in 1492 of Christopher Columbus to find a sea route to East Asia by sailing west across the Atlantic Ocean only to reach the islands of the Caribbean, a truly "new world," or the voyage of Vasco da Gama around the Cape of Good Hope on the southern tip of Africa and across the Indian Ocean to make landfall in 1497 on the Coromandel coast of South Asia. These discoveries and their consequences had an impact that cannot be overestimated. They utterly transformed, directly or indirectly, every single aspect of European society and culture, and the lives of the peoples encountered as well. They brought Europe into more immediate contact with non-European cultures and civilizations. Direct sea routes to Europe's most important trading partners, whether in new worlds or old ones, resulted in intensified trade relations, exotic consumable goods, and vast new wealth. Contact with different, often less advanced civilizations led to conquest and colonization, creating vast empires that forcibly exported European culture, often provoking desperate resistance and brutal oppression, and radically changing the balance of power both within Europe and across the globe. That contact likewise unleashed a flood of new knowledge that would alter the perceived understanding Europeans had of themselves and their world.

The discoveries that followed prompted humanistically trained philosophers such as Thomas More to reconsider fundamental European values and assumptions. The states that underwrote the voyages of exploration, and those that soon followed in their paths, pursued real political power as well as moral or ideological goals. The kingdom of Portugal and the united kingdoms of Aragon and Castile had recently completed the Reconquista of the Iberian peninsula, in the process of which they had subjugated and converted or expelled Muslim and Jewish communities that had resided there since at least the tenth century. The states had experienced a radical increase in their power, authority, and prestige. When they sponsored voyages into the southern and western Atlantic, therefore, they did so not only in the hope of converting non-believers to Christianity and spreading the benefits of European society, but also with the clear intention of further expanding their supremacy and stature.

Thus briefly described, the expansion of European power and influence beyond its own boundaries to a wider world, which begins at the end of the fifteenth century and shapes global history to the present day, has roots in a more distant past. Crucial to that longer term is the transformation of Europe that began with the unrest and rebirth of the fourteenth century. Conquest, commerce, and colonization in what would become the first global economy created further currents of change in Europe that would shape all aspects of its history.

VASCO DA GAMA

Round Africa to India, 1497–1498 C.E.

Vasco da Gama (c. 1460–23 December 1524) was a Portuguese explorer, the first European to reach India by sea. His voyage to India via Cape Horn, which occurred between 1497 and 1499, created a sea route that linked Europe and Asia. It is widely credited with making possible an age of European political and economic expansion that resulted in the first exercise in global imperialism on the part of the West with the establishment by the Portuguese of a trading empire in Asia. It is also credited with beginning a long-term shift in the economic and political balance of power in Europe away from the Mediterranean, which gradually declined to the status of a backwater, and toward the Atlantic economies. For centuries, Asian luxury goods, especially textiles and spices, had reached Europe via land and sea routes that terminated on the eastern shores of the Black and Mediterranean Seas. From there, merchants, especially Italians, transhipped them to various entrepôts in Europe. By the late fourteenth century the most valuable luxury commodities from Asia were spices, pepper and cinnamon above all. When da Gama landed near Calicut on the western coast of India, he placed the Portuguese in a position to bring much of this trade into their own hands. It improved the Portuguese economy, which had hitherto depended upon trade with northern and western Africa, by giving it a virtual commercial monopoly of the Asian spice trade. It also inspired competition. Within a century of da Gama's achievement, the Netherlands, England, and France would rise to the point where they could challenge, and ultimately break, Portugal's maritime superiority and commercial dominance in the Indian Ocean basin. This, in turn, would transform and expand European imperialism in Asia and Africa. Rewarded with noble titles in his lifetime and celebrated in the Portuguese epic poem Os Lusíadas, *da Gama remains a key figure in the history of exploration, and his trip marks a turning point in the historical processes of globalization and multiculturalism.*

From *The Library of Original Sources.* Vol. V: 9th to 16th Century, edited by Oliver J. Thatcher (Milwaukee: University Research Extension, 1907), pp. 26–40.

1498. Calicut. [Arrival.] That night (May 20) we anchored two leagues from the city of Calicut, and we did so because our pilot mistook Capna, a town at that place, for Calicut. Still further there is another town called Pandarani. We anchored about a league and a half from the shore. After we were at anchor, four boats (*almadias*) approached us from the land, who asked of what nation we were. We told them, and they then pointed out Calicut to us.

On the following day (May 22) these same boats came again alongside, when the captain-major sent one of the convicts to Calicut, and those with whom he went took him to two Moors from Tunis, who could speak Castilian and Genoese. The first greeting that he received was in these words: "May the

Devil take thee! What brought you hither?" They asked what he sought so far away from home, and he told them that we came in search of Christians and of spices. They said: "Why does not the King of Castile, the King of France, or the Signoria of Venice send thither?" He said that the King of Portugal would not consent to their doing so, and they said he did the right thing. After this conversation they took him to their lodgings and gave him wheaten bread and honey. When he had eaten he returned to the ships, accompanied by one of the Moors, who was no sooner on board, than he said these words: "A lucky venture, a lucky venture! Plenty of rubies, plenty of emeralds! You owe great thanks to God, for having brought you to a country holding such riches!" We were greatly astonished to hear his talk, for we never expected to hear our language spoken so far away from Portugal.

The city of Calicut is inhabited by Christians. [The first voyagers to India mistook the Hindus for Christians.] They are of tawny complexion. Some of them have big beards and long hair, whilst others clip their hair short or shave the head, merely allowing a tuft to remain on the crown as a sign that they are Christians. They also wear moustaches. They pierce the ears and wear much gold in them. They go naked down to the waist, covering their lower extremities with very fine cotton stuffs. But it is only the most respectable who do this, for the others manage as best they are able. The women of this country, as a rule, are ugly and of small stature. They wear many jewels of gold round the neck, numerous bracelets on their arms, and rings set with precious stones on their toes. All these people are well-disposed and apparently of mild temper. At first sight they seem covetous and ignorant.

*   *   *

On the following morning, which was Monday, May 28th, the captain-major set out to speak to the king, and took with him thirteen men. On landing, the captain-major was received by the alcaide,[1] with whom were many men, armed and unarmed. The reception was friendly, as if the people were pleased

to see us, though at first appearances looked threatening, for they carried naked swords in their hands. A palanquin was provided for the captain-major, such as is used by men of distinction in that country, as also by some of the merchants, who pay something to the king for this privilege. The captain-major entered the palanquin, which was carried by six men by turns. Attended by all these people we took the road of Calicut, and came first to another town, called Capna. The captain-major was there deposited at the house of a man of rank, whilst we others were provided with food, consisting of rice, with much butter, and excellent boiled fish. The captain-major did not wish to eat, and as we had done so, we embarked on a river close by, which flows between the sea end the mainland, close to the coast. The two boats in which we embarked were lashed together, so that we were not separated. There were numerous other boats, all crowded with people. As to those who were on the banks I say nothing; their number was infinite, and they had all come to see us. We went up that river for about a league, and saw many large ships drawn up high and dry on its banks, for there is no port here.

When we disembarked, the captain-major once more entered his palanquin. The road was crowded with a countless multitude anxious to see us. Even the women came out of their houses with children in their arms and followed us. When we arrived (at Calicut) they took us to a large church, and this is what we saw: The body of the church is as large as a monastery, all built of hewn stone and covered with tiles. At the main entrance rises a pillar of bronze as high as a mast, on the top of which was perched a bird, apparently a cock. In addition to this, there was another pillar as high as a man, and very stout. In the center of the body of the church rose a chapel, all built of hewn stone, with a bronze door sufficiently wide for a man to pass, and stone steps leading up to it. Within this sanctuary stood a small image which they said represented Our Lady. Along the walls, by the main entrance, hung seven small bells. In this church the captain-major said his prayers, and we with him.

*   *   *

---

[1] Governor.

May 28. The king was in a small court, reclining upon a couch covered with a cloth of green velvet, above which was a good mattress, and upon this again a sheet of cotton stuff, very white and fine, more so than any linen. The cushions were after the same fashion. In his left hand the king held a very large golden cup (spittoon), having a capacity of half an almude (8 pints). At its mouth this cup was two palmas (16 inches) wide, and apparently it was massive. Into this cup the king threw the husks of a certain herb which is chewed by the people of this country because of its soothing effects, and which they call atambor. On the right side of the king stood a basin of gold, so large that a man might just encircle it with his arms: this contained the herbs. There were likewise many silver jugs. The canopy above the couch was all gilt.

The captain-major, on entering, saluted in the manner of the country: by putting the hands together, then raising them towards Heaven, as is done by Christians when addressing God, and immediately afterwards opening them and shutting fists quickly. The king beckoned to the captain-major with his right hand to come nearer, but the captain-major did not approach him, for it is the custom of the country for no man to approach the king except only the servant who hands him the herbs, and when anyone addresses the king he holds his hand before the mouth, and remains at a distance. When the king beckoned to the captain-major he looked at the others [i.e., da Gama's men], and ordered them to be seated on a stone bench near him, where he could see them. He ordered that water for their hands should be given them, as also some fruit, one kind of which resembled a melon, except that its outside was rough and the inside sweet, whilst another kind of fruit resembled a fig, and tasted very nice. There were men who prepared these fruits for them; and the king looked at them eating, and smiled; and talked to the servant who stood near him supplying him with the herbs referred to.

Then, throwing his eyes on the captain-major, who sat facing him, he invited him to address himself to the courtiers present, saying they were men of much distinction, that he could tell them whatever he desired to say, and they would repeat it to him (the king). The captain-major replied that he was the ambassador of the King of Portugal, and the bearer of a message which he could only deliver to him personally. The king said this was good, and immediately asked him to be conducted to a chamber. When the captain-major had entered, the king, too, rose and joined him, whilst the rest remained where they were. All this happened about sunset. An old man who was in the court took away the couch as soon as the king rose, but allowed the plate to remain. The king, when he joined the captain-major, threw himself upon another couch, covered with various stuffs embroidered in gold, and asked the captain-major what he wanted. And the captain-major told him he was the ambassador of a King of Portugal, who was Lord of many countries and the possessor of great wealth of every description, exceeding that of any king of these parts; that for a period of sixty years his ancestors had annually sent out vessels to make discoveries in the direction of India, as they knew that there were Christian kings there like themselves. This, he said, was the reason which induced them to order this country to be discovered, not because they sought for gold or silver, for of this they had such abundance that they needed not what was to be found in this country. He further stated that the captains sent out traveled for a year or two, until their provisions were exhausted, and then returned to Portugal, without having succeeded in making the desired discovery. There reigned a king now whose name was Dom Manuel, who had ordered him to build three vessels, of which he had been appointed captain-major, and who had ordered him not to return to Portugal until he should have discovered this King of the Christians, on pain of having his head cut off. That two letters had been intrusted to him to be presented in case he succeeded in discovering him, and that he would do so on the ensuing day; and, finally, he had been instructed to say by word of mouth that he [the King of Portugal] desired to be his friend and brother.

In reply to this the king said that he was welcome; that, on his part, he held him as a friend and brother, and would send ambassadors with him to Portugal. This latter had been asked as a favor, the captain-major pretending that he would not dare to present himself before his king and master unless he was able to present, at the same time, some men of this country. These and many other things passed between the two in this chamber, and as it was already late in the night, the king asked the captain-major with whom he desired to lodge, with Christians or with Moors? And the captain-major replied, neither with Christians nor with Moors, and begged as a favor that he be given a lodging by himself. The king said he would order it thus, upon which the captain-major took leave of the king and came to where the men were, that is, to a veranda lit up by a huge candlestick. By that time four hours of the night had already gone.

*   *   *

May 30. On Wednesday morning the Moors returned, and took the captain-major to the palace. The palace was crowded with armed men. Our captain-major was kept waiting with his conductors for fully four long hours, outside a door, which was only opened when the king sent word to admit him, attended by two men only, whom he might select. The captain-major said that he desired to have Fernao Martins with him, who could interpret, and his secretary. It seemed to him that this separation portended no good. When he had entered, the king said that he had expected him on Tuesday. The captain-major said that the long road had tired him, and that for this reason he had not come to see him. The king then said that he had told him that he came from a very rich kingdom, and yet had brought him nothing; that he had also told him that he was the bearer of a letter, which had not yet been delivered. To this the captain-major rejoined that he had brought nothing, because the object of his voyage was merely to make discoveries, but that when other ships came he would then see what they brought him; as to the letter, it was true that he had brought one, and would deliver it immediately. The king then asked what it was he had come to discover: stones or men? If he came to discover men, as he said, why had he brought nothing? Moreover, he had been told that he carried with him the golden image of a Santa Maria. The captain-major said that the Santa Maria was not of gold, and that even if she were he would not part with her, as she had guided him across the ocean, and would guide him back to his own country. The king then asked for the letter.

The captain-major said that he begged as a favor, that as the Moors wished him ill and might misinterpret him, a Christian able to speak Arabic should be sent for. The king said this was well, and at once sent for a young man, of small stature, whose name was Quaram. The captain-major then said that he had two letters, one written in his own language and the other in that of the Moors; that he was able to read the former, and knew that it contained nothing but what would prove acceptable; but that as to the other he was unable to read it, and it might be good, or contain something that was erroneous. As the Christian was unable to read Moorish, four Moors took the letter and read it between them, after which they translated it to the king, who was well satisfied with its contents.

The king then asked what kind of merchandise was to be found in his country. The captain-major said there was much corn, cloth, iron, bronze, and many other things. The king asked whether he had any merchandise with him. The captain-major replied that he had a little of each sort, as samples, and that if permitted to return to the ships he would order it to be landed, and that meantime four or five men would remain at the lodgings assigned them. The king said no! He might take all his people with him, securely moor his ships, land his merchandise, and sell it to the best advantage. Having taken leave of the king the captain-major returned to his lodgings, and we with him. As it was already late no attempt was made to depart that night.

REVIEW QUESTIONS

1. How would you characterize the first encounter of the Portuguese with non-European indigenous peoples?
2. What technological limits influence both the progress of the Portuguese and their relations with indigenous peoples?
3. How do the Portuguese contend with the problem of communication?
4. What do the Portuguese seek in Calicut and why?
5. Do the Portuguese truly encounter Christians in Calicut?

CHRISTOPHER COLUMBUS

Letter on His First Voyage

*Christopher Columbus (c. 1450–1506) was born somewhere around Genoa and made
his living as a sailor from an early age. Columbus saw much of the Mediterranean
and Atlantic world and acquired real skill as a mapmaker and navigator. Self-taught
in geography, Columbus developed an erroneous theory of the globe's size that made
sailing across the Atlantic to China and Japan a daring but plausible adventure.
After he had spent years looking for a patron among the rulers of Europe, Isabella of
Castile took the lead (along with her husband Ferdinand of Aragon) in sponsoring
Columbus's first voyage. This letter is one of his earliest accounts of this trip in 1492.*

From *Selected Documents Illustrating the Four Voyages of Christopher Columbus*, translated
and edited by Cecil Jane (London: Hakluyt Society, 1930), pp. 3–18.

Sir, As I know that you will be pleased at the great victory with which Our Lord has crowned my voyage, I write this to you, from which you will learn how in thirty-three days, I passed from the Canary Islands to the Indies with the fleet which the most illustrious king and queen, our sovereigns, gave to me. And there I found very many islands filled with people in-numerable, and of them all I have taken possession for their highnesses, by proclamation made and with the royal standard unfurled, and no opposition was offered to me. To the first island which I found, I gave the name *San Salvador,* in remembrance of the Divine Majesty, Who has marvellously bestowed all this; the Indians call it "Guanahani." To the second, I gave the name *Isla de Santa María de Concepción;* to the third, *Fernandina;* to the fourth, *Isabella;* to the fifth, *Isla Juana,* and so to each one I gave a new name.

When I reached Juana, I followed its coast to the westward, and I found it to be so extensive that I thought that it must be the mainland, the province of Catayo. And since there were neither towns nor villages on the seashore, but only small hamlets, with the people of which I could not have speech, because they all fled immediately, I went forward on the same course, thinking that I should not fail to find great cities and towns. And, at the end of many leagues, seeing that there was no change and that the coast was bearing me northwards, which I wished to avoid, since winter was already beginning and I proposed to make from it to the south, and as moreover the wind was carrying me forward, I determined not to wait for a change in the weather and retraced my path as far as a certain harbour known to me. And from that point, I sent two men inland to learn if there were a king or great cities. They travelled three days' journey and found an infinity of small hamlets and people without number, but nothing of importance. For this reason, they returned.

I understood sufficiently from other Indians, whom I had already taken, that this land was nothing but an island. And therefore I followed its coast eastwards for one hundred and seven leagues to the point where it ended. And from that cape, I saw another island, distant eighteen leagues from the former, to the east, to which I at once gave the name "Española." And I went there and followed its northern coast, as I had in the case of Juana, to the eastward for one hundred and eighty-eight great leagues in a straight line. This island and all the others are very fertile to a limitless degree, and this island is extremely so. In it there are many harbours on the coast of the sea, beyond comparison with others which I know in Christendom, and many rivers, good and large, which is marvellous. Its lands are high, and there are in it very many sierras and very lofty mountains, beyond comparison with the island of Teneriffe. All are most beautiful, of a thousand shapes, and all are accessible and filled with trees of a thousand kinds and tall, and they seem to touch the sky. And I am told that they never lose their foliage, as I can understand, for I saw them as green and as lovely as they are in Spain in May, and some of them were flowering, some bearing fruit, and some in another stage, according to their nature. And the nightingale was singing and other birds of a thousand kinds in the month of November there where I went. There are six or eight kinds of palm, which are a wonder to behold on account of their beautiful variety, but so are the other trees and fruits and plants. In it are marvellous pine groves, and there are very large tracts of cultivatable lands, and there is honey, and there are birds of many kinds and fruits in great diversity. In the interior are mines of metals, and the population is without number. Española is a marvel.

The sierras and mountains, the plains and arable lands and pastures, are so lovely and rich for planting and sowing, for breeding cattle of every kind, for building towns and villages. The harbours of the sea here are such as cannot be believed to exist unless they have been seen, and so with the rivers, many and great, and good waters, the majority of which contain gold. In the trees and fruits and plants, there is a great difference from those of Juana. In this island, there are many spices and great mines of gold and of other metals.

The people of this island, and of all the other islands which I have found and of which I have information, all go naked, men and women, as their mothers bore them, although some women cover a single place with the leaf of a plant or with a net of cotton which they make for the purpose. They have no iron or steel or weapons, nor are they fitted to use them, not because they are not well built men and of handsome stature, but because they are very marvellously timorous. They have no other arms than weapons made of canes, cut in seeding time, to the ends of which they fix a small sharpened stick. And they do not dare to make use of these, for many times it has happened that I have sent ashore two or three men to some town to have speech, and countless people have come out to them, and as soon as they have seen my men approaching they have fled, even a father not waiting for his son. And this, not because ill has been done to anyone; on the contrary, at every point where I have been and have been able to have speech, I have given to them of all that I had, such as cloth and many other things, without receiving anything for it; but so they are, incurably timid. It is true that, after they have been reassured and have lost their fear, they are so guileless and so generous with all they possess, that no one would believe it who has not seen it. They never refuse anything which they possess, if it be asked of them; on the contrary, they invite anyone to share it, and display as much love as if they would give their hearts, and whether the thing be of value or whether it be of small price, at once with whatever trifle of whatever kind it may be that is given to them, with that they are content. I forbade that they should be given things so worthless as fragments of broken crockery and scraps of broken glass, and ends of straps, although when they were able to get them, they fancied that they possessed the best jewel in the world. So it was found that a sailor for a strap received gold to the weight of two and a half *castellanos,* and others much more for other things which were worth much less. As for new *blancas,* for them they would give everything which they had, although it might be two or three *castellanos'* weight of gold or an *arroba* or two of spun cotton. . . . They took even the pieces of the broken hoops of the wine barrels and, like savages, gave what they had, so that it seemed to me to be wrong and I forbade it. And I gave a thousand handsome good things, which I had brought, in order that they might conceive affection, and more than that, might become Christians and be inclined to the love and service of their highnesses and of the whole Castilian nation, and strive to aid us and to give us of the things which they have in abundance and which are necessary to us. And they do not know any creed and are not idolaters; only they all believe that power and good are in the heavens, and they are very firmly convinced that I, with these ships and men, came from the heavens, and in this belief they everywhere received me, after they had overcome their fear. And this does not come because they are ignorant; on the contrary, they are of a very acute intelligence and are men who navigate all those seas, so that it is amazing how good an account they give of everything, but it is because they have never seen people clothed or ships of such a kind.

And as soon as I arrived in the Indies, in the first island which I found, I took by force some of them, in order that they might learn and give me information of that which there is in those parts, and so it was that they soon understood us, and we them, either by speech or signs, and they have been very serviceable. I still take them with me, and they are always assured that I come from Heaven, for all the intercourse which they have had with me; and they were the first to announce this wherever I went, and the others went running from house to house and to the neighbouring towns, with loud cries of, 'Come! Come to see the people from Heaven!' So all, men and women alike, when their minds were set at rest concerning us, came, so that not one, great or small, remained behind, and all brought something to eat and drink, which they gave with extraordinary affection. In all the island, they have very many canoes, like rowing *fustas,* some larger, some smaller, and some are larger than a *fusta* of eighteen benches. They are not so broad, because they are made of a single log of wood, but a *fusta* would not keep up with them in rowing, since their speed is a thing incredible. And in these they navigate among all those islands, which are innumerable, and carry their goods. One of these canoes I have seen with seventy and eighty men in her, and each one with his oar.

In all these islands, I saw no great diversity in the appearance of the people or in their manners and language. On the contrary, they all understand one another, which is a very curious thing, on

account of which I hope that their highnesses will determine upon their conversion to our holy faith, towards which they are very inclined.

I have already said how I have gone one hundred and seven leagues in a straight line from west to east along the seashore of the island Juana, and as a result of that voyage, I can say that this island is larger than England and Scotland together, for, beyond these one hundred and seven leagues, there remain to the westward two provinces to which I have not gone. One of these provinces they call "Avan," and there the people are born with tails; and these provinces cannot have a length of less than fifty or sixty leagues, as I could understand from those Indians whom I have and who know all the islands.

The other, Española, has a circumference greater than all Spain, from Colibre, by the seacoast, to Fuenterabia in Vizcaya, since I voyaged along one side one hundred and eighty-eight great leagues in a straight line from west to east. It is a land to be desired and, seen, it is never to be left. And in it, although of all I have taken possession for their highnesses and all are more richly endowed than I know how, or am able, to say, and I hold them all for their highnesses, so that they may dispose of them as, and as absolutely as, of the kingdoms of Castile, in this Española, in the situation most convenient and in the best position for the mines of gold and for all intercourse as well with the mainland here as with that there, belonging to the Grand Khan, where will be great trade and gain, I have taken possession of a large town, to which I gave the name *Villa de Navidad,* and in it I have made fortifications and a fort, which now will by this time be entirely finished, and I have left in it sufficient men for such a purpose with arms and artillery and provisions for more than a year, and a *fusta,* and one, a master of all sea-craft, to build others, and great friendship with the king of that land, so much so, that he was proud to call me, and to treat me as, a brother. And even if he were to change his attitude to one of hostility towards these men, he and his do not know what arms are and they go naked, as I have already said, and are the most timorous people that there are in the world, so that the men whom I have left there alone would suffice to destroy all that land, and the island is without danger for their persons, if they know how to govern themselves.

In all these islands, it seems to me that all men are content with one woman, and to their chief or king they give as many as twenty. It appears to me that the women work more than the men. And I have not been able to learn if they hold private property; what seemed to me to appear was that, in that which one had, all took a share, especially of eatable things.

In these islands I have so far found no human monstrosities, as many expected, but on the contrary the whole population is very well-formed, nor are they Negroes as in Guinea, but their hair is flowing, and they are not born where there is intense force in the rays of the sun; it is true that the sun has there great power, although it is distant from the equinoctial line twenty-six degrees. In these islands, where there are high mountains, the cold was severe this winter, but they endure it, being used to it and with the help of meats which they eat with many and extremely hot spices. As I have found no monsters, so I have had no report of any, except in an island "Quaris," the second at the coming into the Indies, which is inhabited by a people who are regarded in all the islands as very fierce and who eat human flesh. They have many canoes with which they range through all the islands of India and pillage and take as much as they can. They are no more malformed than the others, except that they have the custom of wearing their hair long like women, and they use bows and arrows of the same cane stems, with a small piece of wood at the end, owing to lack of iron which they do not possess. They are ferocious among these other people who are cowardly to an excessive degree, but I make no more account of them than of the rest. These are those who have intercourse with the women of "Matinino," which is the first island met on the way from Spain to the Indies, in which there is not a man. These women engage in no feminine occupation, but use bows and arrows of cane, like those already mentioned, and they

arm and protect themselves with plates of copper, of which they have much.

In another island, which they assure me is larger than Española, the people have no hair. In it, there is gold incalculable, and from it and from the other islands, I bring with me Indians as evidence.

In conclusion, to speak only of that which has been accomplished on this voyage, which was so hasty, their highnesses can see that I will give them as much gold as they may need, if their highnesses will render me very slight assistance; moreover, spice and cotton, as much as their highnesses shall command; and mastic, as much as they shall order to be shipped and which, up to now, has been found only in Greece, in the island of Chios, and the Seignory sells it for what it pleases; and aloe wood, as much as they shall order to be shipped, and slaves, as many as they shall order to be shipped and who will be from the idolaters. And I believe that I have found rhubarb and cinamon, and I shall find a thousand other things of value, which the people whom I have left there will have discovered, for I have not delayed at any point, so far as the wind allowed me to sail, except in the town of Navidad, in order to leave it secured and well established, and in truth, I should have done much more, if the ships had served me, as reason demanded.

This is enough . . . and the eternal God, our Lord, Who gives to all those who walk in His way triumph over things which appear to be impossible, and this was notably one; for, although men have talked or have written of these lands, all was conjectural, without suggestion of ocular evidence, but amounted only to this, that those who heard for the most part listened and judged it to be rather a fable than as having any vestige of truth. So that, since Our Redeemer has given this victory to our most illustrious king and queen, and to their renowned kingdoms, in so great a matter, for this all Christendom ought to feel delight and make great feasts and give solemn thanks to the Holy Trinity with many solemn prayers for the great exaltation which they shall have, in the turning of so many peoples to our holy faith, and afterwards for temporal benefits, for not only Spain but all Christians will have hence refreshment and gain.

This, in accordance with that which has been accomplished, thus briefly.

Done in the caravel, off the Canary Islands, on the fifteenth of February, in the year one thousand four hundred and ninety-three.

At your orders.   El Almirante.

After having written this, and being in the sea of Castile, there came on me so great a south-south-west wind, that I was obliged to lighten ship. But I ran here to-day into this port of Lisbon, which was the greatest marvel in the world, whence I decided to write to their highnesses. In all the Indies, I have always found weather like May; where I went in thirty-three days and I had returned in twenty-eight, save for these storms which have detained me for fourteen days, beating about in this sea. Here all the sailors say that never has there been so bad a winter nor so many ships lost.

Done on the fourth day of March.

REVIEW QUESTIONS

1. What can we learn about Columbus's personality and motives from this letter?
2. Columbus provides here the first Western account of the people he called Indians. What do we learn about his interests and abilities as an ethnographer?
3. Compare this account to those of William of Rubruck (pp. 324–330) and Bartolomeo de Giano (pp. 383–389). What can you conclude from their similiarities and differences?

LEONARDO DA VINCI

FROM *The Notebooks*

Leonardo da Vinci (1452–1519) was born in the countryside of Florence, the illegitimate son of a notary in the town of Vinci. He was self-taught and could read Latin only poorly. He was left-handed, a condition viewed by contemporaries as a deformity. Sometime around 1481, he moved to Milan, where his patrons were the dukes Gian Galeazzo (1476–94) and Ludovico Sforza (1494–1500). During the French invasion of 1499, Leonardo fled Milan and led a peripatetic existence until 1508, when he returned to the city. In 1513, he was taken to France, where he lived the remainder of his days. He is widely acclaimed as a genius, the designer of futuristic machines of many sorts. Among these was a device for grinding concave mirrors and lenses that made possible the invention of the telescope in 1509. He was a great artist in many media as well as a keen observer of nature. His interests ranged from aerodynamics to physics to biology to anatomy to optics. His writings on perspective are drawn from his notebooks, which he wrote backward, in a mirror hand, and in no particular order, and which were never published in his lifetime.

From *Leonardo da Vinci's Notebooks*, translated by Edward MacCurdy (London: Duckworth & Co., 1906).

* * *

Principle of Perspective

All things transmit their image to the eye by means of pyramids; the nearer to the eye these are intersected the smaller the image of their cause will appear.

If you should ask how you can demonstrate these points to me from experience, I should tell you, as regards the vanishing point which moves with you, to notice as you go along by lands ploughed in straight furrows, the ends of which start from the path where you are walking, you will see that continually each pair of furrows seem to approach each other and to join at their ends.

As regards the point that comes to the eye, it may be comprehended with greater ease; for if you look in the eye of anyone you will see your own image there; consequently if you suppose two lines to start from your ears and proceed to the ears of the image which you see of yourself in the eye of the other person, you will clearly recognise that these lines contract so much that when they have continued only a little way beyond your image as mirrored in the said eye they will touch one another in a point.

The thing that is nearer to the eye always appears larger than another of the same size which is more remote.

Perspective is of such a nature that it makes what is flat appear in relief, and what is in relief appear flat.

The perspective by means of which a thing is represented will be better understood when it is seen from the view-point at which it was drawn.

If you wish to represent a thing near, which should produce the effect of natural things, it is impossible for your perspective not to appear false, by reason of all the illusory appearances and errors in proportion of which the existence may be assumed in a mediocre work, unless whoever is looking at this perspective finds himself surveying it from the exact distance, elevation, angle of vision or point at which you were situated to make this perspective. Therefore it would be necessary to make a window of the size of your face or in truth a hole through which you would look at the said work. And if you should do this, then without any doubt your work will produce the effect of nature if the light and shade are correctly rendered, and you will hardly be able to convince yourself that these things are painted. Otherwise do not trouble yourself about representing anything, unless you take your view-point at a distance of at least twenty times the maximum width and height of the thing that you represent; and this will satisfy every beholder who places himself in front of the work at any angle whatever.

If you wish to see a proof of this quickly, take a piece of a staff like a small column eight times as high as its width without plinth or capital, then measure off on a flat wall forty equal spaces which are in conformity with the spaces; they will make between them forty columns similar to your small column. Then let there be set up in front of the middle of these spaces, at a distance of four braccia from the wall, a thin band of iron, in the centre of which there is a small round hole of the size of a large pearl; place a light beside this hole so as to touch it, then go and place your column above each mark of the wall and draw the outline of the shadow, then shade it and observe it through the hole in the iron.

In Vitolone there are eight hundred and five conclusions about perspective.

Perspective

No visible body can be comprehended and well judged by human eyes, except by the difference of the background where the extremities of this body terminate and are bounded, and so far as its contour lines are concerned no object will seem to be separated from this background. The moon, although far distant from the body of the sun, when by reason of eclipses it finds itself between our eyes and the sun, having the sun for its background will seem to human eyes to be joined and attached to it.

Perspective comes to aid us where judgment fails in things that diminish.

It is possible to bring about that the eye does not see distant objects as much diminished as they are in natural perspective, where they are diminished by reason of the convexity of the eye, which is obliged to intersect upon its surface the pyramids of every kind of image that approach the eye at a right angle. But the method that I show here in the margin cuts these pyramids at right angles near the surface of the pupil. But whereas the convex pupil of the eye can take in the whole of our hemisphere, this will show only a single star; but where many small stars transmit their images to the surface of the pupil these stars are very small; here only one will be visible but it will be large; and so the moon will be greater in size and its spots more distinct. You should place close to the eye a glass filled with the water mentioned in chapter four of book 113 'Concerning Natural Things', water which causes things congealed in balls of crystalline glass to appear as though they were without glass.

Of the eye. Of bodies less than the pupil of the eye that which is nearest to it will be least discerned by this pupil—and from this experience it follows that the power of sight is not reduced to a point.

But the images of objects which meet in the pupil of the eye are spread over this pupil in the same way as they are spread about in the air; and the proof of this is pointed out to us when we look at the starry heavens without fixing our gaze more upon one star than upon another, for then the sky shows itself to us strewn with stars, and they bear to the eye the same proportions as in the sky, and the spaces between them also are the same.

Natural perspective acts in the opposite way, for the greater the distance the smaller does the thing seen appear, and the less the distance the larger it appears. But this invention constrains the beholder to stand with his eye at a small hole, and

then with this small hole it will be seen well. But since many eyes come together to see at the same time one and the same work produced by this art, only one of them will have a good view of the function of this perspective and all the others will only see it confusedly. It is well therefore to shun this compound perspective, and to keep to the simple which does not purport to view planes foreshortened but as far as possible in exact form.

And of this simple perspective in which the plane intersects the pyramid that conveys the images to the eye that are at an equal distance from the visual faculty, an example is afforded us by the curve of the pupil of the eye upon which these pyramids intersect at an equal distance from the visual faculty.

Of Equal Things the More Remote Appears Smaller

The practice of perspective is divided into two parts, of which the first treats of all the things seen by the eye at whatsoever distance, and this in itself shows all these things diminished as the eye beholds them, without the man being obliged to stand in one place rather than in another, provided that the wall does not foreshorten it a second time.

But the second practice is a combination of perspective made partly by art and partly by nature, and the work done according to its rules has no part that is not influenced by natural and accidental perspective. Natural perspective I understand has to do with the flat surface on which this perspective is represented; which surface, although it is parallel to it in length and height, is constrained to diminish the distant parts more than its near ones. And this is proved by the first of what has been said above, and its diminution is natural.

Accidental perspective, that is that which is created by art, acts in the contrary way; because it causes bodies equal in themselves to increase on the foreshortened plane, in proportion as the eye is more natural and nearer to the plane, and as the part of this plane where it is represented is more remote from the eye.

THE SCHOOL OF ATHENS (1509–1511)

RAPHAEL

The School of Athens, *by Raphael, is one of the most famous frescoes of the Italian Renaissance. Completed between 1509 and 1511, it formed part of a commission to decorate rooms in the Apostolic Palace in the Vatican.* The School of Athens, *representing Philosophy, has long been considered both a great masterpiece by Raphael and the ideal representation the classical spirit of the Renaissance. What do you imagine Raphael's purpose was in painting* The School of Athens? *What makes this painting particularly representative of Renaissance classicism? Why do you imagine Raphael placed Plato and Aristotle at the exact center of the architectural structure? What do you make of the fact that at the center of an image of classical knowledge is a representation of one of its greats pointing upwards? What may Raphael be arguing about the relationship of classical knowledge and Christianity? What does the architectural structure suggest to the viewer? How does Raphael use posture, gesture, and color to link various figures? Would you describe this painting as secular or religious in theme? Given that this painting was commissioned by the pope, why do you imagine Raphael chose philosophy as his theme?*

*   *   *

REVIEW QUESTIONS

1. According to Leonardo, what is the relationship between perspective in nature and perspective in the human eye?

2. What is the relationship between perspective and mathematical principles?
3. Is perspective a constant or contingent?
4. What implications does this have for painting?
5. How might it shape the enterprise of reading?

BALDESAR CASTIGLIONE

FROM *The Book of the Courtier*

Baldesar Castiglione (1478–1529) was born near Mantua and educated in Milan. He entered the service of the duke of Milan in 1496. After the duke was carried to France as a prisoner, Castiglione returned to Mantua. In 1504, he entered the court of Guidobaldo of Montefeltro, duke of Urbino, where he remained until 1524; this is the setting of The Book of the Courtier. *Although he wrote elegant verse in Latin and Italian, this reflection on courtly life was Castiglione's claim to fame. Fashioned as a discourse among courtiers and ladies of the court, it described the ideal courtier and presented the Renaissance man.*

From *The Book of the Courtier*, by Count Baldesar Castiglione, translated by Leonard Eckstein Opdycke (New York: Charles Scribner's Sons, 1903), pp. 22–23, 25–26, 59, 175–77, 247.

*   *   *

"I wish, then, that this Courtier of ours should be nobly born and of gentle race; because it is far less unseemly for one of ignoble birth to fail in worthy deeds, than for one of noble birth, who, if he strays from the path of his predecessors, stains his family name, and not only fails to achieve but loses what has been achieved already; for noble birth is like a bright lamp that manifests and makes visible good and evil deeds, and kindles and stimulates to virtue both by fear of shame and by hope of praise. And since this splendour of nobility does not illumine the deeds of the humbly born, they lack that stimulus and fear of shame, nor do they feel any obligation to advance beyond what their predecessors have done; while to the nobly born it seems a reproach not to reach at least the goal set them by their ancestors. And thus it nearly always happens that both in the profession of arms and in other worthy pursuits the most famous men have been of noble birth, because nature has implanted in everything that hidden seed which gives a certain force and quality of its own essence to all things that are derived from it, and makes them like itself: as we see not only in the breeds of horses and of other animals, but also in trees, the shoots of which nearly always resemble the trunk; and if they sometimes degenerate, it arises from poor cultivation. And so it is with men, who if rightly trained are nearly always like those from whom they spring, and often better; but if there be no one to give them proper care, they become like savages and never reach perfection.

*   *   *

"But to return to our subject: I say that there is a middle state between perfect grace on the one hand and senseless folly on the other; and those who are not thus perfectly endowed by nature, with study and toil can in great part polish and amend their natural defects. Besides his noble birth, then, I would have the Courtier favoured in this regard also, and endowed by nature not only with talent and beauty of person and feature, but with a certain grace and (as we say) air that shall make him at first sight pleasing and agreeable to all who see him; and I would have this an ornament that should dispose and unite all his actions, and in his outward aspect give promise of whatever is worthy the society and favour of every great lord." . . .

—"But to come to some details, I am of opinion that the principal and true profession of the Courtier ought to be that of arms; which I would have him follow actively above all else, and be known among others as bold and strong, and loyal to whomsoever he serves. And he will win a reputation for these good qualities by exercising them at all times and in all places, since one may never fail in this without severest censure. And just as among women, their fair fame once sullied never recovers its first lustre, so the reputation of a gentleman who bears arms, if once it be in the least tarnished with cowardice or other disgrace, remains forever infamous before the world and full of ignominy. Therefore the more our Courtier excels in this art, the more he will be worthy of praise; and yet I do not deem essential in him that perfect knowledge of things and those other qualities that befit a commander; since this would be too wide a sea, let us be content, as we have said, with perfect loyalty and unconquered courage, and that he be always seen to possess them. For the courageous are often recognized even more in small things than in great;

and frequently in perils of importance and where there are many spectators, some men are to be found, who, although their hearts be dead within them, yet, moved by shame or by the presence of others, press forward almost with their eyes shut, and do their duty God knows how. While on occasions of little moment, when they think they can avoid putting themselves in danger without being detected, they are glad to keep safe. But those who, even when they do not expect to be observed or seen or recognized by anyone, show their ardour and neglect nothing, however paltry, that may be laid to their charge,—they have that strength of mind which we seek in our Courtier.

"Not that we would have him look so fierce, or go about blustering, or say that he has taken his cuirass to wife, or threaten with those grim scowls that we have often seen in Berto; because to such men as this, one might justly say that which a brave lady jestingly said in gentle company to one whom I will not name at present; who, being invited by her out of compliment to dance, refused not only that, but to listen to the music, and many other entertainments proposed to him,—saying always that such silly trifles were not his business; so that at last the lady said, 'What is your business, then?' He replied with a sour look, 'To fight.' Then the lady at once said, 'Now that you are in no war and out of fighting trim, I should think it were a good thing to have yourself well oiled, and to stow yourself with all your battle harness in a closet until you be needed, lest you grow more rusty than you are;' and so, amid much laughter from the bystanders, she left the discomfited fellow to his silly presumption.

"Therefore let the man we are seeking, be very bold, stern, and always among the first, where the enemy are to be seen; and in every other place, gentle, modest, reserved, above all things avoiding ostentation and that impudent self-praise by which men ever excite hatred and disgust in all who hear them."

*   *   *

"I would have him more than passably accomplished in letters, at least in those studies that are called the humanities, and conversant not only with the Latin language but with the Greek, for the sake of the many different things that have been admirably written therein. Let him be well versed in the poets, and not less in the orators and historians, and also proficient in writing verse and prose, especially in this vulgar tongue of ours; for besides the enjoyment he will find in it, he will by this means never lack agreeable entertainment with ladies, who are usually fond of such things. And if other occupations or want of study prevent his reaching such perfection as to render his writings worthy of great praise, let him be careful to suppress them so that others may not laugh at him, and let him show them only to a friend whom he can trust: because they will at least be of this service to him, that the exercise will enable him to judge the work of others. For it very rarely happens that a man who is not accustomed to write, however learned he may be, can ever quite appreciate the toil and industry of writers, or taste the sweetness and excellence of style, and those latent niceties that are often found in the ancients.

"Moreover these studies will also make him fluent, and as Aristippus said to the tyrant, confident and assured in speaking with everyone. Hence I would have our Courtier keep one precept fixed in mind; which is that in this and everything else he should be always on his guard, and diffident rather than forward, and that he should keep from falsely persuading himself that he knows that which he does not know. . . .

Then my lady Duchess said:

"Do not wander from your subject, my lord Magnifico, but hold to the order given you and describe the Court Lady, to the end that so noble a Lady as this may have someone competent to serve her worthily."

The Magnifico continued:

"Then, my Lady, to show that your commands have power to induce me to essay even that which I know not how to do, I will speak of this excellent Lady as I would have her; and when I have fashioned her to my liking, not being able then to have another such, like Pygmalion I will take her for my own.

"And although my lord Gaspar has said that the same rules which are set the Courtier, serve also for the Lady, I am of another mind; for while some qualities are common to both and as necessary to man as to woman, there are nevertheless some others that befit woman more than man, and some are befitting man to which she ought to be wholly a stranger. The same I say of bodily exercises; but above all, methinks that in her ways, manners, words, gestures and bearing, a woman ought to be very unlike a man; for just as it befits him to show a certain stout and sturdy manliness, so it is becoming in a woman to have a soft and dainty tenderness with an air of womanly sweetness in her every movement, which, in her going or staying or saying what you will, shall always make her seem the woman, without any likeness of a man.

"Now, if this precept be added to the rules that these gentlemen have taught the Courtier, I certainly think she ought to be able to profit by many of them, and to adorn herself with admirable accomplishments, as my lord Gaspar says. For I believe that many faculties of the mind are as necessary to woman as to man; likewise gentle birth, to avoid affectation, to be naturally graceful in all her doings, to be mannerly, clever, prudent, not arrogant, not envious, not slanderous, not vain, not quarrelsome, not silly, to know how to win and keep the favour of her mistress and of all others, to practise well and gracefully the exercises that befit women. I am quite of the opinion, too, that beauty is more necessary to her than to the Courtier, for in truth that woman lacks much who lacks beauty. Then, too, she ought to be more circumspect and take greater care not to give occasion for evil being said of her, and so to act that she may not only escape a stain of guilt but even of suspicion, for a woman has not so many ways of defending herself against false imputations as has a man.

"But as Count Ludovico has explained very minutely the chief profession of the Courtier, and has insisted it be that of arms, methinks it is also fitting to tell what in my judgment is that of the Court Lady: and when I have done this, I shall think myself quit of the greater part of my duty.

"Laying aside, then, those faculties of the mind that she ought to have in common with the Courtier (such as prudence, magnanimity, continence, and many others), and likewise those qualities that befit all women (such as kindness, discretion, ability to manage her husband's property and her house and children if she be married, and all those capacities that are requisite in a good housewife), I say that in a lady who lives at court methinks above all else a certain pleasant affability is befitting, whereby she may be able to entertain politely every sort of man with agreeable and seemly converse, suited to the time and place, and to the rank of the person with whom she may speak, uniting with calm and modest manners, and with that seemliness which should ever dispose all her actions, a quick vivacity of spirit whereby she may show herself alien to all indelicacy; but with such a kindly manner as shall make us think her no less chaste, prudent and benign, than agreeable, witty and discreet; and so she must preserve a certain mean (difficult and composed almost of contraries), and must barely touch certain limits but not pass them.

"Thus, in her wish to be thought good and pure, the Lady ought not to be so coy and seem so to abhor company and talk that are a little free, as to take her leave as soon as she finds herself therein; for it might easily be thought that she was pretending to be thus austere in order to hide something about herself which she feared others might come to know; and such prudish manners are always odious. Nor ought she, on the other hand, for the sake of showing herself free and agreeable, to utter unseemly words or practise a certain wild and unbridled familiarity and ways likely to make that believed of her which perhaps is not true; but when she is present at such talk, she ought to listen with a little blush and shame.

"Likewise she ought to avoid an errour into which I have seen many women fall, which is that of saying and of willingly listening to evil about other women. For those women who, on hearing the unseemly ways of other women described, grow angry thereat and seem to disbelieve it and to regard it almost monstrous that a woman should be immodest,—they, by accounting the offence so heinous, give reason to think that they do not commit it. But those who go about continually prying into other women's intrigues, and narrate them so minutely and with such zest, seem to be envious of them and to wish that everyone may know it, to the end that like matters may not be reckoned as a fault in their own case; and thus they fall into certain laughs and ways that show they then feel greatest pleasure. And hence it comes that men, while seeming to listen gladly, usually hold such women in small respect and have very little regard for them, and think these ways of theirs are an invitation to advance farther, and thus often go such lengths with them as bring them deserved reproach, and finally esteem them so lightly as to despise their company and even find them tedious.

"And on the other hand, there is no man so shameless and insolent as not to have reverence for those women who are esteemed good and virtuous; because this gravity (tempered with wisdom and goodness) is as it were a shield against the insolence and coarseness of the presumptuous. Thus we see that a word or laugh or act of kindness (however small it be) from a virtuous woman is more prized by everyone, than all the endearments and caresses of those who show their lack of shame so openly; and if they are not immodest, by their unseemly laughter, their loquacity, insolence and like scurrile manners, they give sign of being so. . . .

"I think then that the aim of the perfect Courtier, which has not been spoken of till now, is so to win for himself, by means of the accomplishments ascribed to him by these gentlemen, the favour and mind of the prince whom he serves, that he may be able to say, and always shall say, the truth about everything which it is fitting for the prince to know, without fear or risk of giving offence thereby; and that when he sees his prince's mind inclined to do something wrong, he may be quick to oppose, and gently to make use of the favour acquired by his good accomplishments, so as to banish every bad intent and lead his prince into the path of virtue. And thus, possessing the goodness which these gentlemen have described, together with readiness of wit and pleasantness, and shrewdness and knowledge of letters and many other things,—the Courtier will in every case be able deftly to show the prince how much honour and profit accrue to him and his from justice, liberality, magnanimity, gentleness, and the other virtues that become a good prince; and on the other hand how much infamy and loss proceed from the vices opposed to them. Therefore I think that just as music, festivals, games, and the other pleasant accomplishments are as it were the flower, in like manner to lead or help one's prince towards right, and to frighten him from wrong, are the true fruit of Courtiership.

"And since the merit of well-doing lies chiefly in two things, one of which is the choice of an end for our intentions that shall be truly good, and the other ability to find means suitable and fitting to conduce to that good end marked out,—certain it is that that man's mind tends to the best end, who purposes to see to it that his prince shall be deceived by no one, shall hearken not to flatterers or to slanderers and liars, and shall distinguish good and evil, and love the one and hate the other.

*   *   *

REVIEW QUESTIONS

1. What does Castiglione mean by "grace"? How is it created?
2. To what extent is grace the product of birth or nature?
3. How is grace gendered?
4. What does a courtier's conduct tell others about his status?
5. If status was once thought to reside in one's birth and lineage, how does the courtier alter that notion?
6. How does Castiglione's courtier differ from a medieval monk or knight?
7. Is the courtier's virtue the expression of his nature, cultivation, or education?

PORTRAIT OF POPE LEO X AND TWO CARDINALS (1518)   RAPHAEL

This intriguing portrait of Pope Leo X and two of his cardinals, relatives elevated through acts of nepotism, reveals the full sophistication of Raphael's artistry. He created an attractive painting of his patron in full papal regalia. At the same time, he subtly included less attractive hints about the subject's office and character. What might this portrait tell us of Leo's character? What does the portrait tell us about Renaissance values? Is Raphael exercising a subtle criticism of the church through his portrait of its head? If so, what elements of his criticism are explicit in the painting?

GIOVANNI PICO DELLA MIRANDOLA

FROM "Oration on the Dignity of Man"

Giovanni Pico della Mirandola (1463–1494) is a singular figure in the history of Renaissance humanism. Although the corpus of his published works remained small as a result of his early death, the breadth of his learning won him the admiration of scholars past and present. He received a thorough classical education in Greek and Latin, and studied the scholastic tradition of the Middle Ages as well as Jewish and Arabic philosophy. His conception of the dignity of man and harmony among philosophers found expression in his "Oration on the Dignity of Man." In 1486, Pico published his 900 theses, inviting all scholars to a public debate in January 1487. Before it could take place, however, Pope Innocent VIII appointed a commission to examine the theses, some of which were found to be heretical. An attempt to defend the incriminated points plunged Pico into a conflict with ecclesiastical authorities that lasted several years. The oration, never published in its author's lifetime, was written as an introductory speech for the disputation.

From *Reflections on the Philosophy of the History of Mankind*, by J. G. Herder and F. E. Manuel (Chicago: University of Chicago Press, 1968).

I have read in the records of the Arabians, reverend Fathers, that Abdala the Saracen, when questioned as to what on this stage of the world, as it were, could be seen most worthy of wonder, replied: "There is nothing to be seen more wonderful than man." In agreement with this opinion is the saying of Hermes Trismegistus: "A great miracle, Asclepius, is man." But when I weighed the reason for these maxims, the many grounds for the excellence of human nature reported by many men failed to satisfy me—that man is the intermediary between creatures, the intimate of the gods, the king of the lower beings, by the acuteness of his senses, by the discernment of his reason, and by the light of his intelligence the interpreter of nature, the interval between fixed eternity and fleeting time, and (as the Persians say) the bond, nay, rather, the marriage song of the world, on David's testimony but little lower than the angels. Admittedly great though these reasons be, they are not the principal grounds, that is, those which may rightfully claim for themselves the privilege of the highest admiration. For

why should we not admire more the angels themselves and the blessed choirs of heaven? At last it seems to me I have come to understand why man is the most fortunate of creatures and consequently worthy of all admiration and what precisely is that rank which is his lot in the universal chain of Being—a rank to be envied not only by brutes but even by the stars and by minds beyond this world. It is a matter past faith and a wondrous one. Why should it not be? For it is on this very account that man is rightly called and judged a great miracle and a wonderful creature indeed.

But hear, Fathers, exactly what this rank is and, as friendly auditors, conformably to your kindness, do me this favor. God the Father, the supreme Architect, had already built this cosmic home we behold, the most sacred temple of His godhead, by the laws of His mysterious wisdom. The region above the heavens He had adorned with Intelligences, the heavenly spheres He had quickened with eternal souls, and the excrementary and filthy parts of the lower world He had filled with a multitude of animals of every kind. But, when the work was finished, the Craftsman kept wishing that there were someone to ponder the plan of so great a work, to love its beauty, and to wonder at its vastness. Therefore, when everything was done (as Moses and Timaeus bear witness), He finally took thought concerning the creation of man. But there was not among His archetypes that from which He could fashion a new offspring, nor was there in His treasure-houses anything which He might bestow on His new son as an inheritance, nor was there in the seats of all the world a place where the latter might sit to contemplate the universe. All was now complete; all things had been assigned to the highest, the middle, and the lowest orders. But in its final creation it was not the part of the Father's power to fail as though exhausted. It was not the part of His wisdom to waver in a needful matter through poverty of counsel. It was not the part of His kindly love that he who was to praise God's divine generosity in regard to others should be compelled to condemn it in regard to himself.

At last the best of artisans ordained that that creature to whom He had been able to give nothing proper to himself should have joint possession of whatever had been peculiar to each of the different kinds of being. He therefore took man as a creature of indeterminate nature and, assigning him a place in the middle of the world, addressed him thus: "Neither a fixed abode nor a form that is thine alone nor any function peculiar to thyself have we given thee, Adam, to the end that according to thy longing and according to thy judgment thou mayest have and possess what abode, what form, and what functions thou thyself shalt desire. The nature of all other beings is limited and constrained within the bounds of laws prescribed by Us. Thou, constrained by no limits, in accordance with thine own free will, in whose hand We have placed thee, shalt ordain for thyself the limits of thy nature. We have set thee at the world's center that thou mayest from thence more easily observe whatever is in the world. We have made thee neither of heaven nor of earth, neither mortal nor immortal, so that with freedom of choice and with honor, as though the maker and molder of thyself, thou mayest fashion thyself in whatever shape thou shalt prefer. Thou shalt have the power to degenerate into the lower forms of life, which are brutish. Thou shalt have the power, out of thy soul's judgment, to be reborn into the higher forms, which are divine."

O supreme generosity of God the Father, O highest and most marvelous felicity of man! To him it is granted to have whatever he chooses, to be whatever he wills. Beasts as soon as they are born (so says Lucilius) bring with them from their mother's womb all they will ever possess. Spiritual beings, either from the beginning or soon thereafter, become what they are to be for ever and ever. On man when he came into life the Father conferred the seeds of all kinds and the germs of every way of life. Whatever seeds each man cultivates will grow to maturity and bear in him their own fruit. If they be vegetative, he will be like a plant. If sensitive, he will become brutish. If rational, he will grow into a heavenly being. If intellectual, he will be an angel and the son of God. And if, happy in the lot of no created thing, he withdraws into the center of his own unity, his spirit, made one with God, in the solitary darkness of God, who is set above all things, shall surpass them all. Who would not admire this our chameleon? Or who could more greatly admire aught else whatever? It is man who Asclepius of Athens, arguing from his mutability of character and from his self-transforming nature, on just grounds says was symbolized by Proteus in the mysteries. Hence those metamorphoses renowned among the Hebrews and the Pythagoreans.

*   *   *

REVIEW QUESTIONS

1. How does Pico reorder the hierarchy of creation?
2. What does he claim for human nature that sets it apart?
3. How does Pico conceive of human will?
4. What implications does that conception have?
5. What is Pico's understanding of the relationship of humankind to God?
6. What are its implications?

NICCOLÒ MACHIAVELLI

FROM *The Prince*

Niccolò Machiavelli (1469–1527) was the son of a Florentine lawyer. Little is known of him until 1498, when he entered the service of the Florentine Republic of Pier Soderini as secretary to the second chancery, a minor bureaucratic post he held for fourteen years. From this position, Machiavelli observed the political process of his day. A staunch republican, he lost his position in government in 1512, when Soderini's republic was toppled and the Medici of Florence were restored to power by a papal army. He spent the rest of his days in retirement, possibly trying to restore himself to the graces of the Medici and the pope, but certainly engaged in the scholarly and literary pursuits that would establish his reputation as a political analyst. Among the fruits of these labors was The Prince, *written in 1513. Of the many observations and ideas expressed in this short work, two at least became fundamental truths of modern politics. One was the necessity of national unity based on a common language, culture, and economy. The other was the preservation of national unity through the concentration and exercise of power by the state. As controversial as they were prescient in Machiavelli's day, these ideas encouraged later scholars to number him among the first modern students of politics.*

From *The Prince*, by Niccolò Machiavelli, translated by Robert M. Adams, A Norton Critical Edition, 2d ed. (New York: Norton, 1977), pp. 31–32, 44–50.

How to Measure the Strength of Any Prince's State

There is one other consideration to bear in mind regarding these civil principates; that is, whether a prince is strong enough to stand on his own feet in case of need, or whether he is in constant need of help from others. And to make the matter clearer, let me say that in my opinion princes control their own destiny when they command enough money or men to assemble an adequate army and make a stand against anyone who attacks them. I think princes who need outside protection are those who can't take the field against their foes, but have to hide behind their walls and defend themselves there. I've already mentioned the first class, and will save whatever else I have to say about them till later. As for the others, all I can say is that they should keep their cities well fortified and well supplied, and pay no heed to the surrounding countryside. Whenever a man has fortified his city strongly, and has dealt with his subjects as I described above and will describe further below, people will be slow to attack him; men are always wary of tasks that seem hard, and it can't seem easy to attack a prince whose city is in fine fettle, and whose people do not hate him.

*   *   *

Thus a prince who has a strong city and does not earn his people's hatred cannot be attacked, or if he were, that attacker would be driven off to his own disgrace; because the way things keep changing in this world, it's almost impossible for a prince with his armies to devote an entire year to a siege while doing nothing else. Maybe someone will object: when the people see their possessions outside the walls being burnt up, they will get impatient; a long siege and their own self-interest will make them forget the prince. But to this I answer that a brave, strong prince will overcome all these problems, giving his subjects hope at one minute that the storm will soon pass, stirring them up at another moment to fear the enemy's cruelty, and on still other occasions restraining those who seem too rash. Besides, the enemy will generally do his burning and ravishing of the countryside as soon as he begins the siege, when men's minds are still passionate and earnest for the defense; thus the prince has less reason to worry, because, after a few days, when tempers have cooled, the harm will already have been done, the losses inflicted, and there will clearly be no cure. At that point, the people will rally even more strongly behind their prince, because they will feel he owes them something, since their houses were burnt and their fields ravaged in defense of his cause. Indeed, men are so constructed that they feel themselves committed as much by the benefits they grant as by those they receive. Hence, all things considered, it should not be hard for a prudent prince to keep his subjects in good spirits throughout a siege, as long as he does not run short of food or weapons.

*   *   *

On the Reasons Why Men Are Praised or Blamed—Especially Princes

It remains now to be seen what style and principles a prince ought to adopt in dealing with his subjects and friends. I know the subject has been treated frequently before, and I'm afraid people will think me rash for trying to do so again, especially since I intend to differ in this discussion from what others have said. But since I intend to write something useful to an understanding reader, it seemed better to go after the real truth of the matter than to repeat what people have imagined. A great many men have imagined states and princedoms such as nobody ever saw or knew in the real world, for there's such a difference between the way we really live and the way we ought to live that the man who neglects the real to study the ideal will learn how to accomplish his ruin, not his salvation. Any man who tries to be good all the time is bound to come to ruin among the great number who are not good. Hence a prince who wants to keep his post must learn how not to be good, and use that knowledge, or refrain from using it, as necessity requires.

Putting aside, then, all the imaginary things that are said about princes, and getting down to the truth, let me say that whenever men are discussed (and especially princes because they are prominent), there are certain qualities that bring them either praise or blame. Thus some are considered generous, others stingy (I use a Tuscan term, since "greedy" in our speech means a man who wants to take other people's goods; we call a man "stingy" who clings to his own); some are givers, others grabbers; some cruel, others merciful; one man is treacherous, another faithful; one is feeble and effeminate, another fierce and spirited; one humane, another proud; one lustful, another chaste; one straightforward, another sly; one harsh, another gentle; one serious, another playful; one religious, another skeptical, and so on. I know everyone will agree that among these many qualities a prince certainly ought to have all those that are considered good. But since it is impossible to have and exercise them all, because the conditions of human life simply do not allow it, a prince must be shrewd enough to avoid the public disgrace of those vices that would lose him his state. If he possibly can, he should also guard against vices that will not lose him his state; but if he cannot prevent them, he should not be too worried about indulging them. And furthermore, he should not be too worried about incurring blame for any vice without which he would find it hard to save his state. For if you look at matters carefully, you will see that something resembling virtue, if you follow it, may be your ruin, while something else resembling vice will lead, if you follow it, to your security and well-being.

On Liberality and Stinginess

Let me begin, then, with the first of the qualities mentioned above, by saying that a reputation for liberality is doubtless very fine; but the generosity that earns you that reputation can do you great harm. For if you exercise your generosity in a really virtuous way, as you should, nobody will know of it, and you cannot escape the odium of the opposite vice. Hence if you wish to be widely known as a generous man, you must seize every opportunity to make a big display of your giving. A prince of this character is bound to use up his entire revenue in works of ostentation. Thus, in the end, if he wants to keep a name for generosity, he will have to load his people with exorbitant taxes and squeeze money out of them in every way he can. This is the first step in making him odious to his subjects; for when he is poor, nobody will respect him. Then, when his generosity has angered many and brought rewards to a few, the slightest difficulty will trouble him, and at the first approach of danger, down he goes. If by chance he foresees this, and tries to change his ways, he will immediately be labelled a miser.

Since a prince cannot use this virtue [*virtù*] of liberality in such a way as to become known for it unless he harms his own security, he won't mind, if he judges prudently of things, being known as a miser. In due course he will be thought the more liberal man, when people see that his parsimony enables him to live on his income, to defend himself against his enemies, and to undertake major projects without burdening his people with taxes. Thus he will be acting liberally toward all those people from whom he takes nothing (and there are an immense number of them), and in a stingy way toward those people on whom he bestows nothing (and they are very few). In our times, we have seen great things being accomplished only by men who have had the name of misers; all the others have gone under. Pope Julius II, though he used his reputation as a generous man to gain the papacy, sacrificed it in order to be able to make war; the present king of France has waged many wars without levying a single extra tax on his people, simply because

he could take care of the extra expenses out of the savings from his long parsimony. If the present king of Spain had a reputation for generosity, he would never have been able to undertake so many campaigns, or win so many of them.

*   *   *

On Cruelty and Clemency: Whether It Is Better to Be Loved or Feared

Continuing now with our list of qualities, let me say that every prince should prefer to be considered merciful rather than cruel, yet he should be careful not to mismanage this clemency of his. People thought Cesare Borgia was cruel, but that cruelty of his reorganized the Romagna, united it, and established it in peace and loyalty. Anyone who views the matter realistically will see that this prince was much more merciful than the people of Florence, who, to avoid the reputation of cruelty, allowed Pistoia to be destroyed. Thus, no prince should mind being called cruel for what he does to keep his subjects united and loyal; he may make examples of a very few, but he will be more merciful in reality than those who, in their tenderheartedness, allow disorders to occur, with their attendant murders and lootings. Such turbulence brings harm to an entire community, while the executions ordered by a prince affect only one individual at a time. A new prince, above all others, cannot possibly avoid a name for cruelty, since new states are always in danger. And Virgil, speaking through the mouth of Dido, says:

> Res dura et regni novitas me talia cogunt
> Moliri, et late fines custode tueri.[1]

Yet a prince should be slow to believe rumors and to commit himself to action on the basis of them. He should not be afraid of his own thoughts; he ought to proceed cautiously, moderating his conduct with prudence and humanity, allowing nei-

---

[1] "Severe pressures and the newness of the regime compel me to these measures. I must maintain the borders against foreign enemies."

ther overconfidence to make him careless, nor overtimidity to make him intolerable.

Here the question arises: is it better to be loved than feared, or vice versa? I don't doubt that every prince would like to be both; but since it is hard to accommodate these qualities, if you have to make a choice, to be feared is much safer than to be loved. For it is a good general rule about men, that they are ungrateful, fickle, liars and deceivers, fearful of danger and greedy for gain. While you serve their welfare, they are all yours, offering their blood, their belongings, their lives, and their children's lives, as we noted above—so long as the danger is remote. But when the danger is close at hand, they turn against you. Then, any prince who has relied on their words and has made no other preparations will come to grief; because friendships that are bought at a price, and not with greatness and nobility of soul, may be paid for but they are not acquired, and they cannot be used in time of need. People are less concerned with offending a man who makes himself loved than one who makes himself feared: the reason is that love is a link of obligation which men, because they are rotten, will break any time they think doing so serves their advantage; but fear involves dread of punishment, from which they can never escape.

Still, a prince should make himself feared in such a way that, even if he gets no love, he gets no hate either; because it is perfectly possible to be feared and not hated, and this will be the result if only the prince will keep his hands off the property of his subjects or citizens, and off their women. When he does have to shed blood, he should be sure to have a strong justification and manifest cause; but above all, he should not confiscate people's property, because men are quicker to forget the death of a father than the loss of a patrimony. Besides, pretexts for confiscation are always plentiful; it never fails that a prince who starts living by plunder can find reasons to rob someone else. Excuses for proceeding against someone's life are much rarer and more quickly exhausted.

*   *   *

Returning to the question of being feared or loved, I conclude that since men love at their own inclination but can be made to fear at the inclination of the prince, a shrewd prince will lay his foundations on what is under his own control, not on what is controlled by others. He should simply take pains not to be hated, as I said.

The Way Princes Should Keep Their Word

How praiseworthy it is for a prince to keep his word and live with integrity rather than by craftiness, everyone understands; yet we see from recent experience that those princes have accomplished most who paid little heed to keeping their promises, but who knew how craftily to manipulate the minds of men. In the end, they won out over those who tried to act honestly.

You should consider then, that there are two ways of fighting, one with laws and the other with force. The first is properly a human method, the second belongs to beasts. But as the first method does not always suffice, you sometimes have to turn to the second. Thus a prince must know how to make good use of both the beast and the man. Ancient writers made subtle note of this fact when they wrote that Achilles and many other princes of antiquity were sent to be reared by Chiron the centaur, who trained them in his discipline. Having a teacher who is half man and half beast can only mean that a prince must know how to use both these two natures, and that one without the other has no lasting effect.

Since a prince must know how to use the character of beasts, he should pick for imitation the fox and the lion. As the lion cannot protect him-self from traps, and the fox cannot defend himself from wolves, you have to be a fox in order to be wary of traps, and a lion to overawe the wolves. Those who try to live by the lion alone are badly mistaken. Thus a prudent prince cannot and should not keep his word when to do so would go against his interest, or when the reasons that made him pledge it no longer apply. Doubtless if all men were good, this rule would be bad; but since they are a sad lot, and keep no faith with you, you in your turn are under no obligation to keep it with them.

*   *   *

REVIEW QUESTIONS

1. What, according to Machiavelli, is the basis of political authority?

2. How does his theory differ from others of his day?

3. When he claims that a prince must assume many guises, what is Machiavelli saying about his understanding of human nature?

4. What is the role of artifice in political authority?

5. What might Machiavelli's prince have in common with Castiglione's courtier?

DESIDERIUS ERASMUS OF ROTTERDAM

FROM *Ten Colloquies*

Desiderius Erasmus of Rotterdam (1476–1536) was one of the greatest scholars of his day, measured in terms of his writings and their influence. Educated at Deventer in the Netherlands and in Paris, he began his career as an editor, translator, and popularizer of classical texts. In the humanistic tradition, he used classical tropes as models for his own society, a practice that made him not only a great scholar but also a great satirist. His chief intellectual commitment, however, was the renewal of Christian piety through the study of Christian literature, the Bible and church fathers above all. In this context he is often viewed as the great exponent of Christian humanism, the northern European variant of classical Italian humanism. His translation of the Bible inspired the biblical scholarship of sixteenth-century reformers. His editions of patristic sources remain authoritative to this day. His Ten Colloquies *were written as popular texts to inculcate elegant Latin and to inspire Christian conduct.*

From *Ten Colloquies of Erasmus*, by Desiderius Erasmus, translated by Craig R. Thompson (New York: The Liberal Arts Press, 1957), pp. 120–29.

"Cyclops, or the Gospel Bearer"

CANNIUS: What's Polyphemus hunting here?

POLYPHEMUS: What could I be hunting without dogs or spear? Is that your question?

CANNIUS: Some wood nymph, perhaps.

POLYPHEMUS: A good guess. Look, here's my hunting net.

CANNIUS: What a sight! Bacchus in a lion's skin—Polyphemus with a book—a cat in a saffron gown!

POLYPHEMUS: I've painted this little book not only in saffron but bright red and blue, too.

CANNIUS: I'm not talking about saffron; I said something in Greek. Seems to be a soldierly book, for it's protected by bosses, plates, and brass clasps.

POLYPHEMUS: Take a good look at it.

CANNIUS: I'm looking. Very fine, but you haven't yet decorated it enough.

POLYPHEMUS: What's lacking?

CANNIUS: You should have added your coat of arms.

POLYPHEMUS: What coat of arms?

CANNIUS: The head of Silenus peering out of a wine jug. But what's the book about? The art of drinking?

POLYPHEMUS: Be careful you don't blurt out blasphemy.

CANNIUS: What, you don't mean it's something sacred?

POLYPHEMUS: The most sacred of all, the Gospels.

CANNIUS: By Hercules! What has Polyphemus to do with the Gospels?

POLYPHEMUS: You might as well ask what a Christian has to do with Christ.

CANNIUS: I'm not sure a halberd isn't more fitting for the likes of you. If I were at sea and met a stranger who looked like this, I'd take him for a pirate; if I met him in a wood, for a bandit.

POLYPHEMUS: Yet this very Gospel teaches us not to judge a man by appearances. Just as a haughty spirit often lurks under an ash-colored cowl, so a cropped head, curled beard, stern brow, wild eyes, plumed cap, military cloak, and slashed breeches sometimes cover a true Christian heart.

CANNIUS: Of course. Sometimes a sheep lurks in wolf's clothing, too. And if you trust fables, an ass in a lion's skin.

POLYPHEMUS: What's more, I know a man who has a sheep's head and a fox's heart. I could wish him friends as fair as his eyes are dark, and a character as shining as his complexion.

CANNIUS: If a man with a sheepskin cap has a sheep's head, what a load *you* carry, with both a sheep and an ostrich on your head. And isn't it rather ridiculous to have a bird on your head and an ass in your heart?

POLYPHEMUS: That hurt!

CANNIUS: But it would be well if, as you've decorated the Gospels with various ornaments, the Gospels in turn adorned you. You've decorated them with colors; I wish they might embellish you with good morals.

POLYPHEMUS: I'll take care of that.

CANNIUS: After your fashion, yes.

POLYPHEMUS: But insults aside, you don't condemn those who carry a volume of the Gospels about, do you?

CANNIUS: I'd be the last person in the world to do that.

POLYPHEMUS: What? I seem to you the least person in the world, when I'm taller than you by an ass's head?

CANNIUS: I don't believe you'd be that much taller even if the ass pricked up its ears.

POLYPHEMUS: Certainly by a buffalo's.

CANNIUS: I like the comparison. But I said "last"; I wasn't calling you "least."

POLYPHEMUS: What's the difference between an egg and an egg?

CANNIUS: What's the difference between middle finger and little finger?

POLYPHEMUS: The middle one's longer.

CANNIUS: Very good! What's the difference between ass ears and wolf ears?

POLYPHEMUS: Wolf ears are shorter.

CANNIUS: That's right.

POLYPHEMUS: But I'm in the habit of measuring long and short by span and ell, not by ears.

CANNIUS: Well, the man who carried Christ was called Christopher. You, who carry the Gospels, ought to be called Gospel-bearer instead of Polyphemus.

POLYPHEMUS: Don't you think it's holy to carry the Gospels?

CANNIUS: No—unless you'd agree that asses are mighty holy.

POLYPHEMUS: How so?

CANNIUS: Because one of them can carry three thousand books of this kind. I should think you'd be equal to that load if fitted with the right packsaddle.

POLYPHEMUS: There's nothing farfetched in thus crediting an ass with holiness because he carried Christ.

CANNIUS: I don't envy you that holiness. And if you like, I'll give you relics of the ass that carried Christ, so you can kiss them.

POLYPHEMUS: A gift I'll be glad to get. For by touching the body of Christ that ass was consecrated.

CANNIUS: Obviously those who smote Christ touched him too.

POLYPHEMUS: But tell me seriously, isn't carrying the Gospel about a reverent thing to do?

CANNIUS: Reverent if done sincerely, without hypocrisy.

POLYPHEMUS: Let monks have hypocrisy! What has a soldier to do with hypocrisy?

CANNIUS: But first tell me what hypocrisy is.

POLYPHEMUS: Professing something other than what you really mean.

CANNIUS: But what does carrying a copy of the Gospels profess? A gospel life, doesn't it?

POLYPHEMUS: I suppose so.

CANNIUS: Therefore, when the life doesn't correspond to the book, isn't that hypocrisy?

POLYPHEMUS: Apparently. But what is it truly to bear the Gospel?

CANNIUS: Some bear it in their hands, as the Franciscans do their Rule. Parisian porters, and asses and geldings, can do the same. There are those who bear it in their mouths, harping on nothing but Christ and the Gospel. That's pharisaical. Some bear it in their hearts. The true Gospel bearer, then, is one who carries it in hands and mouth *and* heart.

POLYPHEMUS: Where are these?

CANNIUS: In churches—the deacons, who bear the book, read it to the congregation, and have it by heart.

POLYPHEMUS: Though not all who bear the Gospel in their hearts are devout.

CANNIUS: Don't quibble. A man doesn't bear it in his heart unless he loves it through and through. Nobody loves it wholeheartedly unless he emulates the Gospel in his manner of living.

POLYPHEMUS: I don't follow these subtleties.

CANNIUS: But I'll tell you more bluntly. If you carry a jar of Beaune wine on your shoulder, it's just a burden, isn't it?

POLYPHEMUS: That's all.

CANNIUS: But if you hold the wine in your throat, and presently spit it out?

POLYPHEMUS: Useless—though, really, I'm not accustomed to doing that!

CANNIUS: But if—as you *are* accustomed—you take a long drink?

POLYPHEMUS: Nothing more heavenly.

CANNIUS: Your whole body glows; your face turns rosy; your expression grows merry.

POLYPHEMUS: Exactly.

CANNIUS: The Gospel has the same effect when it penetrates the heart. It makes a new man of you.

POLYPHEMUS: So I don't seem to you to live according to the Gospel?

CANNIUS: You can best decide that question yourself.

POLYPHEMUS: If it could be decided with a battle-ax—

CANNIUS: If someone called you a liar or a rake to your face, what would you do?

POLYPHEMUS: What would I do? He'd feel my fists.

CANNIUS: What if someone hit you hard?

POLYPHEMUS: I'd break his neck for that.

CANNIUS: But your book teaches you to repay insults with a soft answer; and "Whosoever shall smite thee on thy right cheek, turn to him the other also."

POLYPHEMUS: I've read that, but it slipped my mind.

CANNIUS: You pray frequently, I dare say.

POLYPHEMUS: That's pharisaical.

CANNIUS: Long-winded but ostentatious praying is pharisaical. But your book teaches us to pray without ceasing, yet sincerely.

POLYPHEMUS: Still, I do pray sometimes.

CANNIUS: When?

POLYPHEMUS: Whenever I think of it—once or twice a week.

CANNIUS: What do you pray?

POLYPHEMUS: The Lord's Prayer.

CANNIUS: How often?

POLYPHEMUS: Once. For the Gospel forbids vain repetitions as "much speaking."

CANNIUS: Can you concentrate on the Lord's Prayer while repeating it?

POLYPHEMUS: Never tried. Isn't it enough to say the words?

CANNIUS: I don't know, except that God hears only the utterance of the heart. Do you fast often?

POLYPHEMUS: Never.

CANNIUS: But your book recommends prayer and fasting.

POLYPHEMUS: I'd recommend them too, if my belly did not demand something else.

CANNIUS: But Paul says that those who serve their bellies aren't serving Jesus Christ. Do you eat meat on any day whatever?

POLYPHEMUS: Any day it's offered.

CANNIUS: Yet a man as tough as you are could live on hay or the bark of trees.

POLYPHEMUS: But Christ said that a man is not defiled by what he eats.

CANNIUS: True, if it's eaten in moderation, without giving offense. But Paul, the disciple of Christ, prefers starvation to offending a weak brother by his food; and he calls upon us to follow his example, in order that we may please all men in all things.

POLYPHEMUS: Paul's Paul, and I'm me.

CANNIUS: But Egon's job is to feed she-goats.

POLYPHEMUS: I'd rather eat one.

CANNIUS: A fine wish! You'll be a billygoat rather than a she-goat.

POLYPHEMUS: I said *eat* one, not *be* one.

CANNIUS: Very prettily said. Are you generous to the poor?

POLYPHEMUS: I've nothing to give.

CANNIUS: But you would have, if you lived soberly and worked hard.

POLYPHEMUS: I'm fond of loafing.

CANNIUS: Do you keep God's commandments?

POLYPHEMUS: That's tiresome.

CANNIUS: Do you do penance for your sins?

POLYPHEMUS: Christ has paid for us.

CANNIUS: Then why do you insist you love the Gospel?

POLYPHEMUS: I'll tell you. A certain Franciscan in our neighborhood kept babbling from the pulpit against Erasmus' New Testament. I met the man privately, grabbed him by the hair with my left hand, and punched him with my right. I gave him a hell of a beating; made his whole face swell. What do you say to that? Isn't that promoting the Gospel? Next I gave him absolution by banging him on the head three times with this very same book, raising three lumps, in the name of Father, Son, and Holy Ghost.

CANNIUS: The evangelical spirit, all right! This is certainly defending the Gospel with the Gospel.

POLYPHEMUS: I ran across another member of the same order who never stopped raving against Erasmus. Fired with evangelical zeal, I threatened the fellow so much he begged pardon on both knees and admitted the devil had put him up to saying what he said. If he hadn't done this, my halberd would have bounced against his head. I looked as fierce as Mars in battle. This took place before witnesses.

CANNIUS: I'm surprised the man didn't drop dead on the spot. But let's go on. Do you live chastely?

POLYPHEMUS: I may when I'm old. But shall I confess the truth to you, Cannius?

CANNIUS: I'm no priest. If you want to confess, find somebody else.

POLYPHEMUS: Usually I confess to God, but to you I admit I'm not yet a perfect follower of the Gospel; just an ordinary fellow. My kind have four Gospels. Four things above all we Gospelers seek: full bellies; plenty of work for the organs below the belly; a livelihood from somewhere or other; finally, freedom to do as we please. If we get these, we shout in our cups, "Io, triumph; Io, Paean! The Gospel flourishes! Christ reigns!"

CANNIUS: That's an Epicurean life, surely, not an evangelical one.

POLYPHEMUS: I don't deny it, but you know Christ is omnipotent and can turn us into other men in the twinkling of an eye.

CANNIUS: Into swine, too, which I think is more likely than into good men.

POLYPHEMUS: I wish there were no worse creatures in the world than swine, oxen, asses, and camels! You can meet many men who are fiercer than lions, greedier than wolves, more lecherous than sparrows, more snappish than dogs, more venomous than vipers.

CANNIUS: But now it's time for you to begin changing from brute to man.

POLYPHEMUS: You do well to warn me, for prophets these days declare the end of the world is at hand.

CANNIUS: All the more reason to hurry.

POLYPHEMUS: I await the hand of Christ.

CANNIUS: See that you are pliant material for his hand! But where do they get the notion that the end of the world is near?

POLYPHEMUS: They say it's because men are behaving now just as they did before the Flood overwhelmed them. They feast, drink, stuff themselves, marry and are given in marriage, whore, buy, sell, pay and charge interest, build buildings. Kings make war, priests are zealous to increase their wealth, theologians invent syllogisms, monks roam through the world, the commons riot, Erasmus writes colloquies. In short, no calamity is lacking: hunger, thirst, robbery, war, plague, sedition, poverty. Doesn't this prove human affairs are at an end?

CANNIUS: In this mass of woes, what worries you most?

POLYPHEMUS: Guess.

CANNIUS: That your purse is full of cobwebs.

POLYPHEMUS: Damned if you haven't hit it!—Just now I'm on my way back from a drinking party. Some other time, when I'm more sober, I'll argue with you about the Gospel, if you like.

CANNIUS: When shall I see you sober?

POLYPHEMUS: When I'm sober.

CANNIUS: When will you be so?

POLYPHEMUS: When you see me so. Meantime, my dear Cannius, good luck.

CANNIUS: I hope you, in turn, become what you're called.

POLYPHEMUS: To prevent you from outdoing me in courtesy, I pray that Cannius, as the name implies, may never be lacking a can!

REVIEW QUESTIONS

1. Why does Erasmus use the dialogue form?
2. What might he be saying, not only about his readers but also about voice and perspective?
3. What is the older mode of Christianity that Erasmus parodies?
4. What is wrong with it?
5. What ideal of Christian behavior emerges in the colloquy?
6. How might it differ from the older form?
7. How might it be better suited to the instabilities of life in Renaissance Europe?

SIR THOMAS MORE

FROM *Utopia*

Sir Thomas More (1478–1535) was born on Milk Street, in London, the "brightest star that ever shined in the via lactea," according to Thomas Fuller. His father, John More, was a butler at Lincoln's Inn, later raised to the knighthood and made a judge first in the court of common pleas and later on the king's bench. The son was educated in the household of John Morton, archbishop of Canterbury, and at Christ Church, Oxford. Compelled by his father to study law, More entered New Inn in 1494 and Lincoln's Inn in 1496. He lived with the monks at the London Charterhouse and developed there the discipline and devotion that would serve him well in later troubles. Yet he decided on married rather than monastic life. He wed Jane Colet in 1505 and they had four children. More was an early advocate of education for women; he insisted that his son and daughters be taught by the best tutors available. Despite his many interests—intellectual, religious, and domestic—the law remained his career. City, monarchy, and church called on his services.

He was part of a London trade delegation to the cities of the Hanse in 1515. During this service, he wrote Book II of Utopia, *describing a pagan, communist city-state in which all policies and institutions were governed by reason. Such a state contrasted notably with the polity of Christian Europe with its greed, self-interest, and violence, as More described it in Book I. The complete work, which drew heavily on descriptions of the new world as well as passages from classical literature, was published in 1516 in Louvain. It established More's international reputation as a man of letters. But public affairs constantly drew him out of his study. In 1523, he served as speaker of the House of Commons, and in 1529, he succeeded Cardinal Wolsey as lord chancellor under Henry VIII. The king favored More, keeping him in attendance, visiting him at home, and enjoying his learned conversation. They fell out over Henry's growing dispute with the Catholic Church. More resigned his office in 1532, the day after the clergy were deprived of the power to enact constitutions without royal consent. Refusal to swear the Oath of Supremacy in 1534, by which he would have recognized Henry as the supreme head of the church in England, made More guilty of treason. He was martyred in 1535, in his own words "the king's good servant but God's first."*

From *Utopia*, by Sir Thomas More, translated by Robert M. Adams, A Norton Critical Edition, 2d ed. (New York: Norton, 1975), pp. 30–33, 40–42, 50–51, 64.

*   *   *

"**B**ut as a matter of fact, my dear More, to tell you what I really think, as long as you have private property, and as long as cash money is the measure of all things, it is really not possible for a nation to be governed justly or happily. For justice cannot exist where all the best things in life are held by the worst citizens; nor can anyone be happy where property is limited to a few, since those few are always uneasy and the many are utterly wretched.

"So I reflect on the wonderfully wise and sacred institutions of the Utopians who are so well governed with so few laws. Among them virtue has its reward, yet everything is shared equally, and all men live in plenty. I contrast them with the many other nations which are constantly passing new ordinances and yet can never order their affairs satisfactorily. In these other nations, whatever a man can get he calls his own private property; but all the mass of laws old and new don't enable him to secure his own, or defend it, or even distinguish it from someone else's property. Different men lay claim, successively or all at once, to the same property; and thus arise innumerable and interminable lawsuits—fresh ones every day. When I consider all these things, I become more sympathetic to Plato and do not wonder that he declined to make laws for any people who refused to share their goods equally. Wisest of men, he easily perceived that the one and only road to the welfare of all lies through the absolute equality of goods. I doubt whether such equality can ever be achieved where property belongs to individual men. However abundant goods may be, when every man tries to get as much as he can for his own exclusive use, a handful of men end up sharing the whole thing, and the rest are left in poverty. The result generally is two sorts of people whose fortunes ought to be interchanged: the rich are rapacious, wicked, and useless, while the poor are unassuming, modest men who work hard, more for the benefit of the public than of themselves.

"Thus I am wholly convinced that unless private property is entirely done away with, there can be no fair or just distribution of goods, nor can mankind be happily governed. As long as private property remains, by far the largest and the best part of mankind will be oppressed by a heavy and inescapable burden of cares and anxieties. This load, I admit, may be lightened a little bit under the present system, but I maintain it cannot be entirely removed. Laws might be made that no one should own more than a certain amount of land or receive more than a certain income. Or laws might be passed to prevent the prince from becoming too powerful and the populace too unruly. It might be made unlawful for public offices to be solicited, or put up for sale, or made burdensome for the office-holder by great expense. Otherwise, officeholders are tempted to get their money back by fraud or extortion, and only rich men can afford to seek positions which ought to be held by wise men. Laws of this sort, I agree, may have as much effect as good and careful nursing has on men who are chronically or even terminally sick. The social evils I mentioned may be alleviated and their effects mitigated for a while, but so long as private property remains, there is no hope at all of effecting a cure and restoring society to good health. While you try to cure one part, you aggravate the disease in other parts. Suppressing one symptom causes another to break out, since you cannot give something to one man without taking it away from someone else."

"But I don't see it that way," I replied. "It seems to me that men cannot possibly live well where all things are in common. How can there be plenty of commodities where every man stops working? The hope of gain will not spur him on; he will rely on others, and become lazy. If a man is driven by want of something to produce it, and yet cannot legally protect what he has gained, what can follow but continual bloodshed and turmoil, especially when respect for magistrates and their authority has been lost? I for one cannot conceive of authority existing among men who are equal to one another in every respect."

*   *   *

"As for the relative ages of the governments," Raphael replied, "you might judge more accurately if you had read their histories. If we believe these records, they had cities before there were even human inhabitants here. What ingenuity has discovered or chance hit upon could have turned up just as well in one place as the other. As a matter of fact, I believe we surpass them in natural intelligence, but they leave us far behind in their diligence and zeal to learn.

"According to their chronicles, they had heard nothing of men-from-beyond-the-equator (that's their name for us) until we arrived, except that once, some twelve hundred years ago, a ship which a storm had blown toward Utopia was wrecked on their island. Some Romans and Egyptians were cast ashore, and never departed. Now note how the Utopians profited, through their diligence, from this one chance event. They learned every single useful art of the Roman civilization either directly from their guests, or indirectly from hints and surmises on which they based their own investigations. What benefits from the mere fact that on a single occasion some Europeans landed there! If a similar accident has hitherto brought any men here from their land, the incident has been completely forgotten, as it will be forgotten in time to come that I was ever in their country. From one such accident they made themselves masters of all our useful inventions, but I suspect it will be a long time before we accept any of their institutions which are better than ours. This willingness to learn, I think, is the really important reason for their being better governed and living more happily than we do, though we are not inferior to them in brains or resources."

*   *   *

Their Occupations

Agriculture is the one occupation at which everyone works, men and women alike, with no exceptions. They are trained in it from childhood, partly in the schools where they learn theory, and partly through field trips to nearby farms, which make something like a game of practical instruction. On these trips they not only watch the work being done, but frequently pitch in and get a workout by doing the jobs themselves.

Besides farm work (which, as I said, everybody performs), each person is taught a particular trade of his own, such as wool-working, linen-making, masonry, metal-work, or carpentry. There is no other craft that is practiced by any considerable number of them. Throughout the island people wear, and down through the centuries they have always worn, the same style of clothing, except for the distinction between the sexes, and between married and unmarried persons. Their clothing is attractive, does not hamper bodily movement, and serves for warm as well as cold weather; what is more, each household can make its own.

Every person (and this includes women as well as men) learns a second trade, besides agriculture. As the weaker sex, women practice the lighter crafts, such as working in wool or linen; the heavier crafts are assigned to the men. As a rule, the son is trained to his father's craft, for which most feel a natural inclination. But if anyone is attracted to another occupation, he is transferred by adoption into a family practicing the trade he prefers. When anyone makes such a change, both his father and the authorities make sure that he is assigned to a grave and responsible householder. After a man has learned one trade, if he wants to learn another, he gets the same permission. When he has learned both, he pursues whichever he likes better, unless the city needs one more than the other.

The chief and almost the only business of the syphogrants is to manage matters so that no one sits around in idleness, and assure that everyone works hard at his trade. But no one has to exhaust himself with endless toil from early morning to late at night, as if he were a beast of burden. Such wretchedness, really worse than slavery, is the common lot of workmen in all countries, except Utopia. Of the day's twenty-four hours, the Utopians devote only six to work. They work three hours before noon, when they go to dinner. After dinner they rest for a couple of hours, then go to work for another three hours. Then they have supper, and at eight o'clock (counting the first hour after noon as one), they go to bed and sleep eight hours.

The other hours of the day, when they are not working, eating, or sleeping, are left to each man's individual discretion, provided he does not waste them in roistering or sloth, but uses them busily in some occupation that pleases him. Generally these periods are devoted to intellectual activity. For they have an established custom of giving public lectures before daybreak; attendance at these lectures is required only of those who have been specially chosen to devote themselves to learning, but a great many other people, both men and women, choose voluntarily to attend. Depending on their interests, some go to one lecture, some to another. But if anyone would rather devote his spare time to his trade, as many do who don't care for the intellectual life, this is not discouraged; in fact, such persons are commended as especially useful to the commonwealth.

*   *   *

But in all this, you may get a wrong impression, if we don't go back and consider one point more carefully. Because they allot only six hours to work, you might think the necessities of life would be in scant supply. This is far from the case. Their working hours are ample to provide not only enough but more than enough of the necessities and even the conveniences of life. You will easily appreciate this if you consider how large a part of the population in other countries exists without doing any work at all. In the first place, hardly any of the women, who are a full half of the population, work; or, if they do, then as a rule their husbands lie snoring in the bed. Then there is a great lazy gang of priests and so-called religious men. Add to them all the rich, especially the landlords, who are commonly called gentlemen and nobility. Include with them their retainers, that mob of swaggering bullies. Finally, reckon in with these the sturdy and lusty beggars, who go about feigning some disease as an excuse for their idleness. You will certainly find that the things which satisfy our needs are produced by far fewer hands than you had supposed.

And now consider how few of those who do work are doing really essential things. For where money is the standard of everything, many superfluous trades are bound to be carried on simply to satisfy luxury and licentiousness. Suppose the multitude of those who now work were limited to a few trades, and set to producing more and more of those conveniences and commodities that nature really requires. They would be bound to produce so much that the prices would drop, and the workmen would be unable to gain a living. But suppose again that all the workers in useless trades were put to useful ones, and that all the idlers (who now guzzle twice as much as the workingmen who make what they consume) were assigned to productive tasks— well, you can easily see how little time each man would have to spend working, in order to produce all the goods that human needs and conveniences require—yes, and human pleasure too, as long as it's true and natural pleasure.

*   *   *

Their Gold and Silver

For these reasons, therefore, they have accumulated a vast treasure, but they do not keep it like a treasure. I'm really quite ashamed to tell you how they do keep it, because you probably won't believe me. I would not have believed it myself if someone had just told me about it; but I was there, and saw it with my own eyes. It is a general rule that the more different anything is from what people are used to, the harder it is to accept. But, considering that all their other customs are so unlike ours, a sensible man will not be surprised that they use gold and silver quite differently than we do. After all, they never do use money among themselves, but keep it

only for a contingency which may or may not actually arise. So in the meanwhile they take care that no one shall overvalue gold and silver, of which money is made, beyond what the metals themselves deserve. Anyone can see, for example, that iron is far superior to either; men could not live without iron, by heaven, any more than without fire or water. But gold and silver have, by nature, no function that we cannot easily dispense with. Human folly has made them precious because they are rare. Like a most wise and generous mother, nature has placed the best things everywhere and in the open, like air, water, and the earth itself; but she has hidden away in remote places all vain and unprofitable things.

If in Utopia gold and silver were kept locked up in some tower, foolish heads among the common people might well concoct a story that the prince and the senate were out to cheat ordinary folk and get some advantage for themselves. They might indeed put the gold and silver into beautiful plateware and rich handiwork, but then in case of necessity the people would not want to give up such articles, on which they had begun to fix their hearts, only to melt them down for soldiers' pay. To avoid all these inconveniences, they thought of a plan which conforms with their institutions as clearly as it contrasts with our own. Unless we've actually seen it working, their plan may seem ridiculous to us, because we prize gold so highly and are so careful about protecting it. With them it's just the other way. While they eat from pottery dishes and drink from glass cups, well made but inexpensive, their chamber pots and stools—all their humblest vessels, for use in the common halls and private homes—are made of gold and silver. The chains and heavy fetters of slaves are also made of these metals. Finally, criminals who are to bear through life the mark of some disgraceful act are forced to wear golden rings on their ears, golden bands on their fingers, golden chains around their necks, and even golden crowns on their heads. Thus they hold gold and silver up to scorn in every conceivable way. As a result, when they have to part with these metals, which other nations give up with as much agony as if they were being disemboweled, the Utopians feel it no more than the loss of a penny.

*   *   *

Slaves

The Utopians enslave prisoners of war only if they are captured in wars fought by the Utopians themselves. The children of slaves are not automatically enslaved, nor are any men who were enslaved in a foreign country. Most of their slaves are either their own former citizens, enslaved for some heinous offense, or else men of other nations who were condemned to death in their own land. Most are of the latter sort. Sometimes the Utopians buy them at a very modest rate, more often they ask for them, get them for nothing, and bring them home in considerable numbers. These kinds of slaves are kept constantly at work, and are always fettered. The Utopians deal with their own people more harshly than with others, feeling that their crimes are worse and deserve stricter punishment because, as it is argued, they had an excellent education and the best of moral training, yet still couldn't be restrained from wrongdoing. A third class of slaves consists of hardworking penniless drudges from other nations who voluntarily choose to become slaves in Utopia. Such people are treated well, almost as well as citizens, except that they are given a little extra work, on the score that they're used to it. If one of them wants to leave, which seldom happens, no obstacles are put in his way, nor is he sent off empty-handed.

*   *   *

REVIEW QUESTIONS

1. Why did More choose to call the place *Utopia*, literally "Nowhere"?
2. What possibilities created by the discovery of a new world does More explore in *Utopia?*
3. How are More's Utopians different from what medieval Europeans would have considered Christian?
4. How does More's attitude toward the people of Utopia reflect attitudes of the Renaissance?
5. How might *Utopia* be critical of Renaissance society?
6. What do More's Utopians have in common with the kind of Christian Erasmus described in his colloquy "Cyclops, or the Gospel-Bearer"?

13   THE AGE OF DISSENT AND DIVISION, 1500–1564

The year 1492 marked both the end of the expansion of Christianity in Europe, with the final expulsion of the Jews and Muslims from the Iberian Peninsula, and the beginning of the expansion of European Christianity across the globe. So, too, it marked the nadir of papal ambition, venality, and corruption, and thereby the medieval Christian hierarchy. In that year, the Borgia pope, Alexander VI, whom contemporaries such as Machiavelli knew to be rapacious, murderous, treacherous, and ambitious, was elected.

Within a generation of the Reconquista of Spain, the German lands of the grandson of Ferdinando and Isabella of Spain would be split between two very different understandings of Christianity: what it meant to be a Christian, what the Church was and how it was to be constituted, and what the nature of worship was. In part, the Reformation arose in response to perceptions of papal bellicosity and immorality; it belonged to an older tradition of reformatio. Equally, however, the Reformation was heir to the Renaissance: the philological skills and discoveries of fifteenth-century humanists enabled new approaches to the study of the Bible, and the humanist emphasis on historical accuracy led to a call for a return to apostolic Christianity. That return to the text of Scripture, along with a new sensitivity to historical periods, brought theologians such as Martin Luther to reconsider not only devotional practices but the very structure of authority of medieval Christendom—the papal hierarchy—and others, such as John Calvin, to return to the Acts of the Apostles for a vision of the true church.

Even as Christendom divided against itself in Europe, it expanded through the persons of conquistadores to create worlds unimagined in the European tradition. Reformation and expansion both came through bloodshed. In Germany, peasants and artisans fought lords and emperor to institute the godly law they found in the Bible, only to be massacred. In France, the Low Countries, and England, as well as the Holy Roman Empire, Christians executed Christians over questions of the Eucharist, the place of images in worship, and the cult of the saints. Churches divided from one another, each defining itself against the others, even as all confronted worlds for which neither the Bible nor the classical tradition had prepared them.

MARTIN LUTHER

FROM *The Large Catechism,* 1530

Martin Luther (1483–1546), one of the founders of Protestantism, was born of peasant stock. His father had left his fields for the copper mines of Mansfeld in Saxon, where he flourished economically and rose to the status of town councilor. His son, Martin, received a primary education from the Brethren of the Common Life and enrolled at the University of Erfurt in 1501, where he earned his bachelor of arts in 1502 and his master of arts in 1505. His father hoped that his son would continue the family's rise to prominence by pursuing a legal career. These aspirations were shattered when Luther unexpectedly entered a monastery in 1505. As a member of the order of Augustinian Hermits, he began formal training in theology. Selected for advanced training in theology, he made his way to the University of Wittenberg, where he received his doctorate in 1512 and occupied the chair of biblical theology. Even as his academic career prospered, his inner life suffered. Luther was beset by doubts about his own salvation, the result of a consciousness both of his own weakness and of divine righteousness. Long study and meditation led him to a resolution that became the basis for his theology of justification. Salvation was the result of divine grace, freely given; the forgiven conscience could be at peace; the soul could serve God joyfully. Luther having experienced this new conviction, it is not surprising that the extravagant claims surrounding the sale of indulgences in 1517 provoked him to public protest. The form and text of that protest became known as the "95 Theses." His objection to the claim that the pope could remit the temporal punishment of sins led him deeper and deeper into controversy and ultimately to schism. By 1520, the rift between Luther and the Catholic Church had become irreparable and extended to far more issues than papal power. His The Large Catechism, *whose Preface follows, reveals another dimension of Luther's reform: his engagement in the care of souls. Through catechism, a process of recitation and repetition, young people were to be brought to a proper understanding of God's Will and Word. It reveals Luther's familiarity with the Christian Church's past and his hope for its future.*

From *The Large Catechism of Martin Luther*, translated by Robert H. Fischer (Philadelphia: Augsburg Fortress Press, 1959).

Martin Luther's Preface[1]

It is not for trivial reasons that we constantly treat the Catechism and strongly urge others to do the same. For we see to our sorrow that many pastors and preachers[2] are very negligent in this respect and despise both their office and this teaching itself. Some because of their great and lofty learning, others because of sheer laziness and gluttony, behave in this matter as if they were pastors or preachers for their bellies' sake and had nothing to do but live off the fat of the land all their days, as they used to do under the papacy.

Everything that they are to teach and preach is now available to them in clear and simple form in the many excellent books which are in reality what the old manuals claimed in their titles to be: "Sermons That Preach Themselves," "Sleep Soundly," "Prepared!" and "Treasury."[3] However, they are not so upright and honest as to buy these books, or if they have them, to examine and read them. Such shameful gluttons and servants of their bellies would make better swineherds or dogkeepers than spiritual guides and pastors.

Now that they are free from the useless, bothersome babbling of the Seven Hours,[4] it would be fine if every morning, noon, and evening they would read, instead, at least a page or two from the Catechism, the Prayer Book,[5] the New Testament, or something else from the Bible and would pray the Lord's Prayer for themselves and their parishioners. In this way they might show honor and gratitude to the Gospel, through which they have been delivered from so many burdens and troubles, and they might feel a little shame because, like pigs and dogs, they remember no more of the Gospel than this rotten, pernicious, shameful, carnal liberty. As it is, the common people take the Gospel altogether too lightly, and even our utmost exertions accomplish but little. What, then, can we expect if we are sluggish and lazy, as we used to be under the papacy?

Besides, a shameful and insidious plague of security and boredom has overtaken us. Many regard the Catechism as a simple, silly teaching which they can absorb and master at one reading. After reading it once they toss the book into a corner as if they are ashamed to read it again. Indeed, even among the nobility there are some louts and skinflints who declare that we can do without pastors and preachers from now on because we have everything in books and can learn it all by ourselves. So they blithely let parishes fall into decay, and brazenly allow both pastors and preachers to suffer distress and hunger. This is what one can expect of crazy Germans. We Germans have such disgraceful people among us and must put up with them.

As for myself, let me say that I, too, am a doctor and a preacher—yes, and as learned and experienced as any of those who act so high and mighty. Yet I do as a child who is being taught the Catechism. Every morning, and whenever else I have time, I read and recite word for word the Lord's Prayer, the Ten Commandments, the Creed, the Psalms, etc. I must still read and study the Catechism daily, yet I cannot master it as I wish, but must remain a child and pupil of the Catechism, and I do it gladly. These dainty, fastidious fellows would like quickly, with one reading, to become doctors above all doctors, to know all there is to be known. Well, this, too, is a sure sign that they despise both their office and the people's souls, yes, even God and his Word. They need not fear a fall, for they have already fallen all too horribly. What they need is to become children and begin learning their ABC's, which they think they have outgrown long ago.

Therefore, I beg these lazy-bellies and presumptuous saints, for God's sake, to get it into their heads that they are not really and truly such learned

---

[1] In the German edition of the Book of Concord, 1580, this Longer Preface (which dates from 1530) appeared after the Shorter Preface in accordance with the order observed in the fourth German volume of the Jena edition of Luther's Works (1556).

[2] Preachers (*Prediger*) were limited to preaching; pastors (*Pfarrherren*) exercised the full ministerial office.

[3] Titles of medieval sermon books.

[4] The seven canonical hours, daily prayers prescribed by the medieval Breviary.

[5] Luther published the "Little Prayer Book" (*Betbüchlein*) in 1522 to replace Roman Catholic devotional books.

and great doctors as they think. I implore them not to imagine that they have learned these parts of the Catechism perfectly, or at least sufficiently, even though they think they know them ever so well. Even if their knowledge of the Catechism were perfect (though that is impossible in this life), yet it is highly profitable and fruitful daily to read it and make it the subject of meditation and conversation. In such reading, conversation, and meditation the Holy Spirit is present and bestows ever new and greater light and fervor, so that day by day we relish and appreciate the Catechism more greatly. This is according to Christ's promise in Matt. 18:20, "Where two or three are gathered in my name, there am I in the midst of them."

Nothing is so effectual against the devil, the world, the flesh, and all evil thoughts as to occupy oneself with the Word of God, talk about it, and meditate on it. Psalm 1 calls those blessed who "meditate on God's law day and night."[6] You will never offer up any incense or other savor more potent against the devil than to occupy yourself with God's commandments and words and to speak, sing, and meditate on them. This, indeed, is the true holy water, the sign which routs the devil and puts him to flight.[7]

For this reason alone you should eagerly read, recite, ponder, and practice the Catechism, even if the only blessing and benefit you obtain from it is to rout the devil and evil thoughts. For he cannot bear to hear God's Word. God's Word is not like some empty tale, such as the one about Dietrich of Bern,[8] but as St. Paul says in Rom. 1:16, it is "the power of God," indeed, the power of God which burns the devil and gives us immeasurable strength, comfort, and help.

Why should I waste words? Time and paper would fail me if I were to recount all the blessings that flow from God's Word. The devil is called the master of a thousand arts. What, then, shall we call

God's Word, which routs and destroys this master of a thousand arts with all his wiles and might? It must, indeed, be master of more than a hundred thousand arts. Shall we frivolously despise this might, blessing, power, and fruit—especially we who would be pastors and preachers? If so, we deserve not only to be refused food but also to be chased out by dogs and pelted with dung. Not only do we need God's Word daily as we need our daily bread; we also must use it daily against the daily, incessant attacks and ambushes of the devil with his thousand arts.

If this were not enough to admonish us to read the Catechism daily, there is God's command. That alone should be incentive enough. Deut. 6:7, 8 solemnly enjoins that we should always meditate upon his precepts whether sitting, walking, standing, lying down, or rising, and keep them before our eyes and in our hands as a constant token and sign. Certainly God did not require and command this so solemnly without good reason. He knows our danger and need. He knows the constant and furious attacks and assaults of the devil. So he wishes to warn, equip, and protect us against them with good "armor" against their "flaming darts,"[9] and with a good antidote against their evil infection and poison. O what mad, senseless fools we are! We must ever live and dwell in the midst of such mighty enemies as the devils, and yet we despise our weapons and armor, too lazy to give them a thought!

Look at these bored, presumptuous saints who will not or cannot read and study the Catechism daily. They evidently consider themselves much wiser than God himself, and wiser than all his holy angels, prophets, apostles, and all Christians! God himself is not ashamed to teach it daily, for he knows of nothing better to teach, and he always keeps on teaching this one thing without varying it with anything new or different. All the saints know of nothing better or different to learn, though they cannot learn it to perfection. Are we not most marvelous fellows, therefore, if we imagine, after reading or hearing it once, that we know it all and need

---

[6] Ps. 1:2.

[7] I.e., the Word of God really does what holy water was formerly believed to accomplish.

[8] Luther frequently cited the legend of Dietrich of Bern as an example of lies and fables.

[9] Eph. 6:11, 16.

not read or study it any more? Most marvelous fellows, to think we can finish learning in one hour what God himself cannot finish teaching! Actually, he is busy teaching it from the beginning of the world to the end, and all prophets and saints have been busy learning it and have always remained pupils, and must continue to do so.

This much is certain: anyone who knows the Ten Commandments perfectly knows the entire Scriptures. In all affairs and circumstances he can counsel, help, comfort, judge, and make decisions in both spiritual and temporal matters. He is qualified to sit in judgment upon all doctrines, estates, persons, laws, and everything else in the world.

What is the whole Psalter but meditations and exercises based on the First Commandment? Now, I know beyond a doubt that such lazy-bellies and presumptuous fellows do not understand a single Psalm, much less the entire Scriptures, yet they pretend to know and despise the Catechism, which is a brief compend and summary of all the Holy Scriptures.

Therefore, I once again implore all Christians, especially pastors and preachers, not to try to be doctors prematurely and to imagine that they know everything. Vain imaginations, like new cloth, suffer shrinkage! Let all Christians exercise themselves in the Catechism daily, and constantly put it into practice, guarding themselves with the greatest care and diligence against the poisonous infection of such security or vanity. Let them continue to read and teach, to learn and meditate and ponder. Let them never stop until they have proved by experience that they have taught the devil to death and have become wiser than God himself and all his saints.

If they show such diligence, then I promise them—and their experience will bear me out—that they will gain much fruit and God will make excellent men of them. Then in due time they themselves will make the noble confession that the longer they work with the Catechism, the less they know of it and the more they have to learn. Only then, hungry and thirsty, will they truly relish what now they cannot bear to smell because they are so bloated and surfeited. To this end may God grant his grace! Amen.

Preface[10]

This sermon has been undertaken for the instruction of children and uneducated people. Hence from ancient times it has been called, in Greek, a "catechism"—that is, instruction for children. Its contents represent the minimum of knowledge required of a Christian. Whoever does not possess it should not be reckoned among Christians nor admitted to a sacrament,[11] just as a craftsman who does not know the rules and practices of his craft is rejected and considered incompetent. For this reason young people should be thoroughly instructed in the various parts of the Catechism or children's sermons and diligently drilled in their practice.

Therefore, it is the duty of every head of a household to examine his children and servants at least once a week and ascertain what they have learned of it, and if they do not know it, to keep them faithfully at it. I well remember the time when there were old people who were so ignorant that they knew nothing of these things—indeed, even now we find them daily—yet they come to Baptism and the Sacrament of the Altar and exercise all the rights of Christians, although those who come to the sacrament ought to know more and have a fuller understanding of all Christian doctrine than children and beginners at school. As for the common people, however, we should be satisfied if they learned the three parts[12] which have been the heritage of Christendom from ancient times, though they were rarely taught and treated correctly, so that all who wish to be Christians in fact as well as

---

[10] The Shorter Preface is based on a sermon of May 18, 1528.

[11] This was not only a proposal of Luther, but also a medieval prescription; cf. John Surgant, *Manuale Curatorum* (1502), etc.

[12] Ten Commandments, Creed, Lord's Prayer. From 1525 on catechetical instruction in Wittenberg was expanded to include material on Baptism and the Lord's Supper.

in name, both young and old, may be well-trained in them and familiar with them.

I. THE TEN COMMANDMENTS OF GOD

1. You shall have no other gods before me.
2. You shall not take the name of God in vain.
3. You shall keep the Sabbath day holy.
4. You shall honor father and mother.
5. You shall not kill.
6. You shall not commit adultery.
7. You shall not steal.
8. You shall not bear false witness against your neighbor.
9. You shall not covet your neighbor's house.
10. You shall not covet his wife, man-servant, maid-servant, cattle, or anything that is his.[13]

II. THE CHIEF ARTICLES OF OUR FAITH

I believe in God, the Father almighty, maker of heaven and earth:

And in Jesus Christ, his only Son, our Lord: who was conceived by the Holy Spirit, born of the virgin Mary, suffered under Pontius Pilate, was crucified, dead, and buried; he descended into hell, the third day he rose from the dead, he ascended into heaven, and sits on the right hand of God, the Father almighty, whence he shall come to judge the living and the dead.

I believe in the Holy Spirit, the holy Christian church,[14] the communion of saints, the forgiveness of sins, the resurrection of the body, and the life everlasting. Amen.

III. THE PRAYER, OR OUR FATHER, WHICH CHRIST TAUGHT

Our Father who art in heaven, hallowed be thy name. Thy kingdom come, thy will be done, on earth as it is in heaven. Give us this day our daily bread; and forgive us our debts, as we also have forgiven our debtors; and lead us not into temptation, but deliver us from evil. For thine is the kingdom and the power and the glory, forever. Amen.[15]

These are the most necessary parts of Christian instruction. We should learn to repeat them word for word. Our children should be taught the habit of reciting them daily when they rise in the morning, when they go to their meals, and when they go to bed at night; until they repeat them they should not be given anything to eat or drink. Every father has the same duty to his household; he should dismiss man-servants and maid-servants if they do not know these things and are unwilling to learn them. Under no circumstances should a person be tolerated if he is so rude and unruly that he refuses to learn these three parts in which everything contained in Scripture is comprehended in short, plain, and simple terms, for the dear fathers or apostles, whoever they were,[16] have thus summed up the doctrine, life, wisdom, and learning which constitute the Christian's conversation, conduct, and concern.

When these three parts are understood, we ought also to know what to say about the sacraments which Christ himself instituted, Baptism and the holy Body and Blood of Christ, according to the texts of Matthew and Mark at the end of their Gospels where they describe how Christ said farewell to his disciples and sent them forth.

BAPTISM

"Go and teach all nations, and baptize them in the name of the Father and of the Son and of the Holy Spirit" (Matt. 28:19). "He who believes and is baptized will be saved; but he who does not believe will be condemned" (Mark 16:16).

It is enough for an ordinary person to know this much about Baptism from the Scriptures. The

---

[13] Ex. 20:2–17; cf. Deut. 5:6–21.

[14] The translation of *ecclesiam catholicam* by *eine christliche Kirche* was common in fifteenth-century Germany.

[15] Matt. 6:9–13; cf. Luke 11:2–4.

[16] Luther was not interested in defending the apostolic authorship of the Creed.

other sacrament may be dealt with similarly, in short, simple words according to the text of St. Paul.

THE SACRAMENT [OF THE ALTAR]

"Our Lord Jesus Christ on the night when he was betrayed took bread, gave thanks, and broke it and gave it to his disciples, saying, 'Take and eat, this is my body, which is given for you. Do this in remembrance of me.'

"In the same way also the cup, after supper, saying, 'This cup is the new testament in my blood, which is shed for you for the forgiveness of sins. Do this, as often as you drink it, in remembrance of me'' (I Cor. 11:23–25).

Thus we have, in all, five parts covering the whole of Christian doctrine, which we should constantly teach and require young people to recite word for word. Do not assume that they will learn and retain this teaching from sermons alone. When these parts have been well learned, you may assign them also some Psalms or some hymns,[17] based on these subjects, to supplement and confirm their knowledge. Thus our youth will be led into the Scriptures so that they make progress daily.

However, it is not enough for them simply to learn and repeat these parts verbatim. The young people should also attend preaching, especially at the time designated for the Catechism,[18] so that they may hear it explained and may learn the meaning of every part. Then they will also be able to repeat what they have heard and give a good, correct answer when they are questioned, and thus the preaching will not be without benefit and fruit. The reason we take such care to preach on the Catechism frequently is to impress it upon our youth, not in a lofty and learned manner but briefly and very simply, so that it may penetrate deeply into their minds and remain fixed in their memories.

Now we shall take up the above-mentioned parts one by one and in the plainest possible manner say about them as much as is necessary.

REVIEW QUESTIONS

1. Why is the catechism so important to Martin Luther?
2. To whom is the catechism to be taught, and by whom is it to be taught?
3. What matters, issues, or ideas does the catechism teach?
4. What purposes does the catechism serve in the reformation of Luther?
5. What concerns on the part of Luther do these purposes reflect?

---

[17] Luther himself wrote six hymns based on the parts of the Catechism.

[18] Preaching and instruction on the Catechism especially during Lent.

SEBASTIAN LOTZER

The Twelve Articles of the Peasants of Swabia

The Twelve Articles of the Peasants of Swabia, adopted at the free imperial city of Memmingen in 1525, is one of the signal documents of the great agrarian revolt known as the Peasants' War of 1525. More than any other such document, it specifically linked the social and political grievances of the peasants with the evangelical

THE WITTENBERG ALTARPIECE (1547)   LUCAS CRANACH THE ELDER

Created in 1547 by the German Renaissance painter Lucas Cranach the Elder (1472–1553), the Wittenberg altarpiece stands in the City Church of Wittenberg, Luther's own church. Cranach was a court painter to the Electors of Saxony as well as an important figure, at times serving as both a city councilman and mayor, of the city of Wittenberg. In this context, the work came into being. It shows leading figures of the Lutheran Reformation as they perform the "sacraments." On the left front panel, a minister baptizes an infant into the faith; the right panel depicts a minister hearing confession; the center panel shows communion, depicted as the Last Supper of Christ with the leaders of the Lutheran movement as the apostles. The altarpiece seems to suggest, as seems appropriate, given its content and place, that the Lutheran confession is the true church of Christ. In fact, however, it stands in ambiguous relationship to the reformer. Painted after his death, the altarpiece takes a firmer position on the sacramentality of confession than did Luther himself. How do the frames affect your understanding of the three sacraments? Why is the Supper at center? Why is preaching in the predella, or foundation, of the altarpiece? Considering the composition of each panel, what do the postures and gestures of the various figures tell us about their relationship to one another? As ministers play a central role in the altarpiece, what does it communicate about the function of an ideal minister? Comparing this work of Lutheran art to Rubens's The Miracle of St. Ignatius of Loyola, *(see page 447) how would you characterize the intended message of the altarpiece to those people, regardless of confession, who might view it? Why do you think Cranach placed Luther in the Last Supper, and what might be the significance of Luther passing the cup to the knight to our right? Again, comparing the work of Cranach to that of Rubens, why do you suppose the architectural elements are relatively minimal in the former? Are they part of the "message"?*

*principles of the Reformation. Ironically, this document was not composed by a peas-
ant but by a townsman, the journeyman furrier and lay preacher Sebastian Lotzer.
To do so, he summarized and condensed the long (several hundred articles) list of
demands put forward by the peasants of Baltringen. The Memmingen preacher
Christoph Schappeler added a preamble and supplied biblical references in the mar-
gins. This document acquired its importance because it was quickly printed and
widely disseminated. In many areas of the revolt, it was adopted as the basis for lists
of grievances and proposals for settlement.*

From *The Revolution of 1525: The German Peasants' War from a New Perspective*, translated
by Thomas A. Brady Jr. (Baltimore: Johns Hopkins University Press, 1981), pp. 195–201.

The Just and Fundamental Articles of All the Peasantry and Tenants of Spiritual and Temporal Powers by Whom They Think Themselves Oppressed

To the Christian reader, the peace and grace of God through Jesus Christ.

There are many antichrists who, now that the peasants are assembled together, seize the chance to mock the gospel, saying, "Is this the fruit of the new gospel: to band together in great numbers and plot conspiracies to reform and even topple the spiritual and temporal powers—yes, even to murder them?" The following articles answer all these godless, blasphemous critics. We want two things: first, to make them stop mocking the word of God; and second, to establish the Christian justice of the current disobedience and rebellion of all the peasants.

First of all, the gospel does not cause rebellions and uproars, because it tells of Christ, the promised Messiah, whose words and life teach nothing but love, peace, patience, and unity. And all who believe in this Christ become loving, peaceful, patient, and one in spirit. This is the basis of all the articles of the peasants (as we will clearly show): to hear the gospel and to live accordingly. How then can the antichrists call the gospel a cause of rebellion and of disobedience? It is not the gospel that drives some antichrists and foes of the gospel to resist and reject these demands and requirements, but the

devil, the deadliest foe of the gospel, who arouses through unbelief such opposition in his own followers. His aim is to suppress and abolish the word of God, which teaches love, peace, and unity.

Second, it surely follows that the peasants, whose articles demand this gospel as their doctrine and rule of life, cannot be called "disobedient" or "rebellious." For if God deigns to hear the peasants' earnest plea that they may be permitted to live according to his word, who will dare deny his will? Who indeed will dare question his judgment? Who will dare oppose his majesty? Did he not hear the children of Israel crying to him and deliver them out of Pharaoh's hand? And can he not save his own today as well? Yes, he will save them, and soon! Therefore, Christian reader, read these articles diligently, and then judge for yourself.

These are the Articles.

THE FIRST ARTICLE

First of all, we humbly ask and beg—and we all agree on this—that henceforth we ought to have the authority and power for the whole community to elect and appoint its own pastor. We also want authority to depose a pastor who behaves improperly. This elected pastor should preach to us the holy gospel purely and clearly, without human additions or human doctrines or precepts. For constant preaching of the true faith impels us to beg God for his grace, that he may instill in us and confirm in us that same true faith. Unless we have his grace in us, we remain mere, useless flesh and blood. For the Scripture clearly teaches that we may come to God only through true faith and can be saved only through His mercy. This is why we need such a guide and pastor; and thus our demand is grounded in Scripture.

THE SECOND ARTICLE

Second, although the obligation to pay a just tithe prescribed in the Old Testament is fulfilled in the New, yet we will gladly pay the large tithe on grain—but only in just measure. Since the tithe should be given to God and distributed among his servants, so the pastor who clearly preaches the word of God deserves to receive it. From now on we want to have our church wardens, appointed by the community, collect and receive this tithe and have our elected pastor draw from it, with the whole community's consent, a decent and adequate living for himself and his. The remainder should be distributed to the village's own poor, again with the community's consent and according to need. What then remains should be kept in case some need to be called up to defend the country; and then the costs can be met from this reserve, so that no general territorial tax will be laid upon the poor folk.

Wherever one or more villages have sold off the tithe to meet some emergency, those purchasers who can show that they bought the tithe with the consent of the whole village shall not be simply expropriated. Indeed we hope to reach fair compromises with such persons, according to the facts of the case, and to redeem the tithe in installments. But wherever the tithe holder—be he clergyman or layman—did not buy the tithe from the whole village but has it from ancestors who simply seized it from the village, we will not, ought not, and do not intend to pay it any longer, except (as we said above) to support our elected pastor. And we will reserve the rest or distribute it to the poor, as the Bible commands. As for the small tithe, we will not pay it at all, for the Lord God created cattle for man's free use; and it is an unjust tithe invented by men alone. Therefore, we won't pay it anymore.

THE THIRD ARTICLE

Third, it has until now been the custom for the lords to own us as their property. This is deplorable, for Christ redeemed and bought us all with his precious blood, the lowliest shepherd as well as the greatest lord, with no exceptions. Thus the Bible proves that we are free and want to be free. Not that we want to be utterly free and subject to no authority at all; God does not teach us that. We ought to live according to the commandments, not according to the lusts of the flesh. But we should love God, recognize him as our Lord in our neighbor, and willingly do all things God commanded us at his Last Supper. This means we should live according to his commandment, which does not teach us to obey only the rulers, but to humble ourselves before everyone. Thus we should willingly obey our elected and rightful ruler, set over us by God, in all proper and Christian matters. Nor do we doubt that you, as true and just Christians, will gladly release us from bondage or prove to us from the gospel that we must be your property.

THE FOURTH ARTICLE

Fourth, until now it has been the custom that no commoner might catch wild game, wildfowl, or fish in the running waters, which seems to us altogether improper, unbrotherly, selfish, and contrary to God's Word. In some places the rulers protect the game to our distress and great loss, for we must suffer silently while the dumb beasts gobble up the crops God gave for man's use, although this offends both God and neighbor. When the Lord God created man, he gave him dominion over all animals, over the birds of the air, and the fish in the waters. Thus we demand that if someone owns a stream, lake, or pond, he should have to produce documentary proof of ownership and show that it was sold to him with the consent of the whole village. In that case we do not want to seize it from him with force but only to review the matter in a Christian way for the sake of brotherly love. But whoever cannot produce adequate proof of ownership and sale should surrender the waters to the community, as is just.

THE FIFTH ARTICLE

Fifth, we have another grievance about wood-cutting, for our lords have seized the woods for themselves alone; and when the poor commoner needs some wood, he has to pay twice the price for it. We think that those woods whose lords, be they clergymen or laymen, cannot prove ownership by purchase should revert to the whole community. And the community should be able to allow in an orderly way each man to gather firewood for his home and building timber free, though only with permission of the community's elected officials. If all the woods have been fairly purchased, then a neighborly and Christian agreement should be reached with their owners about their use. Where the woods were simply seized and then sold to a third party, however, a compromise should be reached according to the facts of the case and the norms of brotherly love and Holy Writ.

THE SIXTH ARTICLE

Sixth, there is our grievous burden of labor services, which the lords daily increase in number and kind. We demand that these obligations be properly investigated and lessened. And we should be allowed, graciously, to serve as our forefathers did, according to God's word alone.

THE SEVENTH ARTICLE

Seventh, in the future we will not allow the lords to oppress us any more. Rather, a man shall have his holding on the proper terms on which it has been leased, that is, by the agreement between lord and peasant. The lord should not force or press the tenant to perform labor or any other service without pay, so that the peasant may use and enjoy his land unburdened and in peace. When the lord needs labor services, however, the peasant should willingly serve his own lord before others; yet a peasant should serve only at a time when his own affairs do not suffer and only for a just wage.

THE EIGHTH ARTICLE

Eighth, we have a grievance that many of us hold lands that are overburdened with rents higher than the land's yield. Thus the peasants lose their property and are ruined. The lords should have honorable men inspect these farms and adjust the rents fairly, so that the peasant does not work for nothing. For every laborer is worthy of his hire.

THE NINTH ARTICLE

Ninth, we have a grievance against the way serious crimes are punished, for they are constantly making new laws. We are not punished according to the severity of the case but sometimes out of great ill will and sometimes out of favoritism. We think that punishments should be dealt out among us according to the ancient written law and the circumstances of the case, and not according to the judge's bias.

THE TENTH ARTICLE

Tenth, we have a grievance that some people have seized meadows and fields belonging to the community. We shall restore these to the community, unless a proper sale can be proved. If they were improperly bought, however, then a friendly and brotherly compromise should be reached, based on the facts.

THE ELEVENTH ARTICLE

Eleventh, we want the custom called death taxes totally abolished. We will not tolerate it or allow widows and orphans to be so shamefully robbed of their goods, as so often happens in various ways, against God and all that is honorable. The very ones who should be guarding and protecting our goods have skinned and trimmed us of them instead. Had they the slightest legal pretext, they would have grabbed everything. God will suffer this no longer but will wipe it all out. Henceforth no one shall have to pay death taxes, whether small or large.

CONCLUSION

Twelfth, we believe and have decided that if any one or more of these articles is not in agreement with God's Word (which we doubt), then this should be proved to us from Holy Writ. We will abandon it, when this is proved by the Bible. If some of our articles should be approved and later found to be unjust, they shall be dead, null, and void from that moment on. Likewise, if Scripture truly reveals further grievances as offensive to God and a burden to our neighbor, we will reserve a place for them and declare them included in our list. We, for our part, will live and exercise our-selves in all Christian teachings, for which we will pray to the Lord God. For he alone, and no other, can give us the truth. The peace of Christ be with us all.

REVIEW QUESTIONS

1. What do the Twelve Articles tell you about relations between the common man and his lords?
2. What are the priorities of the Twelve Articles?
3. What is most important to the petitioners?
4. Why is it so important?
5. What is second in importance?
6. What changes are the petitioners asking for the tithe?
7. What is Godly Law?
8. What might be its applications?
9. What are the implications of Godly Law for the lords?

JOHN CALVIN

FROM Draft of Ecclesiastical Ordinances, September and October 1541

John (Jean) Calvin (1509–1564) was born of bourgeois parents in the city of Noyon in Picardy. Destined by his father for an ecclesiastical career, he received several benefices to finance his education as early as 1521. In 1523, he transferred to the University of Paris, where he imbibed the spirit of humanism from such teachers as Mathurin Cordier and Guillaume Bude. Calvin earned a master of arts degree at Paris and, without abandoning his study of classical languages and literature, turned to law at Orléans in 1528. By 1532, he had earned a doctorate of law. Sometime during his legal training or shortly thereafter, Calvin converted to Protestantism. The year 1534 was decisive for Calvin. Forced to flee Paris because of the proscription of Protestantism, he made his way to Basel, where he began work on his great systematic theology, Institutes of the Christian Religion *(1536). It was immediately recognized as a superb normative statement of reformed theology and established Calvin's stature as a leader among Protestants despite his youth. As the first edition went to press, Calvin made his way to Geneva, where Guillaume Farel enlisted his aid in the reform of the city. The early years of the Reformation in Geneva were stormy, and the doctrines advocated by Calvin met with considerable opposition. In a dispute over church discipline, the city council banished the*

Protestant pastors. Calvin made his way to Strasbourg, where he remained as a colleague of Martin Bucer and minister to the French refugee church until 1541. Meanwhile, political and religious chaos in Geneva eventually forced the government to seek the return of Calvin. He reluctantly consented, but only with the assurance that his entire original scheme of church polity would be instituted. The ecclesiastical ordinance adopted in 1541 encapsulated that polity and became influential for reformed churches throughout Europe. Written four years later, his Catechism of the Church of Geneva *offers a different vision of the reformer's range of activity. He was no less deeply committed to the inner life of the faithful than he was to the explication of doctrine or the organization of the church. The dedication summarizes the role of education in preserving an embattled and isolated religious community. Calvin remained in Geneva from 1541 until his death in 1564, by which time the city that had accepted reform so reluctantly had been transformed into the center of an international Reformation.*

From *John Calvin*, by G. R. Potter and M. Greengrass (London: Edward Arnold, 1983), pp. 71–76.

First there are four orders of offices instituted by our Saviour for the government of his Church: namely, the pastors, then the doctors, next the elders [*nominated and appointed by the government,*] and fourthly the deacons. If we wish to see the Church well-ordered and maintained we ought to observe this form of government.

The Duty of Pastors

Pastors are sometimes named in the Bible as overseers, elders and ministers. Their work is to proclaim the Word of God, to teach, admonish, exhort and reprove publicly and privately, to administer the sacraments and, with the elders or their deputies, to issue fraternal warnings.

The Examination of Pastors

This consists of two parts. The first concerns doctrine—to find out if the candidate has a good and sound knowledge of the Bible; and, secondly, comes his suitability for expounding this to the people for their edification.

Further, to avoid any danger of his having any wrong ideas, it is fitting that he should profess to accept and uphold the teaching approved by the Church.

Questions must be asked to find out if he is a good teacher and he must privately set forth the teaching of our Lord.

Next, it must be ascertained that he is a man of good principles without any known faults.

The Selection of Pastors

First the ministers should choose someone suitable for the position [*and notify the government*]. Then he is to be presented to the council. If he is approved, he will be accepted and received by the council [*as it thinks fit*]. He is then given a certificate to be produced when he preaches to the people, so that he can be received by the common consent of the faithful. If he is found to be unsuitable and this is demonstrated by evidence, there must be a new selection to find another.

As to the manner of introducing him, because the ceremonies previously used led to a great deal of superstition, all that is needed is that a minister should explain the nature of the position to which he has been appointed and then prayers and pleas should be made that our Lord will give him grace to do what is needed.

After election he must take an oath of allegiance to the government following a written form as required of a minister.

Weekly Meetings to be Arranged

In the first place it is desirable that all ministers should meet together once a week. This is to maintain purity and agreement in their teaching and to hold Bible discussions. Attendance shall be compulsory unless there is good reason for absence. . . . As for the preachers in the villages under the control of the government, it is for the city ministers to urge them to attend whenever possible. . . .

What Should be Done in Cases of Difference About Doctrine

If any differences of opinion concerning doctrine should arise, the ministers should gather together and discuss the matter. If necessary, they should call in the elders and commissioners [*appointed by the government*] to assist in the settlement of any difficulties.

There must be some means available to discipline ministers . . . to prevent scandalous living. In this way, respect for the ministry can be maintained and the Word of God not debased by any minister bringing it into scorn and derision. Those who deserve it must be corrected, but at the same time care must be taken to deal with gossip and malicious rumours which can bring harm to innocent parties.

But it is of first importance to notice that certain crimes are quite incompatible with the ministry and cannot be dealt with by fraternal rebuke. Namely heresy, schism, rebellion against Church discipline, open blasphemy deserving civil punishment, simony and corrupt inducement, intriguing to take over one another's position, leaving the Church without special permission, forgery.

There Follows the Second Order Which We Have Called the Doctors

The special duty of the doctors is to instruct the faithful in sound doctrine so that the purity of the gospel is not corrupted by ignorance or wrong opinion.

As things stand at present, every agent assisting in the upholding of God's teaching is included so that the Church is not in difficulties from a lack of pastors and ministers. This is in common parlance the order of school teachers. The degree nearest the minister and closely joined to the government of the Church is the lecturer in theology.

Establishment of a College

Because it is only possible to profit from such teaching if one is first instructed in languages and humanities, and also because it is necessary to lay the foundations for the future . . . a college should be instituted for instructing children to prepare them for the ministry as well as for civil government.

In the first place suitable accommodation needs to be provided for the teaching of children and others who want to take advantage of it. We also need a literate, scholarly and trained teacher who can take care of the establishment and their education. He should be chosen and paid on the understanding that he should have under his charge teachers in languages and logic, if they can be found. He should also have some student teachers (*bacheliers*) to teach the little ones. . . .

All who are engaged must be subject to the same ecclesiastical ordinances as apply to the ministers.

There is to be no other school in the city for small children, although the girls are to have a separate school of their own as has been the case up to now.

No one is to be appointed without the approval of the ministers—essential to avoid trouble. [*The candidate must first have been notified to the government and then presented to the council. Two members of the 'council of 24' should be present at all interviews.*]

Here Follows the Third Order, or Elders

Their duty is to supervise every person's conduct. In friendly fashion they should warn backsliders and those of disorderly life. After that, where necessary, they should report to the Company [of pastors] who will arrange for fraternal correction. . . .

As our Church is now arranged, it would be most suitable to have two elected from the 'council of 24', four from the 'council of 60' and six from the 'council of 200'. They should be men of good repute and conduct. . . . They should be chosen from each quarter of the city so that they can keep an eye on the whole of it.

Method of Choosing the Elders

Further we have decided upon the machinery for choosing them. The 'council of 24' will be asked to nominate the most suitable and adequate men they can discover. In order to do this, they should discuss the matter with the ministers and then present their suggestions to the 'council of 200' for approval. If they are found worthy [and approved], they must take an oath in the same form as it is presented to the ministers. At the end of the year and after the elections to the council, they should present themselves to the government so that a decision can be made as to whether they shall be re-appointed or not, but they should not be changed frequently and without good cause provided that they are doing their work faithfully.

The Fourth Order of Ecclesiastical Government, Namely, the Deacons

There have always been two kinds of these in the early Church. One has to receive, distribute and care for the goods of the poor (i.e. daily alms as well as possessions, rents and pensions); the other has to tend and look after the sick and administer the allowances to the poor as is customary. [*In order to avoid confusion*], since we have officials and hospital staff, [*one of the four officials of the said hospital should be responsible for the whole of its property and revenues and he should have an adequate salary in order to do his work properly*].

Concerning the Hospital[1]

Care should be taken to see that the general hospital is properly maintained. This applies to the sick, to old people no longer able to work, to widows, orphans, children and other poor people. These are to be kept apart and separate from others and to form their own community.

Care for the poor who are scattered throughout the city shall be the responsibility of the officials. In addition to the hospital for those visiting the city, which is to be kept up, separate arrangements are to be made for those who need special treatment. To this end a room must be set apart to act as a reception room for those that are sent there by the officials. . . .

Further, both for the poor people in the hospital and for those in the city who have no means, there must be a good physician and surgeon provided at the city's expense. . . .

As for the plague hospital, it must be kept entirely separate.

Begging

In order to stop begging, which is contrary to good order, the government should use some of its officers to remove any beggars who are obstinately present when people come out of Church.

And this especially if it should happen that the city is visited by this sourge of God.

Of the Sacraments

Baptism is to take place only at sermon time and is to be administered only by ministers or their assistants. A register is to be kept of the names of the children and of their parents: the justice department is to be informed of any bastard.

Since the Supper was instituted by our Lord to be more often observed by us and also since this was the case in the early Church until such time as

---

[1] The Geneva general hospital had been established in 1535 in one of the series of measures by which the city had broken all connections with the Roman Catholic Church, and which consolidated the various confraternities and eight charitable foundations of the city.

the devil upset everything by setting up the mass in its place, the defect ought to be remedied by celebrating it a little more frequently. All the same, for the time being we have agreed and ordained that it should be administered four times a year, i.e. at Christmas, Easter, Pentecost and the first Sunday in September in the autumn.

The ministers shall distribute the bread in orderly and reverent fashion and no other person shall offer the chalice except those appointed (or the deacons) along with the ministers and for this reason there is no need for many plates and cups.

The tables should be set up close to the pulpit so that the mystery can be more suitably set forth near by.

Celebration should take place only in church and at the most suitable time.

Of the Order Which Must be Observed in Obedience to Those in Authority, for the Maintenance of Supervision in the Church

A day should be fixed for the consistory. The elders should meet once a week with the ministers, on a Thursday, to ensure that there is no disorder in the Church and to discuss together any necessary remedial action.

Since they have neither the power nor the authority to use force, we have agreed to assign one of our officials to them to summon those whom they wish to admonish.

If any one should deliberately refuse to appear, the council is to be informed so as to take action.

If any one teaches things contrary to the received doctrine he shall be summoned to a conference. If he listens to reason, let him be sent back without any scandal or disgrace. If he is obstinate, he should be admonished several times until it is apparent that greater severity is needed: then he shall be forbidden to attend the communion of the Supper and he shall be reported to the magistrates.

If any one fails to come to church to such a degree that there is real dislike for the community of believers manifested, or if any one shows that he cares nothing for ecclesiastical order, let him be admonished, and if he is tractable let him be amicably sent back. If however he goes from bad to worse, after having been warned three times, let him be cut off from the Church and be denounced to the magistrate. . . .

[*All this must be done in such a way that the ministers have no civil jurisdiction nor use anything but the spiritual sword of the word of God as St Paul commands them; nor is the authority of the consistory to diminish in any way that of the magistrate or ordinary justice. The civil power must remain unimpaired. In cases where, in future, there may be a need to impose punishments or constrain individuals, then the ministers and the consistory, having heard the case and used such admonitions and exhortations as are appropriate, should report the whole matter to the council which, in turn, will judge and sentence according to the needs of the case.*]

*   *   *

REVIEW QUESTIONS

1. What is the church according to Calvin?
2. What is its structure?
3. What do the four offices tell us about the function of the church?
4. What is the purpose of the church?
5. What are its goals?
6. What are the practices of the church and the relation of those practices to the process of becoming a Christian?
7. What is the relation between the church and salvation?

John Calvin

FROM Catechism of the Church of Geneva, Being a Form of Instruction for Children in the Doctrine of Christ, 1545

From *Tracts Relating to the Reformation*, vol. 2, by John Calvin, translated by Henry Beveridge (Edinburgh: The Calvin Translation Society, 1844–1851), pp. 34–37.

Dedication.

JOHN CALVIN TO THE FAITHFUL MINISTERS OF CHRIST THROUGHOUT EAST FRIESLAND, WHO PREACH THE PURE DOCTRINE OF THE GOSPEL.

Seeing it becomes us to endeavour by all means that unity of faith, which is so highly commended by Paul, shine forth among us, to this end chiefly ought the formal profession of faith which accompanies our common baptism to have reference. Hence it were to be wished, not only that a perpetual consent in the doctrine of piety should appear among all, but also that one Catechism were common to all the Churches. But as, from many causes, it will scarcely ever obtain otherwise than that each Church shall have its own Catechism, we should not strive too keenly to prevent this; provided, however, that the variety in the mode of teaching is such, that we are all directed to one Christ, in whose truth being united together, we may grow up into one body and one spirit, and with the same mouth also proclaim whatever belongs to the sum of faith. Catechists not intent on this end, besides fatally injuring the Church, by sowing the materials of dissension in religion, also introduce an impious profanation of baptism. For where can any longer be the utility of baptism unless this remain as its foundation—that we all agree in one faith?

Wherefore, those who publish Catechisms ought to be the more carefully on their guard, lest, by producing anything rashly, they may not for the present only, but in regard to posterity also, do grievous harm to piety, and inflict a deadly wound on the Church.

This much I wished to premise, as a declaration to my readers, that I myself too, as became me, have made it my anxious care not to deliver any thing in this Catechism of mine that is not agreeable to the doctrine received among all the pious. This declaration will not be found vain by those who will read with candour and sound judgment. I trust I have succeeded at least so far that my labour, though it should not satisfy, will be acceptable to all good men, as being in their opinion useful.

In writing it in Latin, though some perhaps will not approve of the design, I have been influenced by many reasons, all of which it is of no use to detail at present. I shall only select such as seem to me sufficient to obviate censure.

First, In this confused and divided state of Christendom, I judge it useful that there should be public testimonies, whereby churches which, though widely separated by space, agree in the doctrine of Christ, may mutually recognise each other. For besides that this tends not a little to mutual confirmation, what is more to be desired than that mutual congratulations should pass between them, and that they should devoutly commend each other to the Lord? With this view, bishops were wont in old time, when as yet consent in faith existed and flourished among all, to send Synodal Epistles beyond sea, by which, as a kind of badges, they might maintain sacred communion among the churches. How much more necessary is it now, in this fearful devastation of the Christian world, that the few churches which duly worship God, and they too scattered and hedged round on all sides by the profane synagogues of Antichrist, should mutually give and receive this token of holy union, that they may thereby be incited to that fraternal embrace of which I have spoken?

But if this is so necessary in the present day, what shall our feelings be concerning posterity, about which I am so anxious, that I scarcely dare to think? Unless God miraculously send help from heaven, I cannot avoid seeing that the world is threatened with the extremity of barbarism. I wish our children may not shortly feel, that this has been rather a true prophecy than a conjecture. The more, therefore, must we labour to gather together, by our writings, whatever remains of the Church shall continue, or even emerge, after our death. Writings of a different class will show what were our views on all subjects in religion, but the agreement which our churches had in doctrine cannot be seen with clearer evidence than from catechisms. For therein will appear, not only what one man or other once taught, but with what rudiments learned and unlearned alike amongst us, were constantly imbued from childhood, all the faithful holding them as their formal symbol of Christian communion. This was indeed my principal reason for publishing this Catechism.

A second reason, which had no little weight with me, was, because I heard that it was desired by very many who hoped it would not be unworthy of perusal. Whether they are right or wrong in so judging is not mine to decide, but it became me to yield to their wish. Nay, necessity was almost laid upon me, and I could not with impunity decline it. For having seven years before published a brief summary of religion, under the name of a Catechism, I feared that if I did not bring forward this one, I should cause (a thing I wished not) that the former should on the other hand be excluded. Therefore if I wished to consult the public good, it behoved me to take care that this one which I preferred should occupy the ground.

Besides, I deem it of good example to testify to the world, that we who aim at the restitution of the Church, are everywhere faithfully exerting ourselves, in order that, at least, the use of the Catechism which was abolished some centuries ago under the Papacy, may now resume its lost rights. For neither can this holy custom be sufficiently commended for its utility, nor can the Papists be sufficiently condemned for the flagrant corruption, by which they not only set it aside, by converting it into puerile trifles, but also basely abuse it to purposes of impure and impious superstition. That spurious Confirmation, which they have substituted in its stead, they deck out like a harlot, with great splendour of ceremonies, and gorgeous shows without number; nay, in their wish to adorn it, they speak of it in terms of execrable blasphemy, when they give out that it is a sacrament of greater dignity than baptism, and call those only half Christians who have not been besmeared with their oil. Meanwhile, the whole proceeding consists of nothing but theatrical gesticulations, or rather the wanton sporting of apes, without any skill in imitation.

To you, my very dear brethren in the Lord, I have chosen to inscribe this work, because some of your body, besides informing me that you love me, and that the most of you take delight in my writings, also expressly requested me by letter to undertake this labour for their sake. Independently of this, it would have been reason sufficient, that what I learned of you long ago, from the statement of grave and pious men, had bound me to you with my whole soul. I now ask what I am confident you will of your own accord do—have the goodness to consult for the utility of this token of my goodwill towards you! Farewell. May the Lord increase you more and more in the spirit of wisdom, prudence, zeal, and fortitude, to the edification of his Church.

GENEVA, *2d December*, 1545.

TO THE READER.

It has ever been the practice of the Church, and one carefully attended to, to see that children should be duly instructed in the Christian religion. That this might be done more conveniently, not only were schools opened in old time, and individuals enjoined properly to teach their families, but it was a received public custom and practice, to question children in the churches on each of the heads, which should be common and well known to all Christians. To secure this being done in order, there was written out a formula, which was called a Catechism or Institute. Thereafter the devil miserably rending the Church of God, and bringing upon it fearful ruin, (of which the marks are still too visible in the greater part of the world,) overthrew this sacred policy, and left nothing behind but certain trifles, which only beget superstition, without any fruit of edification. Of this description is that confirmation, as they call it, full of gesticulations which, worse than ridiculous, are fitted only for apes, and have no foundation to rest upon. What we now bring forward, therefore, is nothing else than the use of things which from ancient times were observed by Christians, and the true worshippers of God, and which never were laid aside until the Church was wholly corrupted.

REVIEW QUESTIONS

1. What is the purpose of catechism for John Calvin, and how does his purpose differ from that of Martin Luther?
2. Who, according to Calvin, should be taught catechism, and who should do the teaching?
3. How did Calvin reconcile the unity of faith, which he hoped his catechism would serve, and the diversity of local circumstances and observances, which he expected would be the case?
4. What do this hope for unity and this admission of diversity tell us about the Reformation as Calvin understood it?
5. Use the catechism as a measure of the reformers' concerns and goals to explain how had these changed between 1530, when Luther published his *Large Catechism*, and 1545, when Calvin dedicated the *Catechism of the Church of Geneva*. Do the titles reveal anything?
6. Why did Calvin compose his catechism in Latin rather than a vernacular language, as did Martin Luther?

SAINT IGNATIUS OF LOYOLA

FROM *The Spiritual Exercises*

Saint Ignatius of Loyola (1491–1556), the great mystic and founder of the Society of Jesus, was born into a hidalgo family and spent his early manhood in military service to the king of Spain. Wounded in battle, he spent his convalescence reading the lives of saints, which awoke in him a sense of spiritual inadequacy not unlike those which fired the religious engagements of Martin Luther and John Calvin. His early attempts at reconciliation, in the form of physical austerities practiced on pilgrimage to Montserrat and in the hermitage at Manresa, failed to reassure him of his soul's salvation, just as they failed to ease the spiritual torments of the young Luther. The scholastically trained Luther sought solace in the systematic study of the Bible; the uneducated Loyola found it in visions of God. Loyola spent the next decade educating himself and seeking his mission. After a pilgrimage to the Holy Land in 1523, Loyola began his formal education by studying elementary Latin with schoolboys in Barcelona. He attended the universities in Alcalá and Salamanca, preached in the streets, and was arrested by the Inquisition on suspicion of heresy. He attended the University of Paris from 1528 to 1535 and began to gather around him the companions who would form the initial core of the Society of Jesus. In 1534, he and nine companions swore an oath of poverty and chastity and promised either to undertake a crusade to the Holy Land or, failing that, to offer absolute obedience to the pope. At the center of this group was not only the man Loyola but his series of devotions and meditations that would later be published as The Spiritual Exercises *(1548). These exercises offered a practical and ascetic meditation on the life and death of Christ that drew much from the systematic meditations of the* devotio moderna *("modern devotions"). This system instructed those who made or directed a religious retreat in order to stimulate an imitation of Christ that would be expressed in apostolic action as well as religious devotion. In 1535, Loyola and his company left for Italy. He was ordained in Venice in 1537. Finding no passage to the Holy Land, they continued to Rome, where they preached in the streets and ministered to the poor. Introduced to Pope Paul III by Gasparo Contarini, a great advocate of monastic reform, the company received a charter of foundation as the Society of Jesus in 1540. Constituted an order of clerks regular, devoted to educating the young and propagating the faith, sworn to poverty and obedience, the Jesuits grew quickly to become one of the most influential Catholic orders of the early modern period, a model of piety, discipline, education, and service.*

From *The Spiritual Exercises of St. Ignatius of Loyola,* translated from the *Autograph* by Father Elder Mullen, S. J. (New York: P. J. Kennedy and Sons, 1914).

To Have the True Sentiment Which We Ought to Have in the Church Militant

Let the following Rules be observed.

First Rule. All judgment laid aside, we ought to have our mind ready and prompt to obey, in all, the true Spouse of Christ our Lord, which is our holy Mother the Church Hierarchical.

Second Rule. To praise confession to a Priest, and the reception of the most Holy Sacrament of the Altar once in the year, and much more each month, and much better from week to week, with the conditions required and due.

Third Rule. To praise the hearing of Mass often, likewise hymns, psalms, and long prayers, in the church and out of it; likewise the hours set at the time fixed for each Divine Office and for all prayer and all Canonical Hours.

Fourth Rule. To praise much Religious Orders, virginity and continence, and not so much marriage as any of these.

Fifth Rule. To praise vows of Religion, of obedience, of poverty, of chastity and of other perfections of supererogation. And it is to be noted that as the vow is about the things which approach to Evangelical perfection, a vow ought not to be made in the things which withdraw from it, such as to be a merchant, or to be married, etc.

Sixth Rule. To praise relics of the Saints, giving veneration to them and praying to the Saints; and to praise Stations, pilgrimages, Indulgences, pardons, Cruzadas, and candles lighted in the churches.

Seventh Rule. To praise Constitutions about fasts and abstinence, as of Lent, Ember Days, Vigils, Friday and Saturday; likewise penances, not only interior, but also exterior.

Eighth Rule. To praise the ornaments and the buildings of churches; likewise images, and to venerate them according to what they represent.

Ninth Rule. Finally, to praise all precepts of the Church, keeping the mind prompt to find reasons in their defence and in no manner against them.

Tenth Rule. We ought to be more prompt to find good and praise as well the Constitutions and recommendations as the ways of our Superiors. Because, although some are not or have not been such, to speak against them, whether preaching in public or discoursing before the common people, would rather give rise to fault-finding and scandal than profit; and so the people would be incensed against their Superiors, whether temporal or spiritual. So that, as it does harm to speak evil to the common people of Superiors in their absence, so it can make profit to speak of the evil ways to the persons themselves who can remedy them.

Eleventh Rule. To praise positive and scholastic learning. Because, as it is more proper to the Positive Doctors, as St. Jerome, St. Augustine and St. Gregory, etc., to move the heart to love and serve God our Lord in everything; so it is more proper to the Scholastics, as St. Thomas, St. Bonaventure, and to the Master of the Sentences, etc., to define or explain for our times the things necessary for eternal salvation; and to combat and explain better all errors and all fallacies. For the Scholastic Doctors, as they are more modern, not only help themselves with the true understanding of the Sacred Scripture and of the Positive and holy Doctors, but also, they being enlightened and clarified by the Divine virtue, help themselves by the Councils, Canons and Constitutions of our holy Mother the Church.

Twelfth Rule. We ought to be on our guard in making comparison of those of us who are alive to the blessed passed away, because error is committed not a little in this; that is to say, in saying, this one knows more than St. Augustine; he is another, or greater than, St. Francis; he is another St. Paul in goodness, holiness, etc.

Thirteenth Rule. To be right in everything, we ought always to hold that the white which I see, is black, if the Hierarchical Church so decides it, believing that between Christ our Lord, the Bridegroom, and the Church, His Bride, there is the same Spirit which governs and directs us for the salvation of our souls. Because by the same Spirit and our Lord Who gave the ten Command-ments, our holy Mother the Church is directed and governed.

Fourteenth Rule. Although there is much truth in the assertion that no one can save himself without being predestined and without having faith and grace; we must be very cautious in the manner of speaking and communicating with others about all these things.

Fifteenth Rule. We ought not, by way of custom, to speak much of predestination; but if in some way and at some times one speaks, let him so speak that the common people may not come into any error, as sometimes happens, saying: Whether I have to be saved or condemned is already determined, and no other thing can now be, through my doing well or ill; and with this, growing lazy, they become negligent in the works which lead to the salvation and the spiritual profit of their souls.

Sixteenth Rule. In the same way, we must be on our guard that by talking much and with much insistence of faith, without any distinction and explanation, occasion be not given to the people to be lazy and slothful in works, whether before faith is formed in charity or after.

Seventeenth Rule. Likewise, we ought not to speak so much with insistence on grace that the poison of discarding liberty be engendered. So that of faith and grace one can speak as much as is possible with the Divine help for the greater praise of His Divine Majesty, but not in such way, nor in such manners, especially in our so dangerous times, that works and free will receive any harm, or be held for nothing.

Eighteenth Rule. Although serving God our Lord much out of pure love is to be esteemed above all; we ought to praise much the fear of His Divine Majesty, because not only filial fear is a thing pious and most holy, but even servile fear—when the man reaches nothing else better or more useful—helps much to get out of mortal sin. And when he is out, he easily comes to filial fear, which is all acceptable and grateful to God our Lord: as being at one with the Divine Love.

*   *   *

THE MIRACLE OF ST. IGNATIUS OF LOYOLA (C. 1620)   PETER PAUL RUBENS

The Miracle of St. Ignatius of Loyola *was painted by Peter Paul Rubens (1577–1640) a pro-lific seventeenth-century Flemish Baroque painter, whose works exemplify an exuberant Baroque style, full of movement, color, and sensuality. He is well-known for his Catholic altarpieces, portraits, landscapes, and history paintings on mythological and allegorical themes. In addition to running a large studio in Antwerp, which produced paintings popular with nobility and art collectors throughout Europe, Rubens was a classically-educated humanist scholar, art collector, Catholic diplomat and, it has been speculated, a Protestant spy. This particular painting, commissioned for the Jesuit church in Antwerp, is one of two treatments of the miracle of Saint Ignatius that were completed sometime around 1620. They show the saint, Ignatius of Loyola, founder of the Society of Jesus, standing before the altar and performing miracles, including the casting out of demons to the amazement of his congregation below. How does Rubens capture the spirit of Catholic reform and its response to Protestant criticism in his painting? Given that the Council of Trent authorized the use of images for teaching doctrine, what lessons about doctrine and about the function of saints in religious life might you take away from this image? What do the positions of the various bodies, especially the gesturing of the hands, tell us about the relationship of the human figures to one another? In particular, why did Rubens elevate Loyola above some men and women, but place a row of figures, all in Jesuit habit alongside him? Given that both the Cranach and the Rubens are altarpieces, that is, paintings intended to be place over an altar, what does each tell you about worship in its respective Church? What makes this painting "baroque"? Contrasting Rubens's religious masterpiece with an early masterpiece, for example, Raphael's* The School of Athens *(p. 403), what sets them apart?*

REVIEW QUESTIONS

1. What do you suppose Loyola means by the *Church Militant*?
2. How might the Jesuits have been soldiers of Christ?
3. Loyola asks the members of his order to "praise" in order to be "thinking with the Church." How does this serve the Church?
4. What specifically does Loyola ask the Jesuits to praise?
5. What do the "Rules for Thinking with the Church" tell us about the Church?

SAINT FRANCIS XAVIER

FROM "Letter from India"

Saint Francis Xavier (1506–1552) was one of the original companions of Saint Ignatius of Loyola and one of the original members of the Society of Jesus. The two became friends during their student years at the University of Paris. Shortly after the founding of the Society, Loyola sent Xavier on a mission to Portugal's mercantile empire in South Asia. After a voyage that lasted more than a year, he arrived in Goa on the Coromandel coast of India, accompanied by the Portuguese governor, Don Martin Alfonso de Sousa, and two fellow missionaries, Father Paul and Francis Mancias, not yet in holy orders. It was at Sousa's behest that Xavier turn his attention to the pearl-fishing villages of Cape Comorin, in an effort to spread Christianity among those peoples and, so, bring them more fully into the Portuguese sphere of influence. It was from Comorin that Xavier wrote the following letter. He would remain there two years before spreading his mission to the East Indies and Japan. He died in 1552, waiting to extend his work to China. His was a life of extraordinary hardship and danger as well as extraordinary activity and achievement. To him belongs credit for extending Roman Christianity and Western ideas to Asian peoples.

From *The Life and Letters of St Francis Xavier*, vol. 1, edited by Henry James Coleridge, 2d ed. (London: Burns and Oates, 1890), pp. 151–63.

To the Society at Rome

May the grace and charity of Christ our Lord always help and favour us! Amen.

It is now the third year since I left Portugal. I am writing to you for the third time, having as yet received only one letter from you, dated February 1542. God is my witness what joy it caused me. I only received it two months ago—later than is usual for letters to reach India, because the vessel which brought it had passed the winter at Mozambique.

I and Francis Mancias are now living amongst the Christians of Comorin. They are very numerous, and increase largely every day. When I first came I asked them, if they knew anything about our Lord Jesus Christ? but when I came to the points of faith in detail and asked them what they thought of them, and what more they believed now than when they were Infidels, they only replied that they were Christians, but that as they are ignorant of Portuguese, they know nothing of the precepts and mysteries of our holy religion. We could not understand one another, as I spoke Castilian and they Malabar; so I picked out the most intelligent and well read of them, and then sought out with the greatest diligence men who knew both languages. We held meetings for several days, and by our joint efforts and with infinite difficulty we translated the Catechism into the Malabar tongue. This I learnt by heart, and then I began to go through all the villages of the coast, calling around me by the sound of a bell as many as I could, children and men. I asembled them twice a day and taught them the Christian doctrine: and thus, in the space of a month, the children had it well by heart. And all the time I kept telling them to go on teaching in their turn whatever they had learnt to their parents, family, and neighbours.

Every Sunday I collected them all, men and women, boys and girls, in the church. They came with great readiness and with a great desire for instruction. Then, in the hearing of all, I began by calling on the name of the most holy Trinity, Father, Son, and Holy Ghost, and I recited aloud the Lord's Prayer, the *Hail Mary*, and the Creed in the language of the country: they all followed me in the same words, and delighted in it wonderfully. Then I repeated the Creed by myself, dwelling upon each article singly. Then I asked them as to each article, whether they believed it unhesitatingly; and all, with a loud voice and their hands crossed over their breasts, professed aloud that they truly believed it. I take care to make them repeat the Creed oftener than the other prayers; and I tell them that those who believe all that is contained therein are called Christians. After explaining the Creed I go on to the Commandments, teaching them that the Christian law is contained in those ten precepts, and that every one who observes them all faithfully is a good and true Christian and is certain of eternal salvation, and that, on the other hand, whoever neglects a single one of them is a bad Christian, and will be cast into hell unless he is

truly penitent for his sin. Converts and heathen alike are astonished at all this, which shows them the holiness of the Christian law, its perfect consistency with itself, and its agreement with reason. . . .

*   *   *

The fruit that is reaped by the baptism of infants, as well as by the instruction of children and others, is quite incredible. These children, I trust heartily, by the grace of God, will be much better than their fathers. They show an ardent love for the Divine law, and an extraordinary zeal for learning our holy religion and imparting it to others. Their hatred for idolatry is marvellous. They get into feuds with the heathen about it, and whenever their own parents practise it, they reproach them and come off to tell me at once. Whenever I hear of any act of idolatrous worship, I go to the place with a large band of these children, who very soon load the devil with a greater amount of insult and abuse than he has lately received of honour and worship from their parents, relations, and acquaintances. The children run at the idols, upset them, dash them down, break them to pieces, spit on them, trample on them, kick them about, and in short heap on them every possible outrage.

I had been living for nearly four months in a Christian village, occupied in translating the Catechism. A great number of natives came from all parts to entreat me to take the trouble to go to their houses and call on God by the bedsides of their sick relatives. Such numbers also of sick made their own way to us, that I had enough to do to read a Gospel over each of them. At the same time we kept on with our daily work, instructing the children, baptizing converts, translating the Catechism, answering difficulties, and burying the dead. For my part I desired to satisfy all, both the sick who came to me themselves, and those who came to beg on the part of others, lest if I did not, their confidence in, and zeal for, our holy religion should relax, and I thought it wrong not to do what I could in answer to their prayers. But the thing grew to such a pitch that it was impossible for me myself to satisfy all, and at the same time to avoid their quarrelling among themselves, every one striving to be the first to get me to his own house; so I hit on a way of serving all at once. As I could not go myself, I sent round children whom I could trust in my place. They went to the sick persons, assembled their families and neighbours, recited the Creed with them, and encouraged the sufferers to conceive a certain and wellfounded confidence of their restoration. Then after all this, they recited the prayers of the Church. To make my tale short, God was moved by the faith and piety of these children and of the others, and restored to a great number of sick persons health both of body and soul. How good He was to them! He made the very disease of their bodies the occasion of calling them to salvation, and drew them to the Christian faith almost by force!

I have also charged these children to teach the rudiments of Christian doctrine to the ignorant in private houses, in the streets, and the crossways. As soon as I see that this has been well started in one village, I go on to another and give the same instructions and the same commission to the children, and so I go through in order the whole number of their villages. When I have done this and am going away, I leave in each place a copy of the Christian doctrine, and tell all those who know how to write to copy it out, and all the others are to learn it by heart and to recite it from memory every day. Every feast day I bid them meet in one place and sing all together the elements of the faith. For this purpose I have appointed in each of the thirty Christian villages men of intelligence and character who are to preside over these meetings, and the Governor, Don Martin Alfonso, who is so full of love for our Society and of zeal for religion, has been good enough at our request to allot a yearly revenue of 4000 gold *fanams* for the salary of these catechists. He has an immense friendship for ours, and desires with all his heart that some of them should be sent hither, for which he is always asking in his letters to the King.

*   *   *

We have in these parts a class of men among the pagans who are called Brahmins. They keep up the worship of the gods, the superstitious rites of religion, frequenting the temples and taking care of the idols. They are as perverse and wicked a set as can anywhere be found, and I always apply to them the words of holy David, "from an unholy race and a wicked and crafty man deliver me, O Lord." They are liars and cheats to the very backbone. Their whole study is, how to deceive most cunningly the simplicity and ignorance of the people. They give out publicly that the gods command certain offerings to be made to their temples, which offerings are simply the things that the Brahmins themselves wish for, for their own maintenance and that of their wives, children, and servants. Thus they make the poor folk believe that the images of their gods eat and drink, dine and sup like men, and some devout persons are found who really offer to the idol twice a day, before dinner and supper, a certain sum of money. The Brahmins eat sumptuous meals to the sound of drums, and make the ignorant believe that the gods are banqueting. When they are in need of any supplies, and even before, they give out to the people that the gods are angry because the things they have asked for have not been sent, and that if the people do not take care, the gods will punish them by slaughter, disease, and the assaults of the devils. And the poor ignorant creatures, with the fear of the gods before them, obey them implicitly. . . .

The heathen inhabitants of the country are commonly ignorant of letters, but by no means ignorant of wickedness. All the time I have been here in this country I have only converted one Brahmin, a virtuous young man, who has now undertaken to teach the Catechism to children. As I go through the Christian villages, I often pass by the temples of the Brahmins, which they call pagodas. One day lately, I happened to enter a pagoda where there were about two hundred of them, and most of them came to meet me. We had a long conversation, after which I asked them what their gods enjoined them in order to obtain the life of the blessed. There was a long discussion amongst them as to who should answer me. At last, by common consent, the commission was given to one of them, of greater age and experience than the rest, an old man, of more than eighty years. He asked me in return, what commands the God of the Christians laid on them. I saw the old man's perversity, and I refused to speak a word till he had first answered my question. So he was obliged to expose his ignorance, and replied that their gods required two duties of those who desired to go to them hereafter, one of which was to abstain from killing cows, because under that form the gods were adored; the other was to show kindness to the Brahmins, who were the worshippers of the gods. This answer moved my indignation, for I could not but grieve intensely at the thought of the devils being worshipped instead of God by these blind heathen, and I asked them to listen to me in turn. Then I, in a loud voice, repeated the Apostles' Creed and the Ten Commandments. After this I gave in their own language a short explanation, and told them what Paradise is, and what Hell is, and also who they are who go to Heaven to join the company of the blessed, and who are to be sent to the eternal punishments of hell. Upon hearing these things they all rose up and vied with one another in embracing me, and in confessing that the God of the Christians is the true God, as His laws are so agreeable to reason. Then they asked me if the souls of men like those of other animals perished together with the body. God put into my mouth arguments of such a sort, and so suited to their ways of thinking, that to their great joy I was able to prove to them the immortality of the soul. I find, by the way, that the arguments which are to convince these ignorant people must by no means be subtle, such as those which are found in the books of learned schoolmen, but must be such as their minds can understand. They asked me again how the soul of a dying person goes out of the body, how it was, whether it was as happens to us in dreams, when we seem to be conversing with our friends and acquaintance? (Ah, how often this happens to me, dearest brothers, when I am dreaming of you!) Was this because the soul then leaves the body? And again, whether God was black or white? For as there is so great a variety of colour among men, and the Indians being black themselves, consider their own colour the best, they believe that their gods are

black. On this account the great majority of their idols are as black as black can be, and moreover are generally so rubbed over with oil as to smell detestably, and seem to be as dirty as they are ugly and horrible to look at. To all these questions I was able to reply so as to satisfy them entirely. But when I came to the point at last, and urged them to embrace the religion which they felt to be true, they made that same objection which we hear from many Christians when urged to change their life,— that they would set men talking about them if they altered their ways and their religion, and besides, they said that they should be afraid that, if they did so, they would have nothing to live on and support themselves by.

I have found just one Brahmin and no more in all this coast who is a man of learning: he is said to have studied in a very famous Academy. Knowing this, I took measures to converse with him alone. He then told me at last, as a great secret, that the students of this Academy are at the outset made by their masters to take an oath not to reveal their mysteries, but that, out of friendship for me, he would disclose them to me. One of these mysteries was that there only exists one God, the Creator and Lord of heaven and earth, whom men are bound to worship, for the idols are simply images of devils, The Brahmins have certain books of sacred literature which contain, as they say, the laws of God. The masters teach in a learned tongue, as we do in Latin. He also explained to me these divine precepts one by one; but it would be a long business to write out his commentary, and indeed not worth the trouble. Their sages keep as a feast our Sunday. On this day they repeat at different hours this one prayer: "I adore Thee, O God; and I implore Thy help for ever." They are bound by oath to repeat this prayer frequently, and in a low voice. My friend added, that the law of nature permitted them to have more wives than one, and their sacred books predicted that the time would come when all men should embrace the same religion. After all this he asked me in my turn to explain the principal mysteries of the Christian religion, promising to keep them secret. I replied, that I would not tell him a word about them unless he promised beforehand to publish abroad what I should tell him of the religion of Jesus Christ. He made the promise, and then I carefully explained to him those words of Jesus Christ in which our religion is summed up: "He who believes and is baptized shall be saved." This text, with my commentary on it, which embraced the whole of the Apostles' Creed, he wrote down carefully, as well as the Commandments, on account of their close connection with the Creed. He told me also that one night he had dreamt that he had been made a Christian to his immense delight, and that he had become my brother and companion. He ended by begging me to make him a Christian secretly. But as he made certain conditions opposed to right and justice, I put off his baptism. I don't doubt but that by God's mercy he will one day be a Christian. I charged him to teach the ignorant and unlearned that there is only one God, Creator of heaven and earth; but he pleaded the

obligation of his oath, and said he could not do so, especially as he was much afraid that if he did it he should become possessed by an evil spirit. . . .

REVIEW QUESTIONS

1. What was involved in the conversion of Asian peoples to Christianity?
2. What were the greatest challenges that Xavier and his fellows confronted?
3. How did Xavier's values shape his perception of Asian peoples?
4. How would you describe the reception of Christian missionaries and Christianity among the people of Cape Comorin?
5. How might Xavier and his mission have shaped the interaction and understanding of East and West?

SAINT TERESA OF ÁVILA

FROM *The Life of Teresa of Jesus*

Saint Teresa of Ávila (1515–1582) was a Spanish mystic, spiritual author, and monastic reformer. Her worldly achievements were great, to which the Discalced Carmelites still bear witness; in addition, the beauty of her inner life, as revealed in her writings, earned her recognition as one of the world's great female religious authors. Teresa was born in central Spain, the daughter of a wealthy hidalgo. At age fourteen, she was sent to a boarding school, where she became ill and began to consider her life's vocation. Despite paternal opposition, Teresa became a novice in a Carmelite convent around 1535. Her health collapsed again, leaving her an invalid for three years. During her convalescence, she began the series of meditations that would establish her reputation as a mystic. It took her fifteen years to perfect the prayers and meditations that would lead to her ecstatic visions and conversations with God. Her most celebrated work, The Life, *written in obedience to her confessors and directors, captured this process as the history of a soul, much like Augustine's* Confessions. *They combine religious ardor with human candor, an insistence that her experiences were a gift of God with an unwillingness to claim any spiritual distinction.*

In 1558, Teresa began to consider the restoration of Carmelite life to its original observance of austerity. It required complete separation from the world to promote prayerful meditation, such as was enjoined in the Primitive Carmelite Rule of 1247. In 1562, with the authorization of Pope Pius IV, Teresa and four companions opened the first convent of the Carmelite reform. Despite intense opposition from secular and ecclesiastical officials, her efforts eventually won the approval of the Carmelite general as well as his mandate to extend her reform to men. In 1567, she met a young Carmelite priest, Juan de Yepes, later canonized as Saint John of the Cross, a brilliant friar who helped her initiate the Carmelite reform for men. In her lifetime, she saw sixteen convents and twelve monasteries established. The last decades of her life were given to this work. Forty years after her death, she was canonized; in 1970, she was made a doctor of the Church.

From *The Life of Theresa of Jesus: The Autobiography of Teresa of Avila*, translated by E. Allison Peters (New York: Bantam Doubleday Dell, 1991), pp. 68–71.

*   *   *

I have strayed far from any intention, for I was trying to give the reasons why this kind of vision cannot be the work of the imagination. How could we picture Christ's Humanity by merely studying the subject or form any impression of His great beauty by means of the imagination? No little time would be necessary if such a reproduction was to be in the least like the original. One can indeed make such a picture with one's imagination, and spend time in regarding it, and considering the form and the brilliance of it; little by little one may even learn to perfect such an image and store it up in the memory. Who can prevent this? Such a picture can undoubtedly be fashioned with the understanding. But with regard to the vision which we are discussing there is no way of doing this: we have to look at it when the Lord is pleased to reveal it to us— to look as He wills and at whatever He wills. And there is no possibility of our subtracting from it or adding to it, or any way in which we can obtain it, whatever we may do, or look at it when we like or refrain from looking at it. If we try to look at any particular part of it, we at once lose Christ.

For two years and a half things went on like this and it was quite usual for God to grant me this favour. It must now be more than three years since He took it from me as a continually recurring favour, by giving me something else of a higher kind, which I shall describe later. Though I saw that He was speaking to me, and though I was looking upon that great beauty of His, and experiencing the sweetness with which He uttered those words— sometimes stern words—with that most lovely and Divine mouth, and though, too, I was extremely desirous of observing the colour of His eyes, or His height, so that I should be able to describe it, I have never been sufficiently worthy to see this, nor has it been of any use for me to attempt to do so; if I tried, I lost the vision altogether. Though I sometimes see Him looking at me compassionately, His gaze has such power that my soul cannot endure it and remains in so sublime a rapture that it loses this beauteous vision in order to have the greater fruition of it all. So there is no question here of our wanting or not wanting to see the vision. It is clear that the Lord wants of us only humility and shame, our acceptance of what is given us and our praise of its Giver.

This refers to all visions, none excepted. There is nothing that we can do about them; we cannot see more or less of them at will; and we can neither call them up nor banish them by our own efforts. The Lord's will is that we shall see quite clearly that they are produced, not by us but by His Majesty. Still less can we be proud of them: on the contrary, they make us humble and fearful, when we find that, just as the Lord takes from us the power of seeing what we desire, so He can also take from us these favours and His grace, with the result that we are completely lost. So while we live in this exile let us always walk with fear.

Almost invariably the Lord showed Himself to me in His resurrection body, and it was thus, too, that I saw Him in the Host. Only occasionally, to strengthen me when I was in tribulation, did He show me His wounds, and then He would appear sometimes as He was on the Cross and sometimes as in the Garden. On a few occasions I saw Him wearing the crown of thorns and sometimes He would also be carrying the Cross—because of my necessities, as I say, and those of others—but always in His glorified flesh. Many are the affronts and trials that I have suffered through telling this and many are the fears and persecutions that it has brought me. So sure were those whom I told of it that I had a devil that some of them wanted to exorcize me. This troubled me very little, but I was sorry when I found that my confessors were afraid to hear my confessions or when I heard that people were saying things to them against me. None the less, I could never regret having seen these heavenly visions and I would not exchange them for all the good things and delights of this world. I always considered them a great favour from the Lord, and I think they were the greatest of treasures; often the Lord Himself would reassure me about them. I found my love for Him growing exceedingly: I used to go to Him and tell Him about all these trials and I always came away from prayer comforted and with new strength. I did not dare to argue with my critics, because I saw that that made things worse, as they thought me lacking in humility. With my confessor, however, I did discuss these matters; and whenever he saw that I was troubled he would comfort me greatly.

As the visions became more numerous, one of those who had previously been in the habit of helping me and who used sometimes to hear my confessions when the minister was unable to do so, began to say that it was clear I was being deceived by the devil. So, as I was quite unable to resist it, they commanded me to make the sign of the Cross whenever I had a vision, and to snap my fingers at it so as to convince myself that it came from the devil, whereupon it would not come again: I was not to be afraid, they said, and God would protect me and take the vision away. This caused me great distress: as I could not help believing that my visions came from God, it was a terrible thing to have to do; and, as I have said, I could not possibly wish them to be taken from me. However, I did as they commanded me. I besought God often to set me free from deception; indeed, I was continually doing so and with many tears. I would also invoke Saint Peter and Saint Paul, for the Lord had told me (it was on their festival that He had first appeared to me) that they would prevent me from being deluded; and I used often to see them very clearly on my left hand, though not in an imaginary vision. These glorious Saints were in a very real sense my lords.

To be obliged to snap my fingers at a vision in which I saw the Lord caused me the sorest distress. For, when I saw Him before me, I could not have believed that the vision had come from the devil even if the alternative were my being cut to pieces. So this was a kind of penance to me, and a heavy one. In order not to have to be so continually crossing myself, I would carry a cross in my hand. This I did almost invariably; but I was not so particular about snapping my fingers at the vision, for it hurt me too much to do that. It reminded me of the way the Jews had insulted Him, and I would beseech Him to forgive me, since I did it out of obedience to him who was in His own place, and not to blame me, since he was one of the ministers whom He had placed in His Church. He told me not to worry about it and said I was quite right to obey, but He would see that my confessor learned the truth. When they made me stop my prayer He seemed to me to have become angry, and He told me to tell them that this was tyranny. He used to show me ways of knowing that the visions were not of the devil; some of these I shall describe later.

*   *   *

REVIEW QUESTIONS

1. What distinguishes Teresa's spirituality from that of Ignatius of Loyola?
2. Might we call her spirituality feminine?
3. Is Teresa's piety private or public? In what ways?
4. Are visions portable?
5. Are they entirely private?
6. How does language fail Teresa?

The Council of Trent

The Council of Trent (Latin: Concilium Tridentinum), held between 1545 and 1563 in the cities of Trent and Bologna in northern Italy, was one of the most important ecumenical councils of the Roman Catholic Church. Prompted by the Protestant Reformation, it has been described as the embodiment of the Counter-Reformation. Yet, its actions were as creative as they were reactive. In a series of 25 sessions that extended from 13 December 1545 until 4 December 1563, it declared anathema a wide range of theological, liturgical, and ecclesiological positions adopted by religious reform movements commonly referred to as Protestant. It also defined standard Catholic doctrine on a wide range of subjects including scripture, the biblical canon, sacred tradition, original sin, justification, salvation, the sacraments, the Mass, and the veneration of saints. In the course of its deliberations, the members of the council declared the Vulgate the official, canonical version of the Bible. A year after the council concluded its deliberations, Pope Pius IV issued the Tridentine Creed, and his successor Pius V issued the Roman catechism, both standard works of the Roman Catholic confession. Along with revisions of the Missal and Breviary, issued in the following years, these codified the Tridentine mass, which remained for the next 400 years the principal form of the mass for the Catholic Church. It would be more than three centuries before the next ecumenical council convened, the First Vatican Council. When Pope John XXIII initiated preparations for the Second Vatican Council, he affirmed the decrees issued at Trent, declaring "What was, still is."

From *The Canons and Decrees of the Sacred and Ecumenical Council of Trent, Celebrated under the Sovereign Pontiffs Paul III, Julius III, and Pius IV,* translated by Rev. J. Waterworth (London: C. Dolman, 1848), pp. 152–59.

Session the Twenty-Second,

Being the sixth under the Sovereign Pontiff, Pius IV., celebrated on the seventeenth day of September, MDLXII.

DOCTRINE ON THE SACRIFICE OF THE MASS.

The sacred and holy, ecumenical and general Synod of Trent—lawfully assembled in the Holy Ghost, the same Legates of the Apostolic See presiding therein—to the end that the ancient, complete, and in every part perfect faith and doctrine touching the great mystery of the Eucharist may be retained in the holy Catholic Church; and may, all errors and heresies being repelled, be preserved in its own purity; (the Synod) instructed by the illumination of the Holy Ghost, teaches, declares, and decrees what follows, to be preached to the faithful, on the subject of the Eucharist, considered as being a true and singular sacrifice.

CHAPTER I.

ON THE INSTITUTION OF THE MOST HOLY SACRIFICE OF THE MASS.

Forasmuch as, under the former Testament, according to the testimony of the Apostle Paul, there was no perfection, because of the weakness of the Levitical priesthood; there was need, God, the Father of mercies, so ordaining, that another priest should rise, according to the order of Melchisedech, our Lord Jesus Christ, who might consummate, and lead to what is perfect, as many as were to be sanctified. He, therefore, our God and Lord, though He was about to offer Himself once on the altar of the cross unto God the Father, by means of his death, there to operate an eternal redemption; nevertheless, because that His priesthood was not to be extinguished by His death, in the last supper, on the night in which He was betrayed,—that He might leave, to His own beloved Spouse the Church, a visible sacrifice, such as the nature of man requires, whereby that bloody sacrifice, once to be accomplished on the cross, might be represented, and the memory thereof remain even unto the end of the world, and its salutary virtue be applied to the remission of those sins which we daily commit,—declaring Himself constituted a priest forever, according to the order of Melchisedech, He offered up to God the Father His own body and blood under the species of bread and wine; and, under the symbols of those same things, He delivered (His own body and blood) to be received by His apostles, whom He then constituted priests of the New Testament; and by those words, Do this in

commemoration of me, He commanded them and their successors in the priesthood, to offer (them); even as the Catholic Church has always understood and taught. For, having celebrated the ancient Passover, which the multitude of the children of Israel immolated in memory of their going out of Egypt, He instituted the new Passover, (to wit) Himself to be immolated, under visible signs, by the Church through (the ministry of) priests, in memory of His own passage from this world unto the Father, when by the effusion of His own blood He redeemed us, and delivered us from the power of darkness, and translated us into his kingdom. And this is indeed that clean oblation, which cannot be defiled by any unworthiness, or malice of those that offer (it); which the Lord foretold by Malachias was to be offered in every place, clean to his name, which was to be great amongst the Gentiles; and which the apostle Paul, writing to the Corinthians, has not obscurely indicated, when he says, that they who are defiled by the participation of the table of devils, cannot be partakers of the table of the Lord; by the table, meaning in both places the altar. This, in fine, is that oblation which was prefigured by various types of sacrifices, during the period of nature, and of the law; in as much as it comprises all the good things signified by those sacrifices, as being the consummation and perfection of them all.

CHAPTER II.

THAT THE SACRIFICE OF THE MASS IS PROPITIATORY BOTH FOR THE LIVING AND THE DEAD.

And forasmuch as, in this divine sacrifice which is celebrated in the mass, that same Christ is contained and immolated in an unbloody manner, who once offered Himself in a bloody manner on the altar of the cross; the holy Synod teaches, that this sacrifice is truly propitiatory and that by means thereof this is effected, that we obtain mercy, and find grace in seasonable aid, if we draw nigh unto God, contrite and penitent, with a sincere heart and upright faith, with fear and reverence.

For the Lord, appeased by the oblation thereof, and granting the grace and gift of penitence, forgives even heinous crimes and sins. For the victim is one and the same, the same now offering by the ministry of priests, who then offered Himself on the cross, the manner alone of offering being different. The fruits indeed of which oblation, of that bloody one to wit, are received most plentifully through this unbloody one; so far is this (latter) from derogating in any way from that (former oblation). Wherefore, not only for the sins, punishments, satisfactions, and other necessities of the faithful who are living, but also for those who are departed in Christ, and who are not as yet fully purified, is it rightly offered, agreebly to a tradition of the apostles.

CHAPTER III.

ON MASSES IN HONOUR OF THE SAINTS.

And although the Church has been accustomed at times to celebrate, certain masses in honour and memory of the saints; not therefore, however, doth she teach that sacrifice is offered unto them, but unto God alone, who crowned them; whence neither is the priest wont to say, "I offer sacrifice to thee, Peter, or Paul;" but, giving thanks to God for their victories, he implores their patronage, that they may vouchsafe to intercede for us in heaven, whose memory we celebrate upon earth.

CHAPTER IV.

ON THE CANON OF THE MASS.

And whereas it beseemeth, that holy things be administered in a holy manner, and of all holy things this sacrifice is the most holy; to the end that it might be worthily and reverently offered and received, the Catholic Church instituted, many years ago, the sacred Canon, so pure from every error, that nothing is contained therein which does not in the highest degree savour of a certain holiness and piety, and raise up unto God the minds of

those that offer. For it is composed, out of the very words of the Lord, the traditions of the apostles, and the pious institutions also of holy pontiffs.

CHAPTER V.

ON THE SOLEMN CEREMONIES OF THE SACRIFICE OF THE MASS.

And whereas such is the nature of man, that, without external helps, he cannot easily be raised to the meditation of divine things; therefore has holy Mother Church instituted certain rites, to wit that certain things be pronounced in the mass in a low, and others in a louder, tone. She has likewise employed ceremonies, such as mystic benedictions, lights, incense, vestments, and many other things of this kind, derived from an apostolical discipline and tradition, whereby both the majesty of so great a sacrifice might be recommended, and the minds of the faithful be excited, by those visible signs of religion and piety, to the contemplation of those most sublime things which are hidden in this sacrifice.

CHAPTER VI.

ON MASS WHEREIN THE PRIEST ALONE COMMUNICATES.

The sacred and holy Synod would fain indeed that, at each mass, the faithful who are present should communicate, not only in spiritual desire, but also by the sacramental participation of the Eucharist, that thereby a more abundant fruit might be derived to them from this most holy sacrifice: but not therefore, if this be not always done, does It condemn, as private and unlawful, but approves of and therefore commends, those masses in which the priest alone communicates sacramentally; since those masses also ought to be considered as truly common; partly because the people communicate spiritually threat; partly also because they are celebrated by a public minister of the Church, not for himself only, but for all the faithful, who belong to the body of Christ.

CHAPTER VII.

ON THE WATER THAT IS TO BE MIXED WITH THE WINE TO BE OFFERED IN THE CHALICE.

The holy Synod notices, in the next place, that it has been enjoined by the Church on priests, to mix water with the wine that is to be offered in the chalice; as well because it is believed that Christ the Lord did this, as also because from His side there came out blood and water; the memory of which mystery is renewed by this commixture; and, whereas in the apocalypse of blessed John, the peoples are called waters, the union of that faithful people with Christ their head is hereby represented.

CHAPTER VIII.

ON NOT CELEBRATING THE MASS EVERYWHERE IN THE VULGAR TONGUE; THE MYSTERIES OF THE MASS TO BE EXPLAINED TO THE PEOPLE.

Although the mass contains great instruction for the faithful people, nevertheless, it has not seemed expedient to the Fathers, that it should be everywhere celebrated in the vulgar tongue. Wherefore, the ancient usage of each church, and the rite approved of by the holy Roman Church, the mother and mistress of all churches, being in each place retained; and, that the sheep of Christ may not suffer hunger, nor the little ones ask for bread, and there be none to break it unto them, the holy Synod charges pastors, and all who have the cure of souls, that they frequently, during the celebration of mass, expound either by themselves, or others, some portion of those things which are read at mass, and that, amongst the rest, they explain some mystery of this most holy sacrifice, especially on the Lord's days and festivals.

CHAPTER IX.

PRELIMINARY REMARK ON THE FOLLOWING CANONS.

And because that many errors are at this time disseminated and many things are taught and maintained by divers persons, in opposition to this ancient faith, which is based on the sacred Gospel, the traditions of the Apostles, and the doctrine of the holy Fathers; the sacred and holy Synod, after many and grave deliberations maturely had touching these matters, has resolved, with the unanimous consent of all the Fathers, to condemn, and to eliminate from holy Church, by means of the canons subjoined, whatsoever is opposed to this most pure faith and sacred doctrine.

ON THE SACRIFICE OF THE MASS.

CANON I.—If any one saith, that in the mass a true and proper sacrifice is not offered to God; or, that to be offered is nothing else but that Christ is given us to eat; let him be anathema.

CANON II.—If any one saith, that by those words, Do this for the commemoration of me (Luke xxii. 19), Christ did not institute the apostles priests; or, did not ordain that they, and other priests should offer His own body and blood; let him be anathema.

CANON III.—If any one saith, that the sacrifice of the mass is only a sacrifice of praise and of thanksgiving; or, that it is a bare commemoration of the sacrifice consummated on the cross, but not a propitiatory sacrifice; or, that it profits him only who receives; and that it ought not to be offered for the living and the dead for sins, pains, satisfactions, and other necessities; let him be anathema.

CANON IV.—If any one saith, that, by the sacrifice of the mass, a blasphemy is cast upon the most holy sacrifice of Christ consummated on the cross; or, that it is thereby derogated from; let him be anathema.

CANON V.—If any one saith, that it is an imposture to celebrate masses in honour of the saints, and for obtaining their intercession with God, as the Church intends; let him be anathema.

CANON VI.—If any one saith, that the canon of the mass contains errors, and is therefore to be abrogated; let him be anathema.

CANON VII.—If any one saith, that the ceremonies, vestments, and outward signs, which the Catholic Church makes use of in the celebration of masses, are incentives to impiety, rather than offices of piety; let him be anathema.

CANON VIII.—If any one saith, that masses, wherein the priest alone communicates sacramentally, are unlawful, and are, therefore, to be abrogated; let him be anathema.

CANON IX.—If any one saith, that the rite of the Roman Church, according to which a part of the canon and the words of consecration are pronounced in a low tone, is to be condemned; or, that the mass ought to be celebrated in the vulgar tongue only; or, that water ought not to be mixed with the wine that is to be offered in the chalice, for that it is contrary to the institution of Christ; let him be anathema.

REVIEW QUESTIONS

1. Why did the council find it necessary to redefine the mass?
2. On the basis of your reading, what makes the work of the council creative, as well as reactive?
3. What does the council emphasize as important within the doctrine of the mass?
4. What does the council consider the proper function of the priest to be, when celebrating the mass, and what is his relationship to the laity?
5. How does the council's formulation about the mass differ from those of Luther and Calvin?
6. How would you describe the nature of God as understood by the council?

14   EUROPE IN THE ATLANTIC WORLD, 1550–1660

The challenge to the authority of classical culture that the new worlds posed, combined with the fragmentation of the medieval Christian Church—the "body of all believers"—laid the foundation in the second half of the sixteenth century for profound crises of political and social order and of epistemology, the very foundation of human knowledge. In their efforts to describe what they saw in the Americas, European conquistadores and clergy were forced to adopt analogies: hundreds of species of plants and animals were not to be found in the writings of Pliny, the great and trusted botanist and zoologist of the ancient world, or in the Bible. The cultures of the Americas posed new models of social and political relations, opening new possibilities for the ordering of political relations and calling into question the very nature of political authority.

Within Europe, civil wars arose in the wake of the fragmentation of the Christian Church. The wars of religion in France, 1562–98, led astute observers such as Montaigne to question the claim of each side to know the truth, and to question whether human reason was sufficient to discern the truth. In all the religious wars, beginning with the German Peasants' War of 1525 and culminating in the Thirty Years' War, 1618–48, the social order was overthrown, as peasant killed lord, brother killed brother, son killed father, and neighbor killed neighbor. What was it to be human? To be savage? And where was God while Christian slaughtered Christian?

The crisis of the seventeenth century was not simply intellectual and spiritual but also had real material aspects. The expansion of Europe into new worlds changed patterns of consumption and production, thus contributing to the overthrow of traditional work processes and lifestyles. It created a tremendous influx of wealth that aided the rise of new economic and political powers, both social groups and nation-states, and that contributed to chronic inflation. Changes in society, economy, and politics created tensions that found expression in the violence of the period. Religious wars were seldom entirely religious in cause or in consequence. The almost constant march and countermarch of armies not only destroyed life and property but also disrupted agriculture and spread disease. The struggle for existence, difficult under the best of circumstances in the early modern period, became much more difficult in the age of crisis.

By 1660, peasants had risen in unprecedented numbers against their lords; common Englishmen had executed their king; Europeans had witnessed multiple incidents of cannibalism in their own villages; and the medieval epistemology, that very base by which Europeans could be certain of the veracity of what they knew, had collapsed. New formulations were being tentatively put forward, but they did not yet replace the old certainties that had been irrecoverably lost.

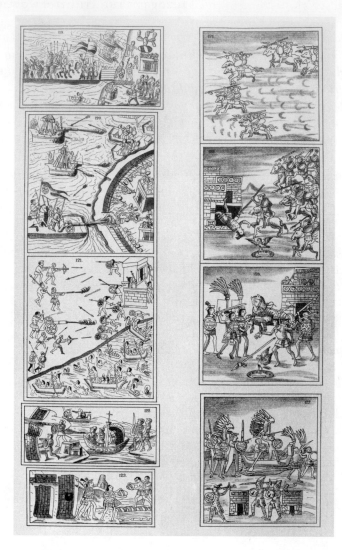

CONQUEST OF MEXICO, FLORENTINE CODEX (C. 1555)

The Franciscan friar Bernardino de Sahagún (d. 1590) directed the team of Nahua artists who produced the Florentine Codex. This book is an account of Cortéz's expedition of 1519, which resulted in the destruction of the Aztec Empire. The story is told in Nahuatl, and is accompanied by over 100 illustrations. Scholars have debated the extent to which the text and pictures allowed the Nahua to express their own views of these events. Sahagún began collecting information in the 1540s, and this chapter may have been composed around 1555. These nine pictures show characteristic battle scenes. Guns and steel certainly played a role in the Spanish conquest of Mexico. What evidence do these pictures provide of this? Perhaps even more striking were the roles of horses. What advantages did these animals provide the Spaniards? Why would indigenous artists have been involved in a project like this? What are the advantages and shortcomings of this historical source?

GIOVANNI MICHIEL

FROM A Venetian Ambassador's Report on the St. Bartholomew's Day Massacre

The struggle for supremacy in northern Italy, which marked the last half of the fifteenth century, gave rise to a new form of diplomacy, including structures and procedures that would be fundamental to relations among all modern states. Requiring continuous contact and communication, Renaissance states turned to permanent diplomacy, distinguished by the use of accredited resident ambassadors rather than ad hoc missions of medieval legates. The tasks of a permanent ambassador were to represent his government at state ceremonies, to gather information, and, occasionally, to enter into negotiations. Nowhere was this system more fully and expertly articulated than by the Republic of Venice in the late fifteenth and sixteenth centuries. Its ambassadors were chosen with unusual care from the most prominent families of the city. They were highly educated, and their duties were carefully defined. Among the latter were weekly dispatches reporting all matters of any interest to Venice. These reports were regularly read and debated in the senate, which replied with questions, instructions, and information of its own. As a result, Venetian ambassadors were among the most skilled and respected in early modern Europe. In this report, Giovanni Michiel interprets the events of St. Bartholomew's Day in 1572. The massacre of Huguenots, instigated by the Queen Mother, Catherine de Medici, outraged Protestant Europe and dashed all hopes for peace in France. Of particular interest is the ambassador's harshly realistic account of the political motives for so violent an act of statecraft.

From *Pursuit of Power: Venetian Ambassadors' Reports on Spain, Turkey and France in the Age of Phillip II, 1560–1600*, by James C. Davis (New York: HarperCollins, 1970), pp. 72–76, 78–79.

*   *   *

Turning to the queen, Admiral de Coligny said, "Madame, the king refuses to involve himself in one war. God grant that he may not be caught up in another which he cannot avoid."

By these words he meant, some say, that if they abandoned the prince of Orange things might go badly for him, and there would be a danger that if the prince failed to win or was actually driven out by the Spanish or for some other reason, then he might enter France with his French and German followers and it might be necessary to drive him out by force. However, everyone understood his words in a very different sense, namely that he was giving notice that he planned to stir up new storms and renew the rioting and civil war. When the queen carefully pondered this it became the chief reason, taken together with the other considerations, why she hurried to prepare that fate for him which he eventually met.

*   *   *

Then, at the dinner hour on Friday, while the admiral was returning on foot from the court to his lodgings and reading a letter, someone fired an arquebus at him. The shot came from a window which faced a bit obliquely on the street, near the royal palace called the Louvre. But it did not strike him in the chest as intended because it so happened that the admiral was wearing a pair of slippers which made walking difficult and, wanting to take them off and hand them to a page, he had just started to turn around. So the arquebus shot tore off a finger on his left hand and then hit his right arm near the wrist and passed through it to the other side near the elbow. If he had simply walked straight ahead it would have hit him in the chest and killed him.

As you can imagine, news of the event caused great excitement, especially at court. Everyone supposed it had been done by order of the duke of Guise to avenge his family, because the window from which the shot was fired belonged to his mother's house, which had purposely been left empty after she had gone to stay in another. When the news was reported to the king, who happened to be playing tennis with the duke of Guise, they say he turned white and looked thunderstruck. Without saying a word he withdrew into his chambers and made it obvious that he was extremely angry.

*   *   *

On Saturday the admiral's dressings were changed and the word was given out—which may or may not have been true—that the wound was not a mortal one and that there was no danger even that he would lose the arm. The Huguenots only blustered all the more, and everyone waited to see what would happen next. The duke of Guise knew he might be attacked, so he armed himself and stuck close to his uncle, the duke of Aumale, and as many relatives, friends and servants as possible.

But before long the situation changed. Late Saturday night, just before the dawn of Saint Bar-tholomew's Day, the massacre or slaughter was carried out. The French say the king ordered it. How wild and terrifying it was in Paris (which has a larger population than any other city in Europe), no one can imagine. Nor can one imagine the rage and frenzy of those who slaughtered and sacked, as the king ordered the people to do. Nor what a marvel, not to say a miracle, it was that the common people did not take advantage of this freedom to loot and plunder from Catholics as well as Huguenots, and ravenously take whatever they could get their hands on, especially since the city is incredibly wealthy. No one would ever imagine that a people could be armed and egged on by their ruler, yet not get out of control once they were worked up. But it was not God's will that things should reach such a pass.

The slaughter went on past Sunday for two or three more days, despite the fact that edicts were issued against it and the duke of Nevers was sent riding through the city along with the king's natural brother to order them to stop the killing. The massacre showed how powerfully religion can affect men's minds. On every street one could see the barbarous sight of men cold-bloodedly outraging others of their own people, and not just men who had never done them any harm but in most cases people they knew to be their neighbors and even their relatives. They had no feeling, no mercy on anyone, even those who kneeled before them and humbly begged for their lives. If one man hated another because of some argument or lawsuit all he had to say was "This man is a Huguenot" and he was immediately killed. (That happened to many Catholics.) If their victims threw themselves in the river as a last resort and tried to swim to safety, as many did, they chased them in boats and then drowned them. There was a great deal of looting and pillaging and they say the goods taken amounted to two million because many Huguenots, including some of the richest of them, had come to live in Paris after the most recent edict of pacification. Some estimate the number who were killed as high as four thousand, while others put it as low as two thousand.

The killing spread to all the provinces and most of the major cities and was just as frenzied there, if not more so. They attacked anyone, even the gentry, and as a result all the leaders who did not escape have been killed or thrown in prison. It is true that Montgomery and some others who were pursued by the duke of Guise escaped to England, but they are not major figures. And the king has terrified them enough so they won't make any trouble.

*   *   *

REVIEW QUESTIONS

1. According to the report, at what level of society did the St. Bartholomew's Day Massacre originate?
2. How was a person identified as Huguenot or Catholic?
3. What does that say about religious identity in early modern France?
4. Do we know from this report who ordered the assassination of Admiral de Coligny?
5. Who caused the massacre?
6. What do we learn about the relation of religion to politics and political action?

REGINALD SCOT

FROM *Discoverie of Witchcraft*

Reginald Scot (1538–1599) was a Kentish squire who witnessed a number of fraudulent accusations of witchcraft in the villages of his shire during the reign of Elizabeth I. In 1584, he wrote his Discoverie of Witchcraft, which contains a remarkable exposition of magical elements in medieval Catholicism and a protest against the persecution of harmless old women. Scot doubted that God could ever have allowed witches to exercise supernatural powers, much less demand that they be persecuted for it. In this regard, he deserves to be ranked among the skeptics on the question of witchcraft, although he never denied the existence of witches. According to Scot, all "witches" fell into one of four categories. First were the innocent, those falsely accused. Second were the deluded, those convinced through their own misery that they were witches. Third were the malefactors, those who harmed people and damaged property, though not by supernatural means. Fourth were imposters, those who posed as witches and conjurers. Scot denied that any of these "witches" had access to supernatural powers. Malefactors and imposters were, in fact, the witches named in the Bible as not being suffered to live. They were the only witches Scot admitted. His work is said to have made a great impression in the magistracy and clergy of his day. Nonetheless, his remained a minority opinion. Most contemporaries understood as tantamount to atheism any denial of the reality of spirits or the possibility of the supernatural. The persecution of witches continued unabated into the eighteenth century; many thousands, mostly harmless old women, fell victim to the rage.

From *Discoverie of Witchcraft*, by Reginald Scot, 1584, edited by Brinsley Nicholson (London: E. Stock, 1886).

* * *

*T*he inconvenience growing by mens credulitie therein, with a reproofe of some churchmen, which are inclined to the common conceived opinion of witches omnipotencie, and a familiar example thereof. But the world is now so bewitched and over-run with this fond error, that even where a man shuld seeke comfort and counsell, there shall hee be sent (in case of necessitie) from God to the divell; and from the Physician, to the coosening witch, who will not sticke to take upon hir, by wordes to heale the lame (which was proper onelie to Christ: and to them whom he assisted with his divine power) yea, with hir familiar & charmes she will take upon hir to cure the blind: though in the tenth of S. *Johns* Gospell it be written, that the divell cannot open the eies of the blind. And they attaine such credit as I have heard (to my greefe) some of the ministerie affirme, that they have had in their parish at one instant, xvii. or xviii. witches: meaning such as could worke miracles supernaturallie. Whereby they manifested as well their infidelitie and ignorance, in conceiving Gods word; as their negligence and error in instructing their flocks. For they themselves might understand, and also teach their parishoners, that God onelie worketh great woonders; and that it is he which sendeth such punishments to the wicked, and such trials to the elect: according to the saieng of the Prophet *Haggai,* I smote you with blasting and mildeaw, and with haile, in all the labours of your hands; and yet you turned not unto me, saith the Lord. And therefore saith the same Prophet in another place; You have sowen much, and bring in little. And both in *Joel* and *Leviticus,* the like phrases and proofes are used and made. But more shalbe said of this hereafter.

* * *

At the assises holden at *Rochester,* Anno 1581, one *Margaret Simons,* the wife of *John Simons,* of *Brenchlie* in *Kent,* was araigned for witchcraft, at the instigation and complaint of divers fond and malicious persons; and speciallie by the meanes of one *John Ferrall* vicar of that parish: with whom I talked about that matter, and found him both fondlie assotted in the cause, and enviouslie bent towards hir: and (which is worse) as unable to make a good account of his faith, as shee whom he accused. That which he, for his part, laid to the poore womans charge, was this.

His sonne (being an ungratious boie, and prentise to one *Robert Scotchford* clothier, dwelling in that parish of *Brenchlie*) passed on a daie by hir house; at whome by chance hir little dog barked. Which thing the boie taking in evill part, drewe his knife, & pursued him therewith even to hir doore: whom she rebuked with some such words as the boie disdained, & yet neverthelesse would not be persuaded to depart in a long time. At the last he returned to his maisters house, and within five or six daies fell sicke. Then was called to mind the fraie betwixt the dog and the boie: insomuch as the vicar (who thought himselfe so privileged, as he little mistrusted that God would visit his children with sicknes) did so calculate; as he found, partlie through his owne judgement, and partlie (as he himselfe told me) by the relation of other witches, that his said sonne was by hir bewitched. Yea, he also told me, that this his sonne (being as it were past all cure) received perfect health at the hands of another witch.

He proceeded yet further against hir, affirming, that alwaies in his parish church, when he desired to read most plainelie, his voice so failed him, as he could scant be heard at all. Which hee could impute, he said, to nothing else, but to hir inchantment. When I advertised the poore woman hereof, as being desirous to heare what she could saie for hir selfe; she told me, that in verie deed his voice did much faile him, speciallie when he strained himselfe to speake lowdest. How beit, she said that at all times his voice was hoarse and lowe: which thing I perceived to be true. But sir, said she, you shall understand, that this our vicar is diseased with such a kind of hoarsenesse, as divers of our neighbors in this parish, not long since, doubted that he had the French pox; & in that respect utterly refused to communicate with him: untill such time as (being therunto injoined by M. D. *Lewen* the

Ordinarie) he had brought frō *London* a certificat, under the hands of two physicians, that his hoarsenes proceeded from a disease in the lungs. Which certificat he published in the church, in the presence of the whole congregation: and by this meanes hee was cured, or rather excused of the shame of his disease. And this I knowe to be true by the relation of divers honest men of that parish. And truelie, if one of the Jurie had not beene wiser than the other, she had beene condemned thereupon, and upon other as ridiculous matters as this. For the name of a witch is so odious, and hir power so feared among the common people, that if the honestest bodie living chance to be arraigned thereupon, she shall hardlie escape condemnation.

A Confutation of the Common Conceived Opinion of Witches and Witchcraft, and How Detestable a Sinne It Is to Repaire to Them for Counsell or Helpe in Time of Affliction

But whatsoever is reported or conceived of such manner of witchcrafts, I dare avow to be false and fabulous (coosinage, dotage, and poisoning excepted:) neither is there any mention made of these kind of witches in the Bible. If Christ had knowne them, he would not have pretermitted to invaie against their presumption, in taking upon them his office: as, to heale and cure diseases; and to worke such miraculous and supernaturall things, as whereby he himselfe was speciallie knowne, beleeved, and published to be God; his actions and cures consisting (in order and effect) according to the power of our witchmoongers imputed to witches. Howbeit, if there be any in these daies afflicted in such strange sort, as Christs cures and patients are described in the new testament to have beene: we flie from trusting in God to trusting in witches, who doo not onelie in their coosening art take on them the office of Christ in this behalfe; but use his verie phrase of speech to such idolators, as com to

seeke divine assistance at their hands, saieng; Go thy waies, thy sonne or thy daughter, &c. shall doo well, and be whole.

*   *   *

In like manner I say, he that attributeth to a witch, such divine power, as dulie and onelie apperteineth unto GOD (which all witchmongers doo) is in hart a blasphemer, an idolater, and full of grosse impietie, although he neither go nor send to hir for assistance.

A Further Confutation of Witches Miraculous and Omnipotent Power, by Invincible Reasons and Authorities, with Dissuasions from Such Fond Credulitie

If witches could doo anie such miraculous things, as these and other which are imputed to them, they might doo them againe and againe, at anie time or place, or at anie mans desire: for the divell is as strong at one time as at another, as busie by daie as by night, and readie enough to doo all mischeefe, and careth not whom he abuseth. And in so much as it is confessed, by the most part of witchmoongers themselves, that he knoweth not the cogitation of mans heart, he should (me thinks) sometimes appeere unto honest and credible persons, in such grosse and corporall forme, as it is said he dooth unto witches: which you shall never heare to be justified by one sufficient witnesse. For the divell indeed entreth into the mind, and that waie seeketh mans confusion.

The art alwaies presupposeth the power; so as, if they saie they can doo this or that, they must shew how and by what meanes they doo it; as neither the witches, nor the witchmoongers are able to doo. For to everie action is required the facultie and abilitie of the agent or dooer; the aptnes of the patient or subject; and a convenient and possible application. Now the witches are mortall, and their power dependeth upon the analogie and consonancie of their minds and bodies; but with their minds they can but will and understand; and with their bodies they can doo no more, but as the bounds and ends of terrene sense will suffer: and therefore their power extendeth not to doo such miracles, as surmounteth their owne sense, and the understanding of others which are wiser than they; so as here wanteth the vertue and power of the efficient. And in reason, there can be no more vertue in the thing caused, than in the cause, or that which proceedeth of or from the benefit of the cause. And we see, that ignorant and impotent women, or witches, are the causes of incantations and charmes; wherein we shall perceive there is none effect, if we will credit our owne experience and sense unabused, the rules of phi-losophie, or the word of God. For alas! What an unapt instrument is a toothles, old, impotent, and unweldie woman to flie in the aier? Truelie, the divell little needs such instruments to bring his purposes to passe.

It is strange, that we should suppose, that such persons can worke such feates: and it is more strange, that we will imagine that to be possible to be doone by a witch, which to nature and sense is impossible; speciallie when our neighbours life dependeth upon our credulitie therein; and when we may see the defect of abilitie, which alwaies is an impediment both to the act, and also to the pre-sumption thereof. And bicause there is nothing possible in lawe, that in nature is impossible; there-fore the judge dooth not attend or regard what the accused man saith; or yet would doo: but what is prooved to have beene committed, and naturallie falleth in mans power and will to doo. For the lawe saith, that To will a thing unpossible, is a signe of a mad man, or of a foole, upon whom no sentence or judgement taketh hold. Furthermore, what Jurie will condemne, or what Judge will give sentence or judgement against one for killing a man at *Ber-wicke;* when they themselves, and manie other sawe that man at *London,* that verie daie, wherein the murther was committed; yea though the partie confesse himself guiltie therein, and twentie wit-nesses depose the same? But in this case also I saie the judge is not to weigh their testimonie, which is weakened by lawe; and the judges authoritie is to

supplie the imperfection of the case, and to mainte-ine the right and equitie of the same.

Seeing therefore that some other things might naturallie be the occasion and cause of such calam-ities as witches are supposed to bring; let not us that professe the Gospell and knowledge of Christ, be bewitched to beleeve that they doo such things, as are in nature impossible, and in sense and reason incredible. If they saie it is doone through the div-els helpe, who can work miracles; whie doo not theeves bring their busines to passe miraculouslie, with whom the divell is as conversant as with the other? Such mischeefes as are imputed to witches, happen where no witches are; yea and continue when witches are hanged and burnt: whie then should we attribute such effect to that cause, which being taken awaie, happeneth neverthelesse?

* * *

What Testimonies and Witnesses Are Allowed to Give Evidence against Reputed Witches, by the Report and Allowance of the Inquisitors Themselves, and Such as Are Speciall Writers Heerein

Excommunicat persons, partakers of the falt, infants, wicked servants, and runnawaies are to be admitted to beare witnesse against their dames in this mater of witchcraft: bicause (saith *Bodin* the champion of witchmoongers) none that be honest are able to detect them. Heretikes also and witches shall be received to accuse, but not to excuse a witch. And finallie, the testimonie of all infamous persons in this case is good and allowed. Yea, one lewd person (saith *Bodin*) may be received to accuse and condemne a thousand suspected witches. And although by lawe, a capitall enimie may be chal-lenged; yet *James Sprenger,* and *Henrie Institor,* (from whom *Bodin,* and all the writers that ever I have read, doo receive their light, authorities and arguments) saie (upon this point of lawe) that The poore frendlesse old woman must proove, that hir capitall enimie would have killed hir, and that hee hath both assalted & wounded hir; otherwise she pleadeth all in vaine. If the judge aske hir, whether she have anie capitall enimies; and she rehearse other, and forget hir accuser; or else answer that he was hir capital enimie, but now she hopeth he is not so: such a one is nevertheles admitted for a witnes. And though by lawe, single witnesses are not admittable; yet if one depose she hath bewitched hir cow; another, hir sow; and the third, hir butter: these saith (saith *M. Mal.* and *Bodin*) are no single witnesses; bicause they agree that she is a witch.

The Fifteene Crimes Laid to the Charge of Witches, by Witchmongers, Speciallie by Bodin, in Dæmonomania

They denie God, and all religion.

Answere. Then let them die therefore, or at the least be used like infidels, or apostataes.

They cursse, blaspheme, and provoke God with all despite.

Answere. Then let them have the law expressed in *Levit.* 24. and *Deut.* 13 & 17.

They give their faith to the divell, and they worship and offer sacrifice unto him.

Ans. Let such also be judged by the same lawe.

They doo solemnelie vow and promise all their progenie unto the divell.

Ans. This promise proceedeth from an unsound mind, and is not to be regarded; bicause they cannot performe it, neither will it be prooved true. Howbeit, if it be done by anie that is sound of mind, let the cursse of *Jeremie,* 32.36. light upon them, to wit, the sword, famine and pestilence.

They sacrifice their owne children to the divell before baptisme, holding them up in the aire unto him, and then thrust a needle into their braines.

Ans. If this be true, I maintaine them not herein: but there is a lawe to judge them by. Howbeit, it is so contrarie to sense and nature, that it were follie to beleeve it; either upon *Bodins* bare word, or else upon his presumptions; speciallie

when so small commoditie and so great danger and inconvenience insueth to the witches thereby.

They burne their children when they have sacrificed them.

Ans. Then let them have such punishment, as they that offered their children unto *Moloch: Levit.* 20. But these be meere devises of witchmoongers and inquisitors, that with extreame tortures have wroong such confessions from them; or else with false reports have beelied them; or by flatterie & faire words and promises have woon it at their hands, at the length.

They sweare to the divell to bring as manie into that societie as they can.

Ans. This is false, and so prooved elsewhere.

They sweare by the name of the divell.

Ans. I never heard anie such oth, neither have we warrant to kill them that so doo sweare; though indeed it be veric lewd and impious.

They use incestuous adulterie with spirits.

Ans. This is a stale ridiculous lie, as is prooved apparentlie hereafter.

They boile infants (after they have murthered them unbaptised) untill their flesh be made potable.

Ans. This is untrue, incredible, and impossible.

They eate the flesh and drinke the bloud of men and children openlic.

Ans. Then are they kin to the *Anthropophagi* and *Canibals.* But I beleeve never an honest man in *England* nor in *France,* will affirme that he hath seene any of these persons, that are said to be witches, do so; if they shuld, I beleeve it would poison them.

They kill men with poison.

Ans. Let them be hanged for their labour.

They kill mens cattell.

Ans. Then let an action of trespasse be brought against them for so dooing.

They bewitch mens corne, and bring hunger and barrennes into the countrie; they ride and flie in the aire, bring stormes, make tempests, &c.

Ans. Then will I worship them as gods; for those be not the works of man nor yet of witch: as I have elsewhere prooved at large.

They use venerie with a divell called *Incubus,* even when they lie in bed with their husbands, and have children by them, which become the best witches.

Ans. This is the last lie, verie ridiculous, and confuted by me elsewhere.

Of Foure Capitall Crimes Objected against Witches, All Fullie Answered and Confuted as Frivolous

First therefore they laie to their charge idolatrie. But alas without all reason: for such are properlie knowne to us to be idolaters, as doo externall worship to idols or strange gods. The furthest point that idolatrie can be stretched unto, is, that they, which are culpable therein, are such as hope for and seeke salvation at the hands of idols, or of anie other than God; or fixe their whole mind and love upon anie creature, so as the power of God be neglected and contemned thereby. But witches neither seeke nor beleeve to have salvation at the hands of divels, but by them they are onlie deceived; the instruments of their phantasie being corrupted, and so infatuated, that they suppose, confesse, and saie they can doo that, which is as farre beyond their power and nature to doo, as to kill a man at *Yorke* before noone, when they have beene seene at *London* in that morning, &c. But if these latter idolaters, whose idolatrie is spirituall, and committed onelie in mind, should be punished by death; then should everie covetous man, or other, that setteth his affection anie waie too much upon an earthlie creature, be executed, and yet perchance the witch might escape scotfree.

Secondlie, apostasie is laid to their charge, whereby it is inferred, that they are worthie to die. But apostasie is, where anie of sound judgement forsake the gospell, learned and well knowne unto them; and doo not onelie embrace impietie and infidelitie; but oppugne and resist the truth erstwhile by them professed. But alas these poore women go not about to defend anie impietie, but after good admonition repent.

Thirdlie, they would have them executed for seducing the people. But God knoweth they have

small store of Rhetorike or art to seduce; except to tell a tale of Robin good-fellow be to deceive and seduce. Neither may their age or sex admit that opinion or accusation to be just: for they themselves are poore seduced soules. I for my part (as else-where I have said) have prooved this point to be false in most apparent sort.

Fourthlie, as touching the accusation, which all the writers use herein against them for their carnall copulation with *Incubus:* the follie of mens credulitie is as much to be woondered at and derided, as the others vaine and impossible confessions. For the divell is a spirit, and hath neither flesh nor bones, which were to be used in the performance of this action. And since he also lacketh all instruments, substance, and seed ingendred of bloud; it were follie to staie overlong in the confutation of that, which is not in the nature of things. And yet must I saie somewhat heerein, bicause the opinion hereof is so stronglie and universallie received, and the fables thereupon so innumerable; wherby *M. Mal. Bodin, Hemingius, Hyperius, Danaeus, Erastus,* and others that take upon them to write heerein, are so abused, or rather seeke to abuse others; as I woonder at their fond credulitie in this behalfe. For they affirme undoubtedlie, that the divell plaieth *Succubus* to the man, and carrieth from him the seed of generation, which he delivereth as *Incubus* to the woman, who manie times that waie is gotten with child; which will verie naturallie (they saie) become a witch, and such one they affirme *Merline* was.

*   *   *

By What Meanes the Common People Have Beene Made Beleevein the Miraculous Works of Witches, a Definition of Witchcraft, and a Description Thereof

The common people have beene so assotted and bewitched, with whatsoever poets have feigned of witchcraft, either in earnest, in jest, or else in derision; and with whatsoever lowd liers and couseners for their pleasures heerein have invented, and with whatsoever tales they have heard from old doting women, or from their mothers maids, and with whatsoever the grandfoole their ghostlie father, or anie other morrow masse preest had informed them; and finallie with whatsoever they have swallowed up through tract of time, or through their owne timerous nature or ignorant conceipt, concerning these matters of hagges and witches: as they have so settled their opinion and credit thereupon, that they thinke it heresie to doubt in anie part of the matter; speciallie bicause they find this word witchcraft expressed in the scriptures; which is as to defend praieng to saincts, bicause *Sanctus, Sanctus, Sanctus* is written in *Te Deum.*

And now to come to the definition of witchcraft, which hitherto I did deferre and put off purposelie: that you might perceive the true nature thereof, by the circumstances, and therefore the rather to allow of the same, seeing the varietie of other writers. Witchcraft is in truth a cousening art, wherin the name of God is abused, prophaned and blasphemed, and his power attributed to a vile creature. In estimation of the vulgar people, it is a supernaturall worke, contrived betweene a corporall old woman, and a spirituall divell. The maner thereof is so secret, mysticall, and strange, that to this daie there hath never beene any credible witnes thereof. It is incomprehensible to the wise, learned or faithfull; a probable matter to children, fooles, melancholike persons and papists. The trade is thought to be impious. The effect and end thereof to be sometimes evill, as when thereby man or beast, grasse, trees, or corne, &c; is hurt: sometimes good, as whereby sicke folkes are healed, theeves bewraied, and true men come to their goods, &c. The matter and instruments, wherewith it is accomplished, are words, charmes, signes, images, characters, &c; the which words although any other creature do pronounce, in manner and forme as they doo, leaving out no circumstance requisite or usually for that action: yet none is said to have the grace or gift to performe the matter, except she be a witch, and so

taken either by hir owne consent, or by others imputation.

Reasons to Proove That Words and Characters Are But Bables, and That Witches Cannot Doo Such Things as the Multitude Supposeth They Can, Their Greatest Woonders Prooved Trifles, of a Yoong Gentleman Cousened

That words, characters, images, and such other trinkets, which are thought so necessarie instruments for witchcraft (as without the which no such thing can be accomplished) are but bables, devised by couseners, to abuse the people withall; I trust I have sufficientlie prooved. And the same maie be further and more plainelie perceived by these short and compendious reasons following.

First, in that *Turkes* and infidels, in their witchcraft, use both other words, and other characters than our witches doo and also such as are most contrarie. In so much as, if ours be bad, in reason theirs should be good. If their witches can doo anie thing, ours can doo nothing. For as our witches are said to renounce Christ, and despise his sacraments: so doo the other forsake *Mahomet,* and his lawes, which is one large step to christianitie.

It is also to be thought, that all witches are couseners; when mother *Bungie,* a principall witch, so reputed, tried, and condemned of all men, and continuing in that exercise and estimation manie yeares (having cousened & abused the whole realme, in so much as there came to hir, witchmongers from all the furthest parts of the land, she being in diverse bookes set out with authoritie, registred and chronicled by the name of the great witch of *Rochester,* and reputed among all men for the cheefe ringleader of all other witches) by good proofe is found to be a meere cousener; confessing in hir death bed freelie, without compulsion or inforcement, that hir cunning consisted onlie in deluding and deceiving the people: saying that she had (towards the maintenance of hir credit in that

cousening trade) some sight in physicke and sur-
gerie, and the assistance of a freend of hirs, called
Heron, a professor thereof. And this I know, partlie of mine owne knowledge, and partlie by the testimonie of hir husband, and others of credit, to
whome (I saie) in hir death bed, and at sundrie
other times she protested these things; and also
that she never had indeed anie materiall spirit or
divell (as the voice went) nor yet knew how to worke
anie supernaturall matter, as she in hir life time
made men beleeve she had and could doo.

*   *   *

Againe, who will mainteine, that common
witchcrafts are not cousenages, when the great and
famous witchcrafts, which had stolne credit not
onlie from all the common people, but from men
of great wisdome and authoritie, are discovered to
be beggerlie slights of cousening varlots? Which
otherwise might and would have remained a per-
petuall objection against me. Were there not three
images of late yeeres found in a doonghill, to the
terror & astonishment of manie thousands? In so
much as great matters were thought to have beene
pretended to be doone by witchcraft. But if the Lord
preserve those persons (whose destruction was
doubted to have beene intended thereby) from all
other the lewd practises and attempts of their
enimies; I feare not, but they shall easilie withstand
these and such like devises, although they should

indeed be practised against them. But no doubt, if
such bables could have brought those matters of
mischeefe to passe, by the hands of traitors, witches,
or papists; we should long since have beene deprived
of the most excellent jewell and comfort that we
enjoy in this world. Howbeit, I confesse, that the
feare, conceipt, and doubt of such mischeefous pretenses may breed inconvenience to them that stand
in awe of the same. And I wish, that even for such
practises, though they never can or doo take effect,
the practisers be punished with all extremitie:
bicause therein is manifested a traiterous heart to
the Queene, and a presumption against God.

*   *   *

REVIEW QUESTIONS

1. What is witchcraft?
2. How does Scot depict it?
3. According to Scot, what characterizes witches
   and witchcraft?
4. How does Scot confound the very notion of
   witchcraft?
5. Where does he locate the source of all power to
   override the laws of nature?
6. What sort of power is left to witches?
7. What, according to Scot, is the relation of
   witches to the natural world?

THE PLUNDERING AND BURNING OF A VILLAGE, A HANGING, AND
PEASANTS AVENGE THEMSELVES (1633)   JACQUES CALLOT

These three prints, often referred to as The Horrors of War, *powerfully reveal commonplace events of the early seventeenth century: the ravages of war on a small village, the punishment of unruly troops, and the violence of the violated. How does Callot portray rural life? What general aspects of the Iron Century does Callot capture in his images? Why do you think Callot decided to reveal the underbelly of seventeenth-century warfare rather than portraying it in more heroic terms?*

FROM The Peace of Westphalia

A series of peace treaties signed over a six-month period in 1648, the Peace of West-
phalia ended both the Thirty Years' War that ravaged the Holy Roman Empire
between 1618 and 1648 and the Eighty Years' War that accompanied the struggle of
the Dutch Republic for independence from the Spanish Empire. A complex process
and treaty, the Peace of Westphalia involved multiple parties, including the Holy
Roman emperor, the king of Spain, the king of France, the king of Sweden, the state-
holder of the Dutch Republic, the princes of the Holy Roman Empire, and the repre-
sentatives of the free imperial cities. It can be denoted by two major events. With the
signing of the Peace of Münster between the Dutch Republic and the kingdom of
Spain on 30 January 1648, which was officially ratified in Münster on 15 May 1648,
Spain recognized the independence of the Dutch Republic. Two further treaties were
signed later in the year, on 24 October 1648: the Treaty of Münster declared peace
between the Holy Roman Emperor and France, and their respective allies; the Treaty
of Osnabrück declared peace among the Holy Roman Empire, the kingdom of France,
the kingdom of Sweden, and their respective allies. Despite their names, the treaties
did not immediately restore peace throughout Europe, but they did create a basis for
national self-determination and a new system of political order, sometimes referred
to as Westphalian sovereignty. Based upon the concept of coexisting sovereign
states, military aggression was to be held in check by a balance of power. A principle
of noninterference in the internal affairs of other states likewise came into being. As
European influence spread across the globe in the course of the seventeenth and
eighteenth centuries, these principles became central to international law and the
world order.

From Treaty of Westphalia, transcribed by the Avalon Project (Yale Law School, Lillian
Goldman Law Library).

In the name of the most holy and individual Trinity: Be it known to all, and every one whom it may concern, or to whom in any manner it may belong, That for many Years past, Discords and Civil Divisions being stir'd up in the Roman Empire, which increas'd to such a degree, that not only all Germany, but also the neighbouring King-doms, and France particularly, have been involv'd in the Disorders of a long and cruel War: And in the first place, between the most Serene and most Puis-sant Prince and Lord, Ferdinand the Second, of famous Memory, elected Roman Emperor, always August, King of Germany, Hungary, Bohemia, Dal-matia, Croatia, Slavonia, Arch-Duke of Austria, Duke of Burgundy, Brabant, Styria, Carinthia, Car-niola, Marquiss of Moravia, Duke of Luxemburgh, the Higher and Lower Silesia, of Wirtemburg and Teck, Prince of Suabia, Count of Hapsburg, Tirol, Kyburg and Goritia, Marquiss of the Sacred Roman Empire, Lord of Burgovia, of the Higher and Lower Lusace, of the Marquisate of Slavonia, of Port Naon and Salines, with his Allies and Adherents on one side; and the most Serene, and the most Puissant Prince, Lewis the Thirteenth, most Christian King of France and Navarre, with his Allies and Adher-ents on the other side. And after their Decease, between the most Serene and Puissant Prince and Lord, Ferdinand the Third, elected Roman Emperor, always August, King of Germany, Hun-gary, Bohemia, Dalmatia, Croatia, Slavonia, Arch-

Duke of Austria, Duke of Burgundy, Brabant, Styria, Carinthia, Carniola, Marquiss of Moravia, Duke of Luxemburg, of the Higher and Lower Silesia, of Wirtemburg and Teck, Prince of Suabia, Count of Hapsburg, Tirol, Kyburg and Goritia, Marquiss of the Sacred Roman Empire, Burgovia, the Higher and Lower Lusace, Lord of the Marquisate of Slavonia, of Port Naon and Salines, with his Allies and Adherents on the one side; and the most Serene and most Puissant Prince and Lord, Lewis the Fourteenth, most Christian King of France and Navarre, with his Allies and Adherents on the other side: from whence ensu'd great Effusion of Christian Blood, and the Desolation of several Provinces. It has at last happen'd, by the effect of Divine Goodness, seconded by the Endeavours of the most Serene Republick of Venice, who in this sad time, when all Christendom is imbroil'd, has not ceas'd to contribute its Counsels for the publick Welfare and Tranquillity; so that on the side, and the other, they have form'd Thoughts of an universal Peace. And for this purpose, by a mutual Agreement and Covenant of both Partys, in the year of our Lord 1641, the 25th of December, N.S. or the 15th O.S. it was resolv'd at Hamburgh, to hold an Assembly of Plenipotentiary Ambassadors, who should render themselves at Munster and Osnabrug in Westphalia the 11th of July, N.S. or the 1st of the said month O.S. in the year 1643. The Plenipotentiary Ambassadors on the one side, and the other, duly establish'd, appearing at the prefixt time, and on the behalf of his Imperial Majesty, the most illustrious and most excellent Lord, Maximilian Count of Trautmansdorf and Weinsberg, Baron of Gleichenberg, Neustadt, Negan, Burgau, and Torzenbach, Lord of Teinitz, Knight of the Golden Fleece, Privy Counsellor and Chamberlain to his Imperial Sacred Majesty, and Steward of his Houshold; the Lord John Lewis, Count of Nassau, Catzenellebogen, Vianden, and Dietz, Lord of Bilstein, Privy Counsellor to the Emperor, and Knight of the Golden Fleece; Monsieur Isaac Volmamarus, Doctor of Law, Counsellor, and President in the Chamber of the most Serene Lord Arch-Duke Ferdinand Charles. And on the behalf of the most Christian King, the most eminent Prince and

Lord, Henry of Orleans, Duke of Longueville, and Estouteville, Prince and Sovereign Count of Neuschaftel, Count of Dunois and Tancerville, Hereditary Constable of Normandy, Governor and Lieutenant-General of the same Province, Captain of the Cent Hommes d'Arms, and Knight of the King's Orders, &c. as also the most illustrious and most excellent Lords, Claude de Mesmes, Count d'Avaux, Commander of the said King's Orders, one of the Superintendents of the Finances, and Minister of the Kingdom of France &c. and Abel Servien, Count la Roche of Aubiers, also one of the Ministers of the Kingdom of France. And by the Mediation and Interposition of the most illustrious and most excellent Ambassador and Senator of Venice, Aloysius Contarini Knight, who for the space of five Years, or thereabouts, with great Diligence, and a Spirit intirely impartial, has been inclin'd to be a Mediator in these Affairs. After having implor'd the Divine Assistance, and receiv'd a reciprocal Communication of Letters, Commissions, and full Powers, the Copys of which are inserted at the end of this Treaty, in the presence and with the consent of the Electors of the Sacred Roman Empire, the other Princes and States, to the Glory of God, and the Benefit of the Christian World, the following Articles have been agreed on and consented to, and the same run thus.

I.

That there shall be a Christian and Universal Peace, and a perpetual, true, and sincere Amity, between his Sacred Imperial Majesty, and his most Christian Majesty; as also, between all and each of the Allies, and Adherents of his said Imperial Majesty, the House of Austria, and its Heirs, and Successors; but chiefly between the Electors, Princes, and States of the Empire on the one side; and all and each of the Allies of his said Christian Majesty, and all their Heirs and Successors, chiefly between the most Serene Queen and Kingdom of Swedeland, the Electors respectively, the Princes and States of the Empire, on the other part. That this Peace and Amity be observ'd and cultivated with such a

Sincerity and Zeal, that each Party shall endeavour to procure the Benefit, Honour and Advantage of the other; that thus on all sides they may see this Peace and Friendship in the Roman Empire, and the Kingdom of France flourish, by entertaining a good and faithful Neighbourhood.

II.

That there shall be on the one side and the other a perpetual Oblivion, Amnesty, or Pardon of all that has been committed since the beginning of these Troubles, in what place, or what manner soever the Hostilitys have been practis'd, in such a manner, that no body, under any pretext whatsoever, shall practice any Acts of Hostility, entertain any Enmity, or cause any Trouble to each other; neither as to Persons, Effects and Securitys, neither of themselves or by others, neither privately nor openly, neither directly nor indirectly, neither under the colour of Right, nor by the way of Deed, either within or without the extent of the Empire, notwithstanding all Covenants made before to the contrary: That they shall not act, or permit to be acted, any wrong or injury to any whatsoever; but that all that has pass'd on the one side, and the other, as well before as during the War, in Words, Writings, and Outrageous Actions, in Violences, Hostilitys, Damages and Expences, without any respect to Persons or Things, shall be entirely abolish'd in such a manner that all that might be demanded of, or pretended to, by each other on that behalf, shall be bury'd in eternal Oblivion.

III.

And that a reciprocal Amity between the Emperor, and the Most Christian King, the Electors, Princes and States of the Empire, may be maintain'd so much the more firm and sincere (to say nothing at present of the Article of Security, which will be mention'd hereafter) the one shall never assist the present or future Enemys of the other under any Title or Pretence whatsoever, either with Arms,

Money, Soldiers, or any sort of Ammunition; nor no one, who is a Member of this Pacification, shall suffer any Enemys Troops to retire thro' or sojourn in his Country.

*   *   *

VI.

According to this foundation of reciprocal Amity, and a general Amnesty, all and every one of the Electors of the sacred Roman Empire, the Princes and States (therein comprehending the Nobility, which depend immediately on the Empire) their Vassals, Subjects, Citizens, Inhabitants (to whom on the account of the Bohemian or German Troubles or Alliances, contracted here and there, might have been done by the one Party or the other, any Prejudice or Damage in any manner, or under what pretence soever, as well in their Lordships, their fiefs, Underfiefs, Allodations, as in their Dignitys, Immunitys, Rights and Privileges) shall be fully re-establish'd on the one side and the other, in the Ecclesiastick or Laick State, which they enjoy'd, or could lawfully enjoy, notwithstanding any Alterations, which have been made in the mean time to the contrary.

*   *   *

XXVIII.

That those of the Confession of Augsburg, and particularly the Inhabitants of Oppenheim, shall be put in possession again of their Churches, and Ecclesiastical Estates, as they were in the Year 1624. as also that all others of the said Confession of Augsburg, who shall demand it, shall have the free Exercise of their Religion, as well in publick Churches at the appointed Hours, as in private in their own Houses, or in others chosen for this purpose by their Ministers, or by those of their Neighbours, preaching the Word of God.

*   *   *

XXXVII.

That the Contracts, Exchanges, Transactions, Obligations, Treatys, made by Constraint or Threats, and extorted illegally from States or Subjects (as in particular, those of Spiers complain, and those of Weisenburg on the Rhine, those of Landau, Reitlingen, Hailbron, and others) shall be so annull'd and abolish'd, that no more Enquiry shall be made after them.

XXXVIII.

That if Debtors have by force got some Bonds from their Creditors, the same shall be restor'd, but not with prejudice to their Rights.

XXXIX.

That the Debts either by Purchase, Sale, Revenues, or by what other name they may be call'd, if they have been violently extorted by one of the Partys in War, and if the Debtors alledge and offer to prove there has been a real Payment, they shall be no more prosecuted, before these Exceptions be first adjusted. That the Debtors shall be oblig'd to produce their Exceptions within the term of two years after the Publication of the Peace, upon pain of being afterwards condemn'd to perpetual Silence.

XL.

That Processes which have been hitherto enter'd on this Account, together with the Transactions and Promises made for the Restitution of Debts, shall be look'd upon as void; and yet the Sums of Money, which during the War have been exacted bona fide, and with a good intent, by way of Contributions, to prevent greater Evils by the Contributors, are not comprehended herein.

*　　*　　*

XLVI.

As for the rest, Law and Justice shall be administer'd in Bohemia, and in all the other Hereditary Provinces of the Emperor, without any respect; as to the Catholicks, so also to the Subjects, Creditors, Heirs, or private Persons, who shall be of the Confession of Augsburg, if they have any Pretensions, and enter or prosecute any Actions to obtain Justice.

*　　*　　*

REVIEW QUESTIONS

1. Why does the peace involve separate treaties for the Holy Roman emperor and the Holy Roman Empire?
2. When the peace refers to "entertaining a good and faithful Neighbourhood," what is meant?
3. Why is "restitution" a particularly important issue of the peace?
4. What becomes of the constitution of the Holy Roman Empire as a result of the peace?
5. How does the treaty define sovereignty?
6. What internal affairs of states does the peace specifically address?

MICHEL EYQUEM DE MONTAIGNE

FROM "Of Cannibals"

Michel Eyquem de Montaigne (1533–1592) originated the essay as a literary form. Born of a wealthy family at the Château de Montaigne, near Libourne, he was first educated by a tutor who spoke to him in Latin but no French. Until he was six years old, Montaigne learned the classical language as his native tongue. He was further educated at the Collège du Guyenne, where his fluency intimidated some of the finest Latinists in France, and studied law at Toulouse. In 1554, his father purchased an office in the Cour des Aides of Périgeaux, a fiscal court later incorporated into the Parlement of Bordeaux, a position he soon resigned to his son. Montaigne spent thirteen years in office at work he found neither pleasant nor useful. In 1571, he retired to the family estate. Apart from brief visits to Paris and Rouen, periods of travel, and two terms as mayor of Bordeaux (1581–85), Montaigne spent the rest of his life as a country gentleman. His life was not all leisure. He became gentleman-in-ordinary to the king's chamber and spent the period 1572–76 trying to broker a peace between Catholics and Huguenots. His first two books of the Essais *appeared in 1580; the third and last volume appeared in 1588. These essays are known for their discursive, conversational style, in which Montaigne undertook explorations of custom, opinion, and institutions. They gave voice to his opposition to all forms of dogmatism that were without rational basis. He observed life with a degree of skepticism, emphasizing the limits of human knowledge and the contradictions in human behavior. Indeed, Montaigne's essays are often cited as examples of an epistemological crisis borne of the new discoveries, theological debates, and social tensions that marked the early modern period.*

From *The Complete Essays of Montaigne,* translated by Donald M. Frame (Stanford: Stanford University Press, 1958).

When King Pyrrhus passed over into Italy, after he had reconnoitered the formation of the army that the Romans were sending to meet him, he said: "I do not know what barbarians these are" (for so the Greeks called all foreign nations), "but the formation of this army that I see is not at all barbarous." The Greeks said as much of the army that Flamininus brought into their country, and so did Philip, seeing from a knoll the order and distribution of the Roman camp, in his kingdom, under Publius Sulpicius Galba. Thus we should beware of clinging to vulgar opinions, and judge things by reason's way, not by popular say.

I had with me for a long time a man who had lived for ten or twelve years in that other world which has been discovered in our century, in the place where Villegaignon landed, and which he called Antarctic France. This discovery of a boundless country seems worthy of consideration. I don't know if I can guarantee that some other such discovery will not be made in the future, so many personages greater than ourselves having been mistaken about this one. I am afraid we have eyes bigger than our stomachs, and more curiosity than capacity. We embrace everything, but we clasp only wind.

*   *   *

This man I had was a simple, crude fellow—a character fit to bear true witness; for clever people observe more things and more curiously, but they interpret them; and to lend weight and conviction to their interpretation, they cannot help altering history a little. They never show you things as they are, but bend and disguise them according to the way they have seen them; and to give credence to their judgment and attract you to it, they are prone to add something to their matter, to stretch it out and amplify it. We need a man either very honest, or so simple that he has not the stuff to build up false inventions and give them plausibility; and wedded to no theory. Such was my man; and besides this, he at various times brought sailors and merchants, whom he had known on that trip, to see me. So I content myself with his information, without inquiring what the cosmographers say about it.

*   *   *

Now, to return to my subject, I think there is nothing barbarous and savage in that nation, from what I have been told, except that each man calls barbarism whatever is not his own practice; for indeed it seems we have no other test of truth and reason than the example and pattern of the opinions and customs of the country we live in. There is always the perfect religion, the perfect government, the perfect and accomplished manners in all things. Those people are wild, just as we call wild the fruits that Nature has produced by herself and in her normal course; whereas really it is those that we have changed artificially and led astray from the common order, that we should rather call wild. The former retain alive and vigorous their genuine, their most useful and natural, virtues and properties, which we have debased in the latter in adapting them to gratify our corrupted taste. And yet for all that, the savor and delicacy of some uncultivated fruits of those countries is quite as excellent, even to our taste, as that of our own. It is not reasonable that art should win the place of honor over our great and powerful mother Nature. We have so overloaded the beauty and richness of her works by our inventions that we have quite smothered her. Yet wherever her purity shines forth, she wonderfully puts to shame our vain and frivolous attempts:

> Ivy comes readier without our care;
> In lonely caves the arbutus grows more fair;
> No art with artless bird song can compare.
>
> Propertius

All our efforts cannot even succeed in reproducing the nest of the tiniest little bird, its contexture, its beauty and convenience; or even the web of the puny spider. All things, says Plato, are produced by nature, by fortune, or by art; the greatest and most beautiful by one or the other of the first two, the least and most imperfect by the last.

These nations, then, seem to me barbarous in this sense, that they have been fashioned very little by the human mind, and are still very close to their original naturalness. The laws of nature still rule them, very little corrupted by ours; and they are in such a state of purity that I am sometimes vexed that they were unknown earlier, in the days when there were men able to judge them better than we. I am sorry that Lycurgus and Plato did not know of them; for it seems to me that what we actually see in these nations surpasses not only all the pictures in which poets have idealized the golden age and all their inventions in imagining a happy state of man, but also the conceptions and the very desire of philosophy. They could not imagine a naturalness so pure and simple as we see by experience; nor could they believe that our society could be maintained with so little artifice and human solder. This is a nation, I should say to Plato, in which there is no sort of traffic, no knowledge of letters, no science of numbers, no name for a magistrate or for political superiority, no custom of servitude, no riches or poverty, no contracts, no successions, no partitions, no occupations but leisure ones, no care for any but common kinship, no clothes, no agriculture, no metal, no use of wine or wheat. The very words that signify lying, treachery, dissimulation, avarice, envy, belittling, pardon—unheard of. How far from this perfection would he find the republic that he imagined: *Men fresh sprung from the gods.*

These manners nature first ordained.

Virgil

For the rest, they live in a country with a very pleasant and temperate climate, so that according to my witnesses it is rare to see a sick man there; and they have assured me that they never saw one palsied, bleary-eyed, toothless, or bent with age. They are settled along the sea and shut in on the land side by great high mountains, with a stretch about a hundred leagues wide in between. They have a great abundance of fish and flesh which bear no resemblance to ours, and they eat them with no other artifice than cooking. The first man who rode a horse there, though he had had dealings with them on several other trips, so horrified them in this posture that they shot him dead with arrows before they could recognize him.

Their buildings are very long, with a capacity of two or three hundred souls; they are covered with the bark of great trees, the strips reaching to the ground at one end and supporting and leaning on one another at the top, in the manner of some of our barns, whose covering hangs down to the ground and acts as a side. They have wood so hard that they cut with it and make of it their swords and grills to cook their food. Their beds are of a cotton weave, hung from the roof like those in our ships, each man having his own; for the wives sleep apart from their husbands.

They get up with the sun, and eat immediately upon rising, to last them through the day; for they take no other meal than that one. Like some other Eastern peoples, of whom Suidas tells us, who drank apart from meals, they do not drink then; but they drink several times a day, and to capacity. Their drink is made of some root, and is of the color of our claret wines. They drink it only lukewarm. This beverage keeps only two or three days; it has a slightly sharp taste, is not at all heady, is good for the stomach, and has a laxative effect upon those who are not used to it; it is a very pleasant drink for anyone who is accustomed to it. In place of bread they use a certain white substance like preserved coriander. I have tried it; it tastes sweet and a little flat.

The whole day is spent in dancing. The younger men go to hunt animals with bows. Some of the women busy themselves meanwhile with warming their drink, which is their chief duty. Some one of the old men, in the morning before they begin to eat, preaches to the whole barnful in common, walking from one end to the other, and repeating one single sentence several times until he has completed the circuit (for the buildings are fully a hundred paces long). He recommends to them only two things: valor against the enemy and love for their wives. And they never fail to point out this obligation, as their refrain, that it is their wives who keep their drink warm and seasoned.

There may be seen in several places, including my own house, specimens of their beds, of their ropes, of their wooden swords and the bracelets with which they cover their wrists in combats, and of the big canes, open at one end, by whose sound they keep time in their dances. They are close shaven all over, and shave themselves much more cleanly than we, with nothing but a wooden or stone razor. They believe that souls are immortal, and that those who have deserved well of the gods are lodged in that part of heaven where the sun rises, and the damned in the west.

They have some sort of priests and prophets, but they rarely appear before the people, having their home in the mountains. On their arrival there is a great feast and solemn assembly of several villages—each barn, as I have described it, makes up a village, and they are about one French league from each other. The prophet speaks to them in public, exhorting them to virtue and their duty; but their whole ethical science contains only these two articles: resoluteness in war and affection for their wives. He prophesies to them things to come and the results they are to expect from their undertakings, and urges them to war or holds them back from it; but this is on the condition that when he fails to prophesy correctly, and if things turn out otherwise than he has predicted, he is cut into a thousand pieces if they catch him, and condemned as a false prophet. For this reason, the prophet who has once been mistaken is never seen again.

*   *   *

They have their wars with the nations beyond the mountains, further inland, to which they go quite naked, with no other arms than bows or wooden swords ending in a sharp point, in the manner of the tongues of our boar spears. It is astonishing what firmness they show in their combats, which never end but in slaughter and bloodshed; for as to routs and terror, they know nothing of either.

Each man brings back as his trophy the head of the enemy he has killed, and sets it up at the entrance to his dwelling. After they have treated their prisoners well for a long time with all the hospitality they can think of, each man who has a prisoner calls a great assembly of his acquaintances. He ties a rope to one of the prisoner's arms, by the end of which he holds him, a few steps away, for fear of being hurt, and gives his dearest friend the other arm to hold in the same way; and these two, in the presence of the whole assembly, kill him with their swords. This done, they roast him and eat him in common and send some pieces to their absent friends. This is not, as people think, for nourishment, as of old the Scythians used to do; it is to betoken an extreme revenge. And the proof of this came when they saw the Portuguese, who had joined forces with their adversaries, inflict a different kind of death on them when they took them prisoner, which was to bury them up to the waist, shoot the rest of their body full of arrows, and afterward hang them. They thought that these people from the other world, being men who had sown the knowledge of many vices among their neighbors and were much greater masters than themselves in every sort of wickedness, did not adopt this sort of vengeance without some reason, and that it must be more painful than their own; so they began to give up their old method and to follow this one.

I am not sorry that we notice the barbarous horror of such acts, but I am heartily sorry that, judging their faults rightly, we should be so blind to our own. I think there is more barbarity in eating a man alive than in eating him dead; and in tearing by tortures and the rack a body still full of feeling, in roasting a man bit by bit, in having him bitten and mangled by dogs and swine (as we have not only read but seen within fresh memory, not among ancient enemies, but among neighbors and fellow citizens, and what is worse, on the pretext of piety and religion), than in roasting and eating him after he is dead.

*   *   *

So we may well call these people barbarians, in respect to the rules of reason, but not in respect to ourselves, who surpass them in every kind of barbarity.

Their warfare is wholly noble and generous, and as excusable and beautiful as this human disease can be; its only basis among them is their rivalry in valor. They are not fighting for the conquest of new lands, for they still enjoy that natural abundance that provides them without toil and trouble with all necessary things in such profusion that they have no wish to enlarge their boundaries. They are still in that happy state of desiring only as much as their natural needs demand; anything beyond that is superfluous to them.

They generally call those of the same age, brothers; those who are younger, children; and the old men are fathers to all the others. These leave to their heirs in common the full possession of their property, without division or any other title at all than just the one that Nature gives to her creatures in bringing them into the world.

If their neighbors cross the mountains to attack them and win a victory, the gain of the victor is glory, and the advantage of having proved the master in valor and virtue; for apart from this they have no use for the goods of the vanquished, and they return to their own country, where they lack neither anything necessary nor that great thing, the knowledge of how to enjoy their condition happily and be content with it. These men of ours do the same in their turn. They demand of their prisoners no other ransom than that they confess and acknowledge their defeat. But there is not one in a whole century who does not choose to die rather than to relax a single bit, by word or look, from the grandeur of an invincible courage; not one who would not rather be killed and eaten than so much as ask not to be. They treat them very freely, so that life may be all the dearer to them, and usually entertain them with threats of their coming death, of the torments they will have to suffer, the preparations that are being made for that purpose, the cutting up of their limbs, and the feast that will be made at their expense. All this is done for the sole purpose of extorting from their lips some weak or base word, or making them want to flee, so as to gain the advantage of having terrified them and broken down their firmness. For indeed, if you take it the right way, it is in this point alone that true victory lies:

> It is no victory
> Unless the vanquished foe admits your mastery.
> Claudian

The Hungarians, very bellicose fighters, did not in olden times pursue their advantage beyond putting the enemy at their mercy. For having wrung a confession from him to this effect, they let him go unharmed and unransomed, except, at most, for exacting his promise never again to take up arms against them.

We win enough advantages over our enemies that are borrowed advantages, not really our own. It is the quality of a porter, not of valor, to have sturdier arms and legs; agility is a dead and corporeal quality; it is a stroke of luck to make our enemy stumble, or dazzle his eyes by the sunlight; it is a trick of art and technique, which may be found in a worthless coward, to be an able fencer. The worth and value of a man is in his heart and his will; there lies his real honor. Valor is the strength, not of legs and arms, but of heart and soul; it consists not in the worth of our horse or our weapons, but in our own. He who falls obstinate in his courage, *if he has fallen, he fights on his knees.* He who relaxes none of his assurance, no matter how great the danger of imminent death; who, giving up his soul, still looks firmly and scornfully at his enemy—he is beaten not by us, but by fortune; he is killed, not conquered.

*   *   *

To return to our story. These prisoners are so far from giving in, in spite of all that is done to them, that on the contrary, during the two or three months that they are kept, they wear a gay expression; they urge their captors to hurry and put them to the test; they defy them, insult them, reproach them with their cowardice and the number of battles they have lost to the prisoners' own people.

I have a song composed by a prisoner which contains this challenge, that they should all come boldly and gather to dine off him, for they will be eating at the same time their own fathers and grandfathers, who have served to feed and nourish his body. "These muscles," he says, "this flesh and these veins are your own, poor fools that you are. You do not recognize that the substance of your ancestors' limbs is still contained in them. Savor them well; you will find in them the taste of your own flesh." An idea that certainly does not smack of barbarity. Those that paint these people dying, and who show the execution, portray the prisoner spitting in the face of his slayers and scowling at them. Indeed, to the last gasp they never stop braving and defying their enemies by word and look. Truly here are real savages by our standards; for either they must be thoroughly so, or we must be; there is an amazing distance between their character and ours.

The men there have several wives, and the higher their reputation for valor the more wives they have. It is a remarkably beautiful thing about their marriages that the same jealousy our wives have to keep us from the affection and kindness of other women, theirs have to win this for them. Being more concerned for their husbands' honor than for anything else, they strive and scheme to have as many companions as they can, since that is a sign of their husbands' valor.

*   *   *

Three of these men, ignorant of the price they will pay some day, in loss of repose and happiness, for gaining knowledge of the corruptions of this side of the ocean; ignorant also of the fact that of this intercourse will come their ruin (which I suppose is already well advanced: poor wretches, to let

THE "ARMADA PORTRAIT" OF QUEEN ELIZABETH (C. 1588)　　　　　　　　　　　　　GEORGE GOWER

The English portraitist George Gower (1540–1596) became Sergeant Painter to Queen Eliz-abeth I of England in 1581. This—his most famous painting—notwithstanding, we know little of the artist or his career. A number of portraits survive from the period before his court appointment. Thereafter, he created portraits of many English aristocrats and supervised the decoration of the royal palace at Hampton Court. The "Armada Portrait" commemorates the defeat of the Spanish Armada in 1588. What elements of the painting indicate the importance of the sea and of naval power for England? Given that warfare was commonly understood to be "man's work," how does Gower handle the apparent contradiction of a warrior queen? How does he signal his patroness's firmness of command without making her masculine? How does he glorify Glorianna?

themselves be tricked by the desire for new things, and to have left the serenity of their own sky to come and see ours!)—three of these men were at Rouen, at the time the late King Charles IX was there. The king talked to them for a long time; they were shown our ways, our splendor, the aspect of a fine city. After that, someone asked their opinion, and wanted to know what they had found most amazing. They mentioned three things, of which I have forgotten the third, and I am very sorry for it; but I still remember two of them. They said that in the first place they thought it very strange that so many grown men, bearded, strong, and armed, who were around the king (it is likely that they were talking about the Swiss of his guard) should submit to obey a child, and that one of them was not chosen to command instead. Second (they have a way in their language of speaking of men as halves of one another), they had noticed that there were among us men full and gorged with all sorts of good things, and that their other halves were beggars at their doors, emaciated with hunger and poverty; and they thought it strange that these needy halves could endure such an injustice, and did not take the others by the throat, or set fire to their houses.

I had a very long talk with one of them; but I had an interpreter who followed my meaning so badly, and who was so hindered by his stupidity in taking in my ideas, that I could get hardly any satisfaction from the man. When I asked him what profit he gained from his superior position among his people (for he was a captain, and our sailors called him king), he told me that it was to march foremost in war. How many men followed him? He pointed to a piece of ground, to signify as many as such a space could hold; it might have been four or five thousand men. Did all his authority expire with the war? He said that this much remained, that when he visited the villages dependent on him, they made paths for him through the underbrush by which he might pass quite comfortably.

All this is not too bad—but what's the use? They don't wear breeches.

*   *   *

REVIEW QUESTIONS

1. What lessons does Montaigne draw from accounts of the New World?
2. Why do you suppose Montaigne chose cannibalism, of all possible topics, to compare European and American cultures?
3. How do Montaigne's ideas reflect the crisis of the iron century?
4. Are there any human constants for Montaigne?
5. Does he believe in a single human nature, a single ideal of virtue?

HUGO GROTIUS

FROM *On the Law of War and Peace*

Hugo Grotius (1583–1645) was a Dutch statesman, jurist, theologian, poet, philologist, and historian, a man of all-embracing knowledge whose writings were of fundamental importance in the formulation of international law. He was born in Delft, the son of the burgomaster and curator at the University of Leiden. Grotius was precocious; he matriculated at the University of Leiden at age eleven. By age fifteen, he had edited the encyclopedia of Martianus Capella and accompanied a diplomatic mission to the king of France, who described Grotius as the "miracle of Holland." He earned his doctorate in law at the University of Orléans and became a distinguished jurist at The Hague. In 1601, he was appointed historiographer of the States of Holland.

He wrote a number of minor but memorable legal treatises before publishing his great work, On the Law of War and Peace, in 1625. Grotius argued that the entire law of humankind was based on four fundamental precepts: neither a state nor an individual may attack another state or individual, neither a state nor an individual may appropriate what belongs to another state or individual, neither a state nor an individual may disregard treaties or contracts, and neither a state nor an individual may commit a crime. In the case of a violation of one of these precepts, compensation might be sought either by war or by individual action. These principles and the arguments that surrounded them significantly aided the development of a theory of state sovereignty and international relations in the early modern period. During the remainder of his life, Grotius remained involved in the political as well as the intellectual affairs of his day. Besides creating a vast corpus of written works, he participated in the government of the United Provinces of the Netherlands. He was eventually imprisoned for his support of Arminianism and managed to escape hidden in a trunk. He spent the rest of his life in exile, honored as one of the great intellectuals of the seventeenth century but unacknowledged by his own country.

From *The Rights of War and Peace*, by Hugo Grotius (Washington and London: M. Walter Dunne, 1901).

*   *   *

VIII

And here is the proper place for refuting the opinion of those, who maintain that, every where and without exception, the sovereign power is vested in the people, so that they have a right to restrain and punish kings for an abuse of their power. However there is no man of sober wisdom, who does not see the incalculable mischiefs, which such opinions have occasioned, and may still occasion; and upon the following grounds they may be refuted.

From the Jewish, as well as the Roman Law, it appears that any one might engage himself in private servitude to whom he pleased. Now if an individual may do so, why may not a whole people, for the benefit of better government and more certain protection, completely transfer their sovereign rights to one or more persons, without reserving any portion to themselves? Neither can it be al-

ledged that such a thing is not to be presumed, for the question is not, what is to be presumed in a doubtful case, but what may lawfully be done. Nor is it any more to the purpose to object to the inconveniences, which may, and actually do arise from a people's thus surrendering their rights. For it is not in the power of man to devise any form of government free from imperfections and dangers. As a dramatic writer says, "you must either take these advantages with those imperfections, or resign your pretensions to both."

Now as there are different ways of living, some of a worse, and some of a better kind, left to the choice of every individual; so a nation, "under certain circumstances, when for instance, the succession to the throne is extinct, or the throne has by any other means become vacant," may choose what form of government she pleases. Nor is this right to be measured by the excellence of this or that form of government, on which there may be varieties of opinion, but by the will of the people.

There may be many reasons indeed why a people may entirely relinquish their rights, and surrender them to another: for instance, they may have no other means of securing themselves from the danger of immediate destruction, or under the pressure of famine it may be the only way, through which they can procure support. For if the Campanians, formerly, when reduced by necessity surrendered themselves to the Roman people in the following terms:—"Senators of Rome, we consign to your dominion the people of Campania, and the city of Capua, our lands, our temples, and all things both divine and human," and if another people as Appian relates, offered to submit to the Romans, and were refused, what is there to prevent any nation from submitting in the same manner to one powerful sovereign? It may also happen that a master of a family, having large possessions, will suffer no one to reside upon them on any other terms, or an owner, having many slaves, may give them their liberty upon condition of their doing certain services, and paying certain rents; of which examples may be produced. Thus Tacitus, speaking of the German slaves, says, "Each has his own separate habitation, and his own household to govern. The master considers him as a tenant, bound to pay a certain rent in corn, cattle, and wearing apparel. And this is the utmost extent of his servitude."

Aristotle, in describing the requisites, which fit men for servitude, says, that "those men, whose powers are chiefly confined to the body, and whose principal excellence consists in affording bodily service, are naturally slaves, because it is their interest to be so." In the same manner some nations are of such a disposition that they are more calculated to obey than to govern, which seems to have been the opinion which the Cappadocians held of themselves, who when the Romans offered them a popular government, refused to accept it, because the nation they said could not exist in safety without a king. Thus Philostratus in the life of Apollonius, says, that it was foolish to offer liberty to the Thracians, the Mysians, and the Getae, which they were not capable of enjoying. The example of nations, who have for many ages lived happily under a kingly government, has induced many to give the preference to that form. Livy says, that the cities under Eumenes would not have changed their condition for that of any free state whatsoever. And sometimes a state is so situated, that it seems impossible it can preserve its peace and existence, without submitting to the absolute government of a single person, which many wise men thought to be the case with the Roman Republic in the time of Augustus Cæsar. From these, and causes like these it not only may, but generally does happen, that men, as Cicero observes in the second book of his offices, willingly submit to the supreme authority of another.

Now as property may be acquired by what has been already styled just war, by the same means the rights of sovereignty may be acquired. Nor is the term sovereignty here meant to be applied to monarchy alone, but to government by nobles, from any share in which the people are excluded. For there never was any government so purely popular, as not to require the exclusion of the poor, of strangers, women, and minors from the public councils. Some states have other nations under them, no less dependent upon their will, than subjects upon that of their sovereign princes. From whence arose that question, Are the Collatine people in their own power? And the Campanians, when they submitted to the Romans, are said to have passed under a foreign dominion. In the same manner Acarnania and Amphilochia are said to have been under the dominion of the Aetolians; Peraea and Caunus under that of the Rhodians; and Pydna was ceded by Philip to the Olynthians. And those towns, that had been under the Spartans, when they were delivered from their dominion, received the name of the free Laconians. The city of Cotyora is said by Xenophon to have belonged to the people of Sinope. Nice in Italy, according to Strabo, was adjudged to the people of Marseilles; and the island of Pithecusa to the Neapolitans. We find in Frontinus, that the towns of Calati and Caudium with their territories were adjudged, the one to the colony of Capua, and the other to that of Beneventum. Otho, as Tacitus relates, gave the cities of the Moors to the Province of Baetia. None of these instances, any more than the cessions of other conquered countries could be admitted, if it were a received rule that the rights of sovereigns are under the controul and direction of subjects.

Now it is plain both from sacred and profane history, that there are kings, who are not subject to the controul of the people in their collective body; God addressing the people of Israel, says, if thou shalt say, "I will place a king over me"; and to Samuel "Shew them the manner of the king, who shall reign over them." Hence the King is said to be anointed over the people, over the inheritance of the Lord, over Israel. Solomon is styled King over all Israel. Thus David gives thanks to God, for subduing the people under him. And Christ says, "the Kings of the nations bear rule over them." There is a well known passage in Horace, "Powerful sovereigns reign over their own subjects, and the supreme being over sovereigns themselves." Seneca thus describes the three forms of government, "Sometimes the supreme power is lodged in the people, sometimes in a senate composed of the leading men of the state, sometimes this power of the people, and dominion over the people themselves is vested in a single person." Of the last description are those, who, as Plutarch says, exercise authority not according to the laws, but over the laws. And in Herodutus, Otanes describes a monarch as one whose acts are not subject to controul. Dion Prusaeensis also and Pausanias define a monarchy in the same terms.

Aristotle says there are some kings, who have the same right, which the nation elsewhere possesses over persons and property. Thus when the Roman Princes began to exercise regal power, the people it was said had transferred all their own personal sovereignty to them, which gave rise to the saying of Marcus Antoninus the Philosopher, that no one but God alone can be judge of the Prince. Dion. L. liii. speaking of such a prince, says, "he is perfectly master of his own actions, to do whatever he pleases, and cannot be obliged to do any thing against his will." Such anciently was the power of the Inachidae established at Argos in Greece. For in the Greek Tragedy of the Suppliants, Aeschylus has introduced the people thus addressing the King: "You are the state, you the people; you the court

from which there is no appeal, you preside over the altars, and regulate all affairs by your supreme will." King Theseus himself in Euripides speaks in very different terms of the Athenian Republic; "The city is not governed by one man, but in a popular form, by an annual succession of magistrates." For according to Plutarch's explanation, Theseus was the general in war, and the guardian of the laws; but in other respects nothing more than a citizen. So that they who are limited by popular controul are improperly called kings. Thus after the time of Lycurgus, and more particularly after the institution of the Ephori, the Kings of the Lacedaemonians are said by Polybius, Plutarch, and Cornelius Nepos, to have been Kings more in name than in reality. An example which was followed by the rest of Greece. Thus Pausanias says of the Argives to the Corinthians, "The Argives from their love of equality have reduced their kingly power very low; so that they have left the posterity of Cisus nothing more than the shadow of Kings." Aristotle denies such to be proper forms of government, because they constitute only a part of an Aristocracy or Democracy.

Examples also may be found of nations, who have not been under a perpetual regal form, but only for a time under a government exempt from popular controul. Such was the power of the Amimonians among the Cnidians, and of the Dictators in the early periods of the Roman history, when there was no appeal to the people, from whence Livy says, the will of the Dictator was observed as a law. Indeed they found this submission the only remedy against imminent danger, and in the words of Cicero, the Dictatorship possessed all the strength of royal power.

It will not be difficult to refute the arguments brought in favour of the contrary opinion. For in the first place the assertion that the constituent always retains a controul over the sovereign power, which he has contributed to establish, is only true in those cases where the continuance and existence of that power depends upon the will and pleasure of the constituent: but not in cases where the power, though it might derive its origin from that constituent, becomes a necessary and fundamental part of the established law. Of this nature is that authority to which a woman submits when she gives herself to a husband. Valentinian the Emperor, when the soldiers who had raised him to the throne, made a demand of which he did not approve, replied; "Soldiers, your election of me for your emperor was your own voluntary choice; but since you have elected me, it depends upon my pleasure to grant your request. It becomes you to obey as subjects, and me to consider what is proper to be done."

Nor is the assumption true, that all kings are made by the people, as may be plainly seen from the instances adduced above, of an owner admitting strangers to reside upon his demesnes on condition of their obedience, and of nations submitting by right of conquest. Another argument is derived from a saying of the Philosophers, that all power is conferred for the benefit of the governed and not of the governing party. Hence from the nobleness of the end, it is supposed to follow, that subjects have a superiority over the sovereign. But it is not universally true, that all power is conferred for the benefit of the party governed. For some powers are conferred for the sake of the governor, as the right of a master over a slave, in which the advantage of the latter is only a contingent and adventitious circumstance. In the same manner the gain of a Physician is to reward him for his labour; and not merely to promote the good of his art. There are other kinds of authority established for the benefit of both parties, as for instance, the authority of a husband over his wife. Certain governments also, as those which are gained by right of conquest, may be established for the benefit of the sovereign; and yet convey no idea of tyranny, a word which in its original signification, implied nothing of arbitrary power or injustice, but only the government or authority of a Prince. Again, some governments may be formed for the advantage both of subjects and sovereign, as when a people, unable to defend themselves, put themselves under the protection and dominion of any powerful king. Yet it is not to be denied, but that in most governments the good of the subject is the chief object which is regarded: and that what Cicero has said after Herodotus, and Herodotus after Hesiod, is true, that Kings were appointed in order that men might enjoy complete justice.

Now this admission by no means goes to establish the inference that kings are amenable to the people. For though guardianships were invented for the benefit of wards, yet the guardian has a right to authority over the ward. Nor, though a guardian may for mismanagement be removed from his trust, does it follow that a king may for the same reason be deposed. The cases are quite different, the guardian has a superior to judge him; but in governments, as there must be some dernier resort, it must be vested either in an individual, or in some public body, whose misconduct, as there is no superior tribunal before which they can be called, God declares that he himself will judge. He either punishes their offences, should he deem it necessary; or permits them for the chastisement of his people.

This is well expressed by Tacitus: he says, "you should bear with the rapacity or luxury of rulers, as you would bear with drought, or excessive rains, or any other calamities of nature. For as long as men exist there will be faults and imperfections; but these are not of uninterrupted continuance, and they are often repaired by the succession of better times." And Marcus Aurelius speaking of subordinate magistrates, said, that they were under the controul of the sovereign: but that the sovereign was amenable to God. There is a remarkable passage in Gregory of Tours, where that Bishop thus addresses the King of France, "If any of us, Sir, should transgress the bounds of justice, he may be punished by you. But if you exceed them, who can call you to account? For when we address you, you may hear us if you please; but if you will not, who can judge you, except him, who has declared himself to be righteousness?" Among the maxims of the Essenes, Porphyry cites a passage, that "no one can reign without the special appointment of divine providence." Irenaeus has expressed this well, "Kings are appointed by him at whose command men are created; and their appointment is suited to the condition of those, whom they are called to govern." There is the same thought in the Constitutions of Clement, "You shall fear the King, for he is of the Lord's appointment."

Nor is it an objection to what has been said, that some nations have been punished for the offences of their kings, for this does not happen, because they forbear to restrain their kings, but because they seem to give, at least a tacit consent to their vices, or perhaps, without respect to this, God may use that sovereign power which he has over the life and death of every man to inflict a punishment upon the king by depriving him of his subjects.

*   *   *

REVIEW QUESTIONS

1. What is the relation between political power and will according to Grotius?
2. How does Grotius define the state? The sovereign state?
3. Where does Grotius locate sovereignty?
4. Does sovereignty have a moral component?
5. What is sovereignty's relation to property? To the good of the people?

FROM The Religious Peace of Augsburg

On September 25, 1555, the Religious Peace of Augsburg officially ended the religious struggle between the Catholic authorities, led by the Holy Roman Emperor Charles V, and the forces of the Schmalkaldic League, an alliance of Lutheran princes. It made permanent the division of Christian church within the Holy Roman Empire by establishing the principle that each ruling authority could determine the official religion of its realm, either Lutheranism in accordance with the Augsburg Confession or Catholicism. This principle was later referred to as cuius regio, eius religio. *Subjects had to submit or migrate.*

From *Select Documents*, edited by E. Reich (London: P. S. King: 1905), pp. 230–32.

*   *   *

15. In order to bring peace to the Holy Roman Empire of the Germanic Nation between the Roman Imperial Majesty and the Electors, Princes and Estates, let neither his Imperial Majesty nor the Electors, Princes, etc., do any violence or harm to any estate of the empire on the account of the Augsburg Confession, but let them enjoy their religious belief, liturgy and ceremonies as well as their estates and other rights and privileges in peace; and complete religious peace shall be obtained only by Christian means of amity, or under threat of punishment of the Imperial ban.

16. Likewise the Estates espousing the Augsburg Confession shall let all the Estates and Princes who cling to the old religion live in absolute peace and in the enjoyment of all their estates, rights, and privileges.

17. However, all such as do not belong to the two above named religions shall not be included in the present peace but be totally excluded from it.

18. And since it has proved to be a matter of great dispute what was to happen with the bishoprics, priories and other ecclesiastical benefices of such Catholic priests who would in course of time abandon the old religion, we have in virtue of the powers of Roman Emperors ordained as follows: where an archbishop, bishop or prelate or any other priest of our old religion shall abandon the same, his archbishopric, bishopric, prelacy and other benefices together with all their income and revenues which he has so far possessed, shall be abandoned

by him without any further objection or delay. The chapter and such [as] are entitled to it by common law or the custom of the place shall elect a person espousing the old religion who may enter on the possession and enjoyment of all the rights and incomes of the place without any further hindrance and without prejudging any ultimate amicable transaction of religion.

19. Some of the abbeys, monasteries and other ecclesiastical estates having been confiscated and turned into churches, schools, and charitable institutions, it is herewith ordained that such estates which their original owners had not possessed at the time of the Treaty of Passau [1552] shall be comprised in the present treaty of peace.

20. The ecclesiastical jurisdiction over the Augsburg Confession, dogma, appointment of ministers, church ordinances, and ministries hitherto practiced (but apart from all the rights of Electors, Princes and Estates colleges and monasteries to taxes in money or tithes) shall from now cease and the Augsburg Confession shall be left to the free and untrammeled enjoyment of their religion, ceremonies, appointment of ministers, as is stated in a subsequent separate article, until the final transaction of religion will take place.

*   *   *

23. No Estate shall try to persuade the subjects of other Estates to abandon their religion or protect them against their own magistrates. Such as had from olden times the rights of patronage are not included in the present article.

24. In case our subjects whether belonging to the old religion or the Augsburg Confession should intend leaving their homes with their wives and children in order to settle in another, they shall be hindered neither in the sale of their estates after due payment of the local taxes nor injured in their honor.

REVIEW QUESTIONS

1. Why do we call this document a "religious peace"?
2. What does the Religious Peace specifically allow?
3. What does the Religious Peace specifically disallow?
4. Does the Religious Peace constitute an act of toleration?
5. What is the particular significance of Article 18, the so-called ecclesiastical reservation?
6. What grounds for future conflicts does this "religious peace" contain?

15 ❧ EUROPEAN MONARCHIES AND ABSOLUTISM, 1660–1725

The word transition *best characterizes the economy and society of early modern Europe. Although the forms of production and exchange remained corporatist and traditional, elements of individualism and capitalism exerted increasingly strong influence. Accordingly, European society, which remained in large part hierarchical and patriarchal, showed signs of an emergent class structure. Evidence of these changes remained regional, being more marked in certain places and times than in others. Nonetheless, the evidence of such a transition can be seen nearly everywhere in Europe, driven by forces that gripped the entire continent.*

For much of this period, the population remained locked in a struggle to survive. Beset by periodic famine and disease, life seemed tenuous and expectancies were short. Given high and early mortality, marriages occurred relatively late in life, and truncated families were commonplace. Beginning in the late seventeenth century, however, mortality began to decline. By the eighteenth century, populations were expanding across Europe.

The principal cause of the change in demographic dynamics was an increase in food supply that can be attributed in turn to a gradual change in agricultural techniques. Throughout the early modern period, traditional agricultural practices gradually yielded to techniques known generally as scientific farming. Landowners who sought gain in the marketplaces of Europe needed more direct control over land use and the ability to respond flexibly to market conditions. As a result, they enclosed communal lands and turned to the kinds of husbandry that would increase harvests and profits. The result was an increased food supply that eventually freed Europe from its age-old cycle of feast and famine.

An increasing population put new pressures on industry by raising the demand for manufactured goods and supplying a ready labor force to produce them. Rural manufacturing in the form of extensive production networks, known as the putting-out system, increased industrial productivity and captured surplus population in industrial work processes. Those who could not find such employment fled to the cities, which also grew rapidly. It is interesting that urban manufacturing remained largely traditional, that is, highly regulated and guild based, throughout the early modern period.

The greatest single force for change between 1500 and 1800 was the expansion of long-distance commerce based on the development of overseas empires and the consolidation of central states. Capitalist practices had existed since the late fourteenth century at least, but the possibility of large profits from direct trade with Asia and the Americas offered new scope for their application. The development of mercantilist theories, which advocated the expansion of trade as a source of political power, combined with capitalist ambitions to facilitate global commerce. As a result, enterprises such as charter companies emerged on a larger scale. The supplies of goods traded and their profitability promoted the refinement of commercial facilities such as commodity exchanges, stock markets, and banking techniques. Moreover, the activities of these enterprises introduced new commodities in such volumes that new tastes emerged and old patterns of consumption were transformed.

Growing populations and expanding economies notwithstanding, the society of early modern Europe remained traditional. It was hierarchical in structure; each individual's place was fixed by birthright. Authority was patriarchal in nature, modeled on the supposedly absolute authority of the father within his family. Yet transition was also evident here. Economic change created mobility. New wealth encouraged social and political aspirations as bourgeois everywhere chafed under the exclusivity of the aristocracy and sought admission to their ranks. New poverty created a class of have-nots that challenged the established order and threatened its security.

Observers and theorists viewed the transformation of Europe's economy and society with some trepidation. In most instances, their responses were reactionary. They returned to notions of fatherhood for a model of authority that could withstand the changing times. As the period progressed, however, more and more theorists turned to philosophical reason to find general laws of human interaction that might be applied to govern economic and social behavior.

Absolutism refers to a particular conception of political authority that emerged in the wake of this transition and its attendant disorders in the later sixteenth century. It asserted order, where Europeans felt order had been undermined in political and social relations, by positing a vision of a society that had its apex in the person of a single ruler. At the center of all conceptions of absolutism was the will of the ruler: For all theorists, that will was absolute, not merely sovereign but determinative of all political relations. Such an understanding of the nature and operation of political power required a number of developments, not the least of which were a military and a bureaucracy to carry out the king's will.

By the end of the period, there would be calls for enlightened absolutism, whereby reason guided the will of the sovereign, but the will of the monarch was still the agent of political life. Among theorists, several emerged who countered the notion of absolute monarchy with that of sovereignty placed in the hands of property owners. Moreover, they argued persuasively that the exercise of sovereignty was limited in accordance with the principles of natural law.

No monarch in this period was truly absolute—such an effective expression of the will of the ruler requires greater technological and military support than any ruler prior to the nineteenth century could have. Many, however, were largely successful in representing themselves as the center of all political life in their states, nurturing courts and bureaucracies that reflected images of omniscient and powerful rulers. These same courts provided both a milieu and the financial support for philosophes such as Voltaire and scientists such as Galileo, even as those intellectuals were calling into question the ethics of and the social bases for absolutism.

JEAN BODIN

FROM *On Sovereignty*

Jean Bodin (1529–1596) was born a bourgeois in Angers. He entered a Carmelite monastery in 1545, apparently set on an ecclesiastical career, but obtained release from his vows around 1549. He pursued a course of study at the royal Collège de Quatre Langues in Paris. By 1550, he was well trained in humanist studies and went on to become one of the greatest scholars of his day. His continual search for religious truth placed him repeatedly under suspicion of heresy, but no clear evidence exists to support a conversion to Calvinism. Bodin continued his studies and attended the University of Toulouse, where he studied law during the 1550s. In 1561, he launched his public career by serving as an advocate before the parliament in Paris. Bodin soon came to the attention of high officials and dignitaries and received special commissions from the king as early as 1570. In 1571, he entered the service of Francis, duke of Alençon, a prince of the blood. During his service to Alençon, and in the aftermath of the St. Bartholomew's Day massacre, Bodin published his great work, Six livres de la république (1576), a systematic exposition of public law. It included an absolutist theory of royal government, from which the following selection is drawn. Bodin's theory was based on the controversial notion, which proved highly influential in the development of royal absolutism, that sovereignty was indivisible and that high powers of government could not be shared by separate agents or agencies. His notion that all governmental powers were concentrated in the king of France can be seen as a direct response to the anarchy of civil war that gripped the kingdom during the second half of the sixteenth century. In 1576, Bodin was chosen as a deputy for the Third Estate of the Estates-General of Blois. Though a royalist, Bodin opposed the civil wars that raged in France and became a leading spokesperson against royal requests for increased taxation and religious uniformity. It cost him royal favor and high office. With the death in 1584 of his patron, the duke of Alençon, Bodin's career in high politics ended. He retired to Laon, where he died.

From *On Sovereignty*, by Jean Bodin, edited by Julian H. Franklin (Cambridge: Cambridge University Press, 1992), pp. 46–50.

Book I

*   *   *

CHAPTER 8
ON SOVEREIGNTY

Sovereignty is the absolute and perpetual power of a commonwealth, which the Latins call *maiestas;* the Greeks *akra exousia, kurion arche,* and *kurion politeuma;* and the Italians *segnioria,* a word they use for private persons as well as for those who have full control of the state, while the Hebrews call it *tomech shévet*—that is, the highest power of command. We must now formulate a definition of sovereignty because no jurist or political philosopher has defined it, even though it is the chief point, and the one that needs most to be explained, in a treatise on the commonwealth. Inasmuch as we have said that a commonwealth is a just government, with sovereign power, of several households and of that which they have in common, we need to clarify the meaning of sovereign power.

*   *   *

We shall conclude, then, that the sovereignty of the monarch is in no way altered by the presence of the Estates. On the contrary, his majesty is all the greater and more illustrious when all his people publicly acknowledge him as sovereign, even though, in an assembly like this, princes, not wishing to rebuff their subjects, grant and pass many things that they would not consent to had they not been overcome by the requests, petitions, and just complaints of a harassed and afflicted people which has most often been wronged without the knowledge of the prince, who sees and hears only through the eyes, ears, and reports of others.

We thus see that the main point of sovereign majesty and absolute power consists of giving the law to subjects in general without their consent. Not to go to other countries, we in this kingdom have often seen certain general customs repealed by edicts of our kings without hearing from the Estates when the injustice of the rules was obvious. Thus the custom concerning the inheritance by mothers of their children's goods, which was observed in this kingdom throughout the entire region governed by customary law, was changed without assembling either the general or local estates. Nor is this something new. In the time of King Philip the Fair, the general custom of the entire kingdom, by which the losing party in a case could not be required to pay expenses, was suppressed by an edict without assembling the Estates.

*   *   *

CHAPTER 10
ON THE TRUE MARKS OF SOVEREIGNTY

Since there is nothing greater on earth, after God, than sovereign princes, and since they have been established by Him as His lieutenants for commanding other men, we need to be precise about their status so that we may respect and revere their majesty in complete obedience, and do them honor in our thoughts and in our speech. Contempt for one's sovereign prince is contempt toward God, of whom he is the earthly image. That is why God, speaking to Samuel, from whom the people had demanded a different prince, said "It is me that they have wronged."

To be able to recognize such a person—that is, a sovereign—we have to know his attributes, which are properties not shared by subjects. For if they were shared, there would be no sovereign prince. Yet the best writers on this subject have not treated this point with the clarity it deserves, whether from flattery, fear, hatred, or forgetfulness.

We read that Samuel, after consecrating the king that God had designated, wrote a book about the rights of majesty. But the Hebrews have written that the kings suppressed his book so that they could tyrannize their subjects. Melanchthon thus went astray in thinking that the rights of majesty were the abuses and tyrannical practices that Samuel pointed out to the people in a speech. "Do you wish to know," said Samuel, "the ways of tyrants? It is to seize the goods of subjects to dispose of at his pleasure, and to seize their women and their children in order to abuse them and to make them slaves." The word *mishpotim* as it is used in this passage does not mean rights, but rather practices and ways of doing things. Otherwise this good prince, Samuel, would have contradicted himself. For when accounting to the people for the stewardship that God had given him, he said, "Is there anyone among you who can say that I ever took gold or silver from him, or any present whatsoever?" And thereupon the whole people loudly praised him for never having done a wrong or taken anything from anyone no matter who.

*   *   *

We may thus conclude that the first prerogative of a sovereign prince is to give law to all in general and each in particular. But this is not sufficient. We have to add "without the consent of any other, whether greater, equal, or below him." For if the prince is obligated to make no law without the con-

sent of a superior, he is clearly a subject; if of an equal, he has an associate; if of subjects, such as the senate or the people, he is not sovereign. The names of grandees that one finds affixed to edicts are not put there to give the law its force, but to witness it and to add weight to it so that the enactment will be more acceptable. For there are very ancient edicts, extant at Saint Denys in France, issued by Philip I and Louis the Fat in 1060 and 1129 respectively, to which the seals of their queens Anne and Alix, and of Robert and Hugh, were affixed. For Louis the Fat, it was year twelve of his reign; for Adelaide, year six.

When I say that the first prerogative of sovereignty is to give law to all in general and to each in particular, the latter part refers to privileges, which are in the jurisdiction of sovereign princes to the exclusion of all others. I call it a privilege when a law is made for one or a few private individuals, no matter whether it is for the profit or the loss of the person with respect to whom it is decreed. Thus Cicero said, *Privilegium de meo capite latum est.* "They have passed," he said, "a capital privilege against me." He is referring to the authorization to put him on trial decreed against him by the commoners at the request of the tribune Clodius. He calls this the *lex Clodia* in many places, and he bitterly protests that privileges could be decreed only by the great Estates of the people as it was laid down by the laws of the Twelve Tables in the words: *Privilegia, nisi comitiis centuriatis irroganto, qui secus faxit capital esto.*[1] And all those who have written of regalian rights agree that only the sovereign can grant privileges, exemptions, and immunities, and grant dispensations from edicts and ordinances. In monarchies, however, privileges last only for the lifetime of the monarchs, as the emperor Tiberius, Suetonius reports, informed all those who had received privileges from Augustus.

*   *   *

---

[1] "Let no privileges be imposed except in the *comita centuriata;* let him who has done otherwise be put to death."

Book II

CHAPTER 5
WHETHER IT IS LAWFUL TO MAKE AN ATTEMPT
UPON THE TYRANT'S LIFE AND TO NULLIFY AND
REPEAL HIS ORDINANCES AFTER HE IS DEAD

Ignorance of the exact meaning of the term "tyrant" has led many people astray, and has been the cause of many inconveniences. We have said that a tyrant is someone who makes himself into a sovereign prince by his own authority—without election, or right of succession, or lot, or a just war, or a special calling from God. This is what is understood by tyrant in the writings of the ancients and in the laws that would have him put to death. Indeed, the ancients established great prizes and rewards for those who killed tyrants, offering titles of nobility, prowess, and chivalry to them along with statues and honorific titles, and even all the tyrant's goods, because they were taken as true liberators of the fatherland, or of the motherland, as the Cretans say. In this they did not distinguish, between a good and virtuous prince and a bad and wicked one, for no one has the right to seize the sovereignty and make himself the master of those who had been his companions, no matter what pretenses of justice and virtue he may offer. In strictest law, furthermore, use of the prerogatives reserved to sovereignty is punishable by death. Hence if a subject seeks, by whatever means, to invade the state and steal it from his king or, in a democracy or aristocracy, to turn himself from a fellow-citizen into lord and master, he deserves to be put to death. In this respect our question does not pose any difficulty.

*   *   *

At this point there are many questions one may ask, such as whether a tyrant, who I said may be justly killed without form or shape of trial, becomes legitimate if, after having encroached upon sovereignty by force or fraud, he has himself elected by the Estates. For it seems that the solemn act of election is an authentic ratification of the tyranny, an indication that the people have found it to their liking. But I say that it is nevertheless permissible to

kill him, and to do so by force unless the tyrant, stripping off his authority, has given up his arms and put power back into the hands of the people in order to have its judgment. What tyrants force upon a people stripped of power cannot be called consent. Sulla, for example, had himself made dictator for eighty years by the Valerian law, which he got published with a powerful army camped inside the city of Rome. But Cicero said that this was not a law. Another example is Caesar, who had himself made permanent dictator by the Servian law; and yet another is Cosimo de Medici who, having an army inside Florence, had himself elected duke. When objections were raised, he set off a volley of gunfire in front of the palace, which induced the lords and magistrates to get on with it more quickly.

*   *   *

So much then for the tyrant, whether virtuous or wicked, who makes himself a sovereign lord on his own authority. But the chief difficulty arising from our question is whether a sovereign prince who has come into possession of the state by way of election, or lot, or right of succession, or just war, or by a special calling from God, can be killed if he is cruel, oppressive, or excessively wicked. For that is the meaning given to the word tyrant. Many doctors and theologians, who have touched upon this question, have resolved that it is permissible to kill a tyrant without distinction, and some, putting two words together that are incompatible, have spoken of a king-tyrant (*roi tyran*), which has caused the ruin of some very fine and flourishing monarchies.

But to decide this question properly we need to distinguish between a prince who is absolutely sovereign and one who is not, and between subjects and foreigners. It makes a great difference whether we say that a tyrant can be lawfully killed by a foreign prince or by a subject. For just as it is glorious and becoming, when the gates of justice have been shut, for someone, whoever he may be, to use force in defense of the goods, honor, and life of those who have been unjustly oppressed—as Moses did when he saw his brother being beaten and mistreated and had no way of getting justice—so is it a most beautiful and magnificent thing for a prince to take up arms in order to avenge an entire people unjustly oppressed by a tyrant's cruelty, as did Hercules, who traveled all over the world exterminating tyrant-monsters and was deified for his great feats. The same was done by Dion, Timoleon, Aratus, and other generous princes, who obtained the title of chastisers and correctors of tyrants. This, furthermore, was the sole cause for which Tamerlane, prince of the Tartars, declared war on Bajazet, who was then besieging Constantinople, Tamerlane saying that he had come to punish him for tyranny and to deliver the afflicted peoples. He defeated Bajazet in a battle fought on the plateau of Mount Stella, and after he had killed and routed three hundred thousand Turks, he had the tyrant chained inside a cage until he died. In this case it makes no difference whether this virtuous prince proceeds against a tyrant by force, deception, or judicial means. It is however true that if a virtuous prince has seized a tyrant, he will obtain more honor by putting him on trial and punishing him as a murderer, parricide, and thief, rather than acting against him by the common law of peoples (*droit des gens*).

But as for subjects, and what they may do, one has to know whether the prince is absolutely sovereign, or is properly speaking not a sovereign. For if he is not absolutely sovereign, it follows necessarily that sovereignty is in the people or the aristocracy. In this latter case there is no doubt that it is permissible to proceed against the tyrant either by way of law if one can prevail against him, or else by way of fact and open force, if one cannot otherwise have justice. Thus the Senate took the first way against Nero, the second against Maximinus inasmuch as the Roman emperors were no more than princes of the republic, in the sense of first persons and chief citizens, with sovereignty remaining in the people and the Senate.

*　　*　　*

But if the prince is sovereign absolutely, as are the genuine monarchs of France, Spain, England, Scotland, Ethiopia, Turkey, Persia, and Moscovy—whose power has never been called into question and whose sovereignty has never been shared with

subjects—then it is not the part of any subject individually, or all of them in general, to make an attempt on the honor or the life of the monarch, either by way of force or by way of law, even if he has committed all the misdeeds, impieties, and cruelties that one could mention. As to the way of law, the subject has no right of jurisdiction over his prince, on whom all power and authority to command depends; he not only can revoke all the power of his magistrates, but in his presence, all the power and jurisdiction of all magistrates, guilds and corporations, Estates and communities, cease, as we have said and will say again even more elaborately in the proper place. And if it is not permissible for a subject to pass judgment on his prince, or a vassal on his lord, or a servant on his master—in short, if it is not permissible to proceed against one's king by way of law—how could it be licit to do so by way of force? For the question here is not to discover who is the strongest, but only whether it is permissible in law, and whether a subject has the power to condemn his sovereign prince.

A subject is guilty of treason in the first degree not only for having killed a sovereign prince, but also for attempting it, advising it, wishing it, or even thinking it. And the law finds this so monstrous [as to subject it to a special rule of sentencing]. Ordinarily, if someone who is accused, seized, and convicted dies before he has been sentenced, his personal status is not diminished, no matter what his crime, even if it was treason. But treason in the highest degree can never be purged by the death of the person accused of it, and even someone who was never accused is considered in law as having been already sentenced. And although evil thoughts are not subject to punishment, anyone who has thought of making an attempt on the life of his sovereign prince is held to be guilty of a capital crime, no matter whether he repented of it. In fact there was a gentleman from Normandy who confessed to a Franciscan friar that he had wanted to kill King Francis I but had repented of this evil wish. The Franciscan gave him absolution, but still told the king about it; he had the gentleman sent before the Parlement of Paris to stand trial, where he was condemned to death by its verdict and thereupon executed. And one cannot say that the court acted from fear, in view of the fact that it often refused to verify edicts and letters patent even when the king commanded it. And in Paris a man, named Caboche, who was completely mad and out of his senses, drew a sword against King Henry II without any effect or even attempt. He too was condemned to die without consideration of his insanity, which the law ordinarily excuses no matter what murder or crime the madman may have committed.

*   *   *

As for Calvin's remark that if there existed in these times magistrates especially constituted for the defense of the people and to restrain the licentiousness of kings, like the ephors in Sparta, the tribunes in Rome, and the demarchs in Athens, then those magistrates should resist, oppose, and prevent their licentiousness and cruelty—it clearly shows that it is never licit, in a proper monarchy, to attack a sovereign king, or defend one's self against him, or to make an attempt upon his life or honor, for he spoke only of democratic and aristocratic states. I have shown above that the kings of Sparta were but simple senators and captains. And when he speaks of the Estates, he says "possible," not daring to be definite. In any event there is an important difference between attacking the honor of one's prince and resisting his tyranny, between killing one's king and opposing his cruelty.

We thus read that the Protestant princes of Germany, before taking up arms against the emperor, asked Martin Luther if it were permissible. He frankly replied that it was not permissible no matter how great the charge of impiety or tyranny. But he was not heeded; and the outcome of the affair was miserable, bringing with it the ruin of some great and illustrious houses of Germany. *Quia nulla iusta causa videri potest,* said Cicero, *adversus patriam arma capiendi.*[2] Admittedly, it is quite certain that the sovereignty of the German Empire does not lie in the person of the emperor, as we shall explain in due course. But

since he is the chief, they could have taken up arms against him only with the consent of the Estates or its majority, which was not obtained. It would have been even less permissible against a sovereign prince.

I can give no better parallel than that of a son with respect to his father. The law of God says that he who speaks evil of his father or his mother shall be put to death. If the father be a murderer, a thief, a traitor to his country, a person who has committed incest or parricide, a blasphemer, an atheist, and anything else one wants to add, I confess that the entire gamut of penalties will not suffice for his punishment; but I say that it is not for his son to lay hands on him, *quia nulla tanta impietas, nullum tantum factum est quod sit parricidio vindicandum,*[3] as it was put by an orator of ancient times. And yet Cicero, taking up this question, says that love of country is even greater. Hence the prince of our country, being ordained and sent by God, is always more sacred and ought to be more inviolable than a father.

I conclude then that it is never permissible for a subject to attempt anything against a sovereign prince, no matter how wicked and cruel a tyrant he may be. It is certainly permissible not to obey him in anything that is against the law of God or nature—to flee, to hide, to evade his blows, to suffer death rather than make any attempt upon his life or honor. For oh, how many tyrants there would be if it were lawful to kill them! He who taxes too heavily would be a tyrant, as the vulgar understand it; he who gives commands that the people do not like would be a tyrant, as Aristotle defined a tyrant in the *Politics;* he who maintains guards for his security would be a tyrant; he who punishes conspirators against his rule would be a tyrant. How then should good princes be secure in their lives? I would not say that it is illicit for other princes to proceed against tyrants by force of arms, as I have stated, but it is not for subjects.

*   *   *

---

[2] "Because there can never be a just cause to take up arms against one's country."

[3] "Because there is no impiety so great, and no crime so great that it ought to be avenged by patricide."

REVIEW QUESTIONS

1. What, according to Bodin, is the definition of *sovereignty*?
2. In describing its prerogatives, would Bodin have agreed with Machiavelli?

3. Can sovereignty be mixed? Why?
4. Is it permissible to resist a tyrant?
5. Can a sovereign ruler be a tyrant?
6. May one resist a sovereign?

THOMAS MUN

FROM *England's Treasure by Forraign Trade. or The Ballance of our Forraign Trade is The Rule of our Treasure*

One of the chief exponents of the economic doctrine known as mercantilism, Sir Thomas Mun (1571–1641) was an English merchant, who served as director of the British East India Company and wrote on economic policy. A strong believer in state support for and direction of commerce, Mun strongly advocated its intervention to relieve the economic depression of the 1620s. He wrote his A Discourse of Trade from England unto the East-Indies *to defend the East India Company and its role in British economic stability. A second pamphlet,* England's Treasure by Forraign Trade, *stands as one of the first expressions of mercantilist principle. In it Mun proposed a set of "means to enrich a kingdom," which centered around ensuring that exports exceeded imports. Mun argued that a positive balance of trade would cause England's wealth steadily to increase. Published posthumously, this concise statement of mercantilist principle made Mun's reputation as a sophisticated economic thinker and became an important contribution to the development of economic theory.*

From *England's Treasure by Forraign Trade*, by Thomas Mun (New York: Macmillan, 1895), pp. ix–13, 22–27, 43–60.

*   *   *

Chapter II

THE MEANS TO ENRICH THIS KINGDOM, AND TO ENCREASE OUR TREASURE.

Although a Kindom may be enriched by gifts received, or by purchase taken from some other Nations, yet these are things uncertaim and of small consideration when they happen. The ordinary means therefore to encrease our wealth and treasure is by Forraign Trade, wherein wee must ever observe this rule; to sell more to strangers yearly than wee consume of theirs in value. For suppose that when this Kingdom is plentifully served with the Cloth, Lead, Tinn, Iron, Fish and other native commodities, we doe yearly export the overplus to forraign Countries to the value of twenty two hundred thousand pounds; by which means we are enabled beyond the Seas to buy and bring in forraign wares for our use and Consumption, to the value of twenty hundred thousand pounds; By this order duly kept in our trading, we may rest assured that this order duly kept in our trading, we may rest assured that the Kingdom shall be enriched yearly two hundred thousand pounds, which must be brought to us in so much Treasure; because that part of our stock which is not returned to us in wares must necessarily be brought home in treasure.

For in this case it cometh to pass in the stock of a Kingdom, as in the estate of a private man; who is supposed to have one thousand pounds yearly revenue and two thousand pounds of ready money in his Chest: If such a man through excess shall spend one thousand five hundred pounds per annum, all his ready mony will be gone in four years; and in the like time his said money will be doubled if he take a Frugal course to spend but five hundred pounds per annum; which rule never faileth likewise in the Commonwealth, but in some cases (of no great moment) which I will hereafter declare, when I shall shew by whom and in what manner this ballance of the Kingdoms account ought to be drawn up yearly, or so often as it shall please the State to discover how much we gain or lose by trade with forraign Nations. But first I will say something concerning those ways and means which will encrease our exportations and diminish our importations of wares; which being done, I will then set down some other arguments both affirmative and negative to strengthen that which is here declared, and thereby to shew that all the other means which are commonly supposed to enrich the Kingdom with Treasure are altogether insufficient and meer fallacies.

Chap. III.

THE PARTICULAR WAYS AND MEANS TO ENCREASE THE EXPORTATION OF OUR COMMODITIES, AND TO DECREASE OUR CONSUMPTION OF FORRAIGN WARES.

The revenue or stock of a Kingdom by which it is provided of forraign wares is either Natural or Artificial. The Natural wealth is so much only as can be spared from our own use and necessities to be exported unto strangers. The Artificial consists in our manufactures and industrious trading with forraign commodities, concerning which I will set down such particulars as may serve for the cause we have in hand.

1. First, although this Realm be already exceeding rich by nature, yet might it be much encreased by laying the waste grounds (which are infinite) into such employments as should no way hinder the present revenues of other manufactured lands, but hereby to supply our selves and prevent the importations of Hemp, Flax, Cordage, Tobacco, and divers other things which now we fetch from strangers to our great impoverishing.

2. We may likewise diminish our importations, if we would soberly refrain from excessive consumption of forraign wares in our diet and rayment, with such often change of fashions as is used, so much the more to encrease the waste and charge; which vices at this present are more notorious amongst us than in former ages. Yet might they easily be amended by enforcing the observation of such good laws as are strictly practised in other Countries against the said excesses; where likewise by commanding their own manufactures to be used, they prevent the coming in of others, without prohibition, or offence to strangers in their mutual commerce.

3. In our exportations we must not only regard our own superfluities, but also we must consider our neighbours necessities, that so upon the wares which they cannot want, nor yet be furnished thereof elsewhere, we may (besides the vent of the Materials) gain so much of the manufacture as we can, and also endeavour to sell them dear, so far forth as the high price cause not a less vent in the quantity. But the superfluity of our commodities which strangers use, and may also have the same from other Nations, or may abate their vent by the use of some such like wares from other places, and with little inconvenience; we must in this case strive to sell as cheap as possible we can, rather than to lose the utterance of such wares. For we have found of late years by good experience, that being able to sell our Cloth cheap in Turkey, we have greatly

encreased the vent thereof, and the Venetians have lost as much in the utterance of theirs in those Countreys, because it is dearer. And on the other side a few years past, when by excessive price of Wools our Cloth was exceeding dear, we lost at the least half our clothing for forraign parts, which since is no otherwise (well neer) recovered again than by the great fall of price for Wools and Cloth. We find that twenty five in the hundred less in the price of these and some other Wares, to the loss of private mens revenues, may raise above fifty upon the hundred in the quantity vented to the benefit of the publique. For when Cloth is dear, other Nations doe presently practise clothing, and we know they want neither art nor materials to this performance. But when by cheapness we drive them from this employment, and so in time obtain our dear price again, then do they also use their former remedy. So that by these alterations we learn, that it is in vain to expect a greater revenue of our wares than their condition will afford, but rather it concerns us to apply our endeavours to the times with care and diligence to help our selves the best we may, by making our cloth and other manufactures without deceit, which will encrease their estimation and use.

4. The value of our exportations likewise may be much advanced when we perform it our selves in our own Ships, for then we get only not the price of our wares as they are worth here, but also the Merchants gains, the changes of ensurance, and fraight to carry them beyond the seas. As for example, if the Italian Merchants should come hither in their own shipping to fetch our Corn, our red Herrings or the like, in the case the Kingdom should have ordinarily but 25s for a quarter of Wheat, and 20s for a barrel of red herrings, whereas if we carry these wares our selves into Italy upon the said rates, it is likely that wee shall obtain fifty shillings for the first, and forty shillings for the last, which is a great difference in the utterance or vent of the Kingdoms stock. And although it is true that the commerce ought to be free to strangers to bring in and carry out at their pleasure, yet nevertheless in many places the exportation of victuals and munition are either prohibited, or at least limited to be done onely by the people and Shipping of those places where they abound.

5. The frugal expending likewise of our own natural wealth might advance much yearly to be exported unto strangers; and if in our rayment we will be prodigal, yet let this be done with our own materials and manufactures, as Cloth, Lace, Imbroderies, Cutworks and the like, where the excess of the rich may be the employment of the poor, whose labours notwithstanding of this kind, would be more profitable for the Commonwealth, if they were done to the use of strangers.

6. The Fishing in his Majesties seas of England, Scotland and Ireland is our natural wealth, and would cost nothing but labour, which the Dutch bestow willingly, and thereby draw yearly a very great profit to themselves by serving many places of Christendom with our Fish, for which they return and supply their wants both of forraign Wares and Mony, besides the multitude of Mariners and Shipping, which hereby are maintain'd, whereof a long discourse might be made to shew the particular manage of this important business. Our Fishing plantation likewise in New England, Virginia, Groenland, the Summer Islands and the New-found-land, are of the like nature, affording much wealth and employments to maintain a great number of poor, and to encrease our decaying trade.

7. A Staple or Magazin for forraign Corn, Indico, Spices, Raw-silks, Cotton wool or any other commodity whatsoever, to be imported will encrease Shipping, Trade, Treasure, and the Kings customes, by exporting them again where need shall require, which course of Trading, hath been the chief means to raise Venice, Genoa, the low-Countreys, with some others; and for such a purpose England stands most commodiously, wanting nothing to this performance but our own diligence and endeavour.

8. Also wee ought to esteem and cherish those trades which we have in remote or far Countreys, for besides the encrease of Shipping and Mariners thereby, the wares also sent thither and receiv'd from thence are far more profitable unto the kingdom than by our trades neer at hand: As for example; suppose Pepper to be worth here two Shillings the pound constantly, if then it be brought from the Dutch at Amsterdam, the Merchant may give there twenty pence the pound, and gain well by the bargain; but if he fetch this Pepper from the East-indies,

he must not give above three pence the pound at the most, which is a mighty advantage, not only in that part which serveth for our own use, but also for that great quantity which (from hence) we transport yearly unto divers other Nations to be sold at a higher price: whereby it is plain, that we make a far greater stock by gain upon these Indian Commodities, than those Nations doe where they grow, and to whom they properly appertain, being the natural wealth of their Countries. But for the better understanding of this particular, we must ever distinguish between the gain of the Kingdom, and the profit of the Merchant; for although the Kingdom payeth no more for this Pepper than is before supposed, nor for any other commodity bought in forraign parts more than the stranger receiveth from us for the same, yet the Merchant payeth not only that price, but also the fraight, ensurance, customes and other charges which are exceeding great in these long voyages; but yet all these in the Kingdoms accompt are but commutations among our selves, and no Privation of the Kingdoms stock, which being duly considered, together with the support also of our other trades in our best Shipping to Italy, France, Turkey, and East Countreys and other places, by transporting and venting the wares which we bring yearly from the East Indies; It may well stir up our utmost endeavours to maintain and enlarge this great and noble business, so much importing the Publique wealth, Strength, and Happiness. Neither is there less honour and judgment by growing rich (in this manner) upon the stock of other Nations, than by an industrious encrease of our own means, especially when this later is advanced by the benefit of the former, as we have found in the East Indies by sale of much of our Tin, Cloth, Lead and other Commodities, the vent whereof doth daily encrease in those Countreys which formerly had no use of our wares.

9. It would be very beneficial to export money as well as wares, being done in trade only, it would encrease our Treasure; but of this I write more largely in the next Chapter to prove it plainly.

10. It were policie and profit for the State to suffer manufactures made of forraign Materials to be exported custome-free, as Velvets and all other wrought Silks, Fustians, thrown Silks and the like, it would emply very many poor people, and much encrease the value of our stock yearly issued into other Countreys, and it would (for this purpose) cause the more forraign Materials to be brought in, to the improvement of His Majesties Customes. I will here remember a notable increase in our manufacture of winding and twisting only of forraign raw Silk, which within 35 years to my knowledge did not employ more than 300 people in the City and suburbs of London, where at this present time it doth set on work above fourteen thousand souls, as upon diligent enquiry hath been credibly reported unto His Majesties Commissioners for Trade. and it is certain, that if the raid forraign Commodities might be exported from hence, free of custome, this manufacture would yet encrease very much, and decrease as fast in Italy and in the Netherlands. But if any man allege the Dutch proverb, Live and let others live; I answer, that the Dutchmen notwithstanding their own Proverb, doe not onely in these Kingdoms, encroach upon our livings, but also in other forraign parts of our trade (where they have power) they do hinder and destroy us in our lawful course of living, hereby taking the bread out of our mouth, which we shall never prevent by plucking the pot from their nose, as of late years too many of us do practise to the great hurt and dishonour of this famour Nation; We ought rather to imitate former times in taking sober and worthy courses more pleasing to God and suitable to our ancient reputation.

11. It is needful also not to charge the native commodities with too great customes, lest by indearing them to the strangers use, it hinder their vent. And especially forraign wares brought in to be transported again should be favoured, for otherwise that manner of trading (so much importing the good of the Commonwealth) cannot prosper nor subsist. But the Consumption of such forraign wares in the Realm may be the more charged, which will turn to the profit of the kingdom in the Ballance of the Trade, and thereby also enable the King to lay up the more Treasure out of his yearly incomes, as of this particular I intend to write more

fully in his proper place, where I shall shew how much money a Prince may conveniently lay up without the hurt of his subjects.

12. Lastly, in all things we must endeavour to make the most we can of our own, whether it be Natural or Artificial, And forasmuch as the people which live by the Arts are far more in number than they who are masters of the fruits, we ought the more carefully to maintain those endeavours of the multitude, in whom doth consist the greatest strength and riches both of the King and Kingdom: for where the people are many, and the arts good, there the traffique must be great, and the Countrey rich. The Italians employ a greater number of people; and get more money by their industry and manufactures of the raw Silks of the Kingdom of Cicilia, than the King of Spain and his Subjects have by the revenue of this rich commodity. But what need we fetch the example so far, when we know that our own natural wares doe not yield us so much profit as our industry? For Iron oar in the Mines is of no great worth, when it is compared with the employment and advantage it yields being digged, tried, transported, brought, sold, cast into Ordnance, Muskets, and many other instruments of war for offence and defence, wrought into Anchors, bolts, spikes, nayles and the like, for the use of Ships, Houses, Carts, Coaches, Ploughs, and other instruments for Tillage. Compare our Fleece-wools with our Cloth, which

requires shearing, washing, carding, spinning, Weaving, fulling, dying, dressing and other trimmings, and we shall find these Arts more profitable than the natural wealth, whereof I might instance other examples, but I will not be more tedious, for if I would amplify upon this and the other particulars before written, I might find matter sufficient to make a large volume, but my desire in all is only to prove what I propound with brevity and plainness.

REVIEW QUESTIONS

1. Why does Mun emphasize the importance of the state as an economic actor?
2. What qualities comprise the perfect merchant and do these differ from the qualities we expect today?
3. By what means might a state by enriched by trade?
4. What "forraign wares" does Mun consider and what "forraign wares" does he ignore?
5. How might a state increase its exports, and what would the consequences be?
6. Why are export prohibitions and trade barriers futile?
7. Are individuals unimportant in Mun's conception of economic practice?

THOMAS HOBBES

FROM *Leviathan*

Thomas Hobbes (1588–1679) was an English philosopher whose mechanistic and deterministic theories of political life were highly controversial in his own time. Born in Malmesbury, Hobbes attended Magdalen Hall, Oxford, and became tutor to William Cavendish, later the Earl of Devonshire, in 1608. With his student, he undertook several tours of the Continent, where he met and spoke with leading intellectual lights of the day, including Galileo and Descartes. Around 1637, he became interested in the constitutional struggle between Parliament and Charles I and set to work writing a "little treatise in English" in defense of the royal prerogative. Before its publication in 1650, the book circulated privately in 1640 under the title Elements of Law, Natural and Politic. *Fearing arrest by Parliament, Hobbes fled to Paris, where he remained for the next eleven years. While in exile, he served as math tutor to the Prince of Wales, later Charles II, from 1646 to 1648. His great work,* Leviathan *(1651), was a forceful argument for political absolutism. Its title, taken from the horrifying sea monster of the Old Testament, suggested the power and authority Hobbes thought necessary to compel obedience and order in human society. Strongly influenced by mechanical philosophy, he treated human beings as matter in motion, subject to certain physical, rational laws. According to Hobbes, people feared one another and lived in a state of constant competition and conflict. For this reason, they must submit to the absolute, supreme authority of the state, a social contract among selfish individuals moved by fear and necessity. Once delegated, that authority was irrevocable and indivisible. Ironically, these theories found favor neither with royalists nor with antiroyalists. Charles II believed that it was written in justification of the Commonwealth. The French feared its attacks on the papacy. After the Restoration, Parliament added* Leviathan *to a list of books to be investigated for atheistic tendencies. Despite frustrations over the reception of his political theories, Hobbes retained his intellectual vigor. At age eighty-four, he wrote an autobiography in Latin and translated the works of Homer into English. He died at age ninety-one.*

From *Leviathan*, by Thomas Hobbes, edited by E. Hershey Sneath (Needham, Eng.: Ginn Press, 1898).

*   *   *

Of the Causes, Generation, and Definition of a Commonwealth

The final cause, end, or design of men, who naturally love liberty and dominion over others, in the introduction of that restraint upon themselves in which we see them live in commonwealths is the foresight of their own preservation, and of a more contented life thereby; that is to say, of getting themselves out from that miserable condition of war which is necessarily consequent…to the natural passions of men when there is no visible power to keep them in awe and tie them by fear of punishment to the performance of their covenants, and observation of the laws of nature. . . .

For the laws of nature, as "justice," "equity," "modesty," "mercy," and, in sum, "doing to others as we would be done to," of themselves, without the terror of some power to cause them to be observed, are contrary to our natural passions, that carry us to partiality, pride, revenge, and the like. And covenants without the sword are but words, and of no strength to secure a man at all. Therefore, notwithstanding the laws of nature, which every one has then kept when he has the will to keep them, when he can do it safely, if there be no power erected, or not great enough for our security; every man will, and may lawfully rely on his own strength and art, for protection against all other men. And in all places where men have lived by small families, to rob and spoil one another has been a trade, and so far from being reputed against the law of nature that the greater spoils they gained, the greater was their honor; and men observed no other laws therein but the laws of honor; that is, to abstain from cruelty, leaving to men their lives and instruments of livelihood. And as small families did then, so now do cities and kingdoms, which are but greater families, for their own security enlarge their dominions upon all pretenses of danger and fear of invasion or assistance that may be given to invaders, and endeavor as much as they can to subdue or weaken their neighbors by open force and secret arts, for lack of other protection, justly; and are remembered for it in later ages with honor.

Nor is it the joining together of a small number of men that gives them this security, because in small numbers small additions on the one side or the other make the advantage of strength so great as is sufficient to carry the victory; and therefore gives encouragement to an invasion. The multitude sufficient to confide in for our security is not determined by any certain number but by comparison with the enemy we fear; and is then sufficient when the advantage of the enemy is not so visible and conspicuous to determine the event of war as to move him to attempt it.

And should there not be so great a multitude, even if their actions be directed according to their particular judgments and particular appetites, they can expect thereby no defense nor protection, neither against a common enemy nor against the injuries of one another. For being distracted in opinions concerning the best use and application of their strength, they do not help but hinder one another, and reduce their strength by mutual opposition to nothing; whereby they are easily not only subdued by a very few that agree together, but also, when there is no common enemy, they make war upon each other for their particular interests. For if we could suppose a great multitude of men to consent in the observation of justice and other laws of nature without a common power to keep them all in awe, we might as well suppose all mankind to do the same; and then there neither would be, nor need to be, any civil government or commonwealth at all, because there would be peace without subjection.

Nor is it enough for the security which men desire should last all the time of their life that they be governed and directed by one judgment for a limited time, as in one battle or one war. For though they obtain a victory by their unanimous endeavor against a foreign enemy, yet afterwards, when either they have no common enemy or he that by one group is held for an enemy is by another group held for a friend, they must needs, by the difference of their interests, dissolve, and fall again into a war among themselves.

It is true that certain living creatures, as bees and ants, live sociably one with another, which are therefore by Aristotle numbered among political creatures, and yet have no other direction, than their particular judgments and appetites; nor speech whereby one of them can signify to another what he thinks expedient for the common benefit; and therefore some man may perhaps desire to know why mankind cannot do the same. To which I answer:

First, that men are continually in competition for honor and dignity, which these creatures are not; and consequently among men there arises on the ground envy and hatred and finally war, but among these not so.

Secondly, that among these creatures the common good differ not from the private; and being by nature inclined to their private, they procure thereby the common benefit. But man, whose joy consists in comparing himself with other men, can relish nothing but what is eminent.

Thirdly, that these creatures, having not, as man, the use of reason, do not see nor think they see any fault, in the administration of their common business; whereas among men, there are very many that think themselves wiser and abler to govern the public better than the rest; and these strive to reform and innovate, one this way, another that way, and thereby bring it into distraction and civil war.

Fourthly, that these creatures, though they have some use of voice in making known to one another their desires and other affections, yet they lack that art of words by which some men can represent to others that which is good in the likeness of evil; and evil in the likeness of good; and augment or diminish the apparent greatness of good and evil, making men discontented and troubling their peace at their pleasure.

Fifthly, irrational creatures cannot distinguish between "injury" and "damage"; and, therefore, as long as they be at ease they are not offended with their fellows; whereas man is then most troublesome when he is most at ease; for then it is that he loves to show his wisdom and control the actions of them that govern the commonwealth.

Lastly, the agreement of these creatures is natural, that of men is by covenant only, which is artificial; and therefore, it is no wonder if there be somewhat else required besides covenant to make their agreement constant and lasting, which is a common power to keep them in awe and to direct their actions to the common benefit.

The only way to erect such a common power which may be able to defend them from the invasion of foreigners and the injuries of one another, and thereby to secure them in such sort so that by their own industry and by the fruits of the earth they may nourish themselves and live contentedly, is to confer all their power and strength upon one man, or upon one assembly of men that may reduce all their wills, by plurality of voices, unto one will; which is as much as to say, to appoint one man or assembly of men to bear their person; and every one to accept and acknowledge himself to be author of whatsoever he that so bears their person shall act or cause to be acted in those things which concern the common peace and safety, and therein to submit their wills every one to his will, and their judgments to his judgment. This is more than consent or concord; it is a real unity of them all in one and the same person, made by covenant of every man with every man, in such manner as if every man should say to every man, "I authorize and give up my right of governing myself to this man, or to this assembly of men, on this condition, that you give up your right to him and authorize all his actions in like manner." This done, the multitude so united in one person is called a "commonwealth," in Latin *civitas*. This is the generation of that great "leviathan," or rather, to speak more reverently, of that "mortal god," to which we owe, under the "immortal God," our peace and defense. For by this authority, given him by every particular man in the commonwealth, he has the use of so much power and strength conferred on him that, by terror thereof, he is enabled to form the wills of them all to peace at home and mutual aid against their enemies abroad. And in him consists the essence of the commonwealth, which, to define it, is "one person, of whose acts a great multitude, by mutual covenants one with another, have made themselves the author, to the end he may use the strength and means of them all as he shall think expedient for their peace and common defense."

And he that carries this person is called "sovereign" and said to have "sovereign power"; and every one besides, his "subject."

The attaining to this sovereign power is by two ways. One, by natural force, as when a man makes his children to submit themselves and their children to his government, as being able to destroy them if they refuse; or by war subdues his enemies to his will, giving them their lives on that condition. The other is when men agree among themselves to submit to some man or assembly of men voluntarily, on confidence that they will be protected by him against all others. This latter, may be called a political commonwealth, or commonwealth by "institution," and the former, a commonwealth by "acquisition." . . .

*   *   *

Of the Office of the Sovereign Representative

The office of the sovereign, be it a monarch or an assembly, consists in the end for which he was trusted with the sovereign power, namely, the securing of "the safety of the people"; to which he is obliged by the law of nature, and to render an account thereof to God, the author of that law, and to none but him. But by safety here is not meant a bare preservation but also all other contentments of life which every man by lawful industry, without danger or hurt to the commonwealth, shall acquire to himself.

And this is to be done, not by care applied to individuals further than their protection from injuries when they shall complain, but by a general provision contained in public instruction, both of doctrine and example, and in the making and executing of good laws to which individual persons may apply their own cases.

And because, if the essential rights of sovereignty . . . be taken away, the commonwealth is thereby dissolved and every man returns into the condition and calamity of a war with every other man, which is the greatest evil that can happen in this life; it is the office of the sovereign, to maintain those rights entire, and consequently against his duty, first, to transfer to another or to lay from himself any of them. For he that deserts the means deserts the ends; and he deserts the means when, being the sovereign, he acknowledges himself subject to the civil laws and renounces the power of supreme judicature, or of making war or peace by his own authority; or of judging of the necessities of the commonwealth; or of levying money and soldiers when and as much as in his own conscience he shall judge necessary; or of making officers and ministers both of war and peace; or of appointing teachers and examining what doctrines are conformable or contrary to the defense, peace, and good of the people. Secondly, it is against his duty to let the people be ignorant or misinformed of the grounds and reasons of those his essential rights, because thereby men are easy to be seduced and drawn to resist him when the commonwealth shall require their use and exercise.

And the grounds of these rights have the need to be diligently and truly taught, because they cannot be maintained by any civil law or terror of legal punishment. For a civil law that shall forbid rebellion (and such is all resistance to the essential rights of the sovereignty), is not, as a civil law, any obligation, but by virtue only of the law of nature that forbids the violation of faith; which natural obligation if men know not, they cannot know the right of any law the sovereign makes. And for the punishment, they take it but for an act of hostility which when they think they have strength enough, they will endeavor by acts of hostility, to avoid.

*   *   *

To the care of the sovereign belongs the making of good laws. But what is a good law? By a good law I mean not a just law; for no law can be unjust. The law is made by the sovereign power, and all that is done by such power is warranted and owned by every one of the people; and that which every man will have so, no man can say is unjust. It is in the laws of a commonwealth as in the laws of gaming; whatsoever the gamesters all agree on is injustice to none of them. A good law is that which is "needed" for the "good of the people" and "perspicuous."

For the use of laws, which are but rules authorized, is not to bind the people from all voluntary actions but to direct and keep them in such a motion as not to hurt themselves by their own impetuous desires, rashness, or indiscretion; as hedges are set not to stop travellers, but to keep them in their way. And, therefore, a law that is not needed, having not the true end of a law, is not good. A law may be conceived to be good when it is for the benefit of the sovereign, though it be not necessary for the people, but it is not so. For the good of the sovereign and people cannot be separated. It is a weak sovereign, that has weak subjects, and a weak people, whose sovereign lacks power to rule them at his will. Unnecessary laws are not good laws but traps for money; which, where the right of sovereign power is acknowledged, are superfluous, and where it is not acknowledged, insufficient to defend the people. . . .

It belongs also to the office of the sovereign to make a right application of punishments and rewards. And seeing the end of punishing is not revenge and discharge of anger, but correction, either of the offender, or of others by his example; the severest punishments are to be inflicted for those crimes that are of most danger to the public; such as are those which proceed from malice to the government established; those that spring from contempt of justice; those that provoke indignation in the multitude; and those which, unpunished, seem authorized, as when they are committed by sons, servants, or favorites of men in authority. For indignation carries men not only against the actors and authors of injustice, but against all power that is likely to protect them; as in the case of Tarquin, when for the insolent act of one of his sons he was driven out of Rome and the monarchy itself dissolved. But crimes of infirmity, such as are those which proceed from great provocation, from great fear, great need, or from ignorance, whether the fact be a great crime or not, there is place many times for leniency without prejudice to the commonwealth; and leniency, when there is such place for it, is required by the law of nature. The punishment of the leaders and teachers in a commotion, not the poor seduced people, when they are punished, can profit the commonwealth by their example. To be severe to the people is to punish that ignorance which may in great part be imputed to the sovereign, whose fault it was that they were no better instructed.

In like manner it belongs to the office and duty of the sovereign, to apply his rewards so that there may arise from them benefit to the commonwealth, wherein consists their use, and end; and is then done when they that have well served the commonwealth are, with as little expense of the common treasure as is possible, so well recompensed as others thereby may be encouraged both to serve the same as faithfully as they can and to study the arts by which they may be enabled to do it better. To buy with money or preferment from a popular ambitious subject to be quiet and desist from making ill impressions in the minds of the people has nothing of the nature of reward (which is ordained not for disservice, but for service past), nor a sign of gratitude, but of fear; nor does it tend to the benefit but to the damage of the public. It is a contention with ambition like that of Hercules with the monster Hydra which, having many heads, for every one that was vanquished there grew up three. For in like manner, when the stubbornness of one popular man is overcome with reward there arise many more, by the example, that do the same mischief in hope of like benefit; and as all sorts of manufacture, so also malice increases by being salable. And though sometimes a civil war may be deferred by such ways as that, yet the danger grows still the greater and the public ruin more assured. It is therefore against the duty of the sovereign, to whom the public safety is committed, to reward those that aspire to greatness by disturbing the peace of their country, and not rather to oppose the beginnings of such men with a little danger than after a longer time with greater.

*   *   *

When the sovereign himself is popular, that is, revered and beloved of his people, there is no danger at all from the popularity of a subject. For soldiers are never so generally unjust as to side with their captain though they love him, against their sovereign, when they love not only his person but also his cause. And therefore those who by violence have at any time suppressed the power of their lawful sovereign, before they could settle themselves in his place have been always put to the trouble of contriving their titles to save the people from the shame of receiving them. To have a known right to sovereign power is so popular a quality as he that has it needs no more, for his own part, to turn the hearts of his subjects to him but that they see him able absolutely to govern his own family; nor, on the part of his enemies, but a disbanding of their armies. For the greatest and most active part of mankind has never hitherto been well contented with the present.

Concerning the offices of one sovereign to another, which are comprehended in that law which is commonly called the "law of nations," I need not say anything in this place because the law of nations and the law of nature is the same thing. And every sovereign has the same right, in securing the safety of his people that any particular man can have in securing the safety of his own body. And the same law that dictates to men that have no civil government what they ought to do and what to avoid in regard of one another dictates the same to commonwealths, that is, to the consciences of sovereign princes and sovereign assemblies, there being no court of natural justice but in the conscience only; where not man but God reigns whose laws, such of them as oblige all mankind, in respect of God as he is the author of nature are "natural," and in respect of the same God as he is King of kings are "laws."

*   *   *

REVIEW QUESTIONS

1. What is Hobbes's view of human nature?
2. What, according to Hobbes, motivates human beings?
3. What, according to Hobbes, is the purpose of the state?
4. Why do human beings come together to form a political society?
5. What are the responsibilities of the sovereign?
6. What is the sovereign's highest obligation?
7. Does Hobbes hold out any hope that the state can improve human nature?

Ambassadeurs Siamois devant Louis XIV.
Ambasciatori di Siam dinanzi a Luigi XIV.   Embajadores de Siam delante de Luis XIV.

SIAMESE EMBASSY TO LOUIS XIV, IN 1686 (1686)

This unattributed engraving commemorates the Siamese embassy to the court of Louis XIV in 1686. It may be a copy of a similar image, created by Nicolas III Larmessin (c. 1640–1725), a member of the de Larmessin (also: de L'Armessin) family, a famous French dynasty of engravers, printers, and booksellers who were active during the seventeenth and eighteenth centuries. It portrays at once the increasing range of international relations and diplomacy, and the centrality of European imperial pretentions in the seventeenth century. What might have made this event a fit subject for an engraving? How does the artist glorify the French king? What elements of court ritual in an age of absolutism are readily visible? In a period of burgeoning imperialism, what propaganda purposes might this image have served?

Coffee House Society

Coffee is an example of the impact of overseas trade and colonial empire on the con-
sumption and lifestyle of ordinary Europeans. The bean's historical origins are
shrouded in legend. What seems clear is that they were taken to Arabia from Africa
during the fifteenth century and placed under cultivation. Introduced into Europe
during the sixteenth and seventeenth centuries, they gained almost immediate popu-
larity. Served at coffeehouses, the first of which was established in London around
1650, coffee's consumption became an occasion for transacting political, social, com-
mercial, or literary business. So great was the demand for coffee that European mer-
chants took it from the Arabian Peninsula to Java, Indonesia, and the Americas. The
following descriptions by two anonymous authors give some sense of the ways in
which colonial products shaped European culture in the seventeenth century.

From *Selections from the Sources of English History*, edited by Charles W. Colby (New York:
Longmans, Green, 1899), pp. 208–12.

*   *   *

1673

A coffee-house is a lay conventicle, good-fellowship
turned puritan, ill-husbandry in masquerade,
whither people come, after toping all day, to purchase, at the expense of their last penny, the repute
of sober companions: A Rota [club] room, that, like
Noah's ark, receives animals of every sort, from the
precise diminutive band, to the hectoring cravat
and cuffs in folio: a nursery for training up the
smaller fry of virtuosi in confident tattling, or a
cabal of kittling [carping] critics that have only
learned to spit and mew; a mint of intelligence,
that, to make each man his pennyworth, draws out
into petty parcels, what the merchant receives in
bullion: he, that comes often, saves twopence a
week in Gazettes, and has his news and his coffee
for the same charge, as at a threepenny ordinary
they give in broth to your chop of mutton; it is an
exchange, where haberdashers of political small-
wares meet, and mutually abuse each other, and
the public, with bottomless stories, and headless
notions; the rendezvous of idle pamphlets, and per-

sons more idly employed to read them; a high
court of justice, where every little fellow in a cam-
let cloak takes upon him to transpose affairs both
in church and state, to show reasons against acts of
parliament, and condemn the decrees of general
councils.

*   *   *

As you have a hodge-podge of drinks, such too
is your company, for each man seems a leveller, and
ranks and files himself as he lists, without regard to
degrees or order; so that often you may see a silly
fop and a worshipful justice, a griping rook and a
grave citizen, a worthy lawyer and an errant pick-
pocket, a reverend nonconformist and a canting
mountebank, all blended together to compose an
oglio [medley] of impertinence.

If any pragmatic, to show himself witty or
eloquent, begin to talk high, presently the further
tables are abandoned, and all the rest flock round
(like smaller birds, to admire the gravity of the
madge-howlet [barn-owl]). They listen to him
awhile with their mouths, and let their pipes go
out, and coffee grow cold, for pure zeal of attention, but on the sudden fall all a yelping at once

with more noise, but not half so much harmony, as a pack of beagles on the full cry. To still this bawling, up starts Capt. All-man-sir, the man of mouth, with a face as blustering as that of Æolus and his four sons, in painting, and a voice louder than the speaking trumpet, he begins you the story of a sea-fight; and though he never were further, by water, than the Bear-garden, . . . yet, having pirated the names of ships and captains, he persuades you himself was present, and performed miracles; that he waded knee-deep in blood on the upper-deck, and never thought to serenade his mistress so pleasant as the bullets whistling; how he stopped a vice-admiral of the enemy's under full sail; till she was boarded, with his single arm, instead of grappling-irons, and puffed out with his breath a fire-ship that fell foul on them. All this he relates, sitting in a cloud of smoke, and belching so many common oaths to vouch it, you can scarce guess whether the real engagement, or his romancing account of it, be the more dreadful: however, he concludes with railing at the conduct of some eminent officers (that, perhaps, he never saw), and protests, had they taken his advice at the council of war, not a sail had escaped us.

He is no sooner out of breath, but another begins a lecture on the Gazette, where, finding several prizes taken, he gravely observes, if this trade hold, we shall quickly rout the Dutch, horse and foot, by sea: he nicknames the Polish gentlemen wherever he meets them, and enquires whether Gayland and Taffaletta be Lutherans or Calvinists? *stilo novo* he interprets a vast new stile, or turnpike, erected by his electoral highness on the borders of Westphalia, to keep Monsieur Turenne's cavalry from falling on his retreating troops: he takes words by the sound, without examining their sense: Morea he believes to be the country of the Moors, and Hungary a place where famine always keeps her court, nor is there anything more certain, than that he made a whole room full of fops, as wise as himself, spend above two hours in searching the map for Aristocracy and Democracy, not doubting but to have found them there, as well as Dalmatia and Croatia.

1675

Though the happy Arabia, nature's spicery, prodigally furnishes the voluptuous world with all kinds of aromatics, and divers other rarities; yet I scarce know whether mankind be not still as much obliged to it for the excellent fruit of the humble coffee-shrub, as for any other of its more specious productions: for, since there is nothing we here enjoy, next to life, valuable beyond health, certainly those things that contribute to preserve us in good plight and eucrasy, and fortify our weak bodies against the continual assaults and batteries of disease, deserve our regards much more than those which only gratify a liquorish palate, or otherwise prove subservient to our delights. As for this salutiferous berry, of so general a use through all the regions of the east, it is sufficiently known, when prepared, to be moderately hot, and of a very drying attenuating and cleansing quality; whence reason infers, that its decoction must contain many good physical properties, and cannot but be an incomparable remedy to dissolve crudities, comfort the brain, and dry up ill humours in the stomach. In brief, to prevent or redress, in those that frequently drink it, all cold drowsy rheumatic distempers whatsoever, that proceed from excess of moisture, which are so numerous, that but to name them would tire the tongue of a mountebank.

*   *   *

Lastly, for diversion. It is older than Aristotle, and will be true, when Hobbes is forgot, that man is a sociable creature, and delights in company. Now, whither shall a person, wearied with hard study, or the laborious turmoils of a tedious day, repair to refresh himself? Or where can young gentlemen, or shop-keepers, more innocently and advantageously spend an hour or two in the evening, than at a coffee-house? Where they shall be sure to meet company, and, by the custom of the house, not such as at other places, stingy and reserved to themselves, but free and communicative; where every man may modestly begin his story, and propose to, or answer another, as he thinks fit. Discourse is *pabulum animi, cos ingenii;*

the mind's best diet, and the great whetstone and incentive of ingenuity; by that we come to know men better than by their physiognomy. *Loquere, ut te videam,* speak, that I may see thee, was the philosopher's adage. To read men is acknowledged more useful than books; but where is there a better library for that study, generally, than here, amongst such a variety of humours, all expressing themselves on divers subjects, according to their respective abilities?

*   *   *

In brief, it is undeniable, that, as you have here the most civil, so it is, generally, the most intelligent society; the frequenting whose converse, and observing their discourses and department, cannot but civilise our manners, enlarge our understandings, refine our language, teach us a generous confidence and handsome mode of address, and brush off that *pudor rubrusticus* (as, I remember, Tully somewhere calls it), that clownish kind of modesty frequently incident to the best natures, which renders them sheepish and ridiculous in company.

So that, upon the whole matter, spite of the idle sarcasms and paltry reproaches thrown upon it, we may, with no less truth than plainness, give this brief character of a well-regulated coffee-house (for our pen disdains to be an advocate for any sordid holes, that assume that name to cloak the practice of debauchery), that it is the sanctuary of health, the nursery of temperance, the delight of frugality, an academy of civility, and free-school of ingenuity.

*   *   *

REVIEW QUESTIONS

1. How would you describe coffeehouse society in the late seventeenth century?
2. What is the attitude of each of our two anonymous authors? How and why do they differ?
3. What is the significance of reading the gazette?
4. What are the virtues of coffee?
5. How could coffee drinking be considered a vice in early modern Europe?

JOHN LOCKE

FROM *Two Treatises of Government*

John Locke (1632–1704) was an English philosopher whose thought contributed to the Enlightenment. He grew up in a liberal Puritan family, the son of an attorney who fought in the civil war against Charles I, and attended Christ Church College, Oxford. He received his bachelor of arts in 1656, lectured in classical languages while earning his master of arts, and entered Oxford's medical school to avoid being forced to join the clergy. In 1666, Locke attached himself to the household of the Earl of Shaftesbury and his fortunes to the liberal Whig Party. Between 1675 and 1679, he lived in France, where he made contact with leading intellectuals of the late seventeenth century. On his return to England, he plunged into the controversy surrounding the succession of James II, an avowed Catholic with absolutist pretensions, to the throne of his brother, Charles II. Locke's patron, Shaftesbury, was imprisoned for his opposition, and Locke went into exile in 1683. Though he was involved to some extent in the Glorious Revolution of 1688, he returned to England in 1689, in the entourage of Mary, Princess of Orange, who would assume the throne with her husband, William. The Two Treatises of Government *(1690) were published anonymously, although readers commonly assumed Locke's authorship. More interesting is the time at which they were written. Most scholars assume that they were written immediately before publication, as a justification of the revolution just completed. Other scholars believe, however, that the treatises were written from exile as a call to revolution, a riskier, much more inflammatory project. The first treatise comprises a long attack on Robert Filmer's* Patriarcha, *a denial of the patriarchal justification of the absolute monarch. The second treatise constructs in the place of patriarchy a theory of politics based on natural law, which provides the foundation of human freedom. The social contract creates a political structure by consent of the governed and designed to preserve those freedoms established in natural law. Locke's treatises inspired the political theories of the Enlightenment.*

From *First Treatise* in *Two Treatises of Government*, by John Locke (London: Whitmore and Fenn, 1821).

*   *   *

Chapter VI
Of Paternal Power

It may perhaps be censured an impertinent criticism in a discourse of this nature to find fault with words and names that have obtained in the world. And yet possibly it may not be amiss to offer new ones when the old are apt to lead men into mistakes, as this of paternal power probably has done, which seems so to place the power of parents over their children wholly in the father, as if the mother had no share in it; whereas if we consult reason or revelation, we shall find she has an equal title, which may give one reason to ask whether this might not be more properly called parental power? For whatever obligation Nature and the right of generation lays on children, it must certainly bind them equal to both the concurrent causes of it. And accordingly we see the positive law of God everywhere joins them together without distinction, when it commands the obedience of children: "Honour thy father and thy mother"; "Whosoever curseth his father or his mother"; "Ye shall fear every man his mother and his

father"; "Children, obey your parents" etc., is the style of the Old and New Testament.

*   *   *

Though I have said above "That all men by nature are equal," I cannot be supposed to understand all sorts of "equality." Age or virtue may give men a just precedency. Excellency of parts and merit may place others above the common level. Birth may subject some, and alliance or benefits others, to pay an observance to those to whom Nature, gratitude, or other respects, may have made it due; and yet all this consists with the equality which all men are in in respect of jurisdiction or dominion one over another, which was the equality I there spoke of as proper to the business in hand, being that equal right that every man hath to his natural freedom, without being subjected to the will or authority of any other man.

Children, I confess, are not born in this full state of equality, though they are born to it. Their parents have a sort of rule and jurisdiction over them when they come into the world, and for some time after, but it is but a temporary one. The bonds of this subjection are like the swaddling clothes they are wrapt up in and supported by in the weakness of their infancy. Age and reason as they grow

PALACE AND GARDENS OF VERSAILLES (1668)   PIERRE PATEL

Patel's famous print of the palace at Versailles captures the grand scale of monarchy in the seventeenth century. Note not only the size of the palace but also its location in the center of carefully planned gardens, boulevards, and buildings. Versailles was truly a theater for the display of political power. Why was such a theater of power necessary? What can be learned from the iconography of power that was built into Versailles, such as the function of gardens or the location of boulevards or alleys or broad open spaces? How might Versailles have functioned not only as a theater of power but also as a prison for the powerful?

up loosen them, till at length they drop quite off, and leave a man at his own free disposal.

Adam was created a perfect man, his body and mind in full possession of their strength and reason, and so was capable from the first instance of his being to provide for his own support and preservation, and govern his actions according to the dictates of the law of reason God had implanted in him. From him the world is peopled with his descendants, who are all born infants, weak and helpless, without knowledge or understanding. But to supply the defects of this imperfect state till the improvement of growth and age had removed them, Adam and Eve, and after them all parents were, by the law of Nature, under an obligation to preserve, nourish and educate the children they had begotten, not as their own workmanship, but the workmanship of their own Maker, the Almighty, to whom they were to be accountable for them.

The law that was to govern Adam was the same that was to govern all his posterity, the law of reason. But his offspring having another way of entrance into the world, different from him, by a natural birth, that produced them ignorant, and without the use of reason, they were not presently under that law. For nobody can be under a law that is not promulgated to him; and this law being promulgated or made known by reason only, he that is not come to the use of his reason cannot be said to be under this law; and Adam's children being not presently as soon as born under this law of reason, were not presently free. For law, in its true notion, is not so much the limitation as the direction of a free and intelligent agent to his proper interest, and prescribes no farther than is for the general good of those under that law. Could they be happier without it, the law, as a useless thing, would of itself vanish; and that ill deserves the name of confinement which hedges us in only from bogs and precipices. So that however it may be mistaken, the end of law is not to abolish or restrain, but to preserve and enlarge freedom. For in all the states of created beings, capable of laws, where there is no law there is no freedom. For liberty is to be free from restraint and violence from others, which cannot be where

there is no law; and is not, as we are told, "a liberty for every man to do what he lists." For who could be free, when every other man's humour might domineer over him? But a liberty to dispose and order freely as he lists his person, actions, possessions, and his whole property within the allowance of those laws under which he is, and therein not to be subject to the arbitrary will of another, but freely follow his own.

The power, then, that parents have over their children arises from that duty which is incumbent on them, to take care of their offspring during the imperfect state of childhood. To inform the mind, and govern the actions of their yet ignorant nonage, till reason shall take its place and ease them of that trouble, is what the children want, and the parents are bound to. For God having given man an understanding to direct his actions, has allowed him a freedom of will and liberty of acting, as properly belonging thereunto within the bounds of that law he is under. But whilst he is in an estate wherein he has no understanding of his own to direct his will, he is not to have any will of his own to follow. He that understands for him must will for him too; he must prescribe to his will, and regulate his actions, but when he comes to the estate that made his father a free man, the son is a free man too.

This holds in all the laws a man is under, whether natural or civil. Is a man under the law of Nature? What made him free of that law? what gave him a free disposing of his property, according to his own will, within the compass of that law? I answer, an estate wherein he might be supposed capable to know that law, that so he might keep his actions within the bounds of it. When he has acquired that state, he is presumed to know how far that law is to be his guide, and how far he may make use of his freedom, and so comes to have it; till then, somebody else must guide him, who is presumed to know how far the law allows a liberty. If such a state of reason, such an age of discretion made him free, the same shall make his son free too. Is a man under the law of England? what made him free of that law—that is, to have the liberty to dispose of his actions and possessions, according to his own will, within the permission of that law? a capacity of knowing that law. Which is supposed, by that law, at the age of twenty-one, and in some cases sooner. If this made the father free, it shall make the son free too. Till then, we see the law allows the son to have no will, but he is to be guided by the will of his father or guardian, who is to understand for him. And if the father die and fail to substitute a deputy in this trust, if he hath not provided a tutor to govern his son during his minority, during his want of understanding, the law takes care to do it: some other must govern him and be a will to him till he hath attained to a state of freedom, and his understanding be fit to take the government of his will. But after that the father and son are equally free, as much as tutor and pupil, after nonage, equally subjects of the same law together, without any dominion left in the father over the life, liberty, or estate of his son, whether they be only in the state and under the law of Nature, or under the positive laws of an established government.

*   *   *

The freedom then of man, and liberty of acting according to his own will, is grounded on his having reason, which is able to instruct him in that law he is to govern himself by, and make him know how far he is left to the freedom of his own will. To turn him loose to an unrestrained liberty, before he has reason to guide him, is not the allowing him the privilege of his nature to be free, but to thrust him out amongst brutes, and abandon him to a state as wretched and as much beneath that of a man as theirs. This is that which puts the authority into the parents' hands to govern the minority of their children. God hath made it their business to employ this care on their offspring, and hath placed in them suitable inclinations of tenderness and concern to temper this power, to apply it as His wisdom designed it, to the children's good as long as they should need to be under it.

But what reason can hence advance this care of the parents due to their offspring into an absolute, arbitrary dominion of the father, whose power reaches no farther than by such a discipline as he finds most effectual to give such strength and

health to their bodies, such vigour and rectitude to their minds, as may best fit his children to be most useful to themselves and others, and, if it be necessary to his condition, to make them work when they are able for their own subsistence; but in this power the mother, too, has her share with the father.

Nay, this power so little belongs to the father by any peculiar right of Nature, but only as he is guardian of his children, that when he quits his care of them he loses his power over them, which goes along with their nourishment and education, to which it is inseparably annexed, and belongs as much to the foster-father of an exposed child as to the natural father of another. So little power does the bare act of begetting give a man over his issue, if all his care ends there, and this be all the title he hath to the name and authority of a father. And what will become of this paternal power in that part of the world where one woman hath more than one husband at a time? or in those parts of America where, when the husband and wife part, which happens frequently, the children are all left to the mother, follow her, and are wholly under her care and provision? And if the father die whilst the children are young, do they not naturally everywhere owe the same obedience to their mother, during their minority, as to their father, were he alive? And will any one say that the mother hath a legislative power over her children that she can make standing rules which shall be of perpetual obligation, by which they ought to regulate all the concerns of their property, and bound their liberty all the course of their lives, and enforce the observation of them with capital punishments? For this is the proper power of the magistrate, of which the father hath not so much as the shadow. His command over his children is but temporary, and reaches not their life or property. It is but a help to the weakness and imperfection of their nonage, a discipline necessary to their education. And though a father may dispose of his own possessions as he pleases when his children are out of danger of perishing for want, yet his power extends not to the lives or goods which either their own industry, or another's bounty, has made theirs, nor to their liberty neither, when they are once arrived to the enfranchisement of the years of discretion. The father's empire then ceases, and he can from thenceforward no more dispose of the liberty of his son than that of any other man. And it must be far from an absolute or perpetual jurisdiction from which a man may withdraw himself, having licence from Divine authority to "leave father and mother and cleave to his wife."

*   *   *

Chapter VII
Of Political or Civil Society

God, having made man such a creature that, in His own judgment, it was not good for him to be alone, put him under strong obligations of necessity, convenience, and inclination, to drive him into society, as well as fitted him with understanding and language to continue and enjoy it. The first society was between man and wife, which gave beginning to that between parents and children, to which, in time, that between master and servant came to be added. And though all these might, and commonly did, meet together, and make up but one family, wherein the master or mistress of it had some sort of rule proper to a family, each of these, or all together, came short of "political society," as we shall see if we consider the different ends, ties, and bounds of each of these.

Conjugal society is made by a voluntary compact between man and woman, and though it consist chiefly in such a communion and right in one another's bodies as is necessary to its chief end, procreation, yet it draws with it mutual support and assistance, and a communion of interests too, as necessary not only to unite their care and affection, but also necessary to their common offspring, who have a right to be nourished and maintained by them till they are able to provide for themselves.

For the end of conjunction between male and female being not barely procreation, but the continuation of the species, this conjunction betwixt male and female ought to last, even after procreation, so long as is necessary to the nourishment and support of the young ones, who are to be sustained by those that got them till they are able to shift and provide for themselves. This rule, which the infinite wise Maker hath set to the works of His hands, we find the inferior creatures steadily obey. In those vivaporous animals which feed on grass the conjunction between male and female lasts no longer than the very act of copulation, because the teat of the dam being sufficient to nourish the young till it be able to feed on grass, the male only begets, but concerns not himself for the female or young, to whose sustenance he can contribute nothing. But in beasts of prey the conjunction lasts longer, because the dam, not being able well to subsist herself and nourish her numerous offspring by her own prey alone (a more laborious as well as more dangerous way of living than by feeding on grass), the assistance of the male is necessary to the maintenance of their common family, which cannot subsist till they are able to prey for themselves, but by the joint care of male and female. The same is observed in all birds (except some domestic ones, where plenty of food excuses the cock from feeding and taking care of the young brood), whose young, needing food in the nest, the cock and hen continue mates till the young are able to use their wings and provide for themselves.

And herein, I think, lies the chief, if not the only reason, why the male and female in mankind are tied to a longer conjunction than other creatures—viz., because the female is capable of conceiving, and, *de facto*, is commonly with child again, and brings forth too a new birth, long before the former is out of a dependency for support on his parents' help and able to shift for himself, and has all the assistance due to him from his parents, whereby the father, who is bound to take care for those he hath begot, is under an obligation to continue in conjugal society with the same woman longer than other creatures, whose young, being able to subsist of themselves before the time of procreation returns again, the conjugal bond dissolves of itself, and they are at liberty till Hymen, at his usual anniversary season, summons them again to choose new mates. Wherein one cannot but admire the wisdom of the great Creator, who, having given to man an ability to lay up for the future as well as supply the present necessity, hath made it necessary that society of man and wife should be more lasting than of male and female amongst other creatures, that so their industry might be encouraged, and their interest better united, to make provision and lay up goods for their common issue, which uncertain mixture, or easy and frequent solutions of conjugal society, would mightily disturb.

But though these are ties upon mankind which make the conjugal bonds more firm and lasting in a man than the other species of animals, yet it would give one reason to inquire why this compact, where procreation and education are secured and inheritance taken care for, may not be made determinable, either by consent, or at a certain time, or upon certain conditions, as well as any other voluntary compacts, there being no necessity, in the nature of the thing, nor to the ends of it, that it should always be for life—I mean, to such as are under no restraint of any positive law which ordains all such contracts to be perpetual.

But the husband and wife, though they have but one common concern, yet having different understandings, will unavoidably sometimes have different wills too. It therefore being necessary that the last determination (i.e., the rule) should be placed somewhere, it naturally falls to the man's share as the abler and the stronger. But this, reaching but to the things of their common interest and property, leaves the wife in the full and true possession of what by contract is her peculiar right, and at least gives the husband no more power over her than she has over his life; the power of the husband being so far from that of an absolute monarch that the wife has, in many cases, a liberty to separate from him where natural right or their contract allows it, whether that contract be made by themselves in the state of Nature or by the customs or laws of the country they live in, and the children, upon such separation, fall to the father or mother's lot as such contract does determine.

For all the ends of marriage being to be obtained under politic government, as well as in

the state of Nature, the civil magistrate doth not abridge the right or power of either, naturally necessary to those ends—viz., procreation and mutual support and assistance whilst they are together, but only decides any controversy that may arise between man and wife about them. If it were otherwise, and that absolute sovereignty and power of life and death naturally belonged to the husband, and were necessary to the society between man and wife, there could be no matrimony in any of these countries where the husband is allowed no such absolute authority. But the ends of matrimony requiring no such power in the husband, it was not at all necessary to it. The condition of conjugal society put it not in him; but whatsoever might consist with procreation and support of the children till they could shift for themselves—mutual assistance, comfort, and maintenance—might be varied and regulated by that contract which first united them in that society, nothing being necessary to any society that is not necessary to the ends for which it is made.

*   *   *

Let us therefore consider a master of a family with all these subordinate relations of wife, children, servants and slaves, united under the domestic rule of a family, with what resemblance soever it may have in its order, offices, and number too, with a little commonwealth, yet is very far from it both in its constitution, power, and end; or if it must be thought a monarchy, and the paterfamilias the absolute monarch in it, absolute monarchy will have but a very shattered and short power, when it is plain by what has been said before, that the master of the family has a very distinct and differently limited power both as to time and extent over those several persons that are in it; for excepting the slave (and the family is as much a family, and his power as paterfamilias as great, whether there be any slaves in his family or no) he has no legislative power of life and death over any of them, and none too but what a mistress of a family may have as well as he. And he certainly can have no absolute power over the whole family who has but a very limited one over every individual in it. But how a family, or any other society of men, differ from that which is properly political society, we shall best see by considering wherein political society itself consists.

Man being born, as has been proved, with a title to perfect freedom and an uncontrolled enjoyment of all the rights and privileges of the law of Nature, equally with any other man, or number of men in the world, hath by nature a power not only to preserve his property—that is, his life, liberty, and estate, against the injuries and attempts of other men, but to judge of and punish the breaches of that law in others, as he is persuaded the offence deserves, even with death itself, in crimes where the heinousness of the fact, in his opinion, requires it. But because no political society can be, nor subsist, without having in itself the power to preserve the property, and in order thereunto punish the offences of all those of that society, there, and there only, is political society where every one of the members hath quitted this natural power, resigned it up into the hands of the community in all cases that exclude him not from appealing for protection to the law established by it. And thus all private judgment of every particular member being excluded, the community comes to be umpire, and by understanding indifferent rules and men authorised by the community for their execution, decides all the differences that may happen between any members of that society concerning any matter of right, and punishes those offences which any member hath committed against the society with such penalties as the law has established; whereby it is easy to discern who are, and are not, in political society together. Those who are united into one body, and have a common established law and judicature to appeal to, with authority to decide controversies between them and punish offenders, are in civil society one with another; but those who have no such common appeal, I mean on earth, are still in the state of Nature, each being where there is no other, judge for himself and executioner; which is, as I have before showed it, the perfect state of Nature.

And thus the commonwealth comes by a power to set down what punishment shall belong to the several transgressions they think worthy of it, committed amongst the members of that society (which is the power of making laws), as well as it has the power to punish any injury done unto any of its members by any one that is not of it (which is the power of war and peace); and all this for the preservation of the property of all the members of that society, as far as is possible. But though every man entered into society has quitted his power to punish offences against the law of Nature in prosecution of his own private judgment, yet with the judgment of offences which he has given up to the legislative, in all cases where he can appeal to the magistrate, he has given up a right to the commonwealth to employ his force for the execution of the judgments of the commonwealth whenever he shall be called to it, which, indeed, are his own judgments, they being made by himself or his representative. And herein we have the original of the legislative and executive power of civil society, which is to judge by standing laws how far offences are to be punished when committed within the commonwealth; and also by occasional judgments founded on the present circumstances of the fact, how far injuries from without are to be vindicated, and in both these to employ all the force of all the members when there shall be need.

Wherever, therefore, any number of men so unite into one society as to quit every one his executive power of the law of Nature, and to resign it to the public, there and there only is a political or civil society. And this is done wherever any number of men, in the state of Nature, enter into society to make one people one body politic under one supreme government: or else when any one joins himself to, and incorporates with any government already made. For hereby he authorises the society, or which is all one, the legislative thereof, to make laws for him as the public good of the society shall require, to the execution whereof his own assistance (as to his own decrees) is due. And this puts men out of a state of Nature into that of a commonwealth, by setting up a judge on earth with authority to determine all the controversies and redress the injuries that may happen to any member of the commonwealth, which judge is the legislative or magistrates appointed by it. And wherever there are any number of men, however associated, that have no such decisive power to appeal to, there they are still in the state of Nature.

And hence it is evident that absolute monarchy, which by some men is counted for the only government in the world, is indeed inconsistent with civil society, and so can be no form of civil government at all. For the end of civil society being to avoid and remedy those inconveniencies of the state of Nature which necessarily follow from every man's being judge in his own case, by setting up a known authority to which every one of that society may appeal upon any injury received, or controversy that may arise, and which every one of the society ought to obey. Wherever any persons are who have not such an authority to appeal to, and decide any difference between them there, those persons are still in the state of Nature. And so is every absolute prince in respect of those who are under his dominion.

For he being supposed to have all, both legislative and executive, power in himself alone, there is no judge to be found, no appeal lies open to any one, who may fairly and indifferently, and with authority decide, and from whence relief and redress may be expected of any injury or inconveniency that may be suffered from him, or by his order. So that such a man, however entitled, Czar, or Grand Signior, or how you please, is as much in the state of Nature, with all under his dominion, as he is with the rest of mankind. For wherever any two men are, who have no standing rule and common judge to appeal to on earth, for the determination of controversies of right betwixt them, there they are still in the state of Nature, and under all the inconveniencies of it, with only this woeful difference to the subject, or rather slave of an absolute prince. That whereas, in the ordinary state of Nature, he has a liberty to judge of his right, according to the best of his power to maintain it; but whenever his property is invaded by the will and order of his monarch, he has not only no appeal, as those in society ought to have, but, as if he were degraded from the common state of rational crea-

tures, is denied a liberty to judge of, or defend his right, and so is exposed to all the misery and inconveniencies that a man can fear from one, who being in the unrestrained state of Nature, is yet corrupted with flattery and armed with power.

*   *   *

Chapter VIII
Of the Beginning of Political Societies

Men being, as has been said, by nature all free, equal, and independent, no one can be put out of this estate and subjected to the political power of another without his own consent, which is done by agreeing with other men, to join and unite into a community for their comfortable, safe, and peaceable living, one amongst another, in a secure enjoyment of their properties, and a greater security against any that are not of it. This any number of men may do, because it injures not the freedom of the rest; they are left, as they were, in the liberty of the state of Nature. When any number of men have so consented to make one community or government, they are thereby presently incorporated, and make one body politic, wherein the majority have a right to act and conclude the rest.

For, when any number of men have, by the consent of every individual, made a community, they have thereby made that community one body, with a power to act as one body, which is only by the will and determination of the majority. For that which acts any community, being only the consent of the individuals of it, and it being one body, must move one way, it is necessary the body should move that way whither the greater force carries it, which is the consent of the majority, or else it is impossible it should act or continue one body, one community, which the consent of every individual that united into it agreed that it should; and so every one is bound by that consent to be concluded by the majority. And therefore we see that in assemblies empowered to act by positive laws where no number is set by that positive law which empowers them, the act of the majority passes for the act of the whole, and of course determines as having, by the law of Nature and reason, the power of the whole.

And thus every man, by consenting with others to make one body politic under one government, puts himself under an obligation to every one of that society to submit to the determination of the majority, and to be concluded by it; or else this original compact, whereby he with others incorporates into one society, would signify nothing, and be no compact if he be left free and under no other ties than he was in before in the state of Nature. For what appearance would there be of any compact? What new engagement if he were no farther tied by any decrees of the society than he himself thought fit and did actually consent to? This would be still as great a liberty as he himself had before his compact, or any one else in the state of Nature, who may submit himself and consent to any acts of it if he thinks fit.

*   *   *

Whosoever, therefore, out of a state of Nature unite into a community, must be understood to give up all the power necessary to the ends for which they unite into society to the majority of the community, unless they expressly agreed in any number greater than the majority. And this is done by barely agreeing to unite into one political society, which is all the compact that is, or needs be, between the individuals that enter into or make up a commonwealth. And thus, that which begins and actually constitutes any political society is nothing but the consent of any number of freemen capable of majority, to unite and incorporate into such a society. And this is that, and that only, which did or could give beginning to any lawful government in the world.

*   *   *

Every man being, as has been showed, naturally free, and nothing being able to put him into subjection to any earthly power, but only his own consent, it is to be considered what shall be understood to be a sufficient declaration of a man's consent to make him subject to the laws of any government. There is a common distinction of an express and a tacit consent, which will concern our present case. Nobody doubts but an express consent of any man, entering into any society, makes him a perfect member of that society, a subject of that government. The difficulty is, what ought to be looked upon as a tacit consent, and how far it binds—*i.e.*, how far any one shall be looked on to have consented, and thereby submitted to any government, where he has made no expressions of it at all. And to this I say, that every man that hath any possession or enjoyment of any part of the dominions of any government doth hereby give his tacit consent, and is as far forth obliged to obedience to the laws of that government, during such enjoyment, as any one under it, whether this his possession be of land to him and his heirs for ever, or a lodging only for a week; or whether it be barely travelling freely on the highway; and, in effect, it reaches as far as the very being of any one within the territories of that government.

To understand this the better, it is fit to consider that every man when he at first incorporates himself into any commonwealth, he, by his uniting himself thereunto, annexes also, and submits to the community those possessions which he has, or shall acquire, that do not already belong to any other government. For it would be a direct contradiction for any one to enter into society with others for the securing and regulating of property, and yet to suppose his land, whose property is to be regulated by the laws of the society, should be exempt from the jurisdiction of that government to which he himself, and the property of the land, is a subject. By the same act, therefore, whereby any one unites his person, which was before free, to any commonwealth, by the same he unites his possessions, which were before free, to it also; and they become, both of them, person and possession, subject to the government and dominion of that commonwealth as long as it hath a being. Whoever therefore, from thenceforth, by inheritance, purchases permission, or otherwise enjoys any part of the land so annexed to, and under the government of that commonweal, must take it with the condition it is under—that is, of submitting to the government of the commonwealth, under whose jurisdiction it is, as far forth as any subject of it.

But since the government has a direct jurisdiction only over the land and reaches the possessor of it (before he has actually incorporated himself in the society) only as he dwells upon and enjoys that, the obligation any one is under by virtue of such enjoyment to submit to the government begins and ends with the enjoyment; so that whenever the owner, who has given nothing but such a tacit consent to the government will, by donation, sale or otherwise, quit the said possession, he is at liberty to go and incorporate himself into any other commonwealth, or agree with others to begin a new one *in vacuis locis,* in any part of the world they can find free and unpossessed; whereas he that has once, by actual agreement and any express declaration, given his consent to be of any commonweal, is perpetually and indispensably obliged to be, and remain unalterably a subject to it, and can never be again in the liberty of the state of Nature, unless by any calamity the government he was under comes to be dissolved.

But submitting to the laws of any country, living quietly and enjoying privileges and protection under them, makes not a man a member of that society; it is only a local protection and homage due to and from all those who, not being in a state of war, come within the territories belonging to any government, to all parts whereof the force of its law extends. But this no more makes a man a member of that society, a perpetual subject of that commonwealth, than it would make a man a subject to another in whose family he found it convenient to abide for some time, though, whilst he continued in it, he were obliged to comply with the laws and submit to the government he found there. And thus we see that foreigners, by living all their lives under another government, and enjoying the privileges and protection of it, though they are bound, even in conscience, to submit to its administration as far forth as any denizen, yet do not thereby come to be subjects or members of that commonwealth. Noth-

ing can make any man so but his actually entering into it by positive engagement and express promise and compact. This is that which, I think, concerning the beginning of political societies, and that consent which makes any one a member of any commonwealth.

Chapter IX
Of the Ends of Political Society and Government

If man in the state of Nature be so free as has been said, if he be absolute lord of his own person and possessions, equal to the greatest and subject to nobody, why will he part with his freedom, this empire, and subject himself to the dominion and control of any other power? To which it is obvious to answer, that though in the state of Nature he hath such a right, yet the enjoyment of it is very uncertain and constantly exposed to the invasion of others; for all being kings as much as he, every man his equal, and the greater part no strict observers of equity and justice, the enjoyment of the property he has in this state is very unsafe, very insecure. This makes him willing to quit this condition which, however free, is full of fears and continual dangers; and it is not without reason that he seeks out and is willing to join in society with others who are already united, or have a mind to unite for the mutual preservation of their lives, liberties and estates, which I call by the general name—property.

The great and chief end, therefore, of men uniting into commonwealths, and putting themselves under government, is the preservation of their property; to which in the state of Nature there are many things wanting.

Firstly, there wants an established, settled, known law, received and allowed by common consent to be the standard of right and wrong, and the common measure to decide all controversies between them. For though the law of Nature be plain and intelligible to all rational creatures, yet men, being biased by their interest, as well as ignorant for want of study of it, are not apt to allow of it as a law binding to them in the application of it to their particular cases.

Secondly, in the state of Nature there wants a known and indifferent judge, with authority to determine all differences according to the established law. For every one in that state being both judge and executioner of the law of Nature, men being partial to themselves, passion and revenge is very apt to carry them too far, and with too much heat in their own cases, as well as negligence and unconcernedness, make them too remiss in other men's.

Thirdly, in the state of Nature there often wants power to back and support the sentence when right, and to give it due execution. They who by any injustice offended will seldom fail where they are able by force to make good their injustice. Such resistance many times makes the punishment dangerous, and frequently destructive to those who attempt it.

*   *   *

REVIEW QUESTIONS

1. According to Locke, what is the nature of political society?
2. How does political society come into being?
3. How does Locke's notion of a social contract compare with that of Hobbes?
4. What are the ends of political society?
5. What are the implications of Locke's reasoning for early modern economic thinking?

ADAM SMITH

FROM *The Wealth of Nations*

Though best remembered for his towering system of political economy, An Inquiry into the Nature and Causes of the Wealth of Nations *(1776), Adam Smith (1723–1790) was one of the most important social philosophers of the eighteenth century. His economic writings constitute only a part of his larger view of social and political development. Born the son of a minor government official, he entered the University of Glasgow in 1737, already a center of what became known as the Scottish Enlightenment, where he was deeply influenced by another great moral and economic philosopher, Francis Hutcheson. After completing his education at Oxford, he returned to Scotland, where he embarked on a series of public lectures in Edinburgh. In 1752, he was appointed professor of logic at Glasgow, and in 1754, he assumed the chair in moral philosophy. He would look on his tenure as the happiest and most honorable of his life. It was certainly the most productive. There he made the acquaintance of some of the leading intellectual lights of his day: James Watt, of steam-engine fame; David Hume, the great philosopher; and Andrew Cochrane. The last was the founder of the Political Economy Club and the likely source of much of Smith's information on business and commerce. In 1759, Smith published his first important work,* The Theory of Moral Sentiments, *in which he attempted to describe universal principles of human nature. His answer to the question of moral judgment was the thesis of the "inner man," or "impartial spectator," which is the conscience in each human being and whose pronouncements cannot be ignored. Thus, human beings can be driven by passions and self-interests and simultaneously capable of ethics and generosity. This principle foreshadowed the "invisible hand" that would guide economic behavior in* The Wealth of Nations. *He began work on this classic text after resigning his post at Glasgow to serve as tutor to the young Duke of Buccleuch. When it finally appeared, it continued the themes first addressed in* The Theory of Moral Sentiments, *the resolution of passion and reason in human behavior, and now, human history. According to Smith, society evolves through four broad stages, each with appropriate institutions: simple hunters, nomadic herders, feudal farmers, and commercial workers. The guiding force in this development is human nature, motivated by self-interest but guided by disinterested reason. Most of the book is given over to a discussion of the function of the invisible hand in the final, current stage. Whereas conscience provided the necessary guidance in* The Theory of Moral Sentiments, *competition assumes that function in* The Wealth of Nations. *Competition rendered markets self-regulating and ensured that prices and wages never stray far from their "natural" levels. Much of the book, especially Book IV, where he places his discussion of colonies, is given over to a polemic against restriction, through both regulation and monopoly, in economic life. The* Wealth of Nations *appeared to great acclaim and earned its author fame and fortune. He published nothing more.*

From *An Inquiry into the Nature and Causes of the Wealth of Nations*, by Adam Smith (Edinburgh: Thomas Nelson, 1838).

*   *   *

Of the Motives for Establishing New Colonies

The interest which occasioned the first settlement of the different European colonies in America and the West Indies, was not altogether so plain and distinct as that which directed the establishment of those of ancient Greece and Rome.

GREEK COLONIES WERE SENT OUT WHEN THE POPULATION GREW TOO GREAT AT HOME.

All the different states of ancient Greece possessed, each of them, but a very small territory, and when the people in any one of them multiplied beyond what that territory could easily maintain, a part of them were sent in quest of a new habitation in some remote and distant part of the world; the warlike neighbours who surrounded them on all sides, rendering it difficult for any of them to enlarge very much its territory at home. * * *

THE MOTHER CITY CLAIMED NO AUTHORITY.

The mother city, though she considered the colony as a child, at all times entitled to great favour and assistance, and owing in return much gratitude and respect, yet considered it as an emancipated child, over whom she pretended to claim no direct authority or jurisdiction.

The colony settled its own form of government, enacted its own laws, elected its own magistrates, and made peace or war with its neighbours as an independent state, which had no occasion to wait for the approbation or consent of the mother city. Nothing can be more plain and distinct than the interest which directed every such establishment.

ROMAN COLONIES WERE SENT OUT TO SATISFY THE DEMAND FOR LANDS AND TO ESTABLISH GARRISONS IN CONQUERED TERRITORIES.

Rome, like most of the other ancient republics, was originally founded upon an Agrarian law, which divided the public territory in a certain proportion among the different citizens who composed the state. The course of human affairs, by marriage, by succession, and by alienation, necessarily deranged this original division, and frequently threw the lands, which had been allotted for the maintenance of many different families into the possession of a single person. To remedy this disorder, for such it was supposed to be, a law was made, restricting the quantity of land which any citizen could possess to five hundred jugera, about three hundred and fifty English acres. This law, however, though we read of its having been executed upon one or two occasions, was either neglected or evaded, and the inequality of fortunes went on continually increasing. The greater part of the citizens had no land, and without it the manners and customs of those times rendered it difficult for a freeman to maintain his independency. . . . The people became clamorous to get land, and the rich and the great, we may believe, were perfectly determined not to give them any part of theirs. To satisfy them in some measure, therefore, they frequently proposed to send out a new colony.

THEY WERE ENTIRELY SUBJECT TO THE MOTHER CITY.

But conquering Rome was, even upon such occasions, under no necessity of turning out her citizens to seek their fortune, if one may say so, through the wide world, without knowing where they were to settle. She assigned them lands generally in the conquered provinces of Italy, where, being within the dominions of the republic, they could never form any independent state; but were at best but a sort of corporation, which, though it had the power of enacting bye-laws for its own government, was at all times subject to the correction, jurisdiction, and legislative authority of the mother city. The sending out a colony of this kind, not only gave some satisfaction to the people, but often established a sort of garrison too in a newly conquered province, of which the obedience might otherwise have been doubtful. A Roman colony, therefore, whether we consider the nature of the establishment itself, or the motives for making it, was altogether different from a Greek one. The words accordingly, which in the original languages denote those different establishments, have very different meanings. The Latin word (*Colonia*) signifies simply a plantation. The Greek word (αποικια), on the contrary, signifies a separation of dwelling, a departure from home, a going out of the house. But, though the Roman colonies were in many respects different from the Greek ones, the interest which prompted to establish them was equally plain and distinct. Both institutions derived their origin either from irresistible necessity, or from clear and evident utility.

THE UTILITY OF THE AMERICAN COLONIES IS NOT SO EVIDENT.

The establishment of the European colonies in America and the West Indies arose from no necessity: and though the utility which has resulted from them has been very great, it is not altogether so clear and evident. It was not understood at their first establishment, and was not the motive either of that establishment or of the discoveries which gave occasion to it; and the nature, extent, and limits of that utility are not, perhaps, well understood at this day.

THE VENETIANS HAD A PROFITABLE TRADE IN EAST INDIA GOODS.

The Venetians, during the fourteenth and fifteenth centuries, carried on a very advantageous commerce in spiceries, and other East India goods, which they distributed among the other nations of Europe. They purchased them chiefly in Egypt, at that time under the dominion of the Mammeluks, the enemies of the Turks, of whom the Venetians were the enemies; and this union of interest, assisted by the money of Venice, formed such a connection as gave the Venetians almost a monopoly of the trade.

THIS WAS ENVIED BY THE PORTUGUESE AND LED THEM TO DISCOVER THE CAPE OF GOOD HOPE PASSAGE.

The great profits of the Venetians tempted the avidity of the Portuguese. They had been endeavouring, during the course of the fifteenth century, to find out by sea a way to the countries from which the Moors brought them ivory and gold dust across the Desart. They discovered the Madeiras, the Canaries, the Azores, the Cape de Verd islands, the coast of Guinea, that of Loango, Congo, Angola, and Benguela, and finally, the Cape of Good Hope. They had long wished to share in the profitable traffic of the Venetians, and this last discovery opened to them a probable prospect of doing so. In 1497, Vasco de Gama sailed from the port of Lisbon with a fleet of four ships, and, after a navigation of eleven months, arrived upon the coast of Indostan, and thus completed a course of discoveries which had been pursued with great steadiness, and with very little interruption, for near a century together.

COLUMBUS ENDEAVOURED TO REACH THE EAST INDIES BY SAILING WESTWARDS.

Some years before this, while the expectations of Europe were in suspense about the projects of the Portuguese, of which the success appeared yet to be doubtful, a Genoese pilot formed the yet more daring project of sailing to the East Indies by the West. The situation of those countries was at that time very imperfectly known in Europe. The few European travellers who had been there had magnified the distance; perhaps through simplicity and ignorance, what was really very great, appearing almost infinite to those who could not measure it; or, perhaps, in order to increase somewhat more the marvellous of their own adventures in visiting regions so immensely remote from Europe. The longer the way was by the East, Columbus very justly con-

cluded, the shorter it would be by the West. He proposed, therefore, to take that way, as both the shortest and the surest, and he had the good fortune to convince Isabella of Castile of the probability of his project. He sailed from the port of Palos in August 1492, near five years before the expedition of Vasco de Gama set out from Portugal, and, after a voyage of between two and three months, discovered first some of the small Bahama or Lucayan islands, and afterwards the great island of St. Domingo.

COLUMBUS MISTOOK THE COUNTRIES HE FOUND FOR THE INDIES.

But the countries which Columbus discovered, either in this or in any of his subsequent voyages, had no resemblance to those which he had gone in quest of. Instead of the wealth, cultivation and populousness of China and Indostan, he found, in St. Domingo, and in all the other parts of the new world which he ever visited, nothing but a country quite covered with wood, uncultivated, and inhabited only by some tribes of naked and miserable savages. He was not very willing, however, to believe that they were not the same with some of the countries described by Marco Polo, the first European who had visited, or at least had left behind him any description of China or the East Indies; and a very slight resemblance, such as that which he found between the name of Cibao, a mountain in St. Domingo, and that of Cipango, mentioned by Marco Polo, was frequently sufficient to make him return to this favourite prepossession, though contrary to the clearest evidence. In his letters to Ferdinand and Isabella he called the countries which he had discovered, the Indies. He entertained no doubt but that they were the extremity of those which had been described by Marco Polo, and that they were not very distant from the Ganges, or from the countries which had been conquered by Alexander. Even when at last convinced that they were different, he still flattered himself that those rich countries were at no great distance, and in a subsequent voyage, accordingly, went in quest of them along the coast of Terra Firma, and towards the isthmus of Darien.

HENCE THE NAMES EAST AND WEST INDIES.

In consequence of this mistake of Columbus, the name of the Indies has stuck to those unfortunate countries ever since; and when it was at last clearly discovered that the new were altogether different from the old Indies, the former were called the West, in contradistinction to the latter, which were called the East Indies.

THE COUNTRIES DISCOVERED WERE NOT RICH.

It was of importance to Columbus, however, that the countries which he had discovered, whatever they were, should be represented to the court of Spain as of very great consequence; and, in what constitutes the real riches of every country, the animal and vegetable productions of the soil, there was at that time nothing which could well justify such a representation of them.

*   *   *

SO COLUMBUS RELIED ON THE MINERALS.

Finding nothing either in the animals or vegetables of the newly discovered countries, which could justify a very advantageous representation of them, Columbus turned his view towards their minerals; and in the richness of the productions of this third kingdom, he flattered himself, he had found a full compensation for the insignificancy of those of the other two. The little bits of gold with which the inhabitants ornamented their dress, and which, he was informed, they frequently found in the rivulets and torrents that fell from the mountains, were sufficient to satisfy him that those mountains abounded with the richest gold mines. St. Domingo, therefore, was represented as a country abounding with gold, and upon that account (according to the prejudices not only of the present times, but of those times), an inexhaustible source of real wealth to the crown and kingdom of Spain.

THE COUNCIL OF CASTILE WAS ATTRACTED BY THE GOLD, COLUMBUS PROPOSING THAT THE GOVERNMENT SHOULD HAVE HALF THE GOLD AND SILVER DISCOVERED.

In consequence of the representations of Columbus, the council of Castile determined to take possession of countries of which the inhabitants were plainly incapable of defending themselves. The pious purpose of converting them to Christianity sanctified the injustice of the project. But the hope of finding treasures of gold there, was the sole motive which prompted to undertake it; and to give this motive the greater weight, it was proposed by Columbus that the half of all the gold and silver that should be found there should belong to the crown. This proposal was approved of by the council.

*   *   *

THE SUBSEQUENT SPANISH ENTERPRISES WERE ALL PROMPTED BY THE SAME MOTIVE.

All the other enterprises of the Spaniards in the new world, subsequent to those of Columbus, seem to have been prompted by the same motive. It was the sacred thirst of gold that carried Oieda, Nicuessa, and Vasco Nugnes de Balboa, to the isthmus of Darien, that carried Cortez to Mexico, and Almagro and Pizzarro to Chile and Peru. When those adventurers arrived upon any unknown coast, their first enquiry was always if there was any gold to be found there; and according to the information which they received concerning this particular, they determined either to quit the country or to settle in it.

*   *   *

IN THIS CASE EXPECTATIONS WERE TO SOME EXTENT REALISED, SO FAR AS THE SPANIARDS WERE CONCERNED.

In the countries first discovered by the Spaniards, no gold or silver mines are at present known which are supposed to be worth the working. The quantities of those metals which the first adventurers are said to have found there, had probably been very much magnified, as well as the fertility of the mines which were wrought immediately after the first discovery. What those adventurers were reported to have found, however, was sufficient to inflame the avidity of all their countrymen. Every Spaniard who sailed to America expected to find an Eldorado. Fortune too did upon this what she has done upon very few other occasions. She realized in some measure the extravagant hopes of her votaries, and in the discovery and conquest of Mexico and Peru (of which the one happened about thirty, the other about forty years after the first expedition of Columbus), she presented them with something not very unlike that profusion of the precious metals which they sought for.

A project of commerce to the East Indies, therefore, gave occasion to the first discovery of the West. A project of conquest gave occasion to all the establishments of the Spaniards in those newly discovered countries. The motive which excited them to this conquest was a project of gold and silver mines; and a course of accidents, which no human wisdom could foresee, rendered this project much more successful than the undertakers had any reasonable grounds for expecting.

BUT THE OTHER NATIONS WERE NOT SO SUCCESSFUL.

The first adventures of all the other nations of Europe, who attempted to make settlements in America, were animated by the like chimerical views; but they were not equally successful. It was more than a hundred years after the first settlement of the Brazils, before any silver, gold, or diamond mines were discovered there. In the English, French, Dutch, and Danish colonies, none have ever yet been discovered; at least none that are at present supposed to be worth the working. The first English settlers in North America, however, offered a fifth of all the gold and silver which should be found there to the king, as a motive for granting them their patents. In the patents to Sir Walter Raleigh, to the London and Plymouth companies, to the council of

Plymouth, &c. this fifth was accordingly reserved to the crown. To the expectation of finding gold and silver mines, those first settlers too joined that of discovering a north-west passage to the East Indies. They have hitherto been disappointed in both.

Causes of the Prosperity of New Colonies

The colony of a civilized nation which takes possession either of a waste country, or of one so thinly inhabited, that the natives easily give place to the new settlers, advances more rapidly to wealth and greatness than any other human society.

COLONISTS TAKE OUT KNOWLEDGE AND REGULAR GOVERNMENT.

The colonists carry out with them a knowledge of agriculture and of other useful arts, superior to what can grow up of its own accord in the course of many centuries among savage and barbarous nations. They carry out with them too the habit of subordination, some notion of the regular government which takes place in their own country, of the system of laws which supports it, and of a regular administration of justice; and they naturally establish something of the same kind in the new settlement. But among savage and barbarous nations, the natural progress of law and government is still slower than the natural progress of arts, after law and government have been so far established, as is necessary for their protection.

LAND IS PLENTIFUL AND CHEAP.

Every colonist gets more land than he can possibly cultivate. He has no rent, and scarce any taxes to pay. No landlord shares with him in its produce, and the share of the sovereign is commonly but a trifle. He has every motive to render as great as possible a produce, which is thus to be almost entirely his own. But his land is commonly so extensive, that with all his own industry, and with all the industry of other people whom he can get to employ, he can seldom make it produce the tenth part of what it is capable of producing.

WAGES ARE HIGH.

He is eager, therefore, to collect labourers from all quarters, and to reward them with the most liberal wages. But those liberal wages, joined to the plenty and cheapness of land, soon make those labourers leave him, in order to become landlords themselves, and to reward, with equal liberality, other labourers, who soon leave them for the same reason that they left their first master.

*   *   *

Of the Advantages Which Europe Has Derived from the Discovery of America, and from That of a Passage to the East Indies by the Cape of Good Hope

THE ADVANTAGES DERIVED BY EUROPE FROM AMERICA ARE (1) THE ADVANTAGES OF EUROPE IN GENERAL, AND (2) THE ADVANTAGES OF THE PARTICULAR COUNTRIES WHICH HAVE COLONIES.

Such are the advantages which the colonies of America have derived from the policy of Europe.

What are those which Europe has derived from the discovery and colonization of America?

Those advantages may be divided, first, into the general advantages which Europe, considered as one great country, has derived from those great events; and, secondly, into the particular advantages which each colonizing country has derived from the colonies which particularly belong to it, in consequence of the authority or dominion which it exercises over them.

(1) THE GENERAL ADVANTAGES TO EUROPE ARE
(A) AN INCREASE OF ENJOYMENTS.

The general advantages which Europe, considered as one great country, has derived from the discov-

ery and colonization of America, consist, first, in the increase of its enjoyments; and secondly, in the augmentation of its industry.

The surplus produce of America, imported into Europe, furnishes the inhabitants of this great continent with a variety of commodities which they could not otherwise have possessed, some for conveniency and use, some for pleasure, and some for ornament, and thereby contributes to increase their enjoyments.

(B) AN AUGMENTATION OF INDUSTRY NOT ONLY IN THE COUNTRIES WHICH TRADE WITH AMERICA DIRECTLY, BUT ALSO IN OTHER COUNTRIES WHICH DO NOT SEND THEIR PRODUCE TO AMERICA OR EVEN RECEIVE ANY PRODUCE FROM AMERICA.

The discovery and colonization of America, it will readily be allowed, have contributed to augment the industry, first, of all the countries which trade to it directly; such as Spain, Portugal, France, and England; and, secondly, of all those which, without trading to it directly, send, through the medium of other countries, goods to it of their own produce; such as Austrian Flanders, and some provinces of Germany, which, through the medium of the countries before mentioned, send to it a considerable quantity of linen and other goods. All such countries have evidently gained a more extensive market for their surplus produce, and must consequently have been encouraged to increase its quantity.

*   *   *

Those great events may even have contributed to increase the enjoyments, and to augment the industry of countries which, not only never sent any commodities to America, but never received any from it. Even such countries may have received a greater abundance of other commodities from countries of which the surplus produce had been augmented by means of the American trade. This greater abundance, as it must necessarily have increased their enjoyments, so it must likewise have augmented their industry. A greater number of new equivalents of some kind or other must have been presented to them to be exchanged for the surplus produce of that industry. A more extensive market must have been created for that surplus produce, so as to raise its value, and thereby encourage its increase. The mass of commodities annually thrown into the great circle of European commerce, and by its various revolutions annually distributed among all the different nations comprehended within it, must have been augmented by the whole surplus produce of America. A greater share of this greater mass, therefore, is likely to have fallen to each of those nations, to have increased their enjoyments, and augmented their industry.

*   *   *

(2) THE PARTICULAR ADVANTAGES OF THE COLONISING COUNTRIES ARE (A) THE COMMON ADVANTAGES DERIVED FROM PROVINCES, (B) THE PECULIAR ADVANTAGES DERIVED FROM PROVINCES IN AMERICA.

The particular advantages which each colonizing country derives from the colonies which particularly belong to it, are of two different kinds; first, those common advantages which every empire derives from the provinces subject to its dominion; and, secondly, those peculiar advantages which are supposed to result from provinces of so very peculiar a nature as the European colonies of America.

The common advantages which every empire derives from the provinces subject to its dominion, consist, first, in the military force which they furnish for its defence; and, secondly, in the revenue which they furnish for the support of its civil government.

*   *   *

(A) THE COMMON ADVANTAGES ARE CONTRIBUTIONS OF MILITARY FORCES AND REVENUE, BUT NONE OF THE COLONIES HAVE EVER FURNISHED MILITARY FORCE.

The European colonies of America have never yet furnished any military force for the defence of the mother country. Their military force has never yet been sufficient for their own defence; and in the different wars in which the mother countries have been engaged, the defence of their colonies has generally occasioned a very considerable distraction of the military force of those countries. In this respect, therefore, all the European colonies have, without exception, been a cause rather of weakness than of strength to their respective mother countries.

AND THE COLONIES OF SPAIN AND PORTUGAL ALONE HAVE CONTRIBUTED REVENUE.

The colonies of Spain and Portugal only have contributed any revenue towards the defence of the mother country, or the support of her civil government. The taxes which have been levied upon those of other European nations, upon those of England in particular, have seldom been equal to the expence laid out upon them in time of peace, and never sufficient to defray that which they occasioned in time of war. Such colonies, therefore, have been a source of expence and not of revenue to their respective mother countries.

(B) THE EXCLUSIVE TRADE IS THE SOLE PECULIAR ADVANTAGE.

The advantages of such colonies to their respective mother countries, consist altogether in those peculiar advantages which are supposed to result from provinces of so very peculiar a nature as the European colonies of America; and the exclusive trade, it is acknowledged, is the sole source of all those peculiar advantages.

THE EXCLUSIVE TRADE OF EACH COUNTRY IS A DISADVANTAGE TO THE OTHER COUNTRIES.

In consequence of this exclusive trade, all that part of the surplus produce of the English colonies, for example, which consists in what are called enumerated commodities, can be sent to no other country but England. Other countries must afterwards buy it of her. It must be cheaper therefore in England than it can be in any other country, and must contribute more to increase the enjoyments of England than those of any other country. It must likewise contribute more to encourage her industry. For all those parts of her own surplus produce which England exchanges for those enumerated commodities, she must get a better price than any other countries can get for the like parts of theirs, when they exchange them for the same commodities. The manufactures of England, for example, will purchase a greater quantity of the sugar and tobacco of her own colonies, than the like manufactures of other countries can purchase of that sugar and tobacco. So far, therefore, as the manufactures of England and those of other countries are both to be exchanged for the sugar and tobacco of the English colonies, this superiority of price gives an encouragement to the former, beyond what the latter can in these circumstances enjoy. The exclusive trade of the colonies, therefore, as it diminishes, or, at least, keeps down below what they would otherwise rise

to, both the enjoyments and the industry of the countries which do not possess it; so it gives an evident advantage to the countries which do possess it over those other countries.

*   *   *

REVIEW QUESTIONS

1. How, according to Smith, did the colonial empires of early modern Europe differ from those of the ancient world?
2. What was the motive force of empire?
3. How does Smith explain the eventual success of the colonies in America?
4. What benefits does he think derive from empire? What costs?
5. How do we explain Smith's apparent indifference to the exploitation of native or slave populations?

CATHERINE THE GREAT

FROM Proposals for a New Code of Law

Catherine II (1729–1796), a German princess who became Tsarina of Russia after disposing of her ineffectual husband, was one of the most successful European monarchs of the eighteenth century and one of the most remarkable female rulers of all time. She followed Peter the Great in regarding Russia as a European power. Among her many achievements was the addition of some 200,000 square miles to the territory of the Russian Empire. Nor were her interests limited to expansion. She also took effective measures to modernize the empire's administration and improve its society. In 1767 Catherine summoned an assembly to draft a new code of laws for Russia and gave detailed instructions to the members about the principles they should apply. The proposed code never went into effect, but the proposal breathes the spirit of the Enlightenment.

From *Documents of Catherine the Great: The Correspondence with Voltaire and the Instruction of 1767 in the English Text of 1768*, translated by W. F. Reddaway (Cambridge: Cambridge University Press, 1931), pp. 216–17, 219, 231, 241, 244, 256, 258.

*   *   *

6. Russia is a European State.

7. This is clearly demonstrated by the following Observations: The Alterations which *Peter the Great* undertook in Russia succeeded with the greater Ease, because the Manners, which prevailed at that Time, and had been introduced amongst us by a Mixture of different Nations, and the Conquest of foreign Territories, were quite unsuitable to the Climate. *Peter the First*, by introducing the Manners and Customs of Europe among the European People in his Dominions, found at that Time such Means as even he himself was not sanguine enough to expect. . . .

8. The Possessions of the Russian Empire extend upon the terrestrial Globe to 32 Degrees of Latitude, and to 165 of Longitude.

9. The Sovereign is absolute; for there is no other Authority but that which centers in his single Person, that can act with a Vigor proportionate to the Extent of such a vast Dominion.

10. The Extent of the Dominion requires an absolute Power to be vested in that Person who rules over it. It is expedient so to be, that the quick Dispatch of Affairs, sent from distant Parts, might make ample Amends for the Delay occasioned by the great Distance of the Places.

11. Every other Form of Government whatsoever would not only have been prejudicial to Russia, but would even have proved its entire Ruin.

12. Another Reason is: That it is better to be subject to the Laws under one Master, than to be subservient to many.

13. What is the true End of Monarchy? Not to deprive People of their natural Liberty; but to correct their Actions, in order to attain the *supreme Good*.

14. The Form of Government, therefore, which best attains this End, and at the same Time sets less Bounds than others to natural Liberty, is that which coincides with the Views and Purposes of rational Creatures, and answers the End, upon which we ought to fix a steadfast Eye in the Regulations of civil Polity.

15. The Intention and the End of Monarchy, is the Glory of the Citizens, of the State, and of the Sovereign.

16. But, from this Glory, a Sense of Liberty arises in a People governed by a Monarch; which may produce in these States as much Energy in transacting the most important Affairs, and may contribute as much to the Happiness of the Subjects, as even Liberty itself. . . .

*   *   *

33. The Laws ought to be so framed, as to secure the Safety of every Citizen as much as possible.

34. The Equality of the Citizens consists in this; that they should all be subject to the same Laws.

35. This Equality requires Institutions so well adapted, as to prevent the Rich from oppressing those who are not so wealthy as themselves, and converting all the Charges and Employments entrusted to them as Magistrates only, to their own private Emolument. . . .

*   *   *

37. In a State or Assemblage of People that live together in a Community, where there are Laws, Liberty can only consist *in doing that which every One ought to do*, and *not to be constrained to do that which One ought not to do*.

38. A Man ought to form in his own Mind an exact and clear Idea of what Liberty is. *Liberty is the Right of doing whatsoever the Laws allow:* And if any one Citizen could do what the Laws forbid, there would be no more Liberty; because others would have an equal Power of doing the same.

39. The political Liberty of a Citizen is the Peace of Mind arising from the Consciousness, that every Individual enjoys his peculiar Safety; and in order that the People might attain this Liberty, the Laws ought to be so framed, that no one Citizen should stand in Fear of another; but that all of them should stand in Fear of the same Laws. . . .

*   *   *

123. The Usage of Torture is contrary to all the Dictates of Nature and Reason; even Mankind itself

cries out against it, and demands loudly the total Abolition of it. . . .

*   *   *

180. That Law, therefore, is highly beneficial to the Community where it is established, which ordains that every Man shall be judged by his Peers and Equals. For when the Fate of a Citizen is in Question, all Prejudices arising from the Difference of Rank or Fortune should be stifled; because they ought to have no Influence between the Judges and the Parties accused. . . .

*   *   *

194. (1.) No Man ought to be looked upon as *guilty*, before he has received his judicial Sentence; nor can the Laws deprive him of *their* Protection, before it is proved that he *has forfeited all Right* to it. What Right therefore can Power give to any to inflict Punishment upon a Citizen at a Time, when it is yet dubious, whether he is *Innocent* or *guilty*? . . .

*   *   *

250. A Society of Citizens, as well as every Thing else, requires a certain fixed Order: There ought to be *some to govern*, and *others to obey*.

251. And this is the Origin of every Kind of Subjection; which feels itself more or less alleviated, in Proportion to the Situation of the Subjects. . . .

252. And, consequently, as the Law of Nature commands Us to take as much Care, as lies in *Our* Power, of the Prosperity of all the People; we are obliged to alleviate the Situation of the Subjects, as much as sound Reason will permit.

253. And therefore, to shun all Occasions of reducing People to a State of Slavery, except the *utmost* Necessity should *inevitably* oblige us to do it; in that Case, it ought not to be done for our own Benefit; but for the Interest of the State: Yet even that Case is extremely uncommon.

254. Of whatever Kind Subjection may be, the civil Laws ought to guard, on the one Hand, against the *Abuse* of Slavery, and, on the other, against the *Dangers* which may arise from it. . . .

*   *   *

269. It seems too, that the Method of exacting their Revenues, *newly* invented by the Lords, diminishes both the *Inhabitants*, and the *Spirit of Agriculture* in Russia. Almost all the Villages are *heavily* taxed. The Lords, who seldom or never *reside* in their Villages, lay an Impost on every Head of one, two, and even five Rubles, without the least Regard to the *Means* by which their Peasants may be able to *raise* this Money.

270. It is highly necessary that the Law should prescribe a Rule to the Lords, for a more judicious Method of raising their Revenues; and oblige them to levy *such* a Tax, as *tends least* to separate the Peasant from his House and Family; this would be the Means by which Agriculture would become more extensive, and Population be more increased in the Empire.

REVIEW QUESTIONS

1. Which articles and which instructions, coincide with the liberal or enlightened principles that were spreading across Europe in the late seventeenth and eighteenth centuries?

2. These liberal sentiments notwithstanding, what makes this document a classic exercise in absolute monarchy?

3. Why does Catherine include the curious instruction in Article 6?

4. How does Catherine understand such concepts as "society" and the "laws of nature"?

5. How does Catherine understand monarchy? How do her ideas differ from those of other absolute monarchs you may have studied?

Credits

Photo Credits

Page 5: Teomancimit/Wikimedia Commons; **p. 55:** De Agostini Picture Library/S. Vannini/Bridgeman Images; **p. 120:** University of Pennsylvania Museum neg. #S8-120800; **p. 142:** Art Resource, NY; **p. 176:** The British Museum; **p. 196:** Bridgeman Images; **p. 222 (top):** Archivo Iconografico, S.A./Corbis; **p. 222 (bottom):** Archivo Iconografico, S.A./Corbis; **p. 256:** Berig/Wikimedia Commons; **p. 257:** Berig/Wikimedia Commons; **p. 307 (left):** Foto Marburg/Art Resource, NY; **p. 307 (right):** Foto Marburg/Art Resource, NY; **p. 341 (top):** Erich Lessing/Art Resource, NY; **p. 341 (bottom):** Erich Lessing/Art Resource, NY; **p. 403:** Erich Lessing/Art Resource, NY; **p. 409:** Erich Lessing/Art Resource, NY; **p. 433:** Foto Marburg/Art Resource, NY; **p. 447:** Erich Lessing/Art Resource, NY; **p. 462:** The Granger Collection, New York; **p. 473 (top):** Art Gallery of New South Wales; **p. 473 (middle):** Bettmann/Corbis; **p. 473 (bottom):** Art Gallery of New South Wales; **p. 483:** The Gallery Collection/Corbis; **p. 509:** © Mary Evans Picture Library/age footstock; **p. 514:** Gianni Dagli Orti/The Art Archive at Art Resource, NY.

Text Credits

Ibn al-Athir: "Arab Account of the Crusade," from *Arab Historians of the Crusades*, Arabic sources translated by Francesco Gabrieli, translated from the Italian by E. J. Costello. Copyright © 1969 by Routledge & Kegan Paul Ltd. Published by the University of California Press. Reprinted by permission of the University of California Press.

Leon B. Alberti: Reprinted by permission of Waveland Press, Inc., from *The Family in Renaissance Florence, Book Three: I Libri Della Famiglia*, translated by Renée Neu Watkins. Long Grove, Ill.: Waveland Press, Inc., 1994. All rights reserved.

Ahmed Ali: From *Al-Qur'an: A Contemporary Translation*, by Ahmed Ali. Karashi, Pakistan: Akrash Publishing. Copyright © 1995, Akrash Publishing. Reprinted by permission of Orooj Ahmed Ali.

Dante Alighieri: "Canto V, Circle Two: The Carnal," pp. 25–28, from *The Divine Comedy*, by Dante Alighieri, translated by John Ciardi. Copyright 1954, 1957, 1959, 1960, 1961, 1965, 1967, 1970 by the Ciardi Family Publishing Trust. Used by permission of W. W. Norton & Company, Inc.

American Bible Society: Scripture taken from the Contemporary English Version © 1991, 1992, 1995 by American Bible Society. Used by Permission.

W. P. Barrett: From *The Trial of Jeanne d'Arc*, edited and translated by W. P. Barrett. Copyright © 1931 by Routledge. Reproduced by permission of Taylor & Francis Books UK.

Ibn Battuta: From *The Travels of Ibn Battuta, A.D. 1325–1354*, edited and translated by H. A. R. Gibb. London: Hakluyt Society, 1958, pp. 41–53. Reprinted by permission.

J. A. Black (ed.): "The Instructions of Shuruppag," from *The Electronic Text Corpus of Sumerian Literature 1998–2006*. Edited by Black, J. A.; Cunningham, G.; Ebeling, J.; Flückiger-Hawker, E.; Robson, E.; Taylor, J.; and Zólyomi, G. Reprinted by permission of the Department of Oriental Studies, Oxford University.

Giovanni Boccaccio: From *The Decameron* by Giovanni Boccaccio, translated by Mark Musa and Peter Bondanella. Copyright © 1982 by Mark Musa and Peter Bondanella. Used by permission of W. W. Norton & Company, Inc.

Jean Bodin: From *On Sovereignty*, pp. 46–50. Copyright © Cambridge University Press 1992. Reprinted with the permission of Cambridge University Press.

S. A. J. Bradley (ed.): "Anglo-Saxon translation of Genesis," from *Anglo-Saxon Poetry: An Anthology of Old English Poems in Prose Translations with Introduction and Headnotes*, by S. A. J. Bradley, pp. 25–32. Copyright © 1982 New York: Everyman's Library.

John Calvin: *Theological Treatises* From *John Calvin*, by G. R. Potter and M. Greengrass. London: Edward Arnold, 1983.

Catherine the Great: "Proposals for a New Code of Law," from *Documents of Catherine the Great: The Correspondence with Voltaire and the Instruction of 1767 in the English Text of 1768*, translated by W. F. Reddaway. Copyright © 1931 Cambridge University Press. Reprinted with permission from Cambridge University Press.

Geoffrey Chaucer: From *The Canterbury Tales: Nine Tales and the General Prologue: A Norton Critical Edition*, by Geoffrey Chaucer, edited by V. A. Kolve and Glending Olson, pp. 192–207. Copyright © 1989 by W. W. Norton & Company, Inc. Used by permission of W. W. Norton & Company, Inc.

Robert Chazan: "Anonymous Mainz Account," from *European Jewry and the First Crusade*, by Robert Chazan, pp. 225–242. Copyright © 1987 Regents of the University of California. Published by the University of California Press. Reprinted by permission of the publisher.

Cicero: Reprinted by permission of the publishers and the Trustees of the Loeb Classical Library from *Cicero: Volume XV–De Republica/De Legibus*, Loeb Classical Library Vol. 213, translated by Clinton W. Keyes, pp. 311–391. Cambridge, Mass.: Harvard University Press. Copyright © 1928, by the President and Fellows of Harvard College. The Loeb Classical Library® is a registered trademark of the President and Fellows of Harvard College.

Columbia: "The Twelve Tables," from *Roman Civilization, Selected Readings, Vol. 2*, edited by Naphtali Lewis and Meyer Reinhold. Reprinted by permission of Columbia University Press.

Christopher Columbus: "The First Voyage of Christopher Columbus," from *Selected Documents Illustrating the Four Voyages of Columbus, Vol. 1*, edited and translated by Cecil

Council of the Churches of Christ in the USA. All rights reserved.

Perpetua: "The Martyrdom of Perpetua," from *A Lost Tradition: Women Writers of the Early Church*, by Patricia Wilson-Kastner, G. Ronald Kastner, Ann Millin, Rosemary Radar, Jeremiah Reedy, pp. 19–32. United Press of America, 1981.

Clyde Pharr: *The Theodosian Code and Novels and the Sermondian Constitutions*, pp. 440–451. Copyright © 1952 in the name of the author, 1980 renewed in name of Roy Pharr, executor. Reprinted by permission of Princeton University Press.

Giovanni Pico: "Oration on the Dignity of Man," from *Reflections on the Philosophy of the History of Mankind*, by Johann Gottfried Herder, edited by Frank Edward Manuel. Copyright © 1968 by The University of Chicago. Reprinted by permission of the University of Chicago Press.

Plato: Excerpts from pp. 146–151, 209–215, *The Republic*, by Plato, translated by Richard W. Sterling and William C. Scott. Copyright © 1985 by Richard W. Sterling and William C. Scott. Used by permission of W. W. Norton & Company, Inc. "Apology," from *The Last Days of Socrates*, by Plato, translated with an introduction by Hugh Tredennick. Penguin Classics 1954, Third edition 1969. Copyright © Hugh Tredennick, 1954, 1959, 1969. Reproduced by permission of Penguin Books Ltd.

Plutarch: From *The Age of Alexander: Nine Greek Lives*, by Plutarch, translated and annotated by Ian Scott Kilvert, introduction by G. T. Griffith. Penguin Classics, 1973. Translation and notes copyright © Ian Scott-Kilvert, 1973. Introduction copyright © G. T. Griffith, 1973. Reproduced by permission of Penguin Books Ltd.

Pope Gregory VII: From "Letter to Bishop Herman of Metz," from *The Correspondence of Pope Gregory VII*, edited by Ephraim Emerton, pp. 166–75. Reprinted by permission of Columbia University Press.

James Pritchard (ed.): "The Book of the Dead," translation by H. L. Ginsburg, and "Treaty between Ramesses II of Egypt and Hattusilis III of Hatti," from *Ancient Near Eastern Texts Relating to the Old Testament—Third Edition with Supplement*. Copyright © 1950, 1955, 1969, renewed 1978 by Princeton University Press. Reprinted by permission of Princeton University Press.

Procopius: *Secret History*, translated by Richard Atwater, pp. 35–36, 39–49. Copyright © by the University of Michigan 1961. Reprinted by permission of The University of Michigan Press.

Martha T. Roth (ed.): Excerpts from "The Code of Hammurabi" and "Middle Assyrian Laws," from *Law Collections from Mesopotamia and Asia Minor*, edited by Martha T. Roth. Scholars Press, 1997, pp. 76–135. Reprinted by permission of Society of Biblical Literature.

St. Augustine: From *Concerning The City of God Against the Pagans*, by St. Augustine, translated by Henry Bettenson, introduction by David Knowles. Pelican Books, 1972. Translation © Henry Bettenson, 1972. Introduction copyright © David Knowles, 1972. From *Confessions*, by St. Augustine, translated with an introduction by R. S. Pine-Coffin. Penguin Classics, 1961. Copyright © R. S. Pine-Coffin, 1961. Reproduced by permission of Penguin Books Ltd.

St. Teresa of Ávila: From *The Life of Teresa of Jesus: The Autobiography of Teresa Avila*, translated by E. Allison Peters. New York: Bantam Doubleday Dell, 1991. Reprinted by permission of the publisher.

Thucydides: From *The Peloponnesian Wars: A New Translation*, translated by Walter Blanco, edited by Walter Blanco and Jennifer Tolbert Roberts, pp. 71–76, 227–231. Reprinted by permission of W. W. Norton & Company, Inc.

Tyrtaeus: "The Spartan Creed," from *Greek Lyrics*, translated by Richmond Lattimore. Copyright © 1949 by The University of Chicago. Reprinted by permission of the University of Chicago Press.

Xenophon: "The Laws and Customs of the Spartans," From *Xenophon's Minor Works*, translated by J. S. Watson, Bohn Classical Library, 1878.

Every effort has been made to contact the copyright holder of each of the selections. Rights holders of any selection not credited should contact Permissions Department, W. W. Norton & Company, Inc., 500 Fifth Avenue, New York, NY, 10110, in order for a correction to be made in the next reprinting of our work.